On the Home Front

The Cold War Legacy of the Hanford Nuclear Site

Third Edition

Michele Stenehjem Gerber

Introduction to the New Bison Books Edition by
John M. Findlay

With a new epilogue by the author

University of Nebraska Press, Lincoln and London

First Nebraska paperback printing: 1997

Library of Congress Cataloging-in-Publication Data
Gerber, Michele Stenehjem, 1948–
On the home front: the cold war legacy of the Hanford nuclear site / Michele Stenehjem
Gerber; introduction to the New Bison Books edition by John M. Findlay; with a new
epilogue by the author. — 3rd ed.
p. cm.
Includes bibliographical references and index.
ISBN-13: 978-0-8032-5995-9 (pbk.: alk. paper)
ISBN-10: 0-8032-5995-6 (pbk.: alk. paper)
1. Nuclear weapons plants—Waste disposal—Environmental aspects—Washington
(State)—Hanford Site. 2. Hanford Site (Wash.) 3. Hazardous waste site
remediation—Washington (State)—Hanford Site. I. Title.
TD898.12.W2G47 2007
363.72'890979751—dc22   2007004538

BISON
BOOKS

Introduction to the New Bison Books Edition
John M. Findlay

When *On the Home Front* was initially published in 1992, it represented the first scholarly, book-length history on production and pollution at a major U.S. nuclear weapons manufacturing site. Its appearance was made possible by a decision by the U.S. government to become more transparent about how decades of making and testing nuclear weapons had affected those who worked and lived in the vicinity of Hanford. The U.S. Department of Energy (DOE) launched this new phase of the Atomic Age by releasing previously classified records; in 1986 documents from Hanford were the very first to be made public on a large scale. Taking advantage of these newly available primary sources in researching and writing *On the Home Front*, Michele Stenehjem Gerber created a narrative for understanding Hanford that had no real counterpart for other major plants devoted to the manufacture of nuclear weapons. Her book was unique in itself, but it also contributed to a larger trend of revising the way Americans understood the nation's engagement with the atom.

Prior to the 1980s, most histories of U.S. nuclear weapons programs were not very critical. Studies tended to emphasize either the successes of the organizations that had overseen the production of American nuclear weapons such as the Army Corps of Engineers and the Atomic Energy Commission, or the lives and contributions of leading scientists from Europe and North America. They also tended to highlight the role of atomic weapons in bringing World War II to an end favorable to the Allies. While some academic historians vigorously debated the decision to drop bombs on Hiroshima and Nagasaki, the prevailing popular view was that the new weapon was a triumph because it shortened the war, saved American lives, and represented a scientific and technological triumph.

After 1980 or so, historical accounts of America's nuclear weapons became more diverse and more ambivalent. This transition partly reflected people's increasing questioning of nuclear technologies and their alarm at the seemingly intractable problems presented by nuclear wastes. Moreover, changes in government policies have made available many more sources than before, not all of which are flattering to the activities of earlier periods. DOE sites involved with producing nuclear weapons, such as Hanford, have not only released previously classified documents (usually under substantial legal and political pressure), but also produced numerous scientific reports and studies, particularly as they moved forward with the mission of clean-up.

Historians thus have had more materials to work with than ever before, but few have paid close attention to the nuts-and-bolts issues of production and pollution. Scholars working independently of the DOE have paid substantial—and less celebratory—attention to the society and culture of the different places associated with making atomic bombs during World War II and the Cold War. We now have histories of community and society in Los Alamos, Oak Ridge, and uranium mining towns; of the politics behind the Nevada Test Site and the personalities of University of California physicists; and of language and culture at various weapons facilities. But we do not have many accessible, technically informed accounts by independent historians of how weapons production in the United States generated radioactive and chemical wastes that threatened and continue to threaten the environment and public health. While scientists, clean-up experts, activists, litigants, journalists, and others are doing so much to publicize the domestic legacy of nuclear bombs, historians' accounts of production and pollution by the U.S. weapons manufacturing complex remain relatively rare. One reason is that, as the experience of writing *On the Home Front* attests, such works are difficult to complete. They require the appropriate mixture of training, resources, and determination.

That Michele Gerber happened to be in the right place at the right time with the right set of skills to produce *On the Home Front* was fortuitous. She earned a PhD in history at the State University of New York–Albany in 1975, writing her dissertation on the New York chapter of the America First Committee and its opposition to U.S. entry into World War II.

For family reasons, Dr. Gerber moved in 1987 to the Tri-Cities region of Washington, next door to the Hanford Site. Her arrival coincided with two local trends. First, she arrived at a time when the local economy was severely depressed. The U.S. Department of Energy had just halted production of weapons-grade plutonium at Hanford, and it had also removed the site from consideration as a national nuclear waste repository. But it had not yet committed to spend the money and time needed to deal with more than forty years' worth of industrial wastes at and around Hanford. There were few jobs to be had for historians such as Dr. Gerber or for anyone else. Furthermore, the government had just begun to release previously classified information about the Hanford production process and the discharge of radioactive and chemical wastes into the surrounding environs. Most of the newly available documents were placed on file in the Public Reading Room operated by the Department of Energy in Richland, Washington. Journalists and activists were sifting through these papers, but their tendency was to publicize specific episodes of waste release. In response, the DOE and its contractors usually suggested that individual, problematic incidents were anomalous and claimed that Hanford had generally been a safe neighbor. Dr. Gerber wondered whether the diverse events under discussion were part of a larger pattern. She decided to undertake a systematic historical study of what had happened at Hanford, focusing in particular on how the site's production of weapons-grade plutonium had affected the environment and public health.

Besides the daunting amount of primary-source material that the recently declassified documents represented, Dr. Gerber faced a series of obstacles to the successful completion of her project. One was monetary. Apart from a small grant from the American Association of State and Local History, she had no financial sponsor for her research and writing. This point deserves emphasis. Some reviewers of the first edition of On the Home Front noted that Dr. Gerber had by the time the book appeared in 1992 worked for one of the DOE's clean-up contractors; they speculated that her interpretation of the site's history was influenced in some fashion by her employment at Hanford. But in fact, she held no job with Hanford during the time she was researching and writing the book. She completed the manuscript in 1990 (more than two years before it appeared in print), and only then went to work at Hanford. The local economy by that point was turning around, in part because of the DOE's new commitment to clean-up, so there were jobs available. It must have been apparent that Dr. Gerber's historical expertise, acquired through months of unpaid research in the Public Reading Room, could assist in accomplishing the site's new mission. So she was hired by one of the DOE contractors at Hanford. But On the Home Front had already been finished and shipped off to a publisher.

Other obstacles were more technical in nature. While Dr. Gerber brought certain historical skills to the Hanford record, she had had no sustained training in science or in environmental history. To succeed with On the Home Front, she had to teach herself about nuclear technologies and their implications for public health. Dr. Gerber read widely in the fields of nuclear weapons and radiation

safety, took courses in chemistry and statistics, and interviewed dozens of people. She recalls feeling that some of her interviewees underestimated her, perhaps
doubting that a newcomer—particularly a woman—could put the entire story
together. Dr. Gerber remembers doing little to try to alter their impression.

There were additional hurdles. While the DOE had released thousands upon
thousands of pages of documents in the later 1980s, it still withheld many pieces
of the puzzle. Dr. Gerber filed dozens of requests under the U.S. Freedom of
Information Act in order to obtain more of the primary sources she needed.
Processing these requests naturally took time, during which Dr. Gerber feared
that others would show up at the Public Reading Room in Richland and write
the story more quickly than she could. She remembers feeling a sense of urgency as she worked on the book, and at the same time—like many historians—she felt isolated. Researching and writing a book can be lonely. She had
every right to be apprehensive, too, about how the book would be received.
Although profound changes were coming to Hanford, people in the vicinity
remained deeply defensive about what the site had done during wartime. Dr.
Gerber was telling a story that some would not like because it would cast Hanford in a negative light. Moreover, she was highlighting the site's history not
during its World War II phase, which almost everyone regarded as triumphal,
but during the Cold War, an era that wrote a more complicated ledger of profits
and losses. How would her neighbors react?

Dr. Gerber took as her first obligation telling the story as accurately as possible. Writing *On the Home Front* required immersion in the thousands of pages
available in the Public Reading Room, most of which are written in the bland,
often passive style of bureaucrats. One of the book's key contributions is its
ability to penetrate, translate, and synthesize the government's dry, technical
reports and memoranda for a general readership. Dr. Gerber aimed to present her account without doing much to insert her own opinions between the
evidence and the reader, and without speculating about the things to which her
primary sources did not appear to speak directly, including the motivation or
reasoning of the officials responsible for discharging Hanford wastes. Indeed,
On the Home Front hews very closely to its base of impersonal, technical documents concerning production and pollution at the Hanford Site, as evinced
by its more than 1,100 endnotes. The book's accomplishments culminate in
a sequence of crucial chapters, each argued closely from sources in the Public
Reading Room: chapter 4 on airborne pollution, chapter 5 on waste discharges
into the Columbia River, chapter 6 on the contamination of the site's soil and
groundwater, and chapter 7 on the evolving knowledge of radiobiology and
monitoring programs at Hanford (or: what the government and its contractors

knew and when they knew it). These pages offer an invaluable summary of the production processes at Cold War Hanford, their effect on the environment, and the uneven efforts undertaken to monitor, manage, and conceal the pollution generated by the site.

By presenting a scholarly, historical narrative about the fate of wastes at one Cold War plant devoted to nuclear weapons manufacture, Dr. Gerber provided readers a glimpse of what the production of nuclear weapons had meant for environs, for public health, and for government officials at DOE sites across the country. When it appeared in 1992, *On the Home Front* joined Barton C. Hacker's 1987 study of radiation safety during the Manhattan Project as one of the few carefully researched, book-length histories of the domestic impact of America's nuclear weapons programs. Now, fifteen years later, additional comparable studies have appeared, including in particular Hacker's *Elements of Controversy* (1994), on radiation safety during nuclear weapons testing by the AEC from 1947 to 1974, and Len Ackland's *Making a Real Killing: Rocky Flats and the Nuclear West* (1999), the work most similar to Gerber's. Still, *On the Home Front* and its companions can fit on a very short shelf of book-length histories documenting the environmental and health impact of America's nuclear weapons programs.

Apart from chapters 4–7, which may be regarded as the book's core, *On the Home Front* includes two other sections that deserve particular attention. First, Dr. Gerber has used the epilogue to keep her book up to date. Tracking the many twists and turns of the DOE clean-up effort at Hanford since 1989 is no simple matter; readers are fortunate to have Dr. Gerber's chronicle of developments, many of which she has observed or participated in firsthand. By the time of the second edition, published in 2002, the epilogue (supported by 162 more endnotes) had become the longest chapter of the book. It provided a relatively rare commodity—a historian's perspective on quite recent trends and events. Dr. Gerber has further updated the epilogue for the current edition.

Second, in chapter 8 ("Truth and Rebirth") and the epilogue, *On the Home Front* pays close attention to the moods of Richland, Pasco, and Kennewick, the Tri-Cities adjacent to the site that serve as home to so many employees and former employees of Hanford. Dr. Gerber has been particularly interested in the fate of these communities, whose populations not only helped create and were exposed to Hanford's pollution, but who also experienced the economic and emotional turbulence following the transition from production to clean-up. As the local economy contracted and expanded, as Hanford's mission changed, as criticism of Hanford increased, as groups debated the future of the nearby rivers and lands, and as the communities' reputation and self-image came into question, many residents of the Tri-Cities felt beleaguered. Living in one of the communities surrounding Hanford, Dr. Gerber has been especially sensitive to the significance of history to the towns' future. Her story certainly has proved difficult for some to hear, but Dr. Gerber has been adamant that the Tri-Cities needed to face up squarely to the past in order to proceed toward the future. In her view, *On the Home Front*, which has sold well in the towns around Hanford, has been therapeutic for communities in the region. Few scholars can make such a claim for the histories that they produce.

Dr. Michele Gerber has helped to illuminate a place and a series of events about which Americans remain enormously unsettled. Fifteen years after the first edition of *On the Home Front* appeared, there remains much interest in what she has had to say.

Contents

Maps

Illustrations

Acknowledgments

Many people and organizations have been helpful in the research and writing of this book. I would like to thank in particular the East Benton County Historical Society in Kennewick, Washington; the Washington State Historical Society in Tacoma; the American Association for State and Local History in Nashville, Tennessee, for their belief in the project and the award of a research grant; and the staff of the Richland Public Library, who efficiently and professionally processed my seemingly endless document searches and who also encouraged me to persevere. The maps and photographs are all courtesy of the Department of Energy.

My family has supported me with their pride and encouragement through years of research. I would like to thank my husband, Eric, particularly, for his constant faith in my abilities and for his extra help with child care and family chores. Without him this book would not have been possible.

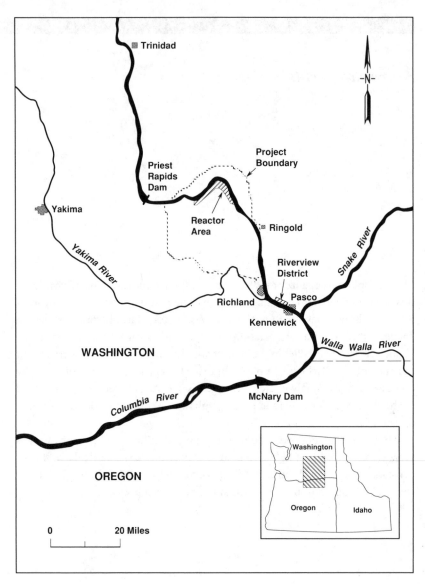

The Hanford Plant vicinity

Introduction:
The Legacy

No one would ever have to exaggerate the Hanford experience. The facts, just as they were, were amazing all by themselves! The whole project was so big, so different, so urgent . . . When people found out about the bomb, they couldn't believe it . . . Being there, watching it all happen, was the experience of a lifetime!—Robley Johnson, Photographer for the original Hanford project and later for the Atomic Energy Commission, Richland, Washington, May 1990

The production reactors all display symptoms of acute aging that could affect safety and are likely to limit the useful lives of these reactors . . . There are significant uncertainties in the abilities of production reactor confinements to mitigate radionuclide releases that would be expected to occur during severe accidents . . . The Department [of Energy's] safety oversight of the production reactors is ingrown and largely outside the scrutiny of the public.—National Academy of Sciences, National Research Council, "Safety Issues at the Defense Production Reactors," 1987

The Hanford Engineer Works (the original name for the Hanford Site) was constructed to produce plutonium for America's first atomic weapons. The facility succeeded far beyond the hopes of its builders, the Manhattan Engineer District (MED) of the Army Corps of Engineers. Only twenty-nine months after ground was broken at the 640-square-mile desert site in March 1943, the Hanford project had produced and delivered the plutonium in the bomb that was dropped on Nagasaki, Japan, and that ended World War II. The Hanford facility also had made the plutonium for the world's first atomic explosion, the Trinity test detonated at Alamogordo, New Mexico, in July 1945. These facts represented pioneering technological achievements and the largest scale-up in the history of the engineering craft. They instigated whole new fields of scientific inquiry. They also changed national defense strategy and altered the course of global politics and world history for at least two generations. For forty years afterward, the Hanford enterprise was praised by politicians, scientists, historians, journalists, and, it seemed, everyone else who was involved or interested in atomic energy.[1]

However, as it turned out, the enormous engineering, chemical, and atomic puzzles that were solved to make the reactors run were not the most difficult ones. Less glamorous but more vexing long-term challenges were thrust on the Hanford endeavor by the Columbia Basin, the host region to the project. Its loose, porous soil, its flat, open topography, its dry winds, and its big, swift rivers presented intransigent problems to site operators. In reality, the toughest Hanford dilemmas began after the manufacturing plant achieved its first successes.

In addition to brilliant breakthroughs in reactor physics and chemical technologies, the Hanford Site pioneered the science of environmental monitoring. At the time that this concept was being developed, most cities throughout the world discharged raw sewage into nearby lakes and rivers. Steel mills, chemical plants, and other industries routinely sent their wastes up smokestacks, or into bodies of water, trenches, and sewers for seepage into the ground. The Hanford Site was unique for measuring contamination levels in stack gases, vegetation, river water, fish and ducks, and groundwater. Hanford's environmental-monitoring records were among the most complete ones in the world. Unfortunately, they do disclose that at many times the huge atomic facilities discharged radioactive and chemical wastes far in excess of the allowable levels and tolerable limits of the National Committee on Radiation Protection (NCRP) and the International Commission for Radiological Protection (ICRP).

In February 1986, the Department of Energy (DOE, the successor agency to the Atomic Energy Commission, AEC) released approximately nineteen thousand pages of reports pertaining to the early history of Hanford. These documents, many of which were newly declassified, consisted of environmental-monitoring surveys, engineering reports, office memoranda and correspondence, and other miscellaneous pieces of the historical record. From these documents, and from nearly fifty thousand additional pages of documentation released in the next six years, the world learned of immense waste discharges from the Hanford facility.[2] In his memoirs, General Leslie Groves, the MED chief, pointed to a partial explanation: "Not until later would it be recognized that chances would have to be taken that in more normal times would be considered reckless in the extreme." The builders and operators at Hanford did "proceed vigorously on major phases of the work despite large gaps in basic knowledge . . . While normally haste makes waste, in this case haste was essential."[3]

The thousands of pages of documents released by the DOE starting in 1986 have disclosed that, at Hanford, haste *did* make waste. Radioactive and chemical wastes totaling into the billions of gallons of liquids, and billions of cubic meters of gases, were emitted from the plant beginning with start-up in late 1944. While going about the business of containing communism, the Hanford Site was spreading millions of curies of radioactivity into the Columbia River and into the air and soil of the Columbia Basin. Furthermore, until recent years, area residents were not informed of the discharges nor warned of any potential dangers, even when releases far exceeded the tolerable limits and "maximum permissible concentrations" (MPCs) defined as safe at the time. In fact, Hanford scientists and managers, on numerous occasions throughout the first four decades of operation, specifically told the public that the plant's workings and wastes were well controlled and harmless.

In the hectic months of 1945 alone, 345,000 curies of radioiodine (I-131), generated by the chemical separation of plutonium from the irradiated fuel rods, was released into the atmosphere. This gas blew down the wind streams ("downwind") of eastern Washington: to the east, northeast, and southeast. The radioiodine also deposited on vegetation throughout the region where it was available to cows and goats, which produced milk drunk by humans. As a carrier of radiation to the thyroid, the milk pathway is many times more potent than simple inhalation of I-131. Discharges of radioiodine in quantities high enough to be of concern to Hanford's scientists and managers occurred repeatedly, and at times almost constantly, for at least a decade after World War II ended. Major releases of radioruthenium (Ru-103 and Ru-106) in airborne particulate form occurred from 1952 to 1954.[4]

The environmental-monitoring documents released in the late 1980s also disclose that just as the airborne problems were slowing down at Hanford in the mid-1950s, waterborne discharges to the Columbia River and to the ground were rising. By 1955, eight single-pass (open-coolant) nuclear reactors operated continuously at Hanford, producing the plutonium that America's leaders deemed essential to winning the cold war. These reactors discharged billions of gallons of cooling water, laden with fission and activation products, to the river and to the ground. Through the rich aquatic life in the Columbia, as well as through the insects and waterfowl that bred in and fed on it, these radioactive wastes entered the food chain. Burdens often concentrated thousands of times before they reached higher mammals. By 1952, three large chemical plants also functioned at the atomic complex. They extracted weapons-grade plutonium from fission products and other impurities by means of precipitation and solvent extraction. They then daily released millions of gallons of low-level radioactive wastes with added chemical constituents (*mixed waste* as now defined by the U.S. Environmental Protection Agency), through trenches and cribs, to the soil. By the late 1950s, underground tanks holding the most toxic, concentrated, and long-lived radionuclides at Hanford had begun to leak into the ground. Sometimes these releases have reached the water table.[5]

At the same time that Hanford's legacy of radioactive and chemical discharges was being made public, the American nation discovered that it had a systemwide problem. Chemical, radioactive, and mixed wastes, accumulated since the first atomic weapons were made during World War II, were leaking from inadequate containers and burial sites across the chain of production. Additionally, the weapons plants themselves were aging. Most had been built either during the hectic years of World War II or during the era of national fear that followed the first atomic explosion of the Soviet Union in 1949 and the outbreak of the Korean War in 1950. In many cases, embrittlement and overuse were causing these old facilities to crack, thereby permitting the seeping and leaching of some of the most dangerous substances known to man. Rivers, streambeds, soils, and underground aquifers near U.S. nuclear production facilities were becoming contaminated with wastes that would remain dangerous for hundreds to thousands of years. Some plants could not function at all. American defense chiefs worried about the possibility of "unilateral disarmament" if stores of tritium, an initiator for the nation's nuclear warheads, could not be replenished.[6] In October 1988, thirty-one members of the House Armed Services Committee stated, "This crisis has not arisen suddenly, but over a long period, and it stems from inadequate attention to maintenance, safety and operating conditions."[7] In June 1989, Admiral James D. Watkins, the new secretary of energy, agreed, "I am certainly not proud or pleased with what I have seen over my first few months in office." He promised to "chart a new course," away from previous DOE failures to protect the environment and the health and safety of residents. He estimated the national repair bill for the aging weapons plant sites at $130 billion.[8] Late that year, the Senate Governmental Affairs Committee released a report that found that in the early years of atomic weapons production, "high-level . . . AEC officials were made aware of serious public health problems stemming from exposure to . . . radioactive particles and gasses emanating from AEC facilities and overexposure of uranium process workers." According to the committee chairman, John Glenn, the AEC had "done nothing . . . and swept the problem under the carpet."[9]

At the three-hundred-square-mile Savannah River Plant (SRP), a nuclear reservation in South Carolina, the safety situation in the late 1980s was precarious. Five weapons-production reactors and two chemical-reprocessing plants were built at the site beginning in the early 1950s. In a special review by the National Academy of Sciences (NAS) in 1987, the three reactors still functioning (P, K, and L) did not fare well: "We are not able to conclude with confidence that significant core damage [with resultant release of radionuclides] would be avoided if there were a severe loss of cooling." Furthermore, the NAS suspected stress-corrosion cracks, criticized the confinement systems, and called the components of a new fuel being developed for the SRP reactors "inherently incompatible."[10] Even normal operations soon were censured. In August 1988, when plant operators attempted to restart a reactor that had been shut down for routine maintenance, an unexpected power spike occurred. Instead of tamping down the nuclear reactor, in compliance with established safety procedures, SRP personnel boosted it. DOE summarily closed the reactor and condemned the irregular and dangerous behavior of the operators.[11] In subsequent months, like the nuclear waste itself, revelations of past radioactive releases seeped out. In September, a 1985 memo of the DuPont Corporation, site contractor at Savannah River since 1951, was made public. The document detailed thirty serious safety events and/or violations at the site, kept secret from the public and even from the DOE, during the previous thirty years. Senator Glenn, DOE Safety Chief Richard Starostecki, and many others were quick to condemn the practices.[12]

In December, serious new cracks and other structural problems were discovered in the aging reactors. Reviews of internal procedures disclosed a myriad of safety violations, including broken and disengaged radiation-monitoring instruments, and sprinkler systems disconnected because they might drench files and computers. In January 1989, a geologic fault running the full twenty-mile length of the complex was found beneath the Savannah River Site.[13] Five months later, when South Carolina Congressman Butler Derrick proposed to exempt the K reactor from discharge specifications of the 1977 Clean Water Act, he met with sharp public criticism. Throughout the ensuing months, cost estimates for the repair and restart of the Savannah River facility have continued to rise, and additional safety and environmental violations have come to light.[14] As of late 1991, the plant was still idle.

At Rocky Flats, the plutonium bomb-trigger manufacturing site located sixteen miles from Denver, safety and contamination are also major areas of concern. The plant was partially closed in October 1988 after two employees and a DOE inspector inhaled radioactive particles. Soon afterward, the General Accounting Office (the investigative arm of Congress) released a report that cited a pervasive attitude of carelessness and numerous safety violations at Rocky Flats. Among the infractions were uncalibrated radiation monitors and antiquated fire-alarm systems. In December, the DOE reported that toxic wastes leaching into the groundwater near Denver made Rocky Flats the department's worst environmental problem. Three years earlier, local citizens had won a lawsuit that forced the DOE to buy a $9-million parcel of land adjacent to the ten-square-mile atomic site. Evidence revealed that Rocky Flats operations had released plutonium and toxic chemicals to the surrounding air and soil for nearly thirty-five years. In the 1970s, spreading contamination had prompted the plant to add thousands of acres to its "buffer zone."[15]

In the late 1980s, health and safety difficulties mounted at Rocky Flats. In June 1989, the Justice Department initiated unprecedented criminal charges against Rocky Flats operators for environmental violations.[16] In December 1989, Secretary Watkins acknowledged that Rocky Flats had been "mismanaged" by his "own department."[17] In early 1990, a special DOE advisory panel recommended further delays in restarting production at the small complex.[18] A year later, the Colorado Department of Health, the federal Environmental Protection Agency (EPA), and the DOE signed a landmark agreement to remediate and monitor 178 contaminated sites at Rocky Flats.[19]

Near Cincinnati, the Fernald Feed Materials Production Center has also been the focus of worrisome disclosures and an aroused public. The 1,050-acre uranium-processing complex opened in 1952 and was operated until 1986 by National Lead of Ohio. (Since that time, Westinghouse Materials Company of Ohio has been the site contractor.) In December 1984, the Fernald plant was shut down after the DOE disclosed that excessive amounts of uranium dust and oxides had been released through ventilating systems in a recent three-month period. Hearings by the Senate Governmental Affairs Committee in 1985 and 1987 revealed that over 230 tons of radioactive material from Fernald had leaked into the Greater Miami River valley during the preceding three decades. The whereabouts of another 337 tons of uranium hexafluoride processed at the Fernald site could not be documented. Thousands of kilograms (kg) of uranium dust had been discharged to the atmosphere and to surface water. Five million kg of radioactive and hazardous (mixed) substances had been released to pits and swamps, permitting percolation into groundwater. Concrete silos containing solid radioactive wastes had vented radon gas. Additionally, about two hundred thousand canisters and barrels at Fernald held mixed and hazardous wastes that had not been identified precisely.[20]

As the result of two lawsuits filed in 1986, the state of Ohio was awarded $1 million and a major oversight role in Fernald's cleanup. In October 1989, a citizens' class-action settlement gathered $78 million in a court-supervised fund to compensate Fernald's neighbors for lost property values and for health screenings (and health care, if needed). The last point held special significance, although specific radiogenic health effects were not claimed in the suit. Widespread public fear and suspicion of health effects was deemed sufficient to award compensation.[21]

During the same period, remediation agreements were concluded for other Ohio atomic facilities. In December 1988, the DOE agreed to clean up soil and groundwater contamination at the small, thirty-four-year-old Portsmouth Gaseous Diffusion Plant in Piketon.[22] In September 1990, the EPA and the DOE endorsed a pact to remediate the Mound Applied Technologies Site near Miamisburg and to provide public documentation of past and present contamination.[23]

In Idaho, a state long known for its support of the Idaho National Engineering Laboratory (INEL), 1988 was a pivotal year. The DOE announced its selection of INEL as the site for a Special Isotopes Separations (SIS) plant, a plutonium recovery and refining facility, and for other new production facilities. However, public hearings on the SIS and the new production plants brought forth surprising opposition based on environmental, safety, and health considerations. Among others, the Twin Falls Chamber of Commerce wanted "any environmental ramifications that have occurred to date by the discharge of water at the INEL" to be "resolve[d] . . . before any further facilities are authorized and constructed."[24] At the same time, Idaho Governor Cecil Andrus boldly banned further nuclear waste shipments to INEL from the Rocky Flats plant. "I'm not in the garbage business anymore," Andrus declared.[25] In February 1989, the DOE agreed to pay $456 million for an accelerated, five-and-one-half-year cleanup of buried waste at the 890-square-mile atomic site.[26] By the following January, public and political pressures had stopped the SIS plant, and no funds for it were included in the 1991 defense budget.[27]

At the thirty-seven-thousand-acre Oak Ridge Reservation in Tennessee, mixed and radioactive contamination also was discovered in the 1980s. In 1983, documents disclosing the discharge of 2.4 million pounds of mercury from the Y-12 Nuclear Weapons Components Plant at Oak Ridge were made public. A landmark 1984 federal court decision resulted, making the DOE subject to the requirements of the Resource Conservation and Recovery Act.[28] Three years later, the DOE reported that polychlorinated biphenyls (PCBs), heavy metals, and radioactive substances all were present in groundwater samples beneath Y-12.[29] In 1988, the department also disclosed that toxic and radioactive wastes from the X-10 Oak Ridge (formerly Clinton) Laboratory and the K-25 Gaseous Diffusion Plant had drained into White Oak Creek, a tributary of the Clinch River. The K-25 plant also had spread radioactive particulates and gases into the regional environment between its start-up in 1945 and its closure in 1964.[30] In May 1990, traces of plutonium were found in a lake forty miles downstream (along several creeks) from the Oak Ridge Site. Although the quantity was minute, it raised disturbing questions about the slow migration of long-lived contaminants from the aging atomic complex.[31]

Likewise during the late 1980s and early 1990s, nuclear wastes were found at other sites across the U.S. defense-production chain. In 1988, dimethylformamide and acetone were discovered in the soil and the Ogallala aquifer beneath the Pantex plant near Amarillo, Texas. Both chemicals are used in the final bomb-assembly processes at Pantex.[32] That same year, the city of St. Louis and several suburbs to the west negotiated with the DOE on how to clean up millions of cubic yards of soil contaminated with thorium, uranium, radium, and other radioactive materials. The substances had been generated at two Mallinckrodt Chemical Works plants that processed uranium for nuclear weapons, from the earliest Manhattan project experiments until 1966.[33] In 1988 and 1989, the soil, parking lots, plant buildings, and the Mohawk River around the Knolls Atomic Power Laboratory (KAPL) near Schenectady, New York, were found to contain radioactive waste (principally cesium-137). Beginning in 1947, KAPL, a General Electric Company facility, performed reactor design and other experimental work for the AEC.[34] In 1991, some Schenectady-area residents also voiced opposition to a proposal by the U.S. Navy to site another trial submarine reactor vessel at the nearby West Milton test facility. They requested declassification of safety and monitoring documents pertinent to the thirty-five-year history of experimental naval reactor programs in the region.[35] By 1989, the DOE's Kansas City plant (Missouri), as well as waste-disposal sites at Maxey Flats (Kentucky), Sheffield (Illinois), and West Valley (New York), were found to have leaked radioactivity into soil and groundwater.[36] In January 1991, the National Oceanic and Atmospheric Administration began tests to determine whether plutonium, cesium-137, and other nuclear wastes were seeping from

47,500 barrels disposed by the Manhattan Project and the AEC in the Gulf of the Farallones National Marine Sanctuary, just west of San Francisco Bay.[37]

Safety hazards surfaced in the 1980s at the Nevada Test Site (NTS). In 1984, twenty-four representative clients won a class-action suit brought by residents near the location of America's continental weapons test explosions. Their suit, the *Allen* case, charged wrongful deaths and radiogenic health effects from the years of atmospheric bomb trials at the NTS. In 1987, a federal circuit court of appeals reversed the *Allen* decision. The appeals court noted "ample evidence" of poor safety planning and knowledge of risks by AEC and NTS officials, but it stated that culpability was not a pertinent issue. The discretionary-function exception precluded government liability. In January 1988, the U.S. Supreme Court upheld the latter ruling. In 1990, Congress established a $100-million trust fund to compensate affected NTS neighbors, as well as uranium miners (and their survivors) of the four-state Colorado Plateau region. In 1989, a lawsuit was filed against the federal government on behalf of NTS workers who cleared rubble and retrieved instruments shortly after detonations in site areas that were heavily contaminated with radioactivity.[38]

How did the United States, the world's first and strongest nuclear power, reach the point where structure dilapidation and public anger came to characterize endeavors that had once been so bright and exemplary? At the huge Hanford Site, for many decades the core of the U.S. "atomic shield," the state and image of decomposition was especially vivid.[39] Perhaps the paradox of history was particularly striking there because the complex was so massive. Its achievements had been so immense, and now its waste volume was so overwhelming. It had done so much good, and it had done so much damage. Also, the Hanford Site was the first to disclose its problems openly. It revealed its historical record at a time when other facilities in the weapons complex held the darker portions of their past as tight secrets. For all of these reasons, the story of the Hanford complex has emerged as one of the most important and riveting ones in modern American history.

Now that much is known about Hanford's radioactive and chemical wastes, what can be learned? Certainly, the evidence that such wastes were discharged in large quantities without public knowledge or warning raises fundamental questions about American democracy. These issues do not have simple and ready answers. They were born in the dusty expanses of the Columbia Basin, but all Americans must ponder them and reach conclusions that make sense to us. Chief among these questions is that of secrecy and national security, juxtaposed with the right of an individual living and working in a contaminated environment to have access to basic health and safety data. How could an individual or a parent in early post–World War II America obtain enough information about atomic production and its wastes to choose the levels of risk he or she was willing to accept, or to move away from? How could the American system have better regulated or supervised a technology so new, so secret, and so little understood that radioactive and chemical wastes far in excess of tolerable limits and MPCs defined as safe by committees of national and international scientific experts, were released to the Columbia Basin with no law or public policy requirement that the public be informed?

Among other salient public-policy questions raised by a study of Hanford's waste emissions are these: How much should local and state governments participate in policy decisions regarding federal activities within their borders? What happens to scientific peer review when much of the pertinent data from an emerging science is classified? Is a population that lives near a major atomic defense production site actually living in a combat zone? If, in the 1940s and 1950s, the Hanford facilities *needed* to pollute in order to produce, should the government have forbidden workers to bring their families? Should it have bought up immense buffer zones around this installation and prohibited farming, ranching, hunting, fishing, and recreational water use for hundreds of miles? Should it have brought in all the food from the outside? Who should have made those decisions? What were the effects in the Pacific Northwest of fallout from American, Russian, English, and French atomic bomb trials? What was the state of biomedical knowledge about various radionuclides during the years of Hanford's major releases? What is the legacy of contamination today? To what extent can the soil and groundwater of the Hanford Site be reclaimed? What uses are appropriate for those physical resources today, and what cost levels justify reclamation? How can the American nation build oversight systems that work, so that risks and options are openly presented to affected people? Finally, and most basically, how and by whom are decisions made in America about what is "best" for all of us?

At the Hanford Site today, a renaissance is in progress. An extensive waste cleanup effort, pioneering innovative technologies, has begun. The open disclosure of Hanford's historical record has facilitated this cleanup. It has also involved state and local officials, a wide range of federal agencies, and the public. The past now serves the present, and makes possible positive change. Once again, the Hanford Site leads the nation. Today the new frontiers are in waste remediation, environmental restoration, and the preservation of democratic principles through public involvement.

"Pop—how far are we from the United States?" Cartoon from Dick Donnell, *You Asked for It: The* Richland Villager *Collection of Dupus Boomer Cartoons,* © Dick Donnell, 1946. Courtesy of Richard L. Donnell, Jr. (*Dupus* stood for *DuPont, U.S.,* and *Boomer* was the name given to workers who traveled from one booming government project to another.)

The "face" of an early Hanford reactor, c. 1945. Aluminum-clad, uranium fuel rods were inserted in long process tubes that ran horizontally back from the face.

Hanford's B Reactor Building, c. 1945. This structure has now been nominated for the National Register of Historic Places. It was designated a Landmark of the American Society of Mechanical Engineers in 1976.

Reactor water intake system, HEW, 1944. The Columbia River's pure and abundant water was one reason the Hanford Site location was chosen.

"NOT NEARLY AS DUSTY NOW THAT EVERYONE HAS THEIR LAWN IN."

"Not nearly as dusty now that everyone has their lawn in." Cartoon from Dick Donnell, *You Asked for It: The* Richland Villager *Collection of Dupus Boomer Cartoons*, © Dick Donnell, 1946. Courtesy of Richard L. Donnell, Jr.

Colonel Franklin T. Matthias, wartime commander of the Hanford Engineer Works, in 1944. He scouted the location for the Hanford Site in December 1942 and served as HEW commander from early 1943 through January 1946.

A Richland neighborhood takes shape, 1943. The presite village of approximately 400 people would house 17,500 people by the end of World War II.

Cells in Hanford chemical separations plant, 1945. The intensely radioactive processes conducted in these cells made remote operation mandatory.

Hanford chemical separations plant, 1945. The two-hundred-foot-high stack (291 structure) prominent in the foreground was constructed to ensure safe atmospheric dispersion of airborne wastes.

HEW 300 Area, 1944. This area contained fuel-fabrication and "process improvement" (research and development) operations.

Hanford "tank farm" under construction, 1944. Sixty-four single-shell, underground tanks for the storage of high-level wastes were built in four such tank farms during World War II.

Hanford Camp, which housed fifty thousand construction workers by late 1944. The camp was evacuated as the work force diminished in February 1945.

Hanford Engineer Work's meteorology tower (622 structure) under construction, 1944. Complete enough for use on December 7, 1944, this structure provided detailed "dissolving forecasts" at wartime HEW. It is still in use as part of an official U.S. weather station.

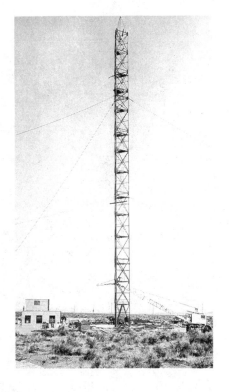

Hanford REDOX (reduction-oxidation) plant, 1952. Utilizing a methyl isobutyl ketone ("hexone") chemistry, this reduction-oxidation plant was the first large-scale, continuous, solvent extraction chemical plant of its kind in the world.

Herbert Parker, c. 1950. The first and most prominent manager of Health Physics at the Hanford Site, Parker established radiation work procedures for two and one-half decades, beginning in 1944.

Gable Mountain Storage Vaults, 1945. These vaults stored the HEW "product" (plutonium nitrate) for shipment to laboratories at Los Alamos, New Mexico.

Forty-two-year-old drums containing methyl isobutyl ketone ("hexone") from REDOX process development in the late 1940s are retrieved in the modern waste cleanup at the Hanford Site, March 1991.

Hanford Site employees discover a cache of World War II signs, August 1991. Such artifacts, protected under the National Historic Preservation Act, bring a sense of identity, fun, and pride to employees engaged in the modern waste cleanup. National, state, and local museums have requested some of the signs for their collections.

Beginnings:
The Land and the Place

The northern portion of the interior Columbia Basin, known as the Great Plain of the Columbia . . . is known in popular parlance as the "Bunch-Grass Country," from the fact that nearly all the plains and hills throughout its extent are covered with this most hardy and nutritious grass . . . The soil is good, though light, and the only drawback to its successful cultivation is the lack of rains in the summer and the facility with which it becomes powdery and dry.

—Thomas W. Symons, *The Symons Report: On the Upper Columbia and the Great Plain of the Columbia*, 1882

First Impressions, 1942

One surprisingly temperate day in late December 1942, Colonel Franklin T. Matthias stood on the lowland desert plain of the Columbia Basin in south-central Washington State. He let the powdery earth sift through his fingers. With him were two men from the DuPont Corporation, Gilbert Church and A.E.S. Hall. The three young engineers were all strangers to the sandy territory. They did not talk with any of the local people but quickly moved through the area, scouting for a secret military project. They drove and walked around in the tract that lay west of three tiny, dusty towns called White Bluffs, Hanford, and Richland.[1] Newcomers almost always thought these towns looked lean and dilapidated. Yet, to those who chose to stay and try to wrest a living from this open land, its comforts became sufficient. There was the bounty of the grains and fresh fruits that the ashy, volcanic soil could produce, the closeness of caring friends, and the beauty of the giant rivers and the tiny desert flowers. The little towns, according to one settler, came to seem "pleasant and comfortable . . . It was a wonderfully free sort of place to live. The buildings weren't elegant but they were adequate . . . the view seemed to be limitless, and the expanses of sky and clouds were unsurpassed in beauty." Neighbors in these villages and on the surrounding farms have recalled their easy sociability.[2] Besides, they always said, "We had the river."[3]

As Matthias, known to his friends as Fritz, and the DuPont engineers explored the triangular tract, they bent over and probed the sandy amalgam. Analytically, they noted the presence of gravel, shale, and sandstone, underlain by hard basalt. In their airplane they flew low over the huge Columbia River. It rushed in a big, southeastward arc past all three of the tiny towns. The men followed the waterway past Richland to trace its confluence with the large, winding Snake River. They observed the deep, wide channels of these two waterways and noted the extreme swiftness of the colder Columbia. It was winter, and yet the ground was not snow covered, and the rivers were not blocked with ice. Near the Columbia-Snake juncture, they checked the big loading docks and warehouses along the Columbia at Pasco, a larger town of thirty-nine hundred inhabitants. They noted the profusion of railroad and electric power lines from Spokane and Grand Coulee Dam to the north, and from Portland and Seattle to the south and west. This district, though remote and nearly empty, was obviously well connected to the outside world.

Then, well pleased, they left. On New Year's Eve, back in Washington, D.C., Matthias told Lieutenant General Leslie R. Groves, chief of the top-secret Manhattan Project: "We were unanimously enthusiastic about the Hanford area . . . We studied and looked . . . and recommended the . . . Hanford site . . . as being far more favorable in virtually all respects than any other."[4] Groves had to see for himself, however. Visiting the neighborhood two weeks later, he recalled: "I was pleased . . . Most of the area was sagebrush suitable only for . . . sheep . . . the total population was small and most of the farms did not appear to be of any great value." He ordered government real estate appraisers to assess the costs of buying out the farms and moving the people.[5] Back in Washington, he told colleagues that the Hanford region was "the best site in general and, more specifically, best in regard to safety."[6] Thus, in only a month's time, and by only a few men, one of the most significant decisions in American history was made.

Geology and Geography of the Hanford Region

The Columbia Basin is a very beautiful place. But it is not an easy land to live on, and it is unforgiving of the mistakes of those who do not make allowances for its chief characteristics—the very dry, sandy volcanic soil and the clouds of dust that are raised from this powdery amalgam when the winds blow across the Cascade Mountains to the west. The Cascades form a "rain shade" to this arid land, so that the moisture from strong and frequent Pacific storms is dropped in the mountains. Then, the winds rush on virtually unobstructed for nearly another two hundred miles before they are swept up into the Bitterroot Range in Idaho, just east of the Washington State line. The Columbia Basin itself surrounds the confluence of the Columbia and the Snake rivers. The flat land tilts in long, sloping angles toward the wide cuts of the swift-flowing rivers. The smaller Yakima River also joins its waters with those of the Columbia, about fifteen miles upstream from the latter's junction with the Snake. All three waterways are rich with salmon, sturgeons, steelhead trout, bass, whitefish, and suckers, as well as bottom-dwelling river life. Nearby, also dependent on the waters, live beaver, muskrat, coyotes, raccoon, deer, skunks, cliff swallows, golden and bald eagles, hawks, and owls. The region is bordered to the south by the Blue Mountains of northeastern Oregon. About 120 miles to the north of the Columbia-Snake confluence lies the vast Grand Coulee of the Columbia, embedded by glaciers that pushed the giant river out of its track during the Pleistocene age. The earliest non-Indian explorers and fur traders who passed through the district named it in various ways that reflected its characteristics. The "Great Forks" or the "Three Rivers" called to mind the junction of the waterways, and the "Great Columbia Desert" indicated the dryness of the level plain.

The ashy soil of the Columbia Basin is underlain by basalt, a gift from the preglacial lava flows. However, there are seams and rifts in the hard, black rock. The substrata are cut into a crazy quilt of confined and unconfined aquifers, and the water table varies from a few feet to 250 feet under the surface. The surface itself, the face that the Columbia Basin presents to the world, looks deceptively sparse and desolate. Actually, it is a mixture of thriving desert flora, including sagebrush, ryegrass, wheatgrass, bluegrass, saltgrass, bunchgrass, cheatgrass, thyme buckwheat, bitterbrush, Russian thistle, prickly pear, and willow. Amid the nonflowering plants, at certain times of the year, bloom the purplish-blue camas, lupine, penstemon, and blue thistle, the yellow ornaments of the black-eyed Susan, sunflower, and yellow toadflax, as well as hop clover, baby's breath, and many others. Tiny, delicate white flowers, and a few red, also can be seen. Despite these colors, this desert appears mostly brown and bleached gray, unlike the panoramic deserts of the American Southwest. It does not give the impression of abundance.

The region boasts relatively mild winters for a location so far north. Partly due to the frequent chinook winds, the area is sometimes called the "Banana Belt" of the Northwest. These winds carry warm Pacific air that usually melts all of the snow by mid-February. By early March, the natural desert cover is sprouting, about a month earlier than in other districts in the same latitude. In the years before the late nineteenth century, soft, billowy bunchgrass covered the territory, before huge cattle herds overgrazed it and plows uprooted it. The settlers said that once torn up, the bunchgrass wouldn't come back. Then the tougher, fibrous sagebrush claimed even more of the desert. However, whether or not there is ground cover, dust storms are a natural phenomenon in the Columbia Basin. Even now, there are days when those who love the region and feel lucky to live there wish that the dust would stop swirling and the gritty mist would cease its buffeting. On these days, there is nothing to do in the Columbia Basin but go inside and wait for nature, the governor of this land, to allow the humans to resume their activities.[7]

Impressions of the Earliest Visitors

The omnipresent dust of the flat, sandy expanses, the whistling winds, and the abundant life in the rivers were chief among the features mentioned by the earliest visitors to record impressions of the Columbia Basin. Meriwether Lewis and William Clark, traversing the highways of the Snake and Columbia rivers in 1805 and 1806, observed "a continued plain, which is low near the water . . . There is through this plain no tree and scarcely any shrub." They noted with discouragement the high winds, the ubiquitous dust, and "the fine sand of the plains," which made overland travel difficult.[8] Lewis also remarked on the "unusually nutritious . . . [and] abundant supply of low grass." Clark, the hunter, commented on the plentiful supply of grouse, ducks, rattlesnakes, and lizards. The salmon impressed him the most, however. "The multitudes of this fish are almost inconceivable." He recounted that the river water was so clear that the fish could "readily be seen at a depth of fifteen to twenty feet."[9] Upstream along the Columbia about forty-five miles from its union with the Snake, Robert Stuart, scouting the territory for John Jacob Astor's Pacific Fur Company in 1811, passed through a dramatic series of seven swirling rapids. Along the shore, the Wanapum Indians were conducting a religious ceremony, demonstrating their reverence for the earth and the river that provided such plenty. Seeing their careful attention to their leader, Stuart named the stretch Priest Rapids.[10]

Other fur traders and military men who crossed through the Columbia Basin in the early to mid-nineteenth century also told of the profusion of fish, waterfowl, rattlesnakes, lizards, grasshoppers, and the "remarkably stout and

long-winded horses . . . [which ranged] in droves in the most fertile plains" of
the lowland desert.[11] They never failed to mention the sandy soil, the winds,
and the dust that the two created when they combined.[12] Samuel Parker, a
wealthy businessman, left his horses in the care of Wallawalla Indians during the
winter of 1835–36. In the spring, he was amazed to find the animals "in fine
condition." He noted, "This shows the superior mildness of the climate and the
nutritive quality of the prairie grass." Although the natural desert cover impressed him, he correctly identified the chief obstacle to successful farming. He
commented, "There is such a want of summer rains that some kinds of grain
cannot flourish."[13]

Earliest Non-Indian Settlement: The Whitman Mission

The first non-Indians to try to colonize and farm the Columbia Basin had
agricultural success, but Indian conflicts drove their settlement from the region.
Marcus and Narcissa Whitman, missionaries from a Protestant organization in
Boston, came to the banks of the Walla Walla River, about forty miles east of the
Snake-Columbia confluence, in 1836. They established Waiilatpu (meaning
"place of the rye grass," in the Cayuse language) Mission and planted two
hundred acres to grains and fruit. The level land and mild winters, as well
as Whitman's waterwheel irrigation system, brought bountiful harvests. The
neighboring Wallawalla and Cayuse Indians grew angry, however. Smallpox
brought by the whites had decimated their tribes. Whitman, a physician, tried
to help but did not seem to cure the sick and dying. The Cayuses lashed out. On
November 29, 1847, they killed the Whitmans and twelve other people at the
mission.[14]

Native American Subjugation

Seven years later, Washington's territorial governor, Isaac Stevens, met with the
principal eastern Washington tribes on council grounds just a few miles from
the abandoned Waiilatpu Mission. Stevens wanted to open the region to
widespread non-Indian settlement, railroad building, and development. He
devised a reservation system, which did not fit the traditional food-gathering
habits nor the tribal groupings of the Yakima, Cayuse, Wallawalla, Umatilla,
and Nez Perce Indians or of various smaller bands. The Indians rebelled against
the new system, and three years of Indian wars occurred in the territory. In
September 1858, these wars were terminated by Colonel George Wright. He led
a decisive expedition that crushed Indian resistance and brought most tribal
leaders and members into the reservation system. The following month, the
military orders that had closed the Columbia Basin to non-Indian settlement

were revoked. The region, covered with its waving bunchgrass, lay open for colonization.[15]

Gold Discoveries in the Region

Still however, the flat, desert land was not highly prized by homesteaders traveling west. Many thousands glimpsed portions of it as they passed along the Oregon Trail to the south. However, they were discouraged by the dusty heat, the lack of wood for fuel and for home and fence building, the scarcity of rainfall, and the absence of railroads to ship their grain. Most took up lands in Oregon's Willamette Valley or in lush, wet, western Washington. It was gold discoveries in British Columbia and present-day Idaho, to the north and east of the Columbia Basin, in 1858 and 1860 respectively, that brought the first substantial numbers of non-Indian visitors to the district. Prospectors came and explored. However, rumors that this area would contain bountiful ore were false.[16] The prospecting surge, as it turned out, did not result in the establishment or growth of any of the major regional towns except Walla Walla and White Bluffs.[17]

The White Bluffs landing, located on the Columbia just south of the Saddle Mountains, had long been one of the central crossing and debarkation points for local Indians. By 1860, a ferry was operated by a non-Indian at the highly prized place. Cattlemen trailing and swimming their herds north from Oregon to provision the miners in British Columbia and present-day Idaho favored the smooth, wide contours of the river at the high bluffs. The soil there, they said, was more solid than the powdery amalgam of sand and volcanic ash at nearby crossings such as Vernita, Wahluke, and the foot of Priest Rapids. But late in the 1860s, the distant mines were abandoned and traffic declined. Still, a ferry and small store at the location operated continuously from 1870.[18]

The Cattle Ranching Period

The Northwest gold discoveries did cause the first large ranches to be established in the Columbia Basin and the Yakima and Walla Walla valleys. Benjamin Snipes, later known as the "Northwest cattle king," came north from The Dalles in 1855 to explore the thick, seemingly endless bunchgrass. He mapped out a trail that ran diagonally northeastward from the middle of the Yakima Valley to the chalky White Bluffs crossing and then north into Canada. Later, as the mines in present-day Idaho became important, ranchers moving stock eastward into the Bitterroots and the Montana Rockies would cross the Columbia at White Bluffs, then veer northeastward to their destinations. Snipes's paths became the most important ones in the region during the years from the late 1850s to the early 1880s, when ranching was the predominant activity in the Columbia Basin.[19]

Other stockmen, similarly drawn by the bountiful, empty grasslands, soon followed. One of Ben Snipes's range riders labeled the expanse "the cattle man's paradise."[20] During the 1860s and 1870s, sparse, unfenced ranches were established in the territory. A few stockmen had very large holdings. Snipes was the biggest, with about twenty-five thousand head of cattle and twenty thousand horses by the late 1860s. However, most of the herds in the district consisted of only a few hundred head each, and the ranching life was lean and primitive.[21]

Nature governed the stock business in the Columbia Basin. Ranchers there often learned, to their peril, that they were not in control. Although chinook winds frequently swept away the snow to expose vital forage to the cattle and to produce open and mild winters, the wind was not an unmitigated blessing. It could drive snow into the eyes in winter. During other months, there was the surprising vehemence of the dust blizzards. As an 1860 visitor affirmed, "If by chance . . . you get caught in a sand storm you get nearly suffocated and blinded whilst the sand pricks your face like so many needles going in."[22] Winters could be extremely harsh, and the ones of 1861–62, 1871–72, and 1880–81 were inordinately frigid and snowy. Up to three-quarters of the cattle in the area perished during each of those killing years.[23] Additionally, the cattle business in the flat, arid territory was hurt by changing demand patterns when more cattle began arriving by ship and railroad in California, Portland, Seattle, Utah, and Wyoming.

Arrival of the Railroads
The most telling blow to Columbia Basin stockmen was dealt by the Northern Pacific Railroad (NPRR) in the early 1880s. The railway, constructed between Spokane and the Columbia-Snake confluence between 1879 and 1884, carried enough homesteaders to the northern tier of the nation that six new states were carved out of the region and admitted to the union in 1889 and 1890. The NPRR brought waves of settlers interested in farming and fencing. Additionally, the railway corporation had enough money to finance irrigation projects to make the land productive and salable.[24] The "iron horse," according to one perceptive rancher, was the "advance agent of a great migration of settlers, which signalled the beginning of the end of that vast cattle range which had been ours for so many years."[25]

Founding of the Columbia Basin Towns
The Northern Pacific, like every other newcomer to the Columbia Basin, had to learn to live with the land. Searching for flat space on which to anchor a major

Columbia River bridge, NPRR engineers founded the region's two principal villages. North and west of the Columbia-Snake confluence, they surveyed and platted two towns to serve as administrative and construction headquarters for their Cascade Division. Pasco, just north of the meeting point of the two giant waterways, was named, during a sand blizzard, for a dusty, windy Andes mountain point called Cerro de Pasco.[26] The site of Kennewick was chosen for its low, open accessibility. Its name is a derivation of the Indian word *Kin-I-Wak,* meaning "a grassy place."[27] The railroad then placed nationwide advertisements geared to attract settlers to the Pasco-Kennewick district. Leaflets, fliers, and newspaper notices throughout the East and Midwest emphasized the mild and positive features of the land: a temperate climate with a long growing season and little rainfall, beautiful and useful rivers, and cheap and plentiful land with good drainage and accessible well water. These promotions termed Kennewick "the Italy of Washington . . . the most like California of any [place] in the Northwest . . . the vales . . . stretch . . . in pensive quietness between the sagebrush fields . . . [along the] lordly Columbia."[28]

The lavish campaigns, combined with aggressive local salesmanship, worked. Prices for farm lots in Pasco jumped in the late 1880s. At White Bluffs, so many families were attracted by the flowery promotions that there was no room for them at the original townsite. The village of White Bluffs, first located between the river and the bluffs on the east (north) bank of the waterway, actually had to move to the west (south) bank. Likewise, farmsteads sprouted on the Wahluke (meaning "soaring up like birds," in the Wanapum language) Slope, on the north side of the Columbia about forty miles north of Pasco.[29]

Early Irrigation Efforts and Failures

As soon as the Northern Pacific Railroad began to fill the Columbia Basin with settlers, the most urgent need of the newcomers was water for their crops. Wheat, barley, hops, alfalfa, cabbages, onions, potatoes, and fruits were the most successful foodstuffs. Soon, farmsteaders diversified into early fruits, vegetables, berries, flowers, maize, peanuts, and even sugarcane. Clearly, in this region that received only about six inches of precipitation per year, organized irrigation efforts would be needed.[30] Reclamation companies and farmers' cooperatives began in the area in 1888. However, meager financial resources, construction delays, and the obstacles imposed by the Columbia Basin itself ruined most of these endeavors. The land was so thirsty that it drained away over 25 percent of the water passing through all but the most expensive concrete ditches. Wooden canals cracked and leaked under the scorching sun of the district as the fine ashy soil shifted in its own natural responses to wind and construction disturbances. Nature broke open the man-made waterways. Tough, fibrous desert weeds and the blowing sand clogged the ditches so badly that water could not pass through them. When the national financial panic of 1893 hit, only one of the irrigation companies in the region survived. All of the farmers' cooperatives went bankrupt. Land values dropped sharply, local businesses closed, and a Portland newspaper predicted the demise of the small towns of the arid territory.[31]

Irrigation Revival and Regional Boom

The 1902 passage of the Newlands Reclamation Act revived the development of the reclamation systems and the consequent settlement of the Columbia Basin. The statute authorized the federal government to participate directly in irrigation projects, with the costs to be repaid over time by the water users. Indeed, the period from 1900 to 1910 saw the greatest population booms, in terms of percentages, in the towns and cities of the district, with the exception of the later boom associated with the establishment of the Hanford Nuclear Reservation. Working with adequate capital, new companies quickly built reclamation canals. They advertised the region throughout the nation, and land prices jumped.[32] By 1905, promoters had constructed irrigation ditches on two large ranches just north of the mouth of the Yakima River on the Columbia's west side. They assembled a thriving community and named the town Richland, in honor of the fertile soil and of the pioneer rancher Nelson Rich.[33]

That same year, Judge Cornelius Hanford of Seattle saw what he believed to be a lucrative business opportunity in eastern Washington. He and a group of other Puget Sound investors formed the Priest Rapids Irrigation and Power Company to reclaim acreage on the south (west) bank of the Columbia River about thirty miles north of Richland. They bought land at White Bluffs and at an undeveloped site about six miles downriver. At the latter place, they platted the town of Hanford. Between 1907 and 1910, a boomlet occurred in the triangular tract encompassing Richland, White Bluffs, and Hanford.[34] A second major railroad, the Spokane, Portland, and Seattle, added to growth when it built a line from Spokane to Pasco between 1904 and 1908. A third route, the Chicago, Milwaukee, and St. Paul, was constructed through the region, about fifty miles north of Pasco, between 1907 and 1909.[35]

Environmental and Agricultural Problems

Once in the Columbia Basin, settlers quickly learned that disturbing the fine, powdery soil was not similar to dealing with more solid ground. There were the dust storms that the powdery soil could raise, the wholesale raids on irrigation water that the parched ground could make, the grass fires that could race across the land and engulf a cabin or a herd or a plowed field before it could be saved, the man-traps that could hide in the swift rivers. There were the millions of jackrabbits that could strip fruit trees of bark and could ruin an entire orchard, and there were the other omnipresent predators and nuisances, such as crows, hawks, magpies, coyotes, pocket gophers, and rattlesnakes, that could destroy crops.[36] The Northern Pacific trains, carrying wheat to the hopeful farmers, also dropped the seeds of the Russian thistle. This stubborn, prickly weed spread like a wildfire across the dry expanses, crowding out even more of the softer grasses. Cheatgrass, so called because its durable, fast-growing root system robs other grasses of water, also proliferated. After the sagebrush, Russian thistle and thirsty cheatgrass became predominant. The fine, sandy soil was never again anchored as well as it had been before; the dust storms, which even the first travelers had described with vehemence, became nightmarish. The earliest farm fields were sometimes literally swept away, the wind bearing all of the seeds, so that entire crops grew in incongruous, unexpected places. The home-steaders learned a few tricks. They planted their wheat crops only biennially. They plowed shallowly during the fallow year to increase absorption of the meager rainfall into the friable topsoil.

Additionally, river flows in the district could vary by as much as a factor of six. Big floods in 1894 and 1907 washed out many of the early irrigation canals. The worst difficulties with the ditches, however, came from the ashy earth itself. It blew into the reclamation systems and plugged the pumps and other facili-ties. Men were hired to shovel out the ditches when they were dry, but after water was running through them, heavy chains, pulled by teams of horses, would have to be dragged along the bottoms to clear the canals. Ditch riders, hired to patrol the length of the reclamation systems in search of ruinous clogs, became essential.[37] The sandy soil's craving for water, along with the arid climate, caused financial difficulties for irrigation companies. A 1922 state survey noted, "65 percent of the water which goes into the ditch [the Hanford irriga-tion canal] is lost by evaporation and leakage."[38] Repeatedly, Judge Hanford's reclamation company and others had to "puddle" the canals (line them with a heavy clay soil) to prevent seepage. Still, the powdery earth refused to pack and seal, forcing the struggling businesses to line their ditches with cement.[39]

The situation in Franklin County, extending above Pasco as if that city were the base of a funnel, was even worse. There, perhaps the driest area in Wash-ington State, reclamation projects had to be large and expensive in order to be workable. The porous earth frustrated growers who tried to irrigate with wooden pipes and flumes coming from the Snake and Walla Walla rivers. Their systems desiccated and split in the dehydrated air. Franklin County growers tried to attract outside capital to develop irrigation projects, but there was little interest in taking the risks required to build on the inordinately thirsty soil. Although a few thrifty "dryland" farmers survived in the parched county, many became disheartened and left. As a result of these conditions, the county north of Pasco remained sparsely populated.[40]

Among those who came to the Columbia Basin in the early twentieth century and stayed, a close sense of community developed. The men harvested wheat together, and the women canned produce together in their homes and worked on joint community projects. Neighbors bartered specialized services and shopped and brought back mail for each other on infrequent trips to larger cities. They dug firebreaks together to turn the grass fires away from their homes. Whole communities participated in annual predator drives that would kill thousands of jackrabbits, gophers, and other nuisance animals.[41] Columbia Basin settlers remember the dust storms and the hard work, and they remember the feeling of being surrounded by caring friends. A Benton County wheat farmer recalled: "The sand blew so much that a person could barely see the tops of the fence posts . . . As the ground drifted, the growing grain was cut off . . . The dust drowned you out. You couldn't see to drive down the road at times."[42] At first, a moldboard plow was used, but later the settlers switched to disc plows to try to keep clods and stubble on top of the powdery ground. Still later, the "Cheney" (rod) weeder, invented for eastern Washington conditions, proved helpful in controlling dust by removing weeds while working clods up to the surface. Orchardists learned to plant alfalfa between rows of trees to anchor the soil. Growers of row crops interspersed asparagus or alfalfa to serve the same function.[43] Despite these struggles with the elements, and despite the sense of isolation that the howling winds could bring, one Richland woman declared: "My earliest recollection was the dust . . . but I never would have changed my growing up in Richland for any other place. It was a small town and everyone knew everyone else."[44]

Interwar Years

The years from 1910 to 1943 brought much slower growth, and in some cases actual decline, to the Columbia Basin. World War I brought a worldwide food shortage that raised agricultural commodity prices throughout the United States. Thus, the war benefited the small family farms and agricultural supply and shipping businesses that formed the backbone of the Columbia Basin's economy.[45] However, drought began in the 1920s, and the Great Depression of the 1930s then lowered farm commodity prices and pinched credit to a point that devastated the region's economy. Over half of the acreage in Franklin County was either abandoned or foreclosed during the 1920s and 1930s. Substantial failure rates prevailed throughout the district. Abandonment of land combined with the drought to produce severe dust storms. The parched region suffered in a dusty, hazy misery until President Franklin Roosevelt came to visit in 1934. Aides called the place "the land of abandoned hopes."[46] Roosevelt promised money for a gigantic dam at Grand Coulee, and this pledge brought the hope of irrigation canals and pumps and the hydroelectric power to run them.[47] The dam created extensive employment, and it supplied the enormous electrical power and irrigation water that made possible the Hanford Engineer Works (later Hanford Site) and the Columbia Basin Irrigation Project, the two largest enterprises in the history of the district.[48]

The Coming of World War II

The coming of World War II brought unmistakable signs of returning prosperity to the Columbia Basin. The war caused an immediate demand for agricultural products.[49] It also brought direct military spending into eastern Washington. In 1942, the navy selected Pasco as the site for a training base for primary, or inexperienced, pilots and purchased 2,285 acres of land on the northern edge of the city. The navy rented three other large tracts of land in the region for gunnery and other exercises.[50] The army placed three bases in or near the Columbia Basin in 1941 and 1942—two pilot-training stations at Ephrata and at Moses Lake in Grant County and a large infantry maneuvers and gunnery range sited between the upper Yakima and Kittitas valleys.[51] However, the overall region, as it stood in the early years of World War II, was not highly developed or populated. Prosperity, where it existed, was moderate. The two counties centrally located in the basin, Benton and Franklin, contained only about nineteen thousand people. Nearly a fourth of these lived in the railroad center of Pasco.[52] Life was relatively lean and cash-poor.[53] Yet, those who made the Columbia Basin their home felt a bond to their windy expanses, and their roots grew as deep and tenacious as those of the sagebrush.

Surprise of the Site Selection

In December 1942, when Leslie Groves and Fritz Matthias reached the decisions that would change the Columbia Basin forever, no one in the region even knew that the men had visited the area. Yet, behind the scenes, events moved quickly. The federal appraisers evaluated the lowland soil as "mediocre to poor in quality and condition . . . low in organic matter." The costs of condemning this land and moving out the approximately fifteen hundred people living within the tract of interest, they believed, would not be prohibitive.[54] The necessary legal procedures were instigated in February. On March 6, 1943, the affected residents learned that history and geography had come together in an unpredictable nexus and that they would have to leave their homes. The next weekly issue of the *Kennewick Courier-Reporter* proclaimed: "RICHLAND, WHITE BLUFFS AND HANFORD AREA TO BE TAKEN BY HUGE WAR INDUSTRY . . . MASS MEETING CALLED AT RICHLAND TO EXPLAIN THE WAR PROJECT TO RESIDENTS."[55] Shock was the common reaction.[56] People also felt a powerful curiosity as to why the federal government would want this arid, windblown, difficult place. They hoped for answers from the Richland meeting; however, they were told that the military plans for the region could not be disclosed. In subsequent discussions with the army engineers who were taking their homes, explanations remained elusive. Matthias, affable yet forceful, disarmed questioners with a smile and the simple answer, "If I told you what the government is doing, I'd be court-martialed tomorrow."[57]

Years later, of course, the residents of the Columbia Basin, along with the rest of the world, learned why the region seemed ideal to the military planners of World War II. The secret endeavor quickly became the Hanford Engineer Works.

Genesis of the Manhattan Project

The project conducted at the Hanford Site had its genesis in early 1940s research carried out by the federal Office of Scientific Research and Development (OSRD). The earliest OSRD studies in atomic physics concentrated on the highly fissionable (divisible), but rare, isotope uranium 235 (U-235). However, in March 1941, a research group headed by the physicist Glenn T. Seaborg at the University of California produced the first, submicroscopic amounts of plutonium 239 (Pu-239).[58] Soon after the United States entered World War II, the OSRD recommended that the Army Corps of Engineers construct industrial plants that could produce the U-235 and Pu-239. Roosevelt agreed and formed a new engineer district, the MED, within the Corps of Engineers in June 1942. In September, Leslie Groves, the veteran procurement, site selection, and supplies officer, was named to head the MED.[59]

The operating procedure of Groves, a direct and efficient man, had a great deal of influence on the entire MED and specifically on the Hanford project. The series of checks and balances that normally guard the American government against excesses was, in the case of the MED under Groves, virtually inoperative. Groves stated that he organized his office to enable him "to make fast, positive decisions." He added, "I am, and always have been, strongly opposed to large staffs, for they are conducive to inaction and delay."[60] At a late 1942 conclave of a few of the highest-ranking men supervising America's war effort, it was decided that a very streamlined committee of three would oversee the MED. In practice, Groves became an executive administrator with enormous power, making many decisions quickly and without consulting the busy men of the oversight committee. Thus, in his words, the governing principle of "keeping authority and responsibility together" within the MED "never changed." He did not "permit the decentralization of authority." Only a few people, and in some cases only Groves, privy to highly secret information, made almost all of the crucial decisions regarding atomic energy installations and their practices during the war years. This continued through 1946, when the civilian AEC was established.[61] For the Columbia Basin and its uninformed populace, there would be serious repercussions from this policy.

As the fragile, dusty territory of eastern Washington lay waiting to discover the reason that the army engineers were so attracted to it, scientific developments were proceeding rapidly. Most of the nation's prestigious pioneers in physics had been assembled by the MED at the University of Chicago's Metallurgical Laboratory (Met Lab). As soon as he assumed command of the MED, Groves visited the Met Lab. He later recalled that he was frankly "horrified" at the information he received. "It seemed as if the whole endeavor was founded on possibilities rather than probabilities." Major uncertainties faced the plutonium project. There were various possible methods for cooling the pile (reactor) in which the uranium would be irradiated as the first step in the production process. The means of subsequent chemical separation was unfixed. Usually, the equipment needed was not even designed, much less manufactured. And, there was the question of maintaining health and safety in the presence of large quantities of new, deadly, and poorly understood radioactive substances. Additionally, Met Lab scientists could not even guess to "within a factor of ten" the amount of fissionable material needed to make each atomic bomb. Despite these huge uncertainties, it was Groves's philosophy that "nothing would be more fatal to success than to try to arrive at a perfect plan before taking any important step." The MED plunged ahead.[62]

Safety and Isolation Govern Site Selection for the Plutonium Project

A series of decisions were made by the MED in late 1942 and 1943, leading to the determination to come to the Columbia Basin. The resolution to seek out the open expanses of eastern Washington was based on safety considerations. In August 1942, the physicist and key bomb developer J. Robert Oppenheimer emphasized to MED officials the extraordinarily hazardous and toxic nature of the gases generated in plutonium's chemical separations phase. In October, these same officials and scientists, as well as representatives of contractors, conferred again.[63] The scientists described the intensely radioactive gases that were generated by all of the processes under consideration. The need for a remote, isolated site was discussed.[64] At the same time, the DuPont Corporation, the large, Delaware-based chemical and engineering firm, was considering General Groves's urgent request that it become the prime industrial contractor for the Hanford project. In November, the company president Walter S. Carpenter reluctantly accepted the assignment but stated that, "for safety's sake . . . because of . . . unknown and unanticipated factors" in the plutonium production process, the plants that would manufacture this deadly substance and its toxic by-products should be located far from the populous East Coast or Midwest.[65]

DuPont also insisted on full indemnification by the U.S. government from "any damages . . . incurred in the course of the work."[66] The company worried about the "moral considerations" involved in a practice of "possibly . . . exposing employees to radiation hazards without revealing the full risks to them," due to wartime security restrictions. The company insisted that a special, $20-million claims fund, at the time a huge amount of money, be established by the government to benefit employees who might experience medical problems resulting from radiation. Groves agreed to provide such a fund because "no one had any reasonable idea what the hazards might be [and] . . . no one could predict the duration of the hazards."[67] According to Deputy MED Chief Kenneth Nichols, Groves assented to all of the DuPont conditions due to "concerns of safety."[68]

In his memoirs, Groves was very candid about the radiological dangers that were known to MED officials. "Reactor theory at this time did not overlook the possibility that once a chain reaction was started, it could . . . get out of control and increase . . . to the point where the reactor would explode . . . We knew, too, that in the separation of plutonium we might release into the atmosphere radioactive and other highly toxic fumes which would constitute a distinct hazard . . . I was more than a little uneasy myself about the possible dangers to the surrounding population."[69] Additionally, the War Department's first public report on the Manhattan Project confirmed the early knowledge of danger. According to this August 1945 document, the Hanford Site was selected partly for its "isolation . . . [because] at that time [late 1942], it was conceivable that conditions might arise under which a large pile might spread radioactive material over a large enough area to endanger neighboring centers of population."[70]

As soon as the decision was made in December 1942 to move the plutonium production facilities far from the densely populated eastern corridor, DuPont officials, Nichols, and Matthias met to develop site criteria. The place would have to be very large and remote, with a hazardous manufacturing area in a rectangle of at least twelve miles by sixteen miles. Laboratory facilities would have to be situated at least eight miles away from the nearest pile or separations plant, and there could be no existing towns of more than one thousand people closer than twenty miles to these structures. There could be no main highway or railway within ten miles of the facilities, and there would have to be space for an employees' village no less than ten miles "upwind" from them. The engineering requirements demanded abundant working water (estimated at twenty-five thousand gallons per minute) and a dependable electric power supply of at least one hundred thousand kilowatts.[71] In most of the crucial areas discussed, the open, arid Columbia Basin seemed ideal. When Matthias and the DuPont engineers found the place two weeks later, they also realized that the tract's composition of shale and sandstone underlain by hard basalt would make a strong foundation for the massive concrete piles. Additionally, they noted that the plentiful gravel could be used for road building and concrete.[72]

Previous History of Radiation Dangers

When Fritz Matthias reported to Leslie Groves that the "Columbia Valley" was the ideal location for the Hanford plant, and when the MED decided to seize the land and build the nation's plutonium manufacturing facilities on it, the MED was also resolving to generate there the largest amounts of radioactivity, and radioactive waste, produced thus far on earth.[73] Before, only minute amounts of plutonium had been produced under controlled laboratory conditions. Now, thousands of pounds of it would be fabricated. In 1950, Dr. Abel Wolman, a frequent AEC scientific consultant, put the massive manufacture of radioactive materials into perspective. He stated: "Less than ten years ago, approximately three pounds of radium were under human control. Now, radioactive substances are being produced and used to the equivalent of millions of pounds of radium."[74]

Before the atomic research sponsored by the MED in the early 1940s, the world had learned some painful lessons about radioactivity.[75] In 1895, the German physics professor Wilhelm C. Roentgen published his discovery of X rays, along with an explanation of how to produce them. Within a year, a medical X-ray center had been founded in nearly every American city, and there were many X-ray machines in private physicians' offices. Doses were measured by guesswork, and many quack practitioners also used the machines. Very quickly, users reported side effects such as hair loss and skin burns. By 1903, the medical community knew that X rays sometimes produced deeper side effects such as cancer, sterility, and "damage to the bloodforming organs." World War I greatly expanded the demand for medical X-ray services. Soon afterward, concern about the dangers of X rays infected the public as a series of news reports documented a disproportionate number of deaths among radiologists.[76]

The first steps in protection were taken by the professional organizations of X-ray workers. In 1921, the American Roentgen Ray Society formed a committee to study X-ray dangers. In the same year, the British X-Ray and Radium Protection Committee was established. Three years later, the German physicist Arthur Mutscheller made the first effort to calculate a "tolerance dose." Based on X-ray intensity at a given distance from an unshielded cathode tube, Mutscheller asserted that X-ray workers should not exceed one-hundredth of an "erythema dose" (which caused a severe reddening of the skin) every thirty days. The following year, the first International Congress of Radiology (ICR) convened in London and adopted Mutscheller's tolerance dose. In 1928, this group established the rad, measured by the ionization of air, as the international X-ray unit. As such, the rad was a measure of exposure from a source of ionizing radiation. It was not a measure of dose, or radiation absorbed, but this differentiation was ignored until the mid-1950s. At the 1928 convention, the ICR also established the International Committee on X-Ray and Radium Protection (later the International Commission on Radiation Protection—the ICRP). Shortly thereafter, the ICRP's American delegate, Lauriston Taylor, formed the (U.S.) National Committee on Radiation Protection and Measurements (NCRP). In 1931, the ICRP changed Mutscheller's tolerance dose from fractions of an erythema dose to roentgens, but the dose level remained the same. Since an erythema dose was calculated to be six hundred roentgens (r), the tolerance dose became six roentgens monthly or two-tenths (0.2) roentgen daily. Three years later, the American committee halved this dose to one-tenth (0.1) roentgen per day. This figure remained in effect throughout World War II. The ICRP continued to utilize the figure of two-tenths roentgen per day.[77] At Hanford, project health physicists accepted the American standard of one-tenth roentgen per day. According to a 1946 DuPont report, however, this figure was considered to be conservative, especially with regard to "hand exposure." Thus, exposures "were permitted to rise . . . without alteration of the work load."[78]

Damaging health effects from radium were recognized first in the mid-1920s. Radium, a naturally radioactive element that undergoes spontaneous atomic disintegration ("decay" or stabilization) into lead, was discovered by Marie and

Pierre Curie in Paris in 1898. Although Marie Curie, as well as her daughter, Irene, later developed cataracts and died of leukemia, no connection was traced to the work with radium. Throughout the early twentieth century, radium was hailed as a miraculous, medical restorative. It was used widely in patented tonics as a cure for ailments including rheumatism, indigestion, hemorrhoids, high blood pressure, diabetes, baldness, and nervousness. It also was used to produce watch dials that glowed in the dark. The coming of World War I increased the demand for these luminous dials. Most of the watches were made by the U.S. Radium Corporation of Orange, New Jersey, and most of the dial painting was done by young women working in home "studios." They painted by hand and pointed the tips of their brushes by moistening the tips between their lips. At the end of the war, the company sought to sustain itself by switching to the manufacture of novelties such as luminous doorbells, light switches, and clocks. By the end of 1924, at least nine of the young women painters employed in this work were dead. The number may have been higher, since the symptoms of radium-induced cancer were not distinguished from many other illnesses. Autopsies performed on two of the dead women showed their bones to be highly radioactive. The lungs of painters still alive contained radon 222, arising from the decay of radium 226. Thus, public awareness of the hazards of radium increased greatly. In 1934, Robley Evans, an MIT researcher, began studies with rats to determine radium tolerance doses. When the coming of World War II again elevated the demand for luminous instruments, the National Bureau of Standards (NBS) pressed Evans for a tolerance figure. He settled on one-tenth microcurie (μCi) of residual radium burden. This figure was published in the NBS handbook of May 27, 1941, and it remained the accepted tolerance dose throughout World War II.[79]

MED Research Leads to New Science of Health Physics

When the Manhattan Engineer District was formed in 1942, it sought to expand the basic knowledge about the health effects of radiation. It also strove to develop methods of shielding workers and the public from the puzzling hazards.[80] The MED established a small medical and health section, which expanded greatly as the major atomic plant construction projects got under way in early 1943. Additionally, the MED, along with the University of Chicago, created a special division at its plutonium pilot plant (semiworks, known as the SMX) at the Clinton Engineer Works (now Oak Ridge) in Tennessee. This group specifically studied the health hazards posed by the plutonium production process. It developed monitoring instruments and trained doctors and "health physicists" to work at the huge Hanford facility. The new field of health physics researched the biomedical effects of ionizing radiation and devised methods of shielding and monitoring radiation workers.[81]

Radiation Studies Still Held Many Unknowns

The Met Lab scientists themselves were products of the prewar era. They expressed everything in terms of X-ray and radium "equivalents," because the world had had no experience with the array of fission products generated in an atomic reactor or in the chemical separations processes that refined and concentrated plutonium. Despite the intense research efforts of the MED and the Met Lab, a dizzying amount about the biomedical hazards and effects of radioactivity simply was not understood in the World War II era. The scientists realized this, as a 1946 DuPont report confirmed: "At the time the [Hanford] Project began, there were no established tolerance limits for certain of the hazards which would be encountered . . . Product hazards were not completely understood."[82] They had an overall, but not a specific, knowledge of danger. They had not even clearly categorized all of the various radionuclides that would be produced by the process at Hanford. MED scientists did not know how these isotopes would interact and compound nor how they would behave in soluble versus insoluble form. Scientists did not comprehend how the isotopes would concentrate in the food chain in plants and in the tissues of insects, river plankton and algae, fish, birds, and mammals. They did not know if, or to what extent, it mattered whether various radionuclides entered living organisms by inhalation, ingestion through food, or contact with the skin, nor what the excretion curves would be. They did not know the dilution factors of wind and river water, and they did not know the adsorption rates or capacity of the sandy earth at the Hanford Site.

The Delicate Balance

Manhattan Project officials, moving swiftly to seize the dusty, triangular tract in the Columbia Basin, weighed a delicate balance. Yes, there were far fewer people living in all of eastern Washington than in Knoxville, Tennessee, alone, and yes, Enrico Fermi had maintained control of the world's only self-sustaining atomic chain reaction achieved thus far. And, the scientists assembled at the Met Lab were brilliant—they were aware of, and working on, the problems of protecting people from the effects of radiation. They tried very hard within the confines of their limited knowledge. All of those affirmatives stood in the assets column of the hard decision. Yet, the hazards were very large while the knowledge base was small. And the Columbia Basin is deceptively complex.[83] In this fragile place, you do not slit and displace whole segments of the desert without causing the land to swirl up to punish and confound. You do not pump and dump huge volumes of liquids where only a few inches of water had entered or left in the past without causing the water table and the drainage patterns to shift. You do not bring thousands of people and immense tonnage in materials and equipment onto this stark and lovely desert without changing, perhaps forever, the delicate balances of life.

Building the Plants:
Nuts, Bolts, and Chaos

The wartime builders of these [atomic] plants worked without any precedent or pattern . . . Considerations of maximum yield or durability did not govern the planning for plants. Time was the governing requirement: The single over-riding necessity was to get pure uranium 235 and plutonium in a hurry. The builders knew that if these substances actually did release atomic energy in useful quantity, the concentrated efforts of scientists and technologists all over the world would probably be able to develop better processes and plants. Even if they succeeded, therefore, they believed that most of the giant structures they built were expendable. —U.S. Atomic Energy Commission, "Fifth Semiannual Report of the AEC," January 1949

Four Construction Booms

As soon as the Manhattan District of the Army Corps of Engineers arrived in force in the Columbia Basin in March 1943, a huge construction boom began. In just over two years, the MED built the massive Hanford plutonium produc-tion complex, as well as the new, government-owned village of Richland. After World War II ended in August 1945, atomic policy drifted. In 1946, the General Electric Company (GE) relieved the DuPont Corporation as the prime operat-ing contractor at Hanford. On January 1, 1947, the civilian Atomic Energy Commission (AEC) took over from the military Manhattan Engineer District (MED). The AEC simplified the name Hanford Engineer Works (HEW) to the

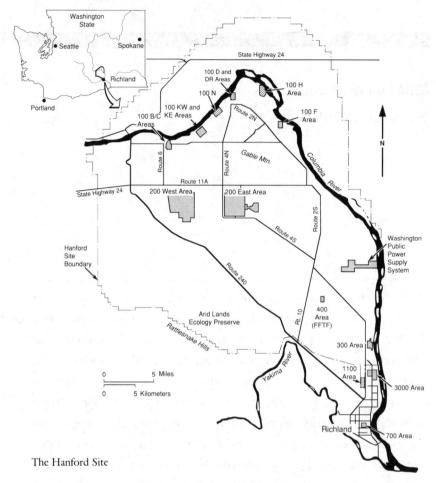

The Hanford Site

Map 100 areas: Reactor areas; 100 B/C Areas means the B reactor and C reactor areas.

200 areas: Chemical-processing and high-level waste-storage areas. 200-East and 20-West areas originally were almost identicak but now contain a variety of facilities in-volved in various ways with chemical processing and high-level waste storage.

300 Area: Research and development area; formerly also housed fuel-fabrication opera-tions.

400 Area: Built during the 1970s, this area houses the Fast Flux Test Facility (FFTF), a modern test reactor, and its supporting and ancillary facilities.

1100 and 3000 areas: Administrative offices and support services for the Hanford Site.

700 Area: Richland offices for the hanford Site. Richland was an official part of the Hanford Site from 1943 to 1958

Arid Lands Ecology Preserve: An experimental botanical and observational area operated by Pacific Northwest Laboratories.

Gable Mountain: A natural "mountain" or upthrust hill. Officially, it is part of the 200-N Area and houses vaults originally used to store plutonium nitrate.

Washington Public Power Supply System (WPPSS)): Commersial nuclear power utility that operates one nuclear reactor (WNP-1) on Han-ford Site land and is custodian for two other un-finished nuclear reactors (WNP-2 and WNP-4)

Hanford Works (HW). Still, the new agency needed time to clarify its priorities and objectives. The entire Columbia Basin, which had developed economic dependence on the Hanford project, felt the uncertainty.

Then, in August 1947, GE and the AEC announced plans for a gigantic expansion of the Hanford plutonium manufacturing capabilities. The new endeavors, the largest peacetime construction project in American history up to that time, cost more than had the erection of the entire wartime Hanford complex. This building boom, which took place in the Columbia Basin from 1947 to 1949, had no sooner ended than two additional growth surges occurred. Known as the first and second Korean War expansions, these latter swells took place in 1950–52 and 1953–55. In total, the Korean War years (1950–53) witnessed a doubling of the plutonium production facilities at Hanford.

During the 1949–55 era, the AEC also enlarged its capacities nationwide. New manufacturing, fuel fabrication, assembly testing, and electrical generation plants were sited at Savannah River, South Carolina; Paducah, Kentucky; Denver (Rocky Flats), Colorado; Idaho Falls (National Reactor Testing Station), Idaho; and Amarillo (Pantex), Texas. Additionally, American atomic bomb testing facilities were enlarged.[1] After the almost frantic construction years of 1947–55, the exigencies of the cold war accelerated weapons-production rates at Hanford and at the other American atomic defense plants. Power levels and output at the Hanford complex remained high through at least 1964.

Speed, Innovation, and Secrecy Characterize Hanford Works

At Hanford, the intense activity carried out for two decades beginning in 1943 was characterized by several features. Chief among these were speed and boldness, innovation, secrecy, and the strict yet oblique handling of radiological hazards in the workplace. The nearby public was not so well protected nor informed as were Hanford workers. The plants generated immense amounts of radioactive and chemical wastes, some of which spread into regional ecosystems.[2]

The Production Cycle

During World War II, three reactors (called *piles*) were built along the Columbia River at HEW. Strung along sixteen miles of the waterway's west bank, reactors B, D, and F composed the "100 Areas" at Hanford. Each reactor core consisted of a cube of graphite bars bored to receive approximately two thousand narrow, aluminum-clad, uranium fuel rods (*slugs*). Concrete and steel walls many feet thick surrounded the core as radiation shields.[3] River pump houses, each containing facilities large enough to supply water to a city of four hundred thousand people, provided cooling water to the reactors.[4] Water treatment plants mixed incoming river water with chlorine to inhibit algal growth, lime to regulate pH, sodium dichromate to inhibit corrosion and film buildup on the aluminum fuel jackets, and ferric or aluminum sulfate and activated silica as coagulants. In general however, the Columbia's water was pure enough that extensive treatment was not needed.[5] At the rear of each reactor sat large retention basins designed to hold effluent (cooling water exiting the piles) long enough for the short-lived radionuclides to "decay," or stabilize.[6]

After the uranium fuel slugs were irradiated, they were "pushed" out the rear of the HEW reactors and dropped into thickly shielded casks filled with twenty feet of water. Here and at special "cooling" areas about five miles away, the rods sat while their radioactivity partially decayed. Decay time was the prime determinant in how much radioiodine (I-131) gas was generated by their subsequent chemical dissolution.[7] After a variable cooling period, the irradiated slugs were transported by rail to Hanford's "200 Areas," two chemical separations complexes located near the center of the vast reservation. The huge separations buildings, officially termed *cell buildings* but dubbed *canyons* or *Queen Marys* by Hanford workers, were eight hundred feet long, sixty-five feet wide, and eighty feet high. Each contained a row of forty thickly shielded concrete cells. Each separations area, 200 East and 200 West, also contained plutonium bulk reduction or concentration buildings, as well as a network of underground tanks (*tank farms*) and test wells for the storage and monitoring of high-level atomic wastes. Sixty-four such tanks were built during World War II. Less concentrated liquid wastes were at first poured directly on low spots on the ground and later entered the ground through open-bottomed structures called *cribs*. At 200 West, one plutonium finishing building refined the final HEW product, a wet plutonium nitrate paste, for shipment to Los Alamos.[8]

The Hanford complex also contained a smaller "300 Area." It contained fuel and equipment fabrication shops, repair and maintenance buildings, and "process improvement" (research and development) structures. At various times it also housed administrative offices, construction personnel, military police units, libraries, and other facilities. This area was located only eight to ten miles north of Richland. Radiation and security risks were lower in the 300 Area than in the major production reactors and canyons. However, the fuel slug jacketing process conducted there did discharge wastes bearing uranium and heavy metals to the groundwater and the Columbia River.[9]

Radioactivity Complicates Design and Waste Products

The unique factor of radioactivity complicated the design and construction of all facilities at HEW. Remote operation and repair capabilities were essential, and extremely precise engineering tolerances were necessary. The bismuth phosphate, peroxide, nitric acid, and other chemicals used in the separations processes were very corrosive, so a high grade of Colombian (austenitic) stainless steel was utilized wherever possible. Because radioactivity could escape through the smallest leaks, nails had lead-covered heads, and lead sheeting was overlapped at the joints. All of the areas where radiation would be present were equipped with special ventilation systems that drew air inward in an attempt to prevent the spread of airborne radioactivity.[10]

In terms of sheer volume, Hanford's 200 Area wastes posed the greatest potential risks to the environment and to the nonworker population of the Columbia Basin. Wastes were mixed with a variety of compounds and acids used in the dissolving and extraction processes. These chemicals often were toxic and/or carcinogenic themselves, and they sometimes changed the adsorption (ion exchange) ratios of radionuclides in regional soil and substrata.[11] Nitric acid and sodium hydroxide were present in huge quantities in all of the chemical separations processes used over the years at the Hanford Site. Copious amounts of organic extractants such as bismuth phosphate, tributyl phosphate, methyl isobutyl ketone (known as hexone), and dibutyl butyl phosphonate were utilized, along with diluents that included saturated kerosene (NPH) and carbon tetrachloride. The latter chemical, along with acetone, 2-butanone, trichloroethylene, and, later, perchloroethylene and iii-trichloroethane also were used as degreasers in machinery repair and fabrication processes across the Hanford Site. The 100-Areas reactors produced effluent (spent cooling water) laden with over sixty radionuclides. Most significant among these were isotopes of phosphorus (P-32), zinc (Zn-65), chromium (Cr-51), arsenic (As-76), iron (Fe-59), and neptunium (Np-239). In the 300 Area, the chief hazards to workers were posed by contact with uranium metal and heavy metals such as chrome, lead, mercury, and others and by inhalation of uranium dust. To the region, the greatest 300-Area risk was the slow seepage of liquid wastes into the Columbia River through trenches located in porous areas near the shore.[12]

Unprecedented Scale
The scale of the original Hanford complex was unprecedented in its time. Army engineers and DuPont's TNX Division, a division created specifically for HEW construction, built over five hundred structures in addition to those for living requirements. Workers laid 158 miles of railroad and 386 miles of automobile roadway. Over 50 miles of electrical transmission lines and four step-down substations were constructed. Hundreds of miles of fencing were emplaced, and 40,000 tons of structural steel and 780,000 cubic yards of concrete were

utilized. During 1944 and early 1945, a peak of about fifty thousand construction workers were housed at a barracks and trailer camp at the old Hanford townsite. The wartime construction of Hanford cost about $230 million.[13] The 1947–49 expansion cost $350 million. The latter cost included the building of two new reactors (DR and H) and the research and design expenses for the REDOX chemical processing facility. The 1947–49 expansion also nearly doubled the size and services of Richland, and it caused tremendous growth in towns and cities throughout the Columbia Basin.[14] The first Korean War expansion cost just over $200 million. The REDOX plant was completed, and construction was begun on C reactor. The second Korean War expansion, part of an overall AEC program costing $4 billion, included the completion of 100-C, as well as jumbo reactors KE and KW and the PUREX (plutonium-uranium extraction) chemical separations facility.[15] Eighty-one additional high-level waste-storage tanks were built during the three postwar expansions, and four more were added in 1963–64. In 1949, the original Plutonium Finishing Plant (Z-Plant) was completed, enabling the Hanford Site to make a finished plutonium metal product. Various new plutonium finishing capabilities also were built at Z-Plant in the 200 West Area. In 1955, the RECUPLEX function was added to reclaim plutonium from various scraps and wastes in site operations. A larger and more complex plutonium reclamation facility, known as PRF, began operating at Z-Plant in 1964.

Postwar Production Lull

National policy drove actions at the Hanford Site in peacetime, just as it had in World War II. One of America's priorities during the early postwar period was to transfer control of atomic energy to an international agency. President Harry S. Truman proposed a phased, atomic disarmament plan to the United Nations (UN). However, the Soviet Union, racing to develop its own atomic bomb, vetoed the plan.[16] The United States then sought to formulate legislation to place its atomic facilities under civilian control. Delays and indecision characterized these efforts throughout 1946. The MED adopted essentially a caretaker position and instituted cost-savings measures that reduced the output of fissionable materials at Hanford and at America's other atomic production facility, the Clinton Engineer Works (now Oak Ridge) in Tennessee. At Hanford, B reactor was temporarily retired in December 1945, and power levels also were decreased at D and F reactors.[17] Throughout the MED, the scientific staff became discouraged by the lack of new research challenges, and many left. The number of contractor personnel at Hanford fell from ten thousand in September 1945 to about five thousand in December 1946.[18]

The confused state of American atomic policy and the stagnation of weapons production worried many government officials and members of the public. In 1946, William L. Borden, a young World War II veteran and law student, published an influential book on defense strategy in the atomic age. In *There Will Be No Time,* Borden emphasized that the appearance of "rockets and atomic bombs" had ended America's military security forever. Soon, he asserted, other nations would obtain atomic weapons. He argued that war preparedness, meaning a large stockpile of atomic weapons, was the only reasonable defense strategy. "The cost of entering an atomic war unprepared is unimaginable . . . since an atomic struggle may last only a few hours or days." He declared, "Our national policy should give precedence over all internal problems to defense." In the stark tones characteristic of that era, he concluded, "There is only one fundamental issue: whether or not the nation will survive."[19]

In 1946, the MED stepped into the leadership vacuum in U.S. atomic policy. Groves added an Advisory Committee on Research and Development, composed of prominent scientists. This group recommended a much expanded, fundamental research program. Strongly endorsing the committee's suggestions, the MED expanded its research budget for fiscal year 1947. Before the end of 1946, Groves had contracted for the construction of the nation's first three national atomic laboratories—Argonne in Illinois, Brookhaven in New York, and Oak Ridge in Tennessee.[20]

During this period, the American atomic weapons cache was very small. Although the exact number of weapons is uncertain, it was very likely less than ten operable plutonium bombs. The AEC's General Advisory Committee (GAC) of prominent scientists, meeting in early 1947, faced a dilemma. Exciting research ideas beckoned. However, the GAC decided that weapons had to be the top priority. Its first goal was to improve the plutonium production reactors at Hanford. According to two historians of the AEC, these decisions were made "from a sense of duty, not enthusiasm."[21] In March, the Joint Chiefs of Staff (JCS) of the American service branches agreed: "The present supply of atomic weapons . . . [is] not adequate to meet the security requirements of the United States." On April 2, President Truman was galvanized by AEC Chairman David Lilienthal's blunt briefing, a turning point in subsequent decisions to increase weapons production.[22]

The Cold War Begins

During the same period, international tension was rising sharply. The long, taut internecine struggle with the Soviet Union was commencing. On March 12, 1947, in response to crises in Greece and Turkey, the president "declared" the cold war: "It must be the policy of the United States . . . to support free peoples who are resisting attempted subjugation by armed minorities or outside pressure." Both houses of Congress approved the Truman Doctrine by large majorities and voted economic and military assistance to Greece. A program of greatly increased U.S. defense spending and the exercise of power in world affairs was begun.[23] In July, U.S. Policy Planning Staff Chief George F. Kennan stated that the United States should adopt a position of "long-term, patient, but firm and vigilant containment" of the USSR and of communism.[24] Later that month, Truman signed the National Security Act. It reorganized the military services and created the Central Intelligence Agency, the National Security Council (NSC), and the National Security Resources Board.[25]

Hanford's First Postwar Expansion

In the Columbia Basin, these new directions in national policy combined to push plutonium production to record levels. At Hanford, some of the wartime design and operational difficulties of the plants were yet to be solved. "Wigner's disease," a swelling of the graphite cores, plagued the reactors. Additionally, the bismuth phosphate chemical separations process wasted large amounts of scarce uranium, and new, domestic sources of high-grade uranium ore had yet to be discovered. Tough decisions had to be made. In March, AEC Production Chief Walter J. Williams directed GE, the site contractor, to concentrate its efforts on research and development for the new "REDOX" process and on plans for new production reactors.[26] Because the reactors would take at least two years to build and because it was unknown whether the existing units would last that long, even this rapid construction schedule might not result in increased plutonium output. With haste as the driving criterion, the AEC firmly told GE to build new reactors that would be similar in most respects to the three original units (B, D, and F). Innovative new reactor proposals would have to be saved for a calmer, future time.[27]

GE was disappointed. It wanted to explore the peaceful and commercial uses of atomic energy, particularly breeder reactor development.[28] Unlike DuPont, GE had never been a heavy construction firm. It simply had not expected that it would have to direct building booms such as those that took place in the Columbia Basin from 1947 to 1955. By 1949, construction cost overruns at Hanford were so excessive that the endeavor was investigated for "incredible mismanagement" by a subcommittee of the Joint Committee on Atomic Energy (JCAE). No fiscal mismanagement was found. However, according to AEC Chairman Lilienthal and others, the company was just "not equipped" to handle the huge expansions.[29] Slow progress in the spring and summer of 1947 worried

AEC Production Chief Williams. In the late summer, he brought a new AEC manager to the Columbia Basin.[30] Carleton Shugg, known as a "hard-hitting expediter," arrived at Hanford Works on Labor Day, 1947.[31] Two days later, he instituted mandatory overtime work for construction designers. In November, he cancelled the fifth "Nucleonics Day" banquet, held each year to commemorate Enrico Fermi's first self-sustained nuclear chain reaction of December 2, 1942. "This year," Shugg exhorted Hanford project employees, "consider our expansion program as our Nucleonics Day program and let everyone dig another shovel of dirt; accomplish one more task; or begin another detail of assignment."[32] The hectic pace of construction and plutonium production that had prevailed at Hanford during World War II was reinstituted.

The Cold War Worsens

The cold war escalated throughout the three postwar expansions at Hanford. In early 1948, a coup in Czechoslovakia brought that country under Soviet domination. The U.S. Congress reacted by funding the Marshall Plan, a huge aid program to rebuild western Europe. In May, the Senate overwhelmingly approved a resolution to "exercise the right of individual or collective self-defense . . . should any armed attack occur affecting . . . national security." This signaled the end of isolationism as a significant factor in American politics. Clearly, the United States was assuming the role of protector of the noncommunist world. In June, the Soviet Union responded by imposing a blockade on all supplies traveling to West Berlin. Truman ordered all provisions delivered by air until the siege ended, eleven months later. In November 1948, the president was reelected on a strong "containment" platform. Although Benton County (home of the Hanford Works) was normally Republican, it gave Truman an overwhelming, three-thousand vote margin in the election.[33] In April 1949, the North Atlantic Treaty Organization (NATO) pact, a mutual defense agreement among the United States and eleven other noncommunist nations, was ratified by Congress. The Soviet Union then formed a similar Warsaw Pact with the communist governments of eastern Europe, although this alliance was not formalized until 1955. In July 1949, Secretary of State Dean Acheson expressed confidence that the "position of the West [had] grown greatly in strength, and that the position of the Soviet Union . . . [had] changed from the offensive to the defensive."[34] The first major postwar expansion at the Hanford Site was winding down.

Hanford's Second Postwar Expansion

However, that September the American nation was shocked when the USSR tested its first atomic bomb. Most U.S. scientists had not anticipated this development so soon. On October 31, Senator Brien McMahan, the author of the Atomic Energy Act of 1946 and an influential member of the JCAE, met with AEC Chairman Lilienthal. According to Lilienthal, McMahan argued that nuclear war with the Soviet Union was inevitable and that the United States should "blow them off the face of the earth, quick," before the USSR did the same to the United States. McMahan added, "We haven't much time." Lilienthal noted: "This was not an impulsive action of one Senator alone . . . The solution of 'drop the A-bomb and have it over with' had not a little public verbal support."[35] Within eight months of the first Soviet atomic detonation, developments in Asia further added to the cold war tensions. In mid-1949, the communist forces of Mao Tse-tung drove the Nationalist army of Chiang Kai-shek off the Chinese mainland. Two months later, Mao and Stalin signed a mutual assistance pact. Mao's government labeled the United States "the Chinese people's implacable enemy."[36] On June 25, 1950, the communist North Korean Army crossed the 38th parallel, a line dividing Korea between U.S. and Russian occupation areas. Truman, seeing the invasion as a clear case of Soviet aggression carried out by a "puppet" government, convened the United Nations Security Council. Taking advantage of a Soviet boycott of that body, he obtained a resolution committing United Nations (UN) troops against North Korea. For the next thirty-seven months, the Korean War raged. Ostensibly it was fought by the UN, but American troops, in fact, constituted approximately 90 percent of the forces battling North Korea. Many people in the highest echelons of the U.S. government, including AEC Chairman Gordon Dean, believed that the Soviet Union might enter the war. Bloody and well-publicized battles such as those at Heartbreak Ridge and Bloody Ridge in 1951 contributed to official and public support for greater defense spending.[37]

Developments at home also increased cold war pressures and the consequent push for more arms production. Some of the most prominent spy cases in American history developed in 1950. Alger Hiss, a former State Department official, in January was convicted of perjury for his denial that he had passed classified documents to the USSR. One month later, Klaus Fuchs, a prominent German scientist who had worked at Los Alamos Laboratory, confessed to betraying atomic secrets to the Soviet Union. That summer, Fuchs's American associates, Harry Gold and Julius and Ethel Rosenberg, were arrested, as was David Greenglass. In February 1950, "McCarthyism," a four-year ordeal of suspicion and fear, commenced when Senator Joseph R. McCarthy of Wisconsin first stated that many key government agencies were "infested" with communists. Though McCarthy's charges were unfounded, they helped arouse a groundswell of distrust that contributed to the perceived need for more atomic weapons.[38]

U.S. atomic weapons production soared. In the autumn of 1949, in response to the initial Soviet atomic bomb test, Congress appropriated $1.5 billion to arm NATO. President Truman released budget reserves in order to advance atomic plant expansions. At that time, Hanford already employed about 70 percent of the construction workers at American atomic plants and approximately 30 percent of those in atomic production work. In February 1950, it received $67 million more than its original $175-million appropriation for the current fiscal year.[39] By October 10, 1949, less than three weeks after the Russian blast, the AEC had proposed an expanded research program for larger and more sophisticated weapons and specifically for the development of the hydrogen (known as the "Super") bomb. In January 1950, Truman decided to proceed with the weapon. Three months later the National Security Council (NSC) asserted that America should spend "upward of 50 percent of its gross national product" for security. NSC Resolution 68 recommended an increase in annual defense funding from $13 billion to $45 billion.[40]

The expansion of American atomic production facilities was particularly rapid from mid-1950 through 1955. A July 1950 supplementary appropriations expanded U.S. weapons facilities. The following January, an additional $1.6-billion defense appropriation was passed. During 1951, construction and equipment accounted for nearly three-fourths of the more than $2-billion AEC budget. The second half of the year, according to the commission, witnessed even more "intense activity" than the first. Existing production plants operated at "full capacity," and over 3 percent of total U.S. building expenditures went into new construction of atomic energy facilities. Nearly 2 percent of the entire American construction force was employed in AEC jobs. Still, in January 1952 the commission and the U.S. Department of Defense (DOD) issued a joint recommendation for "a further important expansion."[41]

Hanford's Third Postwar Expansion

The election of Dwight D. Eisenhower as president in late 1952 brought the third major postwar expansion at the Hanford Site. Eisenhower was alarmed at the huge growth in American defense spending. Under his leadership, the nation's conventional forces and equipment decreased, and defense spending dropped back to $40 billion by 1954. However, the stockpiles of atomic weapons and strategic bombers expanded greatly. This "new look" in armaments underlay his policy of "massive retaliation," announced in 1954. That year, a *New York Times* reporter who visited several AEC installations noted that "the sense of something big—big plants, big ideas, big future—exists."[42] The following year, the development of long-range ballistic missiles became an important goal in both the United States and the Soviet Union. In 1955, Nikita Khrushchev, a bellicose and aggressive cold warrior, emerged as the victor in the two-year Soviet power struggle that had followed the death of Joseph Stalin. Many of Khrushchev's militant statements, as well as the 1957 launching of *Sputnik,* the first artificial satellite to orbit the earth, contributed to policy decisions that further raised weapons production at Hanford.[43]

Speed, Shortcuts, and New Methods

Throughout the wartime construction period and the three expansions of 1947–55, speed and innovation defined the Hanford complex. Chief Army Engineer Franklin Matthias, the original site scout, stated, "Under normal conditions, the [original] Hanford project would have taken more then ten years to complete, even if considered an important national goal."[44] The MED deputy chief, Colonel Kenneth D. Nichols, succinctly stated, "In the Hanford project, time always was of the essence."[45] Walter O. Simon, DuPont's wartime production chief at HEW, has similar memories of wartime pressures shortening the time frame for major accomplishments. Likewise, the innovative designs of the Hanford plants, undertaken with such speed, have been noted by many of the principals. General Groves pointed out, "It is essential . . . to keep in mind the truly pioneering nature of the plutonium development . . . gigantic steps [were taken] . . . moving rapidly . . . from the idea stage to an operating plant."[46] Henry D. Smyth, a Princeton physicist close to the MED, acknowledged in 1945 that the "proposed extrapolations [from experiments to production plants] . . . were staggering. In peacetime no engineer or scientist in his right mind would consider making such a magnification in a single stage."[47]

The scale had to be huge. A crucial consideration was the minuscule amount of plutonium that could be expected from even full-scale operations. The Hanford prototype, the plutonium semiworks at Clinton, Tennessee, was designed to separate one-tenth gram of plutonium per ton of reactor output. Groves later stated that when MED scientists spoke of "quantity production" of plutonium from the Hanford complex, they "did not mean tons per hour, but rather a few thimblefuls per day."[48]

Throughout the war years, the problems of materials and manpower were the most pressing. Among the important materials needed were heavy-gauge railroad track, stainless steel, cement, barracks, copper, lumber, iron, electrical wire, graphite, and aluminum.[49] Sometimes, shortcuts had to be taken in the interests of speed and the ultimate objective of producing plutonium. In the spring of 1944, the Morrison-Knudson Company (M-K), the subcontractor hired to build the underground waste storage tanks, experienced welding difficulties. The tank bottoms, Matthias noted, were "in a rough and deformed condition . . . and progress in the tanks" was "not satisfactory." According to the site commander, the army, fearful that the tanks would not be ready when needed, "determined that X-ray inspection [of the welding] was too rigorous." He reported: "Arrangements have been made to change inspection standards . . . This will permit Morrison-Knudson to go ahead with construction and should reduce the re-welding." In August, M-K complained again that its tank work was "being inspected too rigorously by the X-Ray Department," and arrangements were altered.[50]

An acute shortage of stainless steel and other materials in the wartime economy also prompted the army, in June 1944, to authorize "adjustments" in the DuPont contract. It allowed earthenware instead of chemical stoneware piping for the drains in the 231 (plutonium finishing) building. Also permitted in the interest of speed was the substitution of mild steel for unavailable stainless steel in the water jacketed portions of tank equipment in two other buildings. In the high-level waste storage tank piping systems, according to DuPont, "it was necessary to change the specifications . . . from seamless to welded steel tubing because the delivery of seamless tubing was unfavorable." According to Matthias, such changes were made "to insure . . . maximum production" to meet "construction and erection requirements."[51] As one physicist at the site during World War II has recalled: "We were in such a hurry . . . to construct and operate Hanford in wartime . . . that the stainless steel [*sic*] storage tanks could not wait for stainless steel pipes and, instead, were connected with cast-iron pipes. Consequently, an electric battery was set up in the interface between the different metals, with the result that corrosion began and continued for some 33 years until leakage set in."[52]

The Rush to Produce

Production of the first batches of plutonium at Hanford was rushed. The chief shortcut taken in the initial nine months of operations was that of cooling the irradiated fuel slugs for very brief periods before dissolving them in the chemical separations facilities. The first batch of irradiated slugs was dissolved in the chemical separations area just five weeks after it was pushed from B reactor in late 1944. In late February, MED officials ordered a "schedule acceleration . . . with the idea of getting out product as quickly as practicable." Cooling times for irradiated slugs were shortened, and the three reactors operated at top capacity almost continuously. In one day in early March 1945, at B Reactor, ten tons of irradiated fuel rods were pushed and new slugs reloaded, so that operating power was resumed within twenty-four hours. Production sped ahead. About two weeks later, Matthias recounted, 13.3 tons of irradiated material was pushed from the same reactor, and recharging (reloading) operations at the facility began less than six hours later. On March 28, for the first time, all three Hanford reactors were functioning at 250 megawatts of power.[53]

A month later, Matthias reported that MED officials wanted a further "speed-up and increase in the program" of metal requirements. "The gain," he explained, would be "made in the reduction of process time cycle and in the time of storage before solution" (dissolving). In mid-May, he again spoke of the "reduction of cooling periods between the 100 and 200 Areas," and he noted plans to continue "the shortening of the cooling period," which would "permit processing of pushed material at an earlier date than scheduled." Uranium enrichment also was increased in late May.[54] Even though, according to Du-Pont, "there were . . . many uncertainties with regard to the operability of the separations process," a series of experiments in "increasing charge content" was carried out between March 29 and June 9, 1945. The amounts of plutonium-bearing liquids that were processed were increased, and the process time itself was decreased. No one knew "the maximum amount of product [plutonium] which might be processed in a single charge without danger from a chain reaction." Nevertheless, "appreciably greater" quantities were processed in single batches as the race to produce bomb material drove the hectic work schedules.[55]

In June and early July, production sped up for the Trinity bomb test. Another "accelerated" manufacturing push occurred in late July, to ready the material for the Nagasaki bomb. The exact length of cooling time during this period is unknown or is classified, but it was less than thirty days.[56] Concurrently, in the 200 Area "canyons," the large amounts of plutonium-bearing solutions being worked made the "transfer of a precise quantity of solution . . . difficult." According to DuPont officials, "It was impossible to obtain representative samples of storage solutions for the determination of plutonium content." Finally, an acid wash of process vessels showed "that large quantities of plutonium . . . could accumulate in the Canyon Building . . . Such quantities were considered dangerous from the standpoint of batch size control." The possibility of the buildup of critical mass (explosive) amounts of Pu-239 existed until "several manipulative changes were made during July and August."[57]

After the Japanese surrender, the production rate of the Hanford reactors was cut nearly in half. Still, however, the manufacture of plutonium went forward, and cooling times for the hot fuel rods were kept under fifty days.[58] Previously irradiated slugs awaited chemical dissolving, and the number of charges processed per month in Hanford's 200 Area actually increased through December 1945.[59] For the Columbia Basin, the unfortunate legacy of the rapid and intensive production rate of 1945 was the fact that a total of 340,000 curies of radioiodine were released into the atmosphere in that year alone. In 1946, with a somewhat slower manufacturing schedule but still inadequate cooling periods, 76,000 curies of I-131 were discharged from Hanford.[60]

Secrecy

Secrecy was another extremely important constant in the conduct of affairs at Hanford. In Washington, D.C., the original Hanford project was so strictly classified that even the Joint Chiefs of Staff, as an organization, was not told about it, and the State Department was not informed until shortly before the Yalta Conference in February 1945.[61] Senator Harry S. Truman, many other members of Congress, the American Federation of Labor (AFL), and anyone else who tried to investigate the Hanford endeavor were contacted by Secretary of War Henry Stimson and told not to proceed with their probes. Even after Truman became vice president, he was not informed about the secret undertaking until President Franklin D. Roosevelt's death.[62]

News coverage about Hanford was censored tightly, and everything was placed within the restricted clauses of the wartime Code of Fair Practices. Even the amounts of beer and food consumed by workers at the plant's construction camp were classified so that enemy agents could not guess the scope of the project by the size of the work force. Newspaper editors throughout the Northwest were contacted during 1943 and asked to "cooperate . . . by not asking questions . . . or speculating" in print about the huge and mysterious structures being erected in the south-central Washington desert. The editor of the *Pasco Herald* complained to his family that this was "the biggest story" of his life. He added, "And I can't write it." In mid-1944, the MED hired Lieutenant Milton Cydell, a former *Seattle Times* writer, and briefed him confidentially. He traveled the nation almost constantly, quashing press stories that mentioned the Hanford project.[63]

The real purposes of the Hanford endeavor also were hidden from most of the engineers and all of the construction and support personnel who worked there. Franklin Matthias's wife, Reva, recalled that, even among the few high-level officials who did understand the plant's mission, the "famous HEW [Hanford Engineer Works] line was 'I can't tell you' or 'don't say anything to anyone.'"[64] A DuPont production manager at Hanford remembered not being allowed to keep diaries or private notes. When DuPont left, all its files and working papers stayed at the Hanford Site. Recruiting firms scouring the country for the understaffed enterprise were directed by the MED to use advertisements that were vague as to location and job description. At the site, work was kept compartmentalized. According to Groves, construction drawings were "broken down to disclose as little as possible."[65] When prominent scientists came to Hanford to consult on problems of engineering and physics, they used code names. Enrico Fermi was Mr. Farmer, Arthur Compton was Mr. Comas, and Eugene Wigner was Mr. Winger.[66] Lack of knowledge about the work they were doing led some employees to quit. On the wall of the HEW placement office hung lyrics that expressed this frustration:

There is something about really knowing
The thing that you're trying to do . . .
And that is the reason I'm leaving . . .
The thing is I just want to know.[67]

Activities and goals at wartime Hanford also were kept secret from local and state selective service boards, courts, other government agencies, civic leaders, stockholders, and some officials of the subcontractor companies involved. Matthias negotiated a special agreement wherein the Washington State Draft Board would honor "any certifications [Hanford officials] made or letters" they wrote requesting deferments for men with certain skills. In total, 80 percent of the approximately fourteen thousand draft-deferment requests made for Hanford work during the war were granted.[68] Even on-site construction thefts were not prosecuted in court, in order to avoid entering purchase orders into the public record. Matthias noted that in late 1943, to maintain "Exclusion Authority and for security," the Hanford project got its own justice of the peace and jail.[69] Federal policymakers, according to Matthias, "would not accept concurrent jurisdiction with the State or County over the Hanford area." He emphasized to all other government agencies that the Hanford enterprise was "completely a War Department function and responsibility."[70]

The mystery surrounding the giant undertaking gave rise to a number of jocular or grim wartime rumors. Among these were stories that Hanford was a chemical or germ warfare facility, a prisoner-of-war camp, a nylon and experimental synthetics plant, a conventional munitions factory, a series of mines where valuable ores had been discovered, a bombing range, or a make-work refuge for privileged draft evaders. Some humorous rumors dubbed the project a "summer house" for President and Mrs. Roosevelt or a factory making fifth-term reelection buttons for Roosevelt. One persistent story of human experimentation circulated. It theorized that people were being killed and their bodies brought out to Washington under the ruse that Indian graves were being moved.[71]

As soon as the first atomic bomb was dropped on Hiroshima, Japan, on August 6, 1945, reporters rushed to Richland. "Richland is News Center of World: Army Lifts Curtain on Village Plant," enthused the *Richland Villager,* the community newspaper of the government town. Yet, the media learned very little except the basic fact that Hanford existed to produce the material for atomic weapons. Postwar, the policy of strict secrecy hardly changed. Reporters were given a limited tour of the Hanford Site, and information was presented on the general functions of the plant's three basic sectors (100, 200, and 300 areas). However, General Groves instructed, "Discussion of process, production or the employment of the Atomic Bomb should be limited."[72] On August 9, President Truman stated that "information on weapon design and production" would not be released to the rest of the world until adequate means of control had been formulated.[73]

Anticipating the insatiable public curiosity that atomic weaponry would generate, General Groves had commissioned a special wartime report, entitled *Atomic Energy for Military Purposes*. It was released to the public on August 12, 1945, just three days after the Nagasaki bomb was dropped. The document, written by the Princeton physics professor Henry D. Smyth, became known as "The Smyth Report." Public inquisitiveness about atomic energy was indeed voracious; the Smyth Report's first edition sold out immediately, and it was reprinted and excerpted in thousands of newspapers and periodicals throughout the nation. Late in 1945, it was published as a book. Still, the work did not reveal much about Hanford's secrets. "Nothing in this report discloses necessary military secrets as to the manufacture or production of the weapon. It does provide a summary of generally known scientific facts and gives an account of the history of the [bomb development] work."[74] As one historian of the MED has affirmed, project leaders, in generating the Smyth Report, formulated a deliberate policy that "the release of some selected information would make it easier to maintain the secrecy of the highly classified . . . [protected] aspects of the project."[75]

At postwar Hanford, secrecy continued to reign. At the war's end, Matthias privately wondered whether the suspension of the War Powers Act would "critically handicap any of our [secret] activities." His worries were soon resolved. Plant employees signed statements that obliged them not to discuss, even with their families, most aspects of what they saw, heard, and did at the site. They carried cards that specified the subjects about which they were entitled to have information. To be safe, they hardly spoke of the huge complex at all. Richland became a town where people simply never talked about their work.[76] A San Francisco reporter who visited the government city in September 1945 observed, "There is no shop talk in Richland."[77] Four months later, the *Richland Villager* affirmed: "Regarding security, it's the status quo ante . . . The H.E.W. will remain one of the most closely guarded spots in the country."[78] On plant walls and gates, in the company newsletters, and in stores in Richland, posters and cartoons featuring "Security Jane" were prominent. She and "Corporal Paddy" continually warned employees and residents: "Don't Be Caught With Your Mouth Open," "Don't Talk Shop," and "For Security 'Freeze Up' This Winter."[79] Agents of the Federal Bureau of Investigation (FBI) periodically questioned Richlanders about their neighbors, searching for weaknesses, such as alcoholism or infidelity, that might make Hanford workers targets for blackmail.[80]

When it came time for the AEC to announce Hanford's huge expansion in the summer of 1947, secrecy considerations maintained a high priority. Commission Chairman Lilienthal recounted that "as simple and limited a statement as possible" was issued about the expansion.[81] The terse, closed character of news reports about Hanford was maintained. At that time, GE's Hanford manager, David H. Lauder, reminded workers and residents, "Security regulations are as rigid at Hanford today as at any time during the war." He urged them not to spread rumors about the expansion or increased production.[82] This lid of secrecy stood as "standard operating procedure" at the site for decades to come.

Radiation Information and Policies
Information policies about radiation were formulated in the summer of 1944. At that time, the small group of men who would have primary responsibility for health and safety at the Hanford complex arrived after five months of intensive training at Clinton, Tennessee. They were headed by the English radiologist Herbert M. Parker and his senior assistant, the X-ray defraction scientist Carl C. Gamertsfelder. Approximately fifteen others composed the initial health physics and instrumentation teams. These groups subsequently consolidated and grew into Hanford's large Health Instruments (H.I.) Section.[83] Parker has been described by longtime associates as a stiff and correct man who was aloof but not necessarily cold. Employees tended to be on their toes when around him.

Parker and his staff worked closely with Dr. William D. Norwood, DuPont's medical chief at Hanford, and with the Public Health Department head Dr. Ralph Sachs, a physician and public health graduate of the University of Michigan. These leaders also consulted frequently with some of the leading figures of the era in radiation protection, including Drs. Karl Z. Morgan and Simon Cantril of the Clinton Laboratories, and Drs. Giaochinni Failla and

Robert F. Stone of the Met Lab at the University of Chicago. Hanford's health physicists were charged with defining and measuring the unique and puzzling radiological hazards, establishing procedures to make the jobs in plutonium production safe for workers, and developing and calibrating instrumentation. Later, they expanded into monitoring the workers themselves and surveying the Hanford Site and surrounding environs for radioactive contamination.[84]

Soon after their arrival at the Hanford site, Parker, Gamertsfelder, and Norwood met with other DuPont officials, as well as with Colonel Matthias and Dr. Stone, to define radiation protection policies. The question of how much information about radioactivity would be given to atomic workers was an important one. Strict MED security regulations prevented disclosure even of the existence of radioactivity to most employees. Yet precautionary rules and procedures had to be instituted in the workplace to guard against a danger that employees could not see, smell, taste, or feel. Hanford's policies were strict in terms of regulations governing worker exposure, but they leaned heavily in the direction of secrecy. Information was given only on a "need to know" basis. Physicians, industrial nurses, and medical technicians received "certain hazard disclosures . . . in order to work intelligently."[85] People who worked within the 100 and 200 Areas buildings were "told in general what the hazards" were. At the time, Matthias noted: "People working close to these areas will be told that there is a hazard and people who normally work away from . . . [these areas] will not be given any specific warning. This information will be given them [100 and 200 Area employees] as part of the classified information connected with the project and they will be specifically prohibited from discussing it even with their families."[86] Parker met with his staff and emphasized strict secrecy. The words *plutonium* and *uranium* were forbidden. Uranium was "base metal," and plutonium was "product." Other code words were also used.

Overall secrecy about radiological health was maintained by the MED through an agreement with the U.S. Office of the Surgeon General (OSG). The OSG provided support and personnel to the Manhattan Project. However, the MED retained in its own files all reports that might reveal the "nature or scope" of its endeavor, and responsibility for project health matters was delegated to the district engineer, General Groves.[87] In early 1944, the MED health chief, Dr. Stafford Warren, met with Washington's director of public health. They arranged that all public health records from Hanford would be sent only to Dr. Arthur M. Ringle, the state's public health officer in Walla Walla. As Colonel Matthias explained this agreement, "By this method we could retain control over the information submitted to and on file with the State."[88]

The wartime policies of secrecy and of information given only on a "need to

50

know" basis had their roots not only in fears of enemy sabotage. Matthias expressed the widespread MED fear that workers would become concerned about the hazards of radioactivity, "This might be disastrous to the project as it might cause a large number of people to leave." In August 1944, DuPont wanted to hold practice evacuations at some Hanford facilities. Matthias worried, "This might . . . be sufficiently upsetting so that we could expect a serious effect both on security and manpower facilities to finish the job." He contacted Groves and Nichols to try to "stop" the drills. Eventually, at DuPont's insistence, practice evacuations were held in the plant areas. However, for the Hanford construction camp, only a compromise "headquarters test" was conducted.[89]

Radiation Safeguards

Procedures developed at the Hanford Site for safeguarding workers were rigid and thorough. Thick concrete and lead shielding, distance, and Special Work Permits (SWPs) for intervals as short as thirty seconds per worker were the primary protective features instituted. Periscopes, mirrors, and remote handling devices controlled much of the equipment monitoring and operations. Victoreen integrons, ionization chambers and survey meters, gas sampling vessels, air-monitoring filters with suction devices, mica window Geiger-Müller (G.M.) tubes, and Lauritsen electroscopes measured structures, liquid and gaseous wastes, tools, and clothing. Many of these unfamiliar and unnerving devices were given familiar and even silly names by H.I. staff members and plant workers. Among these designations were the Betty Snoop, Cutie Pie, Zeus, Zeuto, Juno, Queenie, Big Sucker, Little Sucker, Hot Dog Grill, Walkie-Talkie, and Horizontal Pig. Such names seemed to render the gadgets commonplace instead of weird and frightening. Film badges and two small, thin ionization chambers (known as *pencils*) were worn by every employee on every shift. The pencils were read once a day, and the film badges once a week. Finger rings and packets were used in SWP jobs where hand exposure could be high. Alpha monitors, known as *poppies,* also were utilized in personnel monitoring. Urine samples, a joking matter in Richland, were collected at the plant and from the home doorsteps of HW employees. Hanford scientists believed that checks of the rate of excretion of certain radioisotopes, particularly plutonium, could be an index of exposure.[90] Dr. Norwood later confirmed that the urine tests at Hanford were "looking for plutonium. Plutonium did show up, but well below the permissible limits . . . The amount allowed, total whole body, was .04 microcuries."[91]

The magnitude of the surveying job at Hanford can be grasped when it is realized that between January and August 1945 alone, over one million pencils had been measured, over 170,000 film badges had been processed, 52,000 instrument checks and 157,000 hand checks had been made, and over 31,000 surveys of operating conditions had been performed in only the 200 Area.[92] By mid-1950, Hanford's H.I. Section had expanded into a division that employed over 100 professional people and 153 technicians and support personnel. It was larger than the monitoring staff at any other American atomic installation, and it accounted for approximately 4 percent of the Hanford plant's total operating budget.[93]

In many buildings, especially the Plutonium Isolation facility (231 Building), health precautions had to be extreme. In this structure, as well as in some others, smoking, eating, and drinking coffee were prohibited except in certain designated lunchrooms. Clothing had to be changed and hands checked before entering or leaving the work areas. Because of the hazards of absorbing plutonium through open cuts, *every* nick or skin abrasion had to be reported to First Aid. No one with even the smallest hand scratch was permitted to work.[94]

Hanford employees from the 1940s have recalled that although workers respected both radiation and the rules, they often did not understand the oblique plant procedures. Most had absolutely no experience with, nor knowledge of, occupational radiation hazards.[95] But there was a general respect for radiation, and for the most part, safety rules were obeyed. Employees wore radiation gear and carried monitors, believing that H.I. Division regulations would help protect them.

However, some workers at Hanford voiced mixed feelings. A laboratory worker, Yvette Berry, claimed that many ordinary workers wondered "what-how-when—all very frustrating when one knew so little." She stated that when "hot spots" or "spills" occurred, "rumors flew" about the toxicity and health hazards associated with working at Hanford. However, she recounted, "Our confidence grew as we found ourselves continuing in a state of good health." She explained her feelings about daily life at the Hanford plant: "Rules were simply stated but rigidly enforced . . . we all washed our hands so many times a day I thought I was Lady Macbeth . . . At the slightest break in the skin we were questioned about where and how it happened . . . Wash it, scrub it, paint it, check it, and sometimes dispose of it. I never cleaned so much stuff that already looked clean . . . Contamination was the big word . . . when we couldn't get our hand count down, we dunked them in a solution of 'goop' . . . It was supposed to take off a very thin layer of skin. Sometimes it took three or four dunkings."[96]

In fact, it was official MED policy to require the "immediate high amputation" of any human limb with a cut contaminated by plutonium.[97] At Hanford, special hazards bulletins covered "Procedures for Injuries in a Product Work Zone." Continuous cold-water washings and the application of tight tourniquets were required for all injuries sustained in a plutonium work area. If wound contamination was found, removal to Kadlec Hospital in Richland was required.[98]

Isolation and Challenges

The extreme secrecy, the rigid rules and unfamiliar procedures, and the remoteness of the Columbia Basin itself combined to produce a chronic shortage of labor at wartime Hanford. Construction employee turnover varied between 8 and 21 percent at any given point over the life of the project. Workers stated their reasons for leaving as isolation, lack of recreation, and the fierce dust storms of the arid tract. The work was hard, rushed, and remote. Yet, due to secrecy, the commendations received by soldiers and workers at other war production plants could not be issued.[99] "Highlights of Hanford," a small recruiting booklet used during World War II, termed the region "a little on the rugged side." Still, most workers were not prepared for the full effect of the Columbia Basin. A Denver ordnance employee who arrived at Hanford on a hot, windy day recalled his heartsick feeling: "It was so darned bleak. If I'd had the price of a ticket I wouldn't have stayed."[100]

Project managers sought to overcome the feelings of loneliness and privation by building a huge recreation hall in June 1944. Then they brought in popular swing bands, such as the famed Kay Kyser, as well as smaller bands and circuses, to entertain the construction workers. Hanford also received official designation as an "isolated area," allowing generous food rations and extra "hardship gasoline."[101] In early 1944, in another effort to boost morale, Matthias led a campaign to encourage Hanford workers to contribute a day's wages and buy a bomber for the air force. Employees responded enthusiastically. A B-17 named *Day's Pay,* which later served with the Eighth Air Force in England, was purchased.[102]

The stinging windstorms of the Columbia Basin, however, presented problems that administrators could not solve. As the huge construction project tore up the sagebrush and anchoring grasses, the sandy soil rose up in retribution. The dust storms became ferocious. According to a local newspaper: "The land laid bare by the mass excavation swirled to the skies in dust storms to end all dust storms. Busses put on lights and stopped by the side of the road."[103] Some war workers recalled running from one telephone pole to another, seeking "cover from the dirt-laden winds." Another recounted: "Your face would get black in the storms, and you felt grit in the food, on your hands and clothes, and everywhere. Everything felt like real fine sandpaper." The endemic storms became known as "termination winds," and the dust itself as "termination powder," because so many employees quit every time a big blow occurred.[104] Even on quiet days, many have recalled, there was still a fine dust in the air.

To some employees, however, the secrecy and obvious urgency of the wartime work at Hanford provided a challenge sufficient to overcome the isolation, the wind, the dust, and the drudgery. Some, like other newcomers before them, even came to love the arid Columbia Basin. The fact that the manufacturing plant had the highest priority for all resources limited community services. The supply never caught up with demand during the war period. The challenge of living without many services or conveniences inspired some workers and kept them in remote, windy Richland. When it was time to leave in late 1945, the wife of a prominent production manager voiced regrets: "We hate to leave our front room view of Rattlesnake Mountain, the Columbia River at our back door, the wonderful fruit and vegetables."[105]

Ironies: Busy but Quiet

The years 1943–55 witnessed four building booms at the Hanford atomic complex. The initial wartime construction phase was followed by three giant expansions between 1947 and 1955. The land was cleared, leveled, pumped, and blasted away at a frenzied pace. At the same time, plutonium production operations accelerated amid the building. By early 1956, eight reactors and five massive separations facilities stood on the eastern Washington site. Through 1963, the exigencies of the cold war competitions with the Soviet Union pushed plutonium manufacturing even higher. For two decades, then, the Hanford plants hastened through their work. The facilities that the MED had conceived as only temporary and expedient grew and became entrenched.

Hanford was busy and noisy and industrious, and yet, to the outside world, it was silent. Policies of strict secrecy prevailed throughout the period, just as they had during wartime. Thousands of workers streamed into and out of the plant every day, and yet many did not know much about their work, except that it was important to follow some rigid and basic procedures. They were proud of their work in national defense and excited about the enormous buzz of activity in their region. Those who chose to come and stay in the Columbia Basin, like many newcomers before them, often fell in love with the windy, isolated place. They did not question the secrecy, and they came to trust that the complicated operations of the plant would not hurt them. As the years went on, more and more people filled the neighborhood.

"Tell 'Em You're from Richland":
Regional Growth in the Columbia Basin

The entire [Tri-Cities] area is booming . . . One of the proudest boasts of Hanford management is the complete success of safeguards against radiation injuries. The health instrument divisions of Hanford Works provide detection instruments . . . recommend maximum exposure levels, and conduct research on the effect of radiation on living tissue.—Industry Analysis Section, Seattle First National Bank, "Pacific Northwest Industries: The Hanford Works," December 1948

Columbia Basin Population Booms

The construction booms that occurred as the Hanford atomic complex was built and then expanded between 1943 and 1955 brought thousands of new people to the Columbia Basin. When World War II ended, Richland, the city restricted by federal edict to the operating personnel of the Hanford Engineer Works, bustled with 13,000 people. The 1947–49 expansion at the plant increased this population to 23,000, and the two subsequent expansions stabilized the figure at about 25,000. The decision by the Atomic Energy Commission to release Richland from government control sent much of the population growth in the 1950s to Pasco and Kennewick, the other two large cities in the immediate region. By 1949, the Tri-Cities area was home to about 65,000 people. At that time, the Hanford plants employed more than one-fourth of all persons engaged in operating U.S. atomic facilities and two-thirds of all construction personnel engaged in atomic work.[1] At the same time, the building of McNary Dam at Umatilla Rapids, approximately thirty miles downstream from Pasco along the Columbia River, and constant expansions to the generating capacity of the Grand Coulee Dam to the north also swelled the work force in the Tri-Cities vicinity. Pasco's population jumped from 3,900 in 1942 to 10,228 in 1950 and to 15,300 in 1955. During the same years, Kennewick's figures swelled from 1,918 to 10,100 to 12,900 people. The trailer village of North Richland, an enclave for construction workers and their families located about five miles north of Richland, was established early in the 1947–49 expansion. It was thrown together hastily with barracks and trailers brought from the old Hanford construction camp and from the Pasco Naval Air Station. In late 1947, Richland's weekly newspaper, the *Richland Villager,* described North Richland as the scene of the "most intense construction activity and population growth of the entire Hanford Works expansion program."[2] Its population peaked in 1948 at about 25,000 people, including about 12,000 actual workers. Its subsequent high population was approximately 7,500 workers, plus their families, in mid-1954.[3] The Columbia Basin, chosen as the site of the Hanford project partly because it was sparsely inhabited, had been transformed by that very endeavor into the third most populous region in Washington State.

After the three massive expansions of 1947–55 were completed at Hanford, new projects continued to come to the area. The Columbia Basin Irrigation Project (CBP) began to water the dry counties north and east of the Hanford Site in the mid-1950s. Whole new towns were platted and established. In 1958, funds were released to begin construction of the unique N reactor at Hanford. Dedicated in 1963, this plant produced plutonium at the same time that it generated steam heat for electric power. In the early 1960s, Priest Rapids and Wanapum dams were constructed along the Columbia River just upstream from the Hanford Site. Ice Harbor, Lower Monumental, and Little Goose dams also were erected within sixty-five miles upstream from Pasco along the Snake River. The region, it seemed, just could not catch up with itself. Everywhere, new schools, hospitals, roads, houses, businesses, and other facilities were erected. By 1963, the population of Benton and Franklin counties combined stood at just over 100,000. Within fifty miles of the Hanford Site, there were about 250,000 people.[4]

Hanford's Impact on Columbia Basin Cities, Counties, Native Americans, and Farms

The major postwar expansions at Hanford overcrowded schools and housing in Pasco, Kennewick, and other area towns. The MED and the AEC were slow to help. Wartime MED officials stated their position: "[We] are not responsible for taking care of the war conditions in areas not directly on government property."[5] In the autumn of 1947, AEC-Hanford Manager Carleton Shugg admitted to Pasco and Kennewick officials that it was "plain" that the Hanford activity was the cause of the bulging conditions. However, he maintained, the commission could "not spend money" for housing except in government-owned Richland and North Richland. In late 1947, the *Portland Oregonian* editorialized: "The Atomic Energy Commission has revived operations at . . . Hanford . . . on a 'wartime scale.' But the government had made no provision for the tremendous overflow of population in Pasco and Kennewick, where housing and sanitation conditions have become the worst in the nation . . . Pasco and Kennewick [are] tak[ing] the rap" for the expansion program.[6] In early 1948, the AEC agreed to disburse temporary funds to the schools of six communities (in addition to Richland and North Richland) located near the Hanford Site. Pasco, Kennewick, Benton City, Prosser, Grandview, and Sunnyside all received money for extra teachers, temporary halls and huts to be used as classrooms, and concomitant services. Request for AEC funds to build larger, permanent school buildings continued to be rejected, as did pleas by surrounding towns for improvements to their sewage systems and other municipal services.[7] In late 1949, the AEC finally agreed that its activities in the Columbia Basin were "of a permanent character." It pledged financial aid, to begin in 1951, for the construction of new school facilities in seven districts surrounding Hanford and Richland.[8]

The wartime Hanford enterprise created many other dislocations in the tax base, wage scales, and land development plans in the Columbia Basin. Counties, especially Benton (home to the Hanford Site), suffered from increased expenses with a decreased tax base caused by federal acquisition of much of the land.[9] Additionally, the Hanford wage scale was higher than that which area farms and businesses were accustomed to paying. Still, with the chronic manpower shortages at Hanford, Matthias saw "no possible action that could be taken to alleviate this condition."[10]

Traditional Indian food and worship practices on the land and waters from Priest Rapids to Pasco were disrupted by the Hanford project. An agreement reached between Matthias and the Wanapum tribe in 1944 limited fishing near White Bluffs to daylight only. After plutonium production began in late 1944, Indian access to the White Bluffs area was prohibited for safety reasons. The MED agreed not to interfere with Yakima fishermen working at the Yakima River's horn on the southern boundary of the Hanford reserve. However, the Yakima were precluded from fishing along the Columbia within the project boundaries.[11]

The Hanford enterprise also disrupted agricultural patterns and plans in the

58

Columbia Basin. Immediately, the massive project aggravated the already severe shortage of farm labor in the district.[12] The regionally famous fruit orchards at the towns of Hanford, White Bluffs, and Richland presented a special problem. During the 1943 growing season they were tended by a DuPont agriculture specialist. Then a cost-saving decision was made to allow Prison Industries, a section of the McNeil Island Prison near Tacoma, to operate and harvest the orchards. However, beginning in December 1944, DuPont prohibited these activities because of radiological hazards associated with the start-up of plutonium production. The orchards on the atomic site were abandoned.[13] Perhaps the most significant of Hanford's effects on agricultural land use in the region, however, concerned the Columbia Basin Irrigation Project. Portions of the land for this vast federal reclamation undertaking, which had been planned for decades, were pulled out of the design when HEW was sited. The Hanford project also upset plans for various roads designed to connect sections of the CBP.[14]

Richland Population Unique

Among the many people who came to the Columbia Basin in the two decades beginning in 1943, Richlanders most defined the "new image" of the region. Richland residents on the whole were well educated, prosperous, healthy, and relatively young. They had the highest birth rate in the nation and displayed an optimistic, active, and outgoing community spirit. They came to symbolize the huge atomic complex itself. Richlanders were proud of their role in national defense and believed that their work contributed to world peace. Unless it annoyed them, their environment often did not compel much of their attention. Still, in their own casual way, many residents of the government town developed a good fit with the Columbia Basin. Many came to feel comfortable and connected to the arid, windy, seemingly inhospitable place.

The first house in Richland was occupied in late July 1943. MED construction efforts were so efficient that, by the end of World War II, there was a surplus of housing in Richland.[15] The 1947–49 expansion immediately filled these, and by early 1948, 1,800 employees waited for homes. GE, the prime operating contractor, began work on 1,000 new, permanent homes and 250 prefabricated dwellings. Officials of GE and the AEC pleaded with residents to rent out extra bedrooms and living space in the bulging town.[16]

Pride in the atom became evident in Richland in August 1945, as soon as residents learned of the role of their city in producing the world's first atomic weapons. The Japanese surrender of August 14 produced rejoicing in Richland. The village newspaper enthused: "PEACE! OUR BOMB CLINCHED IT."

Richland's victory celebrations were covered in newspapers and on radio programs throughout the nation. The little city basked in the praise of the entire country. National reporters who came to cover the jubilation noted the "combination of confidence, efficiency, warmth and contentment" in the government town.[17] Matthias expressed the local feelings succinctly: "We of the Hanford Engineer Works are proud of our job. We are proud of our community." After the dramatic victory, General Groves appeared in Richland and lauded the Hanford employees. He presented the army-navy "E" award, the highest civilian production commendation, to all of them. Many other high-ranking military officers came to offer praise and citations. The War Department authorized "A-Bomb pins," bearing mushroom clouds, for all Manhattan District employees. Matthias received the Distinguished Service Medal, and the army's on-site production chief, Major J. F. Sally, was given the Legion of Merit Award. At the close of the year, the Associated Press, *Time* magazine, and the *Portland Oregonian* named the "story of Richland and the making of the atomic bomb" the most newsworthy story of 1945. They said it was even more important than the German and Japanese surrenders. *Time* paid tribute to all Hanford workers: "To each and every man and woman who made the slightest contribution to the project in Richland, a SALUTE."[18] "The Atom-Bustin' Village of the West," Richland dubbed itself in 1947. The town began a "Tell 'Em You're from Richland" campaign and featured buttons emblazoned with a swirling atom and a mushroom cloud. The next year, it named its annual community celebration "Atomic Frontier Days." GE's Hanford manager christened Richland "Atom Town, U.S.A."[19]

Reaction to Atomic Power a Mixture of Pride and Fear

However, despite pride in the development of atomic bombs, a pervasive sense of unease about the terrible power of these weapons quickly became evident.[20] In its first postwar issue, *Time* asserted that the terrors associated with the new weapon made "the knowledge of victory . . . as charged with sorrow and doubt as with joy and gratitude." Within days of the war's finish, news media throughout the United States spoke openly of a "Great Fear" in America. Theologians discussed "the 'strange disquiet' and the 'very great apprehension' the atomic bomb had left in its wake."[21] The key bomb development physicist, J. Robert Oppenheimer, felt the anxiety too. Shortly after the bombs were dropped, he wrote, "This undertaking has not been without its misgivings . . . the future . . . is yet only a stone's throw from despair."[22] In Richland, Reva Matthias expressed some of the pride, mixed with ambivalence, felt by many. In 1945, she stated, "God, wearying of this long and tortuous war, had finally reluctantly given us the terrible weapon with which to end it."[23]

The Peaceful Atom

To help quiet the anxieties and fears raised by the emergence of atomic bombs, many ordinary Americans and national leaders quickly focused their hopes on the "peaceful atom." The first AEC chairman, David Lilienthal, later explained: "Somehow or other the discovery that had produced so terrible a weapon simply *had* to have an important peaceful use—[People] resolved that we *must* prove that the Atom has a nonmilitary use of very great importance."[24] In his first major speech as AEC chairman, Lilienthal focused on the "human benefit" of atomic energy. "This intense radiation is a means whereby we can expand our knowledge of nature, push back the frontiers of darkness in a hundred fields—in medicine . . . in industry, in nutrition, in agriculture. It uncovers new concepts of the nature of the universe, brings new skills, new professions, new ideas into being."[25]

Certainly, Hanford's early postwar leaders stressed the concept of the peaceful atom. Shortly after the war's end, Matthias stated, "Atomic energy makes it possible for us to face the future of industrial development without fear of diminishing natural resources now used for energy." The *Richland Villager* editorialized: "Most of [the Hanford project workers] would like to have a hand in the exciting adventure of discovering the 'why and how' of atomic energy and its application to industrial use. They know that atomic energy will change the world of tomorrow and they want to help in that, too."[26]

Richland residents, aware of their village's highly visible, symbolic status, enthusiastically reached out for peace. Colonel Frederick Clarke, the second army commander at Hanford, recalled later: "I think the people felt very proud of their accomplishment in . . . end[ing] the war—[Richlanders] were awe-struck by the atom's power and wondered how nuclear energy could be used for peace."[27] In mid-1946, the village sponsored its own "Win-the-Peace" movement. In symposia, speeches, and other public forums, Richlanders addressed the question: "What are we, the atomic bomb workers who helped win the war, now doing in an effort to help win the peace?" In response, the wife of a DuPont production manager expressed her "Atomic Philosophy As Understood by a Villager." She asked: "Are our hearts as big as our brains? Are we capable of accepting the responsibility we have thrust upon ourselves? . . . Our problem is how to make nuclear physics contribute to human comfort, human knowledge and hence to human dignity."[28] The *Richland Villager* succinctly termed Hanford Works "an arsenal of peace."[29]

Postwar Richland, Vigorous and Extroverted

In Richland, a town praised for its war work and exuberant about its role in a bright new technology, life seemed good. Virtually all Richlanders were newcomers, and almost immediately they formed an unprecedented number of social, cultural, and professional groups.[30] Municipal services such as garbage collection, water, electricity, and even appliance repair and medical and dental care were provided free to residents. Richlanders were well paid and generally well educated and healthy. Their birth rate hovered at record highs throughout the middle and late 1940s, and their death rate (especially the infant mortality rate) was well below average. In 1946, one-sixth of the entire population of Richland was under the age of six. By late 1948, the atomic village had the highest birth rate in the nation. Confounding the national averages, Richland had no maternal deaths in childbirth in 1949 and almost none throughout the late 1940s. Fund drives to combat cancer, polio, and other diseases were usually oversubscribed in the prosperous town. In 1946, Richland became the first American city to "adopt . . . a sister city" in Europe on an ongoing, charitable basis. For many years at Christmas, thousands of pounds of clothing and other goods were collected in the government village and sent to Tiel, Holland.[31]

Visitors were enchanted by the optimism and vigor of Richland. In late 1945, a *San Francisco Chronicle* journalist enthused about the "shiny new village . . . isolated, self-contained . . . happy." He added: "Everyone is . . . between 30 and 40. Their children have playgrounds and good schools . . . [There is a] high level of intelligence . . . and . . . wages are high . . . [It is] paradise."[32] In 1949, *Time* magazine termed Richland a "model residential city . . . an atomic-age utopia."[33]

Plant's Future Focus of Concern

Before the 1947–49 expansion, Richlanders were bothered most by the Hanford plant's uncertain future. By January 1946, according to the community newspaper, a "grapevine" of rumors was flourishing. "Not knowing whether tomorrow will find them 'on the road' or safe in their homes in Richland has left most people at loose ends." Many DuPont officials expected that the Hanford plant would be shut down when the war ended. This occurred at other wartime plants, such as those producing smokeless powder and TNT.[34] The June 1946 announcement that GE would replace DuPont as the prime Hanford contractor, the *Richland Villager* stated, brought "a strong feeling of relief, a let-up of the tension and uncertainty of not knowing what was going to happen." Business in the village, which had been slumping due to doubts about the town's future, revived during the summer of 1946. The September 1 transition between the two giant operating corporations was very smooth. Most of the approximately fifty-five hundred DuPont employees were given the opportunity to stay and work for GE. Most did so.[35] The transition from MED to AEC control four months later was also unruffled. Most of the nonarmy employees of the War Department automatically transferred to the AEC payroll.[36]

However, the community did not really feel secure about its future until plans for the huge postwar expansion were announced in August 1947. AEC Chairman Lilienthal reinforced these feelings by terming the future of the Hanford plants "very permanent."[37] Two years later, he reiterated, "Hanford Works [is] . . . a permanent enterprise as far ahead as anyone can see."[38] The September 1949 explosion of the first Soviet atomic bomb seemed to further solidify Richland's future. The *Richland Villager* proclaimed, "The Russian news has . . . added weight to the previously stated policy that Hanford Works is a permanent installation and will continue to be one of the key links in national defense."[39]

Rapid Growth Besets Richland

After the question of the plant's future was settled, at least for the foreseeable era, the problems that bothered Richlanders became the mundane ones that affected any area beset by rapid development. Electricity and water became scarce, swarms of mosquitoes arose, and construction dust swirled.[40] The water supply at Richland had been problematic since the army engineers had built the village. Storage reservoirs, tanks, and domestic water wells located in the city's southwest quadrant served Richland and North Richland. However, because of the arid climate and the loose, porous soil of the Columbia Basin, city water quickly percolated away. Extra water had to be held in retention basins from the irrigation ditches, and well fields had to be flooded in the dry summers to raise groundwater high enough to pump. Despite the inconvenience of this procedure, Columbia River water was not tapped until April 1949. At that time, a new intake system that pumped water from the Columbia north of Richland went into service as a supplement to domestic well water. The river water then was pumped into a recharging basin (gravel pit) and filtered through the ground into a new well field before it became available for use in the village.[41]

The growth of Richland and the Hanford project caused a mosquito problem in the Columbia Basin. Mosquitoes had never been a problem in the region before because swiftly moving water and arid land gave them no place to breed. However, the Hanford production complex brought effluent retention basins in the 100 Areas, huge waste-water cribs in the 200 Areas, waste-water drainage ponds in the 300 Area, and various other trenches and liquid disposal areas filled with still water. In the spring and summer of 1945, according to the community newspaper, a "mosquito plague" arose with "force." For the first time, children could not be sent to play in city parks. The village public health (P.H.) chief, Dr. Ralph Sachs, arranged for an aerial spraying of a solution of 10 percent DDT (dichloro-diphenyl-trichloroethane) and 90 percent diesel oil along the Columbia River near the parks. Altogether, about twenty-five square miles were sprayed. Despite heavy dousings by the potent DDT solution, the scourge of biting insects did not end until killing frosts arrived in October.[42] The following year, army and DuPont officials, now organized as a Mosquito Control Committee, again used planes and trucks to spray Richland and nearby environs with the DDT compound. They applied the DDT every seven to ten days to interrupt the insects' breeding cycle. Repeatedly, the health department exhorted residents to paint their screens with a DDT/kerosene solution sold prominently in neighborhood stores.[43] Similar sprayings, as well as screen paintings, were carried out in the Richland vicinity throughout the springs and summers of 1947–49. In each of those expansion years, about ninety-five hundred gallons of diesel oil and twenty-three hundred pounds of DDT were used on the town. In April 1949, criticism of DDT as an environmental hazard and a carcinogen appeared in scientific journals. However, GE's Hanford medical chief and head of the Mosquito Control Committee, Dr. William D. Norwood, dismissed the warnings, and the spraying program in Richland went forward with vigor.[44]

Dust Blizzards Rage

Although electrical, water, and insect difficulties were troublesome in the Hanford vicinity throughout the construction periods, no problem was more difficult than the blowing sand and dust. Powder blizzards rose up with a fury. Tree, shrub, and grass planting programs were undertaken by DuPont engineers in Richland beginning in 1945, but it would be years before the plants anchored the loose, ashy soil.[45] Indeed, at the time of the expansion announcements in 1947, GE's Hanford manager, David H. Lauder, remarked that the growth would bring "lots of dust." He explained, "We're going to churn it up and churn it up fast."[46] Lawns had to be seeded over and over before they took root.[47] Dust seeped through windowsills, even those plugged with towels. Many residents have recalled a gritty taste in food for three to four days after each major dust storm. Dick Donnell, a Hanford engineer, became locally famous for creating the cartoon character Dupus Boomer (named for DuPont, U.S., and *boomer*—the term applied to migrating, government project workers). The Dupus Boomer drawings humorously depicted life in growing Richland, amid the wind, the construction clutter, and the water and electrical shortages. One of the most renowned themes was blowing dust. "On a clear day you can see the new houses across the street," quipped Boomer in August 1948.[48]

As legions of construction vehicles excavated homes, roads, commercial and service buildings, and the huge plutonium manufacturing structures, no residential area was affected more heavily by the blowing dust than North Richland. This trailer and barracks community was closest to the plant area, and it had the least ground cover and the most hastily built facilities. Additional amounts of airborne debris and smoke were generated when large sections of the chalky cliffs on the Columbia River's north bank above the Hanford Site were dynamited to provide rock for plant construction.[49] Grass seed was not available until the summer of 1948, and a housewife interviewed that September noted especially the "wind, sand and stark bleakness." Another woman who lived in North Richland as a child recalled, forty years later: "Mostly, I remember the sand, lots of sand. Everything was built on sand." Even the rare prefabricated homes, she recounted, "were no match for the infamous Hanford dust storms." She added, "We could see daylight between the ceiling and walls."[50] Not without good reason was the newsletter of North Richland's school (John Ball School) called the *Sandy City News*. Similarly, Richland's Columbia High School entitled its newsletter the *Sandstorm*.

In a fashion similar to their attack on mosquitoes, Hanford's AEC and GE officials formed a Dust and Pollen Committee in Richland. In early 1947, this committee recommended intensified grass, shrub, and tree cultivation in and around the village. Free grass seed was furnished to all residents who were willing to plant or extend their lawns, and residents were urged to help GE workers with the planting program in block centers and common greenways. In April, a shelterbelt of trees was placed along the western border of Richland as a shield against the prevailing winds.[51] When the huge expansion program began in the autumn of 1947, this shelterbelt had to be uprooted and moved farther west. Then, a record flood of the Columbia River in the late spring of 1948 washed out much of the new greenery. The shelterbelt, where many said the small Pacific rattlesnakes loved to hide, had to be planted again. The cartoon character Dupus Boomer commented often on Richland's ill-fated attempts to grow green. "Nothing shady here," he quipped in 1948 as he viewed a tiny tree lying on its side in his otherwise empty yard.[52] Throughout these years and the early 1950s, GE maintenance crews had to shovel sand from the lawns and flush it down to the streets, where it was picked up and hauled away. Large dunes were stabilized with a coat of gravel. In cases where dump trucks could not get close, cut brush and trees were used to anchor the sand piles in place.[53]

Radioactivity Not Feared by Residents

With such prestigious entities as the Army Corps of Engineers and the DuPont Corporation, and later the Atomic Energy Commission and the General Electric Company, looking after their welfare so assiduously, Richlanders felt confident that they were safe. Many factors seemed to stand as a bulwark between their idyllic town and any possible danger—modern chemicals, the rows of new trees and voluminous sacks of grass seed that arrived by truck and train, the huge earth-moving machinery so prevalent in the town, and the obvious brilliance of the scientists of the MED and the AEC. Radiation and radioactivity seemed mysterious to many of the residents and workers, but they did not fear it. At the time of the bombings of Japan, most Americans had never heard of radiation.[54] However, as soon as atomic energy was unveiled, Americans were told that radioactivity was safely contained in the Hanford project. The Smyth Report of August 1945 averred: "The success of the separation process at Hanford has exceeded all expectations . . . None of the fears expressed [regarding] . . . radiation effects in the chemical processes have turned out to be justified." He concluded, "Factors of safety used in [Hanford] plant design and operation are so great that the hazards of home and the family car are far greater for the personnel than any arising from the plants."[55]

Despite the Smyth Report, news stories appeared on the "health hazards" connected with the Hanford enterprise and on the "heating of the Columbia River" by the project's reactors. There was some early concern that thermal effects of the reactor effluent could produce disease in the valuable salmon and other fish. Matthias, concerned by these reports, collaborated with Parker, the chief health physicist, and Dr. Simon T. Cantril, a prominent Clinton Laboratory health specialist on loan to Hanford.[56] Just ten days after the Japanese surrender, Parker and Cantril issued a special bulletin to all HEW personnel. "We have made this a safe job, and we do not want any misinformation or loose statements . . . to mar either our record or the morale we have built up through confidence in the safety of our operations." No employee, they claimed, had ever received "injurious" exposure to radiation. As for Richland and the surrounding environs, Parker and Cantril were adamant. "We do not live in a 'City of Pluto,' as certain elements of the press describe our Village. Pluto is safely confined behind . . . barriers in the plant. What little of him as does escape is not going to relegate anyone to purgatory." The two health physicists asserted that airborne and waterborne emissions outside the plant were so insignificant that they could not be measured. When radioactive gases did "come to the ground due to certain weather conditions . . . the nitrous fume component [was] the more dangerous one, . . . a hazard similar to one encountered in many industrial plants the country over."[57]

66

Radiological Safety Pledges Continue

Pledges that radioactive emissions were not a health hazard at the Hanford complex, nor in the surrounding environment, continued throughout the postwar years. In November 1945, Richland's community newspaper praised "the healthful environment of the village" and lauded DuPont's "procedures to insure the highest possible health standards." The GE research chief, W. D. Coolidge, toured the Hanford facilities in 1946 and stated: "Protection is remarkably well organized here . . . The health protection in the Hanford plant is outstanding . . . much of the development of protection against radiation has been accomplished here." At nearly the same time, Hanford's chief health physicist, Herbert Parker, also reassured the region's people. "The unknown hazards which were faced in the development of the [plutonium] process resulted in meticulous care being taken with housekeeping, health protection, and industrial safety. Over the . . . life of the H.E.W., the safety and health record has been most outstanding."[58] In early 1947, he boasted: "At the Hanford Engineer Works . . . over 3000 man-years of active exposure have been compiled without a single palpable radiation injury . . . There has been no known instance of the ingestion, inhalation, or other mode of introduction of a damaging amount of radioactive material into any individual."[59] In July 1947, the AEC's Advisory Committee on Biology and Medicine (ACBM) noted, "Outstandingly safe working conditions have been maintained."[60] The following month, GE-Hanford Manager Lauder stated, "There has not been a single injury to date that has been, or can be, charged to radioactivity." Two weeks later, AEC Chairman Lilienthal added, "On the general proposition of health and safety matters . . . the record of everything that I have seen is very good."[61] Throughout 1948 and 1949, representatives of the Richland health department repeated assurances that the community was "a healthy one in which to live"— "superior" to other towns.[62]

Reassurances continued. In mid-1949, the AEC issued a special public report that pledged, "Concentrations of these [waste] gases in the air over Richland, Pasco, and Kennewick . . . [are] too little to be a hazard." High-level, liquid chemical processing wastes, the report stated, were "carefully stored" at Hanford. Lower-level wastes were "temporarily held . . . to permit any radioactivity . . . to die down." The report continued, "After radioactivity fades out, [they] are discharged."[63] Later that year, the AEC again stated: "Discharge standards . . . are at a rate so low that no damage to plants, animals or humans has resulted . . . The methods of safe handling used to date have successfully protected workers and the public."[64] In January 1950, Dr. William Norwood, Hanford's medical chief, told Richlanders, "There is no evidence to date at

Hanford Works of occupational diseases or injury due to radiation."[65] Later
that year, another special AEC report pledged that the Health Instruments
Division at Hanford safeguarded both the workers and "the environs" of the
plant.[66] At nearly the same time, a *New York Times* reporter toured the Hanford
facilities. AEC Manager Fred Schlemmer told him that it was "ten times safer to
work at Hanford as at an average chemical plant."[67]

Promises of healthful operations at Hanford were made again and again
over the years in public AEC reports and other documents. In one such 1951
report, the commission acknowledged its own ultimate responsibility, specified
in the Atomic Energy Act of 1946, to take the "necessary steps to protect life and
property from hazards arising out of its work."[68] In late 1953, the retiring
commission chairman, Gordon Dean, placed the prestige of his position behind AEC promises that Hanford operations were healthful and environmen-
tally sound. At the Hanford plant, "where King Atom reign[ed] supreme,"
Dean declared, man did "control the [atomic] reaction so that it proceed[ed] to
just the right level." The chemical separations process, he averred, was "handled
with the utmost precision and the most painstaking kind of care."[69] In 1955 the
commission's new chairman, Lewis L. Strauss, presented the "assets and deb-
its" of America's atomic programs. He omitted any mention of environmental
contamination.[70] Two years later, in a public report, the AEC vaunted its
extensive and highly technical environmental-monitoring program at Hanford.
"Minute quantities of radioactive contamination in air, vegetation, soil, surface
water and ground water are detected by radiochemical methods . . . All radioactive materials routinely detected beyond the plant perimeter are at or below
one-tenth of the appropriate maximum permissible limits."[71] At nearly the same
time, GE's overall manager at Hanford, W. E. Johnson, termed Richland "a fine,
healthy community . . . a great . . . [place] to learn and to grow."[72]

In September 1958, the United Nations sponsored the Second International
Conference on the Peaceful Uses of Atomic Energy. At this conference, four
leaders from Hanford's H.I. Division noted, "Throughout the history of the
Hanford project, radiation exposures in the environs due to plant contributions . . . have been well within the maximum permissible limits."[73] Two
influential Hanford geologists, with counterparts from the AEC's Oak Ridge
(Tennessee) and Savannah River (South Carolina) production facilities, told
the conference attendees that these plants had "demonstrated the feasibility,
safety and economy in the disposal of . . . liquid wastes" in the soil.[74] That same
year, AEC Chairman John McCone praised General Electric for its "efficient,
safe operation at Hanford."[75]

Industrial, Fire, and Traffic Safety Stressed

At the same time that Hanford's leaders were reassuring the public about radiological health and environmental protection, they were also stressing industrial safety. In fact, the Hanford Site was an extraordinarily safe place to work in terms of common hazards. Broken or worn equipment, unattended trash, leaking pipes, unkempt or slippery roads, loose or frayed electrical connections, and similar perils simply did not exist in the facilities. These excellent conditions resulted from conscious decisions by the MED and the AEC to keep America's atomic production plants as neat, presentable, and efficient as attention to ordinary detail would permit.[76] Throughout the 1940s and 1950s, U.S. atomic plants compiled accident frequency records that were significantly below the national averages for industrial plant construction and operations. Within the Hanford complex itself, safety competitions were held among the various areas and divisions. Well-publicized award ceremonies and other prizes frequently rewarded safe work. Safety slogans and cartoons covered posters, plant stationery, and company newsletters. The final year of the hectic 1940s began at Hanford with the following slogan: "For Your Sake and Mine—Work Safe in Forty-Nine."[77]

The high priorities on safety at the Hanford plant also extended into the government village of Richland. Fire, traffic, and household safety were avidly promoted in the town. No permits at all were granted for weed or trash burning within Richland's boundaries.[78] For atomic officials, the fear of fire, which could spread rapidly and disastrously north from the residential areas to the production districts of the Hanford Site, was significant. A range fire on contaminated land could serve as a "release and transport mechanism" for radioactivity. Contaminated plant foliage could be "volatized" while contaminated sand and dust particles could be "re-entrained by wind erosion" following a fire.[79] As the result of fire safety, fire insurance rates for the entire city were reduced by state and national ratings bureaus. Well-publicized safety campaigns, lectures, proclamations, and award ceremonies were held in the town, and with much success. Traffic accident rates also were kept to record lows.[80]

Medical and Health Protection Stressed

At the same time that MED, AEC, and contractor officials exhorted Richlanders about safety, the officials reminded residents that they enjoyed exceptional medical protection. Richlanders were frequently told that their town had "the most complete medical, dental and public health services in the Northwest."[81] Dr. Norwood and Public Health Chief Dr. Ralph Sachs were featured prominently and often in the *Richland Villager,* telling residents that the village was safe, that the water and milk were safe, and that the Hanford plant was safe. Sometimes, even Chief Health Physicist Parker would grant a public interview. Invariably, he would define health protection at HEW as "excellent."[82] In fact, the Public Health Section of Hanford's Medical Division, run first by DuPont and later by GE, conducted thousands of annual checks of Richland's milk, water, and food. The region from which the Carnation Company drew Richland's milk supply was located to the west of the village, approximately from Prosser to Ellensburg. Tests of the cows, the equipment of the dairies, the processing plant at Sunnyside, and the milk itself were run regularly. Likewise, water checks, including ones made directly from the taps in people's homes, and inspections of food-handling establishments were made on an ongoing basis. Milk, water, and food were analyzed at the bacteriological laboratory at Richland's Kadlec Hospital. Additionally, free chest X rays were offered each year to every Richland resident. Schoolchildren, according to government officials, were "kept, indirectly, under public health supervision through regular examinations by company nurses."[83]

AEC Information Policy Stresses Open Disclosure
In addition to all of the tests and the pledges of radiological and industrial safety and community welfare, the AEC reassured Americans that it practiced open disclosure of information. "In our desire to prevent unauthorized transmission of scientific information of military importance," the commission avowed in 1947, "we must not go to the extreme of . . . locking up all our information . . . the dissemination of scientific and technical information relating to atomic energy should be permitted and encouraged so as to provide that free interchange of ideas and criticisms which is essential to scientific progress."[84] Late that year, the AEC established a small public-information staff and announced the start of a major, ongoing declassification effort. It pledged to work with the American Textbook Publishers' Institute, the Association of Secondary School Principals, the American Society of Newspaper Editors, and many other groups that had formed committees to work for a greater dissemination of knowledge about atomic energy.[85] Nevertheless, of approximately 2,000 research reports prepared at U.S. atomic sites in 1948, only about 500 were unclassified (i.e., nonsecret). At Hanford, only two reports out of 158 were "publishable."[86] That year, an AEC investigative board secretly advised: "A serious obstacle to progress . . . was and still is imposed by wartime security rules . . . some of these rules and the habits they engendered are still a serious and largely unnecessary handicap . . . Free interchange and debate are essential to progress."[87] In 1950, the commission again promised openness. "Basic sci-

ence should be free except where it is directly related to weapons." The commission pledged itself to make public all data and knowledge that did not pertain to "weapons information, including design, production and stockpiles . . . [or any facts that would] help the atomic energy program of a potential enemy."[88]

Regional Newspaper Praises Plutonium Production at Hanford

In the Columbia Basin, Hanford officials and scientists were the most authoritative information source concerning atomic energy and the production site itself. The *Tri-City Herald* was the region's only daily newspaper. Publisher Glenn Lee had a reputation for vocal criticism of the AEC for not providing more aid to area schools, roads, hospitals, police, and other services. However, he never questioned or censured the basic commission policy of pushing plutonium production to the maximum at Hanford. In late 1947, Lee stated with typical enthusiasm: "It certainly makes sense to use every precious minute . . . [in manufacturing plutonium. We] wish . . . those engaged in the current task at Hanford all possible speed in their work."[89]

Regional Confidence High

With the flood of reassurances about health and safety and community protection, with the AEC pledging open disclosure of information not directly related to weapons manufacturing, and with the chief regional newspaper lauding the Hanford operations, few people, if any, doubted that the Columbia Basin was safe. The comforting messages were well received. In mid-1949, Richard Neuberger, a reporter for *The Nation,* visited Richland and questioned inhabitants about "rumors of pits of evil residue, many stories deep . . . so virulent" it could not "even be dumped into the sea." He asked: "Is it unstable? Might it blow up? . . . How dangerous is it?" However, instead of worry, he found confidence and optimism. "I thought the morale of people was high," he concluded.[90] Later in 1949, the University of Michigan Survey Research Center conducted a study of "the attitudes of people toward the radiation hazards . . . in atomic energy developments." Overall, the research project demonstrated, inhabitants near atomic sites, including Hanford, were "taking atomic energy in their stride." According to the study: "They do not fear it more than people elsewhere . . . [There is] no anxiety which could be attributed to fear of radiation or plant disaster." Residents were so confident, the researchers concluded, because they felt "reassured . . . [by the] care and precautions exercised by those in charge."[91]

Others have since endorsed this view that morale was excellent and that people were not fearful. One chemist recalled his own relief at leaving a position with the Seattle Gas Company to work at Hanford. At the Seattle utilities plant, which manufactured gas from oil and water, he had worried about explosions and fire. At Hanford, he remembered, the large and thorough Health Instruments staff put all his fears to rest. A farmwife who lived since the early 1940s in northern Franklin County, across the Columbia River from Hanford's production areas, expressed her feelings succinctly: "You just never gave it [the Hanford plant] a thought. You just thought that if there was anything wrong they'd tell you."[92]

Waste Releases Larger Than Anticipated

But in the Columbia Basin in the years beginning with 1944, there were signs that all was not well. As growth went forward, health physicists, chemists, and other scientists engaged in environmental monitoring at the Hanford Site learned that some wastes were escaping from the atomic plant. Fission and activation products were streaming into the air, ground, and the Columbia River. These emissions were occurring repeatedly, and in some cases continuously, at levels well above those then defined as "permissible" or "tolerable." From the air and the river, these radioactive substances entered the food chain. They contaminated the forage and water of grazing animals. They penetrated the algae, plankton, and benthic populations that lived in the Columbia River and in Hanford's many waste ponds, basins, trenches, and cribs. From these bases, radioactivity spread rapidly through the ecosystem. Milk was contaminated with radioiodine (I-131). Fish and waterfowl were burdened with radioisotopes of phosphorus (P-32), zinc (Zn-65), chromium (Cr-51), neptunium (Np-239), arsenic (As-76), and many other substances. An AEC safety review conducted at the Hanford facilities in 1948 took issue with the 1945 Smyth Report. "Smyth states that Hanford's stack emissions of radioactive iodine and xenon are insignificant and that there is probably no danger of pollution of the Columbia. We question that statement as fact . . . The provoking dust storms of natural origin create not only discomfort, but some problems of atmospheric pollution, involving the transmission of radioactive and toxic products."[93]

Scientists Show Concern

To Hanford scientists, deeply concerned about the data they were collecting, it seemed that the Columbia Basin itself was rising up to do battle with them. They applied new technologies to try to control the radioactive and chemical discharges. Still, the wastes continued their ubiquitous spread through the district. Ironically, many of the same natural features that had attracted army engineers to the neighborhood in the first place now confounded Hanford. The omnipresent wind across the flat open land, the dry and porous soil, the gravelly substrata, and the swift Columbia River all complicated Hanford's operations. The scientists, like many newcomers before them, found the Columbia Basin to be far more complex than it had first appeared.

When evidence of unexpectedly high levels of airborne and waterborne contamination was detected, Hanford scientists tried hard to mitigate the problems. On the atomic site itself, they made strong efforts, even relocating major buildings. They spent a great deal of time and money testing filters, varying temperatures and chemical solutions, and fixing overt leaks.[94] They checked the workers' urine, thyroids, hand counts, and shoe counts; in Richland, they checked the milk, the water, the food, and the people. They battled mosquitoes and fought the dust. They drained and filtered the well fields. However, they put less energy into public information.

Were Some Statements Veiled Warnings?

In view of what we know today, it appears that some public statements made in early Richland may have been based on unvoiced concerns. For example, in formerly classified memos written in mid-1945, health physicists at Hanford discussed experiments that suggested that "the administration of inert [stable] iodine prior to the giving of carrier-free radioiodine very significantly reduced the uptake of the latter by the thyroid." H.I. Chief Parker suggested the "promotion of the use of iodized salt through public education."[95] At nearly the same time, Richland's community newspaper announced, "Medical Department Recommends Use of Iodized Salt." Encouraging dietary intake of iodized salt as "merely a matter of good nutrition," GE physicians advised: "Inland regions with little rainfall [such as the Columbia Basin] tend to have lower iodine content in the water and soil. . . . The body needs a certain amount of iodine . . . we recommend that you use iodized salt."[96]

By mid-1947, Hanford researchers had discovered that airborne radioactive contamination deposited readily on sagebrush. Surprisingly, atmospherically transported gases and particulates could be detected on this hardy plant that was so prevalent in eastern Washington. That summer, Richland's Public Health Section issued warnings to villagers to remove sagebrush plants from their yards. The spindly desert weed, GE officials explained, "aggravates allergies [and] . . . often harbors ticks" that could spread Rocky Mountain spotted fever.[97] Soon afterwards, Hanford researchers discovered that the Russian thistle plant could present an "aerial radiation hazard" because of its pronounced ability to translocate subsurface contamination up through its bracts and stems. In Richland, residents were asked to destroy these plants to decrease the pollen level.[98]

Before the autumn of 1949, large areas near the southern end of the atomic reservation, just west-northwest of Richland, had been open to hunting. This locale was a prime waterfowl habitat, a floodplain between Horn Rapids and the mouth of the Yakima River. However, during the 1947 and 1948 hunting seasons, special assays done by Hanford officials on game birds found the highest radioactivity levels for I-131 in animals taken just north and northwest of Richland.[99] At the start of the 1949 hunting season, the entire Hanford project, including the Yakima floodplain, was closed to hunting. GE announced that increased construction traffic and population growth had made the prized habitat "too crowded to be safe for hunting."[100]

During the time of the insect-control campaigns in the late 1940s, broad-based research at the Hanford complex was beginning to show that many invertebrates have the ability to concentrate radioactivity in their tissues at levels vastly higher than the levels originally discharged into the environment.[101] As I-131 mingled with the blowing construction dust, were the exhortations by Richland's officials to plant and maintain grass and trees simply, as stated, "to beautify the town"? Richlanders were told by GE in January 1948 that air samples were being collected in the village in order to study "pollen concentrations in the air to determine the varieties, abundance and seasonal appearance of hay fever pollens in this locality."[102] At that time, Hanford scientists were establishing a network of air-sampling stations and were expanding the local air-monitoring and animal-assay programs.[103] With radio-iodine being released through the 200 Areas stacks, falling on forage, and raising the radioactivity levels in animal thyroids, was it a coincidence that no chickens or livestock of any kind were allowed in government-owned Richland? Or that no land within the town limits was available for pasture?[104]

During the same years that scientists in the new fields of environmental monitoring and health physics were struggling to understand the multifaceted aspects of radionuclide transfer through the ecosystem and to establish safe tolerance limits, extensive milk-testing and water-testing programs were carried out by health officials in Richland. The milk-testing program was explained to village residents as existing merely to check the milk for "bacterial count and butterfat content . . . seeing that the milk [came] from tuberculin tested cows . . . [and] that the process [of pasteurization] had been properly carried out.[105] Richland's milk supply was brought in from the Ellensburg and Yakima areas. GE officials repeatedly cautioned Richlanders not to drink "poor quality" milk and water from rural regions surrounding the village.[106] Why did Richland officials struggle with the messy and problem-ridden well fields when they could have tapped the Columbia River, as did neighboring cities, for the domestic water supply? Although the huge, regionwide flood of 1948 added domestic sewage burdens from upstream to the Columbia river's waters near Hanford,[107] the village utilities supervisor, Kenneth Leiferman, acknowledged that the river water was generally "low in foreign content; and softer than the well water."[108] Were the frequent tests performed by Public Health officials on the sludge from Richland's sewage disposal simply, as stated, to determine the bacterial content in the waste solution?[109]

Historical Uncertainties

The Hanford Engineer Works brought tremendous growth to the small, dusty towns of the Columbia Basin. The population doubled and redoubled for nearly two decades during major plant expansions and other nearby construction endeavors. These giant expansions attest to a scale of building that was unprecedented and, in fact, nearly unbelievable. We can record much about the early government town of Richland—the optimism, the vigor, the intellectual curiosity, the pride. These qualities, as well as the high birth rate, high education level, patriotism, generosity to charitable causes, and neighborly sociability set the beautiful town apart. However, there is a great deal that we may never know about that time in that place, even though Hanford scientists maintained detailed records of the contamination levels in the Columbia Basin's air, water, vegetation, fish, wild game, and other animals.[110] They undertook to protect public health to the extent that their technology and their limited authority over production schedules allowed. The levels of contaminants that might cause harm in the ecosystem were not yet well understood. The sciences of health physics and environmental monitoring were so new that findings could not possibly be seen as conclusive.

Yet, there was the knowledge that these contaminants were not healthful, and there was concern that they might reach unsafe levels. When Hanford scientists cautioned village residents to use iodized salt, to cut down sagebrush and Russian thistle in the town, to drink only Richland's milk and water, and to hunt far from Hanford, were they actually trying to tell residents how to avoid contact with radioactive and chemical wastes? There is a large, gray area that lies between the asking and the answering of questions about these matters. And there is the timely issue of how a democracy such as the United States can better ensure public access to information about new technologies as they develop.

Does the public need to wait until all the technical questions have been answered conclusively, or is there not a way to have reasonable, ongoing public discussions of potential risks and uncertainties during the period in which newly emerging technologies mature? Amid these uncertainties and questions, the United States as well as the rest of the world has lived its nuclear history.

Blowing in the Wind:
The Airborne Contaminants

"The presence of active xenon and iodine in the vent fumes from the dissolver makes it important to schedule dissolver operations when atmospheric conditions are conducive to maximum dispersion of these active gases. The nitrogen oxides also evolved are a secondary consideration. This situation was realized in the original design, and the Meteorology Station (Bldg. 622) and the Stack Monitor Buildings (292) were provided as aids to safe dissolver operations. Extensive weather and wind studies also were conducted on the site prior to the start of Canyon Building dissolvings . . . These auxiliary facilities were in use from the start of dissolving operations, and weather forecasts were phoned to . . . process dispatchers hourly."—E.I. DuPont de Nemours and Co., *Operation of Hanford Engineer Works,* Book 12: "S Department," 1946, p. 66

Origin, Components, and Effects of Airborne Wastes

For about a decade, from the onset of plutonium manufacturing in late 1944 until approximately 1955, airborne wastes were the emissions of immediate concern at the Hanford Engineer Works. After the mid-1950s, gaseous, aerosol, and airborne particulate releases were brought under relative control. Radio-iodine (I-131), radioxenon (Xe-133), plutonium (Pu-239, released either in particulate form or as an oxide, PuO_2), and radioruthenium (Ru-103 and Ru-106) were the radionuclides of prime concern, and nitrous components were the chemicals of prime concern. All of these materials were released from the chemical separations areas (200 Area). They were emitted when the irradiated uranium fuel rods (*slugs*) were placed into the acidic solutions that dissolved their aluminum jackets and extracted the final product—plutonium 239. Airborne discharges from the reactor stacks and basins (100 Area) were minor. They occurred only sporadically, usually when a retention basin was dried out for repair purposes and the famed eastern Washington wind lifted and carried off the particulate crust.[1] Fires from ruptured fuel slugs or experimental test burns of highly enriched uranium also released radioactivity to the atmosphere. Airborne emissions from the 300 Area were even more minor. Such discharges consisted of uranium dust and the components of the decay cycle of uranium.

Iodine-131 was the airborne radioisotope released from Hanford's 200-Area stacks in greatest quantity. Over 420,000 curies were discharged to the atmosphere of the Columbia Basin during the first two years of plutonium production, even though Hanford's chief health physicist, Herbert Parker, calculated that a maximum emission of one curie per day would keep air and vegetation contamination levels at or below "tolerable limits." By the close of 1955, after a decade of operation, over half a million curies of radioiodine had entered the surrounding atmosphere from Hanford's stacks.[2] In an experiment known as the Green Run in early December 1949, nearly 8,000 curies of I-131 were released in two days.[3] Radioiodine is a beta-emitter with a half-life of approximately 8 days. Its danger lies in its appetite for human and animal thyroid tissue. Radioxenon, a beta-emitter with a half-life of 5.3 days, is not a biochemical hazard. It is an inert gas and does not enter the food chain nor bind with the solutions and tissues of humans or other animals.[4] Plutonium, an alpha-emitter, has a half-life of approximately 24,000 years. In 1946, officials of the prime site contractor, DuPont Corp., termed plutonium "the greatest special hazard."[5]

Emissions of flaky, particulate radioruthenium (Ru-103 and Ru-106) were discharged when the paint and mild steel in the fans and ducts of the 200-Area ventilation systems began to corrode. An "appreciable build-up of radioactivity was noted in the fan casings" by DuPont officials as early as January 1945.[6] However, the "speck problem" was not linked with radioruthenium until autumn 1947. At that time, Parker defined the "specks" as consisting of I-131, Ru-106, and radioisotopes of cerium (Ce-144), strontium (Sr-90), cesium (Cs-137), and yttrium (Y-90 and Y-91).[7] The particulate problem at Hanford reached its most acute stage during the first three years of the operation (1952–54) of the REDOX (reduction-oxidation) chemical-processing plant.[8] Radioruthenium, with a half-life of approximately one year, does not have an affinity for any specific body organ or tissue. Nevertheless, in particulate form it presents a hazard to the lungs and upper gastrointestinal tract, where burning and destruction of surrounding tissue can take place over many months.[9] It is not known whether the presence of airborne radioactive emissions has affected the health of any area residents. Regional Native Americans may have had exposure from the consumption of foods and medicinal herbs derived from contaminated soil and vegetation. Some tribes may have used over seventy foods, and an equal number of medicines, from the ground.[10] Army and contractor security forces at the Hanford Site, as well as area farmers, worked and lived in the path of contaminated gases, sands, and particulates blowing through the region.

Early Meteorological Calculations

The original bismuth-phosphate separations plants operated at Hanford by the Manhattan Engineer District and DuPont operated without any stack filters or airborne waste containment systems. Diluting gas flow with additional volumes of air and venting to the atmosphere under certain meteorological conditions were the standard procedures.[11] A temporary crew of meteorologists brought to the vast desert site by DuPont in June 1943 found that the prevailing winds blew from the northwest, west, and southwest nearly 70 percent of the time.[12] Down from the prevailing wind streams (downwind) lay Pasco, Richland, Walla Walla, Ritzville, and Spokane. However, no one knew what distances and in what concentrations the radioactive gases would travel. According to Hanford's Army Commander Franklin T. Matthias, the DuPont meteorologists were surprised to find a "very large amount of local air circulation within the area with almost exactly opposing winds existing in the valley [Columbia Basin] at points not more than 6 or 7 miles apart." They puzzled over the "almost constantly recurring inversions and the elevation at which the break in inversion occurred." Concerned, Gilbert Church, the company's on-site construction chief, obtained permanent, "official status" for the meteorology studies at Hanford.[13] During 1944, a 350-foot meteorology tower was erected near the 200 Areas.[14]

The level, open appearance of the Hanford Site, like many other features of the Columbia Basin, was deceptively simple. In reality, intense and rapidly changing weather conditions produced three basic trajectories in the stack gases. The more common conditions were "fanning" (a wide, V-shaped path that followed the wind direction in a relatively straight line) and "coning" (a narrow pattern that also followed the wind line straight out from the stack).

DuPont officials termed such circumstances "aloft conditions (process stack discharge . . . not expected to reach the ground)." They meant that the airborne emissions would not fall to the ground within the Hanford Site boundaries themselves. However, when a warm chinook wind or weather front blew over cold ground, as happened often in winter at the atomic complex, a temperature inversion occurred. This condition could cause the off-gases to "loop," or bounce, from ground to stack height several times as they proceeded down the wind line from the two-hundred-foot-high stacks.[15] Looping also occurred, meteorologists found, under "unstable" air conditions.[16] Looping was viewed as the worst possible case, since the primary concern of Hanford officials was to keep fumes from coming to the ground close to the stacks, where workers would receive a concentrated exposure.[17]

By late summer 1944, after only a few months of operation of the plutonium pilot plant (semiworks, or SMX) at the Clinton Engineer Works in Tennessee, DuPont noted, "The radio-active xenon and iodine evolved during the dissolution of the uranium at Hanford Engineer Works may present a health hazard within certain areas around the base of the stack through which the dissolver off-gases are discharged." They reported, in secret, that "calculations indicated" that iodine would "present a greater health hazard" than the xenon. However, they believed that tolerance levels would not be exceeded if the irradiated fuel rods were cooled for "only 30 days, if the normal wind dilution factor" was 1,000. Recognizing that the huge size of Hanford's chemical processing plants, as compared to the SMX, could vary these calculations, they advised review "when additional data . . . from the Hanford Engineer Works dissolver" was available.[18] By August 1945, DuPont chemists had learned that the evolution of radioiodine was "substantially independent" of chemical concentrations in the processing solutions. "Cooling time," the chemist J. L. Dreher reported in secret, "should be sufficiently long so that the activities [I-131] will have decreased through decay."[19] The relationship between longer cooling periods for the irradiated slugs and lowered "radiation intensity from the fission products" was made public in Henry Smyth's War Department report that same month.[20]

Thus, the matter of wind dilution factors assumed considerable importance. In actual operations at Hanford, DuPont scientists measured the normal flow of air and process gases to the internal 200-Area fans at about 40,000 cubic feet per minute (cfm). They augmented this volume with about 20,000 cfm of "additional diluting air," yielding a total stack flow of 60,000 cfm. They believed, "The resultant 50 ft/sec. velocity of discharge . . . assures considerable vertical 'carry' into the atmosphere and assists dispersion."[21] At this stack flow rate, they noted, "Dilution factors greater than 1000:1 are considered favorable, those from 500:1 to 1,000:1 moderately satisfactory, and those less than 500:1 unfavorable."[22] The role of the meteorology group in forecasting wind speeds and conditions was deemed so important that hourly and twelve-hour "dissolving forecasts" were provided for T Plant (the 200 West chemical-processing facility) beginning in November. Similar forecasts were provided for B Plant (200 East) starting in March 1945. After May 1945, according to DuPont, these forecasts "proved too short for effective scheduling of dissolver operations," and Hanford meteorologists switched to a single, daily "dissolving forecast."[23]

The Question of When to Dissolve

Concern with weather forecasting at the Hanford Site centered on a crucial question: could the chemical-dissolving operations be controlled? The answer came soon after start-up. The separations plants operated with batches of material. Within certain broad time constraints, batches could be scheduled when weather conditions were appropriate. There were many variables: the size of the batch, the rate of feed, the temperature. However, if the gases produced by a given run became too large, there was no way to contain them. They exited through the stacks. Many key Hanford officials, including Colonel Matthias, have stated that wind drift, wind changes, weather ceilings, and other meteorological conditions all were important in deciding when to dissolve. Even during the wartime rush to produce plutonium, there were times when the meteorological and environmental-monitoring staffs persuaded Hanford's production managers to postpone dissolving processes until weather conditions improved.

Over time, however, despite attempting to conduct chemical-dissolving operations only under "favorable" conditions, site operators, pushed by urgent production demands, sometimes dissolved under "moderately satisfactory" and even "unfavorable" conditions. Walter O. Simon, DuPont's operations chief at Hanford, confirmed later: "In that period up to June 1945, if there was a good velocity of wind to distribute them [stack gases], we might have taken some chances . . . time was of the essence . . . Some of the first batches of uranium being dissolved left [sic] off a little more gas than we would have liked."[24] From July through December 1945, 25 percent of all dissolving took place under "unfavorable" conditions (i.e., when wind dilution factors were less than 500:1). Another 15 percent of all chemical processing occurred in "moderately satisfactory" conditions (i.e., when wind dilution factors were between 500:1 and 1,000:1).[25] In the first six months of 1946, as the huge wartime inventory of irradiated fuel rods was gradually worked down, dissolving operations also were executed under less than favorable conditions 32 percent of the time.[26]

During July and August 1946, chemical processing took place under "unfavorable" conditions 35 percent of the time and under "moderately satisfactory" conditions another 13 percent of the time.[27]

Early Evidence of Contamination

Evidence of environmental contamination came to the attention of Hanford managers with the processing of the very first charge of metal (batch of irradiated fuel rods) on December 26, 1944. The charge had been cooled thirty-two days, but its radioactivity level was higher, by a factor of ten, than any other metal processed at the SMX. Its dissolving in T Plant, according to DuPont officials, "resulted in the first significant plant discharge of radio xenon and iodine [1,700 curies] into the atmosphere at Hanford."[28] The following spring, as the site rushed to produce plutonium for the Trinity and Nagasaki bombs, "dissolving frequency," as well as "metal activity," increased sharply. Additionally, according to DuPont, the warmer spring weather conditions "caused fumes to be brought to the ground in regions very near to the stacks." In some cases, I-131 concentrations peaked at approximately one hundred times the "permanently tolerable value." In two other cases, some of the heavily burdened "fumes" were drawn into the process buildings. Concerned about worker safety, DuPont decided in June to conduct all dissolving at night. At the same time, regular thyroid checks for the "monitoring of iodine inhalation" by 200-Area workers were begun.[29]

The spring of 1945 also brought evidence of I-131 contamination outside of the Hanford reservation. As early as October 1944, atmospheric monitors (Victoreen integrons) had been emplaced at twenty-nine locations throughout the Hanford Site and the immediately adjacent areas. Richland, Pasco, Kennewick, and Benton City each had a classified monitoring station. By March 1945, according to DuPont, "detectable quantities" had been found at all of these stations. At that time, average monthly readings were as high as 0.8 millirads (mr) per eight-hour period in Richland, 2.9 mr in Benton City, 2.6 mr in Kennewick, and 6.5 mr in Pasco. The company, however, doubted its own data. All readings above 2.0 mr, it reported internally, "included values known to be spurious, but difficult to eliminate with certainty from the written record."[30]

During the summer and autumn of 1945, the monitoring data grew more consistent and harder to dismiss.[31] The H.I. staff was surprised to find contamination on desert flowers that were left on a desk in the office of Deputy Chief Carl Gamertsfelder. The staff expanded vegetation surveys beyond the immediate 200 Area.[32] The H.I. Section, which DuPont had anticipated would "gradually diminish," also expanded. By October, readings of I-131 on vegetation in Richland, Pasco, and Kennewick averaged from 0.57 to 1.2 microcuries per kilogram (μCi/kg).[33] (In January 1946, a level of 0.2. μCi/kg or less was set by Chief Health Physicist Parker as safe and "tolerable.")[34] By December 1945, according to DuPont, a "very decided increase in ground [vegetation] activity [had occurred] . . . The widespread deposition of I-131 on the ground led to a study of its accumulation . . . Surveys of vegetation contamination were extended farther and farther . . . and ranged as far as Pendleton and Walla Walla by December 25."[35]

More Fuel Rods Are Processed

The major increases in ground (vegetation) deposition of I-131 in the Hanford vicinity during the period of June through December 1945 were caused by the large amounts of irradiated slugs being processed and by the shortening of cooling times for these slugs to less than thirty days.[36] The number of charges being processed rose from twenty-two in June to seventy-seven in December. Beginning in September 1945, the month after the Japanese surrender, chemical processing was carried out in "uninterrupted operation." Additionally, according to DuPont, in the interest of "economy . . . an effort was made to reduce the processing cycle time, and to increase the amount of metal processed per charge." By December, the large number of irradiated fuel slugs being stored (cooled) had been reduced to "normal levels." After that time, "as the result of an increase in radioactive iodine deposits on vegetation in outlying districts," the cooling period was lengthened from about thirty-five to about sixty days.[37]

By August 1946, the number of charges being processed had fallen only to sixty-one per month.[38] However, the lengthened cooling times of the dissolved metal allowed vegetation and atmospheric contamination levels to sink somewhat more quickly. In January, these values stood at .64 μCi/kg at Richland and .63 μCi/kg at Pasco. A DuPont report confirmed: "Radioiodine concentrations on the ground in Pasco, Kennewick, and Benton City fell steadily but did not reach the estimated permanently safe level of 0.2 μC/kg until April." In Richland, contamination values did not plunge into the "safe" range until May. In the early spring, the H.I. staff extended its sampling range and found contaminated vegetation in a 150-mile radius.[39] The final quarter of 1946, during which GE, the new contractor company, operated the Hanford Site, witnessed a further rise in vegetation contamination. According to a GE chemist, L. D. Turner, such radioactivity levels "gradually increased during this period in all locations," including those locations that were "Off-Area." In December, sampling locations in Richland, Pasco, Kennewick, Benton City, and at two stations more than fifty miles northeast of Hanford all exceeded the "tolerance condition" of 0.2 μCi/kg.[40]

Radioiodine and the Thyroid

Even during the earliest years of Hanford's operations, some basic facts about the affinity of iodine (both radioactive and stable) for the thyroid gland were known. Almost as soon as the isotope I-131 was discovered in 1942, it was used as a standard medical therapy to slow down (i.e., partially kill) extremely active thyroid function.[41] In 1946, *Time* magazine reported, "The thyroid gland takes up nearly all the iodine fed to the body . . . radioiodine inhibits overactive thyroids."[42] Two years later, another popular U.S. journal affirmed: "The thyroid cannot distinguish between ordinary iodine and radioactive iodine . . . the thyroid . . . commits suicide when it accepts radioactive iodine."[43] At the same time, unclassified (public) AEC research confirmed: "the thyroid gland picks up and utilizes nearly all of the iodine in the human system, normally about 80 times as much as any other tissue . . . Special fission-made iodine [I-131] . . . can . . . destroy human thyroid tissue, if it can get at it. Since it is attracted to thyroid tissue, it can be used to destroy it, whether or not it is diseased."[44] By mid-1948, nearly forty hospitals and laboratories in the United States were engaged in AEC-sponsored studies of radioiodine's effect on the thyroid. One such research project noted, "The human fetal thyroid begins to collect radioiodine after the fourth month of pregnancy."[45]

Radioiodine Concerns and Calculations

At Hanford, Herbert Parker and other health physicists were concerned with radioiodine from the beginning of operations. Almost immediately after the start of dissolving operations at Hanford, the 200-Area stack monitors became so contaminated with I-131 that accurate readings could not be obtained. Efforts to fix this problem continually failed throughout the spring of 1945. On June 1, according to DuPont, "routine operation" of the stack monitors "was abandoned."[46] In October, in conjunction with Dr. Simon Cantril, a health physicist on loan to Hanford from the Clinton Site, Parker and other H.I. officials established a "tentative tolerance concentration of I-131 in the atmosphere." An exposure value of 2.5×10^{-13} curies per cubic centimeter (Ci/c3) was determined for an eight-hour work shift. However, the health scientists knew that the radioactive gas was spreading beyond the site boundaries into the cities where plant workers lived. They set a lower figure based "in actual practice . . . [on] a 24-hour exposure." The continuous exposure quantity was 1×10^{-3} Ci/c3.[47]

In December, due to "recent increases in the amount of radioiodine available for inhalation and ingestion on the reservation and in the surrounding areas," Parker initiated "a critical examination of the current tolerance values." He further noted that medical dosages of I-131 as a therapy for hyperthyroidism had recently been revised downward by nearly 50 percent. Consequently, he lowered the permissible eight-hour inhalation exposure at Hanford to 1.2×10^{-10} Ci/c3.[48] In February 1946, he warned in an internal memo that he "preferred [the] practice of restricting all planned exposure to about one-half of the permissible dose."[49] At the same time, he directed John Healy to study how to contain the I-131 in the separations plants themselves. In April 1946, Healy concluded that the "simplest method" would be to install a "scrubber [stack filter] large enough to handle all of the dissolver off-gases."[50]

Meanwhile Parker, like others at that time, was still confused. He did not know where the primary I-131 hazard lay—whether in drinking water, inhalation, absorption of "vapor" through the skin, or ingestion through the food chain. By January 1946, he was on the right path: "The . . . iodine hazard for farm animals . . . probably arises from the contamination of edible plants." He researched earlier studies on the I-131 uptake rate for the thyroids of animals and humans. Although these rates varied, Parker "assumed that an uptake rate of 20 percent of the ingested amount [was] representative in all cases . . . [and] that the mechanism [was] the same in domestic fowl." Thus, working from the current tolerance dose of one rad per day to the thyroid gland, he arrived at his permissible vegetation contamination level of 0.2 μCi/kg (based on the 20 percent uptake rate).[51] Wanting to determine the amounts of radioactivity collecting in the thyroids of animals in the Hanford vicinity, Parker ordered army and H.I. personnel to capture and test such animals beginning in early 1946. Sheep and cattle grazing near the Hanford Site were "roped from Army jeeps, then thrown and tied" for thyroid checks with Geiger-Müller (G.M.) counters. The tests were done covertly, according to DuPont officials, "under conditions which avoided the excitement of public curiosity." According to the physicist Leona Marshall Libby, the food chain connection was clear: "Great plumes of brown fumes blossomed above the concrete canyons [separations buildings], climbed thousands of feet into the air and drifted sideways as they cooled, blown by the winds aloft . . . The plumes cooled and descended on the desert where the iodine vapor stuck to the artemisia leaves: these leaves were eaten by the rabbits, which in turn were eaten by the coyotes . . . the increasing radioactive content of . . . coyotes' thyroids was regularly monitored."[52] During 1946, the radioactive content (assumed to be predominantly I-131) of the thyroids of tested stock fell within the tolerance limits believed to be safe at that time, and the covert checks were stopped. Thereafter, measurements of ground contamination were used to "deduce the average activity of farm animals."[53]

A few years later, the animal thyroid situation looked much different to Parker and his colleagues. By mid-1949, Hanford biologists had discovered thyroid "concentration factors" in rabbits of twenty to forty times that of the vegetation. Some rabbits that were allowed to browse on 200-Area vegetation, as "bio-indicators" of contamination, showed thyroid activity levels of 100 μCi/kg. Thus, the scientists were forced to question their assumption that animal thyroids would remain safe if the vegetation contamination level was held at the "tolerable level."[54] The following year, Herbert Parker acknowledged, in a secret memo, that the results of the "furtive" 1946 measurements of stock thyroids had been "dubious." Tolerance values had been revised downward. In light of this and other new knowledge, Parker estimated "that range animals were heavily overexposed [to I-131] . . . by a factor of about 1,000 in midwinter 1945–46 . . . [and] by a factor of about 100 in midwinter 1946–47."[55] Likewise, by 1951, developing information had cleared up some of the confusion about the primary sources of I-131 contamination. Radioiodine present in water, Hanford biologists had learned, was not "critical . . . toward influencing thyroid activity densities."[56]

Plutonium in Stack Gases

The year 1947 brought concern over plutonium in the Hanford Site stack gases. Pu-239, on the average of one milligram (mg) per day, had been detected in the 200-Area off-gases at Hanford in mid-1946. A maximum quantity of one mg in ten hours had been discharged, along with other "mixed fission activity" averaging less than two millicuries (mCi) per day.[57] By December, the H.I. chemist F. P. Seymour reported to Parker that the level of Pu-239 in the stack emissions was down to "about 20 mg" per month. The total amount released thus far, he estimated, was "on the order of 0.5 grams."[58] The following summer, Seymour's colleague Robert Thorburn devised a chemical method for separating and evaluating alpha contamination on vegetation. He found Pu-239 on samples of Hanford vegetation but did not test for uranium.[59] At the end of 1950, however, the H.I. Division placed the atmospheric discharge rate for plutonium between 50 and 30 micrograms per twenty-four hours (ug/Pu/24 hrs).[60]

Early "Speck" Problem

In the meantime, in the autumn of 1947, Herbert Parker reported the presence of a definite particulate or "speck problem" at Hanford. Particulate matter containing I-131, as well as longer-lived isotopes such as Ce-144, yttrium, Sr-90,

Ru-106, and Cs-137 (in descending order of percentages), had been found near the 200-Area stacks. The particles also contained chemicals such as carbon, iron, silicon, and hydrogen, components of the resin paint that coated the insides of some of the ducts and fans of the processing facilities. The specks were being emitted at the heavy rate of approximately 10^7–10^8 per month from each of the two separations plants (T and B). The highest areas of deposition, near the stacks, received as much as 50 particles per square foot (psf). According to a Hanford chemist Frank Adley, the deposited material contained radioactivity ranging from .10 to 3.0 μCi and had an "effective half-life of about 300 days."[61] A secret staff report produced in November 1947 warned that the particles were sufficiently radioactive to "cause minor damage to external surfaces of the body if retained, and to cause serious damage to the body if deposited internally."[62] Parker informed GE officials that, even with "no visible reaction on the skin . . . radiation damage could occur."[63]

GE Facilities Manager W. K. MacCready reacted as soon as he was informed of the situation. "The condition described is not consistent with accepted operating standards of contamination control . . . and therefore constitutes a serious health hazard requiring the utmost expediency in its correction." He ordered the immediate replacement of painted iron ductwork and fans with stainless steel equipment. He also directed the installation of both temporary and permanent air filter systems in all exhaust ducts, tank vent piping, stacks, and fans of the T, U, and B (separations) buildings.[64] However, the problem proved to be more intransigent than officials imagined. By January 1948, Parker was identifying "droplets" or "acid mists" from condensed or coalesced processing gases. Like the particles, these mists contained activation products and oxides of nitrogen. They also resulted from the corrosion of the painted and masonry surfaces inside the 200-Area structures. However, their components were so small and soluble that they could pass right through the new filters being installed. The mists possessed, in fact, the "minimal settling qualities . . . [of] smoke and gases." As such, they could be carried long distances into the areas neighboring the plant.[65]

In March, GE officials therefore decided to relocate the planned REDOX (separations) site south and slightly west of its anticipated location.[66] Additionally, during the eight months beginning in April 1948, eleven major air-monitoring stations, designed especially to measure particulate contamination, were established. Three of these stations were in the immediate off-site vicinity, at Richland, Pasco, and Benton City. Eight others stretched in a large trapezoid from Great Falls, Montana, to Boise, Idaho, to Klamath Falls, Oregon, to Stampede Pass, Washington. Many smaller stations were established at post

88

offices as far away as Juneau, Alaska.[67] Also begun, according to a GE report, was the "routine liberation of no-lift theodolite balloons from the 200 Areas . . . [to] indicate whether certain areas are located in a concentration of winds from the Project."[68]

In October 1948, "sand filters" (simply blocks of sand through which gases were forced) were installed at T and B plants.[69] At first, the sand filters were hailed as a great success. Meeting in early 1949, the AEC Advisory Committee on Biology and Medicine (ACBM) termed the filters "99.7% efficient." It declared that the filters had ended the "immediate . . . health hazard." However, the committee unanimously recommended that "in connection with the particle problem," cancer research funds should be used "for studies on cancer of the lung."[70] Throughout 1950, according to Parker, "high radioactive particle content" in the air remained a problem. The sand filters were replaced in late 1950 with smaller, less expensive fiber-glass filters. Nevertheless, the particulate problem continued, and even worsened, at Hanford through 1954.[71]

Iodine Levels Vary, 1947–1949

The most troubling atmospheric problems at Hanford throughout the late 1940s and early 1950s, at least in terms of sheer volume and constancy of occurrence, continued to be those involving I-131. In early 1947, metal cooling times at Hanford ranged between sixty and ninety days. In January, vegetation contamination levels at Richland, Pasco, and Benton City again rose above the "tolerable concentration" of 0.2 μCi/kg. A "trend of contamination spread toward the northeast" was noted by the H.I. chemists Healy and Turner, in a secret memo.[72] Additionally, H.I. Deputy Chief Gamertsfelder admitted in secret that the tolerance dose for I-131 in the human thyroid was simply theoretical and that its accuracy could be only "estimated within a factor of two."[73] Nevertheless, Herbert Parker reported to the AEC in early 1947 that Hanford had "successfully accomplished [solved the problem of] . . . the emission of active gases, particularly radio-xenon and radio-iodine, into the atmosphere."[74] The commission disagreed, reporting on a health and safety survey of its eastern Washington facilities the following year. "The discharge of certain radioactive and chemically toxic materials, such as iodine, fluorine and argon, is not infrequent. Oxides of nitrogen are also discharged in substantial quantities . . . In some instances the factors of safety are low."[75] Vegetation contamination levels in the Tri-Cities dropped into the "tolerable" range during the second and third quarters of 1947 but rose again with the expansion that began late that year. According to the biologist Kenneth Herde, fourth-quarter rises in I-131 contamination on vegetation occurred throughout "a rather wide expanse of privately owned agricultural lands of Washington, Idaho and Oregon." Herde was worried: "In some cases thyroids of game birds probably are eaten by man and this may [constitute a] . . . hazard." Upland wildfowl seemed to be particularly at risk, since they nested on, and derived their food and water from, both river and land vegetation sources. By that time, levels of radioactive contamination in the Columbia River had begun to climb, worrying Hanford biologists.[76] Additionally, construction plans recently developed for McNary Dam at Umatilla Rapids, about thirty-five miles downstream along the Columbia from Richland, would soon flood wildfowl nesting and feeding areas in the vicinity of McNary Dam. Site scientists knew that more birds would come to consume vegetation along the Hanford Reach. Radiation assays done on game birds taken in the territory from forty miles west to seventy miles east of the Hanford Site during the 1947 hunting season found thyroid activity values ranging from .04 to 5.0 μCi/kg. The highest concentrations, far above the "tolerable limit," were found in birds taken from 4 to 8 miles north and northwest of Richland.[77]

As a result of this evidence, and of a tentative decision by the internal hazards subcommittee of the National Committee on Radiation Protection to reduce the MPC for I-131 in humans by a factor of ten, Parker proposed an increase in metal cooling time at Hanford.[78] In the spring of 1948, cooling times were extended beyond ninety days. Meanwhile, scientific consultants, including Enrico Fermi, traveled to Hanford to seek technical solutions. In mid-1948, the AEC appointed an Advisory Stack Gas Problem Working Group, consisting of national experts in industrial health and ventilating problems. The team was charged with the "improvement of existing filters and development of other types of equipment for removing radioactivity from air and gases."[79] Although their studies were to be directed toward aiding all AEC installations, Hanford was given "priority in the efforts of the working group."[80]

In June 1948, the stack gas group reported that, in view of the impending installation of sand scrubbers at Hanford, a return to ninety-day metal cooling times might be safe.[81] Parker disagreed. The efficiency of the filters could not be guaranteed, he asserted, adding that a "fraction of the total iodine" appeared "to escape during process stage rather than dissolving." In the meantime, the NCRP as a whole had voted to reduce the MPC for I-131 not by a factor of ten but by a factor of twenty-five. Parker informed the stack gas group that, using the new NCRP guidelines for vegetation limits for I-131, "the Hanford operations would fail to conform even in distant areas." Parker lowered his tolerable vegetation contamination level to 0.1 μCi/kg, but still confused about the I-131/vegetation pathway, he told the group that there seemed to be "no natural absorption of iodine by leafy vegetation." Nevertheless, he recommended a further extension of fuel slug decay time to "the maximum consistent with [the Production Department's] being able to meet operating obligations until further study of the I-131 deposition in the surrounding area [could] be made."[82]

Throughout most of 1948 and 1949, metal cooling times at Hanford varied between 90 and 125 days. Vegetation samples in the Tri-Cities hovered in the "tolerable" range (near 0.04 μCi/kg), and bird tissue activity declined slightly.[83] Nonetheless, in late 1948, the AEC's Advisory Committee on Reactor Safeguards (ACRS) reported in secret that it would not consider the atmosphere of the Columbia Basin safe until "the stack discharges from the chemical processing plants . . . [were] sufficiently freed of radioactive and chemically toxic materials."[84] In 1949, increased amounts of metal were processed, albeit after relatively long cooling periods. Vegetation contamination levels rose early in 1949 to an average of 0.2 μCi/kg at Richland.[85] These levels represented relative success over the contamination amounts of 1945–47. Only about 1.2 curies of I-131 per day were discharged from the 200-Area stacks during the second and third quarters of 1949.

The Green Run

December 1949 brought the largest single known incident of atmospheric contamination in the history of the Hanford Site. The operation was known as the "Green Run" because it was said to have taken place on raw, or "green," uranium fuel slugs. They had been cooled only sixteen days.[86] Although the specific reasons for the Green Run still are classified by the U.S. Department of Defense, several factors and partial explanations are accessible. In late September 1949, the Soviet Union detonated its first atomic bomb. The blast was not announced but was detected first by Hanford's atmospheric-monitoring equipment throughout the Pacific Northwest and Alaska. Early H.I. personnel have recalled their confusion when fallout from the test first registered at their survey stations. They readily deduced that the source of the contamination could not be Hanford facilities, since monitoring stations in widely divergent locations all showed comparable deposition. Two GE chemists, Robert Thorburn and John Healy, were flown to Washington, D.C., to explain the findings. Two months later, the Green Run, a Department of Defense operation, took place. A DOD meteorologist went to the Hanford plant and defined the conditions under which the Green Run took place and gave the order to proceed. H.I. Deputy Chief Gamertsfelder later recounted that the AEC had assumed that the Soviets' rush to make atomic weapons was causing them to use short-cooled fuel (about twenty days out of the reactor). Such "hot" fuel would be subject to detection at considerable distances from the USSR. The AEC and military officials, he explained, decided to test their assumptions by creating similar conditions and emission levels in eastern Washington. Michael Lawrence, the DOE manager at Hanford in 1986, agreed that the Green Run's purpose was "related to the development of monitoring methodology for intelligence efforts regarding the emerging Soviet nuclear program."[87] At the same time, a Hanford monitoring scientist, Keith Price, concurred that the experiment "was for the purpose of testing instrumentation." He added, "Reading between the lines, this was the Cold War, and they were wondering if they could speed up production of plutonium."[88]

The question of whether the Green Run was a radiological warfare experiment, designed to test harm to foodstuffs and living creatures, is still open. However, according to many early H.I. scientists, the real purpose of the Green Run was not to see how damaging would be the dissolving of metal cooled such a short time nor to determine whether such a brief cooling period could be used safely to speed plutonium production. H.I. scientists already knew, from their experiences, that such a dissolving would produce extremely high amounts of radioactivity in the off-gases.

At least two individuals in knowledgeable positions have stated that the Green Run went awry. Meteorological conditions were defined to include high wind dispersion. When light winds and a cloud cover were forecast for the planned date, Gamertsfelder recalled, he and other Hanford scientists "recommended it not be run at the time . . . The time was wrong."[89] The wind shifted radically, although not completely unexpectedly, after the I-131 was in the air. DOE Manager Lawrence later confirmed, "The total quantity of iodine 131 released was somewhat more than expected . . . the weather turned out to be less favorable . . . resulting in less dilution than expected."[90]

The results of the Green Run, in terms of air and vegetation contamination levels in the Columbia Basin and throughout large stretches of the Pacific Northwest, were extreme. Beginning on the evening of December 2, 7,780 curies of I-131, along with 4,750 curies of Xe-133, were released. Rain and snow moved in quickly, with heavy deposits "raining out" in a pattern northwest and southwest from the 200-Area stacks. Vegetation samples taken in the Tri-Cities and Benton City immediately after the Green Run and continuing until Christmas 1949 averaged I-131 contamination levels ranging between 8.3 and 61.7 μCi/kg. The highest recorded value was 107.3 μCi/kg at Kennewick. (This reading was nearly one thousand times the then-tolerable limit.) Communities up to seventy miles form Hanford demonstrated readings from 2.0 to 5.0 μCi/kg. Walla Walla displayed values between 5.0 and 10.0 μCi/kg.[91] Carl Gamertsfelder has stated that along the Columbia River between Hanford and

The Dalles, Oregon, the radioiodine cloud "probably got as many people as it could."[92] Two weeks after the Green Run, thyroid activity levels in wildfowl taken within seventy miles of Hanford had jumped to an average of nearly fourteen times the levels of October.[93]

Experiments with Shortened Metal Cooling Times

After the Green Run, I-131 airborne discharge levels at Hanford temporarily returned to the range of 1.2–1.3 curies per day. However, worried about the developing Russian atomic program, GE scientists experimented with various decreases in cooling times. Although they never approached the raw Green Run conditions, they did shorten metal cooling periods to 43 days in a series of 1950–51 tests. Commenting on the plan to reduce fuel slug cooling times below the prevailing standards of 88 to 90 days, H.I. Chief Parker observed that the most significant hazard would be the ingestion of I-131 vegetation depositions by grazing animals, particularly in the "belt Benton City-Richland-Kennewick-Pasco . . . [the] representative area of maximum contamination outside the reservation." Over the previous 18 months, except for the weeks after the Green Run, average values in the "reference belt" had been .02–.03 μCi/kg, with occasional samples about five times the average. Cooling the fuel rods at Hanford for only 75 days, Parker estimated, would bring vegetation contamination averages to .08–.12 μCi/kg. Cooling the rods for only 50 days, he calculated, would increase "all exposure values by a factor of 32." Vegetation contamination would be "about 6.0–10.0 μC/kg, with isolated locations at times 30.0–50.0 μC/kg." The condition, he emphasized, would "properly require a willingness on the part of the AEC to compensate for possible injury to animals over a wide area." This was considered "unjustifiable overexposure without arrangements for compensation." However, it "would be safe with respect to humans off the reservation."[94] (From this statement, it is clear that Parker had not made the connection between the consumption of the milk of cows contaminated with I-131 and damage to the human thyroid.)

Silver Reactor Filters

In the meantime, in 1949, Technical Division chemists at Hanford had become interested in new "silver reactor" filters. They theorized that the silver nitrate bed in the filters would chemically react with radioiodine to form silver iodide, thus binding the I-131 more tightly than could physical capturing devices. The "water" (caustic) scrubbers and sand filters, in use at Hanford since 1947 and 1948, had proved to have maximum efficiency rates of 85 percent and 50 percent, respectively. In October and December 1950, amid great hope, silver reactor filters were installed at B and T plants.[95] In September 1950, anticipating good results from these filters, experiments in shortened metal cooling periods got under way at Hanford. That month, cooling time was reduced to just under 70 days. With only the caustic scrubbers and sand filters in place, daily discharge rates for I-131 rose to about 25 curies. During the following two months, the cooling period was increased to approximately 78 days, and about 10 curies per day were released. Beginning in December, with the new silver reactors in place and with the cooling time held near 78 days, the atmospheric emission level for radioiodine fell to about 1 curie per day. This rate held steady for two and one-half months.[96] An initial report, delivered in January 1951, placed the efficiency level of the silver reactor filters at 99.9 percent.[97]

In view of the significant successes of the new filters, Hanford scientists dropped the cooling time to 67 days in mid-February and to an average of 60 days in March. By early April, they shortened it to 48 days, with a minimum period of 43 days. During these months, the average emission level of I-131 hovered at only 2–5 percent of that evolved. However, aggregate quantities discharged to the atmosphere of the Columbia Basin rose significantly, to 16 curies per day in early April, with a maximum of 39 curies in one twenty-four-hour period. GE scientists explained: "As expected, the total curies emitted per day increased with the significant increase in the amount of I-131 involved in the dissolvers."[98] Later in April, according to the H.I. monitors Herman Paas and Joseph Soldat, a "material change in the efficiency of the silver reactor . . . was noted." By early May, with cooling times ranging from 44 to 55 days, the average fraction of I-131 released to the atmosphere had risen to 25 percent, with a maximum of 34 percent released. Throughout May and June, the average fraction of radioiodine emitted to the air leveled off at 10–15 percent, with a maximum of 28 percent. Nevertheless, with the greatly elevated throughput of metal, made possible by decreased cooling periods, the amounts of total curies released soared to a daily average of 181. A one-day maximum of 425 curies was reached. By late July, experimental evidence caused Hanford scientists to report in secret, "Emission on the order of 20 to 30 percent of the dissolved I-131 may be expected for any individual dissolving." Clearly, there was a problem with the silver reactor filters. Metal cooling periods again were lengthened to 80 to 100 days, and the atmospheric emissions of I-131 dropped to an overall average of five curies per day for the fourth quarter of 1951.[99]

Other Iodine Research

At the same time, beginning with the idea of "complexing the I-131 in solution with mercury salts," Hanford researchers initiated a long series of chemical trials designed to reduce radioiodine in the off-gases. Chemists learned that the silver reactor filters became saturated quickly. Cooling periods had to be maintained between 90 and 100 days at the B and T plants built in wartime and at U Plant, a metal recovery processing facility opened in 1952. At REDOX, the newer separations facility that opened in 1952, cooling times varied between 76 and 97 days, but difficulties and emissions above tolerance levels persisted there into the mid-1950s. From February through April 1955, according to Hanford chemists, REDOX discharged "significant quantities" of radioiodine. Emissions average 7.9 curies per day and "exceeded the amount of I-131 which [could] be tolerated." Attempts to understand and solve the problems, site scientists admitted in a secret document, "resulted in several theories which were hard to prove or disprove." At the same time, GE production managers proposed shortening the metal cooling period to 70 days. They suggested revising Hanford's then-current permissible release limit of 1 curie per day, up to a new level of 10 curies per week (with not more than 3 curies per day). H.I. chemists calculated that, at least for the wartime bismuth-phosphate separations plants, the drop to a 70-day cooling time would result in the unacceptable emission rate of 2.8 curies per day.[100]

The "iodine problem" remained troublesome at Hanford throughout the mid-1950s. Throughout the years 1952–54, quarterly averages of I-131 releases did not exceed 4.2 curies per day and usually stayed below 2.8 curies per day. Nevertheless, norms never held at the rate of 1 curie per day, the level necessary to meet the permissible vegetation contamination level.[101] In an August 1955 symposium, none of the speakers could affirm the safety of reducing the holding time to 70 days. Dependable measures to counter the high emission rates generated by shortened cooling times were not at hand.[102] Additionally, projections of the expected 1961 power and enrichment levels created worrisome scenarios. Even with filters operating at 99.5 percent efficiency, the Hanford engineer R. E. Smith calculated that cooling times of 105 days would produce the atmospheric release of 7–8 curies per day. Cooling periods of 90 days or 75 days would yield the respective discharges of 25–30 or 90–110 curies per day.[103]

In early 1956, the new PUREX (plutonium-uranium extraction) separations plant achieved full production, and the wartime T Plant was retired. The average daily release of I-131 from the Hanford stacks dropped to 1.0015 curies per day during 1956–57. However, individual incidents of significant contamination occurred sporadically in January, February, November, and December 1956.[104] Similar incidents occurred in December 1957 and April 1958.[105] A summer 1957 study by a scientist brought to Hanford to research the radioiodine problem confirmed: "Excess amounts of I-131 are sometimes allowed to escape in the off-gases. Why the silver reactors fail to contain the I-131 at these irregular intervals is not known."[106] Intermittent emissions of high levels of I-131 took place, although with decreasing frequency, through 1963. In September of that year, according to a Hanford engineering report, one such emission was caused by the inadvertent charging of "short-cooled" fuel at PUREX.[107]

Vegetation and Animal Thyroid Levels Reflect I-131 Fluctuations

During the 1950s, throughout the period of experimentation with shortened metal cooling times and silver reactor filter technology at Hanford, I-131 deposition levels on vegetation and in animal thyroids clearly reflected the fluctuations in safe and "intolerable" emission quantities. In 1950, the H.I. Division doubled the total number of air samples and augmented the quantity of sampling stations. Throughout 1950 and the first two months of 1951, activity density on vegetation in Richland averaged .16 μCi/kg, slightly above the then "tolerable" level of .10 μCi/kg. However, decreased cooling times and filter difficulties brought levels to an average of .40 μCi/kg in early April. Norms spiked to 2.5 μCi/kg two months later. One sample collected southwest of Kennewick peaked at 23.0 μCi/kg.[108] During 1950, in the territory up to two hundred miles from Hanford, the thyroids of all pheasants assayed contained "detectable levels of I-131." Within thirty miles of the 200-Area stacks, according to Parker, "nearly all specimens . . . exhibit[ed] levels above the permanent MPC for I-131." Early 1951 values were comparable, but they soared in the second quarter of 1951. In the third quarter, according to Parker, a full 92 percent of all wildlife assayed still "exhibited thyroid activities in excess of the . . . chronic MPC of I-131 in man."[109] The periodic PUREX and REDOX problems from 1955 through 1958 caused spikes in thyroid activity in jackrabbits in the Hanford vicinity. In June 1957 and April 1958, these concentrations reached nearly 100 μCi/kg.[110]

Thyroid Medical Information Accumulates

Throughout the 1950s, more biomedical data on the effects of radioiodine on the thyroid accumulated. In 1951, *The American Journal of Roentgenology and Radium Therapy* again emphasized the "amazing greediness" of the thyroid for any kind of iodine.[111] In early 1952, Parker's H.I. Division at Hanford reported in secret that 99 percent of the radioactivity contained in I-131 was retained on the leaves of exposed forage and was not translocated within the plants.[112] Despite these findings, and the excessive I-131 values in regional flora and fauna, no information about the contamination was given to the population of eastern Washington. In fact, in a public report describing events of the second half of

1951, the AEC stated, "The escape of these materials [radioiodine and other fission products] . . . is held to such low limits that they are not a hazard to animal and vegetable life in the vicinity."[113] Hunting for wildfowl remained a popular and locally promoted sport in the Columbia Basin throughout this period.[114]

Experiments with large animals at Oak Ridge National Laboratory in 1954 confirmed severe thyroid damage after I-131 administration. That same year, in a symposium entitled "The Thyroid," scientists discussed in detail the relationships between radioiodine and atypical thyroid activity.[115] In 1954, University of Indiana researchers linked hypothyroidism with increased tooth decay, and doctors were warned of the recent discovery that I-131 could pass through the milk of nursing mothers into babies.[116] The following year brought the ominous news that two patients treated with radioiodine for thyroid cancer had developed leukemia. Other evidence linked hypothyroidism and impaired reading ability.[117] By this time, the ability of animal thyroids to concentrate the I-131 levels on vegetation to vastly higher levels than those on the leaves themselves was well known.[118] Likewise, the path of radioiodine, through the food chain from vegetation into animal milk and in turn to the human thyroid, had been determined. In 1954, the AEC's Division of Biology and Medicine suggested in a secret report, "Doses to the thyroid from iodine radioisotopes may be a greater hazard than Sr89-90."[119] Herbert Parker stated publicly in 1956: "Human breathing of I-131 . . . turns out not to be the final relevant problem . . . One must be concerned with the secondary hazards set up . . . the hazard to grazing animals eating vegetation contaminated with I-131 and the additional possibilities of . . . [deposition] over truck-farming land where [vegetation] products are used by man or used directly as in milk from cows on contaminated pasture."[120]

The Windscale Accident
The linkage among the deposition of gaseous radioiodine on vegetation, its subsequent uptake by range animals, and its ultimate passage through their milk to the humans drinking the milk came to the world's attention in an unmistakable way in 1957. At that time, Pile no. 1 at the Windscale plutonium production facility in England overheated, and radioactive fission products spewed from its stacks. Within twenty-four hours, milk samples from area cows jumped to six times the permissible level for I-131. Two days later, the English Atomic Energy Authority imposed a milk quarantine on seven hundred farms over a two-hundred-square-mile area. The condemned milk was dumped into the Irish Sea along thirty miles of British coastline. The wide publicity given to

this accident and its aftermath dramatically underscored the milk-radioiodine link in the public mind.[121] In 1963, the milk connection was irrevocably confirmed by an AEC scientist, Dr. Harold Knapp. His report on the abrupt rise in I-131 in milk and in human thyroids after nuclear bomb tests in Nevada was a landmark biomedical study.[122]

Sheep/I-131 Studies at Hanford

Much of the knowledge that was gained in the 1950s concerning animal uptake of radioiodine and food chain transfer mechanisms was learned through the pioneer sheep studies of Dr. Leo Bustad at Hanford. The idea for the study was conceived in 1948, and in the spring of 1950 the veterinarian Bustad, with associates in biology and related disciplines, initiated "Problem 690.02." They fed pellets, containing varying dosages of I-131, to sheep kept at a new Experimental Animal Farm on the atomic site. Dosages ranged from 0.005 to 1,800 microcuries per day (μCi/d). According to Parker, the lowest feeding level was designed to approximate "the amount required to effect a deposition in the thyroid equal to the accepted permissible limit." A control group received no radioiodine. Evident within one season were the findings that lambs born to ewes fed radioiodine showed decreased thyroid activity at birth and that I-131 concentration in the ewes' milk was as high as one-third of the daily dose given to those animals. By the end of the second year's lambing, in mid-1951, there was clear evidence that thyroid damage, caused by I-131, produced concomitant problems throughout the body. According to Parker, animals fed high dosages of radioiodine demonstrated "a stupid and lethargic attitude, a stiffness in gait, muscular weakness . . . difficulty in prehension and mastication . . . ulcers . . . [and] one ewe lamb was completely blind." Autopsies revealed multiple changes in blood, hormone, and mineral levels. At that time, the two sheep groups being fed the highest dosages were eliminated from the study. Their thyroids, and those of their offspring, showed virtually complete destruction. A concurrent experiment by Bustad's group determined that, once thyroid damage had occurred, the gland's function did not repair or regenerate even after I-131 ingestion was discontinued.[123] This finding, together with all of Bustad's data, was classified.

In mid-1951, new dosage levels for test groups of sheep were established, ranging from 0.15 to 135 μCi/d. As the Bustad studies progressed, data showed that dosages of radioiodine were harmful at much lower levels than had been thought. As early as 1952, gross deformities were demonstrated in sheep fed amounts of only 45 μCi/d.[124] In August of that year, Parker affirmed these findings to the AEC.[125] However, in November 1953, Bustad, acting as an AEC consultant in an investigation of Utah sheep deaths after atmospheric atomic bomb tests, reported, "Radioactive iodine . . . must be administered in quantities in excess of 480 μC/d to adult sheep in order to produce an impairment of health."[126]

By 1956, Bustad's seminal sheep studies at Hanford had revealed that dosages as low as 1.5 μCi/d for "extended periods" resulted in "diminished [thyroid] avidity . . . [and] lesions that proved to be adenomas." Harm, the veterinary group reported in secret, began to appear at an estimated "cumulative dose of 2,000 rads."[127] Yet, in an early 1957 article in *Nature* magazine, Bustad stated that in his project, the sheep that were exposed to dosages of 15 μCi/d or less showed no "evidence of thyroid tumors." Tumor involvement, he asserted, occurred at an estimated dose of 30,000 rads.[128] In early 1959, a document prepared by Harry Kornberg, the manager of Hanford's Biology Operation, disclosed that six out of seven sheep maintained on the 5 μCi/d dosage had developed "multiple adenomas . . . further confirming the tumorigenicity of this level."[129] Later that year, Bustad revealed to AEC biomedical directors that even sheep fed at levels of 1 μCi/d evidenced "a decrease of thyroid function with time, and at sacrifice 4 to 5 years later show[ed] frank adenomas and/or highly abnormal thyroid function: fibrosarcomas were also found."[130] In 1963, however, he disputed Harold Knapp's evidence of the concentrated passage of ground-deposited I-131 through range animals and into their milk. Bustad claimed a much lower level of transfer.[131]

Airborne Particulate Problems at REDOX

The years 1952–54 also witnessed significant particulate releases from the new REDOX chemical-processing plant. The flaky particles contained high concentrations of radioruthenium (Ru-103 and Ru-106). They were opaque, sometimes black or reddish in color, of irregular shape, but often convex or concave. They could appear as white specks and sometimes as fragile flakes up to several inches in diameter and ranging from one sixty-fourth to one thirty-second of an inch thick. Often, they were large enough to be perceived by the unaided eye. When the stacks were flushed with water, the radioactive particles appeared on the surrounding ground as "bubble-like masses." According to a secret 1954 report, "Operation of Redox separation facility has resulted, almost from the very first, in frequent emission of varying quantities of radioruthenium in excess of desired limits." The REDOX stack air monitor was not installed until June 1952, so quantities released before that time cannot be determined with precision. However, contamination problems began to be noted as early as March of that year. Air activity concentrations rose as high as 1 rad per hour (r/hr). Some instances of heavy emissions may have gone undetected, however. In at least one case in September 1952, a thirtyfold increase in the number of particles appeared on the glass wool-control frames around the REDOX stacks, whereas the stack monitors indicated no abnormally large discharges of ruthenium.[132]

Available evidence shows that releases of Ru-103 and Ru-106 remained at tolerable levels for nearly a year after this September 1952 episode. In August 1953, large fragments or chunks of material, some several inches long and one-half to three-fourths of an inch thick, were seen on the ground around the REDOX stacks. Testing revealed that the active component was radioruthenium. The dose rate was 15 r/hr (full rads) at the particle surface and 300 mr/hr at a distance of two inches. At the same time, stack monitors indicated emissions of only 2 to 3 curies per day, an amount vastly lower than that necessary to produce the visible proliferation of the very active material. These same monitors showed release levels of 35 curies on September 5 and 80 curies on September 6.[133]

In 1954, the radioruthenium particulate problem worsened and spread to produce some of the most acute, specific incidences of off-site contamination in Hanford's history. Stack flushing and caustic scrubber failure at REDOX caused the release of 260 curies of Ru-103 and Ru-106 on January 2–3. An additional 70 curies was discharged to the atmosphere on January 5. Vegetation surveys revealed contamination stretching in a northeastward arc from the 200-W Area to Spokane and Davenport, Washington. At distances as far as 150 miles, samples as high as 10 μCi/kg (or one hundred times the permissible level of .10 μCi/kg) were found. On farm and range land up to 30 miles from the Hanford Site boundary, vegetation samples contained 100 μCi/kg.[134] Further contamination episodes occurred in April and May but were confined to on-site locations and to the Wahluke Slope, uninhabited rangeland across the Columbia River from the 100 Area. The REDOX plant was shut down from June 10 to July 18 in order to install improvements to the stack air systems. However, stack flushings and particle redeposition from previous releases, according to Herbert Parker, caused contamination to spread "outside [the] perimeter barricade in [the] direction of Richland" in late June.[135]

Biomedical Information and Discussion of Particulates

During the year of the initial REDOX particulate releases, Hanford officials and the AEC's Advisory Committee on Biology and Medicine (ACBM) discussed them in secret. As early as January 1951, a Hanford official told the committee, "The particle problem still remains, in my opinion, a very serious health problem." In December of that year, Dr. Earnest W. Goodpasture, vice-chairman of the ACBM, advised AEC Chairman Gordon Dean: "Cancer is a specific industrial hazard of the atomic energy business . . . This significant fact justifies, in the opinion of the Committee . . . special facilities for radiation cancer research, diagnosis and therapy . . . The cancer program [should] be pursued as a humanitarian duty to the nation."[136] By mid-1954, public, AEC-sponsored research had shown that "inhalation of radioactive dust particles in high concentrations" was "one of the chief potential radiological hazards to animal life." Radioactive particles below five microns in size, studies demonstrated, were "deposited in the terminal parts of the lung . . . the bulk of these particles was subsequently carried to the gastrointestinal tract."[137] Secret biological studies performed at Hanford in the summer of 1954 found that the radioruthenium particles being discharged locally had "variable and fairly high solubility" in serums and solutions mixed to "simulate lung conditions . . . [and] gastric juice."[138]

Largest REDOX Particulate Releases

In August 1954, more severe emissions occurred at REDOX. Parker estimated that, in Richland, these stack discharges had resulted in deposition rates of approximately 1 particle per 1,000 square feet on grassy areas and 1 particle per 3,000 square feet on bare surfaces. He calculated maximum dose rates in the government town to be 180 mr/hr. In "all other local communities . . . contamination [was] probable but not yet measured." Experiments with rats and pigs led Parker to compute that some of the particles could deliver a radiation dose of up to 60 rems per hour to the lungs or 160,000 rems in twenty-four hours at contact with the skin. Based on known standards and data, he admitted to GE officials, "Particles of the activity found in Richland and other neighboring communities can give skin contact doses well above conventional safe limits." On the Hanford Site itself, the unquantified risks to personnel from exposure to the particles was deemed serious enough that travel was restricted to main roads for all but work crews and monitoring teams.[139]

Off-site residents were not warned nor restricted in any way. Although he kept AEC officials "fully informed" of the radioruthenium particulate problems, Parker asserted, "Nothing is to be gained by informing the public." He added, "Not all residents will be as relaxed as the one who was recently quoted as saying, 'Living in Richland is ideal because we breathe only tested air!'" The cost of complete removal of the off-site particles was "prohibitive" and not "feasible," Parker stated. Shortly thereafter, Dr. John Bugher, the director of the AEC's Division of Biology and Medicine, reviewed the radioruthenium problems. He, along with other AEC and GE-Hanford managers, confirmed

Parker's recommendation not to tell residents of the contamination. Information on the situation did not become public until many years later.[140]

Subsequent Particulate Releases
In the years after 1954, the Hanford reservation experienced only a few significant episodes of particulate discharge. Contamination events involving radio-ruthenium occurred in December 1955, January and June 1956, July and November 1957, and during the winters of 1958–59 and 1959–60. Only in the case of the November 1957 REDOX release was radioactivity distributed outside of the 200 Areas. In that incident, according to Hanford scientists, "high winds on following days were responsible for extensive spread of the contamination."[141] In a few other cases, fires in the 300-Area waste burial grounds and in ruptured fuel slugs in the 100 Area, spread active particulate matter. In almost all of these cases, contamination stayed within the Hanford Site boundaries. Sometimes, radioactive particulates were spread by the wind when reactor retention basins were dried out for repair work. The most significant unplanned releases of this type occurred in 1957, when basins of 100-C and 100-D scattered particulate matter containing mixed activation products. Even though the areas were flushed repeatedly with water, high wind speeds and velocities caused redeposition in an east and northeast arc.[142]

AEC Reviews of Airborne Consequences of Potential Reactor Accidents
Throughout the 1940s and 1950s, Hanford and AEC officials sometimes discussed the airborne consequences of potential reactor accidents. In early 1947, Carl Gamertsfelder reported on the probable atmospheric effects of an explosion of one of the Hanford piles (reactors). He estimated that the greatest airborne dangers would come from "the broadcasting of fairly sizeable amounts of plutonium, and of radioactive iodine." The deposition of Pu-239 on vegetation, he stated, "could very well introduce a greater potential hazard than that brought about by direct breathing of contaminated air." He added, "Similar considerations apply to the radioactive iodine." Gamertsfelder postulated, "Maximum contamination on the order of 0.4 C/kg [full curies] could exist several miles from the explosion." Such an area "would have to be evacuated immediately because radiation levels near contaminated vegetation would be on the order of 20 rep/hr."[143]

In mid-1948, the ACRS, meeting to review the Hanford situation, made an even more dire evaluation. Commenting on potential explosions, the committee stated, "It is clear that the piles cannot be considered as definitely safe." The group computed a formula for establishing safe distances from the reactors. A "completely controlled area" from which the public should be excluded, they decided, should exist for a distance one one-hundredth of the square root of the operating kilowatt level of each reactor. Applying this formula at Hanford, the "controlled area" would extend for a five-mile radius around each reactor. Outside of this control area, the committee asserted, that there was a "region of real but much smaller hazard." The group stated, "It seems to us reasonable that this area be inhabited, but we recommend that it not contain any large center of population." The group would not set a "definite radius" for this tract. However, it stated in secret, "We estimate that this 'hazard area' extends far enough to include the city of Spokane." The ACRS added: "Thought should be given to further safeguards [for the reactors]. By this we do not mean mere duplication or pyramiding of safety devices, but rather . . . safeguards operated on somewhat different principles and designed for new purposes . . . the potential usefulness of [the Hanford] piles depends in great measure on further safety devices."[144]

This report remained classified for twenty-six years. In 1949, in another secret document, Herbert Parker elucidated for top Hanford managers more about the 1948 ACRS findings. A reactor meltdown, caused by a total water loss, explosion, or enemy bombing or sabotage, he estimated, would create a triangle of air and ground contamination one to two miles wide at its base at the reactors. It would extend thirty to eighty miles outward at an angle "determined by wind direction." The inhabitants of this zone, Parker affirmed, would be "potentially killed by the inhalation hazard, unless previously evacuated."[145]

By 1955, eight reactors lined the Columbia River on the Hanford Site, and all operated at significantly elevated power and exposure levels. These levels continued to rise throughout the remainder of the decade.[146] Still, no metal shells or other safety domes existed to contain fission products in case of a severe reactor accident. This situation continued to worry the ACRS. Meeting in 1955, this committee recommended a series of experiments to determine the "rate of release of fission products from melted fuel elements" in case of a reactor accident at Hanford.[147] Tests in heating unclad uranium fuel rods at varying temperatures and irradiation levels were conducted from mid-1958 through 1961. During these tests, uranium oxide particles, and the radioisotopes of several gases such as xenon, iodine, ruthenium, tellurium, zirconium, and barium, were released in moderate amounts.[148]

By January 1958, the safety questions posed by potential explosions or meltdowns of the Hanford reactors had become the subject of intense debate within the AEC in Washington, D.C. At that time, the ACRS concluded: "In allowing the Hanford reactors to operate at present or increased power levels the AEC is accepting a degree of risk which is greater than in any other existing plant. The Committee . . . [recommends] against increase in power or exposure levels until additional measures are taken to restrain the spread of fission products if they should escape from the reactor in an accident."[149] The ACRS wanted a completely "air-tight container . . . enclosing the entire reactor plant . . . the final safety device in protection of the environment."[150] On receipt of the ACRS recommendations, the commission's Director of Production, Edward J. Bloch, placed a temporary moratorium on planned augmentations in power and exposure levels at Hanford. GE engineers, however, argued for removal of these limitations, "even though the [limits] . . . did not jeopardize the production forecast previously provided to the DOD." They explained, "Whereas the *severity* of a reactor accident would be enhanced incrementally with each increase in power and exposure levels, the *probability* of accident would not be increased." Bloch concurred. In mid-1958, he recommended the removal of "current restrictions" in the Hanford reactors. He noted, "The contribution to national security through gains in plutonium production . . . appear to out weigh the . . . consequences . . . [of] the unlikely event of a major reactor accident."[151]

Throughout the remainder of 1958, the AEC debated Bloch's report and advice. At the same time, $4 million worth of filters and fog sprays were installed as interim safety measures in Hanford's reactors. A feasibility study completed that year showed that $40 million would be needed to "completely encase" the reactor buildings in metal shells.[152] In early 1959, the AEC approved the accretion of power and exposure levels at Hanford. Some commissioners disagreed, asserting, "In providing a completely safe situation, there should be no consideration of funds involved."[153] In early 1960, GE proposed further increases in maximum permissible power levels at Hanford. At that time, ACRS Chairman Leslie Silverman warned in secret, "The advisibility of continuing to raise Hanford power levels . . . remains as questionable as it did . . . several years ago."[154] Nevertheless, power accretions went forward. In 1964, the AEC admitted: "Dependence [at Hanford] was placed on strict administrative control of operations and the engineered safety features of the reactors to prevent . . . a major release of radioactivity . . . Studies showed that containment domes similar to those on power reactors could be built but would be extremely costly."[155] None of the eight reactors operating at Hanford at the time were ever encased in a protective dome.

Airborne Waste and Army and Company Security Forces at Hanford

During the years of Hanford's heaviest airborne emissions, one group with high potential exposure was the army and company security force that guarded the site. These sentries, especially those patrolling the complex and constructing and manning the antiaircraft defenses, were near the atmospheric wastes and the contaminated sand and vegetation. They slept out overnight on the atomic reservation, often in open-air tents or hastily built huts and barracks. While the construction dust swirled from 1943 through 1955, while tests of various particulate and gas filters went forward throughout the late 1940s and 1950s, while the 1950–51 experiments with shortened metal cooling times were conducted, and while the radioruthenium flakes whirled from 1952 to 1954, they walked, stood, dug, ate, and slept on the contaminated site.

A small force of Military Police (MPs) and Military Intelligence (army G-2) personnel guarded the Hanford Site at the start-up of plutonium manufacturing in late 1944. In June 1945, the MP allotment was increased to forty soldiers. Their chief role was to patrol the miles of fences, roads, shoreline, and river of the Hanford Site. Additionally, the Bonneville Power Authority (BPA), a federal entity, provided a few patrolmen of its own to protect the Midway electrical substation and power transmission lines. The substation was located near Vernita, approximately seven miles west of B reactor. Because of this proximity, Matthias stated that the army would "accept no responsibility" for the safety of these guards.[156] Army MPs remained at Hanford until April 1947, when the new AEC assigned guard duties to company patrolmen of the site contractor, GE.[157] However, the huge production expansion initiated in late 1947 brought new concerns about security. In early 1948, General Mark Clark, commander of the Sixth Army (Western Defense), asserted, "Troops should be there [Hanford] permanently—and immediately."[158] In both the spring and the fall of that year, Clark sent troops from Fort Lewis (near Tacoma) to the atomic complex on prolonged maneuvers. However, according to Senator Henry M. Jackson, the congestion and lack of housing in the 1947–49 expansion prevented the troops from staying permanently.[159] In the meantime, GE's security patrols were issued M-8 light armored tanks.[160] Although this equipment was useful for ground actions, the antiaircraft defense crucial to Hanford was still missing.

Finally, in March 1950, in the biggest convoy in Washington State's history, troops arrived at the Hanford Site from Fort Lewis. They brought 120-mm antiaircraft guns, each protected by four 50-mm machine guns. Their headquarters and temporary housing was at North Richland. In 1951, "Camp Hanford" was officially designated by the army. Eventually, three battalions, the 501st, 518th, and 519th, served at the station. In late 1952, the antiaircraft guns were replaced by Nike missiles. These in turn were supplanted by more advanced Nike Ajax missiles in 1954. Still later, Nike Hercules missiles, bigger and faster

weapons with a nuclear option, were emplaced. The 1st and 83rd missile battalions, along with support services groups, served at Camp Hanford during
the Nike years. By the late 1950s, however, the development of intercontinental
ballistic missiles had rendered Hanford's missiles obsolete. On July 1, 1959,
Camp Hanford became a subpost of Fort Lewis. The Camp was deactivated in
1960, and the North Richland offices were transferred to the AEC in 1961.[161]

Very little written material about Camp Hanford has been preserved by the
army.[162] The one booklet that is available, and the statements of several veterans, attest to the rugged, outdoor life of the troops who staffed the gun and
missile emplacements. Furthermore, the same sources reveal that the troops
were not given special radiation equipment, information, training, protective
clothing, nor warnings of potential or real hazards.[163] Many of the MPs and
Camp Hanford soldiers have similar memories of life outdoors on the atomic
site. One MP has recalled his service during 1946, the year that 76,000 curies of
I-131 swirled out from the plant's stacks. The main MP base was located between
Richland and the production areas. He has recounted: "We lived and ate there
except when we were at the sub-station which had Quonset huts where we slept
and a separate one . . . [where] we ate. We had almost daily duty at some sentry
position. There were the Richland, Yakima and Prosser barricades, the sub-
station, the desert patrols, the airport and motor pool, and camp sentry duties . . . I do not recall any . . . radiation training . . . Clothing was regular Army
issue . . . We did not have any radiation dosimeters, film badges or geiger
counters . . . We were never told that we were subject to any radiation exposure."[164]

In addition to the main base at North Richland, Camp Hanford maintained
sixteen weapons emplacements around the production areas. Three of these
bunkers were across the Columbia River, on the Wahluke Slope. This region
was very prone to gaseous drift and deposition from the Hanford plant stacks.
Veterans of the original army detachment that came in the spring of 1950 have
recounted that when they arrived at Hanford, the army told them nothing of
their mission or of the nature of the Hanford plants. The young men were
driven in open vehicles across the sandy, unpaved roads of the Hanford Site and
deposited about two miles west of the 200-W Area. There were no facilities.
The sagebrush had been bulldozed away shortly before the troops arrived, and
the former soldiers remember that the sandstorms were terrible. The men were
told to build gun emplacements and to fill hundreds of sandbags around them.
For about two and one-half months, they were picked up each evening and
driven back to North Richland to sleep. After that time, they moved into tents
near the gun bunkers. They did calisthenics in the sand each morning and were

required to stay out of their tents, near the guns, all day. They got three days' leave every fifteen days. On this leave, they were restricted to the Tri-Cities area, and they generally slept in the North Richland barracks. They also received thirty days of furlough per year, when they were free to leave the region. They watched the excavation and early construction of the REDOX plant and lived amid the billowing dust of that project. In 1951, with no explanation, they were ordered to move their entire position about four miles to the west. Once again, the sagebrush was bulldozed and they dug their camp and gun emplacements in the sand. They wore regular army clothing and had no radiation equipment, dosimeters, nor information.

Veterans of the later, missile years at Camp Hanford have told of similar conditions. However, as the years went on, more of the roads were paved on the Hanford Site, and the forward missile bases got concrete buildings with tile floors, windows, and running water. Also, the missiles were stored underground, so that soldiers were not required to fill and emplace as many sandbags. Some of the demolition troops spent their time dynamiting sections of the White Bluffs to stabilize crumbling overhangs and to provide rock for construction crews on the Hanford Site. None can recall receiving any special radiation training, clothing, equipment, or information. According to one veteran: "I was never told anything in particular about the Atomic Plant. I understood that it produced parts and/or materials for atomic bombs and that was about it . . . Upon my discharge, I had to sign a form . . . that I would never tell anyone what I knew about the Atomic Plant. I thought that was funny because I didn't know anything about it!"[165]

Although some people worried about the silent and invisible risks in the air, sand, and desert vegetation at Hanford, no steps were taken to warn or protect the soldiers. A GE engineer assigned to design filters to trap the radioactive particulates spewing from the 200-Area ductwork and fans between 1946 and 1950 recalled later that he was especially worried about the guards who circled the canyon buildings about one thousand yards out. "I suggested that [Hanford officials] reveal to everybody what the situation was, and have them wear respirators; my group wore them . . . But they didn't tell anybody . . . The reason was alarm."[166] As Camp Hanford itself was created and enlarged in 1950–51, AEC officials in Washington, D.C., and in Richland secretly discussed possible dangers to military personnel. Early in the camp's history, AEC-Hanford Manager David F. Shaw recommended to the ACBM that soldiers spend no more than one-third of their time in plant areas. The troops should be "exposed to airborne particles to the same or lesser degree as plant personnel." However, he stated in early 1951 that the new silver reactor filters in the separations plant stacks had reduced the external radiation dose to a "negligible" level. Current emission levels, he told the AEC, "should not be a limiting factor in the military personnel duty."[167] At nearly the same time, Herbert Parker's H.I Division established three new air-monitoring stations "to evaluate the dosage to which military personnel" were exposed. Radioactivity values at these locations, H.I. staffers reported in June, "were among the higher dosage rates outside of the operating areas."[168]

Environmental-monitoring surveys conducted over the ensuing years of the 1950s continued to demonstrate airborne radiation levels that were higher at Camp Hanford's forward positions than at off-project or 300-Area locations. In fact, readings at some of the military sites often were comparable to measurements within five miles of the 200 Area.[169] During the 1954 radioruthenium particulate releases from REDOX, Parker told Shaw, "The appropriate control of military forces within the [Hanford] reservation introduces special problems." A month later, evaluating the external (beta burn) radiation hazards from the particles, Parker again flagged the exposure risks of the soldiers. "The military personnel on the site appear to be at greatest risk."[170] On at least three occasions between 1956 and 1958, army positions on the Hanford Site, especially those at Rattlesnake Mountain, demonstrated the highest radiation readings of all locations at the atomic complex.[171] Yet, the monitoring data and internal GE communications were classified, and the troops were never informed.

Airborne Wastes and the Columbia Basin Irrigation Project

Growers of the Columbia Basin Irrigation Project came to the Hanford region beginning in 1948. Their outdoor occupations and the fact that they disturbed and worked amid the contaminated vegetation and sand, as well as their position to the east of the atomic site ("downwind"), may have placed them at augmented risk. Additionally, many farm families drank milk from backyard cows and ate leafy produce from backyard gardens. Both of these diet factors increased the amounts of radioactivity that were ingested. If a family's life-style also included hunting and fishing, quantities of radioactivity rose still further.

The CBP was a long-postponed dream by the time World War II began. The idea for a huge dam at the Columbia River's Grand Coulee, about 120 miles north of Pasco, had been proposed as early as 1892. The concept of building a dam at the head of this huge, empty flood channel and running irrigation water down it to bring life to the parched soils of eastern Washington came to life in the Rivers and Harbors Act of 1935. Water began to fill the partially completed reservoir (Lake Roosevelt) behind the dam in 1939. The first priority of the project, the generation of electrical power, commenced in October 1941. American entry into World War II two months later drained manpower and money from the irrigation aspects of the Grand Coulee enterprise. During the years of battle, only preliminary reclamation surveys and engineering studies could be done.[172]

The main portions of the CBP actually developed between 1946 and 1960. Progress was not uniform. Budget constraints, the huge Columbia River flood of 1948, and the ongoing postwar operations of the Hanford project intervened. Nevertheless, in a phased, albeit somewhat spotty fashion, new farms crept southward from the Grand Coulee to Pasco. There were two notable exceptions. Block I, about fifty-four hundred acres just north of Pasco, was the first to be occupied and tilled in May 1948. Conversely, the Wahluke Slope, a huge area just north of the Columbia River from the Hanford Site, was withdrawn from the CBP when the atomic complex was established. In early 1947, the U.S. Department of the Interior, Bureau of Reclamation (BOR), reported to the AEC a "prospective increase in per acre construction costs on the remainder of the project . . . and an added burden for operation of the rest of the project." However, "by far the most serious loss," according to the BOR, was the "blocking of agricultural production valued at . . . $22.5-million, based on 1946 farm prices."[173]

The land and the favorable credit terms of the CBP were popular. The decision was made to allocate farm plots on a lottery basis, with preferences given to World War II veterans. Additionally, farming experience and cash assets were firm requirements. Still, callers abounded.[174] Many of the hopeful young veterans submitted their names year after year to be matched with a piece of the flat, dry Columbia Basin. By the end of 1958, water was available on nearly four hundred thousand acres of CBP land. In about 1960, with demand for land still strong but declining slightly, the veteran preference was dropped.[175]

The CBP was divided into three major segments: the Quincy, East, and South districts. The South District, extending roughly fifty miles north from Pasco, was the one closest to the Hanford Site. This district also included the Wahluke Slope. With the exception of Block I near Pasco, the Quincy and East districts developed sooner than the South District. Intense construction activity and overcrowding in the Pasco area (due to postwar Hanford expansions) and uncertainties over the availability of Wahluke land caused delays in the southern CBP sector. In the Quincy and East districts, encompassing major chunks of Grant and Adams counties, construction activity, land values, and town growth leaped between 1948 and 1955. From 1954 to 1959, the farm blocks on the east side of the Columbia River, just across from Hanford, filled with families.[176]

The Wahluke Slope issue continued to vex the CBP. In July 1948, the AEC announced its decision to permanently restrict farming in a "central zone" of about 88,000 acres (45,000 irrigable) on the slope. It also set aside "secondary zones" on either side of the central sector, where irrigation was "indefinitely deferred." The secondary zones consisted of approximately 173,000 acres, of which 107,000 were irrigable. "Security needs and possible dangers to inhabitants" were the reasons given by the AEC.[177] In fact, the upsloping Wahluke terrain caused concentrated quantities of 200-Area off-gases to come to ground there. The furtive sheep, cattle, jackrabbit, and wildfowl thyroid checks of 1946–47, as well as the secret, ongoing air and vegetation monitoring by Hanford scientists, had shown very heavy wind drift and contamination along the slope. One such survey in February 1947 found at least twenty-seven spots on Wahluke land where vegetation contamination exceeded Herbert Parker's "tolerable concentration" of 0.2 μCi/kg.[178] Furthermore, when the AEC's Reactor Safeguards Committee evaluated the risks of Hanford's operations in 1948, its classified report affirmed: "The main hazards to prospective residents of Wahluke Slope is the violent increase in pile activity leading to fire and dispersal of fission products and plutonium through the countryside. For a person just across the river from the pile the danger would indeed be most acute." With regard to the 200-Area stack emissions, the committee asserted: "The distribution of these stack materials over the Wahluke Slope and over many other areas to great distances is a cause of much concern. Their elimination is essential."[179] In December 1948, the AEC reaffirmed its decision to close the slope to farming and stated that it was "highly improbable" that these lands could be opened for settlement "within the foreseeable future."[180] In 1953, the AEC did grant right-of-way acreage on the Wahluke Slope for certain roads, canals, and power lines of the CBP.[181]

The issue of opening Wahluke Slope lands to agriculture and settlement was raised again in 1958 as the ACRS was evaluating the question of increasing power and exposure levels in Hanford's reactors. GE scientists reported to the ACRS: "in the absence of gross accidents . . . the general contamination of the Wahluke Slope is comparable with that of the Tri-City area . . . Restriction of the occupancy of the Slope against normal contamination is thus not plausible." In the case of a reactor meltdown or explosion, however, they stated that a "release of reactor contents" might "exercise its effect mainly over the Wahluke Slope."[182] As the AEC discussed the power level throughout the remainder of 1958, the question of settlement at Wahluke Slope was raised over and over.[183] In December 1958, when the AEC decided to allow the increase of reactor power and exposure levels at Hanford, it also agreed to release the secondary zones of the Wahluke Slope to the BOR for farm development. Additionally, about thirty-two thousand acres in the control zone were transferred to the custody of the bureau, but no agriculture was permitted.[184]

The first farm blocks on the Wahluke Slope were occupied in 1961 and 1963. In mid-1965, the AEC announced its intention to release approximately thirty-nine thousand acres of the control zone to the BOR for "daylight farming" (nonresidential) only. However, drainage studies completed by the bureau in 1967 demonstrated that irrigation there would contribute to underground pressures that could increase the potential for landslides toward the White Bluffs and the Columbia River. They decided not to develop the land.[185] In November 1971, the AEC issued permits to the U.S. Fish and Wildlife Service and to the Washington State Department of Wildlife to divide the control zone into two wildlife refuges. The western portion became the federal Saddle Mountain National Wildlife Refuge and the eastern (larger) portion became the state Wahluke Wildlife Recreation Area.[186]

Aside from the Wahluke Slope, settlement of the CBP's South District did go forward between 1953 and 1958. The farm families who came to live across from the Hanford plant in Franklin County and southern Adams County, along with the 1948 settlers of Block I near Pasco, struggled hard with the dusty Columbia Basin. In the mid-1950s, a Washington State College survey of CBP families found that family labor, including labor by wives and children, typified the lives of CBP settlers.[187] All CBP settlers, whether they came in 1948 or a decade later, remember the dust and wind. Settlers who bought farms in the region in the mid-1950s quipped that a person could "sneeze and create a dust storm."[188] A 1957 newcomer spoke for others by stating simply, "Our land was powder."[189] Leo Vogel, who wrote a book about his late 1950s farm settlement in Franklin County, described the Columbia Basin ground: "Even the heavier soils will blow with a little encouragement, and the lighter soils are treacherous indeed . . . Wetting down the soil does little good. As soon as the top layer of molecules gets dry the wind will lift it and send it on its way." The year 1959, he recalled, was an especially windy one.[190]

As CBP farms were platted, surveyors "staked" the fields. Every one hundred feet, they placed a stake marked "cut" or "fill" a certain depth (usually one to four feet). Surface irrigation demanded level land. Next, "levelers" came in huge tractors dragging scrapers behind them. Throughout the 1950s and early 1960s, BOR tractors had open cabs. One driver recalled, "You ate a lot of dirt." Leveling went on all year long, unless the ground was frozen. Next, dirt irrigation ditches two to three feet deep were dug on each farm. "Corrugates," three to twelve inches deep, were cut through the fields perpendicular to the ditches. One mid-1950s farmwife has stated, "Maintaining the ditches and corrugates, keeping them clear of weeds, kept you outside all the time, kept you lean." In the 1960s, cement ditches came to the CBP. In 1976, most of the land was re-leveled for push-button "circle" (sprinkler) irrigation.[191]

As the CBP was filling the counties north and east of Hanford with families, site scientists studied and discussed hazards connected with farm settlement. In the late 1940s, they worried especially about the development of Block I because the irrigation water for that tract was drawn directly from the Columbia River about twenty miles downstream from 100-F Reactor.[192] Crop tests in 1949 showed radioactivity values in soil two miles north of the old Hanford townsite to be "higher by a factor of ten than the average given for non-irrigated land on the east bank of the Columbia." During the 1950 growing season, levels of beta radioactivity in the crops and soil of the test station increased by 25 percent over the length of the season. Still, Hanford scientists termed the amounts "only minor," adding that "none was significantly high to cause concern."[193]

Over the ensuing years, many crop studies were undertaken at Hanford. The susceptibility to, and uptake rates of, radioactivity in various plants were determined. In 1950, Hanford researchers found that tomato plants grown in sand through which reactor effluent had been passed concentrated the radioactivity three to ten times over the level of the sand. In the following two years, Herbert Parker's H.I. Division tested the translocation of yttrium, and radioisotopes of cesium (Cs-137), strontium (Sr-90), and cobalt (Co-60) in barley, wheat, and red kidney bean plants. Again, they found higher concentrations in the plants themselves than in the activated nutrient solutions. In one experiment, vegetables and meat were boiled in water containing reactor effluent; as the liquid evaporated, the uptake of radionuclides in the vegetables was "greatly accelerated." Absorption of radioactivity by the meat also occurred, but at a lesser level.[194] The results of these experiments were usually classified and were not shared with BOR officials nor with the Columbia Basin farmers. For reasons of economy, the bureau did not conduct its own tests for radioactive contamination in the vegetation, soil, or water. Also, the bureau did not believe that it had sufficient expertise in radiological science. It accepted the AEC's assurances of radiological safety.

During the heaviest radioruthenium particulate emissions of 1954, growers working the wheat harvest were not informed of any problems, even when Herbert Parker calculated dose rates of 700 mr/hr, every six hundred feet, in the farming areas of Benton and Franklin counties. Even though, according to Parker, "ground contamination was found in orchard and field crop areas," crops from the affected areas were "allowed to proceed to market." Meat supplies from area cattle likewise went to market.[195]

Following the 1954 radioruthenium releases, GE scientists devoted intense study to the problems of wind pickup, erosion, and impaction of particles and contaminated sand. They quickly realized the chief dangers. In this windy, arid region, according to the engineer John Healy, a difficulty came from "recirculation and re-deposition . . . [of] particles from desert soils and sands." All meteorological equations and theories, he reported in secret, might "well be outweighed . . . by the disturbance of the top surface of the ground during work in the region."[196] The meteorologist G. R. Hilst was even more specific: "The problem of migration of these noxious particles is intimately related to the erodibility of the natural surface upon which they lie . . . Tilling of soil so as to form troughs and ridges increased the erosion rate dramatically." On the Hanford Site, Hilst's group experimented with methods of "fixing" activated particles in place. They tried irrigation, paving, chemical binders, and artificial obstacles such as snow fences, shelterbelts, rock courses, plowed furrows, and cover crops. They found that erosion and "diffusion" of particles was the most severe from furrowed areas.[197] However, the farmers and equipment operators of the CBP were not informed.[198]

In 1959 and 1960, and again in 1964, major "off-project exposure" studies were done by Hanford scientists on selected population groups. Residents of Pasco, and especially residents of a few farms in the Ringold-Riverview area just north of Pasco, were chosen for intensive investigation. Dietary habits and lifestyle (primarily occupation, recreation habits, and amount of time spent outdoors), the researchers found, were the most important factors in determining radiation exposure. In these studies, the life-style of the "maximum individual" profiled by Hanford scientists and the outdoor life-style of CBP families were often in close approximation. The "average individual" in these studies typically held an indoor job, did not have a backyard milk cow, and did not grow or capture a great deal of his own food.[199]

Airborne waste emissions were heaviest throughout the first decade of operations at the Hanford Engineer Works. For at least ten years after that, isolated incidents of atmospheric contamination occurred. After about 1955, with increases in power and fuel-exposure levels in the reactors, river-borne contamination began to rise sharply, and Hanford officials turned their attention to wastes in the Columbia River.

"Hail Columbia":
The River-borne Contaminants

Conservative practice would never condone the *planned* pollution of a national asset such as the Columbia River with a long-lived contaminant such as plutonium . . . [Such pollution would] greatly lower public morale in the Columbia Basin [and] it would be a poor business risk.—Herbert M. Parker, "Speculations on Long-Range Waste Disposal Hazards," January 26, 1948

Columbia River and Its Fish Were Objects of Early Concern

The safety of the Columbia River from atomic wastes was among the earliest concerns raised by the Manhattan Project officials who built the Hanford Engineer Works. The economic value of the fishing industry, particularly the salmon catch, in the Columbia was affirmed by General Leslie R. Groves, who served as the overall Manhattan Engineer District chief, and by many others associated with the project. Colonel Franklin T. Matthias, the army commander at Hanford also noted the great love of the people of the Northwest for the big river. The Columbia, the largest river flowing into the Pacific Ocean from the North American coast, is approximately 1,200 miles long. It drains some 259,000 square miles. The Hanford Reach of the river, that stretch encompassing the HEW, runs from about 300 to 350 miles upstream from the mouth. It is a principal hatchery and fishery for salmon and steelhead trout and, to a lesser extent, for whitefish.

Salmon and steelhead, as the earliest Hanford aquatic biologists knew, thrive best in cold water. The eggs and fingerlings could be vulnerable to thermal increases produced by Hanford's reactors. Additionally, there was concern that the radionuclides in reactor effluent could harm all of the fish species in various, unknown ways.[1] Would radiation cause certain species to fail to reproduce, or to reproduce in wild abundance, thereby upsetting the river's natural balance? Would the water itself be unfit to drink, even after filtration, at Pasco and Kennewick?[2] Or would the food chain connection to humans prove to be the most dangerous? Would the tissues of fish and waterfowl that lived in and around the Hanford Reach attain radiation levels that were unsafe for consumption?

As early as the start of HEW construction in March 1943, the MED posed questions about the amounts of radiation a fish would receive in water containing radioactive material. Scientists could calculate only probable absorption ratios, based on the performance of an air-filled ionization chamber in water. No biological data was available.[3] General Groves proposed such experiments, and in a complicated contractual agreement between the federal Office of Scientific Research and Development (OSRD) and the University of Washington (UW), an ichthyologist, Lauren Donaldson of UW, was retained to direct the fish project. In August 1943, the university created the Applied Fisheries Laboratory under the sponsorship of OSRD (later MED, then AEC).[4]

Reactor Effluent Components and Effects

The Hanford Engineer Works used the waters of the Columbia River under the "reserved rights" doctrine of American jurisprudence. Any of the natural resources, including water, of the Hanford Site could be utilized by the project as long as the use was "consistent with the primary statutory purposes" for which the site was created. The mission was to "produce plutonium for nuclear weapons." According to federal officials, the Columbia River could be utilized to whatever extent was necessary to accomplish that mission.[5] However, the atomic energy acts of 1946 and 1954 required production, processing, and utilization operations to be conducted so as "to protect the health and safety of the public."[6] The question of how to balance the needs of plutonium production with the protection of the great public resource of the Columbia was one without an answer during the first years of Hanford's operations. As Hanford's Chief Health Physicist Herbert Parker pointed out in 1952: "At the time that the Hanford reactors were first energized, appropriate limits for the radioactivity of the effluent water to be returned to the Columbia River were not known . . . It was recognized from the start that a realistic limit would have to be based on a knowledge of . . . radiobiological consequences in the river. These were almost completely unpredictable, except as to gross order of magnitude."[7]

By 1955, eight "single-pass" (open-coolant) reactors operated along the Columbia on the Hanford Site. River water, used for cooling, flowed through the
reactors and back into the Columbia. Spent reactor cooling water (effluent) was
the largest avenue by which HEW wastes, containing fission and activation
products, entered the waterway. The fundamental strategy of Hanford scientists was to hold the effluent in retention basins (107 structures) for periods
ranging from thirty minutes to six hours, to allow short-lived radionuclides to
decay (stabilize). Nevertheless, significant quantities of radionuclides with half-
lives longer than a few hours were released to the river. Additionally, fuel slug
ruptures, chemicals added to the cooling water, and activated particulates and
debris from reactor purging (cleansing) operations entered the Columbia. Of
particular concern among the over sixty radioisotopes in Hanford's reactor
effluent (waste water) were phosphorus (P-32), arsenic (As-76), zinc (Zn-65),
chromium (Cr-51), and neptunium (Nr-239).[8] These radionuclides, primarily
beta-emitters, affected the gastrointestinal tract, bones, and reproductive and
blood-forming organs.[9] Additional worries developed in 1959, when evidence
of these isotopes was found in shellfish taken from Washington's Willapa Bay
and Oregon's Tillamook Bay. These areas, located not far from the mouth of
the Columbia River, contained important oyster and clam beds and clam and
shrimp fisheries.[10] At the same time, the Washington and Oregon health departments proposed studies to examine the rising radiological burden of the
Columbia.[11] Likewise, the U.S. Public Health Service (PHS), which had been
studying the effects of Hanford's operations in the Columbia for at least a
decade, issued a statement of alarm.[12]

Wartime Fish Research

Like other wartime endeavors at Hanford, aquatic research was carried out in
great secrecy. In 1944, MED officials installed tiny mesh screens to keep salmon
out of the intake structures for reactor pump houses. "Inasmuch as we have
made the definite commitment to . . . protecting the fish," Matthias affirmed, "it
is important that we live up to this . . . even though it costs money."[13] At the
same time, he secured a variance agreement from the Seattle District of the
Army Corps of Engineers specifying that information on river structures and
dredging operations would be maintained solely by the Hanford Project.[14] In
working through the procedures to create the UW fisheries lab and to hire Dr.
Donaldson, OSRD officials and Matthias consistently sought to "disguise" the
link to Hanford. According to Matthias, they even considered the possibility of
not giving Donaldson "any knowledge of the connection between his work and
this project [Hanford]."[15] In early 1945, when MED Medical Chief Stafford

Warren suggested that fish studies be conducted directly at Hanford, Don-aldson's assistant, the ichthyologist Richard L. Foster, was retained. Under classified arrangements, even the president of the university, Matthias affirmed, had "no idea" of what Foster was doing or why he was working.[16]

When he arrived in June 1945, Foster knew that natural salmon eggs from the Columbia would not be available until autumn. Consequently, he stocked his 100F-Area tanks with trout and kept them in concentrations of effluent water varying from 100 percent effluent (as it entered the river) to 1 part effluent in 2,000 parts river water. DuPont officials calculated that dilution of 1 part effluent to 500 parts river water would represent "the average concentration of area effluent water in the river throughout the year." Foster began to monitor respiration and reproductive rates, fungus formation, general activity level, and body burdens of various fish tissues.[17] He issued a daily bulletin to site workers. One physicist has recalled that the bulletin "might read something like this: 'Tuesday: The fish spent a good night and appear to be feeling well.' 'Wednes-day: The fish are doing somewhat poorly today,' . . . and so on."[18] Although the wartime aquatic research was not extensive, Foster later asserted, "The fact that you even initiated a program under the stresses of war is very, very unusual."[19]

Postwar Aquatic Research Continues in Secrecy

Colonel Matthias avidly supported Foster's fish irradiation studies, believing that the biological data would be "of basic and fundamental importance." After the war ended, the Health Instruments organizations of DuPont and of General Electric, and later divisions within Battelle Pacific Northwest Laboratories, continued aquatic biology studies at Hanford for nearly five decades.[20] Al-though research of tremendous importance was generated, much of it was classified (kept secret) over the years. After emergency wartime directives had expired in 1946, Foster's team was required to sign statements swearing "not to divulge to any persons, except those authorized by the U.S. government, any information received on the studies . . . conducted at Hanford Engineer Works relative to the effect of plant operations on fish life in the Columbia River."[21]

Problems associated with reactor effluent in the Columbia River developed early. Fish, both in Foster's experimental tanks and sampled directly from the river, evidenced disease and rising radioactivity levels in their tissues. By late summer 1945, according to DuPont, external parasites and "a bacterial epidemic spread through the fish" in the test troughs. DuPont officials concluded that the tests "seemed to indicate that high concentrations of the area effluent water probably [had] an adverse effect on fingerling salmon."[22] In September, Foster and some colleagues drifted through the Hanford Reach to observe fish life.

Particularly in areas of quiet, shallow water along the bars of Locke Island (near White Bluffs) and in the vicinity of reactor outfall pipes, fish were extremely plentiful. Water at the 100F outfall "had a temperature of 74F," which was very high in comparison to normal Columbia River temperatures, and it "was 'milky' in appearance." It contained a "noticeable quantity of suspended material . . . [that] may have been ferric sulphate" (particulate matter from the filtration system). Foster advised further study of the abundant fish thriving in these unnatural conditions.[23]

Early Findings

During 1946, several basic trends in the responses of fish to various concentrations of reactor effluent became evident. The higher metabolic rates of young trout and salmon caused them to accumulate proportionately more radioactivity in their tissues than did adults. Foster's group also learned that peak absorption of radioactivity by fish occurred in the first twenty-four to forty-eight hours and that accumulation occurred more slowly in cooler water. Radioactivity levels differed among various fish tissues, with livers, kidneys, and gills consistently containing the highest levels and muscle tissue (flesh) demonstrating lesser amounts. Significantly, the researchers found that the radioactivity of the effluent mixed with river water became concentrated at much higher levels in fish bodies than in the water itself. Average concentrations in trout and salmon ranged from six to thirty times that of the water.[24] Furthermore, 99 percent of young salmon raised in straight effluent water from the Hanford reactors died. At levels diluted 1:500, the amount thought to be "average" in the Columbia itself, 6 percent died.[25] Analyzing the dangerous components within the effluent, the aquatic biologists erroneously reported that the majority of radioactivity came from isotopes of manganese (Mn-56, half-life of 25 hours) and sodium (Na-24, half-life of 14.8 hours). They believed that radiophosphorus (P-32) and isotopes with long half-lives (defined in this case as fifty days or more) composed only 1.0 to 3.3 percent of activity in the effluent.[26]

At the same time that Hanford scientists conducted their early fish studies, they also measured radioactivity levels in the Columbia River itself. There was concern because both Kennewick and Pasco, located about twenty and twenty-five miles, respectively, downstream from F Reactor, used the river for sanitary water supplies. The average travel time for river water from the reactor areas to Pasco was estimated to be twenty-four hours. In 1945, HEW policies specified six to eight hours of effluent hold-up time in the reactor retention basins. That September, Herbert Parker declared that the radioactivity of the waste water fell "by a factor of 20" during the time spent in the retention basins. "Mixing and further dilution" in the river dropped it further by a factor of ten in the next two days, he asserted. Although some "channeling" of effluent had been observed in the Columbia, he affirmed, "It is clear that the problem [radioactivity in the river] . . . is definitely limit[ed] . . . to the local area near the plant."[27]

During 1945 and 1946, activity levels in effluent varied with reactor operations. Dosage rates in reactor effluent at the outfall point were measured as ranging from about 1.65 millireps (mrep) per hour from each reactor area in January 1945, up to 3.1 mrep per hour from each in February 1946, and back down to 1.75 mrep per hour from each by August 1946. The then permissible limit was 0.1 mrep per twenty-four hours.[28] However, basin leaks, such as those that occurred in the 100D and 100F structures in autumn 1945 and at the 300-Area waste pond in October 1948, could cause steep rises in radioactivity levels and hence in potential dosage rates at various points within the Columbia River.[29] The latter event discharged approximately 14.5 million gallons of active waste solution to the river.[30] Other significant reactor basin leaks and breaks occurred in 1954 and 1955.[31] An additional source of contamination, beginning in mid-1959, was the injection of tritium into reactor cooling water. A working limit of 20 curies per day was placed on the use of this highly soluble substance. It was used to locate tube leaks during reactor operations, as GE scientists sought to reduce outage time and achieve maximum plutonium production.[32] Periodic reactor purges and nonroutine events such as fuel slug ruptures within the reactors also added sharply to the amounts of radioactivity released to the river.[33] By December 1946, Hanford scientists estimated, in secret, that a total of 40,000 curies had been released via reactor effluent to the Columbia. The current discharge rate was 1,500 curies per month, down considerably from levels of about 900 curies per day reached during the push to maximum plutonium production in mid-1945.[34]

Increased Knowledge in 1947–49

The year 1947 saw a great augmentation of knowledge about radioactive wastes in the Columbia River. Early that year, Herbert Parker told the AEC: "The concentration of activity in algae or in colloidal materials with its possible utilization by fish, later used for food . . . [is] of great consequence to the public health. Up to the present time, these problems have been by-passed by ultra-conservative policy in waste disposal, but [there is a] future . . . need for extensive research on these problems."[35] In May, Kenneth E. Herde, a site biologist, secretly reported that the factor of concentration of radioactivity in fish tissue over that of the river water now ranged as high as 170,000 times, and averaged 100,000 times. "This concentration factor," he noted, "is higher by a factor of several hundred than factors previously reported." Even twenty miles below the nearest operating pile, F Reactor, concentration values were "several thousand times" that of the water. Moreover, these levels had been reached when reactor operations at Hanford had been low. Concentrations were highest in the fish kidneys and livers, organs not widely eaten by man but part of the food chain nonetheless. Concentrations were lowest in directly edible muscle tissue, but seasonal variation was least in muscle tissue because this flesh tended to concentrate the longer-lived fission products such as P-32, Zn-65, Cr-51, Np-239, and, to a lesser extent, As-76. Fish taken from the Yakima River, and from the Columbia upstream of the reactors, contained "miniscule to nonexistent radioactivity levels."[36]

The biology staff at Hanford was galvanized by Herde's report. They noted that although sport fishing was prohibited in the entire Hanford Reach, nothing could prevent contaminated fish from migrating to some of the most popular public fishing areas at Ringold, on the Columbia's east bank just north of Pasco, and at the Richland Dock. With McNary Dam at Umatilla Rapids under construction approximately twenty-five miles downstream from Pasco, Hanford biologists feared a compounding of the problem. The new dam was expected to create a pool of slack water extending up to Richland. Additionally, the Columbia Basin Irrigation Project (CBP) was scheduled to begin withdrawing river water for crop irrigation about twenty miles below 100-F Area in 1948.[37] Almost immediately, GE scientists commenced studies on bottom-living algae and on Pekin ducks living along the river. Herde also began another fish study.[38] The Pekin duck project demonstrated a clear correlation between trends in reactor operations and radioactivity levels in the wildfowl.[39] Herde's new fish study, completed in 1948, traced the root of the problem to algae, the smallest food organisms for both fish and wildfowl. "Algae are probably responsible for the original concentration while progressively more complex organisms in the food chain . . . may contribute quite significant concentrations . . . Waterfowl which . . . are later killed for food are a potential hazard to man."[40]

The limnological studies confirmed Herde's conclusion that algae collected in the Hanford Reach over the winter of 1947–48 demonstrated "an ability to concentrate [radio]activity from the water to the extent of 1,000 times." Extrapolating from the volume of these organisms found in the river, Hanford biologists estimated that the algae "would be capable of accumulating [radio]activity to the extent of two curies per mile of stream bed on the west

[Richland] bank of the river below the pile areas." Plankton collected in the sloughs of the Hanford Reach revealed radiation levels up to 4,000 times that of the river, a "distinctly higher" average than had previously been found, according to R. W. Coopey, a site biologist. Crustacea displayed concentration factors varying from 30 to 800 times that of the river water. Insects showed levels ranging from 130 to 400 times, and aquatic plants contained values of 40 to 200 times. Coopey summarized that this "concentrating ability" of the smallest and most basic organisms in the regional food chain was "in essence, the foundation of the radio-biological problem in the river."[41]

Concurrent studies explored thermal effects, reproductive abilities of the fish, and the "gross genetic" consequences of radiation exposure.[42] During 1948, GE scientists undertook further limnological, fish, and wildfowl studies. By the end of 1948, Dr. Donaldson at the UW Applied Fisheries Laboratory estimated that the overall radioactivity level of algae along the west bank of the Hanford Reach had reached three curies per mile. In early 1949, Chief Aquatic Biologist Foster detailed for Hanford's managers the process by which food chain contamination and concentration took place in the Columbia. Identifying P-32 as the prime radionuclide of concern, he told them that it was concentrating in aquatic organisms "on the order of" 100,000 times.[43]

At the same time that contamination was increasing in Columbia River organisms, radioactivity levels were rising in the water itself. Additionally, complexities within river flow patterns were becoming evident. In May 1947, L. D. Turner, an H.I. scientist, reported in secret, "There is not much mixing of the effluent by the time it reaches Hanford [townsite]." Additionally, John Healy informed Hanford officials that cross-sectional river samples at the old Hanford townsite had shown higher concentrations on the south (west) bank. These levels were "approximately equal to the concentration at the 300 and the 700 [North Richland] Areas."[44] In mid-1947, river water at Pasco and sanitary (city) water at Kennewick first showed detectable levels of gross beta-emitting radiation. To H.I. Deputy Chief Gamertsfelder, the Kennewick situation was "surprising . . . but . . . apparently real." Values in river water at Richland were even higher, reaching up to four times that at Pasco by late 1948.[45] Despite the massive cleansing action of the largest flood in the recorded history of the Columbia River in May and June 1948, radioactive concentration levels in river water continued to climb. H.I. biologists also noted high "accumulation activity" in river mud.[46] In early 1949, Hanford officials raised the MPC for river water at the point of release from the 107 basins from 100 mrep per twenty-four hours (or 4.17 mrep per hour) to 10 mrep per hour. However, according to J. M. Smith, a site scientist, the 10 mrep/hr standard had "little practical meaning" because hazards to river life were "dependent primarily on . . . longer-lived activities released." In 1952, H.I. Chief Parker admitted in secret that the 1949 revision had been based on "early appraisal of incomplete results."[47] In the meantime, plutonium production levels climbed.

CRAG Is Formed

In mid-1949, AEC-Hanford Manager Fred Schlemmer invited officials of the U.S. Public Health Service and the health departments of Washington and Oregon to form the Columbia River Advisory Group (CRAG). The group's announced purposes included education of state and PHS officials in "the health and sanitation aspects of radioactive materials" and collaboration in developing "long-range programs affecting public health."[48] Another purpose was to augment public faith in the safety of HW operations, and another may have been to forestall in-depth water pollution studies made possible under the Water Pollution Control Act of 1948, the nation's first such statute.[49] CRAG met in Richland for the first time in November 1949. Members were given tours and lectures describing waste disposal practices at the Hanford Site. They were assured that waste levels discharged to the Columbia River were not hazardous and that "the toxic [chemical] effect of pile [reactor] water treatment seem[ed] greater than that resulting from radioactive contamination." Regarding the release of long-lived alpha-emitters, such as plutonium, radium, uranium, and polonium, to the Columbia River, H.I. Chief Parker was oblique. "We could put 12 grams by weight of plutonium in Columbia per day under present tolerances. We feel that 1 gram of plutonium per day would be a very conservative amount. This answer is not to be construed to indicate that we put any plutonium into the Columbia River." As for the safety of fish and other aquatic organisms, CRAG members were told, "The river as of today could not possibly be hazardous to life."[50]

Problems Grow in 1950–51

The year of 1950 was a pivotal one in Columbia River contamination. That summer, Parker reported in secret, P-32 bone concentrations above tolerable levels were found for the first time in Hanford-area waterfowl. Activity densities in fish in the Hanford Reach "were two to four times higher than" the previous year, and concentration levels in plankton reached "an all-time high" in December. Contamination of the river water itself also rose. By the beginning of the year, average beta concentrations in the Columbia at the Hanford townsite and at the Richland Dock registered double those of the previous year. River water at Pasco and Kennewick also jumped. Additionally, "peculiar channeling" effects in the river continued to perplex scientists. In one case in July, backup and channeling of the 100-H effluent produced a "hot" area near the White Bluffs, where activity densities of some organisms climbed by a factor of twenty-two.[51] In another case, Hanford scientists noted that higher concentrations of radioactivity in water were "shifted" to the Pasco (north) side by "the Yakima River, which enters the Columbia on the south bank."[52] In the H.I. staff, employees having the Columbia River as their main responsibility performed 1,500 to 2,000 river samples in 1950, up from 980 in 1947. Additionally, design was begun on a modern aquatic biology laboratory at Hanford.[53]

Early in 1951, radioactivity levels in river plankton showed a threefold increase over those of winter 1950 and a fivefold increase over those of winter 1949. Hanford biologists estimated that 5 to 30 percent of the radionuclides contained in the plankton possessed half-lives of 14.7 days or longer.[54] In December, a secret study of the Pasco city water treatment plant was concluded, showing that inlet (river) concentrations at the Pasco plant approximately doubled between November 1950 and October 1951. Outlet (sanitary) water levels, augmented by standard water-treatment methods, were well within safety margins, but Hanford scientists expressed concern about the buildup of high radiological concentrations in the sludge (backwash). Sludge values rose over 42 times from November 1950 to October 1951. By the latter date, the activity density ratio in sludge stood at more than 500 to 1 that of the water.[55]

In January 1951, H.I. biologists completed a major report on aquatic invertebrates in and below the Hanford Reach. Conducted between October 1948 and February 1950, this research project found average concentration factors for radioactivity in the tissues of bottom-dwelling fauna to be 300–2,300 times that of the water over the entire sampling area. Near the Hanford townsite, the area of highest values, concentration factors had risen to 400–3,700 times that of the water (up from the 1947–48 factors of 100–1,000 times that of the water). In secret, Hanford scientists voiced pronounced concern. "Changes . . . which would disturb the natural biological balance . . . though they may initially affect only the most minute and seemingly insignificant organisms, might produce indirect effects of considerable magnitude which could . . . ultimately . . . directly affect the welfare of man."[56] A variety of other studies on aquatic plants, algae, mollusks, crustacea, insects, fish, and waterfowl also pointed to the passage of "radioactive elements . . . from lower to higher organisms through food chains."[57] In September 1951, Chief Health Physicist Parker noted a "marked increase [in river contamination] over the same quarter 1950," which he attributed "to changes in pile operation."[58]

CRAG and the 1951–54 River Studies

In the early 1950s, CRAG adopted less of a listener-observer stance and became more insistent on an oversight role. In 1950, a planned PHS-AEC "radio-biological-ecological" survey of the Columbia River caused tension when GE-Hanford Company argued that it should conduct the survey alone. Duplication of effort and security risks—the possibility that "information obtained on kind and amount of activity in the river could lead to disclosure of the power levels of the piles"—might result from CRAG participation, the company asserted.[59] Nevertheless, CRAG insisted, "The responsibility of the Water Pollution Control Agencies [of the states] lies in the determination of whether or not the corrective measures applied by industry are sufficient to prevent pollution."[60]

The 1951–53 survey did go forward as a joint project, designated officially as the Public Health Service Columbia River Studies. (However, separate reports were later issued.) All of the PHS researchers obtained "Q" clearances—the highest-level AEC security clearances—before beginning the study. However, cooperation remained difficult, according to PHS investigators. The AEC-GE organization at the Hanford Site was reluctant to share much information about reactor and fuel processing operations. In early 1954, the PHS submitted a first-draft report on the river survey. According to Hanford's Herbert Parker, this draft "contained several statements that would have been highly damaging to public relations." The PHS scientists were concerned about hazards to sport fishing. They considered recommending the closure to public fishing of the entire stretch between Priest Rapids and McNary Dam. At that time, the average disposal of radioactive materials to the Columbia had spiked to nearly 7,000 curies per day (after four hours' decay time). Increases in reactor power levels, planned for the later 1950s, were projected by Parker to raise activity density in fish "on the order of 5 to 10 fold." PHS scientists found such levels unacceptable.

The final PHS report, issued in 1954, was mild. According to Parker, "[GE and AEC] efforts . . . led to revisions [in this report] that should tend to preserve the present status."[61] The report concentrated on characterizing basic hydrology and river flow velocities and patterns and on analyzing the effects of the approaching impoundment of water behind McNary Dam.[62] The report carried no authority beyond that of recommendations. It termed the radiophosphorus (P-32) concentration factors in aquatic organisms in the Columbia "a potential public health problem." But the report added, "There are no definite effects yet apparent on the physical, chemical, or bacteriological characteristics of this river as a result of the discharge of reactor effluents." The sanitary water systems of Kennewick and Pasco, the PHS affirmed, were effective in removing

50 to 95 percent of the radioactive materials present at the points of intake. Likewise, the report stated, thermal effects from reactor discharges were not "detectable." Further studies and improved analytical techniques were recommended. The document concluded by advising, "Efforts should be continued toward the reduction of the amounts of radioactive materials that enter the river."[63] The GE Columbia River survey report, issued at nearly the same time, stated no conclusions on the safety or hazards of radiological conditions in the waterway. This document assessed diffusion and dilution rates and recommended "desirable sampling frequencies," locations, and techniques.[64]

Rising Waste Levels in the Columbia Prompt Debate

By the end of 1952, gross beta activity in effluent from the operating Hanford reactors had increased about twenty times over that of May 1947.[65] The following year, the first study to compare river plankton with nannoplankton, those minuscule organisms so small that they slipped through regular plankton collection nets, was completed. This secret survey found that the nannoplankton exceeded other plankton in weight and abundance by a factor of eight and outstripped regular plankton in radioactivity by a factor of sixteen.[66] By 1955, Hanford scientists had found even higher concentration values in the Columbia's invertebrates. A research project completed late that year demonstrated concentration factors in shiners and caddis fly larvae that were "160,000 and 340,000 times, respectively, that of [river] water."[67]

Debates about river-borne waste policy arose among Hanford officials, and the effluent retention policy shifted a number of times. The three original reactors, B, D, and F, each had been equipped with twin six-million-gallon concrete retention (107) basins. DR and H reactors each had nine-million-gallon concrete 107 structures. In the earliest months, the 107 basins were used in parallel (one after another), providing a holdup time of nearly eight hours. In 1946, policy changes resulted in the use of only one of the basins for normal effluent, with holding time varying from four to six hours. The remaining 107 facility was used to handle abnormal effluent such as that from purges (cleansing operations or flushes) or from fuel element ruptures. However, a fundamental question arose as 100-C Area was under construction in late 1951. Parker noted, "The total radioactivity from the Hanford piles is now several times what it was in 1947 and . . . it may ultimately reach several times its present level." He proposed a reduction in effluent retention time "to one-third" of the current four to six hours. Such a reduction, he admitted, would raise "gross radioactivity put into the river at the pile by a factor of two or three." However, he claimed that the short half-lives of some of the radionuclides "would produce no noticeable increase in radioactivity in the vicinity of Richland or Pasco and Kennewick." The cost savings in constructing smaller 107 basins at C Reactor would be about $1 million per basin. CRAG, fearing additional river contamination, rejected Parker's proposal, and the originally planned, ten-million-gallon steel basins were built. In 1952, Parker again advised, "Retention time may be safely reduced."[68]

Subsequently, both KE and KW reactors were equipped with triple nine-million-gallon steel retention basins.[69] During the first few months of operation of these reactors in 1955, the basins adjacent to each of them were used in sequence. Then, policy shifted to provide for parallel use of two of the structures and for the routing of abnormal effluents to the third. By 1958, according to a secret Hanford report, there was "progressive deterioration of concrete retention basins, particularly at B, D, and F Areas." By 1960, average holdup time for normal effluent ranged from thirty minutes to three hours. This period provided for virtually no decay of the isotopes of major concern, including As-76, P-32, and those with longer half-lives. In 1964, site scientists admitted that such retention times did "not effectively reduce the radioactivity of the effluent cooling waters." The chief function of the 107 basins, they said, was to provide some thermal cooling. By that time, systems for handling the very hazardous "unusual effluent" (primarily that from fuel slug ruptures and purges) were faulty or nonexistent. Trenches for such effluent from C, KE, and KW reactors worked by filtration and ion exchange but were located near the riverbank. A classified 1960 report admitted, "The time delay between introduction of effluent into a trench and its emergence at the river shoreline is short, probably a few hours." At the remaining five reactors, there was no mechanism at all for the holdup of abnormal effluent.[70]

The result of these practices, along with vast increases in total reactor activity, was that by 1963, the average release rate of beta-emitters to the Columbia River totaled about 14,500 curies per day (after retention decay time). Amounts climbed by nearly 4,000 curies per day in the twenty-seven months between August 1957 and November 1959. A quantity of 20,300 curies, possibly the all-time high, was attained during one day in April 1959. In the river at the 300 Area, the concentration of gross beta-emitters increased over ninety-five times between 1946 and 1959.[71]

Thermal and Chemical Effects of Reactor Effluent in the Columbia

The rising quantities of reactor effluent in the Columbia also produced thermal and chemical effects. These increases particularly affected the salmon. Studies completed that year showed that salmon, returning to the Hanford Reach to spawn, were "little affected by the pile effluent since [they] cease[d] to feed upon entering fresh water."[72] However, Herbert Parker warned in secret that year: "Current disposal practice increases the river temperature to a point which is conceivably critical in October . . . [Shortened retention times] will aggravate the condition. It is *conceivable* that we may recommend reduced power levels for a period of perhaps two weeks in each year."[73] The fall salmon run in 1951, according to the GE biologist Harry Kornberg, was "substantially less . . . than in 1947."[74]

By 1953, chemicals added to reactor cooling water to prevent slug and tube corrosion and film formation had become the object of careful attention by Hanford engineers. Sodium dichromate, and a diatomaceous earth slurry, were found to be the most helpful in impeding fuel slug ruptures and in maintaining pile reactivity.[75] In a secret 1954 report, Foster and two other biologists stated that chemical toxicity from the sodium dichromate, as well as increased river temperatures caused by the hot effluent, formed the "greatest potential threat to the local salmon."[76] Parker warned in a classified document that same year that the chinook salmon population that spawned in the Hanford Reach was "at risk in the future if adverse natural conditions in a particular year, supplemented by an increment of temperature from reactor water, [drove] the river temperature above the tolerable limit." He added: "High summer temperatures could also promote disease epidemics in transient sock-eye salmon . . . The possibility of damage . . . exists."[77] Likewise, Dr. John Bugher, the director of the Division of Biology and Medicine for the AEC in Washington, D.C., cautioned, "With the coming to full power of the new reactors [KE and KW, in 1955] . . . these problems will become more acute, especially with reference to the . . . survival of the Columbia River salmon."[78]

In early 1956, GE-Hanford Company completed a study of the projected effects in the Columbia of two additional single-pass reactors. Had they been built, these reactors would have been the ninth and tenth open-coolant facilities at the eastern Washington atomic complex. The 1956 report, called a feasibility study (but actually a prototype of the environmental impact statement that would be required under the 1969 National Environmental Policy Act), found that such reactors could raise the hexavalent chromium (sodium dichromate) levels in area river water to concentrations that would "approach the local recommended limit for juvenile fish." Also, they could increase river temperatures to points that would "make control of bacterial disease [in salmon] difficult."[79] Later that year, D. G. Watson, a Hanford biologist, reported on experiments demonstrating that temperatures of five degrees above normal for the Columbia produced "a marked increase in mortality in salmon." Such temperature elevations, he stated, "might result from future increases in reactor operation."[80] As a result of these studies, no more single-pass reactors were built at the site after KE and KW came on line in 1955. However, power levels and total throughput in the existing eight reactors did increase between 1956 and 1963, to the point that these reactors each achieved power levels nearly ten times, in the aggregate, World War II levels.[81]

Problems with salmon rose accordingly. In 1957, Chief Aquatic Biologist Foster reported that proposed new specifications for hexavalent chromium in reactor cooling water would cause "significant retardation of growth and a measurable increase in mortality . . . [in] salmon and trout."[82] The following year, he again warned that the fall run of chinook salmon was "definitely vulnerable to further temperature increases in [the] river." He pointed out that whitefish also were at risk, since thermal increments of only 2–3 degrees C "significantly increased the mortality of both eggs and young of this species."[83] That year, a program of cooling the Hanford Reach by releasing a controlled spill from the bottom levels of Lake Roosevelt, located behind Grand Coulee Dam, was instituted. For periods varying from sixteen to seventy-eight days in the late summer and autumn, average river water temperatures in the vicinity of Hanford were reduced by 0.25–1.50 C. In the severely hot and dry summer of 1961, temperatures were reduced by 7.7 C. After 1965, the gradual shutdown of the eight single-pass reactors reduced the need for special cooling of the river, and this program was discontinued.[84]

Despite the cooling program, salmon runs in the mid-Columbia declined significantly in the late 1950s. In 1959, Hanford biologists reported that the number of chinook salmon spawning in the vicinity was only about 19 percent of that of 1958.[85] In 1960, Priest Rapids Dam, approximately ten miles upstream from the 100 Areas, became fully operational, and the salmon run in the mid-Columbia was similar to the low of 1959. The Hanford biologist D. G. Watson explained, "The rapid change in river level due to dams upstream from HAPO [Hanford Atomic Products Operation] left some salmon nests completely out of water."[86] In 1961, the salmon run was much larger. A general resurgence occurred in the late 1960s, after the single-pass reactors began to close.[87]

Whitefish Accumulate Highest Levels of Radioactivity

In the meantime, as in the mid-1950s, the radioactive contamination of water and whitefish in the Hanford vicinity became worrisome to site and AEC officials. In 1952, Chief Aquatic Biologist Foster and his colleague P. A. Olson reported in secret that the highest "activity densities in fish" in and near the Hanford Reach appeared in bottom feeders such as suckers and in omnivorous species such as whitefish. They noted the tendency of these fish to migrate to popular sport fishing spots off, but near, the Hanford reservation, and they cautioned, "All indications point to the fact that the food chain is by far the most important process by which radioactivity is accumulated." They calculated in July 1952 that, in areas near the Hanford townsite, accumulation of radioactivity could occur such that "one pound of muscle from a sucker caught under peak radioactive conditions would furnish . . . about 20% of the chronic permissible intake [in man] and 1% of a single permissible intake of P32."[88] At that time, and again in 1954, Foster and other site biologists identified P-32 as the prime radionuclide of concern and estimated that it constituted 75–90 percent of the activity in fish tissues.[89] In a visit to Hanford in the summer of 1954, AEC Chairman Lewis Strauss expressed worry over the "Columbia River contamination situation." In a report ordered by Strauss that year, Herbert Parker calculated that the consumption of thirty-five pounds of whitefish per week would be needed to reach man's tolerance limit "in the absence of all other radiation hazards." He added: "Individual fish reach contamination levels appreciably higher than the average on which this limit is based. With projected increases in activity density on the order of 5 to 10 fold, it may be necessary to close public fishing between Priest Rapids and McNary Dam." Parker was adamant, however, that debate of this subject should be conducted in secret. "The public relations impact would be severe . . . The relations situation is always potentially dangerous, and it will be severely taxed if and when actual restrictions . . . are recommended."[90]

Dr. Charles Dunham, deputy director of the AEC's Division of Biology and Medicine, reviewed Parker's calculations and found that Parker had arrived at his limit of thirty-five pounds of whitefish per week because he disagreed with recommended NCRP limitations. Using the maximum permissible rate of intake for P-32 recommended by the NCRP, Dunham estimated that consumption of only seven pounds of whitefish per week would bring an individual to the tolerance limit. He warned, "The quantity of fish eaten by persons who like to fish and to eat fish may average several pounds per week . . . it appears that concentration of P-32 in the fish of the Columbia River may be even nearer the level at which some limiting action is required than the attached report [Parker's] may indicate."[91] However, AEC-Hanford Manager David F. Shaw agreed with Parker's position. "The [NCRP] tolerance values are extremely conservative . . . We doubt that any real human hazard could be positively demonstrated."[92] The AEC decided simply to "keep this potential problem [of sport fish contamination] under close observation."[93] Richard Foster and another prominent GE aquatic biologist, Royal Rostenbach, stated publicly: "Even if game fish were caught in the most radioactive section of the river, a person could eat the improbable amount of 20 pounds daily without exceeding permissible radioactivity levels . . . In the water of the Columbia River below the Hanford reactors, no health hazard to users currently exists."[94]

Contamination levels in Columbia River sport fish continued to climb. Surveys conducted by Hanford scientists among fishers at popular local sport-fishing sites disclosed that steelhead trout, whitefish, and bass were the "most abundant" and that salmon and sturgeon were taken "occasionally." Although suckers and carp were "abundant in the river," the surveys found, these species were "not regarded as food fish in this region." The surveys added "Considerable quantities of carp are consumed by a few individuals, however." Suckers and carp, as bottom feeders, contained some of the highest levels of beta contamination. Radioactivity values in bass, on the other hand, had "pronounced seasonal variations." In 1955–56, levels could jump by 100-fold from spring to late summer and fall.[95] The salient fish of concern, however, was whitefish. In a classified 1956 document, Hanford scientists affirmed that these species presented "the greatest potential radiation hazard as a food fish." The report noted, "They feed voraciously on bottom-dwelling invertebrates throughout the year and . . . acquire relatively high concentrations of radioisotopes."[96] Between 1955 and 1958, average contamination levels in whitefish caught at the popular sport-fishing sites of Ringold and Priest Rapids rose by tenfold. Individual fish often reached even higher maximums. By autumn 1956, Hanford biologists calculated, the consumption of only 2.7 pounds per week of whitefish flesh could "produce maximum permissible limits" for P-32. "It is quite possible that some of the more successful fishermen and members of their families may have eaten more . . . during the peak of the fishing season [autumn]." GE scientists conducted a special study to "determine the effect of cooking on the concentration of radioactive materials in edible whitefish tissues." They obtained a mean decrease of 13 percent in the concentration value of muscle tissue but an increase in activity level in skin, scale, and bones. Changes in the latter tissues, they reported, were "not of major significance," since these tissues generally were not eaten.[97]

In early 1957, the "advisability of closing" Priest Rapids and Ringold to fishing was again discussed secretly at Hanford.[98] That same year, the NCRP followed the lead taken in 1956 by the ICRP and revised downward the MPCs for various radioisotopes (including P-32).[99] By October 1958, based on the new standards, GE biologists calculated that the consumption of just one pound per week of whitefish flesh from the Columbia River could achieve the MPC for P-32 in humans. Additionally, they reported in secret, "The P32 content of the flesh of some ducks which are killed along the river . . . is similar." However, they decided not to issue any warnings to local hunters or fishers.[100] A public Hanford report on the 1958 situation stated only, "During the past three years radioactive contamination levels in . . . river organisms have increased slightly."[101]

Complexities in the Food Web

In the late 1950s, complexities in the food web, including the transfer mechanisms of various radionuclides, became the object of much research at Hanford. In a series of 1957–58 experiments, site researchers found that the concentrating abilities of aquatic animals operated in the same fashion with radiocesium (Cs-137) as with P-32. In fact, Cs-137 concentration by aquatic plants occurred at even higher factors. They noted, "Disposal of Cs 137 at MPC levels for drinking water will . . . produce hazardous levels of contamination in aquatic organisms which may be consumed by man."[102] Chief Aquatic Biologist Foster publicly disclosed that, for P-32, "the limiting situation" was not "the MPC in the drinking water but the accumulation levels" in fish that were caught and eaten.[103] In other words, reactor effluent concentrations in the Columbia's water could be within tolerable limits and still present a biomedical hazard, due to the concentrating abilities of aquatic organisms.[104] In 1959, Foster told a national seminar on biological problems in water pollution: "Measurement of the amount of radioactive material taken up by fish from their environment does not complete the task of appraising the magnitude of the problem . . . In those situations where substantial quantities of radioactive materials are taken up by fish, significant amounts of the isotopes are apt to be present in other components of the environment . . . the situation calls . . . for . . . a comprehensive evaluation of the total exposure to individuals from all significant sources."[105] In 1961, a Hanford aquatic biologist, R. H. Schiffman, confirmed that the compounding mechanisms for radiostrontium (Sr-90) operated much the same as those for Cs-137 and P-32.[106] During 1959, unusually heavy flow rates in the Columbia aided effluent dilution, and activity values in fish dropped off to levels near those of 1956. In the early 1960s, however, concentrations of P-32 and other radioisotopes in Columbia River biota rose to record levels. In 1961, whitefish achieved a concentration value of about 5,000 times that of the river water. Values went even higher in 1964–66.[107]

Population Dosages Become the Focus of Study

In light of developing knowledge about the multifaceted nature of radionuclide uptake and transfer, many studies at Hanford in the late 1950s and early 1960s focused on actual dosages to populations. Diet and life-style became the key avenues of investigation. Profiles of the key habits and consumption patterns of an "average man" and a "maximum individual" were developed.[108] GE-Hanford Company regulations issued in mid-1957 specified that, for individuals outside the reservation boundaries, radioactive contamination be limited to "one-tenth of the maximum permissible body burden for radiation workers." The manual added, "The concentrations of radioisotopes from Hanford in air and water . . . [outside the atomic site] shall be limited to one-twentieth of the maximum permissible concentrations in air and water for radiation workers."[109] Thus, the point of interest became not the concentration levels in reactor effluent, vegetation, aquatic organisms, stack gases, or groundwater but the doses received by populations. By 1960, ALAP—"as low as possible" human radiation exposure—had become a popular concept in the scientific community. Accumulated dose became the focus. GE-Hanford Company stated, "Since an individual's accumulated dose . . . would normally result from exposure to diverse sources and multiple paths of intake of radionuclides, the actual concentration of any one radionuclide in the environs is important only to the degree that it contributes to the potential dose from the particular mixture of radionuclides . . . present."[110]

In 1959, Hanford scientists began to examine dosages to off-site population groups. One study measured the body burdens of persons living near Willapa Bay, Washington, a coastal community not far from the mouth of the Columbia River. The Columbia's plume extended into the Pacific about two hundred miles from the river's mouth. Studies showed that southerly winds in winter transported effluent along the Washington coast and that northerly winds in summer spread the contaminated river water along the Oregon coast. Radioactive contamination was confirmed in fish and shellfish, particularly oysters, in Pacific coastal waters at both Willapa Bay and Tillamook Bay, Oregon, two of the most important regional shellfish beds on the Pacific Coast. In shellfish, radiozinc (Zn-65) was the primary radionuclide of concern, although P-32, Cr-51, and Np-239 (with subsequent decay to Pu-239) also were present in significant amounts. At Willapa Bay in 1959, oysters demonstrated concentration levels of Zn-65 about 250 times those of Chesapeake Bay oysters that had been flagged as having high contamination levels from atmospheric nuclear fallout.[111]

The other important "off-project exposure" study begun in 1959 examined the Pasco area. Pasco was the first city downstream of the reactors to use significant amounts of water from the Columbia River. This public (unclassified) study identified contaminated fish and waterfowl, and farm produce irrigated with raw river water, as the principal pathways of radioactivity to humans. However, Foster and Junkins, site biologists, concluded that "fallout from weapons testing" contaminated local produce more than did Hanford's operations. Even from both sources, they estimated, the radiological body burden achieved as a result of eating such produce would be "considerably less than one per cent of the applicable limit." They based their evaluation of Pasco's water on drinking water MPCs and computed that the maximum permissible exposure to the gastrointestinal tract from this water was about 5 percent. As for immersion doses, they stated that an "enthusiastic swimmer" would have to spend about 240 hours per year in the Columbia to receive ten percent of the permitted total body exposure.[112]

Shortly after Foster and Junkins's study was published, an Oregon citizen questioned it. Dr. Charles Dunham, of the AEC's Division of Biology and Medicine, reassured her: "Quantities of radiophosphorus . . . in fish muscles . . . are far too low to do any damage to the fishes themselves . . . A person who eats 500 pounds of whitefish per year might accumulate enough exposure to reach the maximum permissible level for life long exposure. That a person would consume this much whitefish seems unlikely."[113] At the same time, Herbert Parker testified to Congress about radiation doses to the public in the Hanford environs. For the "average man," he stated, total doses approximated only 9 to 45 percent of the maximum permissible levels. In "exceptional cases where unusual amounts of local fish and leafy vegetables" were eaten, he claimed that doses ranged between 40 and 60 percent "of the limits."[114] Two years later, in additional congressional testimony, Parker emphasized that only "uncommon food habits or other idiosyncracies" could lead to significant radionuclide uptake from the Columbia River.[115] At the same time, two GE biologists, R. B. Hall and R. H. Wilson, publicly acknowledged, "Some few people who eat unusually large amounts of fish may acquire about 30 percent of the appropriate limit."[116] In early 1963, the AEC also publicly reported, "The phosphorus 32 found in locally caught [Columbia River] white fish can be a significant though not hazardous source of exposure to the few persons who eat them in quantity."[117]

Throughout the early 1960s, Parker's H.I. Division continued to monitor a small group of family farms in the Riverview and Ringold districts north of Pasco. Hanford scientists estimated that these neighborhoods contained only thirty families, working thirty-five hundred acres. Site scientists studied this small area intensively throughout the early 1960s and found that contamination levels in milk, produce, and humans were generally within permissible limits.[118]

Fuel Slug Ruptures Are Examined

During the decade from 1955 to 1964, when reactor effluent waste volume in the Columbia River was highest, Hanford scientists spent a great deal of time analyzing and debating specific problems associated with effluent discharges. Fuel slug ruptures, which added a noticeable radionuclide burden to the Columbia, became one primary concern. Such ruptures, or failures, occurred when uneven heat distribution or faulty bonding caused the aluminum jackets covering the fuel rods to split open. As early as 1952, Herbert Parker confirmed that "gross release from ruptured slugs" could be "significantly more hazardous *per rep* than . . . activation products . . . from normal reactor effluent."[119] Hanford chemists identified two types of ruptures. In a side or fragmented split, the quantity of fission products escaping to the river could be as high as "that contained in 150 grams of uranium" (essentially the entire slug). Tip ruptures, they estimated, allowed the discharge of fission products from only about nine grams of uranium. Releases from both types of failures were mostly in the form of "small particulates . . . primarily uranium oxides." Before 1954, site chemists did not account for fuel failures in routine analyses of reactor effluent. However, by that year, six single-pass reactors were operating at Hanford, and reactor flow rates had risen fourfold since 1948. Effluent retention time again became an important question. Hanford scientists reported "concern that further increases would cause the [retention] basins to overflow their sides." They added, "This coupled with increasing leakage from the full basin into the empty one brought about a change in policy whereby the 107 B, D, F, DR, and H basins were operated in parallel permitting unusual effluents from reactor purges and fuel element ruptures to flow into the river." The use of the 107 structures at C Reactor was characterized as "not . . . consistent." The welded seams in the steel basins cracked and caused various procedural changes over the years. "In many cases, but not in every case," the report continued, "unusual effluents are caught and routed to a trench."[120]

In 1954, Hanford scientists tried to calculate the number and effect of past fuel slug ruptures. They estimated that such failures had accounted for the release of about 11,500 curies of gross beta-emitters to the Columbia in 1952. More frequent and severe ruptures, they theorized, had caused the release of approximately 20,100 curies in 1954. Ruptures of enriched uranium-aluminum alloys may have doubled these quantities, they added.[121] By 1958, with increased reactor power levels and total production, as well as aging 107 basins, site scientists estimated that fuel failures contributed 45,000 curies per year to the Columbia. However, they admitted, concentrations could be as high as twelve times these estimates if ruptures were not detected for at least four hours.

"Significant uncertainty still exists concerning actual release." They identified radiostrontium as the chief hazard in slug ruptures, estimating that such failures contributed about 20 percent of the Sr-89-90 content in the Columbia River at Pasco. A sidelong fuel element split, they postulated, could release as much as 75,000 curies (at twenty-four hours' decay). They calculated that "the resulting downstream conditions" could be as high as "280% of the MPC for one hour duration at Pasco." They added, "Lower concentrations of proportionately longer duration may be of greater radiological consequence because of increased chances for exposure." There was, they acknowledged, "a significant lag period between detection, and confirmation, and reactor shutdown."[122]

On May 12, 1963, a nearly total and rapid fuel element rupture did occur at KE Reactor. About a pound of irradiated uranium, with attendant fission products, was released into the river. Daily radiation surveys were undertaken along the nearly 350-mile stretch between the reactor and the waterway's mouth. Chief Aquatic Biologist Foster estimated that, at Pasco, one liter of water consumed during the period of maximum river contamination "would have contributed a dose . . . to the thyroid of an infant" of about one-fourth of the estimated dose (and one-fiftieth of the allowable dose) for a year. This event is thought to be the largest and most catastrophic fuel slug failure in the history of the Hanford Site.[123] In 1964, Hanford officials continued to consider fuel rupture information to be top secret, but they told the U.S. PHS that the number of such ruptures "was still far too many."[124]

300-Area Wastes in the Columbia River

Alpha-emitting radiation, primarily from uranium in the 300 Area, was another source of contamination in the Columbia. Until 1956, alpha-emitters remained below detection limits in all river locations except in the immediate vicinity of the 300 Area.[125] There, wastes bearing "cold" (unirradiated) uranium seeped into the Columbia through the groundwater below a waste pond located near the riverbank. Hanford scientists relied on dispersion and dilution of such wastes in the Columbia. A 1957 study found that by the time the 300-Area wastes reached site boundaries, normal river flow had diluted the wastes by 500 times.[126] However, another research project conducted in 1961 revealed alpha contamination in the river near a proposed Richland sanitary water plant at levels "seven to ten times" what would have been anticipated "if complete dispersion had occurred." Additionally, a Plutonium Recycle Test Reactor (PRTR), containing what GE scientists termed "a large inventory of fission products," now operated in the 300 Area. The scientists cautioned, in secret, that with this facility and other "proposed . . . major . . . future programs located" in that region of the Hanford Site, "the potential for accidentally releasing radioactive materials [into the river] in large quantities [had] increased substantially."[127]

Purging the Reactors

Another factor that assumed increased importance with heightened operations at Hanford throughout the 1950s was reactor purging, or cleansing. In this process, diatomaceous earth, an abrasive, pumice-like material, was circulated through the reactors in order to scrape accumulated film from the cooling pipes. The film, composed mainly of iron oxides, was purged two to three times a month in the early 1950s. In 1952, Hanford chemists analyzed the differences in contamination discharge levels when purges were done with a reactor shut down and with a reactor in operation. "Hot" (operating) purges, they found, were so efficient that they increased total beta releases to the river by a factor of 5.5 over "down" purges, even with four hours of retention time for the effluent. Increases were especially severe for P-32 and Fe-59.[128] In 1956, site scientists again confirmed concentration factors of up to four times for the release of important radionuclides in hot purges. As a result, in early 1957, GE-Hanford Company changed policy to limit purges to those days when temperatures in the Columbia were below 15 degrees C. However, that June, a Hanford chemist, W. N. Koop, pointed out that purge effluent contained more particulate matter and filterable solids than did normal effluent. Such material, he argued, constituted a "relatively insoluble form" of P-32. Therefore, the isotope in this state might be less available to whitefish. As a result of Koop's recommendations, GE-Hanford Company adopted a "less restrictive" limit of ten purges between August 15 and November 1, the time when river temperatures were most likely to exceed 15 degrees C.[129]

In the late 1950s, Hanford chemists hoping to cleanse the reactors without adding a great deal of particulate matter to the Columbia River experimented with a number of detergents. By 1957, they had settled on the commercial reagent Turco 4306-B. Early tests demonstrated that the use of this compound resulted in the release of twenty times the strontium isotopes as were released in normal effluent water. However, GE researchers reported that is use "would not cause significant increase of fission products . . . being sent to the river."[130] Later that year, research showed that Turco 4306-B also augmented the release of other long-lived radionuclides of biomedical concern, including Fe-59 and Np-239. This study also found that the cleanser had entered and affected the drinking water supplies of reactor areas downstream. Additionally, trials with chinook salmon demonstrated that the fish appeared to be able "to detect even low concentrations" and that the fish made "an effort to avoid the reagent." The study added, "At higher concentrations significant mortality resulted."[131]

During the late 1950s, Hanford scientists searched intensively for feasible means of disposing of spent cleansing solutions and of reactor effluent itself. In 1958, they tried passing the concentrated radioactive solutions through trenches and then releasing it to area soils. They also tested the drainage of effluent through beds of aluminum cuttings and the horizontal passage of liquid wastes through permeable dams across retention basins. The following year, a series of tests was begun using beds of different types of aluminum turnings. In 1960, experiments with phosphoric acid cleansing solutions for reactor piping again presented the difficulty of what to do with the activated cleanser itself.[132] By 1964, according to Hanford scientists, approximately 50,000 tons of chemicals (primarily sulfates) per year were added to the Columbia. Clean disposal methods still proved elusive.[133]

In 1956, GE-Hanford Company estimated that it would cost $16 million to convert one reactor to a recirculating cooling system. The "net annual economic gain" was estimated at $3.55 million.[134] Later that year, Hanford engineers toured other U.S. research and production laboratories to investigate organic (chemical) reactor coolants. Such coolants could reduce the metal corrosion caused by hot-water cooling.[135] However, thermal thresholds and radiation effects, as well as cost considerations, were effective barriers to conversion. None of Hanford's eight single-pass reactors were converted to a recirculation, or an organic cooling, system.

Self-Purification Mechanisms in the Columbia

In examining the overall question of the fate of radioactive effluent in the Columbia, Hanford scientists in the late 1950s became intrigued with the river's own purification possibilities. Perhaps, they speculated, "natural self-cleansing" of the river would greatly reduce the need for man-made solutions. In the early 1950s, a Hanford scientist, J. F. Honstèad, had noted "selective isotopic adsorption by clay and silt in the river." A few critical isotopes, such as P-32, Fe-59, Zn-65, Cr-51, and As-76, he said, tended to adhere to particulate matter and to settle into river sediments.[136] By early 1956, GE researchers were mapping and calculating reactor effluent plumes and the "turbulent diffusion pattern" of isotopes in liquid and particulate form in the Columbia.[137] That summer, a special study was conducted on the "mechanism and nature of natural stream purification." The final report argued that "selective isotopic removals" by the riverbed might allow "expanded use of the Columbia River for the disposal of radioactive materials should the need arise."[138] The following year, Hanford researchers again examined the area of heavy radionuclide deposition in river sediments between Hanford and Pasco. They learned that when turbulence disturbed the water in this stretch, radionuclides recirculated and measured at very high levels. Apparently, the isotopes were settling into river silts in only the most transitory way. True adsorption, with ion exchange and stabilization, was not taking place. Therefore, the scientists concluded, the "loss of these radionuclides to the stream bottom" actually could be a source of *increased* contamination through recirculation in the river between the Hanford Site and McNary Dam and "could be . . . indirect routes" to man.[139] Still, a public report issued by site scientists in 1960 stated that an effective mechanism for reducing water contamination downstream from the reactors was "retention of the radionuclides in river sediments, bottom strata, and biological forms."[140]

The River Water Itself

During the same years of the late 1950s, Hanford scientists conducted many studies of the Columbia's water itself. The tendency of reactor effluent to "channel," rather than disperse broadly, was noted frequently. A 1954–55 research project found, "In the immediate vicinity of the discharge points [reactor outfalls] there is quick mixing of the effluent with river water followed by channeling conditions . . . [that] persist . . . in a narrow band for six to ten miles of river flow." Both thermal and radioactivity levels in the river, this study concluded, were "dependent on the mixing and channeling effects."[141] A 1960 report confirmed the "strong tendency for effluent to remain in channels rather than to disperse rapidly across the river."[142] Dye tests conducted in 1963 by the U.S. Geological Survey and the GE-Hanford Company again found "maximum concentrations of . . . [effluent] in mid-channel."[143]

The knowledge that dispersion was incomplete and that waste quantities in the Columbia were rising led Hanford researchers to reexamine the sanitary water systems of Pasco and Kennewick.[144] The filtration systems of the two cities were relatively slow, providing additional time for the decay of short-lived radioisotopes. They also allowed for fairly effective trapping of radioactive particulate matter. Pasco used a conventional treatment plant, with "coagulation followed by filtration through sand or anthrafilt" (a commercial absorbent). The Kennewick system consisted simply of sand infiltration beds along the Columbia "with no further treatment other than chlorination." (In 1957, however, Kennewick switched to collectors beneath the riverbed.) A secret 1955 Hanford study found that the Pasco plant effected a decrease in radioactivity, of nearly seven times, between raw river water and the treated water consumed by residents. However, in their report, the two researchers who conducted the study projected future growth curves in radioactivity levels in river water. According to other Hanford scientists, these projections were "disconcertingly high in comparison to maximum permissible concentrations."[145] In December 1956, a malfunction at D Reactor temporarily brought water samples from the Pasco water plant and the Kennewick treatment reservoir up "about 50 percent in beta activity density."[146]

At the same time, commercial navigation companies were lobbying the AEC to open the Hanford Reach for barge navigation. H. V. Clukey, a Hanford scientist, conducted a special study to examine the "radiation protection aspects" of allowing limited commercial and recreational use of that stretch of the river.[147] His 1956 report highlighted the radiological dangers of reactor effluent bubbles, which often surrounded the outfall points in the center of the river and shallow, shoreline areas on the Hanford Site. He recommended the erection of warning signs and fences and advised that emergency warning procedures be established "in case of gross contamination of the river." In general, however, he felt that immersion dose would be "low" unless a person swam or fell in an effluent bubble or unless foam or algae adhered to the skin "for several hours." Boat contamination, he averred, could be "ignored, since it decay[ed] rapidly." He identified the most serious hazard as that of "common use of river water for drinking on tugs." Restrictions on water use, he concluded, "might cause little inconvenience. However, public relations might suffer from such restrictions."[148]

Washington, Oregon, and the U.S. PHS Again Study the Columbia

In the late 1950s and early 1960s, officials of the states of Washington and Oregon became increasingly concerned about radioactive wastes in the Columbia River. They pressed for more power to regulate atomic discharges. In 1957, the issue of the role of states in managing atomic activities within their borders was raised at both the Western and Southern conferences of governors. After these conclaves, bills were introduced in the Washington and Oregon legislatures, calling for state officials to assume more control over atomic wastes. In conjunction with the PHS, they initiated new Columbia River studies. In early 1961, the PHS scientists E. C. Tsiveglou and M. W. Lammering, working with the states under the auspices of the Columbia River Advisory Group, completed a large "Evaluation of Pollutional Effects of Effluents from Hanford Works." The authors began their final report by noting the "downward and increasingly conservative trend" in radiation protection standards of the NCRP and ICRP. "What was acceptable . . . radioactive waste disposal practice . . . a few years ago may no longer prove acceptable, even though the actual or numerical levels of radiation exposure may not have changed materially in the interim." The researchers used only unclassified data, and they focused on aggregate dosages from all forms of radiation exposure. In view of the compounding effects of accumulated dose, they asserted, "Actual environmental concentrations [of radioactivity] should . . . be kept as far below the M PC's as possible." They concluded somberly: "The average radiation exposure of the near downstream populations is not far removed from the recommended limits at the present time. Thus, in terms of resulting human radiation exposure, the capacity of the Columbia River to receive further radioactive pollution appears to be nearly, if not fully, exhausted . . . at least in the vicinity of the Hanford Works."[149]

At almost the same time, Washington and Oregon issued proposals for new "radiological health studies" of the Columbia from the Hanford Reach to the Pacific Ocean. They began to perform radioassay on samples of "water, shellfish, bottom sediments, algae, plankton, fish, and other environmental materials."[150] In early 1962, Washington Governor Albert D. Rosellini requested that the U.S. Department of Health, Education and Welfare (HEW, the umbrella agency above the PHS) "join with the state of Washington on water pollution enforcement sections involving the Columbia River." Additionally, at a 1962 conference dealing with the Upper Columbia River, Washington, Oregon, and the PHS called on the AEC to take "early action . . . to reduce radioactivity on the Columbia resulting from Hanford Works operations . . . in keeping with the fundamental principle . . . of preventing all possible [ALAP] radioactivity from entering the environment."[151]

Dilemmas

By 1962, a difficult dilemma seemed to be building for the Hanford reservation. Clearly, the states of Washington and Oregon wanted increased regulatory authority over discharges to the Columbia River. The city of Richland was building its new water treatment plant and preparing to take drinking water out of the Columbia at least eleven miles closer to the reactor areas than any other city water system. The population of the Tri-Cities vicinity was booming. N Reactor, a giant production reactor that also would generate electric power, was nearing completion on the Hanford Site, and many families of new operating employees were arriving. The CBP also was filling up the arid stretches of Franklin and adjacent counties, bringing in farm families with outdoor habits and high consumption of fish, wildfowl, and home-grown produce. Picnickers, boaters, and swimmers made increasing, albeit surreptitious, use of the Columbia's east bank and islands for recreation.[152] Hanford officials, still under pressure to produce record amounts of plutonium, faced the predicament of whether, or how, to limit production, reduce the radiological burden of the Columbia River, or warn the public of potential risks. These dilemmas were debated throughout 1963 at Hanford and within AEC headquarters in Washington, D.C.

On January 8, 1964, President Lyndon B. Johnson announced a reduction in plutonium and enriched uranium production. Department of Defense (DOD) and AEC studies had demonstrated, he said, that the long-range national defense and peaceful needs for these special materials could be met at lowered production levels. That same month, the AEC and GE announced their mutual decision to transfer the operating contract at Hanford to an array of other businesses. A program to diversify the local economy of the Hanford region was begun.[153]

In the spring of 1964, at the request of the PHS, officials of that agency and of the Hanford Site conducted a "review of the [radioactive] waste disposal practices" at the atomic facility. The phased shutdown of three of Hanford's old reactors already had been announced. The fate of the other single-pass reactors was undetermined. AEC-GE managers deemed it too costly to convert any of these facilities to recirculating cooling systems. And, according to Portland PHS Chief Richard Poston, treatment of the reactor effluent was "regarded [by AEC-GE] as unreasonably costly because of the large volumes involved." Influent chemical water treatments being used to reduce radionuclide formation in the effluent, he reported, did "not reduce heat loads" to the Columbia. The chief alternative offered by Hanford scientists to lower radioactive contamination in the river was the creation of an "inland lake" (or a two-lake system) on the atomic site. In this plan, effluents would be routed to large, artificial lakes, south and west of the reactors. There, the waste water could undergo about two days of radioactive decay and heat loss before percolating down into Hanford soils. A related plan, involving a trench percolation system, actually was being tried in the K-Reactor area. However, the inland lake concept contained large potential problems. Radioactive materials would be subject to widespread dispersion by the famed eastern Washington wind. Also, the lake beds might clog with particulate matter and diatomaceous slurry contained in the effluent. Importantly, even if the plan succeeded, it would exacerbate groundwater mounding and other related difficulties that were mounting at Hanford. Still, the PHS insisted that measures be found and taken to "improve . . . the radioactive quality of the Columbia River."[154]

Reactor Shutdowns Cause Drop in River Radioactivity Levels

Between 1964 and 1971, all of the eight single-pass reactors at Hanford closed. The first reactor shutdown, DR, occurred in December 1964. The following year, F and H reactors ceased operation. Decreases in radionuclides in the Columbia River became significant in 1966. That summer, a strike by local members of the Oil, Chemical, and Atomic Workers Union closed the reactors for about six weeks. Hanford scientists used this opportunity to conduct intensive study of contamination trends in the regional environment. They found that concentrations of P-32, Cr-51, and Co-60 decreased rapidly in the river's benthic fauna. Other, longer-lived radionuclides such as Zn-65, Fe-59, and Sc-46 declined less. After resumption of reactor operations, concentrations of most radionuclides returned to former, high levels within five weeks.[155] Between 1966 and 1970, the release rate of P-32, Cr-51, Zn-65, As-76, and Np-239 to the Columbia fell dramatically, by an average factor of 7.6.[156]

By 1967, P-32 concentration factors in Hanford-area plankton stood at 5,000–118,000 times that of the river water, a slight decline from the highest values of 1959–64.[157] Thereafter, levels declined with the closure of 100-D in 1967, 100-B in 1968, 100-C in 1969, 100-KW in 1970, and 100-KE in 1971. Studies completed in 1973 demonstrated a large drop in activity levels in river water and aquatic organisms. Hanford scientists observed, "In a river-reservoir complex, the measurable body burden of fission-produced radionuclides decreased to essentially undetectable levels within 18 to 24 months of cessation of input of once-through cooling water." They noted, however, that varying, albeit much lower, levels of isotopes were "still available from the sediments, from N-reactor [recirculation cooling system] seepage effluents, and from residual radioactivity in the different organisms in the food web."[158]

In 1975, Hanford scientists delineated the residual burden of long-lived radioactivity present in Columbia River sediments as the result of twenty-seven years of single-pass reactor operation. The "upper limits" of this burden, they estimated, were comprised of "about 1,000 Ci of 65Zn . . . some 4,000 Ci of 60Co and 2,000 Ci of 152Eu . . . along with about 3,000 Ci of tritium and 10,000 Ci of 99Tc [technetium] and less than 1,000 Ci of all other nuclides."[159]

At the Hanford Site, nearly three decades of operation of eight single-pass reactors produced a large deposition of radionuclides into the Columbia River. After the phased closure of the single-pass reactors between 1964 and 1971, radioactivity levels in the waterway declined dramatically. However, difficulties with chemically complex wastes disposed to the ground were more puzzling. The slow migration of these wastes to and through the groundwater beneath the atomic site became an issue of prime concern during and after the resolution of the river situation.

Laying Waste to the Soil:
The Groundwater Contaminants

At Hanford, we used to have a joke that there was no sense in doing a percolation test because you couldn't drop to your knees fast enough to measure any water before it all disappeared into the ground.—Randall Brown, former Hanford hydrologist, interview with the author, July 18, 1989

Ground and Tank Waste-Disposal Policies and Components at the Hanford Site
For many years, scientists at the Hanford Site thought that area sand and gravel substrata were "a nearly ideal environment for ground disposal of radioactive wastes."[1] They relied on adsorption, in which radioactive substances undergo ion exchange with stable elements in the soil. Thereby, the electron-proton balance of the radioactive materials is stabilized, and the substances bind chemically with each other. In other cases, liquid wastes were discharged to the soil at Hanford on a "specific retention basis." In this instance, waste liquid was thought to be "held against the force of gravity by the molecular attraction between soil particles and the surface tension of water." Chemically complex, intermediate-level wastes, particularly from the U-Plant operations between 1953 and 1956, were discharged on a "specific retention basis" because such wastes did not undergo significant ion exchange with the sediments. According to Hanford scientists, however, this method worked only "if no additional water" was added "to the soil profile."[2] By 1957, Hanford policy recommended this method as an "emergency measure to be resorted to only when lack of tank storage space" threatened "continued operation of separations processes."[3]

Hanford scientists divided site sediments into three zones. These strata were the upper vadose zone (unsaturated region above a depth of about twenty feet), the lower vadose zone (unsaturated layers below twenty feet), and the saturated zone (below the water table). The lower vadose zone was considered to be the most "desirable for the disposal of radioactive wastes." Here, there was "minimal chance of organism contact," as well as some protection against immediate introduction of contaminants into the groundwater.[4] "High-level" liquid wastes (those containing more than 100 microcuries per milliliter [μCi/ml] of radioactivity) produced by Hanford processes were placed in underground storage tanks.

By 1949, difficulties with these waste-disposal practices were noted. "Ground water mounds" had formed south and east of the 200-W Area and south of the 200-E Area, diverting the downward percolation of liquid wastes into new lateral patterns. New studies also revealed wide variations in the gravels, grains, silts, and clay that underlay the huge site. Some of the finer clays and silts beneath some parts of the 200 Area afforded slow, downward trickling of wastes. However, larger and coarser sands and gravels nearby could provide poorer adsorption ratios and faster vertical penetration.[5]

In the 1950s, many studies were done at Hanford to identify and characterize the specific radionuclide content, plumes, and transfer paths of waste percolation. The rapid growth of plutonium production from 1957 to 1964 increased the volume of liquid wastes discharged to 200-Areas soils, expanding groundwater mounds and causing further shifts in underground flow patterns. This sequence heightened the possibility that long-lived radionuclides would reach the groundwater and then travel to the Columbia River before adequate ion exchange or radioactive decay (stabilization) had time to take place. Among the chief radioisotopes of concern were those of strontium (Sr-90), cesium (Cs-137), cerium (Ce-144), iodine (I-129), yttrium (Y-91), and rare earths such as europium (Eu-152 and Eu-154) and technetium (Tc-99). Plutonium (Pu-239) and uranium-bearing wastes also were examined closely.[6] In 1956, the presence of radiocobalt (Co-60, half-life of 5.27 years) in groundwater beneath Hanford was confirmed.[7] During the latter half of the 1950s, leaks were confirmed in the high-level waste-storage tanks. High-level atomic wastes were defined as those containing more than 100 microcuries per milliliter (μCi/ml) of radioactivity. Intermediate or mid-level wastes (a category not designated until the late 1950s) were defined as those containing from 5×10^{-5} to 100 μCi/ml of radioactivity, and low-level wastes were defined as those containing less than 5×10^{-5} μCi/ml of radioactivity.[8]

Throughout the 1950s and later, Hanford scientists tried several technical solutions to both low-level and high-level waste problems. They tried chemical methods of binding up the low-level wastes; they installed air-lift circulators in tanks to mix the contents and thermal couples to measure temperatures. Both of the latter devices were attempts to prevent and detect the formation of "hot spots," which might pose explosion risks within tanks. They built two waste evaporators in 1951, and two larger ones in 1973 and 1976, to concentrate tank wastes to the smallest possible volume. Process condensates boiled off the evaporators were then released to site soils. Additional waste concentrators were built into the newer Hanford processing facilities, such as PUREX and the remodeled B Plant, which operated in the 1960s and 1970s. Small, in-tank stabilization (evaporation) units were tried in two high-level waste tanks in the 1960s. Various methods of partitioning and "fractionating" wastes were utilized, in order to retain valuable isotopes for use in NASA and other programs. Processes to reclaim plutonium from metal conversion wastes and scraps were constructed at Z Plant in 1955 and 1964. And, after the latter date, only double-shelled, high-level waste tanks were built.[9] Solid wastes, such as contaminated equipment, clothing, and utensils, continued to be buried at disposal sites throughout the atomic reservation, but modernized standards required separation, minimization, and more stringent packaging of these wastes.[10] During these years, national concern over radioactive wastes was rising. In 1975, an environmental impact statement concerning Hanford's defense wastes met with substantial public criticism, primarily focused on the buried, high-level waste-storage tanks.[11]

Hanford Site and Area Geology

The Hanford reservation is situated in the central part of the Pasco Basin, a "down-warped" area located near the middle of the Columbia River basalt plateau. Overlying the basalt is the Ringold Formation, a succession of silts and sands interspersed with beds of clay and gravel. This stratum is approximately 1,200 feet thick. Above it is a layer of local silt, clay, and wind-deposited Palouse soils. This zone may average 10 feet thick, but actually its depth is so variable that averages mean little. Topping this stratum is the Touchet Formation, the soil layer through which liquid process wastes discharged from Hanford had to travel to reach groundwater. Again, the depth varies widely, but it averages 100–250 feet thick. The Touchet Formation consists of glacial outwash sands and gravels and many layers of fine volcanic ash. The sand and gravel grains range from very fine to large and coarse, an important factor in ion exchange capacity and in permeation time. Sand and gravel grain sizes in sedimentary materials, as defined at the Hanford Site, conformed to a set of definitions developed in 1947 by the American Geophysics Union. These definitions were based on the sizes of grains of materials that would pass through sieves with various hole sizes.[12]

The water table under the Hanford reservation is extremely variable. It includes a number of confined and unconfined aquifers, sliced by upthrust basaltic ridges. These ridges, combined with the variable depths, weights, and sizes of the underground soil components, have produced a crazy quilt of groundwater levels. Although the average level is 250 feet below the surface at Hanford, the pattern in fact fluctuates from just a few feet to over 300 feet. The aquifers below the site flow in many directions but generally travel either southeastward toward the Columbia River or south-southwestward toward the Yakima River.[13]

Early Surveys of Hanford Site Soils and Substrata

The permeable character of Hanford-area soils, as well as the variable properties of the water table, was well noted by early ranchers and farmers. A 1904 government irrigation survey found that the land drained away over 25 percent of the water passing through wooden and packed sand reclamation canals. Early growers learned that the parched and porous soil often could not hold water long enough to nourish crops.[14] In 1918, 1921, and 1929, additional surveys of the soil and substrata of the Hanford area were conducted by state and federal agencies. All remarked on the "faulted and folded . . . layers" of rock, sand, and silt.[15] All noted the widely varying thickness of the many layers and the high porosity of soils in the entire region. The 1921 study reported losses as high as 65 percent by evaporation and leakage from irrigation canals.[16] Additionally, close connections were reported between Columbia River levels and groundwater levels, with many distinct and indirect flows between the two systems.[17]

When the army engineer Franklin T. Matthias and his DuPont counterpart Gilbert Church first visited the site that would become the Hanford Engineer Works, they noted that the ground appeared to be sturdy enough to bear the weight of massive structures. They also observed that the local soil contained enough aggregate to make much of the needed concrete.[18] A month later, U.S. War Department appraisers visited the tract and stated: "Drainage in most of the area is adequate to excessive . . . [with] high transmission losses."[19] Army and U.S. Geological Survey (USGS) engineers soon arrived and drilled core borings to a depth of 540 feet. DuPont reported, "All holes penetrated sand and gravel of excellent [weight] bearing capacity with some silt and clay layers, also of excellent bearing capacity." Again, the presence of abundant aggregate was noted. The engineers were pleased with the hardy ground.[20]

Earliest Waste Disposals to the Ground

Together, army and DuPont engineers chose a "well-defined gradual sloping flat topped ridge" for the location of the 200 East and West areas. This elevated plateau, they affirmed, formed a "water shed between Cold Creek Valley and the Flats (riverbank areas)." The northerly slope of this ridge, they stated, broke "sharply," whereas the southerly slope was much more gentle.[21] According to Hanford's chief health physicist, Herbert Parker, the decision to dispose of low-level, liquid radioactive wastes in the ground in Hanford's 200 Areas was conceived as a "temporary but necessary expedient . . . pending the development of intrinsically safer and more effective means of ultimate disposal."[22]

The earliest separations activities began at Hanford in late 1944, using a bismuth-phosphate chemistry. This process, and the plutonium concentration process that followed it, utilized nitric acid, oxalic acid, lanthanum fluoride, potassium permanganate, sodium hydroxide, and other solutions.[23] At that time, low-level liquid wastes were simply mixed with uncontaminated water and "disposed of by seepage into and evaporation on the ground surface." DuPont summarized the practice, "When the activity level is sufficiently low, the [200 Area] waste is discharged through an open ditch to the nearest natural depression . . . where it is dispersed by evaporation and settling into the sand."[24] In late January 1945, radiation monitoring of these ditches and "swamp areas" was begun. A month later, the locations demonstrated readings as high as 6.5 millireps (mrep) per hour. Parker, along with Dr. Simon Cantril, of the Clinton Engineer Works in Tennessee, and Dr. Robert F. Stone, of the MED's Metallurgical Laboratory (Met Lab), quickly halted the practice. They pointed out that the eastern Washington wind could pick up dried radioactive residues from these swamp areas and spread them throughout the surrounding territory. The open ditches were flooded with uncontaminated water and posted as "Danger Zones." Beginning at that time, deep "reverse-wells"—dry shafts with holes at the bottom—were dug in the 200-Area to receive low-level liquid waste.[25]

Hanford's reverse-wells were used between early 1945 and mid-1947. According to the site geologists R. E. Brown and H. G. Ruppert, the wells did not provide an ideal disposal method because they allowed the wastes to be discharged closer to the groundwater table than was desirable and made the "behavior of [radio]activity in the ground . . . more difficult to follow than at shallower depths." Additionally, the dry wells and the pipes that transferred wastes to them became plugged by solids and sand, causing a buildup of radioactivity. DuPont measured values as high as 2 full rep per hour in some disposal wells by August 1946. Furthermore, plugs in the transfer lines sometimes caused the wells to rupture. In a June 1946 incident, such an occurrence caused the shutdown of B Plant (200 East). The break was discovered when a depression appeared in the earth over the broken pipe and Russian thistle plants growing in the locale exhibited high radioactivity levels. Hanford scientists then developed the practice of using these plants as "bio-indicators" to monitor for such ruptures.[26]

During this same period, adsorption was first tested at the Hanford Site. In 1946, two series of trials examined plutonium adsorption. Both used "soil columns"—long, narrow vessels layered with the various soils and substrata of the Hanford vicinity, through which volumes of liquids containing radioactive wastes were passed. Both sets of experiments yielded inconclusive results. "The unknown sub-surface characteristics below any waste . . . [disposal site]," wrote the process chemist W. L. Kay in February 1946, "as well as lack of knowledge on the leachability of product [plutonium] from soil by water would hardly justify any definite conclusions as to the safety of introducing sizeable amounts of product into this soil." Factors such as size of gravel and sand grains, depth of water table, and the presence of any lateral channels of flow through the substrata, he noted, could alter the retention patterns under various locations of the atomic site.[27] In another classified report, an H.I. chemist, John W. Healy, confirmed that "general conclusions should not be drawn" from these trials. His experiments demonstrated that an average of 0.2–0.7 percent of the plutonium washed through the soil column and was not adsorbed.[28]

Testing and Characterization of Substrata Expands, 1947–50

The 1947 decision of the Atomic Energy Commission to expand operations prompted Hanford scientists to expand tests on soil adsorption and the movement of liquids underground. Tests for uranium had been positive in 300-Area wells since June 1945 and in wells at Benton City (off site) since mid-1947. In the 300-Area retention pond, alpha counts had reached 300 disintegrations per minute (dis/min) per liter in late 1945. This pond was located near the Columbia River, and from it, wastes bearing uranium and heavy metals percolated to groundwater and the river.[29] In early 1947, Herbert Parker sketched the workings of this pond, as well as 200-Areas ground disposal practices, for the incoming AEC. He concluded, "The required standards for waste disposal of this type constitute one of the most pressing problems for future Health Physics considerations."[30] Later that year, he ordered the replacement of all 200-Areas reverse wells with "cribs" and tile fields. These early cribs were fourteen feet square and seven feet high, consisting of a network of six-inch by six-foot timbers. The tops and sides were wrapped with heavy tar paper to prevent ionizing radiation from escaping to the atmosphere, and the bottoms

were open to the ground. Tile fields were simply filtration beds, approximately
180 feet long, built over coarse gravel.[31] Parker and his staff also began a major
research project to determine whether there was "significant risk of pollution of
potable water sources" and to ascertain whether "additional radioactive li-
quors" (mid-level waste sludges) could be "similarly released." At the same
time, the new prime contractor, the General Electric Company, drilled several
test wells to monitor the results of waste disposal in the 200 Areas.[32]

Herbert Parker's report, completed in early 1948, concluded that plutonium
was held very readily by Hanford subsoils and that other fission products
(except for uranium) were "moderately well held by subsoil." He noted "rapid
percolation to ground water" of uranium-bearing wastes. The downward penetration of plutonium, he estimated, would "not substantially exceed 25 feet in
two years." The percolation of other radionuclides (except for uranium)
"should go at a rate not substantially exceeding 100 feet in two years." The
water table under the "high terraces" of the 200 Areas, he averred, was approximately 250 feet below ground. Thus, that percentage of plutonium not adsorped by ion exchange with the substrata would take twenty-five years to reach
groundwater. Proportions of other fission products not so retained would take
five years to reach groundwater.[33] He warned that substantial increases in the
volume of waste water and/or major physical or chemical changes in the
composition of waste could shorten these ground percolation times. Additionally, Parker identified "distorted spheroids" (groundwater mounds), up to
300 feet in diameter, that were spreading under the 200-Areas disposal sites.
These mounds, he cautioned, posed the risk of lateral "runoff to sloping
terrain . . . [where the] coarser nature of some lower [underground] strata
[could] lead to some acceleration" in the downward penetration of active
liquids. However, overall, he was not fearful. The lateral spheroids, he maintained, included "only a small fraction of the beds . . . [under] the Separations
Plants." He added: "The whole process could be repeated several times from
new local disposal points. This gives capacity for hundreds of years of plutonium disposal, and for perhaps 50 years of [other] fission product disposal."[34]

By January 1948, samples from test wells in and near the separations areas
indicated that plutonium had migrated about two hundred lateral feet from its
point of disposal. Other fission products had migrated about three hundred
feet.[35] Later that year, the AEC's Advisory Committee on Reactor Safeguards
(ACRS) reviewed Hanford and noted the "diffusion of . . . plutonium and long-
lived radioactive substances" through the soil. "Undoubtedly," concluded the
ACRS, "some of such materials . . . will reach the . . . Columbia River and may
affect important uses below Hanford . . . much more extensive study . . . should
be initiated promptly."[36]

During 1948 and 1949, a major study of subsurface characteristics and groundwater movement in and near the 200 Areas was conducted by the U.S. Geological Service. The test-well drilling project begun by GE in 1947 also was expanded. The secret USGS report, issued in mid-1949, concluded that the groundwater mounds beneath 200-E and 200-W could be "controlled as desired, by changing the sites of the disposal sumps . . . [and could] act as ground-water dams behind which contamination [could] be contained." However, the document cautioned that when areas behind the dams eventually filled up, they would "no longer so act." It also noted that "substantially all the aqueous fluid wastes of the Hanford operations [disposed thus far had] percolated downward to an underlying zone of saturation [groundwater]." Groundwater flow, the study found, was "slow and relatively steady" from beneath the 200 Areas to the Columbia River. However, beginning from one to eight miles west of the river, particularly between the old White Bluffs and Hanford townsites, movement toward the Columbia accelerated.[37]

In February 1950, Hanford's own geologists completed one of the most comprehensive surveys of underground characteristics to date. Examining the growing groundwater mounds, they noted that the spread of such a mound was blocked to the west of the 200-W Area by the underground, basaltic Yakima Ridge. Therefore, contaminated subsurface liquids were spreading from 200-W in a lateral, north-south pattern to the east. Larger and coarser sand and gravel grains in that vicinity, the scientists predicted, would afford poorer adsorption ratios and faster vertical penetration. "The rate of movement of the ground water may . . . be expected to increase." However, they insisted, "In no case whatsoever is plutonium known to be traveling in the ground water even though plutonium-bearing wastes were injected directly into the ground in one instance and in another were injected within 75 feet of the water table."[38]

REDOX and U-Plant Operations Alter Waste Patterns

In 1952, B Plant (a wartime bismuth-phosphate separations plant) closed, thereby decreasing waste volumes discharged from 200-E Area. The PUREX (plutonium reduction extraction) facility began to function in that sector in 1955 and became fully operational in 1956. In 200-W Area, the 1952 start-ups of the REDOX (reduction oxidation) processing plant and the U Plant added to waste amounts. The REDOX facility, the first continuous-feed (nonbatch) solvent extraction plant of its kind in the world, used methyl isobutyl ketone (known as hexone) as the organic extractant. This chemical, along with aluminum nitrate, nitric acid, and other dissolving, oxidizing, and reducing solutions, combined with the fission products from the irradiated uranium fuel rods being processed to produce complex new wastes.[39] The volume of low-level waste discharged to the ground rose, while REDOX waste sent to high-level waste-storage tanks was so concentrated with high-heat isotopes that it boiled spontaneously.

The U Plant, sometimes called the Metal Recovery Plant or the TBP Plant, recovered uranium from high-level wastes produced by the old bismuth-phosphate separations plants and lying in Hanford's tank farms. It pioneered a unique separations chemistry that used tri-butyl phosphate (TBP), diluted with saturated kerosene (NPH), as the organic extractant. In the scale-up from laboratory to plant, poorer than expected contact between the organic and aqueous phases of the extraction process was achieved. Because of this, as well as the very act of liquefying tank wastes in preparation for the extraction process, waste volume from the U-Plant operation was greater than expected. Large quantities of radiocobalt (Co-60) were discharged. Also, ferrocyanide salts were added to the new wastes to precipitate cesium (Cs-137), thus making the remaining volumes of this waste available for ground disposal.[40]

Groundwater Mounds Increase in Early 1950s

The operation of REDOX and U Plant, along with the 1951 start-up of two waste concentrators, 242-T in 200-W and 242-B in 200-E, added to the volume of liquid process waste discharged to the ground in the 200 Areas. Water table mounding and lateral migration of the waste increased accordingly. Between 1951 and 1955, approximately 20 billion gallons of such waste issued from the two separations areas, with 88 percent coming from 200-W. This total quantity was more than double that of the seven-year period from 1944 to 1950. Between 1952 and 1956, according to Hanford scientists, "the entire sediment column beneath" at least two cribs in 200-W became "nearly saturated." The scientists noted, "Measurable amounts of strontium and cesium were moved downward from the zone of high concentration immediately below the cribs to points deeper in the soil."[41]

Throughout the early 1950s, GE scientists increased groundwater monitoring. Well drilling operations were transferred to the USGS, in order to allow Herbert Parker's geology, soil science, and other technical groups to concentrate on their monitoring and characterization work. The annual report for Parker's H.I. Division reported in secret in early 1951 that "a zone of ground water contamination" was under surveillance beneath each separations area and beneath the 300 Area.[42] By March 1951, approximately equal amounts (5.5 billion gallons) of waste water had been discharged to the two separations areas. Beneath 200-E, the liquid mound had elevated the groundwater level about fifteen feet. Beneath 200-W, where the spread to the west was blocked, the groundwater level had risen an estimated fifty-five feet. These mounds, Hanford scientists observed, "locally reverse[d] and increase[d] the gradient . . . [allowing] groundwater flow . . . at velocities several times greater than under natural conditions previously . . . the ground water move[d] much more freely . . . and preferentially in northwestward and southeastward directions."[43]

By May 1953, the mound beneath 200-E had subsided five feet (since mid-1951), but there was a ten-foot rise in the mound beneath the northern sector of 200-W. The mound beneath the southern sector of 200-W increased over thirty feet during the two years. Researchers of Herbert Parker's H.I. Division confirmed in secret that some of the contaminated waste water seeped "downward to the ground-water reservoir."[44] By October 1955, the mound under 200-E had dropped an additional five feet, to a level that Hanford scientists termed "only a remnant of . . . its peak." Beneath 200-W, however, the northern mound had risen another twenty-five feet, and the southern mound had climbed an additional twenty feet. These increases had caused the two hillocks to join, forming a single mound that peaked under the northern sector at about 485 feet above mean sea level, or over ninety feet above the normal (preproduction) level. Tests by GE researchers also revealed that the subsidence of the mound under 200-E now was permitting a rapid flow of 200-W wastes to the southeast. Well samples demonstrated "radioactive materials apparently moving with velocities in the order of hundreds of feet per day."[45]

Experiments Test Selective Adsorption

Throughout the period, H.I. scientists experimented with the adsorption and transmitting properties of various substrata in and near the separations areas. They found large variations. In 1952, they reopened the question of whether plutonium "could conceivably move downward and laterally . . . eventually reaching and contaminating the groundwater." Their tests showed that fine sands containing mica and calcite retained and adsorbed approximately 98 percent of plutonium in liquid solution. On the other hand, coarse sand, with less total surface area per grain, adsorped only 46.6 percent of the plutonium.[46] One pumping test that year demonstrated "near instantaneous recovery of water level . . . indicat[ing] a very small storage coefficient." A 1954 trial at a nearby well showed "fairly high transmitting properties . . . [with] stratifications and bedding planes which provide[d] some degree of confinement at different depths."[47]

In a landmark 1953 study, H.I. chemical engineer Healy reported on the selective nature of isotopic adsorption in various substrata. "Plutonium and strontium, fortunately," were "strongly held" by ionic exchange in Hanford soils. Ruthenium (Ru-106), Healy stated, was "the most mobile." He added: "Cesium [Cs-137] is intermediate in mobility . . . This makes cesium one of the more troublesome isotopes because of its high fission yield and the 37 year half-life." Another factor was the continual flushing of 200-Areas soils by new waste discharges. Radionuclides adsorped by ionic exchange, Healy predicted, would be held in the ground only if the material was "not removed by prolonged flushing." Nevertheless, he estimated underground liquid travel time from the 200 Areas to the Columbia River at "from 50 years to 1,500 years." He noted: "On this basis, the contamination of the groundwater with isotopes with half-lives up to 3 years is permitted . . . Past policies may have been conservative, and . . . some increase in the levels [of liquid wastes] cribbed may be allowed."[48]

As the years went on, the continually expanding operations at the Hanford Site, as well as the AEC's commitment to operate the Hanford plant for "a considerable period of time," prompted further research on radionuclide adsorption. J. R. McHenry, a site scientist, explained in 1954 that waste discharge to the ground had to be evaluated in terms of "an attempt to secure maximum economic benefit . . . consistent with the welfare of human and other life." In experiments with Cs-137, McHenry found "adequate" adsorption (approximately 96.6 percent) in the absence of salts. However, in the presence of 20–40 percent sodium nitrate ($NaNO_3$) content, a level contained in many of the separations processing solutions, only 12–14 percent of the radiocesium was retained in the soil.[49] Similarly, tests completed early in 1955 demonstrated that with a 16 percent $NaNO_3$ level in the separations solutions, only 2 percent of radiostrontium (Sr-90) was retained in soils. In the absence of sodium nitrate, 90 percent of the initial Sr-90 was adsorped.[50] A 1954 investigation of the Ru-106 (half-life of one year) being discharged from T Plant, a wartime bismuth-phosphate facility, revealed that the isotope "had penetrated far beyond the . . . sampling point." The report added, "Detectable amounts of ruthenium have been found in ground water."[51]

Groundwater Mounds Shift in Late 1950s

In the latter half of the 1950s, the sheer volume of liquid discharges from both separations areas again rose. Approximately 32 billion gallons of low-level waste waters were released to the ground between 1956 and 1960, a jump of over 50 percent above the quantity released in the previous five years. Operational changes caused shifts in discharge amounts and mounding patterns below the 200-E and 200-W areas. In 200-W, T and U plants shut down in 1956 and 1958, respectively. However, long-lasting drainages from 200-W caused the groundwater mound under this sector to continue to spread to the north and south. The peak of this mound shifted, according to site scientists, "tending to route . . . contaminants toward more permeable zones in the Gable Butte-Gable Mountain area."[52]

In 200-E, PUREX plant operations increased the 1956–60 liquid discharges from 200-E to 52.3 percent of the total volume released from the separations areas. Within the first six months of full operations, PUREX discharges raised the groundwater level east of 200-E to within four feet of the maximum height achieved during all of the years that B Plant functioned (1945–52). Like the U Plant, PUREX chemistry utilized TBP diluted with NPH. However, because PUREX did not mine older wastes out of storage tanks, it did not generate new wastes as chemically complex as those of U Plant. Additionally, the PUREX process used nitric acid as the salting agent, rather than the aluminum nitrate used in REDOX. The nitric acid could be cleansed and reused several times in the PUREX process, thus reducing waste volumes overall. Evaporators built into the process concentrated the wastes that would go into high-level storage tanks but consequently made more wastes available for ground disposal.[53] Increased plutonium production also caused PUREX to generate record amounts of waste.

As a result of PUREX operations, the groundwater mound under 200-E climbed twenty-five feet in just the twenty months between October 1955 and June 1957. It migrated toward the transmissible substrata to the southeast, and water began to fill the underground valley between the two mounds.[54] In December 1956, at the end of PUREX's first year, an H.I. monitor, B. V. Andersen, reported in secret that contaminants from the plant's A-8 crib reached groundwater for the first time, causing "significant increases in beta emitter activity in groundwater samples . . . 106 curies in 55 million gallons of waste."[55] In early 1957, GE chemists warned that soil-column tests indicated that Sr-90 would "probably be the first such [long-lived] isotope to reach the groundwater."[56] Additionally, a mid-1956 survey of the water-bearing formations adjacent to the Columbia River seemed to indicate that PUREX discharges were accelerating the spread of the groundwater mound beneath 200-E to a very transmissible zone. This study found that between 100-K and 100-F areas (the northernmost shoreline of the Hanford Site), substrata were "relatively impermeable" (transmitted water poorly). "In contrast, those adjacent to the river between 100-F Area and 300 Area [those to the east and southeast of PUREX] are quite permeable and transmit water readily."[57]

By mid-1957, liquid discharges from PUREX averaged 9.8 million gallons per day (mgd), up by over 50 percent from the 6.3 mgd average in 1956. Projections envisaged "the eventual discharge of up to 20 . . . mgd to disposal swamps, and up to 4 mgd of low-level radioactive wastes to cribs in and adjacent to 200-East Area." In the meantime, the groundwater mound beneath this sector was continuing to rise, and plumes of contaminated groundwater were spreading north of Gable Mountain and to the east as far as the old Hanford townsite (approximately fifteen miles away). During the first quarter of 1957, groundwater beneath some PUREX cribs demonstrated concentrations of beta activity almost 100,000 times the site's allowable limit.[58] The hydrologist William Bierschenk proposed a plan wherein disposal to swamps located north, south, and southeast of PUREX would be done in a rotating sequence. Thereby, groundwater mounds could be "controlled" and used to block and divert each other.[59] Projects to relocate the PUREX cooling water swamp continued during that time.[60]

However, an early 1958 report revealed that groundwater contaminated by PUREX wastes was continuing to spread along distorted hydraulic gradients toward "permeable glaciofluviatile sands and gravels."[61] That same year, the presence of gamma-emitters was detected for the first time in the water table at depths of 235–240 feet, in at least nine test wells in the vicinity of PUREX. Additionally, it was learned that Ru-106 had traveled southeastward approximately eight miles, or 160 feet per day, from a disposal site in the 200-E Area.[62] During 1959 and 1960, conditions in the groundwater beneath 200-E changed very little.[63] Reports confirmed that the south "and progressively southeastward movement of contaminants" proceeded.[64]

The year 1956 also brought the discovery that beneath 200-W Area, radiocobalt, a byproduct isotope generated by U-Plant operations, was present in "significant concentrations" in groundwater. An April report disclosed that Co-60 concentrations in groundwater had increased twentyfold in the two months ending March 12, 1956, and now exceeded HAPO (Hanford Atomic Products Operation) limits "by a factor of three hundred." Site scientists learned that the Co-60 in U Plant's waste stream "had little or no affinity" for Hanford subsoils. Ion exchange was "poor."[65] Radioruthenium also was present in "significant concentrations" in the U-Plant discharge. However, based on Hanford Site policy defined in 1953, large-scale disposal of Ru-106 was permitted, "since it has a half-life of less than three years." Nevertheless, disposal of the U-Plant wastes to cribs was halted in mid-1956, and fifteen new "specific retention" trenches were dug to receive the supernatant (liquid portions of the waste, suspended above the sludge portions) from the metal-recovery facility. These trenches still did not provide an ideal disposal solution. The Hanford chemist W. A. Haney pointed out in a 1957 study that they occupied "relatively large" pieces of land and presented the "potential . . . for excessive personnel radiation exposures and serious incidents." Also important was the "lack of knowledge relating to the movement of unadsorped radio-isotopes placed in soils."[66] During the first two months of use in early 1957, 2.5 million gallons of supernatant were discharged to the new trenches. Hanford officials raised by tenfold the permissible concentration limit for Co-60 disposal to cribs.[67] Levels of Co-60, cyanide ions, and nitrate ions did not decline until after U-Plant operations ceased in 1958.[68]

In the meantime, test wells located east and southeast of the REDOX facility indicated beta activity densities of up to twenty-five times the official contamination limit in early 1957. By autumn, this level had more than quadrupled, and by December, it had increased more than thirty times again. According to Hanford chemists, contaminants in groundwater were "traveling southeast-ward rather then eastward." In mid-1957, Sr-90 above the contamination limit appeared for the first time in groundwater beneath 200-W.[69] In 1958, gross beta concentration levels under the REDOX locale reached approximately five times the previous high of December 1957. The presence of Sr-90 in groundwater remained constant through 1958 but increased twentyfold in 1959. Concentration levels began to decrease slightly in 1960 as the overall dynamic of liquid movement toward the southeast continued. At the close of 1960, only twenty-two out of sixty-five test wells monitoring 200-W showed gross beta contamination within acceptable limits, and one well demonstrated beta activity about 32,000 times that level. At the same time, half of the fourteen wells sampled in Hanford's 300 Area showed positive analyses of both beta and alpha (uranium) contamination.[70] Alpha contamination was also accumulating in two 200-W-Area cribs that received uranium wastes from the UO_3 (uranium oxide) Plant. This plant received the uranyl nitrate hexahydrate (UNH) product from REDOX and PUREX and calcined (heated) it to form UO_3 powder for shipment to AEC gaseous diffusion plants off the Hanford Site. Tests in later years confirmed uranium at concentrations 120–170 times preoperational levels in groundwater beneath cribs serving the UO_3 facility.[71]

Characterization Studies Expand in the Late 1950s
During the same years of the late 1950s, GE-Hanford's well-drilling program greatly expanded, with as many as sixty new wells sunk per year. Additionally, the company hydrologist Bierschenk reported that controlled pumping tests done in and near the 200 Areas in 1956 revealed "vast differences in the character and extent of the aquifers at Hanford." He noted: "Many such multiple-well tests would be required to complete quantitative study . . . [the water table]

In the early 1960s, Hanford scientists began to track nitrate concentrations in groundwater beneath the site. Plumes containing concentrations above the natural background level of 2–4 ppm approached within one mile of the Columbia River by 1963.[90] Hanford researchers also began to monitor tritium (H³) in site groundwater in 1961. Tritium, with its high solubility, had the ability to travel quickly through water and to penetrate water-based tissues of plants, animals, and humans. In 1962, site chemists mapped H³ patterns in area groundwater and found levels at or below the allowable limit of 1×10^{-5} microcuries per cubic centimeter (μCi/cc). However, beneath the B swamp, which received condenser cooling water and acid fractionator condensate from PUREX, H³ concentrations were one hundred times the allowable limit.[91] Tritium levels in underground water rose and spread during 1963, with average concentrations peaking at 49,000 picocuries (pc, one-trillionth of a curie) per cc below 200-E and 120,000 pc/cc below 200-W. These levels declined slightly in 1964.[92]

Opinions Differ on Ground Disposal Practices

In early 1964, a Hanford study affirmed that "only minor changes were noted in the areal extent of contaminated ground water under 200 West Area." Beneath 200-E, the situation was more complex.[93] That same year, Donald Brown and William Haney, in an important unclassified report, concluded, "The history and current status of low and intermediate-level liquid waste disposal practices . . . attest to the safety and practicality of current and projected . . . operations." They predicted an average travel time of seven to eight years "for Ru-106 contamination in the groundwater to move from the Purex site southeast to the Columbia River," and six to seven years "for tritium following the same path." These travel times, they said, would result in less than 1 percent of the radioruthenium and "about 70 percent" of the H³ that "enter the groundwater beneath Purex . . . reaching the river." Less permeable substrata beneath 200-W Area, they maintained, would result in a twenty-year migration time for the Ru-106 and H³ discharged there. Less than 100 curies of Ru-106 per year would enter the Columbia over the next seven to eight years. Furthermore, the yearly rates of tritium addition to the river would "not increase the present tritium background concentration in river water by more than 50 percent." The majority of all radioactivity from separations area wastes would enter the river just north of the 300 Area, they predicted.[94]

Just after the Brown/Haney report was issued, the U.S. PHS called for a "review of [radioactive] waste disposal practices at Hanford." Conducted jointly with AEC-GE officials, this review used only unclassified data. Even

varies greatly from place to place . . . [and] ranges from less than one to more than 300 feet below the land surface."[72] Other trials by GE chemists found "striking variation" in concentrations among contaminants in the ground. Wastes were "stratified with the highest concentrations near the bottom of the [test] zone . . . probably . . . caused by the sinking of high-density waste solutions."[73]

In late 1957, Hanford geologists completed a major evaluation of ground disposal practices. They found that, in general, soils in and near 200-W had greater capacity than did those in and near 200-E. "Immediately southeast of 200-W area . . . greater volumes of radioactive liquids can be disposed of . . . per unit surface area than at any other sites studied." In the 200-E vicinity, the area "immediately south" of the boundary had "better" adsorption capacity than others.[74] At the same time, geologists calculated that soils artificially saturated by effluents under 200-E held only 7.2 percent of their potential liquid capacity. Beneath 200-W, they estimated, soils held only 60 percent of their potential liquid capacity. Further use of these areas as liquid disposal sites was possible.[75]

In 1958, William Bierschenk conducted a landmark study of groundwater and ground disposal. He calculated that 3.8 billion gallons of low- and intermediate-level wastes, containing a total of 2.5 million curies of gross beta radioactivity, had been discharged to the ground since the 1944 start-up of the Hanford plant. The resultant groundwater mounds, he acknowledged, had "increased and locally reversed natural hydraulic gradients" and consequently had "accelerated the movement of much of the groundwater." Such changes could be expected to continue "in response to continual changes in [natural] water levels . . . and the continuing artificial recharge of the aquifers by plant effluents." Bierschenk also noted the great variations in Hanford substrata: "Each test is merely a guidepost or segment of knowledge . . . there may be considerable deviation from the . . . paths shown [on groundwater maps]." In conclusion, he estimated groundwater travel time from the 200 Areas to the Columbia and Yakima rivers for radionuclides other than Ru-106 at 175–180 years.[76]

By 1960, site geologists understood groundwater migration trends and complexities quite well. They often reiterated that groundwater travel time from the 200 Areas to the Columbia River was 180 years but modified this by adding that "heterogeneity and anisotropy [changes based on direction of measurement] of the aquifers," and the great range in "movement rate" for various waste components, could alter expectations.[77]

Research Examines Ways to Slow or Contain Waste Plumes

As plumes of contaminated groundwater spread from beneath the 200-Areas in the late 1950s, Hanford researchers experimented with methods of containing

158

or slowing the movement. In mid-1957, hoping to capture a good portion of the wastes before they entered the ground, chemists spread aluminosilicate gel over soil columns. Early results indicated that "a considerable amount of free moisture [was] still available for removal by the soil." Additionally, the gelling process cost nine to fourteen cents per gallon of waste.[78] By autumn, tests demonstrated the aluminosilicate gel could hold gross concentration levels in site soils at permissible levels only if "essentially all of the radioactivity (greater than 99%)" was bound to the gel or if the activity in wastes that did drain through was "nearly completely absorbed [sic] by the soil immediately under the gel." Nevertheless, GE scientists decided to study the possibilities of "extending . . . the waste gelling process to include high level wastes."[79] Pursuing trials with high-level PUREX wastes, they learned that the high temperatures of these wastes virtually prohibited the gelling technique. The chemist C. E. Linderoth reported in secret that such a process "would likely develop hazards of unpredictable magnitude." He noted, "A gelling process . . . without a provision for artificial cooling would not be practical."[80]

In the closing years of the 1950s, Hanford scientists investigated other ways to bind or contain the wastes generated by the increase in plutonium production. In late 1957, they tried a drum-drying process on mid-level coating waste that had been reduced by gelation to about 60 percent of its original volume. However, William Haney secretly reported that there were too many "questions concerning inconsistencies in gel formation and stability, radioisotope retention characteristics, and permanency of retention."[81] By 1959, these trials had been abandoned. Other tests sought a chemical barrier that would aid in fastening wastes before they passed into site soils. Particularly, chemical compounds and detergents to bind Cs-137, Sr-90, and Pu-239 were evaluated.[82] In 1960, the Micro Pilot Plant (MPP) was established at Hanford to "explore the ability of various packing bed materials to remove radioisotopes from Purex tank condensate waste." Several inorganic ion exchange materials, such as hydrous silicates of sodium and calcium and granular apatite (calcium fluorophosphate), were tried. However, a workable reactive method remained elusive. The ability of Hanford soils and substrata to adsorb radionuclides in process wastes continued to provide the prime safeguard. By 1960, data on test wells continued to show that radioisotopes of strontium, cesium, and zirconium, as well as plutonium and rare earths, were removed relatively effectively by site soils. The removal of radioruthenium, cobalt (Co-60), and iodine (I-129) was less effective.[83]

Throughout these years, Hanford scientists implemented various new processes to partition, "fractionate," and reclaim wastes. The RECUPLEX facility

LAYING WASTE TO THE SOIL

opened at Z Plant in 200-W Area in 1955, and the larger and m PRF (Plutonium Reclamation Facility) began operations the facilities attempted to reduce the overall quantity of Pu-239 reclaiming it from various process scraps and wastes. Howe tions also added to the Hanford soils quantities of TBP, NPH, acid, carbon tetrachloride, dibutyl butyl phosphonate, and used in the extraction processes. In some cases, plutonium als Z-Plant solutions disposed in the ground.[84] Beginning in 19 recovery program was started at C Plant (known as the Hot S process, which extracted the high-heat Sr-90 component waste from PUREX tank farms, became a full-scale operation B Plant from 1968 to 1978. Cesium-137 also was recovered from ten-year B-Plant mission.[85]

Low-Level Waste Volumes Peak, 1961–65

The years 1961–65 saw the peak volume of liquid waste d ground at Hanford. Slightly over 32 billion gallons of low wastes were so released, of which 64 percent drained thr (PUREX) Area. The groundwater mounds beneath the separ tinued to rise and spread. Hanford scientists, attempting to d flows, discharged 80 percent of them to the Gable Mountain north and west of the alternative choice (B Pond). Still, ground to the south and east of 200-E, and the "valley" between these level over 400 feet above mean sea level. Radionuclide levels also increased. Under 200-W, these levels peaked in 1961, but t rise under PUREX in 1963 and 1964.[86] In 1961, Hanford chemis only about 86 percent of the Cs-137 and 88 percent of the Sr-9 ground was held successfully in the substrata.[87]

The period from 1961 to 1965 also brought extensions of the program at Hanford. New wells were drilled, and many exi deepened so that they reached groundwater and/or basalt. Th ald J. Brown affirmed in December 1964: "Recent analysis samples . . . indicate that contaminated ground water is movi which may ultimately carry it from beneath Hanford into off-To provide . . . a more accurate definition of the flow sy monitoring wells have been proposed . . . within the broa ground-water front near the Columbia River."[88] Experiment ward at the MPP. Apatites, resins, and zeolites (particularly cli tested for their abilities to adsorb plutonium, strontium (Sr-(Cs-137).[89]

though they learned that "75% to 90% of the tritium" went into the groundwa-ter, PHS officials concluded that the crib disposal system was safe. The "large well monitoring program," said Portland PHS Chief Richard F. Poston, had resulted in "an excellent tracing of the movement and retention of the crib wastes in the 200 Area."[95] Later that year, Hanford scientists began using a "neutron soil moisture monitor" to more accurately measure groundwater flow rates.[96] In 1965, AEC Chairman Glenn T. Seaborg asserted that the adsorption process worked so well in Hanford subsoils that "essentially no radioactivity" reached the Columbia River, "except for . . . tritium and ruthenium-106."[97] A 1973 groundwater review at Hanford by AEC environmental monitoring con-tractor Battelle Northwest Laboratories claimed, "Liquid nuclear wastes have been safely discharged to the lower vadose zone for over 20 years."[98] Two years later, Hanford scientists again claimed that most radionuclides were "being held within the soil column and relatively high above the regional water table." The scientists added, "These sediments are expected to remain essentially in this position." However, they stated: "Long-lived radionuclides reaching the water table . . . do migrate slowly with the groundwater . . . an inventory of mostly tritium and ruthenium-rhodium products will remain in the groundwater under the Reservation for 10's of years. Fission products will remain in the soil columns under cribs, trenches and ponds for many centuries. Plutonium . . . [must] be recovered from soil columns at a later date to avoid the need for multicentury control and surveillance of the site."[99]

Other agencies and individuals held different beliefs. In a 1960 study of the Hanford Site, the NAS asserted that ground disposal of low-level liquid process wastes was "of limited application and probably involve[d] unacceptable long-term risks."[100] In 1963, former AEC Chairman David Lilienthal termed ground disposal and burial of radioactive wastes at Hanford "a crude method of dealing with these poisons." He noted, "Surely something better must be devised."[101] In 1966, the NAS again stated that the soil "would no longer be a suitable disposal medium" beyond an equilibrium point where the rate of disposal exceeded the rate of isotopic decay.[102]

In 1975, when a comprehensive waste management plan for the site (an environmental impact statement, EIS) became available for public comment, officials of many government agencies and groups questioned the inherent validity of "storing" low- and mid-level radioactive waste in the vadose zones. The office of the U.S. secretary of the interior commented: "We have found no [soil] section beneath any disposal area described in sufficient detail to suggest that the soil contains a significant amount of clay in the uppermost 150 to 300 feet . . . to make good 'filterbeds' . . . Evidence . . . shows vertical migration of

137-Cs and 90-Sr . . . [with later extensions] laterally and vertically . . . From this evidence, it is doubtful that the radionuclides can be retained in the soil columns for many centuries."[103] Federal Environmental Protection Agency (EPA) Administrator Sheldon Myers noted: "[Hanford's] estimates of gross beta, tritium and nitrate quantities in the zone of saturation (unconfined) . . . presupposes complete mixing, no density stratification, and does not deal with the three-dimensional aspects of the groundwater flow system. The presence of tritium in the basalt aquifer, for example, is indicative of possible deep downward and lateral movement of radionuclides."[104] Further comments questioning Hanford's ground disposal policies were received from the Department of Agriculture, the National Science Foundation, the Department of Health, Education, and Welfare, the states of Washington and Oregon, and other entities.

Discharges to Soils Decrease in the 1960s and 1970s

Beginning in 1965, the volume of low-level waste disposed to the ground at Hanford dropped due to the decrease in plutonium production. Overall, about 27 billion gallons of waste waters were discharged to soils at the site from 1966 to 1970. The REDOX plant closed in 1967, causing the total quantity of liquid wastes released from 200-W Area between 1965 and 1970 to fall to about half that of the previous five-year period.[105] Still, the aggregate volume of fluid waste that had been discharged from the two separations areas by 1970 was massive. That year, Hanford scientists estimated that ponds, ditches, cribs, and specific retention trenches on the site had received a total quantity of about 120 billion gallons. Approximately 3.2 million curies of beta-emitters had been so disposed, along with about 280,000 grams of plutonium and 120,000 kilograms of uranium.[106]

"Isotope campaigns" and waste management decisions at the Hanford Site caused a rise in the volume of low-level process wastes disposed to the ground in the mid-1970s. New processes developed in Hanford's chemistry laboratories in the late 1950s and the 1960s made it possible to extract radioisotopes of cerium, strontium, cesium, neptunium, and rare earth elements such as promethium from high-level waste produced at the atomic complex. The burgeoning U.S. space program was interested in these isotopes and rare earth elements to power Systems for Nuclear Auxiliary Power (SNAP) generators on spacecraft. Also, new medical uses were being developed for some of these materials. At one point during the 1960s, Hanford laboratories produced the world's only supply of promethium-147, a material used in the development of the artificial heart. The waste partitioning and fractionating processes that made the extraction of these materials possible generated large volumes of low-level process fluids. Additionally, the removal of some of these high-heat and high–specific activity materials from high-level waste storage tanks at the site made it feasible to compress remaining tank wastes to smaller volumes, without raising in-tank temperatures to unreasonable levels. Two large evaporators, 242-S and 242-A, began operation at the site in 1973 and 1976, respectively. They concentrated tank waste and then discharged the low-level condensates from this process to the ground. Therefore, the volume of waste water discharged to site soils rose at the same time that plutonium production declined.[107]

Underground High-Level Waste-Storage Tanks

During the first twenty years of operation at the Hanford Site, contaminants reaching groundwater came primarily from low- and mid-level wastes discharged through 200-Area soils. After that period, leaks from buried, single-shelled, high-level waste storage tanks (SSTs) became a concern. A total of 149 SSTs were built at Hanford between 1944 and 1964. During World War II, the army and DuPont constructed 64 such tanks, made of "concrete, with a carbon steel liner on the bottom and side walls." Sixteen of the tanks held only 54,500 gallons each. The rapid postwar expansions that occurred at the Hanford Site between 1947 and 1952 brought the construction of 60 more tanks, 48 of which held 780,000 gallons each and 12 of which held 530,000 gallons each. In the expansion that took place between 1953 and 1955, 21 additional tanks were built, each of which held 1 million gallons. The last 4 million-gallon tanks were built at Hanford in 1963–64.[108] Shortages of high-grade stainless steel during World War II, combined with the rush to complete plutonium production facilities, resulted in the substitution of milder (more corrosive) steels and even earthenware in some of the piping and drains leading to the first 64 tanks.[109] The first chemical-processing operations began at Hanford in T Plant, on December 27, 1944. The following day, according to Matthias, "the run of hot material into high-level waste tanks began."[110]

The earliest operations of the separations facilities demonstrated to DuPont scientists the key role of the pH balance (alkalinity/acidity level) of waste solutions in preventing tank corrosion and leakage. "It is necessary that the contents be maintained alkaline to prevent corrosion," noted a mid-1945 report. DuPont chemists added caustic alkaline solution (sodium hydroxide) to neutralize the highly acidic tank wastes.[111] However, later that year, to reduce waste volume and conserve space in the tanks, scientists reduced the alkalinity of the waste solutions from a pH of 10 to a pH of 7. Supernatant from settled wastes was diverted for direct ground disposal, as Technical Department research had shown that the pH reduction (toward a more acidic balance) decreased "the plutonium content of the wastes . . . to a level comparable to that of . . . wastes normally sent to the dispersal" areas. Thereafter, the wastes sent to the tanks were monitored more frequently "as a check against conditions" that might have corroded the tank liners.[112]

The first several years of Hanford's operations brought only sporadic leaks in some of the water jackets, pipes, and fittings around the high-level tanks. Throughout DuPont's tenure, company officials reported "no operating difficulties" with the tanks. They added, "The number of jacket leaks increased, but the rate of . . . leakage . . . remained so low that no replacements of jacketed vessels were required."[113] A secret 1948 study by Chief Health Physicist Herbert Parker in early 1948 found the buried SSTs to be, for the most part, sturdy and reliable.[114] However, a review by the AEC's Safety and Industrial Health Advisory Board later that year cautioned: "Hundreds of thousands of dollars have been spent and are currently being spent for providing holding tanks for so-called 'hot wastes,' for which no other method of disposal has yet been developed. This procedure . . . certainly provides no solution to a continuing and overwhelming problem. The business of constructing more and more containers for more and more objectionable material has already reached the point both of extravagance and of concern."[115]

Tank Space Quickly Becomes a Problem

The B and T separations plants that operated during World War II each were connected to sixteen underground SSTs. By December 1945, however, tanks serving B Plant were 70.8 percent full, and those receiving T Plant's high-level wastes were 83.5 percent full. Tie-ons were begun to connect these processing plants to the thirty-two other SSTs in U and C tank farms. Six months later, B and T tank farms were 100 percent full, U tank farm was 37.1 percent full, and C tank farm was 45.6 percent full. The need for tank space resulted in decisions to dispose of second-cycle process wastes in cribs and trenches.[116] The initial postwar production lull and then the construction of additional SSTs in the late 1940s and early 1950s temporarily eased the tank space situation.

High-Heat Tank Waste Solves Some Problems, Creates Others

Soon after the start-up of REDOX in 1952, high-heat-generating isotopes such as zirconium-95 and niobium-95 in the wastes from this plant caused solution temperatures within the S tank farm to reach the boiling point. Additionally, sudden thermal releases, called "bumping," sometimes occurred as the hottest areas of sludge concentration in the bottoms of these tanks attempted to achieve equilibrium. "Sludge temperatures . . . just above the tank bottoms," reported the chemist D. W. McLenegan, "have been recorded much higher than those contemplated when the existing tanks were designed." These temperatures, he warned, "raised questions regarding . . . possible effects on the integrity of the tank liners." Hanford scientists were intrigued and saw wastes that boiled spontaneously as a way to concentrate future tank wastes under controlled, "self-boiling" conditions. They designed the SX tank farm (constructed in 1953–54) to accommodate self-boiling wastes, installing air-lift circulators to mix the wastes and thermal couples to monitor temperatures at specific locations within the tanks. They also built interconnected condensers on the tanks, to collect and cool the vapors and then either to drop them back into the high-level waste solutions or to route excess amounts of condensate to cribs. The scientists also retrofitted S tank farm with many of these same features.[117]

As the design of tank farms for the self-boiling wastes from REDOX and PUREX went forward, Hanford scientists studied various construction materials and protective coatings. They found that "mild steel" (not stainless) was subject to pitting and rusting and that the welds cracked in the presence of these intense solutions. All of the various coating materials that were tried became brittle and shrank, developed blisters, or melted and became soluble. None, according to GE researchers, "gave completely satisfactory results."[118] In 1958, tests in PUREX operations demonstrated that all construction materials corroded from ongoing contact with the aqueous wastes. Even stainless steel and titanium could not withstand the hot, highly concentrated chemical and radioactive solutions.[119] At nearly the same time, L. E. Brownell reported "upward dishing" of up to four feet in the bottom liners of some of the tanks. He speculated that "either air, vapor or liquid pressure between the steel liner and the concrete bottom" of the tanks might have caused this "excessive rippling." In the case of one tank, he stated, the bottom had undergone "such a series of severe plastic strains" that he assumed that some of the welds had failed. He noted, "Slow leakage will probably occur through the concrete shell."[120] By the mid-1960s, a special "neutron monitor" had been developed to measure heat dissipation in the soil from the underground tanks.[121]

Process Line and Tank Leaks Increase

In the meantime, leaks in the piping that led to high-level waste tanks became more frequent and severe during the early 1950s, and confirmed tank leaks began in 1956. One 1954 Hanford document "suggested" a tank waste leak that "may have penetrated to groundwater."[122] Through 1960, the largest tank leak in terms of volume occurred in 1956, when 55,000 gallons escaped from the 104-U tank. The most significant leak in terms of amount of radioactivity released took place in 1959, when about 20,000 curies (primarily Cs-137) seeped from the 101-U tank. In many of these early cases, GE scientists added diatomate (an inert, granular substance) to form a plug. In other instances, they simply allowed the precipitates in the waste sludges themselves to cork the ruptures. Field tests in 1958 revealed that the precipitate in the REDOX tank solution (about 75 percent by volume) caused "an insignificant amount (less than 20 gallons) of waste [to] enter . . . the soil before the orifice became plugged by the precipitate."[123] In the decade beginning in 1962, eight important tank leaks occurred at Hanford, the largest in 1971, when 70,000 gallons, containing 50,000 curies of Cs-137, escaped. A significant leak in the cooling coil of a waste-sampling tank occurred in 1964. Three major tank ruptures took place in 1973, the largest of which was the escape of 115,000 gallons, containing 40,000 curies of Cs-137, in June.[124]

Waste Management Plans Vary in Approaches to Tank Wastes

In 1953, the USGS completed a survey of underground conditions and waste-disposal practices at the Hanford Site. Its report noted: "The connection of the storage tanks by rigid or semirigid piping creates a hazardous condition that may allow large quantities of long-lived waste to reach underground. Earthquake or other vibrations might rock the monolithic tanks in unphased oscillation so as to sever those frail connecting pipes."[125] Perhaps spurred in part by this report and also by increases in piping and tank leaks, the AEC increased investigations of new high-level waste treatments. In January 1957, it reported on some of these methods, including adsorption and subsequent fusion of prepared wastes in montmorillonite clay and heat conversion of wastes associated with aluminum nitrate salts to a dry oxide powder (with subsequent packaging of the powder in steel containers). Chemical separation of Sr-90 and Cs-137 from high-level wastes (with subsequent release of some remaining liquids to the environment) and self-sintering (spontaneous heating or welding without melting) of high-activity wastes in a slurry with earthen materials also were examined. High-level radioactive waste storage in the underground tanks, the commission affirmed, was "not a final economical answer."[126]

In late 1958, Hanford officials prepared the site's first comprehensive waste management plan. It advocated the immobilization of high-level wastes in solid ceramic form. The solidification process facilities would be retrofitted into B Plant, the wartime separations canyon in 200-E, and immobilization of the current waste inventory would be completed in seven years.[127] One month after this plan was proposed, Herbert Parker confirmed, in congressional testimony, that, in the thinking of Hanford officials, the use of high-level waste tanks was "generally considered to be waste *storage* rather than waste *disposal*."[128] However, as interest in extracting isotopes for space and medical uses expanded in the late 1950s and early 1960s, the idea of immobilizing Hanford's high-level wastes was questioned. If such wastes could be a source of valuable isotopes, then perhaps solidification was not an ideal solution. Soon, new plans to partition the high-level wastes, extracting Sr-90, Cs-137, and some other components, were developed. The lower-heat wastes that remained would then be condensed into salt cakes within the tanks. This plan was scheduled to begin in 1965, with completion (i.e., no residual liquids in the tanks) by 1975.[129]

Concerns over High-Level Waste Disposal Increase

In the meantime, the issue of how to dispose of atomic wastes began to receive national and international attention. The situation was discussed at the first United Nations Conference on the Peaceful Uses of Atomic Energy, but according to Laura Fermi, wife of the atomic pioneer Enrico Fermi, "no aspects of . . . disposal . . . were without problems."[130] Dr. Abel Wolman, of Johns Hopkins University, a frequent AEC consultant, told the conference that "the disposal of reactor and fuel processing wastes" would be one of "the major controlling factors in determining the extent of" future atomic production.[131] The following year, former AEC Chairman Gordon Dean underscored the importance of the disposal question. "Upon the answer to it [the disposal question]—and no completely satisfactory answer has yet been found—may depend just how far man may ultimately go in realizing the blessings of nuclear fission."[132] In 1958, James Terrill, a Public Health Service official, cautioned that the "environmental factors" of dilution and isolation that had been practiced by the AEC to protect people from radioactivity could have, instead, a compounding effect. Biological accumulation in the food chain, underground aquifers, and river ecosystems, he said, was often the result.[133] During these years, the "soil cycle" became a topic of particular concern. This cycle involved plant uptake of radionuclides deposited in the ground with subsequent transport through the food chain to humans. In this pathway, Sr-90 and Cs-137 were of especial importance.[134] However, the soil cycle did not pose a significant hazard at Hanford, since agriculture was not permitted on the site.

In early 1959, the Congressional Joint Committee on Atomic Energy (JCAE) held hearings on radioactive wastes. Although most of the witnesses who testified agreed that the AEC, thus far, had done a responsible job of safeguarding public health, they concurred that no adequate long-term disposal solution was at hand.[135] That summer, AEC tests in an undersea area twenty miles from Boston, an area that was used for dumping barrels of sealed atomic wastes, found one leaking barrel out of the fourteen tested. Soon afterward, a commission proposal to authorize twenty-two new radioactive waste dump sites in the Atlantic Ocean and the Gulf of Mexico brought protests from several eastern congressmen, citizens' groups, and the Mexican government.[136] According to former AEC Chairman Lilienthal, state and federal health officials were angry that neither they nor marine biologists at the navy's Woods Hole Research Center on Cape Cod had been asked for their approval or advice on sea disposal practices.[137]

In the early 1960s, as questions about the ultimate disposal of radioactive wastes remained unsettled, the U.S. PHS asked Hanford officials for a comprehensive review of waste-disposal practices at the site. After learning of the plans to partition high-heat isotopes from high-level wastes between 1965 and 1975 and to concentrate remaining wastes into salt cakes, Portland PHS Chief Richard Poston responded, "This plan [should] proceed to completion regardless of the marketability of such isotopes as Sr-90 and Cs-137 . . . very long term integrity of the tanks is questionable."[138] Nevertheless, budget strains and contractor changes stalled the high-level waste solidification plans at Hanford. After the passage of the National Environmental Policy Act in 1969, and the highly publicized tank leak in 1973, Hanford officials and other government agencies and groups gave increased attention to the punctures of and seepages from the SSTs. A 1975 ERDA report estimated that approximately 47 million gallons of liquid wastes and 25 million gallons of solidified waste were stored in underground tanks at Hanford. This document acknowledged that, at Hanford, "the largest number of unplanned environmental release incidents [accidents] occurred in the chemical processing (200) areas." As a result of these accidents, and of deliberate ground disposal policies, ERDA concluded that some of the land at the Hanford Site was contaminated "in an irretrievable and irreversible manner" with long-lived radionuclides. The very long half-lives of iodine-129, technetium-99, and Pu-239 made them the prime isotopes of concern. Comments from many sectors of the public, including the federal Departments of Agriculture, the Interior, and Health, Education, and Welfare, the EPA, and the states of Washington and Oregon, all focused on questions of tank reliability.[139]

Burial of Solid Wastes at the Hanford Site

Throughout the years of Hanford's operations, solid objects contaminated with radioactive and chemical wastes were buried at various disposal sites across the reservation. Transuranic wastes (those with atomic numbers above that of uranium in the periodic table of chemical elements) were included in this disposal practice before 1970. Bulldozers simply interred containers filled with contaminated equipment, clothing, and utensils of assorted sizes. In 1956, a 500-foot tunnel, large enough to hold twelve loaded railroad cars, was constructed at the end of a track spur near the PUREX plant. Into this tunnel was rolled apparatus that was too heavy to be hauled away for burial. A huge concrete, water-filled gate barred the tunnel entrance.[140] In 1964, a 1,688-foot tunnel was built to replace the earlier one. Between 1944 and 1970, approximately 5,040,000 cubic feet of unsegregated solid wastes were buried at the Hanford Site. After 1970, over 500,000 cubic feet of transuranic wastes were placed in retrievable storage. To date, a total of over 10 million cubic feet of solid atomic wastes have been buried or stored at Hanford. These materials did not receive much attention during the first twenty years of site operations. Sometimes, however, the collapse of burial containers during backfilling operations spread particulate contamination, and the slow disintegration of some containers after burial made radionuclides available for underground transport.[141]

At the Hanford Engineer Works, the ground disposal of low- and mid-level atomic wastes and the underground tank storage of high-level wastes were first conceived as temporary, wartime expedients. However, increasing volumes of liquid process wastes generated during the ensuing twenty years presented new and unexpected difficulties to site scientists and officials. Beginning in the late 1950s, public concern over nuclear waste increased and became vocal, providing one of the first challenges to AEC hegemony. During the same years, biomedical knowledge of exposure to radioactivity, including fallout from atomic weapons tests, also attracted public notice. Along with radioactive waste, fallout served as a catalyst in generating public insistence on participation in nuclear policy decisions.

Radiobiology:
The Learning Curve

With the dawn of the atomic age, it has become necessary as never before to understand the biologic effects of radiation . . . Changes brought about [by radiation] in the germ plasm are in general harmful and are cumulative.—Shields Warren, M.D., former chief medical officer, Operation Crossroads, and staff member, New England Deaconess Hospital Cancer Research Institute, address to the American Association for the Advancement of Science, October 1956

1944–64: Vast Expansion of Radiobiological Knowledge

At the end of World War II, little precise data existed on the impacts of ionizing radiation on living tissues. However, some fundamental facts about radioactivity's ability to produce harm were known from early experiences with radium and X rays. The Manhattan Engineer District conducted research that vastly expanded the information base. However, the only authentic experience with radiobiological effects came from the cattle that received radiation flash burns as a result of the Trinity bomb test at Alamogordo, New Mexico, and from observations of the Japanese bombing victims in and around Hiroshima and Nagasaki. A significant amount of information also was learned from the Operation Crossroads bomb tests in 1946.

The Advisory Committee on Biology and Medicine (ACBM) of the Atomic Energy Commission held its first meeting in September 1947. It was charged with studying the "basic policies relating to the medical, biological and health aspects of the Atomic Energy Program . . . [including] research on possible health hazards in the development of atomic energy."[1] It soon undertook widespread research programs into the peaceful uses of this powerful new force, including curative and diagnostic medical uses and agricultural applications. Among the findings were that radiation could cause cancer, genetic mutations, cataracts, central nervous system damage, and hypothyroidism with its attendant problems of slowed mental and physical activity, tooth decay, and immune deficiencies. (Hypothyroidism resulting from exposure to radiation comes most often from exposure to radioiodine [I-131].) A search for therapies for these specific radiogenic ailments, as well as for the less precise malaise of "radiation sickness," had been under way since wartime and remained a high priority throughout the 1950s. During the same period, researchers discovered that radiation also affected plant life through the "soil cycle" and therefore could pass radioactivity to humans via food crops. In this era, scientists also strove to establish safe "tolerance doses," or maximum permissible concentrations, for human radiation exposure.

Researchers at the Hanford Atomic Products Operation conducted pioneering radiobiological studies during these years. They examined the effects of I-131 on sheep, the biomedical effects of tritium and plutonium, and the reactions of plant life to radiation, and they participated in the quest for radiation therapies. Hanford's chief health physicist, Dr. Herbert Parker, also helped to establish tolerance doses for various forms of exposure to radiation. Additionally, the Hanford Site played a seminal role in tracking and studying the effects of fallout, from distant atomic bomb tests, on the Pacific Northwest and on other regions, including the South Pacific and Alaska. As information developed about the biomedical effects of ionizing radiation in the two decades after the founding of the Hanford plant, researchers in chemistry, physics, medicine, and agriculture, as well as members of the public who read popular scientific journals, came to recognize the magnitude and intransigence of the effects of radioactivity on living tissues.

Wartime Research Examines Effects of Plutonium and Other Fission Products

In 1944, a U.S. medical physics textbook listed the carcinogenic and mutagenic effects that could come from exposure to radioactivity. Ionizing radiation, stated Paul Henshaw, an MED physician, was "known to cause . . . mutations . . . cell death . . . [or] carcinogenesis."[2] Plutonium (Pu-239), the new substance produced in bulk for the first time at Hanford, was investigated vigorously by Manhattan District scientists. "Product [plutonium] hazards were not completely understood at the start of the Hanford operations," DuPont, the operating contractor, confirmed in 1946.[3] Herbert Parker added that "animal experience" was needed to evaluate the "metabolism" (i.e., assimilation, distribution, and retention) of plutonium and the fission products. MED researchers, he affirmed, strove to find "at least provisional answers on the toxicity of all of these materials before the stage of plentiful supply was reached."[4] Based on "early analogies with radium," Parker first set the Pu-239 whole-body tolerance level at five micrograms (5 μg). However, according to DuPont, "this was found high, due to different modes of bone deposition at about the time that the isolation process was started [early 1945]." The "extremely conservative value of 0.1 ug then was taken as the Hanford permissible level." This was increased to 0.5 ug in May 1945.[5]

MED research, publicly available in 1946, stated: "Inhalation is the most dangerous route of [plutonium] administration . . . The lethal action, even with extremely low doses, is much greater than with comparable doses administered intravenously or intramuscularly." Manhattan Project scientists also learned that "once in the lung," plutonium was "tightly bound." The highest percentages of initial dose remained in the lungs and produced "considerable . . . damage . . . necrosis, and abscess formation . . . widespread scarring . . . and emphysema." The bronchial linings "often showed remarkable proliferative activity" (precancerous cell multiplication). The next most significant site of plutonium deposition was the skeleton. Blood changes, including anemia, lymphopenia, and heteropenia (reductions in lymphocytes and heterophils in the blood) also resulted. Almost all of the experimental animals soon died.[6] Intramuscular and subcutaneous injections of plutonium, radium, and radio-isotopes of yttrium (Y-91), cerium (Ce-144), and strontium (Sr-90), given to mice and rats, produced bone tumors and malignant fibrosarcomas. Aside from these "carcinogenic properties," other "manifestations of radiation damage were observed locally . . . [including] graying of hair, epilation [and] ulceration of the skin, and destruction and atrophy of muscles, often followed by spontaneous amputation of the injected leg." Pu-239 and Ce-144 "showed a consistently high concentration in the liver," and liver damage "was frequently noted." Colon cancer was observed often in animals fed Y-91. MED scientists also remarked on the stealth of radiogenic ailments. "All animals appeared well during the feeding period, and growth was not impaired."[7]

MED research into the metabolism of other fission products also was made public in 1946. The most notable finding, stated the physician Joseph Hamilton, was "prompt deposition and prolonged retention" of radioisotopes in the skeleton. "A number of the fission products and actinide elements . . . possess the curious property of accumulating in the . . . osteoid matrix [of the bones] . . . a thin layer of tissue adjacent to . . . the [bone] marrow cavity." From

174

the osteoid matrix, he said, alpha disintegrations (alpha particle emissions) from the isotopes could result in "the bombardment of the radiosensitive bone marrow . . . the blood-forming tissues." Hamilton reported that lung, liver, and thyroid deposition also were important with certain radioisotopes.[8] Corollary MED studies of external beta radiation found severe skin damage with adjunct spleen, bone, testicular, and lymph node injury, including "the destruction of nearly all the small lymphocytes in . . . the side nearest the [irradiated] surface."[9]

Early in 1947, Herbert Parker reported on previous Manhattan Project research into the "general body effects" of radiation. "Lassitude and fatigue . . . and demonstrable effects upon the leukocytes" (a depression in white blood cell counts), as well as lung cancer, skeletal deposition, and erythema of the skin followed by "ulceration [that] . . . may progress to cancer of the skin," were "well-known" results of exposure. In fruit flies, very low doses of radiation had caused hereditary mutations that were "not only cumulative in the individual but in succeeding generations." Other studies had identified a susceptibility of female reproductive organs to radiation harm, and reduced exposure limits for women radiation workers had been recommended.[10]

The MED had initiated experimental work into the effects of "long-continued exposure at low intensity," Parker told the incoming AEC, but results were not yet available. The extent of "eventual injuries" from such exposure, he reported, was "not known." He did affirm that "repeated exposure [of tissues] initially followed by repair" could "eventually exhaust the regenerative reserve and result in permanent damage." He added, "Exhaustion of the bone marrow reserve is typical."[11]

World's First Atomic Explosions Provide Data

The world's first atomic detonation took place at Alamogordo, New Mexico, on July 16, 1945. Those involved were much more concerned with determining if their bomb would work than with measuring the effects of radioactive fallout on surrounding plants and animals. Observers were surprised that cattle grazing fifteen to twenty miles downwind from the blast suffered burns. Army officials rounded up about forty and later presented them to the AEC, which kept the cattle under study for many years at the experimental farm at Oak Ridge, Tennessee. In 1953, the research director of that facility reported that there had been "no lasting effects" on the Alamogordo cattle, with the exception of grayed hair at the site of the burns. The bomb's fallout, he explained, had damaged the hair follicles and the pigmentation of the skin. "But the effects did not penetrate below the skin." The offspring bred from these cattle, he affirmed, "were no different, either in quantity or quality, from the young of normal cattle from the same general area."[12]

As soon as military occupation forces arrived in conquered Japan, the Allied Public Health Section began to observe, test, and treat survivors of the atomic bombings. In 1947, the AEC formed the Atomic Bomb Casualty Commission (ABCC) to study potential, delayed effects from the radiation exposure. Staffed by 550 Americans, Australians, Chinese, and Japanese medical personnel, the ABCC undertook the largest epidemiological study in world history up to that point. Over the ensuing years, it examined nearly one-half million survivors of the Hiroshima and Nagasaki bombings, as well as a control group of nearly 200,000 people in undamaged Kure, Japan.[13] Early reports indicated that "no significant differences," aside from excessively thick scar tissue, had been discovered among Japanese bomb survivors. However, the AEC cautioned, "Probably it will be 25 years before the first reliable information can be obtained about the hereditary effects of the bomb."[14] Late that year, the first indications of delayed damage became evident when blindness caused by radiation cataracts was discovered among survivors of the bombings. By July 1951, a large ophthalmic survey had found cataracts in about 10 percent of those known to have been within 1,000 meters of the points directly below the two atomic explosions; the normal frequency of that ailment in urban Japan was less than 1 percent. At the same time the AEC revealed, "A very real increase of . . . leukemia, a fatal blood disease, was found among survivors within 2,000 meters of the points below the explosions."[15] By late 1951, according to the commission, "detectable malformations appeared in 1.18 percent of parents who showed no immediate effects of radiation, while among offspring of parents who showed immediate evidences of radiation injury, the figure was 1.40 percent." Additionally, "among women exposed within the 2,000 meter zone, the percentage of male births" had been "significantly lowered."[16]

By January 1954, after more than 60,000 newborns had been examined by the ABCC, the commission upheld the conclusion that "for sex ratio," exposure of the father was shown "to have no effect," but heavy exposure of the mother appeared "to have produced a significant though small decrease (1.3 percent) in the number of male children."[17] Two years later, the ABCC reported no increased rates of dominant mutations such as major malformations, decreased weight in live babies, or increased rates of stillbirths and neonatal deaths in first-generation descendants of survivors.[18] Missing, however, were the notations that dominant mutations are less frequent than recessive (hidden) mutations and that only the dominant ones would be likely to appear in one generation. In the 1980s, the Radiation Effects Research Foundation (RERF), the successor agency to the Atomic Bomb Casualty Commission, confirmed augmented radiogenic disease levels in survivors (and their offspring) of the Hiroshima and Nagasaki bombings.

Operation Crossroads Yields Information

In the meantime, in the years beginning with 1946, important animal data was gained from Operation Crossroads, two atomic bomb trials conducted at Bikini Atoll in the Marshall Islands of the South Pacific. A special Naval Medical Research Section (NMRS) was created, consisting of civilian scientists, naval officers, and personnel from the army's Chemical Warfare Service and Biological Warfare Division. They brought thousands of fruit flies, goats, pigs, and rats to the tests. Pigs were chosen because their skin was thought to be similar to human skin "in its response to radiation." Goats were selected because their blood contained more and smaller red cells than human blood, thereby yielding "more material for studying the effects of radiation on the blood." NMRS physicians, veterinarians, and other scientists conducted observations, measurements, and autopsies on the experimental animals, searching for links to the two major radiogenic maladies: cancer and hereditary defects. They also experimented with radiation remedies, including penicillin, liver extract, iron compounds, various chemicals derived from blood hemoglobin, and folic acid, a recently discovered vitamin. Seeds and soil samples also were transported to the blast area "to learn how atom bomb radiation" could affect "future crop production and habitability."[19]

The two explosions of Operation Crossroads, particularly the underwater blast, Test Baker, brought surprising results. Beforehand, military officials had predicted that the water in Bikini lagoon might retain radioactivity "to a dangerous degree from five to seven days." However, ten days after the explosion, the "Geiger-men" (radiation monitors) of the task force were still detecting high radioactivity levels aboard the target vessels. One physician described a dawning sense of horror among veteran navy officers. They had "braved a world war with . . . complete faith in the old ritual of 'a clean sweepdown fore and aft.'" He noted: "[Now] little seems to be accomplished by repeated scrubbings . . . Fission products . . . cannot be washed off . . . The whole business . . . seem[s] like a very bad dream . . . decks you can't stay on for more than a few minutes . . . air you can't breathe without gas masks . . . water you can't swim in, and good tuna and jacks you can't eat." Tests of coral, algae, fish, shoreline, sand, bottom mud, and ship surfaces all demonstrated "unexpected" levels of radioactivity.[20]

Eighteen days after Test Baker, Operation Crossroads was abandoned as an experiment.[21] In September, Charlie, a deep-water test shot planned to complete the mission, was cancelled by President Harry Truman because of the unexpected radiation burdens already in the area. Of the original target fleet of seventy-six vessels, all but ten had to be scrapped and sunk. Those remaining had to be towed to U.S. ports and decontaminated with acid and sandblasting, in experimental and training work for military safety squads. In 1948, a task force physician, David Bradley, published *No Place to Hide,* in which he concluded: "There are no satisfactory countermeasures and methods of decontamination [for fallout]. There are no satisfactory medical or sanitary safeguards for the people of atomized areas."[22] Dr. Stafford Warren, the head of the Bikini Radiological Safety Service, and J. Robert Oppenheimer, a key bomb development physicist, also commented that there were "no specific countermeasures" to fallout contamination.[23] In 1949, the approximately two hundred Marshallese people of Bikini, who had been moved 109 miles away to Rongerik Island, were told that they could not repopulate their atoll. *Science Illustrated* observed that year, "The animals [of Operation Crossroads] are almost gone, the ships are almost gone, the Marshallese natives are gone—and the radioactivity of the 'Baker' bomb, like the cheese in *The Farmer and The Dell,* stands alone."[24] For at least eleven years after the tests, Hanford scientists and others continued to resurvey the Bikini region and the plant, animal, soil, and water for hundreds of miles around it.[25]

The two Operations Crossroads detonations produced dramatic consequences in the animal test subjects. Approximately 10 percent were killed as a direct result of Test Able, the airdrop. Within a few weeks, another 10 percent died of radiation sickness, and an additional 10 percent were sacrificed for tissue assay and study. Radioactive spray and an irradiated water supply from the underwater blast, Test Baker, killed about 62 percent of the animals. Survivors became restless, aggressive, and hyperirritable for one to two weeks and then became listless. Many later succumbed to various infections, but leukemia was the most frequent specific cause of death.[26] Three years after Operation Crossroads, only twenty-eight of the fifty-five hundred animals conveyed to Bikini were still alive. Ordinary drowning and natural death had befallen some. However, in 1949, Task Force scientists publicly disclosed that the majority of the animals "really did catch a lethal dose of radiation illness at Bikini." Displaying classic indications of "radiation sickness," the animals "lost their appetites and became depressed and cranky." The scientists added: "Then the real atomic death set in. White blood cells disappeared, the animals bled internally and their blood lost its clotting power; skin sluffed off . . . and then one morning they would be found lying dead."[27] Additionally, marine life throughout the Marshall Islands area displayed the same tendency to concentrate waterborne fission products as did the aquatic life of the Columbia River.[28]

Geneticists at the U.S. Naval Research Institute, observing the test animals, found no "monster" offspring in the three ensuing years. Yet they cautioned:

"[Mutations] are usually recessive—that is, they lie hidden in the chromosomes, as long as one of the parents is normal. But let two parents with similar mutated genes breed, and some of the children will be freaks."[29] The following year, researchers at Washington State College and at Texas A&M jointly published the results of four years of study of specimens from the Operations Crossroads tests. "Ionizing radiation . . . can cause breaks in plant chromosomes . . . human and animal chromosomes . . . are also liable to the same kind of injury," stated Dr. Meta Brown. As a result, the AEC and the Department of Defense stated in a handbook released that year, "There is a large body of data which indicates that any dose of radiation, no matter how small, increases the probability of genetic changes."[30]

Media Discuss Radiobiology

Meanwhile, the media in the United States began to inform Americans about the biomedical effects of radioactivity. In January 1947, *Life* magazine reported that weakening, nausea, loss of white blood cells and immunities, internal bleeding, and then a silent, mysterious death often followed exposure to large, single doses of radiation. Smaller doses, the journal stated, could be survived initially. "[But] in a year deepseated organic damage sometimes becomes apparent. Leukemia, a wild overproduction of white blood cells, occurs and internal organs waste away . . . some experimental animals go blind and develop tumors." *Life* concluded, "Many scientists think that people, like rats, may show . . . effects after years of exposure."[31] That summer, the New York City Board of Health banned shoe-fitting devices that used X rays. Soon afterward, calling radiation "the weirdest danger in the world," *Popular Science* magazine cautioned, "No important source [of radioactivity] is weak enough to be wholly harmless."[32] At nearly the same time, the *American Journal of Public Health* published a speech by a prominent University of Rochester radiologist, Andrew H. Dowdy. "All living cells whether of man, animal or plant, are capable of injury from . . . various types [of radiation]. The most sensitive tissues are the reproductive cells of the generative and hematopoietic systems . . . The reproductive function may be temporarily decreased, interrupted, or permanent sterility may ensue . . . A profound leucopenia [abnormally low number of white blood cells] may result followed by a reduction in the number of platelets and red blood cells . . . [and] almost complete destruction . . . [of] the bone marrow and lymph nodes."[33]

Thus began an avalanche of articles on the biomedical effects of radioactivity. Over thirty-five such reports were published in just two years in popular U.S. magazines, and more were reported in professional journals and in classified research documents sponsored by the AEC. Numerous speeches and conferences also discussed the subject. In January 1948, one AEC-funded study on "ionizations in the tissue" published particularly graphic findings. Mice irradiated with alpha-emitters demonstrated consistent weight loss "until death." The article noted: "The effects of radiation on the organs . . . were unmistakable . . . the spleen was small in size . . . paper thin and gray or black in color . . . liver weights were generally below normal . . . [and] appeared pale . . . mottled, some had round necrotic areas, and others looked hemorrhagic . . . The kidneys were pale . . . intraperitoneal hemorrhage was present; lymph nodes were small . . . anemia was apparent."[34]

AEC Funds Further Research

By December 1948, five young physicists had developed cataracts from exposure to neutron rays during wartime atomic research. The AEC established the Committee on Radiation Cataracts to locate and examine approximately six hundred scientists who might have been exposed to a similar hazard. In a year, six more physicists, average age of thirty-one, were found to have cataracts. The National Research Council immediately approved five research contracts to study the process by which neutrons damaged the soft tissues of the eyes.[35] By late 1956, AEC-sponsored biomedical research had demonstrated that exposure to radiation led to "the death of epithelial cells on the surface of the lens [of the eye] which eventually migrated to form opacities."[36]

As public discussion of the health hazards of radioactivity increased in the late 1940s, the AEC funded further research. In January 1949, the commission reported to the public, "The element plutonium, the product of the Hanford Works, can cause serious damage to the liver, kidney, and bone marrow if enough of it gets into the blood stream . . . overexposure to radiation may induce cancer."[37] Six months later, the AEC affirmed its "clear responsibility to inform people . . . about . . . the dangers of radiation." The AEC added: "Radiation attacks, disrupts, and destroys the delicate electro-chemical balance in the atoms . . . within the bodies of living things. As a result, it damages and kills the cells . . . If enough cells are destroyed, the whole organism—plant, animal, man—is severely injured or dies . . . rapidly growing tissues are more sensitive to radiation."[38] In 1950, the commission acknowledged that, in general, "in living tissues the ionizing effect of radiation causes the injury and death of cells."[39]

Beneficial Uses of Radioactive Materials Are Explored

During the same early postwar years, beneficial uses for radioactive materials also were explored. Some proved to be real, but some were unworkable (and sometimes dangerous) theories. The AEC emphasized the use of radioisotopes to "trace" biochemical processes and to diagnose and treat disease.[40] Tales of nearly miraculous cancer cures had surrounded radioactivity since its discovery. Marie Curie was hailed throughout the early 1920s as "the woman who had found the cure for cancer."[41] In the early post–World War II era, Americans heard much about medical treatments and diagnoses performed with common substances followed by mysterious new "atomic numbers." "Phosphorus 32 for Cancer," proclaimed a popular U.S. science magazine in mid-1946, describing the treatment of basal cell carcinoma and hyperkeratosis, two surface-level skin cancers, with P-32. This therapy, stated the article, was "an excellent illustration of the theory of possible treatment of cancer with artificially radioactive substances, and it brighten[ed] the future in this field."[42] At almost the same time, the development of "effective penetrating X-ray treatments for cancer and other ills without the patient suffering radiation sickness" was reported in a widely read journal.[43] Later in 1946, *Time* magazine informed Americans that radiophosphorus (P-32), "with its affinity for blood-forming tissues," was being utilized to slow the overproduction of red blood cells in the ailment polycythemia. Concurrently, medical investigators were considering the use of radioactive sex hormones against breast, uterine, and prostate cancers and the use of radioactive amino acids against other cancers. *Time* termed such treatments "a promising line of attack!"[44] That same year, an MIT physics professor, Robley Evans, stated, "Through medical advances alone, atomic energy has already saved more lives than were snuffed out at Hiroshima and Nagasaki."[45]

In 1948, the AEC related that in the two previous years, 1,010 biomedical research projects in over 90 laboratories and hospital research departments had utilized radioisotopes.[46] The following year, the commission reported on experimental therapies that used yttrium colloids to treat lymphatic cancers and used radioarsenic (As-76) against certain blood diseases and cancers.[47] Soon most of the major atomic energy installations, including Hanford, became involved in biomedical research. Projects investigated radioactive gallium to treat bone cancers, radioruthenium to remedy surface tumors, and radiomanganese to attend thyroid tumors.[48] Radiogold was injected directly into malignant tissues, and a radioactive gold wash was utilized to treat lung, ovarian, and bladder cancers.[49] Cancerous brain tumors were attacked with boron neutron bombardment, and radiocobalt (Co-60) wafers for use against "deep-seated cancers" were developed by Hanford's operating contractor, the GE Company. "Radiation," *Newsweek* magazine told its readers in 1951, "is a classic treatment in stubborn skin diseases, acute infection, inflammations, gas gangrene, and both benign and cancerous growths."[50] At the same time, high-voltage betatrons were used in an increasingly routine manner for cancer therapy at major hospitals in the nation.[51] In 1953, AEC Chairman Gordon Dean termed radio-isotopes "the servants of man."[52] Two years later, the new AEC chairman, Lewis L. Strauss, vaunted the "always interesting and sometimes spectacular progress in the use of radiation in . . . medicine, biology, agriculture, chemistry."[53]

Radioactive Materials Proliferate in American Life

During the late 1940s and early 1950s, radioactive materials proliferated in American life. Radiotracers and X-ray inspections were used to detect flaws, leaks, and inadequate welds in many facets of U.S. industry. Compounds containing radioisotopes were used to fashion metallic alloys in manufacturing processes. Often workers handling the substances were inadequately trained and had little understanding of any hazards.[54] Repeatedly, groups of business-men petitioned the AEC for more participation in the development of atomic technology.[55] At the same time, new devices placed radioactive materials directly into the hands of the public. A mechanism known as the Omegatron brush, using polonium (Po-210, an alpha-emitter with a half-life of 140 days) along with an attendant impurity (Radium D, an alpha-emitter with a half-life of 22 years), was sold as a static charge eliminator for phonograph records. A similar device was used in commercial print shops to remove static from paper and machinery.[56] Radium-dial watches were still in use in the United States.

In 1953, a Washington State College researcher identified multiple applications for radioisotopes in animal husbandry, fertilizer uptake studies, plant breeding, and industry. Isotopes could be used to gauge thickness and volume in paper and pulp industries, he said. They also could trace the diffusion of metals in alloys and the wearing characteristics of engine parts, tires, pavements, and "even car polishes." Radioisotopes also were investigated as tracers to determine insect dispersion paths and the distribution of insecticides within plants, and they were used to kill or sterilize insect populations.[57] In 1954, University of Michigan researchers submitted plans for an irradiation plant that would use wafers of radiocesium (Cs-137) to sterilize hog carcasses.[58] That same year, the new Atomic Energy Act opened further potential avenues for commercial radioisotope use.[59]

Some investigative groups worried about the multiplication of inventions containing radioactive substances. In early 1950, *Consumers' Research Bulletin,* a widely read product-evaluation journal, warned its readers: "Very grave danger involving one's very life can be present and not be felt immediately through the senses . . . don't be lulled into a false sense of security . . . Overexposure to radiation can result in leukopenia (decrease in the number of white blood cells), loss of hair, impairment of vision, sterility, cancer, destruction and death of the bones, anemia, leukemia, and even death."[60] In 1953, the U.S. Food and Drug Administration (FDA) announced that applications for the manufacture of cosmetics containing radioisotopes were being refused "because of the danger associated with their use."[61]

The Cancer Connection

Knowledge about the carcinogenic effects of radioactivity, observed for many years and confirmed by MED research, expanded in the late 1940s and 1950s. In 1947, Dr. Austin Brues, a former MED physician then working at the AEC's Argonne National Laboratory, designated a new "atomic disease" that he called "plutonism." Caused by exposure to large doses of radium or X rays, or to the atomic fission products yttrium, radiocerium (Ce-144), and radiostrontium (Sr-90), the malady produced liver and spleen damage, bone cancer, and greyed and/or lost hair.[62] In 1949, Dr. Egon Lorenz, of the National Cancer Institute, cited "extensive animal research" to declare that exposure to radiation produced earlier and more frequent cancers than were the average in unexposed groups. Sometimes, such damage could result from exposure that was "quite small—so small, in fact, that probably very little immediate effect" was noticed.[63] In 1950, an entire chapter of a landmark medical text was devoted to the cancer-radiation link.[64] At the same time, Dr. Brues flatly stated that the "production of" leukemia and bone, lung, skin, and ovarian tumors by "irradiation" was "well known."[65] By late 1952, radiation's role as a "cancer-maker" was confirmed in a major AEC-sponsored study at the University of Rochester. Exposure to "exceptionally small amounts of radiation" caused lymphocytes with bilobed nuclei to appear in the blood. (Such cells had nuclei shaped like hourglasses. Often, this condition was a precursor to leukemia.)[66] Two years later, University of Illinois medical researchers stated that cancer was "one disease closely connected with radiation."[67]

The most salient evidence came in June 1956. The Committee of the British Medical Research Council and six separate committees of the National Academy of Sciences of the United States simultaneously released large, long-term studies of the human effects of ionizing radiations. The American report was known as BEAR-I. Both documents emphasized evidence of the delayed effects of radiation in damaging blood and blood-forming organs and in leading to leukemia and other cancers. These findings revealed leukemia rates ten times higher than normal in patients treated with X rays for the joint disease ankylosing spondylitis. The British report also pointed out a strong statistical correlation between the inhalation of radioactive particles and the development of lung cancer.[68] Later that year, the AEC added that feeding insoluble radio-isotopes to test animals had resulted in tumor formation in the colon.[69] In 1957, a University of California researcher confirmed that exposure to levels of radiation below those permitted in atomic installations and research laboratories increased the number of binucleated (bilobed) lymphocytes in the blood.[70] A year later, personnel from the U.S. Public Health Service and the University of Rochester found abnormally high incidences of such bilobed cells among uranium miners of the Colorado Plateau and among laboratory workers exposed to low levels of radiation.[71]

During the late 1950s, studies and evidence on the radiation-cancer link became too numerous to cite. In 1957, the chief of research of the Pasteur Institute in Paris reported on his study of carcinogens. He noted that mankind, seeking to "master Nature and to make it work for him . . . has not always foreseen all the consequences of his enterprise." The researcher added, "The very real and immediate risk of cancer caused by radiation is one such consequence."[72] The following year, prominent researchers in the United States, England, and France all reported on the cancer link.[73] A 1958 report of the UN Scientific Committee on the Effects of Chronic Radiation contended that long-term exposure to even low levels of radiation could produce cancers and anemia.[74] In 1960, a second NAS report on the "Biological Effects of Atomic Radiation" (BEAR-II) stated, "A late effect of radiation appears to be leukemia, which may arise years after radiation exposure." Cancers of the gastrointestinal tract, bone, skin, thyroid, lungs, and respiratory tract also were noted as being radiogenic in nature.[75]

Genetic and Hereditary Effects

The accretion of proof that exposure to ionizing radiations could produce genetic mutations in mammals followed the same pattern as the accumulation of evidence about cancer. In 1946, an American geneticist, George Snell, demonstrated an increase in negative genetic mutations in the second, or grandchild, generation of mice exposed to radiation. His work underscored the concept that genetic mutations, carried in recessive genes, could remain unnoticed throughout more than one generation.[76] A University of Chicago biophysicist, Raymond Zirkle, told the Radiological Society of North America in 1948 that the "biological effect" of irradiation could be "the mutation of a gene, the breaking of a chromosome, an increase in permeability of a [cell] membrane, an inhibition of cell division . . . or any one of many other radiobiological phenomena."[77] In 1949, the Nobel Prize–winning zoologist H. J.

Muller stated: "It is . . . well established . . . that the frequency of mutations induced in the genes is exactly proportional to the total dose of radiation, no matter in how concentrated or dilute form the dose was received. There is no dose without at least some . . . risk, commensurate with its size . . . [and] doses of more than 600 roentgens usually result in sterility." Muller confirmed that "probably . . . no important increase in . . . human monsters [would] appear . . . in any succeeding generation" after exposure to radiation. "On the other hand," he warned "this is very far from saying that the ultimate hereditary damage would be negligible . . . The effects of radiation on heredity are more insidious, elusive and delayed . . . Their total magnitude would undoubtedly be very considerable."[78]

At nearly the same time, the AEC acknowledged in a public document that it could "be said with certainty that ionizing radiation . . . greatly increased . . . the rate of mutation in the genes . . . [of] all living things." The report added: "Very small doses of radiation may produce a genetic change. In fact, it is questionable whether there is a dose of radiation so weak that it does not have some effect."[79] In 1950, Oak Ridge National Laboratory's Biology Division agreed that there was "no [radiation] threshold below which" some hereditary effect was not produced.[80] A 1951 Oak Ridge study noted, "So far as genetic effects are concerned, humans are more sensitive to radiation than previous estimates have indicated."[81] That same year, the National Institutes of Health in the United States funded a comparative survey of four thousand radiologists and a control group of four thousand other physicians who did not work with radiation. The project looked at rates of sterility, stillbirths, and hereditary abnormalities. In that study, published in 1955, Drs. Stanley Macht and Philip Lawrence found a small but statistically significant increased rate of fetal deaths and congenital defects and a decreased rate of fertility and male births among radiologists and their offspring. The two researchers cautioned, "Visible first generation effects represent only a small fraction of the total damage that may have been inflicted."[82]

In 1953, the AEC affirmed: "Radiation . . . increases the frequency of mutations above the normal rate, and the increase seems to be in direct proportion to the dosage. Since most mutations are disadvantageous, large increases are considered undesirable."[83] Two years later, in commission-sponsored research, irradiation during pregnancy produced significant deformities in developing mice embryos.[84] Also in 1955, Drs. Eugene Rabinowitch and Henry Quastler, of the University of Illinois, asserted that increasing environmental exposure to radioactivity could increase the number of "genetically underprivileged" people in the world—those with mental deficiencies and/or high susceptibility to disease.[85] At the same time, a California Institution of Technology geneticist, A. H. Sturtevant, declared, "Any increase at all in the number of individuals that are defective either mentally or physically is not to be lightly dismissed."[86]

At the first International Conference on the Peaceful Uses of Atomic Energy, sponsored by the UN in August 1955, geneticists from around the world spoke of increases in mutation rates and "genetic death" (the failure to reproduce in a healthy manner, by individuals who had inherited a mutation) as a result of exposure to radiation.[87] BEAR-I and the accompanying British Medical Research Council report of June 1956 both stressed: "It cannot be assumed that any dose whatsoever of ionizing radiation is without genetic effect . . . there is no threshold . . . there is no disagreement among geneticists as to fundamental conclusions in this area."[88] At nearly the same time, the AEC reported on several studies with important implications for the food chain. Research had shown that the fecundity of fruit flies and lower organisms could remain high even when they carried a large burden of radiation and a "heavy degree of mutation."[89]

The late 1950s brought a further spate of warnings. The UN's World Health Organization reported in 1957: "There are strong grounds for believing that most genetic effects are very closely additive, so that a small amount of radiation received by each of a large number of individuals can do an appreciable amount of damage to the population as a whole . . . In essence, then, all man-made radiation must be regarded as harmful from the genetic point of view."[90] At the same time, Dr. Michael Bender, of Johns Hopkins University, told the American Institute of Biological Sciences, "Many geneticists [believe] that there is no 'safe' dose of radiation."[91] There were many other such warnings, including those contained in the 1960 BEAR-II report.[92]

Other Biomedical Effects of Radiation

Just as knowledge about the role of radioactivity in producing cancer and genetic damage increased in the mid-1950s, so did awareness of more vague and multifaceted injuries. In July 1950, the International Commission on Radiological Protection (ICRP) identified some potential effects of exposure to radiation as "cataract, obesity, impaired fertility . . . reduction of life span . . . superficial injuries, [and] general effects on the body."[93] A 1954 study of alpha-emitting radionuclides in rats and mice found a principal effect to be a shortened life-span.[94] This effect was investigated specifically in other mid-1950s studies.[95] The BEAR-I document of June 1956 emphasized the statistically shorter life-spans (60.5 years, as opposed to 65.6–65.7 years) of radiologists as compared with other physicians and with the general population.[96] The AEC also confirmed that "accelerated aging" and "premature" death could occur even when test animals appeared to suffer no immediate effects from radiation exposure, or when they suffered radiation sickness but appeared to recover fully.[97] In 1957, the principal geneticist at ORNL, Dr. W. L. Russell, added that exposure to radiation not only condensed the life-span of the irradiated individual but also produced a "significant effect . . . on the length of life of the offspring."[98] Former AEC Chairman Dean also spoke of the life-shortening effects of exposure to radiation.[99]

Other health effects became evident. In 1957, the AEC stated, "Irradiated animals are more susceptible to . . . bacteria, viruses, and toxins, and . . . irradiation may stimulate a latent disease infection, such as typhus, to renewed activity."[100] The propensity of radioactivity to disrupt the brain and the central nervous system, investigated as early as 1952, was confirmed in both American and Russian research by 1956. The brains of developing fetuses were found to be especially sensitive. In 1958, a Russian biophysicist, A. M. Kuzin, reported: "Under the chronic influence of low doses of radiation the earliest changes appear in the central nervous system . . . an asthenic [weak] condition . . . inertia, sluggishness . . . serious disturbances . . . in conditional reflex action and in the bioelectrical activity of the cerebral cortex . . . [and depression of] the alpha-rhythm . . . [These dysfunctions] have been established beyond all doubt."[101] In January 1960, the AEC reported, "Radiation produces a basic defect in the transfer of electrolytes across the cell membrane."[102] A year later, the AEC research disclosed that "a nonspecific chronic stress [reaction] was produced" even in unirradiated mice from an irradiated germ line. "The data," concluded the commission, "suggest the inheritance of a genetic burden of recessive and/or sublethal mutants detrimental to survival."[103]

So concerned with the multifaceted effects of exposure to radiation were the NAS scientists who wrote the BEAR-I report that they recommended the reduction of exposure to all forms of radiation, through all possible pathways, including X rays, radioactive waste, bomb test fallout, irradiated components of the food chain, and fission and activation products from atomic reactors.[104] Their highly publicized document, along with the 1956 British report, galvanized public attention. In the two years beginning in March 1957, over fifty articles detailing the biomedical effects of radioactivity appeared in American popular magazines.[105]

Hanford's Role in Biomedical Research

Throughout the 1950s, the Hanford Site contributed much research to the body of knowledge about radiation health effects. H.I. Division scientists under

Herbert Parker explored the carcinogenic effects of active particles, the bone metabolism of radioelements, and the gastrointestinal and percutaneous absorption rates of plutonium and tritium. The radionuclide uptake capacity of bacteria was examined to determine the potential value of these organisms to "scrub" the reactor effluent basins and the waste-water trenches and cribs of the separations areas. Hanford researchers also were involved in monitoring and bioassay work for U.S. atomic bomb testing programs. By late 1951, the Hanford biology staff numbered seventy-seven people, with forty-eight more individuals working on the development of biophysical radiation measurement techniques and instrumentation.[106]

Important data was developed as early as 1950–52. In a gastrointestinal absorption experiment with rats, the Hanford biologist Kenneth Herde found that the highest beta radiation concentrations appeared in the blood and kidneys. Trials revealed that plutonium was most highly concentrated in bones and the spleen. Parker estimated that Pu-239 had a "biological half-life of 50 years." Gastrointestinal tests demonstrated that tritium quickly interacted with bacteria to form "significant quantities of tritium oxide which . . . [became] distributed throughout the animal body." Researchers concluded that the biological half-life of tritium oxide was "surprisingly long . . . on the order of 100 days or more." Apparently, human volunteers were used in some of the Hanford experiments. In percutaneous absorption tests, scientists placed containers of tritium oxide vapor on areas of the human forearm and/or abdomen. Interposing a layer of clothing between the skin and the vapor, they found, "insignificantly affected" the absorption rate.[107] Other Hanford scientists stated, "Tritium may be considered one of the most biologically significant radionuclides in an arid climate because of its rather complete involvement in all levels of the ecosystem."[108]

Some Hanford Site experiments focused on the fission products found most frequently in biological monitoring of wildlife in the local vicinity. Such monitoring demonstrated that bone (P-32) and thyroid (I-131) concentrations were highest.[109] In muscle tissues, Cs-137 accounted for 90 percent of the radioactivity present.[110] After a 1957 study of cesium retention in rats, Hanford scientists concluded, "If one accepts the general picture of cesium metabolism derived from the rat data, but substitutes the longer half-life measured in man, then the MPCs would require reduction from presently recommended values by a factor of approximately ten."[111] H.I. experiments in 1955 with ruthenium and plutonium oxides produced fibrosis in the lungs of mice.[112] Two years later, William Bair, a respiration expert at Hanford, concluded a landmark study of long-term Ru-106 particle retention: 427 days after inhalation, 80–90 percent of the body burden of inhaled radioruthenium remained in the lungs of mice.[113] In 1958, a Hanford researcher learned from an experiment with rats that approximately half of ingested radiozinc (Zn-65) was absorbed from the gastrointestinal tract and retained primarily in the bone and prostate. Very young rats retained up to 5.5 times the adult level.[114]

The previous year, in experiments that utilized audioradiography, site scientists noted: "Plutonium does actually follow the path of the puncture wound, penetrates the skin, and diffuses into the surrounding tissue . . . [It is] evidenced by a diffuse alpha track pattern among cellular elements . . . [Pu-239 in particulate form] is evidenced by microscopic alpha stars originating from a single point."[115] Later that year, Hanford biologists discovered that the gastrointestinal absorption of plutonium by growing rats "exceeded adult absorption by as much as 85 times." Eighty percent of the Pu-239 deposited in the skeleton.[116] In 1958, William Bair found that when plutonium was administered to the lungs of dogs, only about 1 percent of the plutonium translocated to other tissues and only about 10 percent was excreted. The vast majority of the Pu-239 was retained in the lungs. The next year, he observed a slow decrease in the lung burden of PuO_2 (plutonium oxide) as the bone and liver burdens of experimental animals increased. Pulmonary and lymphatic damage was obvious. Then, in 1960, Bair and a colleague, D. H. Willard, demonstrated that the smaller the quantity of Pu-239 inhaled, the greater the percentage of retention in the lungs. Possibly, they reasoned, the small amounts did not trigger the important lung clearance function of "phagocytosis."[117]

By 1959, site researchers were turning their attention to the interactions between pairs of isotopes within living tissue. They learned that such pairs could form compounds that altered the behavior of each. Simple linear equations could not predict the behavior of these compounds, and the complex mixtures often behaved differently in the human body than in laboratory solutions or in the soil.[118]

Botanical and Agricultural Studies

During the same postwar years, data accumulated on the hazards of radioactivity to plant life. As early as 1946, a popular American journal reported, "In plants like corn, barley, and rice, the [X]ray-produced changes resulted in albino plants, lacking in chlorophyll and therefore unable to nourish themselves, or in plants with stalks so weak that they could not support their own weight."[119] The Hanford Site actively participated in botanical and agricultural experiments with radioactive substances. Among the very earliest findings of H.I. researchers was the fact that plants grown in reactor effluent water and activated sand concentrated the radioactivity in their tissues to much higher levels than that of the water itself.[120] In 1951, Hanford botanists discovered that exposure to Sr-89, Sr-90, and Cs-137 resulted in "a decreased growth rate and early senescence of the plant."[121] Almost concurrently, Washington State College researchers found that irradiated barley, wheat, and oat seeds produced plants that "had irregularities in the vital pairing of . . . chromosomes."[122] They also found genetic mutation rates fifteen times as high as the spontaneous rate in barley and wheat seedlings exposed to X rays or to the radiation in the first Operation Crossroads bomb test.[123] At the same time, experiments at the AEC's Brookhaven National Laboratory revealed "no indication that radiation could improve growth rates and yield [of crop plants], but in large doses caused marked damage to both." Plant chromosome breakage, and hence genetic mutation, resulted from irradiation in these tests.[124]

The AEC was very interested in the possible benefits of radioisotopes as tracers in examining plant growth and the uptake of fertilizers, as sterilizing agents in fungicides, as herbicides, and as the initiators of mutations that could produce stronger strains of plants. In early 1952, in reference to plant studies, the commission termed radioisotopes "the most important scientific tool developed since the microscope."[125] That same year, however, AEC researchers stated: "Damage in plants is directly related to the amount and rate of exposure to radiation . . . When radiation is heavy enough, it retards growth, reduces yield, and causes malformations." Lesser amounts of radiation might cause "no readily discernible harm," but they also conferred "no benefits." Plants grown in nutrient solutions containing radioisotopes demonstrated chromosome breakage, cell enlargement, and "definite possibilities of harm." Tests indicated that the level of radiation that damaged plants was "very low." Additionally, exposure to radioactivity "hasten[ed] the maturity" of plants as well as their subsequent "aging and decline."[126]

In 1954, botanical research at the commission's Brookhaven National Laboratory produced the "first report of a tumor in plants induced by gamma radiation."[127] Two years later, other AEC studies suggested that growing tissues were "more sensitive to radiation than . . . nongrowing tissues."[128] Tests performed at Hanford from 1952 onward found many factors that affected plant uptake of various radionuclides. Soil type, pH balance, mixture of nutrients and organic matter in the soil, ion exchange capacity of the soil, temperatures of seeds both before and after irradiation, and soil particle size all were important. Site scientists learned that tritium, iodine, cesium, ruthenium, curium, and cobalt were quite well absorbed by plants. Zirconium, niobium, promethium, americium, and some of the other rare earths, as well as plutonium, were less well absorbed.[129] In the early 1960s, botanical research with radioisotopes continued as scientists hoped to control and adjust mutations to produce more desirable and hardy plants.[130]

Fallout Tracking and Research

The Hanford Site participated in tracking fallout from the 193 announced atmospheric weapons tests conducted by the United States between 1946 and 1958 and from the 137 American underground and atmospheric tests conducted in 1962 and 1963. Additionally, Hanford monitors reported fallout measurements in the Pacific Northwest from tests conducted in those years by the Soviet Union, England, and France. In early 1951, as the atomic trials began at the Nevada Test Site (NTS), Hanford's H.I. Division installed special "active particle air filter monitors" at Richland and at seven new positions in Utah, Colorado, New Mexico, and Idaho. These operated in addition to previously established particle-sampling stations that stretched from Great Falls, Montana, to Stampede Pass, Washington, and from Boise, Idaho, to Klamath Falls, Oregon.[131] Thus, the Hanford Site took the lead in fallout monitoring over a wide band of seven states. Often, in conjunction with the University of Washington's Applied Fisheries Laboratory (later the Laboratory of Radiation Biology), Hanford scientists also surveyed and analyzed the effects of fallout on marine and aquatic organisms, stock and other mammals, crops, and milk.[132] In particular, they investigated levels of Sr-90 through the soil cycle to accumulation in milk.[133]

During the years of atmospheric bomb testing, fallout was deposited on the Hanford region on at least six occasions in significant quantities and on many occasions in lesser amounts. Hanford monitors soon learned that fallout from trials at the NTS arrived in the Pacific Northwest two to five days after the explosions and that debris from Pacific Proving Grounds missions arrived in five to seven days. Fallout from some tests, particularly hydrogen bomb blasts beginning in November 1952, often entered the stratosphere and circulated, depositing slowly, for many weeks. The first test series at the NTS, Operation Ranger, executed in January and February 1951, produced spikes on Hanford-based particle-monitoring devices. At Richland, levels of beta-emitters in the atmosphere increased by one hundred times, seventy-two hours after the initial Ranger-Able shot.[134] As early tests continued, Hanford scientists expressed surprise at the far-reaching effects of fallout and at quirky upper-air currents that sometimes directed the atomic debris "backwards" (westward) from the NTS and then in long, curving arcs to the north. They also learned that "rainouts" (rainfall in conjunction with a fallout cloud) produced heavy localized depositions. On May 26, 1953, such a rainout occurred as the fallout from test Grable, part of the Upshot-Knothole series, passed over Richland. H.I. monitors measured I-131 levels in crops and fruits in the Tri-Cities at over one hundred times the normal amounts, and readings for nonvolatile beta-emitters climbed to over five thousand times the average. Worried, site scientists established "control plots" in Richland, Pasco, and Kennewick to study "the decay of the contamination deposited on May 26." In Franklin and Adams counties to the east of the Hanford Site, rain samples demonstrated up to one thousand times the prevailing averages for overall beta activity. According to H.I. Division calculations, the May 26 rainout produced unshielded, ground-level doses of 25 millirads per hour (mr/hr) in Richland, 9.7 mr/hr in Pasco, and 8.3 mr/hr in Kennewick.[135]

Due to other incidents of high contamination produced in Utah by subsequent tests in the Upshot-Knothole series, and in the South Pacific by the Operation Castle series of 1954, fallout began to attract attention among scientists and the public. Studies increased at Hanford and at other atomic sites and universities throughout the nation.[136] In May 1955, the Hanford region again received heavy fallout deposition from test Zucchini of the Operation Teapot series at the NTS and from Operation Wigwam at the Pacific Proving Grounds. During the week ending May 18, radioactivity on the ground reached 60 particles per square foot (psf) at Pasco and averaged 30 psf at Richland.[137] Operation Redwing, a series of seventeen atomic detonations at the Pacific Proving Ground in mid-1956, produced record particle counts from Great Falls, Montana, to Yakima, Washington. The last two Redwing shots, Tewa and Huron, fired on July 20 and 21, brought so much fallout that the telex hummed with urgent messages between the Hanford Site and the AEC's Division of Biology and Medicine in Washington, D.C.[138] Additionally, Hanford's laboratories performed radiochemical analyses on seawater and marine life collected up to a year after the Redwing tests, over a four-hundred-mile stretch from the Pacific Proving Ground west to the Caroline Islands.[139] On June 1, 1957, fallout from the Boltzman test of Operation Plumbbob at the NTS "rained out" over the Hanford area. Radiation readings spiked in air, water, vegetation, and wildlife thyroid samples.[140] However, it was test Newton of the Plumbbob series that produced the heaviest contamination that year in the Hanford region.[141] In 1958, Operation Hardtack II, a crowded series of thirty-seven detonations in forty-eight days at the NTS in September and October, also raised activity levels in all components of the Columbia Basin ecosystem. H.I. Division monitors noted in secret, "Fallout concentrations increased by several orders of magnitude during the last two weeks of October."[142]

On October 31, 1958, the United States, the USSR, and Great Britain entered into a voluntary moratorium on atmospheric atomic testing. France became a member of the "nuclear club" in early 1960 but exploded only four weapons over the following year and a half.[143] In 1959 and 1960, studies of the effects of fallout on the environment and the food chain burgeoned. Hanford's Biology Operation, part of the H.I. Division, participated extensively in the AEC's Project Chariot, a program that measured "the transfer of radioisotopes through freshwater and terrestrial ecosystems" in the remote Cape Thompson area of northern Alaska. In the summer of 1959, Hanford biologists, performing a survey of the invertebrate fauna, fish, birds, mammals, vegetation, soil, and water at the headwaters of Ogotoruk Creek near Cape Thompson, were surprised to find radiostrontium (Sr-90), radiocesium (Cs-137), and radioisotopic complexes of ruthenium (reported as Ru-106) and cerium (reported as Ce-144), as well as yttrium and rare earths, in all of their samples.[144] Additionally in 1960, Hanford's H.I. Division participated in a large AEC "cross-state fallout transport study." For this project, Hanford established eight new sampling stations roughly in a line across Washington State from Quinault on the west to Coffee Pot Lake (northwest of Sprague).[145]

After the Soviet Union broke the atmospheric testing moratorium on September 10, 1961, the United States executed Operation Nougat (1962) and Operation Storax (1963).[146] Fallout depositions from moderate to heavy were measured by Hanford monitors across the Pacific Northwest through these test series. Shots Eel and Des Moines of the Nougat series, on May 19 and June 13, 1962, most affected the region.[147] In a 1963–64 study, Hanford scientists found significant deposits of radiocesium in humans and caribou in Alaska. That state, as a whole, was situated in a "fallout band," and the central, mountainous Anaktuvuk region was directly down the jetstream from Novaya Zemlya, a large Soviet atomic testing site. The Hanford researchers calculated exposure rates for people in Anaktuvuk villages at thirty-two to fifty-four times higher than that for people living in the coterminous United States.[148]

Over the years of atmospheric atomic testing, no biomedical topic was investigated more intensively than the deposition of Sr-90 through fallout. Sr-90 is a beta-emitting, bone-seeking isotope with a half-life of twenty-eight years. MED researchers had early noted that when it was administered to test animals, "bone tumors were readily produced . . . and in many individuals [experimental animals] widespread metastases occurred."[149] A 1949 study, funded by the AEC, concluded, "Sr-90 is by far the most hazardous isotope resulting from nuclear detonations, and that distribution of this isotope over large areas of the earth's surface constitutes the limiting factor in . . . the long-range hazard from the use of a large number of atomic bombs."[150] As soon as continental weapons tests began in 1951, AEC researchers became concerned with the "soil cycle" of Sr-90. Scientists in Hanford's H.I. Division participated in plant absorption and translocation studies. During the 1951 Buster-Jangle test series, they noted, "Strontium is similar to calcium . . . and plants will draw the one out of the soil as readily as the other." Flora grown in a nutrient solution containing Sr-90 "built up strontium in their leaves until they assayed 5 to 10 times as high a concentration as was present in the nutrient." They reported: "If animals should eat plants containing large quantities of radioactive strontium, the material would lodge in their bones and injure their blood-forming organs. It would appear in cow's milk and, from this source and from leafy vegetables such as spinach, could be taken in directly by human beings."[151] The scientists affirmed in secret to the AEC, "Strontium is potentially the most biologically hazardous of the fission products."[152] In 1955, the Hanford veterinarian Leo Bustad affirmed: "With regard to the toxicity of bone seeking element[s], once absorbed they are usually retained a long time . . . The principal hazard from . . . [bone-seekers] is the increased probability of bone tumors . . . An aplastic anemia may also accompany deposition of radioactive bone seekers."[153]

At Hanford, additional long-term plant experiments with Sr-90 were begun in 1955. By 1959, these tests had yielded the "unexpected" result that radiostrontium deposited in soil was "as fully available" to plants three years after deposition as was Sr-90 added to the soil just before planting. Approximately 10 percent of Sr-90 administered to lactating sheep and cows appeared in the animals' milk.[154] During the years of the nuclear testing moratorium, 1959–61, the issue of milk contamination from Sr-90 rose to the forefront. At Hanford, environmental scientists examined the interaction of dietary radiostrontium with calcium (Ca). They learned, according to the H.I. biologist Harry Kornberg, that pairs of elements could form compounds that altered the behavior of each. Therefore, calculations based on soil ratios could not predict the Sr-90/Ca ratios produced in the body. In rat experiments in 1959, Kornberg concluded that the ingestion of dietary calcium did not necessarily cause a "proportionate decrease in deposition of Sr-90." This finding made doubtful the prevalent theory: "As calcium in the environment goes up, the Sr-90 hazard goes down." Kornberg reported, "The true concentration of the radioelement cannot be obtained from such ratios."[155]

The Search for Radiation Therapies
As the biomedical effects of exposure to radioactivity became known, almost no other research topic was pursued more avidly by the AEC than the search for

194

radiation therapies. In early 1949, the commission affirmed that one of its "most pressing responsibilities, of course," was to find out how to treat "injuries that radiation inflict[ed] upon the human body."[156] After clothing trials held at the 1946 Operation Crossroads, scientists stated, "Synthetic materials are least resistant to atomic effects, and light colors are more resistant than dark . . . [but] no fully protective clothing is feasible now."[157] The following year, Herbert Parker confirmed that no "fundamental advances" had been made in radiation protection. He meant that the physical barriers of shielding, distance, and limited time exposures were the best available means of radiation protection.[158] Neither penicillin, transfusions, nor drugs had proved effective in treating radiation overexposure.[159]

By early 1949, AEC-sponsored research at the University of Rochester was testing "a number of drugs and hormones." A hopeful development, the commission announced, was Argonne Laboratory's demonstration that "the relatively harmless element zirconium" could displace "large amounts of plutonium in the body and thus eliminate it."[160] In other 1949 studies, male and female sex hormones, horse serum, adrenal hormones, "certain steroids or foreign protein," antibiotics, and nitrogen gas were investigated as potential radiation therapies. These treatments sought to "help . . . build up certain white blood cells" and thus counteract the "depression in blood cells and antibodies . . . [that occurred] with radiation injury."[161] That same year, Richland's village newspaper reported that oak bark might be an antidote to radiation damage.[162]

A great deal of research was conducted in the 1950s by Hanford's H.I. Division on "Problem 687.21—Possible Therapeutic Agents for Radiation Damage." Repeatedly, however, H.I. Chief Parker was forced to report "no progress." Experiments in administering zirconium citrate after the ingestion of plutonium in rats seemed promising in 1952, but Hanford biologists soon concluded that the chelated compound "was without significant effect on the amount of plutonium retained in the animal."[163] In the twelve months ending June 30, 1951, the AEC invested approximately $20 million in radiation antidote research. Burn studies continued, as did experiments with cysteine and various chelating agents used to induce more rapid and complete excretion of ingested radionuclides.[164] A promising technique involved shielding the spleen with lead during radiation exposure or transplanting the organ after exposure. However, transplants and shielding were expensive and impractical on a mass basis. Another experiment injected pulverized embryonic mouse tissue into irradiated mice.[165] Still other theories proposed that fatty acids in the diet, particularly linoleic acid, offered "protection against atomic bomb radiation," that extreme heat or cold aggravated the harmful effects of radiation, and that zymosan, the insoluble cell-wall residual from yeast, offered some protection.[166] In 1953, the Naval Medical Research Institute acknowledged that "at the moment" no radiation antidotes held "any real therapeutic benefit, but they [made] hope for therapy rational."[167]

In mid-decade, the AEC announced the most significant discovery to date in the field of radiation therapy: bone marrow transplants combined with liberal doses of antibiotics, given after heavy radiation exposure, produced increased recovery rates in test animals.[168] However, such treatments were impractical on a mass scale.[169] Injections of trypsin, a chemical present in soybeans, was thought to offer some protection to irradiated laboratory mice in 1956, but this hypothesis did not stand up after testing.[170] Scientists also tried applying the synthetic thyroid hormone tri-iodothyronine as an ointment for radiation burns.[171] Nearly concurrently, French researchers reinjected dogs with their own previously irradiated blood.[172] Both of these practices soon fell into disrepute, however. Throughout this period, a scientific debate occurred over the properties of oxygen in either aggravating or aiding recovery from radiation injuries.[173] During 1959, Hanford scientists tested various chelated compounds, such as DTPA and EDTA, for their abilities to remove ingested plutonium oxide (PuO_2).[174] In other research, irradiated rats treated with the antidiuretic hormone pitressin showed improved body fluid retention. However, this therapy addressed only one symptom among the many associated with radiation injury.[175] By 1960, expensive and painful bone marrow transplants were still the best and only effective therapy for radiation damage.[176]

The Tolerance Dose

Throughout the years after World War II (and indeed since Marie Curie's discovery of radium in 1896), scientists searched for and debated the concept of a "tolerance dose" for the exposure of living tissue to ionizing radiations. Herbert Parker stated in 1945 that a tolerance dose was "assumed to be that dose to which the body" could be "subjected without the production of harmful effects."[177] The concept had been introduced in 1924 by the German physicist Arthur Mutscheller.[178] Although many scientists accepted it readily, its inherent value was debated over the ensuing years. "The tolerance dose is never a harmless one," asserted two researchers, H. Wintz and W. Rump, to the League of Nations in 1931.[179] In 1950, Dr. Brues framed the key dilemma: "No true threshold for chronic or delayed effects [of radiation] may exist . . . in no other field is such a wealth of experimental data and exact physical information counterbalanced by such a dearth of clinical experience."[180]

The MED's Plutonium Project subscribed to the 1945 statement of Parker and another prominent health physicist, Simon Cantril, who noted, "The majority of radiation effects are thought to be of the threshold type."[181] Below a "threshold" level, Parker explained, amounts of radioactivity could be absorbed by humans with virtually no ill effects. In early 1947, however, he stated that for genetic effects, there might be no threshold level and "no true tolerance dose, but rather an acceptable injury limit."[182] Later that year, one of Parker's H.I. colleagues stated, "Subtolerance radiations produce certain biological changes; and so, tolerance dose is not what one strives to get but the maximum permissible."[183] At the same time, another H.I. staff member cautioned: "A 'threshold' effect is not measurable by present methods until . . . [it] is exceeded . . . The majority of radiation effects are thought to be of the threshold type. It may be that as more delicate indicators are found to measure effects, more of them will be found to be of the non-threshold type."[184] Parker later stated that the threshold dose was "intended to refer to somatic effects only." For genetic effects, he admitted, it was known as early as World War II that there was no "completely safe dose."[185] In the late 1970s, he added, "The recognition of the probably non-threshold development of a wide variety of late cancers seems in retrospect, to have been slow in coming."[186]

Under Parker, Hanford's H.I. Division strove to establish and monitor tolerable doses of radioactivity for various organs and tissues, time periods, and types of exposure. Parker differentiated sharply between "dose" and "dosage rate." *Dose* referred to single (isolated) or total exposure, whereas *dosage rate* concerned limits for ongoing exposure. He proposed in 1947: "Daily short exposures at high rates may be more damaging than equal doses at normal rates . . . a *daily* tolerance dose . . . is arbitrary . . . One cannot prove that . . . [double] and zero [exposure] on alternate days . . . [is] unacceptable."[187]

Tolerable Levels and MPCS

During the postwar years, radiation protection standards, expressed in terms of tolerable levels, MPCs, or allowable limits, struggled for legal recognition. In the United States, no such standards had the stature of enforceable law. Instead, they derived their credibility from the scientific prestige of the organizations that issued them: the NCRP and the ICRP. Radioactive and chemical emissions at AEC sites were governed solely by the commission's agreement to operate within NCRP and ICRP guidelines. Under this system, the AEC's contractor companies, such as GE at Hanford, applied the scientific guidelines in setting their own discharge limits.[188] These companies, in applying for commission licenses, pledged themselves to maintain health and safety standards based on the amounts of discharge and dosage allowed by the NCRP and the ICRP.

Failure to maintain these standards constituted the violation of a regulation and not of a law.[189] At Hanford, Herbert Parker translated NCRP and ICRP guidelines into site operating standards for exposure to radiations and for discharges of radioactivity. But, as he stated in 1947, these standards were "recommendations only."[190] It was Parker's stated policy to limit the exposure of workers to the NCRP and ICRP recommendations and to confine public exposures to only 10 percent of these standards.[191] In 1948, however, an AEC safety review of the Hanford Site advocated more public health agency involvement. "The establishment of maximum tolerance allowances has been primarily by the producer, and not the guardians of public health . . . it is an unusual deviation from . . . the past . . . In the Atomic Energy operations no . . . external reviews were provided . . . representative agencies of various municipal and state governments [should be involved] so that responsibility in part be shared with those who may be affected."[192]

Throughout the postwar years, the AEC subscribed to the validity of the MPC concept. "Maximum permissible radiation doses . . . are considerably lower than the radiation level which causes any observable bodily change . . . The body may safely receive a small dose of radiation because the effects are repaired virtually as rapidly as they are produced."[193] Repeatedly during this period, the NCRP and the ICRP revised the MPCs downward for radioactivity in humans, other animals, and plants. The NCRP issued major handbooks in 1936 and 1938, on "X-Ray Protection" (external) and "Radium Protection" (internal), respectively.[194] The 1936 recommended level for whole-body external radiation was 10 roentgens per eight-hour day. The ICRP issued similar guidelines in 1937.[195] During the 1940s, no other standards were available because scientists were just becoming familiar with the vast array of fission products that would be produced in nuclear explosions and in reactors.[196]

In 1950, the NCRP recommended a decrease of the whole-body external radiation limit to 3 roentgens per week, and the AEC officially adopted the change. At the same time, the commission established its own permissible concentrations in drinking water, in air, and "fixed in the human body" for radium, plutonium (Pu-239), uranium 233, 234, 235, and 238, iodine (I-131), tritium, strontium (Sr-90), sodium (Na-24), and phosphorus (P-32). The limits were based on 1949 recommendations of representatives of the radiation protection committees of the United States, Canada, and Britain.[197] In 1951, the ICRP also revised its X-ray and radium exposure guidelines and added exposure limits for nine radioisotopes and for natural uranium.[198] A comprehensive listing of MPCs for a wide range of radionuclides in the human body and in air and water was not available until 1953.[199]

By the mid-1950s, scientists had learned that dosage calculations could not be drawn from simple linear equations. J. W. Healy, a Hanford scientist, summed this up in 1955: "The excretion of at least some isotopes is not a constant fraction of the quantity present but rather . . . the excretion rate decreases as a function of time . . . [In the case of] long-lived emitters . . . the quantity of radioisotope in the body increases with time, so that the daily increment must be judged on the life expectancy of the individual." He noted additional factors such as different uptake and retention rates based on age, species, and on method of intake (ingestion, inhalation, percutaneous absorption, etc.).[200] Another important point of discussion within the NCRP, the AEC, and the scientific community became whether to regulate radioactive emissions at the point of release or at the points of contact with (or ingestion by) populations. At least for waste-water disposal, the NCRP decided that the point of discharge was the most important. Too many interactions took place between water and the rest of the environment to be able to calculate meaningful limits away from the emission site.[201]

In April 1956, the ICRP again lowered many of its MPCs and MPDs (maximum permissible accumulated dose for radiation workers), and the NCRP soon followed suit. In the United States, these changes were published first as an NBS Technical News Bulletin in 1957 and later in NBS Handbook no. 69 (1959). They were "officially adopted by the AEC," and the GE-Hanford Company issued its own revised radiation protection manual, based on the new limits, in July 1957. Overall, the guidelines urged "that exposure to radiation be kept as low as practicable in all cases" (the ALAP concept). It recommended that permissible dose levels "for individuals outside of controlled areas" (off site) be kept at one-tenth that allowed for radiation workers.[202] The new off-site limits specified that no person should receive a dose of more than 0.5 rem in any one year.[203] The AEC commented, "The changes in [NCRP levels] are not the results of positive evidence of damage due to the use of the earlier permissible dose levels, but rather are based on the desire to bring . . . [standards] into accordance with the trends of scientific opinion . . . there are still many uncertainties in the available data and information."[204]

The closing years of the 1950s witnessed greatly increased awareness and controversy over radiation protection standards. In 1959, the NCRP again issued a major downward revision of many tolerance doses. However, it doubled the amount of Sr-90 that could be allowed in the human body without causing an "unacceptable" hazard. MPCs of radiostrontium in water, food, and milk also were revised upward, but in lesser proportion. At almost the same time, the ICRP, under its pioneering chairman Rolf Sievert, recommended a lowering of the current MPCs for Sr-90. Discord over the NCRP and ICRP differences soon developed in the scientific community. *Science* magazine explained: "Immediately after the international [ICRP] report became available, criticism of the national [NCRP] report began to mount . . . The suggested possibility [was] that the United States, with its heavy investment in atomic energy, was presenting a misleading view of the dangers involved."[205] In September 1959, the AEC established an Office of Health and Safety to "centralize its responsibilities . . . and develop and recommend health standards for protection of the public." That same year, President Eisenhower established the Federal Radiation Council (FRC) to "study the hazards and use of radiation . . . and [to make] recommendations for the guidance of Federal agencies in the conduct of their radiation protection activities."[206]

The debate over radiation protection standards intensified in 1960. That year, the NAS published its BEAR-II report, in which the genetic hazards of even low doses of radiation were stressed. The FRC produced its first report, containing no specific organ dose recommendations other than for the gonads. It took the laissez-faire position that individual federal agencies should implement for themselves the existing guidelines of the NCRP, the ICRP, and the NAS. In response to public criticism, President Eisenhower announced in September 1960 that he would "reexamine" this policy. The FRC then adopted the viewpoint that radiation exposure standards should be set on a risk/benefit basis. What "risks of exposure may be accepted in order to realize the benefits associated with incurring the exposure?"[207] On January 1, 1961, the AEC adopted new radiation exposure limits consistent with the 1959 NCRP guidelines.[208]

The twenty years beginning with the energizing of the Hanford plants brought a rapid accumulation of information on the biomedical effects of ionizing radiation. As learning developed, debates were conducted within the scientific and medical communities about the amounts of exposure to various radionuclides necessary to produce harm. The concept of a safe, or threshold, dose also was argued. However, the dominant trend assigned greater and greater risk to smaller and smaller dosages of radiation.

Truth and Rebirth

The way we've operated these plants in the past . . . was: This is our business, it's national security, everybody else butt out . . . They're not going to be operated that way anymore.—Henson Moore, U.S. deputy secretary of energy, Washington, D.C., June 1989

Revelations of Hanford's Waste Bring Pain

The last days of February 1986 were shocking ones. The DOE (successor to the AEC) released nineteen thousand pages of documents on the history of the Hanford Site. From these, the public learned that radioactive and chemical wastes had been released far in excess of previously known levels. The state of Washington assembled a Hanford Historical Documents Review Committee and began to prepare abstracts of the voluminous and complex documents. Oregon and Washington, the Indian Health Service, and the Yakima, Umatilla, and Nez Perce Indian nations formed the Hanford Health Effects Review Panel. They called in personnel from the U.S. Centers for Disease Control (CDC) and the Washington State Department of Social and Health Services to calculate potential radiation doses to populations living near Hanford in the 1940s and 1950s. Meetings were held in schools and city halls. Newspapers and other media carried the story for months. In the Pacific Northwest, the community grief process proceeded through all of the roller-coaster emotions of shock and denial, anger, fear, powerlessness, and despair.

In the Tri-Cities of Washington in particular, home to the Hanford complex, the pain was sharp. In this region, known for its patriotism and support of government programs, the news just plain hurt. Added to the distress over the waste emissions was the fact that other areas of the Northwest began to treat the neighborhood surrounding Hanford as a pariah. A mantle of collective historical guilt was laid over the Tri-Cities, as if the residents were somehow to blame for the situation they had just discovered. In the "atomic city" of Richland, many people instinctively defended their homes and their heritage. Some people denied that the documents could be accurate. Perhaps a majority were bitter that the achievements of the Hanford complex as the workhorse of the nation's defense effort now were being devalued. It was as if the news about the radioactive emissions had leached and spread, like the wastes themselves, to sully the accomplishments of the plants. Feelings sunk deeper as nearly fifty thousand additional pages of Hanford historical documents were released over the next five years. Throughout this period, some residents of the Hanford area asked: How could our government have allowed these wastes to be released and have not told us?[1] In his 1963 memoirs, David Lilienthal, the first AEC chairman, offered some pertinent observations. "The production of the atomic bomb was a great big 'scientific success story.' The scientists were given a blank check, and they 'delivered,' with world shaking results. With such credentials, the . . . widely held assumption among laymen was that the scientist was infallible . . . a scientist did not make errors . . . And . . . [scientists'] authority in . . . nonscientific areas was, at least at first, not strongly questioned."[2]

Federal Studies and Groups Coalesce

The investigations that began with the releases of the Hanford historical documents coalesced into two major federal studies. The first study, known as the Hanford Environmental Dose Reconstruction Project (the HEDR Project, or HEDRP), began its work in 1988. It was funded for $15 million by the DOE, and the work was performed by the Pacific Northwest Laboratories of Richland. However, it derived its independence and academic credentials from its Technical Steering Panel of outside experts. John Till, a nuclear physicist from South Carolina and the panel chairperson, stated that the HEDR Project's mission was to "reconstruct the doses that people [might] have received from the releases of radioactive materials from Hanford." He added, "This is an enormous task with a great deal of detail involved."[3] Mary Lou Blazek, the panel vice-chairperson, added the "why" of the concept. "People have a right to know. They have a right to know if they were exposed to radioactive materials from Hanford."[4] The second study, the Hanford Thyroid Disease Study, was funded for $5 million by a special vote of Congress in 1988. In 1989, under the supervision of the U.S. CDC, the Fred Hutchinson Cancer Research Center of the University of Washington began work. Its mission was to determine whether or not there was an increased incidence of thyroid disease among people who had lived near Hanford in the 1940s and 1950s.[5]

During the same years that these studies began, groups of Northwest citizens interested in past and present Hanford issues became organized. In 1985, the Hanford Education Action League (HEAL) formed in Spokane. By 1988, it had grown to about four hundred members. It defined its mission as "help[ing] citizens examine and . . . challenge policies that promote nuclear weapons at the expense of environmental quality, public health and human dignity." HEAL also sought to establish mechanisms for timely, ongoing public access to facts about Hanford emissions. Later, it extended its goals to include the permanent closure of the PUREX (plutonium reduction extraction) plant and to ensure that public involvement and oversight, adequate funding, and safe transport all be addressed in waste cleanup plans.[6] In the same period, some current and former Hanford area residents organized other groups. Known as "Downwinders" because they lived in the pathways of some waste emissions from Hanford, they wanted to bring their stories to public attention, to identify medical resources in radiogenic health effects, and to share emotional sustenance with each other. In 1988, the National Association of Radiation Survivors, a San Francisco–based advocacy group, established a Hanford Downwinders chapter.[7] In mid-1989, the Downwinders Information and Support Group (DISG) formed in Seattle. It announced its "intent to be a clearinghouse for Hanford Downwinders." The group noted, "Our efforts will be directed for our mutual support and relief." In December 1989, the DISG sponsored an exhibit to commemorate the fortieth anniversary of Hanford's Green Run.[8]

Economic Losses Add to Hardship

During the same period that the Hanford historical document releases occurred, that the HEDRP and CDC studies commenced, and that HEAL and the Downwinder organizations formed, the Hanford area underwent other traumas. In January 1987, the last remaining defense production reactor at Hanford, 100-N, was shut down for safety modifications. The surrounding region waited tensely for thirteen months. Then, in February 1988, the DOE announced that this reactor, a major employer and point of pride in the area, would be placed on "cold standby," essentially a defueling and "mothballing." At that time, DOE-Hanford Manager Michael Lawrence announced a nearly unbelievable fact: "This decision essentially closes out the plutonium production mission here at the [Hanford] Site."[9] Just two months earlier, Congress had ended the

Basalt Waste Isolation Project (BWIP) at Hanford, an effort to develop the nation's first geologic repository for commercial, high-level nuclear waste.[10] The N Reactor and BWIP closures brought job losses and economic hardship to the Hanford neighborhood.[11] Then, in August 1988, the DOE announced plans to build new defense production reactors at the Savannah River Plant and at the Idaho National Engineering Laboratory. The conversion of a partially complete Washington Public Power Supply System (WPPSS) reactor (WNP-1), located on the Hanford Site, to a defense (tritium) production plant was considered and rejected in this decision.[12]

Although the N, BWIP, and WNP-1 decisions were reached for ostensibly technical reasons, they were part of a trend. The timing of these projects virtually prohibited their success. In the United States as a whole, nuclear safety and nuclear waste had become major issues. Since 1978, no American utility company had ordered a nuclear power reactor, and all such orders placed since 1974 had been canceled. Although high costs were a factor in these cancellations, public fears about nuclear safety and waste also played a role. The National Academy of Sciences noted this trend in 1988 when it examined safety issues at some DOE reactors. "In the interval since . . . [the 1950s and 1960s] the demands of society for safety of nuclear plants have increased. Thus . . . acceptable risk at . . . [that] time . . . may not be acceptable today."[13] An April 1990 DOE presentation of the "four major obstacles" to nuclear power development listed "public concerns about safety . . . [and] concerns about the disposal of radioactive waste" as the foremost barriers.[14] Polls taken in the United States and Europe confirmed that few people had worried about radioactive wastes before 1970 but that by the mid-1970s, a majority of people saw such wastes as a problem. Furthermore, nearly all surveyed, both those who were "pro-nuclear" and those who were "anti-nuclear," said that they would rather live near a reactor than near a nuclear waste-disposal site. According to the historian Spencer Weart, many people "felt that nuclear wastes were somehow unique, more dreadful than other industrial dangers."[15]

In the late 1980s, the historical tide ran against N Reactor, WNP-1, and BWIP. Safety modifications had essentially been completed at 100-N when the "cold standby" decision was made. Nevertheless, the fact that N's irradiated fuel rods would have to be processed in the aging PUREX plant, with the concomitant generation of high- and low-level nuclear waste, collided with the public renunciation of such wastes.[16] For WNP-1, conversion from its original design raised certain technical questions. The NAS cautioned in 1988, "Operating nuclear reactors in ways that depart from their original design can have serious safety implications."[17] More important, however, was the sensitive issue of public acceptance of switching a "peaceful atom" project to military uses. BWIP, like the geologic repository investigations in Nevada and in Texas, encountered the powerful national revulsion against nuclear waste. Several lawsuits questioning the safe isolation of wastes from groundwater and soil cycles were launched by agencies of Washington and Oregon, the Yakima Indian Nation, and other Northwest groups. When Oregon officials started looking at BWIP's technical basis, they discovered that the real problem was waste in general. A consensus built among many that they did not want the Pacific Northwest to take all of the waste from the nation's nuclear power plants.

Regional Waste Concept Grows

The concept that radioactive waste rightfully belonged in the region that generated it became a potent and emotional one in the late 1980s. The national disposal site for transuranic defense waste, the Waste Isolation Pilot Project (WIPP), was far behind schedule. In October 1988, Idaho Governor Cecil Andrus announced that his state no longer would store nuclear waste from U.S. defense plants. Seven boxcars of waste from the Rocky Flats (Colorado) bomb trigger manufacturing plant sat waiting for a destination, and Rocky Flats was projected to reach its 1,635-cubic-yard limit for temporary waste storage in early 1989.[18] In a February 1989 compromise, Andrus agreed to accept two boxcars of waste per month (nearly all of the normal Rocky Flats amount) for six more months. In exchange, he obtained an eightfold increase in waste cleanup funds for INEL.[19] In October, the DOE asked governors from seven states to accept Rocky Flats waste until the WIPP site could be completed. All seven refused.[20] In February 1990, Secretary of Energy James D. Watkins announced that a program of "waste minimization" at the Colorado facility would allow legal storage of plant wastes on site for six additional months. After that, he said, a special waste compactor would enable Rocky Flats to handle its own wastes until late 1991.[21] Presently, along with other DOE sites that need permitted waste-storage facilities, Rocky Flats awaits the opening of the WIPP site near Carlsbad, N.M. Land withdrawal issues and safety concerns have delayed the use of that defense waste repository.[22]

In the meantime, the issue of regional nuclear waste disposal became more prominent. In 1988, in response to pressure from states hosting disposal sites for low-level, commercial nuclear waste, Congress passed a law requiring each state, or regional consortium of states, to create its own disposal site for such waste by January 1, 1993. A sponsor of this statute, South Carolina Representative Butler Derrick, explained: "It's politics. Nobody wants nuclear waste. It's a matter of the states . . . wanting to dump on someone else."[23] In February 1990, Washington, Nevada, and South Carolina announced that they would bar waste shipments from Rhode Island and Washington, D.C., because those districts had not done enough to develop their own waste-disposal sites.[24] Later that year, Washington State officials barred waste from Michigan for a similar reason and announced that they were considering banning waste from New York, Connecticut, New Jersey, Maine, and Massachusetts.[25] Throughout 1990 and 1991 in some states, particularly Nebraska, bitter disputes raged over where to site their low-level repositories.[26]

In April 1990, the DOE offered financial incentives to states that would accept interim storage of high-level defense wastes. Governor Gardner was "not interested."[27] The following month, when the DOE again asked the Hanford reservation to accept waste from the Rocky Flats plant, this time on a test "certification" basis, an advisor to Gardner conveyed an adamant refusal. "We're not interested in taking any waste . . . when the real [DOE] goal is interim storage."[28] In August 1990, President George Bush appointed David Leroy, former lieutenant governor of Idaho, to negotiate with states and Indian nations for the location of interim and permanent high-level waste repositories. After six months on the job, Leroy reported no progress at all. He stated that nuclear waste was so unpopular that if he even met with any state governor individually, he "would instantly have created the principal issue in that governor's next re-election campaign."[29]

Hanford Region Bewildered by New Concepts

In the Tri-Cities of Washington State, the emphasis on accepting only regional waste, and the concept that Hanford would no longer produce weapons materials, were confusing to many people. The area had so long been proud of its role in weapons manufacturing and in storing decommissioned nuclear submarine parts and other wastes that it did not understand why these missions were being devalued. It had always defended nuclear energy. And, it had always had powerful friends in Congress who were ready to send more nuclear programs to the eastern Washington desert. In 1971, President Richard Nixon had cut all funding for N Reactor for fiscal 1972. However, residents of the Tri-Cities rallied and sent forty thousand letters to the White House in support of N's continued operation. That, along with newspaper editorials in Seattle, Portland, and Spokane, help from labor unions and the Sierra Club, and aid from Washington's senators Warren Magnuson and Henry Jackson, kept the reactor running.[30] The Three Mile Island (Pennsylvania) reactor accident in March 1979 brought only renewed expressions of confidence in nuclear power in the Tri-Cities. A Prosser (Benton County) woman demanded and obtained time on the CBS national news to rebut statements made by the anchorman Walter Cronkite about the risks of nuclear power.[31]

Even earlier, partial disclosures of radioactive releases at Hanford did not shake the dedication of the Tri-Cities to nuclear energy. The 106-T tank leak of June 1973 brought expressions of confidence in letters to the local newspaper.[32] In late April 1979, when newspapers in Seattle and Spokane published partial reports of Hanford's 1952–54 radioruthenium particulate discharges, local feelings still evidenced support for the site. In fact, the editor of the *Tri-City Herald* complained, "This story [in the *Seattle Post-Intelligencer*] . . . demonstrated . . . the potential for sensationalism of almost anything nuclear."[33] Shortly thereafter, the *Herald* denounced the "Great Nuke-In," an antinuclear demonstration of about seventy-five thousand people in Washington, D.C., as "an amorphous, mindless outcry."[34] One week after that, a debate on nuclear energy took place in Richland between the physicist Ralph Lapp and the antinuclear consumer advocate Ralph Nader. Nearly one thousand residents demonstrated against Nader, and billboards in Richland carried slogans such as "Nukes Are Necessary" and "Nuclear Energy Since 1943—We Like It."[35] As late as 1988, at the time of the DOE decision to place 100-N on "cold standby," the *Tri-City Herald* termed the reactor "a national resource." The newspaper, as well as many area citizens, viewed N's closure as "a crisis born in betrayal." It added, "The [Reagan] administration has cynically exploited the patriotism, community spirit and technological know-how of the citizens of the Tri-Cities."[36]

Unexpected Developments Shake Tri-Cities

However, by 1989 and 1990, residents of the Tri-Cities had to face the reality that the DOE contemplated no future defense production missions at Hanford. Secretary Watkins made this intention clear in visits in August 1989 and October 1990. "A logical process . . . of proper evolution," Watkins said, dictated that Hanford should became a center for research and development, especially in waste-remediation technologies. The new DOE-Hanford manager, John Wagoner, reiterated this priority as he assumed command of the site in July 1990. The end of the defense era seemed so gentlemanly, yet so final.[37] In addition to this reality, evidence of radioactive waste emissions from Hanford was undeniable. At quarterly public meetings mandated under cleanup agreements with Washington State and the EPA, Hanford officials openly disclosed and discussed leaking waste-storage tanks and process lines, plumes of contaminated liquids and vapors emanating from old processing buildings and reactor effluent basins, degrading barrels and other buried waste containers, and many other contamination sources.[38]

In the closing years of the 1980s, residents of the Hanford region had seen and heard so much that was difficult, so much that they had never expected. In July 1989, the DOE reported that it was unable to ensure that its nuclear facilities across the nation were meeting state or federal environmental standards.[39] In early 1990, Secretary Watkins expressed dismay at the findings of another DOE report that showed numerous violations, including inadequate radiation control and waste-storage practices that violated environmental laws, at the weapons sites. In May of that year, other internal DOE reports documented equipment failures, worker contamination, theft, drug use, sleeping on the job, and waste-storage transgressions.[40]

Meanwhile, in December 1989, the Senate Governmental Affairs Committee released a report showing that the AEC had known in 1947 that workers at Hanford were being exposed to "significant quantities" of radioactive particles. Commission officials had decided not to warn employees of risk, even though they secretly termed the exposures "a very serious health problem." The 1989 document also cited evidence of dangers over the years to workers at the Oak Ridge, Rocky Flats, Fernald, INEL, SRP, Los Alamos, and Nevada Test Site facilities and at uranium mines and milling sites.[41]

Other findings across the world also seemed to sully the atomic safety record. From Central Australia came evidence of particulate contamination spread by British nuclear tests conducted in the 1950s and early 1960s.[42] Likewise, French atomic bomb tests conducted in the Polynesian islands of Moruroa, Fagataufa, and Tahiti beginning in 1966 had spread radioactive fallout and marine contamination over wide areas as far east as New Zealand and Australia. After hydrogen bomb detonations had commenced in Polynesia in 1968, coral in the area became so damaged that French engineers said it looked like "Swiss cheese." Food-chain effects and ciguatera poisoning, an infection carried through the food chain from damaged coral to fish to man, had ensued.[43] From the Marshall Islands, where the United States had conducted atomic weapons trials between 1946 and 1964, came evidence of elevated levels of radiogenic ailments, congenital defects, and radioactive contamination in food, soil, and humans.[44] The environmental and radiogenic effects of Soviet nuclear production and testing in areas of the Ural Mountains and Siberia, effects first discussed publicly in the late 1980s and 1990, were even more devastating.[45]

In 1988, reports declassified in the United Kingdom revealed that the 1957 fire at the Windscale atomic weapons plant had been worse than previously disclosed.[46] In 1990, a British medical journal published a study that found an increased incidence of leukemia among children whose fathers worked at the Sellafield (formerly Windscale) plant. Because of the research design, the conclusions were associated more with routine work at the nuclear plant than with the 1957 fire itself.[47] In December 1989, the U.S. National Research Council (the research arm of the NAS) released BEIR-V, the most recent in a series of reports begun in 1956 on the biological effects of radiation. BEIR-V reported that the cancer risk from low-level radiation was approximately four times as high as estimated in the 1980 BEIR-IV. A spokesman for the National Committee on Radiation Protection (NCRP) stated that, as a result of the new study, current radiation exposure standards "may be reduced," perhaps by more than half.[48]

During the same years of the late 1980s, independent studies also linked increased incidences of leukemia, lymphomas, multiple myeloma, and cancers of the thyroid, pharynx, esophagus, stomach, small intestine, bile ducts, gallbladder, liver, and breast with American military personnel present at the occupations of Hiroshima and Nagasaki and at U.S. atmospheric nuclear bomb tests. As a result of this data, the Atomic Veterans Compensation Act was passed in 1988, making these ailments and these veterans eligible for service-connected death or disability benefits.[49] Elevated rates of lung cancer also were found in uranium miners of Colorado, Utah, Arizona, and New Mexico. In 1985, thirty-two miners and survivors negotiated a legal settlement for compensation from the company that had bought Vanadium Corporation of America (the former owner of the Utah uranium mine). In late 1990, Congress established a $100-million trust fund to compensate other injured miners or survivors.[50]

With all of these developments, what were residents of the Hanford area to think? In January 1989, William Bequette, the retired editor of the region's newspaper, chronicled much of the new evidence about health hazards, "unreported accidents and intentional radioactive leaks . . . [and] a nuclear weapons complex in shambles." Nuclear workers, he said, felt stunned. "Their world has been knocked askew . . . Most are conservative, patriotic people who think of their jobs not just as a living but as a way to serve their country . . . Now . . . they wonder if the trust they put in their supervisors and in officials in Washington, D.C., was misplaced."[51] A year later, detailing additional evidence, Bequette went further: "The people who worked in those [atomic] plants and [uranium] mines were proud of their contributions to national defense. Now many of them feel betrayed by their own government . . . Declassification of once-secret documents is writing new chapters in the emerging story of working conditions in the nuclear plants and uranium mines . . . At issue is whether the government failed to protect workers from levels of radiation it knew could cause harm."[52]

In the midst of these feelings, as well as the hard realities of economic contraction in the late 1980s, how could the people of the Hanford region feel any hope? In the center of the stark and lovely Columbia Basin lay the largest known mass of radioactive waste in the Western world. Ongoing and new missions at the Hanford complex were disappearing. So was optimism and confidence in the Tri-Cities. There seemed to be nothing left of the bright and busy productivity of the place, of the dynamic and creative energy. A future that consisted simply of the dreary task of guarding and monitoring old wastes (the "muck and truck" business) did not seem to fit the place that had given so much to the national defense effort. The future did not seem to inspire anyone. The depression phase of the community grief process deepened.

Waste Cleanup Brings Hope

However, the 1980s ended with clear signs that the grief process of the Hanford region, and of the Northwest as a whole, had run its course. Hope came in the form of immense waste-cleanup programs at the Hanford Site. These efforts involve not just tedious custodial management of the wastes but new research and technological developments, regional pride, and the promise of an estimated $57 billion of industrial and research activity to an area that has known periodic economic bust since the atomic reactors began to close in 1964.

In May 1989, after much negotiation, posturing, false starts, and tentative trust, the Hanford Federal Facility Agreement and Consent Order (known as the Tri-Party Agreement) was signed. The signatories—the DOE, the EPA, and Washington State—agreed to a detailed, scheduled cleanup of the Hanford Site by the year 2018. Washington State, through its Department of Ecology, assumed a major oversight role in the remedial work. Among the most immediate goals listed in the covenant were to upgrade the liquid effluent discharge systems so that waste releases to Hanford soils would be prevented and to pump out leaking, single-shelled, high-level waste tanks. Any future hazardous waste generated by the decommissioning of Hanford's eight old, single-pass reactors also was included in the Tri-Party Agreement. DOE-Hanford Manager Michael Lawrence praised the Tri-Party Agreement as "good government in action."[53]

In June 1989, following the lead of the Hanford Site, both Watkins and his deputy, Henson Moore, announced a "fundamental change in priorities" within the chain of weapons production, with greatly augmented emphasis on health and safety and the environment.[54] In August, Watkins released the DOE's Environmental Restoration and Waste Management Five-Year Plan. This document officially announced the department's "commitment to a 30-year goal to clean up and restore the environment at its nuclear sites, to revitalize its own internal culture, and to break with the dysfunctional aspects of its past activities and corporate posture." Specifically, the DOE pledged itself to "comply with laws and regulations aimed at protecting human health and the environment . . . contain known contamination at inactive sites and vigorously assess the uncertain nature and extent of contamination at other sites . . . fulfill the requirements of compliance agreements already in place . . . implement programs to minimize current waste generation and future waste disposal requirements . . . [and] release, for scientific analysis, the health records of workers at DOE facilities."[55] On August 29, Secretary Watkins visited Hanford and termed the site the "flagship" of DOE waste-cleanup and environmental-restoration programs.[56]

For the Hanford vicinity, the Tri-Party Agreement and the Five-Year Plan made many things bright. The regional economy began to expand as engineering, drilling, consulting, and construction firms moved in.[57] The area's pride in engineering and technical expertise was bolstered as new ideas in waste vitrification, waste solidification, waste burn, and waste isolation were researched.[58] One of the brightest outgrowths of the waste cleanup, however, was that it fostered state, local, and federal cooperation and public involvement. Meaningful control and joint decision making over Hanford affairs was extremely important to Washington State officials. They were adamant in demanding a new relationship with the DOE and its contractor companies.[59]

The public involvement mandated in the Tri-Party Agreement was, at first, a relatively new and stiff process. However, larger and more interactive, informed crowds began to attend the quarterly community meetings. A DOE summary of public comments received at the autumn 1989 meetings revealed that Northwest residents wanted the DOE to "change its culture from one of secrecy and arrogance to one of openness and responsiveness." Furthermore, stated the summary, the DOE "should work with the States, Indian Nations, the EPA and the public to define cleanup . . . clearly and completely explain to the public its waste problems . . . present to the public an evaluation of wastes that will be produced in the future . . . explain to the public how much money is needed for Hanford cleanup . . . [and] develop new cleanup technologies . . . [that] provide better long-term protection." The public also affirmed that Hanford "should not become a dump for waste from other government nuclear facilities or operations."[60]

DOE Acts on Pledges

In September 1989 and in 1990, Secretary Watkins took further steps to enhance environmental restoration, openness, and credibility. He issued SEN-11-89, a directive entitled "Setting the New Course," in which he defined among his objectives "preserving our environment, protecting public health and safety . . . restart [of] the defense production reactors only after safety of their operations can be assured, and only after health and environmental requirements have been addressed." SEN-II-89 also pledged to "initiate excellence" in the DOE's epidemiological and radiological health studies.[61] DOE health studies had a particularly controversial history, and in August 1989, Watkins had flatly stated that DOE supervision of such work had been "a mess."[62] In early 1990, a special Secretarial Panel for the Evaluation of Epidemiologic Research Activities, created by Watkins, recommended to him that the DOE's long-secret medical and radiation exposure records on nuclear workers be opened to independent scientists. Kristine M. Gebbie, the panel chairperson and Washington State's secretary of health, affirmed: "We feel that this legacy of secrecy and mistrust has got to be broken . . . People who have an interest in studying the status of these workers should be able to make use of the data."[63] In January 1991, the DOE signed a "Memorandum of Understanding," agreeing to transfer research and administrative control of epidemiological studies, including dose reconstructions and exposure-assessment studies, to the Department of Health and Human Services.[64]

FFTF Threat Unites Parties

Dedicating itself to waste cleanup, environmental restoration, and research into peaceful nuclear technologies, the Hanford region began its renewal. However, acrimony over past radioactive releases had left the area politically divided and weakened. In early 1990, Energy Secretary Watkins announced that the only operating reactor on the Hanford Site, the Fast Flux Test Facility (FFTF), would be shut down at the beginning of fiscal 1991. The FFTF, the nation's newest and largest research and test reactor, was the only DOE reactor that met all modern criteria for nuclear safety and environmental protection. Its operations had already been subject to a complete environmental impact statement. It produced no weapons materials but instead conducted profitable irradiation experiments for the United States and other nations. It had developed the capability to produce rare medical isotopes, and it could burn some of the most long-lived, high-level wastes existing at Hanford, including I-129 and Tc-99. It could transmute other actinides, such as americium and neptunium, into isotopes of plutonium (Pu-238 and Pu-239) for use as power sources for radioisotope thermoelectric generators (RTGs) in space and for the FFTF itself.[65] The reactor named in early 1990 to conduct the FFTF's experimental missions was the tiny, aging Experimental Breeder Reactor II (EBR-II), located at INEL.

In a show of unanimity unprecedented in recent years, Washington State's entire congressional delegation, including U.S. House Speaker Thomas Foley, expressed disapproval. In an even more historic display of cooperation, Washington's Governor Booth Gardner worked with technical personnel from Hanford Site contractors and the community, and financed marketing trips to Japan and Europe, to keep the reactor running. The Hanford Site's new policies of cooperation with Washington State bore fruit. Mutual support for a clean and valued industrial asset was a reality. Congress appropriated funds to operate the FFTF in fiscal years 1991 and 1992. In February 1991, the Washington congressional delegation introduced a bill to permit private industry to support FFTF marketing and operations.[66]

Renewal and Sadness Mix with Historical Findings

As of 1990, the massive waste-cleanup endeavor at Hanford was progressing on schedule. The fiscal 1991 budget included $700 million for waste remediation, or half of the total spending at Hanford.[67] New businesses began to come to the region to participate in this immense industrial, technological, and research effort. Ancillary and support businesses, as well as agriculture, also proliferated. However, longtime residents and newcomers in the wide, windy basin experienced new pain in July 1990 when the Technical Steering Panel of the HEDR Project announced the results of Phase I of its study. The news was bad. Emissions of radioiodine (I-131) from the Hanford chemical reprocessing plants from 1945 through 1947, and releases of reactor effluent to the Columbia River from 1964 through 1966 (the Phase I areas of examination), had been huge. Indeed, by the standards of 1990, they had been perilous. The Technical Steering Panel estimated that 5 percent of the people (13,500) living in a ten-county area around Hanford from 1944 to 1947 may have received radiation doses of 33 or more rads to their thyroids. Some infants who drank milk from backyard cows that had eaten contaminated forage may have received doses as high as 2,900 rads. Such doses would be among the highest known to have been received by any American population group.[68]

When the hard scientific data that confirmed the historical doses was announced, the Hanford region struggled to comprehend the evidence. Bewilderment and grief temporarily resurfaced. "Downwind" residents expressed "sorrow, betrayal and relief" at finally learning the truth. Others voiced anger and claimed that they had been used as "guinea pigs."[69] In the ensuing three months, four large class-action lawsuits charging deleterious health effects and decreased property values in the Hanford vicinity were filed against former and current operators of the site.[70] The local newspaper expressed anger at the DOE for keeping the data secret for so many years, terming the secrecy itself "an outrage of huge proportions."[71] It called for timely compensation for radiation victims or for their survivors.[72] Likewise, the Hanford region's congressman, Sidney Morrison, pledged to work for a compensation act if CDC studies demonstrated deleterious health effects from the doses.[73] Kristine Gebbie, Washington State's director of health, stated that the HEDR Project's findings reinforced the need for waste cleanup at Hanford, with state and EPA oversight.[74]

The Challenges of the 1990s

In 1991, the gigantic amounts of nuclear wastes that are part of the heritage of the Hanford vicinity are not seen by area residents as a handicap or a stigma. They are seen as a challenge. Taking "ownership" of this challenge means claiming a regional legacy and a part of national history and completing the production mission that generated these wastes. It means restoring a beautiful stretch of land and river and then building a future upon them. In 1991, the nuts and bolts, the financing, the technology, the priorities, the personalities, and the politics of cleaning up the waste dominate the region. The DOE's fiscal year 1992 budget allocates $1.4 billion to the Hanford Site, over $1 billion of which will fund waste remediation. Three "expedited response action" (ERA) cleanup projects have taken place, to remove drums containing hexone (methyl isobutyl ketone) from development experiments for the old REDOX process from a burial site near the Columbia River, to remove sediments containing uranium and fuel-fabrication solvents from the 300 Area, and to draw carbon tetrachloride vapors from the earth in disposal cribs in the 200-W Area. In May 1991, negotiations among the signatories resulted in changes to the Tri-Party Agreement, delaying by ten months the construction of the Hanford Waste Vitrification Plant (HWVP), the facility planned to solidify pretreated, high-level wastes into immobile "logs." The stabilization of wastes stored in single-shell tanks, the construction of grout vaults to encase low-level waste, and the installation schedule for groundwater-monitoring wells also were delayed slightly. Other changes to the Tri-Party Agreement authorized the construction of four new double-shell tanks, the use of broader "aggregate area studies" to characterize waste sites, and assessments of Hanford's laboratory capabilities and of the structural soundness of B Plant as a waste pretreatment facility.[75]

The Lessons of History

Having examined the first twenty years of operation at the Hanford Site, what lessons can we learn? Clearly, the Hanford experience underscores a need to examine issues of secrecy and openness. As long ago as the victory celebrations of World War II, the physicist Henry Smyth, author of the Manhattan Project's first public report on atomic energy, framed the dilemma. The purpose of his report, Smyth said, was to "inform . . . the people of the country." He stated: "In a free country like ours such questions [of the uses and responsibilities of atomic energy] should be debated by the people and decisions must be made by the people through their representatives . . . Because of the restrictions of military security [in wartime] there has been no chance for the Congress or the people to debate such questions."[76] Smyth fully expected that information on almost all aspects of atomic science, except the nuts and bolts of how to make weapons, would be disseminated widely. Then, he thought, public policies could be formulated as the American democratic system intended, with an examination of various policy alternatives. The majority could decide, but checks and balances within the American system would not allow small groups of people, or remote and sparse places, to bear too heavy a burden.

J. Robert Oppenheimer, the key bomb-development physicist, focused on the scientific parallel to the political structure of checks and balances: peer review. Such examination by equally qualified scientists, he said in 1947, was one of the most "valid and inspiriting" assets of science. "[It] gives us means of detecting error . . . The whole point of science is . . . to invite the detection of error and to welcome it." He applied this principle to Hanford. "To keep completely secret the design of the Hanford piles [reactors] I think has never been a controversial thing. To keep secret the fact that we don't know how to do some things may be controversial because it may be that we really need some ideas, and the classification, or keeping secret, our ignorance of an area in which we haven't been able to make any progress may in some cases be a very serious hindrance to getting the insight, the bright ideas and the progress which would come if a much wider group of people could be interested [allowed access to data]."[77] The AEC agreed, recommending (in secret) in 1948: "The operations of the Atomic Energy Commission have implications for the towns . . . and for the populations external to these reservations . . . It is recommended that . . . liaison with official groups that have been concerned with radiation in the past (Bureau of Standards, U.S. Health Service, etc.) be established . . . One of the most pressing problems is the disposal of radioactive wastes . . . As the industrial and public health applications of AEC's future operations will be increasingly a public and not a secret matter, the sooner the present clumsy secrecy of H-P [Health Physics] technics is modified the better."[78]

At the same time, however, the promise of atomic energy seemed bright. The AEC sped forward, boasting to Congress in 1948 that, through atomic energy, "man's conquest of nature" could proceed "in the pattern of (a) observation, (b) understanding, and (c) control."[79] Hurrying to produce and expand, and believing in a future of technology and progress, the commission spent little time or resources worrying about nuclear waste. In 1949, Herbert M. Parker, the chief health physicist at Hanford, emphasized this confidence in science as he concluded a report on long-range waste-disposal hazards. "Projection of the problem to [the] future . . . appears to be irrelevant in terms of the technological progress in corrective measures that can be anticipated."[80] However, at Hanford and at the other U.S. atomic weapons production installations, the classification of broad categories of data also became part of the future. The stark and strident battle lines of the cold war overtook the American system of checks and balances. The stamps of *Top Secret* and *Classified* and *Confidential* prevented scientific peer review from operating, except within the limited realm of contractor and AEC personnel. Other scientists across the nation, whose combined efforts might have helped solve waste-disposal puzzles sooner, were not even aware that problems existed. In 1956, the Manhattan Project mathematician Norbert Wiener expressed his dismay that the secrecy of wartime had hung on so long and had become so entrenched in the atomic energy infrastructure. "We [MED scientists] had voluntarily accepted a measure of secrecy . . . for the sake of the war . . . We had hoped that this unfamiliar self-discipline would be a temporary thing, and we had expected that after this war . . . we should return to the free spirit of communication . . . which is the very life of science. Now we found that, whether we wished it or not . . . At no time in the foreseeable future could we again do our research as free men."[81]

The former AEC chairman Gordon Dean expressed similar views: "Among the responsibilities of . . . scientists and administrators who do know the facts . . . is the very important one of keeping the public informed. There will always be a temptation, to which they must never accede, to withhold the facts that frighten, and to publicize only the information that tends to mollify and reassure."[82] In 1958, the editor of *Science* magazine, the journal of the American Association for the Advancement of Science, called on the AEC to share its data on health and safety with the U.S. Public Health Service in order to "provide an independent source of information . . . appraised primarily from the standpoint of public health rather than from the standpoint of weapon development."[83] Still, the AEC kept the ring of secrecy around its weapons production plants. In 1963, AEC Chairman Lilienthal blamed a "mystique of secrecy and a misplaced worship of the infallibility of scientists and experts."[84] He identified the solution as more openness, more public discussion and involvement, and more checks and balances with other agencies and views. In 1973, an investigative task force composed of AEC-Hanford Manager Alex Fremling and prominent university professors brought together by the *Portland Oregonian* reaffirmed, "The federal government must find a way to remove its iron curtain that envelops the weapons production side of facilities like Hanford—a wartime secrecy hangover that only enhances the public's mistrust."[85]

In 1990, Horace Busby, a Washington journalist since the 1940s, expressed the enduring importance of checks and balances and of free policy debate. "In the wake of World War II, an attitude permeated Washington [D.C.] that the government is always right. This came out of the war experience, when to think otherwise was almost treason. Presidents, the civilian bureaucracy and the military knew best because they had better information. That is the most important change we've experienced in our history. Today . . . the people don't take the government's word for everything. They make their own judgments. That is not distrust. It is the predicate for freedom."[86] John Till, chairperson of the HEDR Project's Technical Steering Panel, reiterated the importance of scientific peer review on the day of the Phase I announcements. "The word controversy in science is great . . . that's what makes science good . . . one of us criticizing the other . . . making the results better."[87]

It is obvious now that the public-disclosure requirements in the atomic energy acts of 1946 and 1954 were not followed thoroughly in the nearly forty years after their enactment. "The dissemination of scientific and technical information relating to atomic energy should be permitted and encouraged so as to provide that free interchange of ideas and criticisms which is essential to scientific progress," read the 1946 statute. The 1954 law contained a similar provision.[88] These stipulations were an important part of the reason the American nation felt so strongly that atomic energy should be controlled by civilian, not military, authority. It is a venerable aspect of the U.S. tradition that civilian control operates to promote openness and democracy, whereas the military, of necessity, works through secrecy and compulsion.

Throughout those forty years after World War II, environmental monitoring was carried out at Hanford in perhaps the most thorough and technically excellent example in the nation. Yet, this precedent-setting endeavor faltered by classifying most of the data it collected. Early Hanford chemists have recalled a heady feeling among Herbert Parker's pioneering Health Instruments staff. They felt that they were on the cutting edge of science. How much sooner might the problems of airborne, river-borne, and groundwater discharges have been solved had these unique and talented environmental-monitoring scientists shared their data? How much less nuclear waste would lie in the magnificent Columbia Basin today?

The Future

The Hanford story today, like the Hanford achievements of the past, is one that points the way toward our national future. The revelations about the radioactive emissions and operating problems at Hanford have brought emotional pain and a period of economic hardship to the surrounding region. However, the suffering has also brought a cleansing and a new beginning. In June 1990, John Till, the HEDR Project's Technical Steering Panel chairperson, stated: "Hanford is a national resource. It has great talent who can develop new technologies. It's time to stop pointing fingers at what has been done. It's time to credit those trying to solve the problems created for this nation. It's time to build a new future."[89] The current renaissance in the Hanford region is based on admission of problems, careful and open study, and vigorous waste cleanup. In these processes, the Hanford Site now stands on the cutting edge in the preservation of democratic principles. In these achievements, there is glory and honor enough to equal, and perhaps surpass, the dazzling scientific accomplishments of the 1940s.

History is sometimes hard to talk about and hard to hear about. Nevertheless, the past, like a wise grandparent, can point the way to what works and what does not. In the coming years, the Hanford lead will have to be followed at other contaminated DOE and industrial facilities. At some of these sites, historical data is still tightly restricted. Decision makers at these sites forget that the historical record does not belong to companies or to sites or even to the DOE but that its rightful proprietor is the American people. At stake in the issue of information release is the very question of a democracy's right to set its own priorities, to know itself and its common will, with access to the pertinent facts. Possibly, by following the Hanford example, other sites with accumulations of waste can minimize community suffering and acrimony and move quickly and positively into open discourse and cleanup. If these goals are to be achieved, it will take ongoing public involvement and shared decision making among local, state, and federal officials. At Hanford, the painful disclosures about the past have cleared the air and readied the new path. The future is full of promise. The Columbia Basin is lovely and entrancing. The Hanford Site is dynamic and exciting. Together with the willpower of the people of this remarkable place, the entire region can assume its position as a national asset.

Epilogue
Richland, Washington: September 2006

Hanford Site Slips Further into History as Twenty-First Century Opens, but Significance Endures

The twenty-first century announced itself with blaring audacity on September 11, 2001. Just twenty months into the new century, the issues argued in the presidential debates of 2000 were rendered moot—as indeed they had been at the time they were contended. The new century would be defined by its own issues, which, though stark and imperative, did not come with the clarity and sheer undisguised bluntness that characterized those of the twentieth century.

Would the Hanford Site and the study of its history still be relevant in this new era? Did it have anything to teach those who would have to face the challenges of factionalism, hide-and-seek warfare, splintered ethnic and religious identities more powerful—and more elusive—than nationalism? Hanford, after all, represented a time when might could be measured in terms of mass, and when sheer bulk and brawn imposed itself into the power equation with stunning results. Hanford had functioned as Paul Bunyan, the hulking bodyguard to the nation in an era where the bright red telephone "hotline" between Washington, D.C., and Moscow symbolized clear lines of authority. Now, in the era of homemade bombs detonated by shadowy figures with cellular telephones, were the lessons of Hanford still important?

I asked myself these questions on the morning of September 11, 2001, glancing between the astonishing scenes unfolding in real time on a television screen and the dusty tan site where hulking gray concrete monoliths containing defunct nuclear reactors stood silent guard along the rushing Columbia River.

Was Hanford so different from the giant and mysterious statues on the Easter Islands? The Egyptian pyramids? Stonehenge or any number of other ancient sites now quiet but once the very "epicenters" of their cultures?

Hanford is at once emblematic, as well as real and immediate. At Hanford, the bellicose speeches of the Cold War delivered in distant Washington, D.C., or in Moscow were made real in concrete, steel, lead, uranium, and in men's and women's daily lives. In the grand tradition of the American frontier, the "dirty jobs" were sent "out West." The Cold War dominated the twentieth century, and its nexus with the disturbing wars and conflicts of the early twenty-first century runs straight through Afghanistan.

It is possible to make the case that one cannot understand the twentieth century unless one understands the Cold War, and one cannot understand the Cold War without knowing the Hanford Site. The battle that was fought at the Hanford Engineer Works (HEW—the World War II–era name for the Hanford Site) caused the world to turn upside down, and ushered in change as fundamental in American life as that which occurred on another battlefield when "the world turned upside down"—the battlefield at Yorktown, Virginia, where the British Lord Cornwallis surrendered to General George Washington.

In a survey of journalists and scholars taken as the twentieth century ended, the atomic bombings of Hiroshima and Nagasaki were voted the most significant events of that century. That finding, conducted by the Newseum, a news and history museum in Arlington, Virginia, clearly places the Hanford Site at the epicenter of twentieth-century history, because it is where the plutonium (Pu) core of the Nagasaki weapon was manufactured. For this reason and many others, Hanford—the first, most productive, costly, and wasteful plutonium production site in the United States—can be expected to retain its regional, national and international significance for as long as it is practical for humans to imagine.

Pulitzer Prize–winning journalist Charles Krauthammer of the *Washington Post* described a fundamental enigma of the Cold War by saying that the conflict was: "Our war, the war we hardly recognize . . . the long twilight struggle that ended as no other great war in history—with utter silence."[1] But Hanford, one of America's premier battlefields of the Cold War, is not silent. Echoes of the Cold War can be heard in the busy machinery of cleanup, and in the voices of the region's people debating their heritage.

In 2000, the National Research Council completed a study of long-term stewardship at Hanford and twenty-six other Department of Energy (DOE) sites contaminated with nuclear wastes and special nuclear materials (SNM). "Radiological and non-radiological hazardous wastes will remain, posing risks to humans and the environment for tens or even hundreds of thousands of years," the report stated. "Complete elimination of unacceptable risks to humans and the environment will not be achieved, now or in the foreseeable future."[2]

Yet, real human beings, with no choice but to live their lives, must do something with Hanford. They must find practical ways to isolate, contain, repackage, reposition, and keep track of the enormous load (nearly 500 million curies worth) of nuclear wastes and SNM at the site today. Noisy and contentious public dialogue currently rages over how to conduct the largest waste "cleanup" (containment) project ever undertaken by humanity, how to prioritize and spend the available dollars, and how to provide long-term gain a seat at a bargaining table dominated by short-term interests and incremental funding.

Americans working at, studying, funding, or visiting this rugged old Cold War arsenal site struggle to make sense of their history. At this place of dumbfounding contrasts, most of the real threats are silent and invisible, and the only sounds heard for hundreds of square miles are bird songs, the rustle of dry desert grasses, and the whooshing flow of a huge and rapid river. Yet the immediacy of history, the demand to participate and be heard, the fears and hopes expressed, and the constant press of those coming to hear the Hanford story create a cacophony of voices and visitors in this remote place. A silent war in a silent place? Hanford is isolated and deceptively quiet, but even in the new century it has lessons to teach about who we are as Americans, how we exercise power, how we respond to the limitations of our power, who we want to be, and how we want the world to know us.

Legacy of Hanford's World War II Builders

A nearly two-hour silent film made at HEW during late 1944 and early 1945, discovered in archives in 1999, provides a detailed look at construction methods and materials, worker life at HEW, and scenes of some areas and settings for which few or no others are known to exist.

It portrays the unabashed pride of Hanford's builders in the hectic pace of accomplishments during the time when HEW was engaged almost wholly in construction, and none of the ambivalence that would come to some participants later—after the site's fruits had been deployed at Alamogordo and Nagasaki.

The film depicts HEW's construction methods as being on the cutting edge of modern efficiency, the juggling of scarce wartime resources as effective and productive, and the craftsmanship as skillful and precise. To historians, however, the style and sequence of presentation is even more important than the content, for it tells us what the HEW builders thought of themselves and how they wished to be seen by posterity.

Close-up views of the workers and their machinery in the film inspires admiration for the hard work and the high level of skills at HEW. The builders there constructed huge parts and systems to stricter tolerances and standards than had ever been achieved in the world before. Without computers to guide their tools, it is beyond remarkable that they achieved the precise standards that they did. But it is the optimism, the pride, the sureness of purpose, the sweeping "go for the goalpost" energy that provide the most important aspects of the knowledge we gain from this film. To Hanford's early government workers, this home front of science, secrecy, and battle was not unlike the battlefield challenges of the Second World War with their stark necessities, risk mentality, and vast unknowns.

Today, the work methods seem beautiful but quaint. Watching this film is like having the chance to watch a Renaissance builder or artisan at work on a cathedral, and one is struck by how very old the Hanford Site really is. Printed titles and sentences interspersed between segments of film convey a 1920s vaudevillian atmosphere. In our world of cellular phones the size of three fingers, it is jarring to watch a construction supervisor pick up a huge, heavy "squawk box" (a primitive walkie-talkie), and realize that the film's intent is to demonstrate modern efficiency. In the present era of transistors, microchips, and palm-sized computers, it is hard for us to imagine them building a place as macro as the Hanford Engineer Works. Yet, the evidence that they did so is all around us at the Hanford Site of the twenty-first century—in the hulking, contaminated old buildings that stand as stark and gray reminders of past defense imperative, the huge waste volumes, and the new facilities constructed to perform cleanup.

The personalities of HEW also come alive in the old film, in contrast to their sometimes wooden looks in the World War II photos. As lumbering and preposterous old vehicles with headlights bulging like bug eyes begin to move in the film, the men with their slick hair, bulky clothes, and ever-present cigarettes also move and become real human beings. Customs of the era, now relics of a bygone culture, are evident in the film, including segregated work crews and an all-black tavern, men in Fedora hats, references to female workers as "girls," a total absence of seat belts, and the before-meal prayer in the day nursery.

However, the final scenes of the film are the most astonishing in evoking the profound change in world history that came about as a result of HEW's pioneering work. The last minutes of the film deal with the final construction and preparations for operating B-Reactor and T-Plant, the two facilities that actually produced the plutonium core of the Trinity and Nagasaki weapons. Huge equipment that would form the "guts" of T-Plant, mocked up and built in a nearby construction shop, is draped in heavy black material and guided onto a flatbed rail car for a journey of less than half a mile to T-Plant.

As the tall, top-secret load inches along the track, one is reminded of the ringing phrase of then-President Franklin Roosevelt that the American people had a "rendezvous with destiny." Americans, and specifically Hanford workers, were certainly about to change the world. Nine months later, the plutonium they produced would be used on Nagasaki and would end World War II, a war that had lasted fifteen years in some parts of the world, had involved approximately fifty nations, and had cost over fifty million lives. Were these Americans egocentric? Bullying? Good? Bad? Right? Wrong? Whatever the spectrum of answers, it is clear that Hanford still has the power to engage the twenty-first century in daunting debates.

Hanford Retools for Cleanup, and
Deactivates and Demolishes Major Facilities

The Cold War's end in 1991 left people at the Hanford Site temporarily confused and reeling. Missions central to the site's identity ended in rapid succession. The DOE issued formal deactivation orders to the mighty PUREX (plutonium-uranium extraction) Plant in 1992 and to the imposing N-Reactor in 1995. The thousand-foot-long, hundred-foot-high PUREX had processed nearly three-quarters of all Hanford's defense plutonium (yielding nearly forty metric tons of product). Together with N-Reactor, it had formed the cornerstone of Hanford's production arsenal capabilities during long years of tense posturing and building for deterrence.[3]

Other key Hanford defense production facilities closed, including the Uranium Trioxide Plant (in 1995), B-Plant (in 1998), and many others.[4] Still other plants with long service in the production cycle retooled for cleanup work, and "deactivation" became a new science. The passage of these old workhorse facilities into the next phase of their history was met with a wide range of emotions, depending on the viewer's perspective. On the one hand, workers saluted and cried at ceremonies marking the end of the PUREX Deactivation Project in June 1997, recalling a lifetime of camaraderie and proud service to the "Gray Lady."[5] At the end of the B-Plant Deactivation Project, Portland's *Oregonian* wrote: "Although it [B-Plant] fulfilled its purpose of recovering plutonium from reactor fuel, it wreaked havoc with the environment at Hanford, releasing radioactive gases into the air and flushing contaminated process water directly onto the ground, creating open atomic ponds."[6]

Deactivation of the large, aging nuclear processing buildings became a high priority in the early 1990s because many millions of dollars were spent each year just to inspect, monitor, and safeguard them and the hazardous wastes and materials remaining inside. Deactivation is the phase between operations and D&D (decontamination and decommissioning—the actual teardown of building structures). During deactivation, hazardous chemicals and bulk nuclear materials are removed, and contamination on interior surfaces or equipment is fixed with special sealants or isolated so that it cannot migrate into the environment. These measures decrease the need for frequent and expensive monitoring and maintenance, and render the structures essentially "passive."[7]

The PUREX Deactivation Project cost approximately $150 million over a four-year period. Finished in 1997, it has thereafter saved most of the $40–45 million per year that was spent in the early 1990s to monitor potentially mobile contaminants within the huge facility. The plant now rests behind high razor-wire fences erected during the defense build-up under President Ronald Reagan and is entered for monitoring only a few times a year.[8] Deactivation was completed at N-Reactor in September 1998.[9] Deactivation also began in the 1990s in the large fuel-making facilities and some of the experimental laboratories in Hanford's 300 Area.[10]

In the mid-1990s, Hanford's environmental restoration program began "mothballing" or deactivating the old production reactors along the Columbia River. By that time, the ordinary industrial hazards of the aging concrete and concrete block buildings urgently needed to be addressed. A Hanford worker fell to his death through the roof of one World War II reactor while performing a structural inspection in 1992.

Hanford's reactor cores are huge graphite blocks, ranging up to forty-one feet per side in some cases, and surrounded by iron, steel, Masonite, and concrete shields that make them several feet larger. While all of the spent (irradiated) fuel has been removed, the cores are still radioactive because the graphite itself became activated through exposure to the uranium fission reaction years ago.

The Interim Safe Storage (ISS) Project began physical demolition work at C Reactor in 1996. The project—better known as "cocooning"—tore all of the "wings" off the 1952 structure, removing hundreds of tons of asbestos, concrete, steel, copper, and contaminated soil. In addition, the old pumps, tunnels, and other ancillary parts of the facility were razed. In total, approximately 80 percent of C Reactor was eliminated and buried in Hanford disposal facilities. Only the core and the surrounding shields were left. These were then sealed up and given a new steel roof slanted at a sharp angle to facilitate rainwater run-off and extended down over the top portions of the walls for additional sealing.

By 1998 the "cocooned" C Reactor stood as a new form on the Hanford landscape, a hybrid born of production and cleanup. When workers entered the cocoon for the first surveillance in 2003, they found inert, dry, stable conditions, and sealed up the facility for another five years.[11] By 2006, F, H, D, and DR reactors had been cocooned, and cocooning was underway at N Reactor. Plans to cocoon the K East and K West reactors were being developed. Costs declined at each location as the old facilities gave up their secrets and crews learned their way through the maze of tunnels, levels, and service areas.[12]

The full-scale demolition of highly contaminated nuclear structures at Hanford began in 2003, when the 233–S Plutonium Concentration Facility was razed. Much of the 1950s structure had been too radioactive to enter since a fire swept through plutonium processing equipment there in the early 1960s.[13] In 2006, the 232–Z Plutonium Incinerator Facility—per square one of the most difficult, intensely contaminated structures in the nation—was also demolished.[14]

Accelerated Cleanup along Columbia River

Hanford stakeholders (people who feel an ownership stake in the Hanford region, also sometimes called "shareholders"), made it clear early in site cleanup that they wanted to reclaim the Columbia River and its corridor lands. In 2000 a plan was developed to attack cleanup of the Columbia River Hanford shoreline as a fast-track, single-focus project.[15] The contracting method would be a "closure contract" because it would encompass the entire life cycle of the project instead of simply running a standard five-year period.

Hanford's 300 Area, seated hard by the rushing river, was swept into the fast-moving demolition project after earlier plans to reindustrialize the area by attracting private businesses foundered. Although a few commercial businesses came into the 300 Area, most buildings were too contaminated to lease to industry even under relaxed "brownfield" standards.[16] Savings in the project came mainly from not having to maintain and surveil the old 300 Area structures for many years before tearing them down.[17] By September 2006, more than thirty buildings had been demolished in the 300 Area, and the demolition project was ahead of schedule.[18]

In mid-2000, workers began digging up massive quantities of soil in the reactor areas of the Columbia's shoreline. They started with the N Cribs—disposal trenches, drain, cribs, and tile fields where many of N Reactor's liquid wastes had been dumped during the production years. The N Cribs project alone excavated more than 150,000 tons of contaminated soil and debris over the next few years. In the interim, soil cleanup projects began at many more of the sixty-five defined waste sites in Hanford's 100 Areas (reactor areas). By mid-2003 approximately half of the soil cleanup was completed, with nearly 900,000 tons removed from F Reactor Area, 500,000 tons removed from H Reactor Area, and work beginning in the 100–B/C Reactor Area and the K Reactor Area. By spring 2006 nearly six million tons of contaminated soil and debris had been removed, and the project wasn't yet finished![19]

Many unpleasant surprises accompanied the rivershore "digs." Mercury tubes and small pot-bellied furnaces from the world's first tritium production site in 100–B Area were uncovered. Over two tons of elemental mercury were found. Workers had to don impermeable chemical suits and supplied-air respirators to continue the work. Pieces of spent (irradiated) uranium fuel were discovered in the ground in several reactor areas; in some cases these findings halted work for months. In the 300 Area, a lead and concrete safe containing bottles of liquid plutonium solution was dug up, along with many other beakers, gas cylinders, and other dangerous items. In spring 2006 workers began the grisly task of digging up radioactive animal carcasses and manure in the 100–F Area, where the large animal farm for radiobiological experiments operated until 1970. Special respirators to filter out pathogens were offered to the cleanup workers, and all site employees were warned that trucks hauling the exhumed remains to lined reburial areas in central Hanford could give off strong odors.[20]

The government awarded a contract in March 2005 to Washington Closure Hanford, a limited liability company owned by three major cleanup corporations.[21] In this contract, 210 square miles extending along the Columbia's shoreline through the Hanford Site and extending inland to (but not including) Hanford's Central Plateau receive near-term, concentrated attention.[22] The area of focus includes the nine aging production reactors and dozens of their remaining support buildings, about 150 structures in the 300 Area, and nearly 900 contaminated soil and other waste sites (most of them along the river).[23]

Included in the contract is remediation of the 618-10 and 618-11 waste burial grounds located a few miles north and west of the 300 Area. The burial grounds received especially highly concentrated wastes from 300 Area radiochemical and radiometallurgical experiments in the 1960s. Today, wells near them demonstrate extremely high concentrations of tritium.[24] All of the rivershore cleanup work, as well as remediation of the 618-10 and 618-11 burial grounds, is scheduled to be completed by 2012.[25]

Upgrades/New Construction Support Waste Cleanup Mission
In contrast to the deactivations occurring at many old Hanford facilities, some structures were upgraded for new roles in the waste cleanup mission. The World War II T-Plant, processor of the Trinity and Nagasaki plutonium, has bustled

throughout the cleanup years with upgrade activities and then waste-sorting, repackaging, decontamination operations, and other stabilization activities.[26] A long future in site cleanup activities is planned for this structure—the oldest nuclear facility in the world that still operates with a nuclear mission.

Likewise, the 222 S Control Laboratory, built in conjunction with the REDOX facility during 1950–51, was renovated during 1993–94 to analyze waste samples taken from Hanford's high-level waste tanks.[27] The 242–A Evaporator, built in the 1970s to evaporate wastes stored in Hanford's underground, high-level waste-storage tanks, was completely refurbished at nearly the same time. Since then, the evaporator has reduced tank waste volume at Hanford by over twenty-three million gallons.[28]

In addition, new waste-related facilities were constructed. A large new Waste Receiving and Processing (WRAP) facility was completed in 1998. This facility, unique in the world for its range of capabilities, examines, repackages, compacts, and certifies various types of solid nuclear waste for disposal. After assay, low-level waste is disposed of into Hanford's solid waste burial grounds in perpetuity. Transuranic waste (TRU—containing elements and isotopes that have numbers higher than uranium [U] on the Periodic Table of the Elements and that are more radioactive than low-level waste) is shipped to the Waste Isolation Pilot Plant (WIPP) in New Mexico.[29]

Additional facilities constructed for the cleanup at Hanford include the Waste Sampling and Characterization Facility; a laboratory for the analysis of samples containing low levels of radioactivity and other hazardous materials including paint, lead, and asbestos; and the Central Waste Complex for storing solid waste on an interim basis. In addition, the Environmental Restoration Disposal Facility (ERDF), a huge hazardous and mixed waste "super" landfill for Hanford's cleanup rubble, soil, and other debris, opened in 1996 and has since received nearly seven million tons of waste material.[30]

Two other new facilities constructed in the cleanup years are a state-of-the-art chemistry facility named the Wiley Environmental Molecular Science Laboratory (EMSL) and the Volpentest HAMMER (Hazardous Waste Materials Management and Emergency Response) facility. Both EMSL and HAMMER are multiprogram facilities that have roles in research, development, training, and homeland security that stretch far beyond the boundaries of Hanford.[31]

In 1995, two Treatment and Disposal Facilities began operating in Hanford's 200 and 300 Areas, along with a large Liquid Effluent Treatment Facility, ending forever the fifty-two-year practice of discharging untreated, contaminated low-level liquid waste streams into Hanford soils and ponds. Completion of the liquid treatment plants was hailed as a major victory even by regulators and traditional Hanford skeptics. Doug Sherwood, then the Hanford project manager for the U.S. Environmental Protection Agency (EPA), called the cessation of untreated ground discharges "a very important start," and Portland's *Oregonian* termed the milestone a "much-needed morale boost."[32]

Groundwater Remediation Project Is Created and Grows in Visibility

In November 1997 the DOE at Richland confirmed that past leaks from Hanford's single shell tanks had reached groundwater in some cases and constituted "a contributing source of groundwater contamination" beneath the site.[33] Many regional residents, stakeholders, and regulators expressed outrage.[34] A spokesperson for the Oregon Department of Energy (ODOE) called the groundwater situation a "slow-motion disaster."[35]

Investigations showed that 440 billion gallons of contaminated liquids had been intentionally disposed of into Hanford soils during the production years, and from one to two million gallons of tank waste had unintentionally escaped. About a hundred square miles of aquifer under the site was contaminated with long-lived radionuclides and hazardous chemicals. The fear was that these contaminants would, through the groundwater, reach the Columbia River—the eighth-largest river in the world—in substantial amounts.

The early scientific experiments at Hanford that had seemed to show that the most highly radioactive components of these liquids would bind to the soil just below the surface of the land, and thus pose no threat to groundwater, proved to be wrong. Other tests that had predicted that the water containing the most radionuclides would take hundreds of years to seep into the groundwater, losing most of its radioactivity before reaching the Columbia River, also were mostly wrong.

The nascent science had produced overly optimistic predictions. The mismatch between laboratory and real on-site conditions, and the ability of intersecting plumes to combine and mobilize each other, resulted in contamination moving more quickly. Southeastward drainage from Hanford toward the Columbia proved inevitable. Even when some unusual underground formations caused a few plumes to drain westward, they soon channeled back to the stunning river.

However, the good news was that the DOE created Hanford's newest project: the "Groundwater Vadose Zone Integration Project," as it was called then.[36] This project, whose name soon changed to the "Groundwater Remediation Project" (GRP) was directed and funded as an integrated group of site contractors to study, recommend, and implement solutions for contaminant movement in the groundwater, beginning in 1998.[37]

The contaminants that GRP studies found in Hanford's groundwater were daunting. In the 100 Areas, where the Columbia comes in from the west, arches north in a pointed horn, and then sweeps east and south in a giant arc, thousands of gallons per minute of Columbia River water treated with sodium dichromate ran through the reactor cores and became activated. It was pumped into open holding basins and eventually leaked into the surrounding soil and substrata. The dichromate, used to inhibit corrosion in the reactors' tubing, contained hexavalent chromium (also called chromium+6 or Cr+6)—a soluble carcinogen that binds readily to the tissues of living organisms.

Thus, treating hexavalent chromium plumes and changing the chemical to trivalent chromium—a much less soluble form—quickly became a central goal of the GRP in the 100 Areas. The area was documented as an important habitat for salmon, steelhead, and other fish species. Negotiating and communicating constantly with WDOE and EPA, the Hanford GRP drilled several sets of extraction and injection wells, and installed pump-and-treat systems. Contaminated plumes of groundwater were intercepted in the 100 D, H, and K areas, and sent through treatment systems to sorb the hexavalent chromium with sodium dithionate—essentially changing the dangerous chemical to trivalent chromium. The treated water was then re-injected into the groundwater up-gradient (up the hydraulic gradient). In other words, the clean water was injected into groundwater areas at points where it would flow toward the contaminated plume—helping to dilute the plume and drive it to extraction wells.[38]

By mid-2005, and for the first time in nearly fifty years, the levels of Cr+6 in Hanford's 100–H Area were below (within) the drinking-water standard of 100 micrograms per liter (μg/L) established by the EPA. (A microgram is a measure of parts per billion.) The Cr+6 contamination levels held at less than this standard in all parts of 100–H Area and below fifty μg/L in all but a small portion of the area near the river. Hanford workers removed over seventy-five pounds of Cr+6 and remediated seven major chromium liquid waste sites in the soil of the 100–H Area. Further, a major solid-waste site between the 100–H and 100–D Areas, where sodium dichromate drums were crushed and discarded, was cleaned and closed. However, nitrates and strontium 90 (Sr-90) are still detectable in levels above EPA standards in some 100–H Area wells.[39]

In the 100–D Area, just upstream of the 100–H Area, the GRP has operated pump-and-treat systems for over eight years, processing about 350 million gallons of groundwater and removing about 600 pounds of Cr+6. In 1999, the program also installed a passive, underground chemical barrier system. The *InSitu* Redox Manipulation barrier works in the groundwater by converting the Cr+6 into trivalent chromium through a chemical oxidation-reduction process. In 2004, however, GRP scientists detected plumes in the 100–D Area with the highest known concentrations of Cr+6 anywhere at Hanford. The following year, more wells were drilled and the 100–D Area pump-and-treat-systems expanded.[40]

In the 100–K Area, about three miles west of 100–D, standard treatment efforts over the past ten years have been directed at a very large Cr+6 plume associated with a mile-long trench just east of the K Reactors. That plume, which used to stretch in a semicircular arc from a land disposal site just northeast of the KE Reactor nearly all the way to N Reactor (about two lateral miles), has been cut by more than half and split into two parts by remediation efforts.[41]

In 2006, the GRP tested an innovative treatment system in the 100–K Area. The new method, which mixed contaminated groundwater with calcium polysulfide in an above-ground tank, and then re-injected it, soon cut levels of Cr+6 in the groundwater to essentially undetectable levels at the test site. However, some of the water re-injected into the ground had lower concentrations of oxygen than are desirable for fish. While studying the hypo-oxygenation issue, the GRP is now building a new treatment facility, drilling additional wells, and resuming standard—but expanded—pump-and-treat methods in the 100–K Area.[42]

In the 100–N Area, which hugs the Columbia shoreline between the 100–D and 100–K areas, the problem in the groundwater isn't hexavalent chromium but Sr-90. The 100–N Area is home to the largest production reactor ever built at Hanford. The New Production Reactor (or N Reactor) operated longer than any of the other production reactors at Hanford (twenty-three years), had larger fuel assemblies, recirculated its cooling water several times before disposing it, and irradiated its fuel for weeks to months longer.

All of these factors combined to produce a large plume of Sr-90 in the soil and the groundwater. Sr-90 is harmful to living organisms because it concentrates in bones, replacing calcium and weakening the hosts (including humans) that ingest it. In 100–N Area, about ninety-six acres of groundwater are contaminated with strontium at levels more than one thousand times those allowed in drinking water. Strontium also has been found in river plants and clams.[43]

In 1995, pump-and-treat systems were installed to remove Sr-90 from the groundwater. Unfortunately, they removed far less Sr-90 than is naturally removed by radioactive decay and were turned off in 2006. That same year, GRP scientists and engineers implemented a large new test that pumped a solution of a calcium-phosphate compound into 100–N Area soil along a three-hundred-foot grid, to bind the strontium. The calcium compound diffuses through the ground and chemically reacts with the Sr-90 to bind it in place, keeping it from the river while it radioactively decays. Hanford watchers range from cautiously optimistic to very enthusiastic about the test results and prospects.[44]

In Hanford's 200 Areas, a distasteful stew of acids, sodium bismuthate, potassium permanganate, lanthanum fluoride, and sodium hydroxide complexed with plutonium, uranium, and fission products was pumped for decades into unlined trenches and drains, or into tanks that later leaked. As Hanford's postwar role in the arms race grew, new chemicals in even greater amounts were added to the soil and substrata. Tributyl phosphate, methyl isobytyl ketone, aluminum nitrate nonahydrate, and carbon tetrachloride, all contaminated with dissolved radioactive elements, were intentionally and unintentionally disposed of into Hanford's sandy soils.[45]

However, given the Hanford area's low rainfall and thick vadose zone in the 200 Areas (groundwater is found beginning 250–300 feet below the ground surface), groundwater contamination in those areas was not among the highest priorities in early remediation actions. A few plumes of contamination in the 200 Areas were so egregious that they did receive attention. In the Plutonium Finishing Plant (PFP) region of the 200 West Area, a soil-disposed collection of approximately 1.2 million pounds of carbon tetrachloride became an important concern soon after the cleanup mission began in 1989. A vapor-extraction system began operating in 1991, to extract carbon tetrachloride as a vapor from the soil itself.[46] By 2006 this system had removed about 173,000 pounds of the chemical.

Pump-and-treat operations to remove carbon tetrachloride as a liquid from the groundwater began in 1996 and were expanded in 2005. These operations pump contaminated groundwater to a treatment building where an air-stripper tower removes carbon tetrachloride from the water. Contaminated air from the tower is then routed through an activated carbon filter that captures the chemical. Clean water and air are then released into the environment. Even today, concentrations of carbon tetrachloride in the groundwater near PFP sometimes exceed four thousand µg/L—a concentration eight hundred times higher than the EPA drinking water standard of five µg/L for carbon tetrachloride. Another pump-and-treat system in the same area works to remove U and technetium 99 (Tc-99) from the groundwater.[47]

At the U Plant region, also in Hanford's 200 West Area, outsized concentrations of U and Tc-99 in groundwater were discovered in the mid-1980s—as high as 38,000 picocuries (pCi)/L for Tc-99 (more than forty times the EPA's drinking water standards),[48] and 4,000 µg/L for uranium (nearly 135 times the EPA drinking water standard). Ten wells were installed, and pump-and-treat operations began in 1995. Early in 2006, the U Area pump-and-treat systems achieved what many thought was impossible. The heart, or high concentration zone, of the uranium/Tc-99 plume was removed and pumping was stopped. The area has been monitored for rebound ever since, with the results successful. Remediation systems near U Plant removed over 1,900 pounds of U, 119 grams of Tc-99, and 60,000 pounds of nitrates.[49]

In the past few years, as the priority and visibility of groundwater protection programs has risen ever higher, the GRP has ramped up operations in central Hanford. It has launched increasingly invasive tests in the areas in and around tank farms and waste disposal trenches, cribs, French drains, lagoons, and tile fields. The well-drilling program has doubled in the past four years, and deeper and more sophisticated wells and boreholes are penetrating the secrets beneath the high plateau.

In and around tank farms in the 200 East Area, GRP scientists are finding Tc-99 and U as the chief contaminants of concern, although iodine 129 (I-129), tritium, nitrates, Sr-90, manganese, arsenic, chromium, vanadium, and other contaminants are present. Not unexpectedly, they are by-products of dissolving hundreds of thousands of tons of irradiated uranium (spent fuel) in nitric acid and then separating plutonium in a noxious stew of chemicals inside B Plant and PUREX for more than thirty years. Not far away, beneath the unusual collection of trenches known as the B/C Cribs, cobalt 60 and uranium, along with cyanide and chromium are evident in the groundwater. Further drilling, sampling, investigating, mapping, and remediating are underway.[50]

In Hanford's 300 Area, more than twenty million uranium fuel elements were manufactured and coated, or jacketed, for irradiation in Hanford's reactors. It is, therefore, not surprising that uranium is the prime contaminant of concern in groundwater under the small (1.4–square-mile) area. Fuel-making and experimental wastes, including uranium and other heavy-metal dust slicked with acids, trichloroethene, dichloroethene, perchloroethylene, acetone, kerosene, and many other hazardous substances, percolated through shallow soil into ground and surface water. In approximately four-tenths of a square mile under the 300 Area, groundwater concentrations exceed 10 μg/L of uranium, as compared to natural background concentrations of 5–8 μg/L. In 40 percent of the plume there, concentrations exceed the drinking water standard of 30 μg/L. In some places this past year, levels reached 97 μg/L. Organic compounds from the fuel processes, as well as Sr-90, nitrates, tritium, and arsenic are also present in above-standard levels. As a result, an ambitious program is underway to drill fifteen new wells in this area in 2006. In addition, experiments using polyphosphate to bind the uranium are being developed and deployed.[51]

Other key measures to protect Hanford's groundwater from further degradation include decommissioning old wells that were once used to monitor contamination or inject liquid waste. Many of the old wells can be pathways that allow contamination to reach groundwater more rapidly.

More than seven thousand wells were drilled over the years on the Hanford Site. Today, about two thousand are potential candidates for decommissioning. Decommissioning a well essentially means sealing it, usually with special cement called grout. About five hundred Hanford wells have been physically decommissioned since 1995, and another twelve hundred have been administratively decommissioned—a paperwork process.[52]

Along with decommissioning old wells, the GRP works to reduce water recharge into contaminated soil areas by relining leaky water lines, using a process called mortar-lining. Scraping out the buildup of old scale and corrosion and then relining the pipes eliminates leaks that drive contaminants downward to the water table. The application of the mortar-lining technique at Hanford has won national awards. In total, about twenty-six hundred feet of old, leaking pressurized fresh-water lines have been lined at the site in the past three years.[53]

Thus far, 2.7 billion gallons of contaminated groundwater at Hanford have been treated, and multiple drivers of contaminants have been reduced or eliminated. Still, the effort is not sufficient in the eyes of many. The 2.7 billion gallons remediated to date represents just six-tenths of 1 percent of the total 440 billion gallons disposed. Two separate reports by the Energy Department's inspector general, and by the Alliance for Nuclear Accountability (a stakeholder group), in 2004 criticized the GRP for "not effectively remediating Hanford's groundwater."[54]

In 2005 several key agencies and groups, including the WDOE, EPA, ODOE, Hanford Watch, and Columbia Riverkeeper (regional advocacy groups), actively expressed the view that not enough money was being spent and the right technical solutions were not in place to effectively protect the Columbia.[55] Another report critical of the GRP was issued by the Government Accountability Office (GAO) in spring 2006. A draft of a report required by the EPA under the Comprehensive Environmental Response, Compensation and Liability Act (CERCLA), called the CERCLA Five Year Review, issued at nearly the same time, also censured the program.[56] That April, Washington Governor Christine Gregoire told the television show *60 Minutes* that "we [Pacific Northwest residents] are very vulnerable to the groundwater contamination and a plume that we now have moving towards the Columbia River which is the lifeline of our Pacific Northwest. . . . If it [the plume] gets there [to the Columbia River] we have an absolute disaster on our hands."[57]

Congress got the message. In autumn 2005 it passed a special appropriation allocating an extra $10 million for fiscal years (FYs) 2006 and 2007, boosting Hanford's GRP budget about 10 percent over the two years. About half the money is being used to address hexavalent chromium contamination in Hanford's 100–D Area. Much of the remaining funds are allocated to investigating, identifying, and testing programs to bind Sr-90 in the 100–N Area using calcium phosphate, bind uranium in the aquifer under the 300 Area using polyphosphate, sequester Tc-99 and U using a new nanoparticle metal phosphate, and demonstrate in-situ degradation of carbon tetrachloride using a hydrolysis method in the 200 Areas.[58] In September 2006 the GAO reported that DOE and its contractors still did not really understand the extent and location of contamination in the vadose zone and recommended more investigation.[59]

Central Plateau Soil Waste Sites and Structures Begin to Receive Attention

At nearly the same time that Hanford watchers, regulators, and cleanup personnel became restive about groundwater cleanup, they also began paying increasing attention to soil waste sites and structures in Hanford's Central Plateau, the area containing many of the most dangerous, long-lived production leftovers. A focused project conducted during 2003–5 to list, sort, and categorize, as well as plan remediation, found nearly one thousand structures and nearly another thousand soil waste sites that needed attention over approximately sixty square miles.[60]

Project planners quickly realized that grouping the structures and soil sites into "zones" was the best way to make sense of it all. They created twenty-two zones organized around major structures and geographical features. Within the zones, they listed nearly four thousand specific items requiring closure actions. The major constituents of the zones were arranged into five major elements: Hanford's five huge processing "canyons" (major chemical processing buildings); other structures; underground waste tanks; soil waste sites; and wells. Hanford's U Plant canyon, in which a special (and especially messy) uranium recovery mission had taken place during 1952–58, was chosen to pilot the zone closure approach.[61]

Although highly contaminated, U Plant is the least contaminated of Hanford's five canyons because it handled uranium and fission products but never specifically processed plutonium. It also contains waste sites, buried pipelines, groundwater issues, and many other components whose cleanup can be representative of many future cleanup activities required at central Hanford sites.[62] In late 2005, a Record of Decision (ROD, a legally-binding decision resulting from an EIS or other public process) was signed among DOE and its regulatory agencies for the final disposition of U Plant—the first ever for a Hanford canyon.[63] The agreement won a national award from the EPA in 2006 for its complexity, ingenuity, and for the cooperative work it took to achieve.[64]

U Plant closure will include removing all TRU wastes and shipping them to the WIPP facility, disposing some low-level wastes in Hanford's ERDF, and consolidating other contaminated equipment on the canyon deck and in below-grade cells. Then all internal spaces, vessels, cells, and other void space areas in the plant will be filled with grout, the facility's roof and top wall sections will be removed, and an engineered barrier will be constructed over the remnants of the building. The barrier's ability to wick away moisture will be enhanced by planting specially chosen vegetation over it.[65] The finished barrier will still mound up nearly fifty feet, standing as far into the future as can be foreseen as testimony to the frenzied activities that took place in this desert in the mid-twentieth century.

Major cleanup funding to advance U Plant disposition has not been allocated. In the meantime, U Plant Zone cleanup in selected waste sites and small, ancillary structures proceeds slowly, again due to funding limitations. Hanford watchers have begun to worry and wonder aloud about the lack of funds and the snail's pace of Central Plateau cleanup.[66]

Solid Waste Receipt and Disposal Become Major Issues
Hanford's solid waste burial grounds today contain about 915,000 cubic yards (700,000 cubic meters) of radioactive waste, most of it low-level. Much of it is the result of Hanford's own production and experiments, but some was shipped to the site from other government sites—and some commercial nuclear sites—over the years. Once Hanford's Federal Facility Agreement and Consent Order—known as the Tri-Party Agreement or TPA[67]—was signed, signatories began to set priorities and policies for solid waste receipts, ongoing burials, and removals. They decided that low-level solid wastes already disposed of at Hanford—and new wastes generated—could be disposed of at Hanford with no expectation of removal. The post-1970 low-level waste burial sites in the 200 Areas would remain undisturbed. The legacy (pre-1970) burial sites in the 100, 300 and 600 areas would be dug up and their contents removed to either the ERDF or other disposal destinations depending on their radioactivity levels.

Transuranic waste, however, was another matter. TRU waste, they decided, would not be stored at Hanford on anything more than a temporary basis and would be removed to the WIPP facility as soon as practicable. The first shipment of TRU waste was shipped from Hanford's WRAP for disposal at the WIPP facility in July 2000.[68] As of the end of September 2006, 288 shipments had been sent, each carrying about 180 curies worth of radioactive material. Hanford has many more shipments ready to go, but priority shipping was given first to the contents of the DOE's Rocky Flats Site in Colorado. That site closed in 2005, and now priority shipping is given to the DOE's Idaho National Laboratory per an agreement with Idaho's governor in which that state allows spent nuclear fuel from U.S. Navy ships to be stored in Idaho.[69]

WDOE and U.S. DOE further agreed that several post-1970 Hanford trenches identified as containing "suspect TRU waste"[70] would be dug up so that the waste could be examined according to modern criteria and finally categorized as low-level or TRU waste—whichever designation turned out to be accurate. Things seemed to be progressing well when several thorny problems came to a head in 2003. In 2000, the DOE had selected Hanford and the Nevada Test Site as the places it would store low-level wastes from all other DOE sites. Washington state and Oregon officials immediately objected, as did many regional stakeholder groups.[71]

However, by 2002, DOE had adopted and expanded the plan in the draft of a formal solid waste Environmental Impact Statement (EIS—a decision document that, when signed, legally obliges a course of action). The EIS proposed a "megatrench" at Hanford that would contain low-level wastes (from Hanford and elsewhere), mixed low-level waste (containing hazardous chemicals as well as radioactive materials), and some "low-end" transuranic wastes. "Clean up, don't fill up Hanford," said Oregon's senior Senator Ron Wyden.[72] "Hanford's taken enough," editorialized the *Oregonian*.[73] Washington state officials "vehemently" disapproved.[74] The Hanford region's public newspaper, the *Tri-City Herald*, proposed charging DOE to store extra wastes at Hanford. "The biggest worry," it said, is "that Hanford will become a dumping ground for the Energy Department's other nuclear sites. . . . Tri-Citians and other Northwesterners know that DOE's priorities are no more permanent than the politicians who help set them. Despite its [DOE's] assurances, more wastes may end up at Hanford, and for longer periods, than anyone anticipates."[75]

In late 2002, Washington state and the DOE reached an agreement to allow some TRU wastes from the outside to be shipped to Hanford, provided the two sides could reach an accord by March 1, 2003, to add legally enforceable milestones on low-level, mixed, and TRU solid wastes to the Tri-Party Agreement.[76] However, when the March 1 deadline passed with no milestones having been reached, the state sued the DOE and stopped all TRU radioactive waste shipments into Hanford. A month later, DOE sued WDOE for unilaterally setting deadlines and interfering with its cleanup work.[77] A federal judge put a moratorium on the shipments until the litigation could be resolved.[78] Meanwhile,

DOE issued another draft of its solid waste EIS, adding fuel to the fire. The new draft proposed storing solid wastes produced by hardening some of Hanford's lower-activity (albeit still highly radioactive) tank waste into ceramic form.[79] Disposing of Hanford's tank wastes was and is an unimaginably polarizing issue in the region.

As part of the fallout from the state-DOE dispute over solid radioactive wastes, three environmental groups announced plans in mid-2003 to gather signatures to place an initiative barring outside waste shipments to Hanford on the next state-wide ballot. Their plans went forward, becoming Initiative 297 (I-297) in the November 2004 elections. Emotions ran high, with I-297 being called a "political football" and many other things.[80] Not surprisingly, the immediate Hanford region opposed the measure while many environmental/activist groups supported it.[81]

However, the arguments in western Washington and Oregon were nuanced, not monolithic. "The initiative is a false promise fraught with risk for cleanup of the Hanford nuclear reservation," editorialized the *Seattle Times*.[82] Likewise the *Oregonian* editorialized that the initiative "looks like a no-brainer at first glance . . . [but] voter approval . . . in fact, could make it even harder to . . . get Hanford cleaned up. . . . Freeing the region of this radioactive and chemical menace [Hanford's wastes] is too complex to be solved by a well-intentioned but simplistic initiative. Washington voters should reject I-297."[83] Both newspapers believed that backlash from other locations designated to accept Hanford wastes in the future would preclude the ultimate hope of ridding the Pacific Northwest of radioactive and hazardous wastes.

Initiative 297 passed by a wide margin. The federal Justice Department, acting on behalf of the U.S. DOE, immediately went to court to overturn it. Justice Department attorneys argued that the initiative violated existing contracts (with companies supporting DOE's cleanup) and interfered with the federal government's ability and right to direct the national cleanup program. A judge blocked implementation of the initiative until the complete arguments could be heard. Finally in mid-2006, a federal judge struck down I-297 as unconstitutional, upholding the federal arguments. Washington state is appealing that ruling.[84]

In the meantime, however, in that angry spring and summer of 2003 when DOE and Hanford's home state were suing each other, other solid waste issues were raised. A Seattle-based advocacy group called Heart of America Northwest charged that the contractor company that had prepared the draft EIS for solid waste, Battelle,[85] had a conflict of interest since its parent company was trying to ship TRU wastes to Hanford.[86] WDOE and EPA, along with some prominent Hanford public watchdog groups, said that the revised (2003) draft EIS, while better than the 2002 version, was still inadequate.[87] Negotiations continued between the state and DOE to end their lawsuits and establish enforceable Tri-Party Agreement milestones for TRU waste treatment that were acceptable to them and the EPA. WDOE went to court to order DOE to vastly speed the retrieval of about seventy-five thousand drums (or drum-equivalents) of suspect TRU waste from Hanford trenches.[88]

DOE responded by ordering the shutdown of major portions of cleanup operations at Hanford, citing specific clauses in WDOE's order that prohibited generating new TRU and mixed wastes until a disposal path (or plan) for the older wastes had been identified. The *Tri-City Herald* called DOE's action "risky posturing. . . . Hanford's neighbors and its workers are less important to DOE than flexing a few muscles and showing the state exactly who's in charge. The war of wills . . . [is] to no one's benefit." The *Seattle Times* called DOE's position a "tantrum."[89] Both sides modified their stances a few weeks later, and cleanup resumed at Hanford. In autumn 2003, WDOE and DOE reached agreements on several aspects of solid waste retrieval and treatment. Immediately, DOE contractors began digging out the old, suspect-TRU waste drums, working nearly around the clock. As of late 2006, they were meeting schedules agreed to in 2003 to retrieve this waste.[90]

In January 2004, DOE issued its final EIS for solid waste at Hanford and issued Records of Decision for treating and disposing of several types of solid waste later that year. The "megatrench" (by then known as the Integrated Disposal facility—IDF) would be built, TRU waste shipments from off-site to Hanford would be vastly curtailed, and all wastes would thereafter be disposed of in lined trenches. Although many groups and agencies objected to portions of the decisions, compromise was in the air. WDOE didn't like the amounts of low-level solid waste shipments that the DOE intended to send to Hanford, and DOE temporarily halted them in July so that talks could proceed.[91]

Cordial relations soon soured. In September 2004, Washington imposed its largest-ever penalty on DOE for improperly shipping a load of mixed radioactive waste from its Savannah River Site in South Carolina to Hanford.[92] All of the barely submerged animosities resurfaced. In early 2005, a ruling was handed down in the state's still-pending 2003 solid waste lawsuit against DOE. A federal judge found that Washington state did have authority to bar some waste shipments (TRU waste mixed with chemicals—known as TRUM) to Hanford.[93] WDOE called the ruling "an incredible win for the state."[94]

Modifications, exceptions, and other partial rulings followed in the spring of 2005, until an amazing event occurred that July. U.S. DOE headquarters an-

nounced that the Solid Waste EIS finalized in January 2004 was flawed. As part
of the discovery process in the still-ongoing solid waste litigation between DOE
and Washington state, Battelle—the contractor who prepared the EIS document—had identified "discrepancies in the data related to the impact of waste
disposal [at Hanford] on the groundwater." DOE headquarters said it was "very
disappointed . . . [in] Battelle's lack of appropriate quality assurance" and also
excoriated DOE's Richland Operations Office for not providing adequate oversight to Battelle. The planned waste shipments from Battelle's other facility in
Ohio were cancelled.[95]

In January 2006, Washington state and DOE settled their 2003 lawsuit over
TRU waste shipments into Hanford when DOE agreed to prepare an entirely
new Solid Waste EIS for the site. Because solidified, low-activity wastes from
Hanford's high-level waste tanks were being considered for burial in the lined
IDF, the Solid Waste EIS would be combined with another EIS concurrently being prepared for Hanford Tank Closure. The large new EIS would be completed
in 2008, and the state would have a significant role in establishing key analytical parameters and in proving review and input to it. In the meanwhile, DOE
agreed not to ship waste from other sites to Hanford, except in certain specific
instances to which the state had already agreed. The parties agreed that provisions of the 2004 EIS would remain in place until the new EIS was completed,
to allow ongoing Hanford cleanup operations to continue.[96]

In the meantime, the Tri-Parties agreed to allow construction to begin on
the IDF, a twenty-six–acre, lined landfill in central Hanford, for the future
disposal of solidified, mixed low-activity waste from Hanford's underground
tanks. WDOE issued permits in phases, allowing it to keep a careful eye on developing issues with solid waste and tank waste plans at the site. By spring 2006,
the initial two cells of the "megatrench" had been completed.[97]

Plutonium Finishing Plant Stabilization
Brings Accolades as Deactivation Begins

The end of the Cold War brought an abrupt shutdown order to Hanford's
Plutonium Finishing Plant (PFP)—so sudden that nearly eighteen metric tons
(over twenty U.S. tons) of Pu-bearing residues, sludges, liquids, and other
materials were left either "held-up" in plant equipment or stored in unstable
conditions. During the early 1990s, the plant busily performed equipment, instrumentation, and containment upgrades in preparation for a "stabilization
run" to convert and/or solidify its special materials into stable oxide powders
or Pu metal. The Defense Nuclear Facilities Safety Board (DNFSB), a federal
safety oversight body independent of the DOE, encouraged the stabilization of

240

the materials, which posed dangers in their then-current configurations and locations. "The halt in production of nuclear weapons and materials to be used in nuclear weapons froze the manufacturing pipeline in a state that, for safety reasons, should not be allowed to persist," wrote DNFSB Chairman John Conway. He specifically identified Hanford's PFP as a place where "large quantities of plutonium solutions are stored in deteriorating tanks, piping, and plastic bottles."[98]

However, as plans moved forward angry stakeholders confronted DOE, contending that the stabilization run was, or could be, viewed as a "back-door" way to continue plutonium production. They objected to spending money to upgrade key parts of the "production infrastructure" at PFP and said that once facilities such as the Remote Mechanical "C" Line (RMC Line) inside the main PFP building and the Plutonium Reclamation Facility (PRF—a companion facility) were refurbished to conduct stabilization runs safely, DOE might use the modernized condition of these facilities to attract or accept new Pu production missions for the Hanford Site. Such future missions, they stated, were distinctly unwelcome. In 1994, DOE put the RMC and PRF upgrade campaigns on hold.[99]

Although other DOE sites have, at different times, housed more plutonium than Hanford's PFP, no collection in the United States was so unique, varied, and complicated. The PFP complex contained nearly four million curies of alpha radionuclides (generally longer-lived than many other forms of radionuclides) bound up in Pu-bearing materials in forms not suitable for long-term storage. These variegated materials dated from PFP's own operations that began in 1949, and from the years following 1972 when the facility was designated the Central Scrap Management Organization for Pu-bearing scraps for the entire Atomic Energy Commission (AEC). Often the scraps represented the leftovers from experiments conducted long ago, at Hanford and at various government laboratories and sites such as the Argonne National Laboratory in Illinois, the Los Alamos Laboratory in New Mexico, and many other places. Many of these materials arrived with sparse or erroneous characterization data, because long-term storage was never intended.[100]

The composition of the materials changed inexorably over time as certain radioisotopes decayed to become other isotopes and chemical interactions occurred. "Reactive scrap" was the name applied to the materials, because the radiolytic and chemical decay processes produced gases that prevented cans and containers from maintaining a seal. The scraps had to be examined and repackaged on a periodic basis, resulting in ongoing worker exposure, and potential environmental exposure, to plutonium and americium.[101]

Furthermore, the highly contaminated main PFP building, the 234-5Z facility, is a steel shell building—not as sturdy as concrete—and it does not meet seismic or other criteria for new plutonium structures. Plutonium was stored in glove boxes and "hoods" in this and other PFP buildings, vaults, and even in long service tunnels under the structure. In many cases, it was stored in thin metal cans similar to those used in the food packing industry that were never intended to hold corrosive or reactive plutonium-bearing solutions for many years.[102]

Beginning in late 1994, PFP began implementing "interim stabilization" measures to address some of the most urgent risks. Throughout the remainder of the 1990s, they stabilized some of the most reactive materials by heating them to very high sustained temperatures in tiny ovens inside steel glove boxes until the organic materials, water vapors, and other decay products that could support gas or other reactions within the plutonium were driven off. They cleaned Pu dusts out of duct work, filled certain containers bearing Pu process residues with cement, sandblasted and painted to affix surface contamination, and took many other measures. In 1996, they presented a detailed inventory of Pu-bearing materials in the PFP complex to the DNFSB.[103]

That same year, the DOE completed an EIS for PFP Stabilization and signed a Record of Decision (ROD) committing it to stabilize all of the Pu-bearing residues at the plant by 2001, and to finish cleanup of the buildings and structures of the PFP complex by 2004.[104] However, progress was slow in the years immediately after the ROD was signed. The old facilities of the PFP complex proved reluctant to comply with the strict operating processes and procedures of the modern nuclear world.

In late 2000, a new plutonium stabilization schedule had been negotiated between the DOE and the DNFSB. In DNFSB Recommendation 2000-1, the Board was stern in its admonishment of PFP: "The story of the inability to treat plutonium solutions at PFP has been typical of a sequence of ineffective activities at that Plant."[105]

That same year, Hanford's PFP morphed from a stabilization dullard to a super-star. It started up four new processes for plutonium stabilization in 2000.[106] It also designed and built a new system of glove boxes and state-of-the-art equipment in the compound of vaults within the PFP complex, to process plutonium materials of high concentration and purity. In 2001, additional ovens began operating in the 234-5Z Building, and a magnesium-hydroxide precipitation process was launched to stabilize the inventory of forty-three hundred liters of plutonium-bearing solution. (The magnesium-hydroxide precipitation process was later replaced by an oxalate precipitation process.) Nearly each type of material stabilized at Hanford's PFP required a new process.[107]

Altogether, PFP's stabilization rate quadrupled in 2000 and quadrupled again in 2001. In April 2001, PFP became the first facility in the weapons complex to comply with DOE's new standard STD-3013, a set of strict safety and storage requirements for plutonium packages.[108] That same year, a "pipe-and-go" system started up at PFP to transfer plutonium-bearing residues into large, heavily reinforced containers. Residues are those forms of solid, plutonium-bearing scrap that require no thermal stabilization, but only require repackaging into sturdy containers for disposal.[109]

Achievements followed quickly at PFP. In late 2001, a PFP team completed the stabilization and canning of all plutonium metals at the compound. By mid-2002, all of PFP's plutonium-bearing solutions, considered the highest risk form of plutonium, had been stabilized.[110] Workers completed stabilizing approximately one thousand polycubes, a unique form of plutonium-bearing solids in a polystyrene matrix, in early 2003. No stabilization process meeting modern standards had ever before been developed for polycubes.[111]

The engineering and safety aspects of the parts and portions of the PFP stabilization project were complicated almost beyond rational understanding. Nevertheless, in February 2004, the project finished the job by completing repackaging over six tons of plutonium residues and stabilizing a complicated array of alloys and high-chloride oxides. In total, PFP workers packed nearly two thousand large drums of plutonium-bearing residues and 2,239 of the 3,013 containers.[112] In the midst of these first-of-a-kind stabilization activities, Hanford's PFP became the first high-hazard nuclear facility in the nation to be awarded Star Status in the DOE's Voluntary Protection Program, a stringent safety program modeled after that of the Occupational Safety and Health Administration.[113]

Occurring almost exactly fifteen years after defense production ended and cleanup became the central mission at the site, PFP's stabilization accomplishment seemed to embody Hanford's vision, intent, and promise to stabilize and safely manage wastes and SNM in the site's Central Plateau. Completion of plutonium stabilization and packaging was one of the last operational missions at Hanford that involved working mostly with non-waste materials.[114]

The Secretary of Energy offered his congratulations, and Washington's then-Governor Gary Locke called the success "a major accomplishment for Hanford and for the Northwest." The representative of the governor of Oregon gathered with distinguished guests and PFP workers to celebrate. He called PFP's work a "tremendous achievement. . . . This is what every cleanup project at Hanford aspires to." The U.S. EPA, often a critic, stated that "we're all impressed. . . . You've demonstrated that even the toughest jobs at Hanford can be completed with excellence." The Hanford region's Congressman Richard Hastings said that "the progress has been absolutely remarkable. . . . You ought to be very proud of the work you have accomplished."[115]

Even before PFP's stabilization work ended, the old complex was busy with a large D&D project that will bring the sixty-one structures in the fifteen-acre complex to demolition-ready status in the next few years. As of late 2006, seventeen structures had been demolished, and dangerously contaminated equipment was being removed from others.[116]

Unique Spent Nuclear Fuel Project Succeeds at Hanford, Fuel Sludge Tackled Next

On a glorious fall day in 2004, the Hanford Site again made history when the last container of spent nuclear fuel was removed from the K Basins less than a quarter of a mile from the Columbia River. The fuel had contained 95 percent of the radioactivity in Hanford's reactor areas and was the largest concentration of stored nuclear fuel in the United States—over two-thirds of the entire DOE spent fuel inventory.[117]

Workers and dignitaries applauded and cheered as the huge steel container emerged from the old basin where the fuel had stewed and languished for a quarter century.[118] The completion of the Spent Nuclear Fuel (SNF) Project in 2004 stood out as a "cornerstone event" in Hanford's long farewell to arms, and a down payment to the stakeholders, taxpayers, residents, and environment of the magnificent region on the debt incurred when the Manhattan Project seized the land and river for nuclear production over sixty years ago. Congratulations poured in from across the nation.[119]

"The Columbia River and surrounding communities are safer today because of the success of this project," said Secretary of Energy Spencer Abraham. "This high-risk material is now safely contained." The EPA, which had sparred with the spent fuel cleanup project for a decade, was pleased, calling the completion of fuel removal from the K Basins a "monumental achievement. . . . One of the biggest risks to the Columbia River has been abated . . . and the site must be seen as much safer." Likewise, ODOE, also a frequent Hanford critic, termed the success "one of the most significant accomplishments there has been at Hanford."[120]

The achievement was not easy in coming. The project to remove the 105,000 irradiated fuel assemblies—over 4.65 million pounds of fuel—had proven more complex than anyone's planning or imagination could have foreseen. Although spent fuel is dried and stored at nuclear power plants in many parts of the world, the work done in Hanford's SNF Project had never been attempted anywhere before. The Hanford fuel was solid uranium metal (not in sintered oxide powder or pellet forms as is most commercial nuclear fuel), and the cladding (or coating metal) had been breached to some extent on about half of the fuel assemblies. The job was one of the toughest and riskiest in the cleanup universe.[121] Additionally, reactions between uranium and water over the years had produced about fifty cubic meters of radioactive sludge that swirled around the fuel, clouding the water and posing the constant possibility of unsafe concentrations.

Located about thirty-five miles north of Richland, the K Basins are two indoor, rectangular structures 125 feet long, 67 feet wide, and 21 feet deep. The now fifty-four-year-old basins were constructed to store spent fuel from the K East and K West plutonium production reactors on a temporary, rotating basis. They were built to the Uniform Building Code of 1952, with a twenty-year design life, and were not intended for multi-year storage of spent fuel. Yet, the K Basins had provided crude, underwater storage for the huge collection since the mid-1970s. In the late 1970s, the K East Basin leaked approximately fifteen million gallons of contaminated water into surrounding soils and leaked another ninety-four thousand gallons into the environment in 1993.[122]

During 1970–71, the K Reactors and their basins were shut down. However, in 1975 and 1981, the basins were reopened to store spent fuel from Hanford's N Reactor, which remained in operation while the PUREX Plant was shut down for safety and environmental upgrades. The N Reactor's own spent fuel basin had become full, and the fuel began to accumulate in the K Basins. Due to mission changes and other priorities at the PUREX Plant, this spent fuel was never dissolved and reprocessed.

The SNF Project was created at Hanford in 1994, once the dust settled from the Cold War's end and the huge mission changes that came with it. The alternative of sending the fuel to Europe for reprocessing was rejected due to nonproliferation concerns, and reprocessing in the United States would violate existing laws and regulations.[123] Once the path was chosen to remove and dry the fuel assemblies, no one thought that waiting or moving slowly was a good idea.

The process was deceptively "simple" but was beset with Byzantine complexities. During the years between 1994 and the start of fuel removal in 2000, the SNF Project built two new facilities and completely refurbished the K Basins with hundreds of thousands of pounds of new, first-of-a-kind equipment.[124] It also retrofitted the K Basins with remotely operated washing machines, de-capping equipment to open the old fuel canisters, casks, hoists, cranes, elevators, shuttles, giant robotic arms, and other first-of-a-kind equipment. All of the equipment sat in twenty feet of water in the basins. Over four hundred mammoth new storage canisters—called multi-canister overpacks (MCOs)—were procured, each costing $75,000 and manufactured to the strictest engineering codes for nuclear materials.

Nuclear workers stood on grating above the basins, working through slots with long-handled tools to grapple and manipulate each fuel assembly or piece thereof. The basin water provided some shielding from the radiation, but gas bubbles from the fuel brought radioactive contamination to the surface and into the air. Often, the workers had to toil in heavy, bulky radiation protection suits and breathe through air packs and hoses.[125]

Thus encumbered, they loaded the fuel into the large new containers, which were placed into the basin water. The containers, enclosed in casks, were then lifted out of the water and sent to a new Cold Vacuum Drying Facility, where free water and some of the chemically bound water in the fuel was removed in a cyclical drying/pumping/condensation process. The containers were then filled with helium gas, transported to a new Canister Storage Building in Hanford's interior, and moved via a massive, radiologically shielded crane into steel storage tubes that extend forty feet below ground level. There they will rest until, and if, they are moved to a federal repository at some future time.[126]

There were so many questions—so many "what-ifs"—that had to be answered before fuel removal could begin. Then, in mid-stream, more puzzles arose. How would the engineer/designers assure that enough water had been removed from each collection of fuel assemblies inside the MCOs? To limit the generation of hydrogen from the radiolysis of water, they could allow only about one part water in ten thousand parts fuel for the five to six tons of fuel inside each container. Would tiny bits of residual or "bound" water left inside the MCOs react with the uranium in the fuel to produce hydrogen in sufficient quantity to form, with oxygen, a combustible mixture? What amount of fuel scrap (broken bits of irradiated uranium) could safely be stored inside any given MCO? Could an aluminum hydroxide coating found on some of the elements inside aluminum canisters generate oxygen and pressure within the sealed MCOs during long-term storage? Would the uranium oxidation rate, or reaction rate, rise while the fuel was being dried and produce high temperature spikes? Or, would oxidation cause fuel to crumble and then produce unsafe amounts of heat during the drying process?[127]

By 1999, the technical questions had been studied and resolved. Fuel removal began on a chill December day in 2000. Then operational problems arose. The Fuel Transfer System (FTS) that brought fuel from the K East Basin to the K West Basin for processing "had a mind of its own," according to the manager who operated it. It was always quirky and challenging, experiencing problems with its limit switches (electronic "brakes" that allow equipment to move only certain distances), "traveling nuts," and "jackscrews" (large bolts holding key equipment pieces level and on rails). It also suffered persistent alignment issues, demonstrating the difficulties of working with newly engineered systems in aged facilities. Worse yet, radiological contamination built up on its transfer casks, slowing down work for repeated decontamination scrubs.[128]

Nearly thirty years of underwater storage had corroded and degraded much of the fuel to the point that it literally either fell apart when touched or expanded and stuck inside its containers. About 6 percent of the fuel—some six thousand assemblies—was known as "Class D," the worst of the worst. It had gross cladding failure with substantial element dilation and deformation, clad splitting, and void spaces—simply put, no integrity. When they encountered Class D fuel stuck fast inside its aging containers, engineers and craftsmen for contractor Fluor Hanford (FH), who had designed and built many one-of-a-kind tools throughout the course of the Project, created even more eye-popping tools. They mounted a "jaws of life" hydraulic shear on a twenty-foot pole and modified its controls so it could be rotated by operators working on grating far above the submerged fuel. They also altered an underwater rotary cutter, and a chisel tool, to operate from a twenty-foot distant angle.

However, the swollen fuel was so difficult to extricate from the old canisters that workers wrestling with it broke two "jaws of life" tools in just the first month of use. One Basin manager summed it up by saying that "with this fuel, when you would expect things to get worse . . . [they] got even worse than you could imagine."[129]

The SNF Project also experienced cost overruns and schedule delays. In 1999, it became the only Hanford project to be placed on a DOE headquarters "Watch List" for projects with "significant issues." This bad-boy list carried with it more stringent financial controls for the project, and the possibility of loss of funding or other disciplinary actions.[130]

Along the way, the old K Basins proved that they could deliver the kind of surprises that Hanford watchers fear but half expect. In late 1999, newly declassified historical documents revealed that the concrete floors in parts of the K Basins were inches thinner than had been thought. For a time, the finding called into question the safety basis for loading the old floors with the immense tonnage of new equipment.[131] Later, cracks in basin walls were discovered by underwater cameras. Although both issues were quickly investigated and found to pose no significant safety risks, the discoveries underscored the lurking, stomach-churning apprehensions that both the well-informed and the uninformed can never dismiss about Hanford.[132]

When the dangerous, highly radioactive fuel was finally out of the K Basins, one manager spoke for many when he stated: "Not many jobs are as important as this one. We're not making 'slinkies' out here. . . . This is *real* cleanup!"[133]

However, removing the irradiated fuel did not complete the cleanout of the K Basins. Left behind was about seventy cubic yards of sludge, an amalgam of dirt, sand, chemicals, polychlorinated biphenyls, and corrosion products from the metal fuel and its cans and racks, all contaminated with fission products. Although highly radioactive, the sludge contained only about 2 percent of the total radioactivity in the fuel. One factor that made the sludge so dangerous was that its approximately one million curies was contained in such a small volume—a volume only enough to fill about ten standard dump trucks, if the sludge were dry.[134]

The sludge could be dense and heavy, or light and swirling. It coated basin walls and floor areas, as well as tools, equipment, and other items that were discarded in the K Basins over the years. The EPA, as well as state regulatory agencies and stakeholders, emphasized to DOE that recovering and treating the sludge so that it did not leak into the environment was, and is, one of the most important jobs at the Hanford Site.

Capturing the sludge as it swirled through the 1.2 million gallons of water in the basin proved to be extremely challenging. One manager compared the work to "vacuuming under the bed of your child's room with all the toys on the floor and working through a tiny hole in the roof above the room." The analogy refers to the debris hidden within and covering much of the sludge, and to the operators with their long-handled tools standing on grating twenty feet above the basin floor. Sludge retrieval work has also been compared to "capturing smoke," or to the frustration of "driving for nine hours straight in a thick fog, while only being able to see the road through the rear-view mirror," because workers could only "see" the sludge through a camera.

Visibility in the K East Basin water—which contained over 80 percent of the sludge—was especially poor. The water appeared as if chocolate milk and orange dye had been poured into it. Much of the time during sludge retrieval work, workers could not see the bottom of K East Basin. And, to remain safe, they had to work in full radiation suits and breathe with cumbersome air-puri-fying respirators.[135]

The sludge work proved to be so difficult and slow that DOE passed along to its cleanup contractor a large fine from the EPA and threatened to give the work to another company.[136] Retrieval began in mid-2004, but had to pause for several months to remove enormous amounts of debris. As the debris came to the surface, its bulk and variety surprised everyone. Over two hundred tons of debris were removed from the relatively small basins by late 2006—enough to fill more than six maximally loaded, full-sized moving vans. By late 2006, about 95 percent of the sludge in the K East Basin had been captured in underwater containers and was awaiting removal to a treatment building. Containerization of the much smaller volume of sludge in the K West Basin was just beginning.[137]

Waste-Storage Tank Issues Huge, Complex, Controversial

Many successes were packed into the first seventeen years of the Hanford cleanup: PUREX, B-Plant, N Reactor and many 300 Area facilities were deactivated or demolished, additional reactors were "cocooned" or on the way, PFP was finished with plutonium stabilization, twenty-three hundred tons of spent fuel were moved out of the K Basins, and many additional victories were in hand. However, the program to remediate Hanford's 177 underground high-level waste-storage tanks was still experiencing difficulties.

The simple facts in late 2006 were that a cleanup division aimed at remediating Hanford's underground, high-level tank waste had existed for sixteen years, it had spent nearly $5 billion over that time period, it had employed between 1,800 and 5,000 people per year, and yet no tank waste curies had left the Hanford Site except by natural radioactive decay. The "babysitting" aspects of tank waste work were frustrating to all concerned, including Hanford workers and Hanford watchers.

Just keeping the tanks safe each day, monitoring, repairing, ventilating, and sampling were not enough for most of the people concerned, because these activities followed a path that led nowhere. With 68 of Hanford's 177 high-level waste tanks already known or suspected to have leaked, it was an inevitable conclusion that every other tank would leak someday if the waste was not removed and treated.

The stealthy nature of tank leaks, and the gaps where facts are not known, conjure some of the most intrinsic nuclear fears. Viable plans for dealing with tank waste have been produced at Hanford since 1958.[138] Since that time, the site has generated file drawers full of plans that were under-funded, scrapped due to policy changes, lost in the shuffle of contractor and personnel changes, bypassed because a more technological solution beckoned just over the horizon, or still-born for other reasons.

In 1991, the first division in Hanford's history to focus solely on the underground waste-storage tanks was created, signifying that waste management had at last staked a salient claim on time, money, personnel, and physical resources. Renamed repeatedly during its early years, the division was designated the River Protection Project (RPP) in 1998. A special DOE office at Hanford, named the Office of River Protection (ORP), was created to focus on and manage solely the tank issues and work.[139]

Among the daunting early tasks faced by RPP was characterization of the multifaceted wastes, different in each of the 177 tanks due to recurring transfers and treatment schemes over the decades since the 1940s. Characterization efforts ramped up but had been substantially completed and were winding down by 2000.

The central task was to develop *and carry out* plans to empty the tanks of their then sixty-one million gallons of high-level liquid wastes,[140] dispose of these contents in an acceptable manner, figure out what to do with hard salt-cakes and sludges clinging to interior tank surfaces, and decide whether or not (or how) to remove the tanks themselves.

To support these overarching tasks, almost every aspect of day-to-day tank operations needed improvement. Training and safety qualifications for maintenance and operating personnel were crying needs, as were tightening the physical and administrative controls over the work, building databases and a historical library, increasing surveillance and monitoring capabilities, robotizing certain operations, and performing many other ancillary services. When Harry Harmon, the first vice president to head the new tank waste division, took over in the early 1990s, he said, "Everything needs attention."

By FY 1994, tank waste remediation work consumed about one-fifth of the Hanford Site's record budget of nearly $2 billion.[141] By that time, tank workers were pumping wastes out of eight single-shelled tanks into newer, sturdier double-shelled tanks. In 1993, Hanford engineers safely installed a huge pump (seven stories tall, forty inches in diameter, and weighing nineteen thousand pounds) into double-shelled Tank SY-101 in the 200 West Area. The pump represented a major safety improvement, since it stirred the bubbly tank contents and prevented the build-up of flammable hydrogen gases that had caused the tank to periodically "burp," or rapidly vent, several times a year.[142]

However, researchers for the U.S. Senate Committee on Energy and Natural Resources produced a report in March 1995 entitled "Train Wreck along the River of Money," which criticized DOE's cleanup programs as wasteful and unfocused.[143] The *Wall Street Journal* and other major media outlets ran equally critical articles denouncing "what happens if pork gets into play," specifically condemning the uses of DOE dollars in the Hanford Site cleanup.[144] Almost immediately, Hanford's nuclear waste cleanup funding was cut.[145] Pump-out of single-shell tanks and other key work slowed.[146]

In 1999, the TPA signatories met to commemorate and reflect on the ten years of the agreement, and most were complimentary of its flexibility and vibrancy as a living document. Mike Lawrence, who was DOE's Hanford manager at the time the TPA was signed, said that "the reality that we are here tonight [June 29, 1999], celebrating ten years of progress, is a result far better and more positive than what I dared anticipate in 1989." Deputy Director of WDOE Dan Silver pointed to the long and impressive list of cleanup achievements.[147]

Almost every speaker and commentator, however, emphasized that the biggest, most expensive, risky, and important cleanup challenge—that posed by the tank waste—needed to be handled quickly and efficiently, with no further delays.[148] Why, they asked, was it so hard to get on with tank remediation? Even if better technologies might be on the horizon, they said, go forward now using the tools currently at hand.

Key stakeholder and Hanford watcher Todd Martin wrote: "Despite the consensus behind the importance of this program [tank waste remediation], its history is littered with false starts, dramatic changes of direction, and a lack of willingness on the part of DOE to carry the program to success. . . . The time when another false start or failure is an acceptable program outcome is past. . . . Failure is unacceptable."[149] WDOE wrote that "although all other federal sites with liquid high-level waste have treatment facilities, the process to remove and immobilize the wastes is barely underway at Hanford. . . . Citizens of the Northwest must hold the federal government to its commitment to remove this environmental threat."[150]

The RPP has since achieved some important successes. In 1999 it sluiced most of the sludge waste from problematic World War II Tank C-106. The tank had routinely overheated, forcing workers to add six thousand gallons of water to it each month. The water additions were distinctly undesirable over the long term, because the tank has just a single shell, and if it had begun to leak, the constant need to add water would have driven the leaking wastes toward Hanford's groundwater.[151]

Because the tank's waste was a thick sludge, simple pumping would not budge it. A precisely engineered, high-pressure water sluicing operation was adapted from the mining industry, and the hot waste in Tank C-106 was pumped underground into a newer double-shelled tank with an engineered ventilation system capable of cooling it. When the six feet of radioactive sludge, or about 188,000 gallons, were safely inside the double-shelled tank, WDOE called it "a really good success story."[152]

Other key victories in Hanford tank work during the 1990s and early twenty-first century included resolving safety concerns on fifty-three tanks originally placed on a special "Watch List" for problem tanks by Oregon's Wyden in 1991.[153] Additionally, the tank waste program constructed, and in 1998 began to operate, a new set of double-walled, steel, underground transfer lines to pump tank waste from the 200 West Area (populated mostly by single-shelled tanks) to the 200 East Area (which contains twenty-five of Hanford's twenty-eight double-shelled tanks).[154] Other projects constructed and installed new ventilation systems to cool double-shelled tanks, replaced portions of the underground piping running between and among tanks, upgraded instrumentation on these lines, installed berms and drainage improvements to keep runoff away from the tank farms, sealed process pits with polyurea, and performed many other physical improvements.[155]

Another success for the RPP came in 2000, when just over 500,000 gallons of waste were pumped out of the formerly notorious burping Tank SY-101. After the mixer pump was installed in the tank in 1993, the difficulties in that tank seemed to be over. However, by 1998, a distinct crust (dubbed a "nuclear blob" by news media) was thickening to almost ten feet on the waste surface inside the 1.2 million gallon tank.[156] Site scientists knew that the waste in Tank SY-101 was more concentrated than that in any other Hanford tank. They decided to pump about half of the waste out of the problematic tank into a nearby double-shelled tank and then dilute the contents of both.[157] When the pump/dilute operations were completed successfully, the *Tri-City Herald* quipped that "Hanford's infamous burping tank apparently has run out of gas."[158]

However, the most important single achievement in Hanford tank management operations since site cleanup began came in 2004, when engineers completed pumping the liquids out of all 149 single-shelled tanks. By 1998, this issue had become so important that Washington state announced its intent to sue DOE for missing pump-out milestones. DOE's confirmation the year before that wastes from tank leaks had reached groundwater added urgency to the state's desire to see liquids removed from the last thirty tanks that held them. Most newspapers in the state supported the state's action. The *Tri-City Herald* said the "screwy, interminable approach the Department of Energy has to its responsibilities has tested the patience and good humor of state officials and Tri-Citians."[159]

After much discussion, a Consent Decree was signed in 1999 between DOE and Washington state extending the completion deadline for pumping out almost all liquid wastes from single-shell tanks to 2004. As Governor Gregoire said, the agreement targeted the "worst first" in terms of pumping tanks with certain types of wastes known to migrate faster through subsurface formations.[160]

It was with great relief and effusive praise that participants, Hanford watchers, and the state's newspapers greeted the completion of liquids removal from the 149 single-shelled tanks in 2004. The *Seattle Times*, often critical of Hanford, stated that "the threat from those 149 single-shell tanks has been greatly diminished. . . . The removal of pumpable liquid wastes from Hanford's risky single-shell tanks is an important achievement in a long and difficult job."[161] Gregoire returned to Hanford to help celebrate, stating that "we knew they (the single-shell tanks) were literally a threat to the Columbia River. . . . I can't imagine a few years ago thinking we would be here today, but we are."[162]

Following liquids removal, the next crucial task became how to mobilize and remove the hard salt/sludge crust inside each of the single-shelled tanks. It seemed to make sense that most of the mobilization would occur by shooting the crust with high-pressure jets of water and then pumping the slurry out into double-shelled tanks. The wet slurry would then be condensed in Hanford's only operating waste evaporator. However, there were problems with this system. Even under the best of conditions, the technique involved manipulating tank wastes at least three times before they came to rest in a condensed state inside double-shelled tanks. In addition, some of the single-shelled tanks had cracks or holes. Introducing high-pressure water would only drive contaminants out into the ground.

Yet, leaving the waste crust behind in the single-shelled tanks was anathema to environmental groups. When Hanford's tank waste management contractor proposed leaving some waste behind in selected tanks, the groups sued.[163] Washington state tried to join the suit as a "friend of the court" and remained adamantly opposed to leaving waste in the tanks. The 1989 Tri-Party Agreement committed DOE to remove 99 percent of the radioactivity in Hanford's tanks, and that was the standard the state wanted to keep.[164]

In October 2002, DOE announced plans to "close" (remove 99 percent of the waste from) twenty-six single-shell tanks by the end of FY 2006.[165] In January 2003, it announced it would begin a new EIS on tank wastes, based on the working premise that it would vitrify (harden into ceramic glass) 47 percent of all tank wastes and would explore other ways to deal with the remainder.[166] In late 2003, negotiations began among the Tri-Parties to establish new milestones for the single-shelled tanks. The meaning of tank closure loomed as a key issue.[167]

In the meantime, work had begun in spring 2003 to retrieve the salt cake residue inside the first tank. By late autumn of 2006, retrieval had been completed in only six tanks, with the work in three more underway. In the interim, DOE's contractor[168] had developed a "salt mantis" to retrieve wastes in tanks whose integrity was questionable or bad. The salt mantis operated somewhat like a rug-cleaning system, in that it vacuumed away water additions almost immediately after they were introduced. The company also invented and deployed the "sand mantis," a tiny robot that sprayed extremely high-pressure, focused jets of water at the hardest, most stubborn fractions of waste inside the tanks to dislodge them.[169]

Nothing is simple when it comes to handling Hanford's tank waste. Although progress was made, new complications always seemed to appear. Pitting corrosion and thinned wall sections were found during the ultrasonic examination of a double-shelled tank in 1999, exacerbating worries about the safe lifespan of these tanks.[170] Additionally, DOE confirmed in early 2000 that polychlorinated biphenyls (PCBs) existed in trace amounts inside Hanford's waste tanks, further complicating waste treatment, handling, and regulations leading to vitrification.[171] In 2004, work at Hanford's tank farms was halted completely when several workers said they were made ill by chemical vapors coming from the tanks. A quick study and report by the National Institute for Occupational Safety and Health (NIOSH) validated the concerns. All tank work was conducted by employees wearing full supplied-air respirators for over a year until ventilation upgrades were made.[172]

Problems and Delays Multiply in Tank Waste Vitrification Project

Given the unending dilemmas in monitoring, manipulating, and upgrading Hanford's high-level waste tanks and their contents, everyone knew there had to be a better answer. The 1996 EIS for ultimate disposition of Hanford's tank waste adopted a plan simple in concept but devilishly difficult to execute. The plan called for tank waste to be pumped out of single-shelled tanks and collected in double-shelled tanks while a vitrification (sometimes called "glassification") plant was constructed to mix the wastes with silica and bake (melt) them into blocks (or "logs") of solid, hard, borosilicate glass. The glass would still be highly radioactive but would have the advantages offered by solidity—inability to leak through the environment, lower costs to monitor and maintain, and relative ease of safeguarding.[173]

Once the decision was taken to pursue vitrification as the end state for Hanford tank wastes, DOE decided to privatize a demonstration project to construct and operate facilities to vitrify the first 10 percent (by volume) of the waste. The government would not finance the project "up front"—the private contractor would receive no funds until the first vitrified waste logs were produced.[174]

In 1998, the DOE signed a privatized, $6.9 billion contract to design, construct, certify, and operate prototype waste processing and vitrification facilities for initial portions of Hanford's tank waste. The contract was awarded to BNFL, Inc., a subsidiary of British Nuclear Fuels, Ltd., of England, and the start date for waste vitrification was set at 2007.[175] However, in mid-2000, BNFL, Inc. submitted a new cost estimate of $15.2 billion for its vitrification activities at Hanford—more than double its estimate at the time of the contract's award. DOE summarily fired the private contractor, calling its new estimate "outrageously expensive."[176]

Fallout from termination of the huge contract was enormous. In the Hanford region, many felt angry and betrayed that cleanup was further delayed, and that the credibility of the entire cleanup endeavor had suffered. Nearby, Yakima's newspaper declared: "Delays have become so common in meeting cleanup deadlines over the years that it would be easy to be lulled into a sense of resignation. But given the seriousness of the cleanup problem, that cannot be allowed to happen."[177]

The privatization debacle also added strain to the relationship among DOE and its regulators. DOE and WDOE sparred with each other, exacerbating morale and confidence throughout the region. At odds over the timetable for the new vitrification contract up for bid, DOE and WDOE agreed in mid-2000 that a federal judge in Richland would oversee the effort.[178] An exasperated then–State Attorney General Gregoire complained in regard to the waste tanks: "You [DOE] spend a lot of money. You spend a lot of time. You don't clean up squat."[179]

In a back-to-the-future approach, DOE rapidly rebid the contract, structuring it along the lines of old-fashioned, cost-reimbursement government contracting.[180] In late 2000, it awarded a ten-year, $4 billion contract to construct and operate an initial Hanford tank waste vitrification facility to a team comprised of Bechtel National, Inc. and Washington Group International, Inc. (The contractor group was called Bechtel National, Inc. or BNI.) The new contract required that the first wastes be vitrified in 2009.[181]

However, costs escalated continuously, and the schedule slid into the future, frustrating everyone. By spring 2003, the cost estimate stood at $5.6 billion, and the schedule for startup was pegged at 2011. Reluctantly, Washington state accepted the changes.[182] A year later, the GAO criticized the massive vitrification construction project for, among other things, using a "fast-track" approach that allowed construction to begin before designs were finalized. This practice, said the GAO, led to wasteful mistakes that required expensive correction later. A third case of misplaced or inadequate steel reinforcing bars (rebar) in the facility's concrete turned up that same year.[183]

In mid-2005, construction was halted on crucial portions of Hanford's vitrification structures because serious questions were raised about the adequacy of earthquake risk analyses. The price tag then stood at $6.5 billion, with no one willing to commit to a startup date.[184] The Army Corps of Engineers reviewed the project that summer and found "serious management and oversight deficiencies" in DOE's project management office (ORP); cost, performance, and contracting problems; and safety issues. The Corps review team "saw little evidence that BNI has taken steps to minimize and control project costs. . . . There does not appear to be an appropriate sense of urgency regarding such initiatives [to control costs and advance work], and there is no evidence such actions have been routinely taken."[185]

Rumors flew throughout the autumn of 2005 that costs for the vitrification plant were rising further, and that the seismic issues were more serious than had been disclosed. However, DOE would not release its latest reports, prompting the *Tri-City Herald* to opine that the federal agency's "silent treatment [was] getting very, very old. . . . If the Department of Energy had existed during the days of the Manhattan Project, we'd probably still be at war with Japan."[186]

Leaked and redacted versions of the report finally became public, and BNI released new estimates in early 2006 placing the cost of the vitrification project at more than $10 billion, with a startup date of 2017.[187] By spring 2006, still newer estimates placed the cost at $11.3 billion, with a start date of 2018. Congress was incensed. When it was discovered that Bechtel had installed a massive, faulty tank in one of the main vitrification structures, and collected a $15 million progress payment for doing so, public outrage almost could not be contained. The television news show *60 Minutes* aired a segment on the project called "Lethal and Leaking." On it, Washington's Governor Gregoire said that "the chances of a catastrophic event over there [Hanford's tanks] are real. . . . Time is not on our side."[188]

In June, DOE ordered BNI to give back $48 million in performance fees earned on the vitrification plant construction—the largest fine ever levied on a contractor at Hanford. A new formal estimate released later that month placed the cost at $11.5 billion, with a start date of 2019.[189] The following month, rumors placed new cost estimates at $13.2 billion, although in September 2006 the new official estimate stood at $12.2 billion.[190] In August, DOE confirmed that construction on key portions of Hanford's vitrification complex—the "Pre-Treatment" building that will handle all wastes at the beginning of the process, and the "High-Activity" building that will handle the hottest wastes—would remain on hold through FY 2007. The Department's reputation could not stand any more engineering or financial mistakes.[191]

Not surprisingly, since vitrification is proving so difficult at Hanford, site personnel have been investigating alternatives to solidify at least some fractions of the tank waste. After a technology study and selection exercise, a process known as "bulk vitrification" (quite different from the process to be used in Hanford's main vitrification complex) was chosen. Essentially, the bulk vitrification process is intended for portions of the tank waste that have lower radioactivity levels (although all tank waste is classified as "high-level waste"). It mixes these wastes with soil in large containers, then applies high voltage electricity via robust electrodes for several days to harden the waste/soil mixture into solid blocks. The chemistry of this process is not the same as the ceramic melting process, but its result also immobilizes the waste.[192]

Small tests of the bulk vitrification method, conducted in 2004 and 2005, proved successful enough that further tests were authorized.[193] In the summer of 2006, design was completed for a Bulk Vitrification Pilot Plant to be built and operated in central Hanford to treat up to 300,000 gallons of actual tank waste.[194]

Another idea floated by DOE to deal with some of the lower-activity tank wastes at Hanford was to process and harden wastes in eight to twenty specific tanks as sludge and then ship that material to the WIPP facility for disposal. The plan would designate this subset material as TRUM solid waste rather than high-level waste. Hanford's official citizen advisory board approved the plan in 2003, and DOE began discussing it with WDOE. However, a late-2005 report by DOE's Office of Inspector General found that DOE's ORP had not followed the proper legal pathways in New Mexico (the state that would receive the wastes). Therefore, the report concluded, ORP had wasted over $5 million spent by its contractor to design and purchase project systems and equipment to implement the plan, only to ramp down when its legality was questioned.[195]

Designating part of Hanford's tank waste as TRUM was opposed in principle by New Mexico because it was part of a larger dispute over "reclassifying" parts of the high-level waste in tanks at the DOE sites at Hanford, Savannah River, and Idaho. The reclassification issue arose in late 2001, when a confidential staff memo written by then-DOE Assistant Secretary for Environmental Management (EM—the cleanup division) Jessie Roberson was leaked to the public. The memo stated that high among EM's priorities was to "eliminate the need to vitrify at least 75% of the waste scheduled for vitrification today."[196] To accomplish this end, DOE would reclassify several subsets of waste as "incidental to reprocessing" and develop alternate processing and disposal plans. Some of those plans involved shipping solidified tank wastes to WIPP. Among the options most irksome to Washington state was leaving much of the dry waste crust inside Hanford's single-shelled tanks (after liquid removal), filling the tanks with grout, and leaving them in place in perpetuity.[197]

Immediately, several stakeholder groups filed a lawsuit charging DOE with violating the Nuclear Waste Policy Act of 1982. The states of Washington, Oregon, Idaho, and South Carolina filed briefs supporting this position as "friends of the court."[198] In mid-2003, a federal judge supported the plaintiffs and voided DOE's reclassification plans. The Department appealed to Congress to grant it authority to reclassify and also proposed withholding $350 million in cleanup funds in the FY 2005 budget from the affected sites until the reclassification matter was resolved.[199] In the meantime, New Mexico modified the WIPP acceptance permit specifically to prohibit acceptance of any reclassified waste from high-level tanks at Idaho, Hanford, or Savannah River.[200]

Additional backlash in the affected states was huge. "DOE [is] pulling a fast one at Hanford," editorialized the *Seattle Post-Intelligencer*, and it called the Department "arrogant."[201] "The Department of Energy doesn't learn," said the *Tri-City Herald*. "Instead of trying to persuade the public and elected officials that the proposal has merit, the agency is stepping up its back-door attempts to force the change."[202] "A sneaky ploy . . . ill-advised," said the *Seattle Times* about DOE's plan.[203] The *New York Times* editorialized that "the decision [on reclassifying nuclear waste] should not be left to an agency that is desperate to get past a staggeringly difficult waste disposal problem."[204]

In late 2004, however, the 2005 Defense Authorization Act (the law that funds and directs DOE cleanup each year) passed, allowing reclassification of some high-level tank wastes at the Idaho and South Carolina DOE sites, but not at Hanford.[205] The opposition to the plan had been strongest by Washington state's Congressional delegation, who argued that legislation allowing reclassification would violate the Tri-Party Agreement. Idaho's and South Carolina's Congressional delegations were more unified in their desire to seek future DOE projects. Soon after passage of the legislation allowing reclassification, New Mexico reiterated its intention to bar all reclassified tank wastes—including those from Idaho and South Carolina—from the WIPP site.[206]

In early 2005, two National Research Council (NRC) reports backed DOE's technical position that it would be impossible and prohibitively expensive to remove all of the tank wastes from the three sites that have them. However, they stated that DOE should not be the sole agency to make decisions about reclassification. They recommended that an independent regulator be named and that

258

much public involvement be included in such decisions.[207] The NRC also began a new study of tank waste retrieval and disposition, required in the 2005 Defense Authorization Act as part of the reclassification compromise. That study, published in 2006, advocated slowing down tank waste decisions and final actions until better technologies were developed, and specifically asked for more research and testing to prove the bulk vitrification technique being considered at Hanford.[208] Of course, slowing down tank waste actions any further was and is anathema to the Hanford region. "It is becoming impossible to accept more delays," said a spokesperson for WDOE in September 2006.[209] The mind-numbing conundrums and complexities continue to this day.

Fast Flux Test Facility Shut Down

The Fast Flux Test Facility (FFTF), an experimental power reactor in Hanford's 400 Area, was rendered permanently inoperable in the spring of 2005, when its core vessel was drilled as part of a long-debated deactivation. The loss of a "real good friend" was mourned by the Tri-Cities community, which had hoped to see the reactor participate in the nuclear revival sweeping the nation and world.[210] "The fight is over now on all fronts," editorialized the *Tri-City Herald*. "What this community should remember is that the Tri-Cities always recognized FFTF's potential as a national asset and remained a supporter of FFTF's restart until the end . . . despite the stupidity of its [DOE's] decision to abandon the plant."[211]

Opponents of the reactor's restart, mostly based in western Washington and Oregon, rejoiced at its demise. They had long called for DOE to "pull the plug" on the reactor. "Enough is enough," editorialized the *Seattle Times*. "Time is overdue to step beyond the point of no return."[212]

The FFTF—the reactor with nine lives—had received reprieve after reprieve after DOE announced a final decision to decommission it in late 2000.[213]

Built during the 1970s to be the prototype for America's breeder reactor program, the FFTF was a bridge to a newer, non-defense role for Hanford. A highly technical, highly prestigious venture, it seemed to point the way to "clean" energy while employing hundreds of people. However, the nation turned away from the breeder reactor concept in the early 1980s, and the FFTF had to supplement its DOE budget with paid experiments for other nuclear nations. Finally, the finances didn't add up anymore, and DOE issued a deactivation order for FFTF in December 1993.[214]

However, the FFTF's deactivation was placed on hold in 1996, when a private consortium of investors came forward and asked DOE for time to seek ways and means to obtain and operate it.[215] That year, an independent panel of technology experts commissioned by DOE reported that the FFTF could produce enough tritium per year to be a viable provider for DOE weapons-related tritium needs. Since the reactor could produce medical isotopes for commercial uses at the same time, and could rent facility space for experiments, the possibility of continued operation for FFTF temporarily became stronger.[216]

In the meantime, FFTF was also proposed as a potential supplier of plutonium 238 (Pu-238), the isotope used by the National Aeronautics and Space Administration to power deep-space probes. Cleanup and Hanford "watchdog" groups in the Northwest expressed intense opposition to both the tritium and Pu-238 missions for the FFTF. "The history of opposition to any nuclear restart at Hanford," explained Paige Knight, founder and president of Hanford Watch, "stems from the extensive and ominous contamination of land and groundwater from the production of plutonium for atomic bombs over the last 50 years. . . . Keeping the Fast Flux reactor on hot standby robs precious dollars from Hanford's diminishing cleanup budget. . . . The environmental community objects to the addition of any more waste streams that will increase threats to the Columbia River."[217]

In 1998, DOE announced that FFTF would not be used for tritium production.[218] The next year, DOE began preparing an EIS on various means for ensuring an adequate national supply of isotopes for medical, research, and industrial purposes. FFTF once again was a candidate for producing such isotopes, and so the reactor continued on standby. The draft EIS, released in 2000, identified alternatives ranging from restarting the FFTF for isotope production to permanently deactivating it with no new missions.[219]

Groups in the Hanford region, strongly polarized on the FFTF issue, immediately rallied their campaigns once again. "Kill the FFTF," argued the *Seattle Post-Intelligencer*. "Focus on Cleanup at Hanford. . . . Quit mothballing the facility [FFTF] and close it down for good," wrote the *Seattle Times*. Seven Oregon and Washington Congressional representatives and senators sent a letter to DOE protesting the "apparent bias of the EIS for Hanford's FFTF."[220] At the same time, a hearing in Richland brought out hundreds of FFTF supporters, while cancer survivors and others who wanted the reactor to produce isotopes petitioned the DOE.[221] In mid-2000, two DOE analyses deemed FFTF to be a reasonable choice for producing medical isotopes.[222]

Later that year, the DOE bowed to majority pressure in Washington state and announced the permanent deactivation of the FFTF.[223] Medical isotopes, it said, would be produced in other existing facilities.[224] However, the election of President George W. Bush, a supporter of nuclear energy, brought yet another twist in the long, convoluted decision path for FFTF. Bush's new Secretary of

Energy Spencer Abraham in April 2001 announced a ninety-day reprieve for further study of the FFTF. The two sides busily and vociferously joined the debate again.[225] In late 2001, DOE again announced permanent deactivation of the reactor.[226]

The FFTF had become a lightning rod for the rawest of regional feelings about environmental justice, trust and mistrust, nuclear fears and nuclear hopes, and image. The debate was not about facts anymore. In late 2002, DOE transferred the FFTF to its EM Office and began dismantling the reactor.[227] Although supporters fought on, draining of the rector's sodium coolant began in the spring of 2003. Although not a final death blow, sodium draining came close to rendering the facility inoperable. By the time that 40 percent of the coolant was drained in July 2003, the *Oregonian* gloated that the reactor had "passed [the] point that any new use is unlikely."[228]

In late 2005, about six months after the FFTF's core was drilled, permanently killing the machine, an audit by the DOE's Office of Inspector General pointed out a national shortage of medical isotopes. The *Tri-City Herald* said that the audit findings "felt . . . like a slap in the face. . . . The audit is a little like taking flowers to the cemetery. It's a nice gesture, but it doesn't change the past."[229] It was blunt, and it showed the extent to which the FFTF issue had abraded local and DOE partnering.

In April 2006, the FFTF was named a National Nuclear Historic Landmark by the American Nuclear Society. The *Tri-City Herald* called the honor "bittersweet."[230] At about the same time, DOE melded a study of how to dismantle FFTF into the larger EIS being prepared for Hanford's tanks and solid wastes. The question, basically, was whether to demolish the reactor, or simply to deactivate it and leave it in essentially "inert" condition on the landscape. By this time, many stakeholders were advocating spending minimal amounts of money to "mothball" and surveil FFTF, and spending cleanup dollars instead on Hanford's more urgent wastes.[231]

FMEF Closure Also Reflects Regional Debate

Also in Hanford's 400 Area, within yards of the FFTF, is the giant Fuels and Materials Examination Facility (FMEF). A companion facility to the FFTF, the FMEF was built to examine materials and nuclear fuels that had been irradiated in the FFTF. The idea was to check the fuels and materials for cracking, buckling, thinning, bulging, or any other signs of wear that they might show after experiencing the inferno of the fission reaction. In this manner, scientists could learn how to build better alloys and fuel blends that could withstand longer periods of safe irradiation for future world power needs. The ninety-eight-foot-tall FMEF has a footprint of nearly 48,000 square feet and contains nearly 190,000 square feet of operating space. Within that space are several "hot cells," completely enclosed and sealed areas where nuclear materials with radiation levels that deliver doses well beyond lethal levels within seconds can be examined safely.[232]

Because the FMEF's construction coincided with the national decision to suspend the breeder reactor program in the early 1980s, the facility was never quite finished on the inside. The portals and remote manipulators that would work inside the hot cells were not completed, and no radioactive materials were ever brought inside the giant edifice. By 1995, it was devoid of almost all missions, and DOE offered the facility for sale or lease. It was considered as a Hollywood movie set, a prison, and a safe storage facility for various commercial uses.[233]

However, like the FFTF, the FMEF became a lightning rod for controversy. In 1997, it was named in a national DOE ROD on the storage and disposition of weapons-usable fissile materials as a potential place to handle nuclear materials taken out of U.S. weapons that were in excess of need. The ROD specified that the United States would continue to pursue a two-track approach that could allow for immobilization of surplus plutonium in glass or ceramic material (essentially vitrification), and for burning some of the surplus plutonium as mixed oxide (MOX) fuel in existing commercial reactors.

The FMEF was a candidate facility on the latter track, known as the "reactor burn" option, in that its hot cells could house the steps necessary to convert metallic plutonium into oxide powder, blend the powder with other oxide materials, sinter the blend into pellets, and load and weld the pellets into fuel assemblies. The fuel could then be burned in any commercial U.S. reactor to make electric power. DOE's technical evaluation of candidate sites stated that the "FMEF is well suited to accomplish the MOX fabrication mission . . . [because] the facility has adequate space to house fabrication . . . while achieving desirable process flow, operational flexibility and maintenance and operations support."[234]

Around the region, the familiar polarizations became unmistakably evident. A 1997 hearing in Richland drew almost universal praise for the FMEF MOX fabrication and reactor burn option. The "Hanford Communities," an organization consisting of the Tri-Cities, West Richland, and Benton County, lobbied hard to use the FMEF for the MOX mission, basing its arguments on national cost savings and economic benefit to the region. However, the Communities' statement was blunt: "It is not clear that the Department of Energy's decision-making process will appropriately consider the benefits, cost savings and synergy of locating all of these processes in one existing federal facility [the FMEF]. ... In light of our experience in working with DOE ... the Hanford Communities are concerned that a thorough and fair process will be followed."[235]

At a hearing in Portland, much of the crowd expressed the view that a MOX mission for the FMEF simply amounted to another "corporate welfare scheme for a nuclear power industry that is on its last legs." One man stated flatly that such a mission was just a back-door way to build up Hanford's nuclear infrastructure: "All of the incentives will be in place to promote the continuation of a ... plutonium recycling program which can then embody such proposals as reliance on breeder reactors or plutonium separation from backlogged nuclear wastes." The Oregon Legislature voted nearly unanimously to ask then-President Bill Clinton to honor the traditional separation of the commercial nuclear industry and the weapons complex and disallow MOX fuel fabrication from weapons-grade Pu.[236]

In 1998, unsurprisingly, DOE announced that the Hanford Site had been ruled out as a candidate for plutonium disposition work. The FMEF was shut down shortly afterward. In 1999, DOE awarded a contract to a consortium of companies to build a MOX fabrication plant at its Savannah River Site. The MOX would be burned on a test basis at commercial reactors in Virginia and North Carolina.[237] Clearly in the Hanford region, the legacy of fairness and fear, trust and mistrust, still lay at the core of debates and decisions.

Nuclear Resurgence—Will Hanford Have a Role?
It began even before September 11, 2001. In response to unmistakable signs of global warming, the United States, Britain, other European countries, and Canada all began talking about a resurgence in generating and using nuclear power. In early 2001, the powerful New Mexico Senator Peter Domenici introduced legislation to expand research into nuclear power generation, and Vice President Richard Cheney said that constructing new nuclear power plants would reduce the greenhouse gases that cause global warming more effectively than international efforts to cut such emissions. However, critics immediately raised the ugly issue of what to do with nuclear waste.[238]

After September 11, 2001, the tilt toward more nuclear power increased. Dependence on foreign oil seemed a path toward national suicide, and demands for nuclear power grew.[239] By 2005, high gasoline prices, raised by the Iraq War and other market disruptions, added yet another substantial reason to reexamine the nuclear option. That year, real signs of a nuclear renaissance were in the air. The Energy Policy Act of 2005 included some benefits for new nuclear power plants such as insurance, protection against permit delays, and other subsidized advantages. From the political right and left, major leaders placed their support behind new nuclear initiatives.[240]

In 2006, talk of new nuclear power plants was everywhere. Even major environmental groups that had long opposed them, notably Greenpeace, announced support for new nuclear power plants.[241] Did America need to get "up and atom"? Was nuclear power the "atomic balm" for a battered U.S. environment and economy? President Bush earmarked funds in the proposed federal budget for FY 2007 to develop plans and locate facilities to generate power by nuclear means and to recycle the spent fuel into new MOX fuel. The recycling concept—once known as reprocessing—had been rejected soundly during the administration of President Jimmy Carter in the late 1970s and had essentially been banned from debates in the United States ever since.[242]

However, nearly everyone discussing the possibility of a nuclear rebirth in 2006 identified nuclear waste—and the national failure to open a repository to store it—as the Achilles heel of nuclear power. "If nuclear power generation is to have any credibility, the federal government must manage existing waste," editorialized the *Seattle Post-Intelligencer*.[243] "Nuclear power should not be given a free pass in our frantic quest for energy and environmental security," said the *New York Times*.[244] "As the nation rushes back to the future by embracing atomic energy, the industry and government have to solve one . . . problem: . . . how to deal with nuclear waste. . . . The deadly radioactive waste that nuclear power plants produce . . . [has] been a smoldering problem," wrote the *Washington Post*.[245]

As the question of new nuclear power plants rose to prominence, still unremediated sites like Hanford stuck out like "sore thumbs" once again. Although Hanford was not primarily a power plant, but a weapons production site, it and the other polluted old defense sites stood as naked reminders of the failure of the past to grapple effectively with nuclear waste, and of the intransigence of those wastes once they reach the environment. The Hanford region wanted badly to play in the new nuclear arena. But Washington state's senators and governor said firmly that Hanford's wastes must be dealt with first.

In September 2006, the Hanford region's primary economic development organization submitted a grant application to DOE headquarters to study whether a new nuclear power plant and recycling facility could be built on Hanford land. Later that year, President Bush's Global Nuclear Energy Partnership selected the Hanford region's proposal, and those from ten other interested locations around the nation, with community and state support for the proposed facilities as a requirement. The site of Hanford's FMEF and many of the support facilities built for it and the FFTF, as well as other relatively uncontaminated Hanford land and resources, were proposed.[246]

Would Hanford stand a chance? Local citizens pointed to their long experience, training, and comfort level with things nuclear. The greater Pacific Northwest wanted power, but it also wanted waste cleanup to remain Hanford's priority. Like everything else in the Hanford region, the debates and issues were polarizing, daunting, infuriating, and heartfelt. Time would tell whether Hanford could play a role in the nation's nuclear reawakening.

Hanford Carves Role in Post–Cold War Disarmament, Nonproliferation Issues

Without question, one of the most spectacular events of the late twentieth century was the end of the Cold War, the longest and most expensive (in dollars) in modern history. It ended in 1991, when the Soviet Union dissolved into fifteen separate republics. Late that year, U.S. President George H. W. Bush announced the largest cuts in nuclear weapons ever undertaken since such weapons became part of the American arsenal. In January 1993, just before leaving office, Bush signed the second Strategic Arms Reduction Treaty (START II) with Russian President Boris Yeltsin.

In 1994, President Clinton signed a protocol with President Yeltsin to cease plutonium production. At about the same time, Clinton identified nearly 40 percent of the weapons-grade plutonium (Pu-239) produced in total by the United States to exceed the country's needs, including all of the Pu-239 remaining at the Hanford Site. In 1997, Vice President Albert Gore and Russian Prime Minister Viktor Chernomyrdin signed a Plutonium Production Reactor Agreement, and lower-tier officials signed the Core Conversion Implementing Agreement (CCIA). These agreements essentially pledged the United States to assist in converting reactors in the Commonwealth of Independent States (CIS) so that they did not produce weapons-grade plutonium at the same time they provided heat and electricity for domestic consumption. Russia's three remaining, operating production reactors, two near Sversk and one near Zheleznogorsk, were designated for the cooperative conversion project.[247]

Other key U.S. cooperative programs with the Russian Federation, with the government of Kazakhstan (home of the CIS's huge nuclear weapons test site at Semipalatinsk), and with other CIS and former Eastern bloc governments grew in the 1990s. Irony, hope, and history merged dramatically on a stifling July day in 1994, when high-ranking representatives of Russia's Ministry of Atomic Energy (MINATOM) and various scientific and nuclear institutes in Russia toured Hanford's PFP, even entering the tightly guarded Pu storage vaults. During that visit, two Cold Warriors who had been adversaries in the national security business for over thirty years, shook hands in PFP's central alarm station and promised to work together to dismantle the fearful SNM they were inspecting. "We make a good team," said Jack Keliher, then director of DOE's Office of Nonproliferation and National Security, to Nikolai Yegorov, deputy minister of MINATOM. An awe-struck silence filled the control station, as armed guards and plant workers watched former committed adversaries converse as fellow humans interested in a different future.[248]

By that time, the Hanford Site was deeply engaged in new cooperative missions with its former adversaries in the CIS and the East European nations that had formerly been members of the mutual defense Warsaw Pact. The Pacific Northwest National Laboratory (PNNL), located at Hanford, provides technical leadership for many cooperative programs with the CIS and the former Eastern bloc through its Center for Global Security, opened in 1998.[249] PNNL took a leading role in helping to secure the Chornobyl site and safeguard the remains of the reactor where the world's worst nuclear accident took place in 1986.[250] The laboratory also assisted Kazakhstan in oil and gas exploration, helped develop training programs for customs officials to detect nuclear smuggling, helped MINATOM in groundwater contamination studies in Siberia, and invented a nuclear weapons test explosion detection device for treaty-verification purposes.[251] In late 2001, it formed the Institute for Global and Regional Security Studies with the University of Washington in Seattle.[252]

In 2000, the White House signed an agreement between Gore and Russian Prime Minister Mikhail Kasyanov to reduce the excess stockpile of nuclear weapons materials in each of the two nation's reserves by thirty-four tons. The excess materials would be burned in nuclear power reactors or immobilized with radioactive waste for disposition in repositories.[253] At the same time, the Secretary of Energy announced that the United States would help the CSI build two large new storage facilities at Vladivostok, Russia, for SNF from Russian nuclear submarines decommissioned under treaty agreements.[254] Importantly, in 2000, President Clinton reached agreements with President Vladimir Putin of Russia to help the CIS to finance a MOX fabrication plant to convert about thirty-three metric tons of CIS weapons-grade plutonium into reactor fuel.[255]

However, although new pacts for cooperation, reactor conversion, and MOX burning were signed in 2001 and 2002, implementation lagged. By 2003, core conversion of the three plutonium-producing reactors had not begun, and interim upgrades were authorized. PNNL managed the interface with Russian scientists on the upgrades project, although U.S. engineering companies were contracted to perform the physical work.[256] Two issues—the unwillingness of CIS to provide liability protection to U.S. companies working on science and engineering projects in Russia, and disputes over physical inspections of CIS nuclear sites—held back MOX and other cooperative projects.[257] In August 2006, a new agreement to shut down the three Russian reactors by 2010 was finally announced.[258]

Hanford Regional Economy Strong despite Federal Budget Rollercoaster

Since the early 1960s when President Lyndon Johnson announced that Hanford's reactors would begin to close, the economy of the Tri-Cities and the Hanford region has tried to diversify to blunt its dependence on the federal government. In 1963, Tri-Cities bankers, businessmen, and other economic development leaders formed the Tri-Cities Nuclear Industrial Council (TRIC-NIC) and worked with the AEC and Washington's Congressional delegation to require new contractors coming into Hanford to create non-Hanford businesses. Later, when the atom began to lose its glamour and anti-nuclear forces gained strength throughout the United States, Tri-Cities leaders reconfigured TRICNIC as TRIDEC (Tri-Cities Industrial Development Council). Economic diversification efforts produced only marginal results before the 1990s, however. When the DOE announced that N Reactor would remain closed in 1988, dependence on federal dollars was yet so strong that the Hanford area sank into a recession.[259] However, waste cleanup dollars soon flooded in, and by 1994, Hanford's budget stood at $1.88 billion and site employment had soared to nearly 18,000—thousands above the number of workers employed in the highest defense production years.

The budget cuts of FY 1995 then created fear in the region. About six thousand workers were laid off that year alone, and the area's need and desire to diversify its economy away from dependence on DOE became sharp. In 1995, DOE decided to procure a new Hanford Site "management and integration" (M&I) contractor team. The M&I contractor would be selected and financially rewarded partially on the basis of its commitment to create private sector jobs to replace government jobs in the region. In 1996, an M&I team led by the Fluor Daniel Corporation of California was selected and began managing nearly three-fourths of Hanford's cleanup work, partly on the strength of its pledge to create three thousand commercial jobs in the Hanford area.[260]

Fluor brought a new Project Hanford Management Contract (PHMC) structure to Hanford. Under this arrangement, six major companies teamed with Fluor as subcontractors, and six additional companies known as "enterprise companies" (ENCOS) were spun off on the first day of the contract. The ENCOS were to be hybrids, given Hanford Site work during an initial development period but mandated to develop private sector work while being weaned off government work.[261] Hanford's people were intrigued. Yet, their micro-knowledge of their own unique, milestone-driven world made them wary. DOE dollars still dominated. How could it be more efficient to work with thirteen companies, thirteen legal and thirteen human resources departments, and thirteen sets of high-level managers and still meet cleanup milestones driven by tight budgetary constraints?

It was not. In 1999, Fluor announced a massive restructuring at Hanford, ending the PHMC concept and bringing its remaining subcontractors into partnership within "Fluor Hanford, Inc." (FH). At the same time, the subcontractor company that had been performing tank waste remediation work under the PHMC umbrella became an independent contractor to the DOE's newly formed ORP. Some of the ENCOs achieved self-sustaining status and some did not. Essentially, the ENCOs had either become private businesses (albeit with some special contractual ties to FH) by 1999, or they had been reabsorbed into FH.[262] Working with TRIDEC and the local cities, counties, and ports, FH did help create nearly three thousand new jobs by late 2000. When its initial Hanford contract expired in 2001, it was renewed without most of the private business creation provisions.[263]

In the meanwhile, however, the real Cinderella story was the private sector— the Hanford regional economy itself. By late 2000, it was breaking all historical records for employment, housing, retail sales, population growth, school enrollment, housing starts, business starts, apartment occupancy rates, tourism, and every other economic indicator.[264] *Washington CEO* magazine summed up the situation in February 2000 when it wrote: "The federal government's decision to lay off thousands of workers at the Hanford Nuclear Reservation threatened to return the Tri-Cities to desert dust. It didn't happen. Instead, an entrepreneurial spirit has sprung from Hanford's downsizing. Unemployed white collar workers stayed to carve their own destinies in the dry, sunny climate 200 miles from Seattle. Business leaders focused their economic development efforts on attracting private industries such as metals and manufacturing, food processing, and high-tech spinoffs. It seems to be working."[265]

The positive trends continued. In late 2005, the Tri-Cities ranked ninth out of 171 small cities for entrepreneurs in the nation by the National Research Council and *Entrepreneur Magazine*.[266] In early 2006, the Milken Institute of Santa Monica, California, ranked it seventh on a list of 379 smaller metropolitan areas in the United States in terms of job and wage growth.[267] By early 2006, the Tri-Cities population stood at nearly 200,000—astonishingly nearly double that of 1990. There were approximately 99,000 private sector jobs, as compared to 75,700 jobs in September 1994 just before the large Hanford lay-offs began. The Hanford Site budget for FY 2006 stood at $1.7 billion, with $1.8 billion proposed for FY 2007. Hanford workers still average the highest pay in the region.[268]

Public/Tribal Involvement Evolve as Way of Life at Hanford, and Secrecy Abates Somewhat

Opening the doors of secrecy embodied in the creation of citizen advisory boards, Indian tribal consultations, DOE openness initiatives, and document declassifications is a harbinger of palpable change.

In 1991, when the U.S. Senate Committee on Armed Services asked the Office of Technology Assessment (OTA) to conduct an independent evaluation of concerns about and possible solutions to the problems of defense wastes, OTA identified "public skepticism of DOE's decision-making process" as a key barrier. To improve public credibility and trust, OTA recommended the creation of citizen/tribal advisory boards at each DOE site.

That year, DOE formed a citizen/tribal group in the Hanford region to discuss the future uses of site lands that would be freed by cleanup for potential non-DOE uses. Called the "Hanford Future Site Uses Working Group," it had representatives from agriculture, environmental groups, official agencies, local and state governments, regional Indian nations and tribes, economic development and business interests, education, labor, Hanford watchdog/activity groups, and a few members representing the public at large. In late 1992, this group produced a report outlining its values and priorities for the region and then translated those values into specific recommendations for future land uses.[269]

The trend toward public involvement continued. In 1993, then–Energy Secretary Hazel O'Leary came to the Hanford region for the first Hanford Summit. Primarily aimed at economic development and diversification planning, the summit series also served as a forum at which O'Leary heard the views of diverse stakeholders in special sessions. The following year, the Hanford Advisory Board (HAB) was created as an ongoing, funded group of area stakeholders that meets several times a year. Composed of representatives of many of the same interests as the Hanford Future Site Uses Working Group had been, the HAB also has site employee representatives and more representatives from the public at large. The *Tri-City Herald* has called the HAB "a rambunctious, sometimes unwieldy coalition that derives its political strength from the fact that any positions it officially takes require the nearly unanimous support of about thirty different Northwest constituencies."[270]

The HAB reviews all major Hanford Site initiatives, plans, and budgets, and often responds to the DOE and its regulators with advice that is blunt. No matter the specific advice, the intent and message from the HAB to DOE is clear: We exist, we matter, we have a right to know, don't try to leave us out because (or if) we are not "technical." And most of all: We don't want or need the federal government to act like Big Brother in our home anymore! By mid-2006, the HAB had issued 189 letters of advice to the DOE at Hanford and was focusing intently on rivershore cleanup and the timetable for the tank waste vitrification plant.[271]

Beginning in December 1993, O'Leary shocked many when she held a series of nearly breathtaking press conferences. She divulged the amounts and whereabouts of SNM produced throughout the DOE complex, previous weapons tests (including many formerly unannounced tests), and other topics never before made public. In January 1994, she asked the National Academy of Sciences to form a committee to advise the DOE on priorities and methods for declassifying and publicly releasing millions of pages of documents it held in secrecy.[272]

The Academy's report recommended sweeping changes in DOE's basic classification principles. The DOE should, said the report, minimize the areas of information that are classified; shift the burden of proof to those who argue for classification and not place it on those who argue for declassification; change its philosophy from "the current emphasis on 'risk avoidance' to 'risk management'"; enhance openness and public access; and take the initiative to declassify documents and to define information subject to classification.[273]

In response, the DOE launched a major declassification project to review all of the classified documents at its various major sites. At Hanford, turning away from congenital secrecy was hard, but the site's declassification project declassified approximately two million pages of documents, while keeping about another 20 percent classified according to strict guidelines. It also declassified thousands of site photos and in 2000 opened a Web site where it placed an index of nearly 90,000 previously classified photographs.[274] The project then reviewed and declassified many document abstracts that in some cases were the only remaining parts of documents that no longer existed in their entirety.

After the attacks of September 11, 2001, many government websites—including those of the U.S. DOE—either stopped releasing or withdrew documents from the public domain to review the available information. Archives also withdrew thousands of documents. Maps and photographs were especially targeted for review. At Hanford, information about the PFP, reactors, high-level waste tank farms, and spent nuclear fuel storage areas were closely examined. Interest groups wrote to the Energy Secretary, asking DOE to justify the guidelines it was using for the document reviews and warning that legitimate public access to information should not suffer.[275]

By 2006, it was clear that mistakes had been made in the flight from openness after September 11. A General Accountability Office report in March of that year found that DOE needed more oversight in handling, re-marking, and restricting information. The House Committee on Government Reform concurred and unanimously approved a bill for procedures to assure that sensitive—but unclassified—information was not capriciously withheld from the public. The National Archives confirmed that more than one-third of the twenty-five hundred historical documents withdrawn since 1999 did not contain sensitive information justifying classification.[276] In August 2006, the public learned that the numbers of weapons in the U.S. nuclear arsenal during the Cold War—openly shared since 1971—had been redacted by the Pentagon and the DOE.[277]

The balance was and is difficult to achieve. Some Hanford information, although old, is not innocuous. It is of great interest to weapons proliferators and dirty-bomb makers who want simple technologies not reliant on computers that can be assembled in fairly primitive surroundings. Yet, the United States is a democracy and requires broad citizen access to information. Although information about Hanford is more openly available today than it was during the site's first fifty years, vigilance is needed to guard freedom and at the same time guard the site's dangerous old secrets.

Health Studies: The Sad Toll of Wars Fought at Hanford

On the night of February 3, 2000, the tone in Richland's Federal Building Auditorium was hushed, as it is when emotions run deep. Area residents had gathered at the request of Dr. David Michaels, a representative of DOE headquarters on a special assignment to hear testimony about health problems at major sites around the DOE complex. One by one, members of an audience of about five hundred stepped forward to tell Michaels, sometimes haltingly, sometimes tearfully, and occasionally angrily, about old family secrets. Fathers, husbands, sons, wives, mothers, and daughters spoke of seeing strong loved-ones sicken and die from cancers and from ailments more mysterious and hard to diagnose. Miscarriages, stillbirths, infertility, shortness of breath, dizziness, inability to digest food, rashes that tore at the skin, and other afflictions were described by the sick and the family members of those not able to attend or unwilling to talk.

The hearing was historic, because Hanford workers and their families had never told such stories in public before. These people had worked the hazardous jobs everyday feeling that the work was more than just a job, it was a noble and patriotic duty. Yet, this night they opened the curtains to the dark underside of their world. "Hanford Workers Break Silence," said the *Seattle Post Intelligencer* the next day. The *Tri-City Herald* commented: "It breaks no new ground to say a link likely exists between health problems and radiation. . . . But at least the federal government is now joining the chorus of people who see the link."[278]

Just ahead of the hearing, the White House had released a draft report by the National Economic Council stating that America's Cold War nuclear workers "may be at increased risk of illness." Studying workers at the fourteen largest U.S. nuclear weapons sites, the report found "credible evidence" of increased health risks, including increased risks for twenty-two types of cancer, due to exposure to ionizing radiation and chemical and physical hazards. The news, said the *Tri-City Herald*, "hit Hanford like a lightning bolt from one of the sudden summer storms that sweep over the nuclear reservation." The Secretary of Energy stated in late January that "the Department of Energy is coming clean with its workers."[279]

Two months after the Richland hearing, DOE announced a Clinton administration initiative that would compensate workers, former DOE site workers, and/or the survivors of workers who have or had a variety of job-related illnesses. Vice President Gore stated that "for decades, the government ignored mounting evidence that workers who were contributing to our nation's defense were themselves being put at risk. . . . While we cannot undo their suffering, today . . . [we] begin the process of healing by admitting the government's mistakes, designing a process for compensating these workers for their suffering and by becoming an advocate for Department of Energy workers."[280]

The Energy Employees' Occupational Illness Compensation Act (EEOICA) became law on October 30, 2000. Specific provisions provided lump sum payments or a package of benefits including lost wages, medical expenses, and job retraining for workers with radiation related cancers and with illnesses caused by exposure to beryllium, silica, asbestos, heavy metals, chemicals, and other substances. Benefits for survivors, including workers' children and surviving spouses, were added later.[281]

However, the rules and administration of the compensation programs soon drew criticism. By summer 2002, approximately sixty-three hundred claims had been filed by former Hanford workers, but none had been paid. At a hearing in Richland, workers were "angry, confused and frustrated with the . . . program, and not in a mood to listen." They shouted at DOE officials because they had found that their dose and exposure records, and their work histories, were incomplete, nonexistent, or inaccessible. They said that their claims simply languished.[282] In April 2003, the first claim under the EEOICA was paid to a retired Hanford worker. Only twenty-two cancer claims had been paid by early 2004, and late that year the U.S. Congress, fed up, transferred administration of the program away from the DOE to the Department of Labor (DOL).[283]

Complaints about slow service, lost claims, and summary denials of claims surfaced again by mid-2005. A bipartisan group of House representatives and senators wrote to the Secretary of Labor that summer, questioning the program's responsiveness.[284] Complaints continued. In May 2006, the administration of President George W. Bush proposed a 50 percent reduction in the compensation program.[285] In July 2006, in response to financial and other proposed changes by the Bush administration, a bill was introduced in Congress to give that body greater influence over how the program is conducted.[286] By that time, nearly $100 million in claims had been paid to ill Hanford workers.[287]

In the meantime, a number of important health studies that included data and cases from Hanford's work force went forward or were completed. A NIOSH study examining the relationship between multiple myeloma (a cancer of blood-forming tissues) and occupational exposure to ionizing radiation at four DOE sites including Hanford was completed in early 1998. The study found slightly elevated occurrences of multiple myeloma in older workers.[288] Another NIOSH study, this one looking at mortality among female nuclear weapons workers found increased relative risk for leukemia, with less definitive—although "associated"—increased risk for breast cancer and other cancers.[289] Yet another NIOSH study examined the relationship between lung cancer and exposure to external ionizing radiation in Hanford's reactor-area workers as well as workers at other DOE sites. Published in 2005, it found no increased cancer rate when age at exposure was not considered, but "radiation doses [received] at age 55 and above were more strongly associated with lung cancer mortality."[290]

In January 1999, the draft of a long-awaited study funded by the U.S. Centers for Disease Control (CDC) reported no increased incidence of thyroid disease in persons who had lived in the Hanford region as children during the years 1944–57. The draft results, which became a bellwether for views pro and con about Hanford itself, were reviewed by the National Research Council and found to be overstated, although the study design itself was deemed sound. The study's final report in 2002 agreed with the draft results.[291]

Later that year, a beryllium support group was formed at Hanford after initial tests by the University of Washington in 1998 found several cases of beryllium sensitization. By December 1999, two confirmed cases of chronic beryllium disease, along with eight specific cases of heightened sensitivity to beryllium had been confirmed. Beryllium is a light gray metal that was used during uranium fuel fabrication work at Cold War Hanford. Grinding of the metal had led to lung disease or susceptibility to lung disease in the workers identified.[292]

In mid-2006, a study of cancer rates near Hanford, funded by original site contractor DuPont, found no increase in cancer deaths in the counties near Hanford, as compared to control counties. However, that July, the Hanford Birth Cohort Study (funded by the CDC) found "the strongest potential link to date" between growing up near Hanford and having thyroid disease. The study determined a statistically significant increase in hypothyroidism among males who grew up near Hanford.[293]

Historic Lawsuits: Remembering in Anger

In 1990, the lawsuits began. Two major class action lawsuits were filed in Federal Court for the Eastern District of Washington in Spokane, the same location where Judge Schwellenbach had issued the orders of land condemnation that had created the Hanford Site forty-seven years earlier. The 1990 lawsuits were class action charges by many of Hanford's "downwinder" neighbors against the site's operating contractors over the years. The suits alleged that both health and property in the region had been adversely affected by Hanford operations. Since the government cannot be sued for operating facilities deemed to be in the national interest, the contractors were named as defendants.

Later that year, members of the Yakima Indian Nation and some residents of northeastern Oregon filed two more such lawsuits. In 1991, these four lawsuits, along with another similar case, were consolidated by Federal Judge Alan MacDonald. In 1993, two additional huge class action suits were filed by Hanford downwinders, asking for medical care for thousands of eastern Washington and Oregon residents.[294]

By mid-1994, the GAO reported that law firms representing former Hanford contractors were running up massive bills, paid by the federal government (taxpayers), with little or no DOE oversight regarding "allowable costs." Real embarrassment for the agency came in November when the Spokane *Spokesman - Review* called the legal fees charged by defendant firms "corporate welfare." The newspaper wrote: "Of all the people cashing in on the Hanford windfall, few are benefiting as handsomely as the lawyers. . . . Taxpayers paid the contractors who made Hanford's mess, and now pay again to defend the companies against any harm they may have done. . . . The contractors rack up huge bills at premium rates. . . . The result is out-of-control legal costs." New costing rules were implemented and some further consolidation of the suits took place, but the GAO charged again in mid-1996 that more could and should be done to control defendant expenses.[295]

In August 1998, Judge MacDonald dismissed the claims of most of the approximately forty-five hundred plaintiffs in Hanford's historical lawsuits. He ruled that scientific evidence about radiation injury was too complex for a jury to determine and wrote in his 760-page ruling that a jury's consideration could lead to "an erroneous conclusion that exposure to Hanford emissions was a cause in fact of an individual's disease." MacDonald did allow the claims of a small percentage of the plaintiffs to proceed, including some with thyroid cancer and those who could prove they had received a dose of at least five rads[296] of radioiodine when their ages ranged from infancy to age four at the time of exposure, ten rads from ages five to nine, thirty-three rads from ages ten to nineteen, and one hundred rads for those twenty and older.[297] In mid-1999, MacDonald limited the number of plaintiffs in a parallel lawsuit to about one hundred, out of the original group of about thirteen hundred that had filed.[298]

At roughly the same time, another federal judge, Edward Shea, dismissed a suit brought by a group of approximately fourteen thousand downwinders who had asked the DOE to pay about $13 million for medical monitoring. The judge ruled that the plaintiffs, as private citizens, did not have the right to sue the federal government under the "Superfund"[299] law.[300] In mid-2000, however, a new lawsuit asking $100 billion was filed by seventeen selected plaintiffs against thirteen past and present Hanford Site contractors, claiming damages from World War II and Cold War radiation releases. The complaint also asked the judge to expand the lawsuit into a class action claim on behalf of 10,000–14,000 people who lived in or visited the Hanford area during the Second World War and the early Cold War. The complaint alleged that the contractors "irradiated thousands of unsuspecting men, women and children without their consent through their activities" at Hanford.[301]

In 2002, a U.S. District Court of Appeals overturned MacDonald's limitations on the downwinder cases and said the lawsuits could go forward. The new ruling was hailed as a "huge victory" by lawyers for the downwinders.[302] In early 2003, MacDonald came under pressure when it was disclosed that he owned orchard land in the downwind area on the east side of the Columbia River from Hanford. Critics said that MacDonald had a financial interest in showing that the land was not contaminated. He recused himself from the downwinder lawsuits that March.[303]

By spring, the new judge, William Nielsen, ruled that he would move the then twelve-year-old cases along by having attorneys pick a few "bellwether" plaintiffs and begin trial soon. Although this method would resolve only a few cases quickly, it could guide other claims toward settlement or dismissal.[304] Nielsen sold his stock in General Electric—one of the defendant contractor companies—in order to preclude an appearance of bias in the cases.[305] He also ruled that the plaintiffs did not have to prove that the contractor companies who operated Hanford had been negligent—they only had to prove that their health had been harmed substantially by Hanford's emissions. The defendants, he ruled, could not argue that they couldn't be held liable for injuries caused by radioactive releases simply because they were acting on federal orders.[306]

In April 2005, the trial of the bellwether plaintiffs opened to a packed courtroom in Spokane. A month later, the jury ruled that Hanford's emissions had probably caused thyroid cancer in two plaintiffs and awarded them $545,000 collectively. It rejected the claims of three other plaintiffs and deadlocked on the case of one more. Later that year, Nielsen denied a motion for a new trial for a woman on whose case the first jury had deadlocked. The unsuccessful plaintiffs appealed their 2005 decisions, and the defendants offered a settlement to a large group of downwinders waiting to pursue their own cases. As of late 2006, the appeals process and the waiting were still continuing.[307]

Consensus Emerges in Region about Columbia River

The end of DOE's plutonium production mission at the Hanford Site also ended its preeminent right to use the bordering Columbia River to further defense production needs. However, in perhaps the most outstanding example of unintended consequences in a place well known for such surprises, it turned out that the "Hanford Reach" of the Columbia River (the fifty-two-mile stretch from the northwestern site border downstream to just above Richland, Washington) had been preserved as one of the most ideal salmon breeding habitats left in the Pacific Northwest. In a region in love with the tradition and romance of salmon, but unprepared to sacrifice development goals to preserve them, the Hanford Reach in the 1990s came to stand as the last stretch on the fourteen-hundred-mile river that might be able to prevent the extinction of several salmon and other fish, bird, insect, and plant species.

Likewise, the fate of two wildlife preserves occupying nearly ninety thousand acres of border lands just north of the Columbia, across from the site's 100 Areas, became entwined with that of the Reach. These preserves, owned by DOE but managed by state and federal wildlife agencies, also would need to be preserved from economic development in order for the habitat of the Reach to remain viable. Irrigated farming of this North Slope (or "Wahluke Slope") land would cause landslides into the river from the chalky White Bluffs that would destroy salmon spawning and feeding areas. Landslides also could divert the Columbia into Hanford's 100 Areas, destroying important cultural and archeological sites and releasing buried contamination that could pollute the great river all the way to its mouth. The presence of farm chemicals in the water would upset the unique and fragile eco-balance, and any damming or dredging, of course, would be ruinous to salmon habitat.[308]

In the early 1990s, the rapidly changing roles, missions, and rules in the Hanford region set the stage for an intense battle between environmentalists and corporate farm developers. "Save the Reach" bumper stickers, T-shirts, and hats sprouted like the waving bunch grass of the land itself. Deeply rooted in the events of the last sixty years, this debate wore many disguises—most notably that it was a contest over local versus national control. However, it was fundamentally a debate over economic development and heritage and about how—or whether—the two can live in balance in a world of diminishing resources.

Men and women who had become county commissioners in the farm areas had been raised to believe that the Hanford Project upset plans to turn the whole Columbia Basin into a rival of California's Central Valley in food production. Environmentalists pointed to the "time-stood-still" natural heritage of the Hanford Reach and the North Slope in terms of salmon, steelhead, eagles, sage grouse, rare bunch grasses and shrub-steppe habitat, and many other endangered or threatened animal, insect, and plant species. Because the existence of the Hanford Site kept developers and irrigators away, the wildlife of the area appeared as it had decades ago, and as it appeared virtually nowhere else in the American West. Surveys of parts of the Hanford Site in the mid-1990s by the Nature Conservancy of Washington, a private environmental group, identified over eight hundred species that were rare, threatened, of conservation concern, or new to science.[309]

Salmon restoration plans mandated by the federal courts are expensive. Saving the Hanford Reach was seen as the least expensive of all such plans, and the most effective, by regional environmentalists. They maintained that the recreational value and sheer, drop-dead beauty of the river winding past the open Slope was a quality of life issue that could help attract high-tech companies with discerning work forces to diversify the economy of the nearby Tri-Cities as Hanford operations closed down.[310]

State and regional politicians at all levels, and almost every regional group and newspaper, aligned themselves for or against the preservation position. The DOE, after receiving over five hundred comments, petitions, and requests identified the conservation, preservation, habitat, and recreational use for the Slope and river corridor as its preferred alternative in its Final Comprehensive Land Use Plan EIS.[311] However, the question was made moot on June 9, 2000, when President Clinton declared nearly 200,000 acres along the Reach, and on other Hanford border lands, as a National Monument.[312] The Hanford Reach

National Monument is now managed by the U.S. Fish and Wildlife Service (USFWS), by agreement with DOE, just as USFWS has managed approximately 77,000 acres of uncontaminated Hanford land called the Arid Lands Ecology Reserve (ALE) since 1997.[313]

The National Monument designation was hailed by major media and others as good for tourism and for the image of the Hanford region. The *Seattle Post Intelligencer* commented: "Having a national monument resplendent with wild fish, birds and animals—especially adjoining a nuclear site—promises to help counteract the negative public relations image that too long has dogged the Tri-Cities."[314] The "wasteland to treasure" theme was echoed by many others, and even local citizens opposed to preservation had to admit that the image change could only be good for the regional economy.[315]

Less than three weeks after the Hanford Reach National Monument was designated, a huge fire swept across it, devestating the rare shrub-steppe habitat. The entire Hanford Site went into emergency alert status, as the fire burned southeast toward the Tri-Cities and Benton City.

On the night of June 28, 2000, this fire became the fastest-growing wildfire in the United States in the previous ten years, when it jumped from 27,500 acres to 150,000 acres and traveled twenty miles in just ninety minutes. In its fierce progression, the fire became the most intense in Hanford's history. Eventually, the fire gobbled up 164,000 acres of ALE and other National Monument lands managed by USFWS.[316] After the fire, the USFWS received a $6 million federal restoration grant. In late 2004, it completed planting approximately one million sagebrush seedlings and other native plants.[317]

In the meantime, the Service formed a local steering committee representing a wide variety of interests in 2001, to help form a management plan—known as a Comprehensive Conservation Plan—to guide use policies on the vast monument. After much work, the plan was drafted and made available for public comment in 2006.[318]

In 2003, a consortium of groups including the USFWS, the nonprofit Friends of the Reach, the Tri-Cities Visitor and Convention Bureau, a small local museum, and the Richland Public Facilities District broke ground for a dynamic new museum to be called the Hanford Reach National Monument Heritage and Visitors Center. When it opens, this center will interpret the unique history of the Hanford Reach, the campaign to save it, the Ice Age Floods that carved the lovely Columbia Basin, the Hanford Site's significant history, and other regional histories.[319] As such, it already symbolizes a remarkable healing process in the Hanford region, bringing together factions with vastly different views in a common effort to understand and come to terms with their history.

278

Preserving B Reactor as Hanford's Voice

B Reactor (105–B Building) at the Hanford Site is the first full-scale nuclear reactor in the world. It was unlike the only two test reactors built before it—the Chicago Pile I (CP-I) built by Enrico Fermi under the squash court seats at Stagg Field at the University of Chicago in 1942, and the X-10 Reactor at the Manhattan Project's Clinton Engineer Works (now the DOE Oak Ridge Site) in Tennessee in 1943. B Reactor was massive by comparison to the previous two pilot-scale reactors, but it was also different in so many engineering aspects that there is no real basis for comparison.

The most salient difference was that B Reactor was water-cooled. Its cooling water was pumped from the Columbia River, catapulted through the reactor's process tubes to remove heat from the fission reaction, and then, after a brief holding period, sent back into the Columbia River. CP-1 was tiny, not encased in a building, and reached a power level of only one/half watt, so its heat was simply dissipated. The X-10 was designed to operate at 1,000 kilowatts, a power level low enough that air-cooling was sufficient. B Reactor's design power level was 500 million times that of CP-1 and 250 times that of the X-10. Air-cooling would not be sufficient for B Reactor. Cooling a nuclear reactor is essential; if cooling is not sufficient the fuel can instantly melt, burn, and result in a Chernobyl-like disaster.

The fact that B Reactor was water-cooled is a major difference. The difference between air cooling and water cooling affected every aspect of reactor operations, including fuel design and manufacturing, instrumentation, waste generation, the support services required, and the ability to increase power levels over time. Ultimately, the fact that B Reactor was water-cooled became its limiting factor and a primary reason for its permanent closure in 1968.

The operation of B Reactor was also completely unique, due to the thermal hydraulics inherent in the water-cooling system. An entire science was developed around the reactor water delivery system and the technical problems it posed. The system produced a myriad of extremely serious and complex engineering and maintenance challenges to reactor operations that were never before experienced or solved in world history.

Importantly, water-cooling linked B Reactor to the Columbia River, and to liquid waste generation and disposal—issues that stand among the crucial legacies and subjects of historical debate about the reactor today. When cooling water passed through B Reactor's core, all of the trace minerals in the river water became activated, transformed from their stable, natural states into radio-isotopes. Sometimes, the inferno of the fission reaction split the thin "jackets" or coatings on the fuel elements within the reactor.[320] As a result, products of radioactive activation and fission, as well as hazardous chemicals, were dumped into the Columbia River in massive quantities. The problem of how to dispose of B Reactor's contaminated effluent became so intractable after the machines' power levels were raised by engineering changes over the years that it became unmanageable.

B Reactor's water-cooling system also necessitated and led to unique experiments and discoveries in nuclear fuel development. A first-of-a-kind fuel manufacturing and jacketing process was developed at World War II HEW, precisely because the reactors (B Reactor being the first) would be water-cooled. Over time, many other unique modifications in fuel design and fuel manufacturing were tested and implemented at Hanford, all to try and improve the heat-transfer mechanisms, cooling properties, "seating" properties of the fuel inside the reactor as the water flowed over it, and other aspects of fuel performance. This pioneering work in fuel development occurred because B Reactor was water-cooled and because cooling fuel presented new operating challenges each time scientists tried to increase reactor power levels or change operations.

In addition to being water-cooled, B Reactor's other path-breaking aspects included the methods of its construction, the new construction skills that were developed during construction, and the way certain building materials were used. Many new techniques in materials handling and in building, welding, machining, measuring, and protecting components were pioneered and actually invented during the building of B Reactor. It was constructed in an astonishing eleven months, to closer tolerances (variations in measurement) than any other structure in history.

It is not surprising, therefore, that engineers became the first to want to preserve the reactor as an interpreted historic exhibit. B Reactor was designated a National Historic Mechanical Engineering Landmark in 1976, was placed on the National Register of Historic Places in 1992, was named a Nuclear Historic Landmark in 1993, and a National Civil Engineering Landmark in 1994. In late 2000, Historic American Engineering Record documentation of B Reactor was completed, to fulfill obligations of the National Historic Preservation Act as negotiated between the DOE, the Washington State Historic Preservation Office, and the National Council on Historic Preservation.[321] Studies of the feasibility and cost of preserving B Reactor as a museum were conducted during 1995–2000.[322] Safety analyses, hazards studies, and structural analyses of the 105–B Building were conducted throughout 1997–2002.[323]

In 2004, President Bush signed the Manhattan Project Study Act, mandating that the National Park Service study B Reactor and a small number of other "signature facilities" identified at the three key Manhattan Project Sites: Hanford, Los Alamos, and Oak Ridge. The studies, to determine if preservation and public access are feasible, suitable, and manageable, began in 2006. However, even before, a wide and varied group of supporters had already joined the engineers in trying to preserve B Reactor. Motivations ranged across the board. Those who loved the machine for its intricate, exquisite mechanical and physical characteristics were joined by others who wanted to hear the human stories—to know who imagined and built this dazzling device—and by still others who thought the apparatus was a monster and an abomination. If the reactor were not preserved, they all said, how could its lessons be debated and absorbed?

Across the world, people visit sites where important events took place, to learn, touch, remember, and reflect. Why? History, the great guidepost and teacher, fascinates most. Whether it is the White House, the Gettysburg Battlefield, Appomattox Courthouse, Pearl Harbor, the bridge at Lexington and Concord, Auschwitz, or Robben Island where Nelson Mandela was jailed for so many years, people come to learn more about themselves. They want to know who built or dared, or decided or overcame or faced loss in the places that shaped human lives. Coming to these places fulfills part of the human need to be connected.

B Reactor, by making the plutonium material in the cores of the Trinity and Nagasaki weapons, super-sized America and helped lift the nation from isolationism to world-power status in an instant. Its product changed the global balance of power for all time since then. Before B Reactor started up, four one-millionths of one pound of plutonium had been produced in the laboratory in all of world history. Once B Reactor began operating, tons of the deadly and powerful substance became available for humanity to exercise its will in new ways and live with the consequences. Like other significant monuments, B Reactor can speak about those who conceived and constructed it, those who operated its complex parts without computers, those who were displaced and harmed by it, and about the great river into which B Reactor once flushed its wastes.

Requests for B Reactor tours come from all over the world. People want to know what kind of a nation built and operated this machine and how this nation chooses to remember it. If B Reactor is cocooned and destroyed, it is certain that, over time, the debates about it will fall silent and whatever it has to say and teach will be forgotten. If we allow this destruction to happen, it will say more about us than it will about the reactor.

Notes

Abbreviations Used for Document Sources

AEC documents are those generated by the Atomic Energy Commission. Most of the AEC documents cited are located at the DOE Public Reading Room in Richland, Wash., and through the DOE's Coordination and Information Center (CIC) Library in Las Vegas, Nev.

ARH documents are those generated by the Atlantic Richfield Hanford Company, a contractor to the Hanford site from 1971 to 1977.

BNWL documents are those generated by the Battelle Corporation's Pacific Northwest Laboratories (BNWL), the chief environmental-monitoring contractor to the AEC at the Hanford Site beginning in 1965, and later to the ERDA and to the DOE. (Beginning in 1979, a change in the official name of this laboratory led to a change in the designation given to documents; please see PNL below.)

CH documents refer to those generated at the University of Chicago's Metallurgical Laboratory during World War II and continuing until the Manhattan Engineer District was dissolved on December 31, 1946.

CIC documents are those stored at the DOE's Coordination and Information Center Library in Las Vegas, Nev.

CPD documents were generated by the Waste Management Advisory Board, Atomic Energy Commission, Richland Operations Office.

One **DC** document was used in the preparation of this manuscript. It was generated by the General Electric Aircraft Propulsion Department at the Idaho National Engineering Laboratory.

DEL means that portions of the document have been deleted by the classification office in releasing the document to the public.

DUH documents refer only to a few reports so designated by the DuPont Hanford Company, the prime operating contractor for the Hanford Site from 1943 to 1946. Most reports generated by DuPont personnel received HW designations.

ERDA documents are those generated by the U.S. Energy Research and Development Administration.

GEH documents refer to only a few reports so designated by the General Electric Hanford Company, the prime operating contractor for the Hanford Site from 1946 to 1964. Most reports generated by GE personnel received HW designations.

HAN documents are designations of the internal retrieval system of the Hanford Site 300 Area Technical Library, operated by Battelle Pacific Northwest Laboratories.

HAPO is the acronym for Hanford Atomic Products Operation, the name designation for the Hanford Site from 1953 to 1965, by the prime contractor, General Electric Company.

HB documents refer to the earliest designations (pre–World War II) for the handbooks on radiological protection generated by the National Committee on Radiation Protection (NCRP) and printed by the National Bureau of Standards (NBS). After World War II, the designation for these handbooks changed to NBS (please see NBS below).

HEW is the acronym for Hanford Engineer Works, the earliest designation for the Hanford Site.

HW documents refer to reports generated at the Hanford Site between 1944 and 1965 and written by Hanford scientists and managers. (Such personnel were employees of the DuPont or General Electric companies, but reports written by U.S. Army or AEC personnel carried either MDDC or AEC designations.) The HW documents constitute by far the largest single body of sources used in the preparation of this narrative. These documents are housed at the DOE Public Reading Room in Richland, Wash.

MDDC documents refer to those generated by the Manhattan Engineer District and housed in the Manhattan District Records in the National Archives and Records Service in Washington, D.C.

NBS documents refer to the National Bureau of Standards handbooks and policy letters on radiological protection standards. These documents, and the recommendations within them, were devised by the National Committee on Radiation Protection (NCRP) but were printed by the NBS, a part of the U.S. Department of Commerce.

NWD documents refer to those generated by the Nuclear Weapons Data Center of the Natural Resources Defense Council.

PB documents were generated by the U.S. Public Health Service before it became a part of the U.S. Environmental Protection Agency.

PNL documents are those generated by the Battelle Corporation's Pacific Northwest Laboratories (PNL) beginning in 1979, after a change in the official name of the company's Richland Laboratory. The PNL documents followed those designated BNWL and were generated by the same corporate entity. PNL is the current monitoring contractor at the Hanford Site.

RHO documents are those generated by Rockwell Hanford Operations, chemical-processing and waste-management contractor at the Hanford Site, 1977–87.

RL documents refer to some reports generated at the Richland (Hanford) Site of the Atomic Energy Commission in the transitional years of the mid-1960s as General Electric was leaving the site and new contractors were taking over various functions.

RL refers to Richland, Washington.

TD documents are a designation of the internal retrieval system of the U.S. Environmental Protection Agency Library, Robert S. Kerr Environmental Laboratory, Ada, Okla.

TID documents are those generated by the Technical Information Division of the U.S. Atomic Energy Commission.

USDI U.S. Department of the Interior.

USGS documents are those generated by the United States Geological Survey.

Introduction

1 *Richland Villager,* August 9, 1945, pp. 1–2, August 14, 1945, pp. 1–2, August 16, 1945, pp. 1–5; and Franklin T.

Matthias, "Journal and Notes, 1943–45," unpublished diary, March 1943, July 1945, August 1945, Department of Energy Public Reading Room, Richland, Wash.

2 In April 1987, the DOE released approximately another twenty thousand pages of reports pertaining to Hanford's past. In the three years since, about another twenty thousand pages have been released. These reports are known collectively as the Hanford Historical Documents. Their release places the Hanford Site far ahead of any other nuclear defense facility in the world in terms of disclosure.

3 Leslie R. Groves, *Now It Can Be Told: The Story of the Manhattan Project* (New York: Harper and Brothers, 1962), p. 11.

4 Radiation Protection Department, Department of Social and Health Services, State of Washington, and Center for Environmental Health, U.S. Centers for Disease Control, "The Environmental Source Term Data Extracted from Historical Hanford Documents, 1944–57," 000009 (Olympia: State of Washington, 1986), pp. 8–15. See also "Hanford Historical Documents" (Richland: Department of Energy, 1944–89). Two such documents of particular reference are J. M. Selby and J. K. Soldat, "Summary of Environmental Contamination Incidents at Hanford, 1952–1957," HW-54636 (RL: HAPO, January 25, 1958), pp. 7–11; and U.S. Energy Research and Development Administration, "Waste Management Operations Hanford Reservation: Final Environmental Statement," ERDA-1538, vol. 2 (Richland: U.S. Energy Research and Development Administration, December 1975), pp. II. 1-B-26-27, II. 1-C-81-82.

5 "Hanford Historical Documents." Two such documents of particular reference here are ERDA-1538, 2:II. 1-B-26-27, II. 1-C-80-83, II. 1-E-18, and G. E. Backman, "Summary of Environmental Contamination Incidents at Hanford, 1958–1964,"

HW-84619 (RL: HAPO, April 12, 1965), pp. 4–11. For a more detailed discussion of the workings of these chemical plants, please see chapter 6.

6 Irwin Goodwin, "Perils of Aging U.S. Weapons Plants . . . ," *Physics Today*, 41, no. 11 (November 1988): 49–51; Keith Schneider, "Reactor Shutdown Could Impede Nuclear Deterrent, Officials Say," *New York Times*, October 8, 1988, p. A1; Associated Press, "Era of Change Faces Savannah River," *Tri-City Herald*, April 3, 1989, p. A9; and Associated Press, "SRP Restart Back to Late '89, Paper Says," *Tri-City Herald*, December 9, 1988, p. A1, citing Lieutenant Colonel Richard L. Oborn.

7 Bryan Brumley (Associated Press), "Defense A-Plant Problems Came over Long Time," *Tri-City Herald*, October 30, 1988, p. A1, citing Armed Services Committee (U.S. House of Representatives), Letter to John S. Herrington (Secretary of Energy), October 27, 1988.

8 Lee Bandy (Knight-Ridder Newspapers), "Watkins Admits DOE Mistakes," *Seattle Times*, June 28, 1989, p. A1, citing James D. Watkins; and "Dangerous Mind Set," *Time*, 134, no. 1 (July 3, 1989), p. 18. In the past three years, cost estimates have risen sharply.

9 Majority Staff of the Committee on Governmental Affairs, U.S. Senate, *Early Health Problems of the U.S. Nuclear Weapons Industry and Their Implications for Today*, 101st Cong., 1st sess., S. Print 101-63 (Washington, D.C.: U.S. Government Printing Office, December 1989), p. 1; and Senator John Glenn, News Release, December 19, 1989, p. 1.

10 Richard Meserve, Letter to John S. Harrington (Washington, D.C.: National Academy of Sciences—National Research Council), March 9, 1987; and National Academy of Sciences—National Research Council, "Safety Issues at the Defense Production Reactors" (Washington, D.C.: National Academy Press, 1987), pp. 134, 168, 178, 186.

284

11 Associated Press, "S. C. Reactor Shuts after 'Power Spike,'" *Tri-City Herald,* August 18, 1988, p. A1; and "Big Trouble at Savannah River," *Time,* 132, no. 16 (October 17, 1988): 55.

12 Lee Bandy, "Secret Mishaps Revealed," *The State* (Columbia, S.C.), October 1, 1988, p. A1; Keith Schneider, "Severe Accidents at Nuclear Plant Were Kept Secret up to 31 Years," *New York Times,* October 1, 1988, p. A1; and "Big Trouble," p. 55.

13 Associated Press, "Test Finds New Pipe Crack at SRP," *Tri-City Herald,* December 18, 1988, p. A2; Associated Press, "Reactor Pipe Cracks as Old as 30 Years," *Tri-City Herald,* December 21, 1988, p. D3; Associated Press, "Officials Say SRP Reactors Face Late 1989 Restart Date," *Tri-City Herald,* December 26, 1988, p. A4; Wanda Briggs, "Geologic Fault Found Beneath SRP Reactors," *Tri-City Herald,* January 12, 1989, p. A1; and Hal Strauss, "Nuclear Plant Monitoring Devices Left Broken or Untested for Years," *Atlanta Journal and Constitution,* May 13, 1989, p. A6.

14 Carl Langley, "Exemption for K-Reactor Deplored," *Aiken* (S.C.) *Standard,* July 21, 1989, p. A1; Keith Schneider, "Restarting Weapons Reactors to Cost 4 Times Estimate," *New York Times,* July 31, 1989, p. A1; Associated Press, "Westinghouse Denies Date Set for Savannah Restart," *Tri-City Herald,* December 12, 1990, p. C11; Associated Press, "Safety Violations High at Savannah Site, Report Says," *Tri-City Herald,* January 28, 1991, p. A10; and New York Times Service, "DOE Plan Signals Environmental Shift," *Tri-City Herald,* February 1, 1991, p. A11.

15 Matthew L. Wald, "Nuclear Arms Plants: A Bill Long Overdue," *New York Times,* October 23, 1988; Cass Peterson (*Washington Post*), "Plutonium Plant Faces Rocky Times," *Tri-City Herald,* December 12, 1988, p. A8; Carl J. Johnson, "Rocky Flats: Death, Inc.," *New York Times,* December 18, 1988; and "DOE's Guide to Weapons Plant Spills," *Science,* 242, no. 4885 (December 16, 1988): 1500.

16 "A New Scare at Rocky Flats," *Newsweek,* 113, no. 26 (June 26, 1989): 60; and "Dangerous Mind Set," *Time,* 134, no. 1 (July 3, 1989), p. 18. In an additional part of this investigation, inspectors looked for evidence that an uncontrolled nuclear chain reaction had taken place at Rocky Flats. The presence of radioactive isotopes in the soil and water (not normally present unless fission has occurred) led inspectors to suspect that a spontaneous fission reaction had happened. In August 1989, a special team of investigators stated that such an accident had not taken place. See Associated Press, "DOE Finds No Evidence of Any Nuclear Chain Reaction at Rocky Flats," *Tri-City Herald,* August 12, 1989, p. B4.

17 *Washington Post,* "Energy Secretary Says Rocky Flats Was Mismanaged," *Seattle Times,* December 2, 1989, p. A7.

18 Associated Press, "Panel Wants Delay in Production at Rocky Flats," *Tri-City Herald,* June 6, 1990, p. D1.

19 Associated Press, "'Landmark' Rocky Flats Cleanup Plan Inked," *Tri-City Herald,* January 23, 1991, p. C5. The Rocky Flats cleanup agreement was modeled after the historic Hanford Federal Facility Agreement and Consent Order (Tri-Party Agreement) signed in May 1989. For a description of this agreement, see chapter 8.

20 U.S. Congress, Senate, Subcommittee of the Committee on Governmental Affairs, Hearing, *Management and Operations of the U.S. Department of Energy's Fernald, Ohio, Feed Materials Production Center,* 99th Cong. 1st sess. (Washington, D.C.: U.S. Government Printing Office, 1985), pp. 1–20, 250–54; and U.S. Congress, Senate, Committee on Governmental Affairs, Hearing, *Environmental*

Issues at Department of Energy Nuclear Facilities, 100th Cong., 1st sess. (Washington, D.C.: U.S. Government Printing Office, 1987), pp. 1–16.

21 Associated Press, "Nuclear Plant's Closure Sought," *Tri-City Herald,* October 19, 1988, p. D2; Matthew L. Wald, "Nuclear Arms Plants: A Bill Long Overdue," *New York Times,* October 23, 1988; "Nuclear Danger and Deceit," *Time,* 112, no. 8 (October 31, 1988): 28–30; Matthew L. Wald, "U.S. Will Pay Ohio to Settle Charges at Nuclear Plant," *New York Times,* December 2, 1988, p. A1; and Associated Press, "Judge Issue Final Clearance in Fernald Lawsuit," *Tri-City Herald,* October 15, 1989, p. D8.

22 Matthew L. Wald, "U.S. Now to Keep Atom Plant Vow," *New York Times,* December 21, 1988.

23 "DOE, EPA Ink Mound Cleanup Agreement," *Environment Week,* 3, no. 35 (September 6, 1990): 4.

24 David Whitney, "Congressional Split Rules Out Hanford," *Tri-City Herald,* August 4, 1988, p. A1; Dan W. Reicher and Jason Salzman, "High-Tech Protest against Plutonium Plant," *Bulletin of the Atomic Scientists,* 44, no. 9 (November 1988): 27–30; Associated Press, "Idaho Residents Show DOE Distrust at INEL Reactor Hearings," *Tri-City Herald,* November 12, 1988, p. A3; Associated Press, "Protesters Voice Reactor Opposition," *Tri-City Herald,* November 17, 1988, p. A1; and Associated Press, "Idaho Prepares Court Action on A-Waste," *Tri-City Herald,* November 22, 1988, p. A5.

25 "Crisis Brewing in Nuclear Waste Storage," *Tri-City Herald,* November 28, 1988, p. A4, citing Cecil Andrus; and Associated Press, "DOE, 3 Governors Set A-Waste Summit," *Tri-City Herald,* December 16, 1988, p. D1.

26 Mark N. Trahant, "Idaho Is Winner in Nuclear 'War,'" *Arizona Republic,* February 11, 1989, p. A8.

27 Associated Press, "Groups File Suit to Block SIS Plant," *Tri-City Herald,* April 29, 1989, p. A1; Associated Press, "Idaho Plutonium Plant Criticized," *Tri-City Herald,* May 31, 1989, p. A5; and New York Times News Service, "Bush Puts New Idaho Plutonium Plant on Hold," *Tri-City Herald,* January 27, 1990, p. A3.

28 U.S. House of Representatives, Subcommittee on Energy and Production and Subcommittee on Investigations and Oversight, *Impact of Mercury Releases at the Oak Ridge Complex* (Washington, D.C.: U.S. Government Printing Office, July 11, 1983), p. 18.

29 U.S. Department of Energy, *Environmental Survey Preliminary Report, Oak Ridge Y-12 Plant, Oak Ridge, TN* (Washington, D.C.: U.S. Government Printing Office, 1987), pp. 3–139.

30 Ibid., pp. 2–101; and U.S. Department of Energy, *Environmental Survey Preliminary Report, Oak Ridge National Laboratory (X-10), Oak Ridge, TN* (Washington, D.C.: U.S. Government Printing Office, 1988), pp. 4–150.

31 Associated Press, "Plutonium Trace Found in Tennessee Lake," *Tri-City Herald,* May 9, 1990, p. D1.

32 Keith Schneider, "Wide Threat Seen in Contamination at Nuclear Units," *New York Times,* December 7, 1988, p. A22; and "DOE's Guide to Weapons Plant Spills," *Science,* 242, no. 4885 (December 16, 1988): 1500.

33 The New York Times News Service, "St. Louis Area Faces Challenge of Urban Area Nuclear Waste," *Tri-City Herald,* March 24, 1990, p. C5.

34 Mark Hammond, "Parking Lot at Knolls Lab Contaminated at Least 20 Years by Nuclear Waste," *Schenectady* (N.Y.) *Gazette,* June 22, 1988; Mark Hammond, "GE Acknowledges It Knew Knolls Lot Was Contaminated," *Schenectady Gazette,* June 23, 1988; and "KAPL's Radioactive Waste Lingers; Awaiting Final Clean-Up and Grave," *Schenectady Gazette,* March 29, 1989, p. 33.

35 New York Times News Service, "Navy Reactors under Scrutiny," *Tri-City Herald,* January 1, 1991, p. C4.

36 Associated Press, "Low-Level Waste a High-Level Puzzle," *Tri-City Herald,* March 20, 1989, p. A1.

37 New York Times News Service, "Radioactive Wastes Pose Threat to Marine Sanctuary," *Tri-City Herald,* January 20, 1991, p. D6. See also Jane Kay, "Radioactive Threat to Farallones Seen," *San Francisco Examiner,* May 6, 1990, p. A1.

38 Chris Sivula, "'Downwind' Advocate Urges Weapons Test Compensation," *Tri-City Herald,* January 15, 1988, p. B1; Associated Press, "Congress Approves Funding to Victims of Nuclear Testing," *Sun City* (Ariz.) *News-Sun,* September 28, 1990; New York Times News Service, "Officials Knew of Radiation Danger," *Tri-City Herald,* December 14, 1989, p. D2; Associated Press, "Officials Knew Workers Exposed to Radiation," *Sun City News-Sun,* December 14, 1989, p. B8; and Keith Schneider, "Atom Tests' Legacy of Grief: Workers See Betrayal on Peril," *New York Times,* December 14, 1989, p. A1.

39 The term *atomic shield* was used first by President Harry S. Truman's secretary of state, Dean Acheson. It became a common phrase among American politicians throughout the 1940s and 1950s.

Chapter 1

1 Leslie R. Groves, *Now It Can Be Told: The Story of the Manhattan Project* (New York: Harper and Brothers, 1962), pp. 70–71, 74; and Franklin T. Matthias, "Hanford Engineering Works, MED: Early History," address delivered at the Department of Energy Technical Exchange Program, Richland, Washington, January 14, 1987, p. 10.

2 Mary Powell Harris, *Goodbye, White Bluffs* (Yakima, Wash.: Franklin Press, 1972), pp. 136–39, 145.

3 Martha B. Parker, *Tales of Richland,*
White Bluffs, and Hanford, 1805–1943 (Fairfield, Wash.: Ye Galleon Press, 1979), p. 34, citing Hattie Wiehl.

4 Matthias, "Hanford," pp. 7, 10. See also Richard Hewlett and Oscar Anderson Jr., *The New World, 1939/1946* (University Park: Pennsylvania State University Press, 1962), p. 189.

5 Groves, *Now,* pp. 74–75.

6 Kenneth D. Nichols, *The Road to Trinity* (New York: William Morrow and Co., 1987), p. 79, paraphrasing Leslie R. Groves.

7 Information contained in the preceding four pages of this narrative was drawn from many sources, as well as from the author's own hikes and explorations around the Columbia Basin. Among the sources consulted were John A. Alwin, *Between the Mountains: A Portrait of Eastern Washington* (Bozeman, Mont.: Northwest Panorama Publishing, 1984), pp. 12–18; Ross Cox, *Adventures on the Columbia River: An Overland Journey in the Fur Trade Country* (1835; reprint, Portland: Binfords and Mort, n.d.), pp. 22–24; Washington Irving, *Astoria,* Clatsop edition (1835; reprint, Portland: Binfords and Mort, [1967]), pp. 280–90; Gordon B. Dodds, *The American Northwest: A History of Oregon and Washington* (Arlington Heights, Ill.: Forum Press, 1986), pp. 39–51; Paul C. Pitzer, "The Atmosphere Tasted Like Turnips," *Pacific Northwest Quarterly,* 79, no. 2 (April 1988): 50–55; J. Orin Oliphant, *On the Cattle Ranges of the Oregon Country* (Seattle: University of Washington Press, 1968), pp. 62–72, 130–31; Minola C. Phillippay, *As I Remember* (Steamboat Springs, Colo.: Steamboat Pilot, 1972), pp. 1–17; Harris, *Goodbye, White Bluffs,* pp. 108–21; Walter A. Oberst, *Railroads, Reclamation, and the River: A History of Pasco* (Pasco, Wash.: Franklin County Historical Society, 1978), pp. 61–71; David Lavender, *Land of Giants: The Drive to the Pacific Northwest, 1750–1950*

(Garden City, N.Y.: Doubleday and Co., 1958), pp. 434–43; Richard Rhodes, *The Making of the Atomic Bomb* (New York: Simon and Schuster, 1986); George Sundborg, *Hail Columbia: The Thirty-Year Struggle for the Grand Coulee Dam* (New York: Macmillan, 1954); and U.S. Energy Research and Development Administration, "Waste Management Operations Hanford Reservation: Final Environmental Statement," ERDA-1538, vol. 1 (Richland: U.S. Energy Research and Development Administration, December 1975), pp. II. 3-42-46, Appendix II. 3-G.

8 Meriwether Lewis, *The Lewis and Clark Expedition*, vol. 3 (1814; reprint, New York: J.B. Lippincott, 1961), pp. 423–24; and Elliott Coues, ed., *History of the Expedition under the Command of Lewis and Clark* (1893; reprint, New York: Dover Publications, 1965), pp. 973–75, citing Meriwether Lewis.

9 Coues, *History*, p. 968; and Lewis, *Expedition* 3:424–25.

10 Thomas W. Symons, *The Symons Report on the Upper Columbia River and the Great Plain of the Columbia* (Fairfield, Wash.: Ye Galleon Press, 1967). Reprint of 1882 Senate Doc. 186, 47th Cong.

11 Washington Irving, *The Adventures of Captain Bonneville, U.S.A.*, ed. Edgeley Todd (Norman: University of Oklahoma Press, 1961). Original manuscript published in 1837.

12 See Alexander Ross, *The Fur Hunters of the Far West*, ed. Kenneth Spaulding (1855; reprint, Norman: University of Oklahoma Press, 1956), pp. 45, 137; Archie Binn, *Peter Skene Ogden: Fur Trader* (Portland: Binfords and Mort, 1967), p. 51; and B. C. Payette, comp., *Captain John Mullan, His Life: Building the Mullan Road* (Montreal: Payette Radio, 1968), pp. 162–70.

13 Samuel Parker, *Journal of an Exploring Tour beyond the Rocky Mountains* (Minneapolis: Ross and Haines, 1967), pp. 273–74, 121.

14 Lancaster Pollard, *A History of the State of Washington*, vol. 1 (New York: American Historical Society, 1937), pp. 217–24; and Florence E. Sherfey, *Eastern Washington's Vanished Gristmills and the Men Who Ran Them* (Fairfield, Wash.: Ye Galleon Press, 1978), pp. 102–5.

15 Sidney Berland, "Strategy Strike on the Indian War Front," *Columbia*, 2, no. 1 (Spring 1988): 6–8; and Garrett Hunt, *Indian Wars of the Inland Empire* (Spokane, Wash.: Spokane Community College Printing Department, n.d.), pp. 65–71, 83–86.

16 Oliphant, *Cattle Ranges*, pp. 66–68.

17 Ibid., p. 31; Andrew J. Splawn, *Kamiakin—Last Hero of the Yakimas* (1917; reprint, Caldwell, Idaho: Caxton Printers, 1980), pp. 61–82, 195–210; and Pollard, *A History* 1:306–7.

18 Harris, *Goodbye, White Bluffs*, pp. 7–10, 13–45; and Splawn, *Kamiakin*, pp. 150–60, 200–216.

19 Oliphant, *Cattle Ranges*, pp. 71–72; Splawn, *Kamiakin*, pp. 149–51, 216–20; and Roscoe Sheller, *Ben Snipes: Northwest Cattle King* (Portland: Binfords and Mort, 1957), pp. 35–38, 198–205.

20 Charles Ernst, ed., *As Told by the Pioneers: Reminiscences of Pioneer Life in Washington*, vol. 3 (Olympia, Wash.: State Pioneer Project, 1937), p. 130, citing Alexander McNeill.

21 Sheller, *Ben Snipes*, pp. 198–205; Phillippay, *As I Remember*, pp. 5–6; Oliphant, *Cattle Ranges*, p. 187; and Parker, *Tales*, pp. 16–23.

22 George F. Stanley, ed., *Mapping the Frontier: Charles Wilson's Diary of the Survey of the 49th Parallel, 1858–1862* (Seattle: University of Washington Press, 1970), pp. 101–2.

23 Splawn, *Kamiakin*, pp. 145–46, 323; Oliphant, *Cattle Ranges*, pp. 62, 130–31; Sheller, *Ben Snipes*, pp. 210–20; and Ernst, *As Told by the Pioneers* 3:123, citing Charles O. Splawn.

24 Oliphant, *Cattle Ranges,* pp. 74, 113; Sheller, *Ben Snipes,* pp. 200–10; and Dodds, *American Northwest,* pp. 141–44.
25 Splawn, *Kamiakin,* p. 295.
26 Oberst, *Railroads,* p. 6.
27 Martha B. Parker, *Kin-I-Wak, Tehe, Kenewick, Kennewick* (Fairfield, Wash.: Ye Galleon Press, 1986), pp. 1–7.
28 Ibid., pp. 23–24, citing *Northwest Magazine,* January 1893, January 1894, and March 1894.
29 Ibid., pp. 39–41; Oberst, *Railroads,* pp. 3–19; and Harris, *Goodbye, White Bluffs,* pp. 25–46.
30 Ted Van Arsdol, *Desert Boom and Bust: The Story of Irrigation Efforts and Town Building in Benton County, Washington, 1888–1904* (Vancouver, Wash.: Published by the author, 1972), pp. 24, 38–39; and Parker, *Tales,* pp. 19–43.
31 Parker, *Tales,* pp. 18–19; and Van Arsdol, *Desert,* pp. 32–47, 57, 5, citing *Portland Oregonian,* April 9, 1889.
32 Pollard, *A History* 2:45–58; and Van Arsdol, *Desert,* pp. 50–55.
33 Parker, *Tales,* pp. 41–50.
34 Ibid., pp. 43–51, 57–65; and Harris, *Goodbye, White Bluffs,* pp. 90–103.
35 Oberst, *Railroads,* pp. 8–18; Carlos A. Schwantes, "The Milwaukee Road's Pacific Extension, 1909–1929," *Pacific Northwest Quarterly,* 72, no. 1 (January 1981): 30–36; Harris, *Goodbye, White Bluffs,* pp. 35–40; Parker, *Tales,* p. 165.
36 Parker, *Tales,* pp. 47, 158, 183, 260; Parker, *Kin-I-Wak,* pp. 160–61; Phillippay, *As I Remember,* pp. 8–12; and Harris, *Goodbye, White Bluffs,* pp. 145–46.
37 Harris, *Goodbye, White Bluffs,* p. 119; and Phillippay, *As I Remember,* pp. 2–6.
38 Olaf P. Jenkins, "Underground Water Supply of the Region about White Bluffs and Hanford," *Bulletin #26, Washington State Department of Conservation and Development, Division of Geology* (Olympia, Wash.: Frank M. Lamborn, Public Printer, 1922), p. 32.
39 Parker, *Kin-I-Wak,* p. 47; Parker,

Tales, pp. 83–151; and Harris, *Goodbye, White Bluffs,* pp. 104–9.
40 Oberst, *Railroads,* pp. 61–71; Leo Vogel, *Years Plowed Under* (Spokane, Wash.: University Press, 1977), pp. 84–89; and Phillippay, *As I Remember,* pp. 9–17.
41 Parker, *Tales,* pp. 32, 183, 189, 260, 287–89 citing Sybil Garbutt, 329 citing Mary Druse; Harris, *Goodbye, White Bluffs,* pp. 2–6; Minola C. Phillippay, *Kahlotus Is Home* (Steamboat Springs, Colo.: Steamboat Pilot, 1973), pp. 40–50; Parker, *Kin-I-Wak,* pp. 160–61, 172–80; and Phillippay, *As I Remember,* pp. 8–12.
42 Parker, *Tales,* p. 79, citing Wesley Sawyer.
43 Van Arsdol, *Desert,* pp. 59–60, citing A. C. Amon; and Harris, *Goodbye, White Bluffs,* pp. 104–6.
44 Parker, *Tales,* p. 329, citing Mary Druse.
45 Phillippay, *Kahlotus,* pp. 40–50; Parker, *Tales,* p. 189; and Parker, *Kin-I-Wak,* pp. 172–80.
46 David Lavender, *Land of Giants: The Drive to the Pacific Northwest, 1750–1950* (Garden City, N.Y.: Doubleday & Co., 1958), pp. 434–50. See also Frank Friedel, "F.D.R. and the Northwest: Informal Glimpses," *Pacific Northwest Quarterly,* 76, no. 4 (October 1985): 125–28.
47 Parker, *Tales,* pp. 307, 322–29, citing Mary Druse; and Pitzer, "The Atmosphere," pp. 52–53.
48 Lavender, *Land,* pp. 439–43; and Cecil Dryden, *Dryden's History of Washington* (Portland: Binfords and Mort, 1968), pp. 328–29. For a more complete examination of the Columbia Basin Irrigation Project, please see chapter 4.
49 Parker, *Tales,* pp. 365–67, 370.
50 Oberst, *Railroads,* pp. 102–5, 133. The facility built by the navy at Pasco was officially named the Pasco Naval Air Station. A gunnery range just west of Richland was designated the Paterson Ridge Range. Another training range

was located amid the dwarf juniper forests and sand dunes of Franklin County. In the early 1960s, Juniper Flats practice range was the site of ground survival training for the first American astronauts. The other 1942 practice range was located up the Yakima River near Zillah.

51 Rita Seedorf and Martin Seedorf, "Army Air Bases: The Effects of World War II on Grant County, Washington," unpublished paper delivered at Military Influences on Washington History Conference, Camp Murray, Tacoma, Wash., March 29–31, 1984; and DCPA Section, Yakima Firing Center, "Yakima Firing Center History" (Yakima, Wash.: U.S. Army, 1978), pp. 1–2.

52 *Washington State Yearbook* (Eugene, Oreg.: Information Press, 1988), p. 92.

53 Pollard, *A History* 2:45–58, 263–74; and Parker, *Tales*, pp. 149–50.

54 L. C. Chestnut and C. W. Wright, "Gross Appraisal, Gable Project" (Washington, D.C.: U.S. War Department, January 23, 1943), pp. 2–5. See also Office of the Chief of Engineers, "Basic Data on Hanford Engineer Works, Pasco, Washington" (Washington, D.C.: U.S. Army Corps of Engineers, May 19, 1943), pp. 4–8.

55 *Kennewick Courier-Reporter,* March 11, 1943, p. 1.

56 Ted Van Arsdol, *The City That Shook the World* (Vancouver, Wash.: Published by the author, 1972), p. 20, citing C. J. Barnett.

57 Harris, *Goodbye, White Bluffs,* pp. 151–53; Hanford Thayer, letter to the author November 8, 1988. Van Arsdol, *City,* p. 18, cites the statement made by Colonel Matthias to C. J. Barnett of Richland.

58 Groves, *Now,* pp. 6–35.

59 Ibid., pp. 11–39.

60 Ibid., p. 28.

61 Ibid., pp. xi–xiii.

62 Ibid., pp. 19, 39–42.

63 Vincent C. Jones, *Manhattan: The Army and the Atomic Bomb* (Washington,

D.C.: U.S. Center for Military History, 1985), pp. 69–71. Jones cites evidence for the discussions at these meetings from the diary of Colonel James C. Marshall, July–August 1942, and September 13, 1942, contained in the Manhattan District Records, 1942–48, National Archives and Records Center, Washington, D.C. The plutonium pilot plant (semiworks) in Tennessee was very small compared with the reactors built at Hanford. The Tennessee unit operated at 15 kilowatts (kw), whereas the first units at Hanford operated at 300 kw. Still, the Met Lab scientists felt the need of a two-hundred-square-mile buffer area in Tennessee.

64 Glenn T. Seaborg, "Large-Scale Alchemy—25th Anniversary at Hanford-Richland," CIC-0148580 (Washington, D.C.: U.S. Atomic Energy Commission, June 7, 1968), p. 4; and Jones, *Manhattan,* pp. 193–94. Jones cites evidence from the Minutes of the Conference at the Met Lab, October 15, 1942, Manhattan District Records, 1942–48, National Archives and Records Center, Washington, D.C. Scientists present at the conference decided to use the bismuth phosphate method, Seaborg has stated, due to the highly corrosive nature of the lanthanum fluoride. The plutonium semiworks in Tennessee began to operate in early 1944. According to DuPont records, "The early experience at Clinton Laboratories sufficed to define rather clearly the radiation hazards to be expected in the separations process at Hanford." See DuPont Corporation, *Operations of Hanford Engineer Works,* HAN-73212 (Wilmington, Del.: E.I. DuPont de Nemours and Co., 1946), Book VII, p. 87.

65 Groves, *Now,* pp. 55–56.

66 Ibid., pp. 55–57.

67 Ibid., pp. 51–57. See also Nichols, *Road,* p. 82.

68 Nichols, *Road,* p. 77.

69 Groves, *Now,* p. 69.

70 Henry D. Smyth, *Atomic Energy for Military Purposes* (Princeton, N.J.: Princeton University Press, 1945), p. 112.

71 Groves, *Now,* pp. 70–71.

72 Ibid., p. 74; and Hewlett and Anderson, *New World,* p. 189. Much of the concrete used in the construction of the Hanford reactors and other structures was eventually made on the site from the aggregate found locally.

73 David Lilienthal, *Change, Hope and the Bomb* (Princeton, N.J.: Princeton University Press, 1963), p. 135; Simon T. Cantril and Herbert M. Parker, "Status of Health Protection at Hanford," HW-7-2136 (RL: HEW, August 24, 1945), p. 1; and DuPont Corporation, *Operations of Hanford Engineer Works,* HAN-73214 (Wilmington, Del.: E.I. DuPont de Nemours and Co., 1946), Book VII, "Medical Department: Health Instruments," p. 17.

74 Abel Wolman, "Public Health Aspects of Atomic Energy," *American Journal of Public Health,* 40, no. 12 (December 1950): 1502–3. The Atomic Energy Commission was the civilian agency that assumed control of America's atomic energy production from the MED on January 1, 1947. The AEC functioned until it was replaced by the Energy Research and Development Administration (ERDA) in 1974.

75 For a discussion of the state and growth of radiobiological knowledge during these years, see chapter 7.

76 Barton Hacker, *The Dragon's Tail: Radiation Safety in the Manhattan Project, 1942–46* (Berkeley: University of California Press, 1987), pp. 8–12.

77 Ibid., pp. 12–18; and Lauriston Taylor, "Brief History of the National Committee on Radiation Protection (NCRP) and Measurements Covering the Period 1929–1946," in *Health Physics,* vol. 1 (New York: Pergamon Press, 1958), pp. 3–10. Actually, the American dose of 0.1 rad per day and the international dose of 0.2 rad per day were in close agreement. The apparent difference was actually due to differences in methods of measurement. The European (international) method utilized a surface dose that included "backscatter" from the human body, whereas the American method used the dose measured in the air. See Herbert M. Parker (Health Instruments Section), "H.I. Lecture Series," HW-7184, Part I (RL: HEW, July 1, 1947), Lecture XII: "Tolerance Dose," p. 6.

78 DuPont, *Operations,* Book VII, p. 18.

79 Hacker, *Dragon's Tail,* pp. 3, 19–25; Francoise Giroud, *Marie Curie: A Life,* trans. Lydia Davis (New York: Holmes and Meier, 1986); and William Houff, "Silent Holocaust," *Wildfire,* nos. 3–4 (November 1985): 28. Houff's article was originally delivered as a sermon at Spokane Unitarian Church, May 1984. Cataracts can be caused by excessive exposure to radiation. There is some evidence that Marie Curie, by the early 1920s, suspected that her work with radium might have caused the cataracts. See Giroud, *Marie Curie,* p. 235.

80 NCRP, "X-Ray Protection," HB20 (Washington, D.C.: U.S. Government Printing Office, 1936); NCRP, "Radium Protection," HB23 (Washington, D.C.: U.S. Government Printing Office, 1938); and ICRP, "International Recommendations for X-Ray and Radium Protection" (Oxford, England: International X-Ray and Radium Protection Commission, 1937).

81 Jones, *Manhattan,* pp. 410–15.

82 DuPont, *Operations,* Book VII, pp. 17–18.

83 The brief, subsurface investigations made by the U.S. Army Corps of Engineers in 1943 were made only to determine whether the site could bear the weight of the huge planned concrete structures. See L. C. Chestnut and C. W. Wright, "Gross Appraisal, Gable Project"

(Washington, D.C.: U.S. War Department, January 21, 1943); U.S. Army Corps of Engineers, "Basic Data on Hanford Engineer Works" (Washington, D.C.: Office of the Chief of Engineers, May 19, 1943); and DuPont, Corporation, *Construction—Hanford Engineer Works: History of the Project*, HAN-10970, vol. 1 (Wilmington, Del.: E.I. DuPont de Nemours and Co., 1945), pp. 2–3, 103.

Chapter 2

1 U.S. AEC, "Ninth Semiannual Report of the Atomic Energy Commission" (Washington, D.C.: U.S. Government Printing Office, January 1951), pp. 4–5, 9, 16; U.S. AEC "Eleventh Semiannual Report of the Atomic Energy Commission" (Washington, D.C.: U.S. Government Printing Office, January 1952), pp. 19, 23, 35; U.S. AEC, "Seventh Semiannual Report of the Atomic Energy Commission" (Washington, D.C.: U.S. Government Printing Office, January 1950), pp. 10, 18; and U.S. AEC, "Tenth Semiannual Report of the Atomic Energy Commission" (Washington, D.C.: U.S. Government Printing Office, July 1951), foreword, and pp. 1, 29.

2 Chris Sivula, "Hanford Waste Water 346 Billion Gallons," *Tri-City Herald*, April 13, 1991, p. A1.

3 Some of the most accurate and detailed accounts of Hanford's construction can be found in Richard Hewlett and Oscar Anderson, Jr., *The New World, 1936/1946* (University Park: Pennsylvania State University Press, 1962), pp. 86–87, 216–26, 302–10; Army Corps of Engineers, "Manhattan District History, Book IV—Pile Project, X-10, Volume 3—Design," December 31, 1946, pp. 80–90; and DuPont Corporation, *Construction History—Hanford Engineer Works: History of the Project*, vols. 1–4 (Wilmington, Del.: E.I. DuPont de Nemours and Co., August 9, 1945).

4 H.I. Section, "Health Instruments Lecture Series," HW-7184, Part II (RL: HEW, July 1, 1947), Lecture XVII: "The Fundamental Process," p. 12.

5 R. F. Foster, J. J. Davis, and P. A. Olson, "Studies on the Effect of the Hanford Reactors on Aquatic Life in the Columbia River," HW-33366 (RL: HAPO, October 11, 1954), pp. 3–4. Demineralization and deaeration plants designed to remove impurities and gases from the river water were deemed necessary at first. However, it turned out that the Columbia's water was pure enough that problems with the absorption of neutrons by dissolved solids and salts were avoided. Only one demineralization facility was built (at B reactor), and it was never needed.

6 R. B. Hall and P. C. Jerman, "Reactor Effluent Water Disposal," HW-63653 (RL: HAPO, February 1, 1960); and H. W. Heacock, "Adaptation of a Recirculating Water System to 100-H Area—Interim Feasibility Report," HW-40837 (Richland: General Electric Co., January 9, 1956). For a discussion of reactor effluent, retention (107) basins, and the Columbia River, see chapter 5.

7 For a discussion of I-131 in the Columbia Basin, see chapter 4.

8 Hewlett and Anderson, *New World*, pp. 218–24; DuPont, *Construction* 3:812; and H.I. Section, HW-7184, Part II, Lecture XVIII: "200-Area Buildings," pp. 1–15. For a discussion of ground and tank waste-disposal practices, see chapter 6.

9 Hewlett and Anderson, *New World*, pp. 221–24; G. E. Backman, "Dispersion of 300 Area Liquid Effluent in the Columbia River," HW-73672 (RL: HAPO, May 25, 1962), pp. 1–3; and U.S. Energy Research and Development Administration, "Waste Management Operations, Hanford Reservation: Final Environmental Statement," ERDA-1538 (Washington, D.C.: U.S. Energy Research and Development Administration, December 1975), 2: II. 1-E-3-18.

10 Franklin T. Matthias, "Hanford Engineering Works, Manhattan Engineer District: Early History," speech delivered to the Technical Exchange Program, Department of Energy, Richland, Wash., January 14, 1987, p. 13; Leslie R. Groves, *Now It Can Be Told: The Story of the Manhattan Project* (New York: Harper and Brothers, 1962), p. 84; Hewlett and Anderson, *New World*, pp. 218–22; and DuPont, *Construction* 3:877–80.

11 M. J. Klem, "Inventory of Chemicals Used at Hanford Site Production Plants and Support Operations, 1944–1980," WHC-EP-0172 (Richland: Westinghouse Hanford Co., April 1990). For a discussion of radionuclide adsorption in Hanford area soils and substrata, see chapter 6.

12 H.I. Section, HW-7184, Part II, Lecture XX: "H.I. Survey Training—300 Area," pp. 5–7.

13 Ted Van Arsdol, *The City That Shook the World* (Vancouver, Wash.: Published by the author, 1972), pp. 7, 24–25, 32; and *Richland Villager*, September 3, 1945, p. 3.

14 For a discussion of regional growth in the towns and cities of the Columbia Basin, see chapter 3.

15 Silver Anniversary Committee, "Alive: Richland and the Hanford Project" (Kennewick, Wash.: Advance Advertising, 1983), pp. 19–23.

16 Vincent C. Jones, *Manhattan: The Army and the Atomic Bomb* (Washington, D.C.: U.S. Center for Military History, 1985), pp. 569–73; and Robert A. Divine, T. H. Breen, George M. Fredrickson, and R. Hal Williams, *America, Past and Present*, vol. 2 (Glenview, Ill.: Scott, Foresman and Co., 1984), pp. 809–10.

17 Jones, *Manhattan*, pp. 580–81; and Kenneth D. Nichols, *The Road to Trinity* (New York: William Morrow and Co., 1987), pp. 216–17.

18 Jones, *Manhattan*, p. 585. B reactor was activated again in 1948.

19 William L. Borden, *There Will Be No Time: The Revolution in Defense Strategy* (New York: Macmillan and Co., 1946), pp. 170, 110, 123, 127, 209, 212–13, 220–22.

20 Jones, *Manhattan*, pp. 586–93; and Hewlett and Anderson, *New World*, pp. 636–37.

21 Hewlett and Anderson, *New World*, p. 631. See also Richard Rhodes, *The Making of the Atomic Bomb* (New York: Simon and Schuster, 1986), p. 765. A prominent MED official at Hanford, Colonel Frederick Clarke, has stated that at the close of World War II, the United States possessed only enough material for one nuclear bomb. Historical documentation on this topic is still classified. See *Tri-City Herald*, March 24, 1989, p. A3.

22 Richard Hewlett and Francis Duncan, *Atomic Shield, 1947/1952* (University Park: Pennsylvania State University Press, 1969), pp. 31–47, citing JCS memorandum. See also *Richland Villager*, March 20, 1947, p. 1.

23 Divine et al., *America* 2:810–11, partially citing Harry S. Truman.

24 John Spanier, *American Foreign Policy since World War II* (New York: Praeger Publishers, 1973), pp. 36–37, citing X (George F. Kennan, pseudonym) in "Sources of Soviet Conduct," *Foreign Affairs* 25 (July 1947): 566–82.

25 Hewlett and Duncan, *Atomic*, pp. 127–29.

26 Ibid., pp. 39–40.

27 Ibid., pp. 62–63.

28 Hewlett and Anderson, *New World*, pp. 636–37; Nichols, *Road*, p. 231; Hewlett and Duncan, *Atomic*, pp. 39–40, 62–63; David Lilienthal, *The Journals of David Lilienthal* (New York: Harper and Row, 1964), vol. 2, *The Atomic Energy Years, 1945–50*, p. 113, citing diary entry of November 26, 1946; and *Richland Villager*, September 5, 1946, p. 1.

29 *Richland Villager*, May 19, 1946, p. 6, July 8, 1949, p. 1; and Lilienthal, *Journals* 2:488, citing diary entry of March 18, 1949. The JCAE's cost overrun hearings,

chaired by Senator Bourke Hicken-
looper, were an attempt to discredit AEC
Chairman Lilienthal, whom Hicken-
looper believed was "soft" on communism. Although Lilienthal weathered the
hearings, he was replaced in July 1950 by
Gordon Dean, a more hard-line anticom-
munist. See Roger Anders, ed., *Forging
the Shield: The Office Diaries of Gordon E.
Dean* (Chapel Hill: University of North
Carolina Press, 1987), p. 4.
30 Hewlett and Duncan, *Atomic*, pp. 85–
86, citing Walter Williams.
31 Ibid., pp. 85–86, 145.
32 *Richland Villager,* September 4, 1947,
p. 1, November 27, 1947, p. 1, both citing
Carleton Shugg; and Hewlett and Duncan, *Atomic*, pp. 85–86, 145.
33 John A. Garraty and Robert A. Mc-
Caughey, *The American Nation*, 6th ed.,
vol. 2 (New York: Harper and Row,
1987), pp. 833–45, partially citing
Arthur M. Vandenberg; Divine et al.,
America 2:813–27; and Richard Neuberger, "Plutonium and Problems," *Nation* 169 (July 30, 1949): 104.
34 Hewlett and Duncan, *Atomic Shield*,
p. 184, citing Dean Acheson in *Time* 54
(July 4, 1949): 5.
35 Divine et al., *America* 2:813–27; and
David Lilienthal, *Change, Hope, and the
Bomb* (Princeton, N.J.: Princeton University Press, 1963), pp. 143–44.
36 Spanier, *American Foreign Policy*, pp.
96–97, citing official government broad-
cast from Peking, China.
37 Clay Blair, *The Forgotten War: America in Korea, 1950–1953* (New York: Times
Books, 1987); Max Hastings, *The Korean
War* (New York: Simon and Schuster,
1987); and Anders, *Forging*, pp. 19–28.
38 Garraty and McCaughey, *The American* 2:839–46.
39 U.S. AEC, "Seventh Semiannual," pp.
1–9; U.S. AEC, "Eighth Semiannual Report of the Atomic Energy Commission
(Washington, D.C.: U.S. Government
Printing Office, July 1950), pp. vii–x;

Richland Villager, September 1, 1949, p. 1,
October 20, 1949, p. 1, October 27, 1949,
p. 1, February 16, 1950, p. 1; and Neuberger, "Plutonium and Problems,"
p. 105.
40 Leona Marshall Libby, *The Uranium
People* (New York: Crane, Russak, 1979),
pp. 273–79; and Divine et al., *America*
2:815, partially citing NSC-68, April 1950.
See also Lilienthal, *Change*, p. 15. The defense budget did triple between 1950 and
1953.
41 Anders, *Forging*, pp. 4–7; *Richland
Villager,* February 16, 1950, p. 1. The July
1950 supplementary appropriation
amounted to $260 million.
42 E. Abel, "Our Vast Empire of the
Atom," *New York Times Magazine,*
September 5, 1954, pp. 11, 46–49.
43 Divine et al., *America* 2:821–27; U.S.
AEC, "Minutes of Meeting 1392,"
CIC-0001177 (Washington, D.C.: U.S.
Atomic Energy Commission, July 29,
1958), pp. 562–66; and Anders, *Forging*,
pp. xxiv–xxix.
44 Matthias, "Hanford," pp. 12, 15. See
also Franklin T. Matthias, "Journal and
Notes, 1943–45," unpublished diary (located at Richland, U.S. Department of
Energy Public Reading Room), April 23,
1945.
45 Nichols, *Road*, p. 79.
46 Groves, *Now*, p. 38.
47 Henry D. Smyth, *Atomic Energy for
Military Purposes* (Princeton, N.J.:
Princeton University Press, 1945), p. 109.
48 Groves, *Now*, p. 41.
49 Matthias, "Journal," 1943 throughout;
and Groves, *Now*, pp. 19–24.
50 Matthias, "Journal," April 5, 1944,
April 22, 1944, May 27, 1944, August 25,
1944, September 5, 1944. The single-
shelled, high-level waste-storage tanks
built at Hanford during World War II
have been the subjects of considerable
controversy in the 1970s and 1980s. Many
of them have leaked into the surrounding
soils and groundwater. Therefore, their

construction is an important matter. See ERDA-1538, 2: II.1 C-79-83; and U.S. Department of Energy, "Disposal of Hanford Defense High-Level, Transuranic, and Tank Wastes: Final Environmental Impact Statement," DOE/EIS-0113, vol. 1 (Washington, D.C.: U.S. Department of Energy, December 1987), pp. 1.5, 2.1–2.3, 5.64–5.66.

51 DuPont, *Construction* 3:875–76; and Matthias, "Journal," June 1, 1944, August 29, 1944, September 19, 1944, April 23, 1945.

52 Libby, *Uranium*, p. 190.

53 Matthias, "Journal," November 19, 1944, December 29, 1944, January 14–17, 1945, February 2, 1945, February 20–21, 1945, March 8, 1945, March 22–28, 1945.

54 Ibid., April 20, 1945, April 23, 1945, May 3, 1945, May 9, 1945, May 18, 1945, June 1, 1945, June 8, 1945.

55 DuPont Corporation, *Operations of Hanford Engineer Works*, HAN-73214 (Wilmington, Del.: E.I. DuPont de Nemours and Co., 1946), Book XII, pp. 48–50. See also Book XV, pp. 2–11.

56 In one interview, Colonel Frederick Clarke, second HEW commander, stated that cooling times dropped as low as fifteen days in mid-1945. See Mike Lindblom, "Early Hanford Boss Makes Nostalgic Visit," *Tri-City Herald*, March 24, 1989, p. A3. However, available written records are not specific, except to confirm unspecified time periods below thirty days.

57 DuPont, *Operations*, Book XII, pp. 146–47.

58 Matthias, "Journal," July 4, 1945, July 10, 1945, July 30, 1945, August 11–12, 1945, August 14, 1945, December 4, 1945.

59 DuPont, *Operations*, Book XII, S Department, p. 145.

60 Radiation Protection Department, Washington Department of Social and Health Services, and Center for Environmental Health, U.S. Centers for Disease Control, "The Environmental Source Term Data Extracted from Hanford Historical Documents, 1944–57," 000009 (Olympia: State of Washington, September 1986), p. 10; F. P. Seymour, "A Study of Total Amounts of Active Waste Released in All Manners by the HEW Process to Date," HW-7-5463-DEL (RL: HEW, December 5, 1946), p. 3; and R. E. Roberts, "History of Airborne Contamination and Control-200 Areas," HW-55569 RD (RL: HAPO, April 1, 1958), p. 6.

61 Groves, *Now*, pp. xi, 35.

62 Matthias, "Journal," August 9, 1943, December 7, 1943, July 22, 1944, July 26, 1944, January 31, 1945, February 27, 1945, March 5, 1945, June 21, 1945; and Harry S. Truman, "Why I Dropped the Bomb," *Parade Magazine*, December 4, 1988, p. 10.

63 Matthias, "Journal," June 13–14, 1943, June 24, 1943, December 7, 1943, December 14, 1943, December 29, 1943, April 4, 1944, April 11, 1944, June 22, 1944, July 4, 1944, October 6, 1944, December 17, 1944; Van Arsdol, *City*, pp. 44–50; and Hill Williams, "Full Circle," *Seattle Times*, March 31, 1988, p. D2, citing *Pasco Herald* editor.

64 *Richland Villager*, August 16, 1945, p. 5, citing Reva Matthias.

65 Matthias, "Journal," June 14, 1943; and Groves, *Now*, p. 80. In late 1944, a DuPont employee sued the company because he was assigned work at Hanford that was "different from that which . . . [he] had understood . . . [he was] to do when hired." MED officials worried about the future implications of this suit for the secrecy of the Hanford project. See Matthias, "Journal," November 2, 1944, November 4, 1944, November 27, 1944.

66 Matthias, Baker Interview, p. 33; and *Richland Villager*, December 20, 1945, pp. 1, 4.

67 Matthias, "Journal," June 14, 1943; Groves, *Now*, p. 80; and Van Arsdol, *City*, p. 44, citing lyrics.

68 Van Arsdol, *City,* p. 30; and Matthias, "Journal," June 8, 1943, February 16, 1944, February 29, 1944, March 1, 1944, November 21–22, 1944, May 14, 1945.
69 Matthias, "Journal," December 31, 1943, February 17, 1944, October 19, 1944.
70 Ibid., August 18, 1943, January 4, 1944, February 25, 1944, March 31, 1944.
71 Ibid., February 2, 1944, February 27, 1945, May 16, 1945, August 14–17, 1945; and Van Arsdol, *City,* pp. 41–42.
72 *Richland Villager,* August 9, 1945, pp. 1–2, August 14, 1945, pp. 1–2; and Matthias, "Journal," August 6–17, 1945. Even though the fissionable material used in the Hiroshima bomb was U-235, manufactured at the Clinton Engineer Works in Tennessee, the basic facts about the entire Manhattan Project were revealed in the government news releases of August 6 and 7, 1945. Through these press bulletins, reporters learned of Hanford's part in the Manhattan Project, and they rushed there even before the Nagasaki bomb (produced by Hanford's plutonium) was dropped on August 9.
73 Jones, *Manhattan,* pp. 569–70, citing Harry S. Truman.
74 Smyth, *Atomic,* p. 226.
75 Jones, *Manhattan,* p. 554.
76 Matthias, "Journal," June 1, 1945; and Paul Loeb, *Nuclear Culture: Living and Working in the World's Largest Atomic Complex* (New York: Coward, McCann, Geoghegan, 1982), pp. 55–59.
77 *Richland Villager,* September 3, 1945, p. 2, citing Robert DeRoos in *San Francisco Chronicle.*
78 *Richland Villager,* January 24, 1946, p. 1.
79 "Hanford Works News" (Richland: General Electric Co., 1948), August 13, 1948, p. 7, March 26, 1948, p. 7, October 1, 1948, p. 7.
80 Loeb, *Nuclear,* p. 56.
81 Lilienthal, *Journals* 2:214, citing diary entry of June 28, 1947.

82 *Richland Villager,* August 14, 1947, p. 1, citing David H. Lauder.
83 Matthias, "Journal," February 4, 1944, April 17–18, 1944, May 25, 1944; *Richland Villager,* May 6, 1948, pp. 3, 15, May 13, 1948, p. 18; and DuPont, *Operations,* Book VII, "Medical Department, Health Instruments," pp. 3–5.
84 DuPont, *Operations,* Book VII, pp. 3–5, 47–48.
85 Ibid., Book VI, pp. 12–15.
86 Matthias, "Journal," July 12, 1944, August 6–7, 1944.
87 Jones, *Manhattan,* pp. 410–13.
88 Matthias, "Journal," January 24, 1944, January 31, 1944, February 4, 1944.
89 Ibid., August 23, 1944, August 26, 1944, August 28–30, 1944, September 1, 1944, September 4, 1944, September 8, 1944, September 20, 1944.
90 H.I. Section, HW-7184, Lecture XVIII, p. 10, Lecture XIII, pp. 1–10, Lecture X, p. 12; DuPont, *Operations,* Book IV, Instruments Section, pp. 1–22; Carl Dreher, "The Weirdest Danger in the World," *Popular Science* 149, no. 4 (October 1946): 86–90; and Hanson Blatz, ed., *Radiation Hygiene Handbook* (New York: McGraw-Hill, 1959), pp. 11–19. The *"pencils"* covered exposures ranging from 20 to 200 mr. The film badges covered the range from 50 mr to 3 r. See HW-7184, Lecture I, p. 5. Although these devices were useful in determining whether maximum permissible exposure levels were exceeded, they could not record exposure to low-energy beta radiation. Such low-level dosages could have occurred repeatedly over time, with the instruments showing no findings. See Blatz, *Radiation,* section 11, p. 47.
91 William D. Norwood, in S. L. Sanger and R. W. Mull, eds., *Hanford and the Bomb: An Oral History of World War II* (Seattle: Living History Press, 1990), p. 150.
92 DuPont, *Operations,* Book VII, pp. 7–10; and Herbert Parker, "Status of

Health Protection at Hanford Engineer
Works," HW-7-2136, in R. Kathren,
R. Baalman, and W. Bair, *Herbert M.
Parker* (Columbus, Ohio: Battelle Press,
1986), pp. 309–10 (the document was
originally written August 24, 1945).
93 U.S. AEC, "Control of Radiation
Hazards in the Atomic Energy Program," in "Eighth Semiannual," p. 154.
94 DuPont, *Operations,* Book XII, pp.
115–25.
95 Ibid., Book VI, p. 15.
96 Yvette Berry, cited in Van Arsdol,
City, pp. 49–55.
97 David Bradley, *No Place to Hide*
(Boston: Little, Brown and Co., 1948),
pp. 134–35.
98 H.I. Section, HW-7184, Part 1, Lecture
XV, pp. 4–5. See also Lectures XIII, XIV,
and XV (entire).
99 *Richland Villager,* September 3, 1945,
p. 1.
100 Van Arsdol, *City,* pp. 28–33, 37–40,
44.
101 Matthias, "Journal," June 18, 1943,
November 27, 1944.
102 Ibid., July 23, 1944.
103 *Richland Villager,* September 3, 1945,
p. 3, describing 1944 conditions.
104 Van Arsdol, *City,* pp. 37–38; and
Matthias, "Journal," August 21, 1943,
August 23, 1943.
105 *Richland Villager,* September 27,
1945, p. 1, citing Mrs. Walter O. Simon.

Chapter 3
1 Seattle First National Bank, "Pacific
Northwest Industries: The Hanford
Works" (Seattle: Seattle First National
Bank, December 1948), pp. 6, 3.
2 *Richland Villager,* September 4, 1947, p.
1, January 22, 1948, p. 1, February 12,
1948, p. 1.
3 Silver Anniversary Committee, "Alive:
Richland and the Hanford Project"
(Kennewick, Wash.: Advance Advertising, 1983), pp. 9–21; "A Standard Community Industrial Survey, for Kennewick,

Washington" (Olympia: State of Washington, 1974), p. 1; Kennewick Community Planning and Development Department, "Official Population Estimates"
(Kennewick, Wash.: City of Kennewick,
1950, 1955); R. L. Polk, "Polk's Pasco-
Kennewick Directory, 1955" (Seattle:
R. L. Polk and Co., 1955), p. 13; and Ted
Van Arsdol, *Boomers on Wheels: The Story
of Trailers in the Tri-Cities . . . 1943 to 1958*
(Vancouver, Wash.: Published by the author, 1970), pp. 30–38.
4 Technical Steering Panel, "Fact Sheet,"
#5 (Richland: Hanford Environmental
Dose Reconstruction Project, February
1990).
5 Franklin T. Matthias, "Journal and
Notes, 1943–45," unpublished diary (located at Richland, U.S. Department of
Energy Public Reading Room),
March 29, 1944, May 6, 1944, May 10,
1944, May 23, 1944, September 22, 1944.
In January 1945, Matthias noted that
housing conditions in towns surrounding
the Hanford project were "still critical."
See Matthias, "Journal," January 19, 1945.
6 *Tri-City Herald,* November 13, 1947, p.
9, citing Carleton Shugg, p. 4, citing
Portland Oregonian, November 10, 1947;
and Frances T. Pugnetti, *Tiger by the Tail:
Twenty-Five Years with the Stormy* Tri-City
Herald (Pasco, Wash.: *Tri-City Herald,*
1975), pp. 17–59.
7 *Richland Villager,* March 11, 1948, p. 1,
July 1, 1948, p. 1.
8 Ibid., September 15, 1949, p. 11, citing
David Lilienthal. See also *Prosser Record
Bulletin,* May 25, 1950, p. 1, June 1, 1950,
p. 1.
9 Matthias, "Journal," July 17, 1944,
January 31, 1945. The congressional
hearings were held by the Public Lands
Committee.
10 Ibid., February 25, 1944.
11 Ibid., September 15, 1944, April 2,
1944.
12 Ibid., April 17, 1943, April 21, 1943.
World War II as a whole, and the Hanford Project especially, caused such an

agricultural labor shortage in central and eastern Washington that the first Hispanics to populate the district were brought in to harvest the crops. See Erasmo Gamboa, "Mexican Migration into Washington State: A History, 1940–1950," *Pacific Northwest Quarterly* 72, no. 3 (July 1981): 121–31.

13 Matthias, "Journal," March 30, 1943, May 4, 1943, May 20, 1943, September 20, 1943, September 22, 1943, March 31, 1944, November 14, 1944, November 17, 1944, November 29, 1944, December 2, 1944, December 4, 1944, December 16, 1944, February 17, 1945.

14 Ibid., May 26, 1944, June 2, 1944, January 30, 1945, February 1, 1945, September 24, 1945.

15 DuPont Corporation, *Operations of Hanford Engineer Works,* HAN-73214 (Wilmington, Del.: E.I. DuPont de Nemours and Co., 1946), introductory volume, p. 21; and Kenneth D. Nichols, *The Road to Trinity* (New York: William Morrow and Co., 1987), p. 138.

16 *Richland Villager,* August 14, 1947, p. 1, September 11, 1947, p. 1, September 18, 1947, p. 1, October 9, 1947, p. 1, February 5, 1948, p. 1.

17 Ibid., August 14, 1945, pp. 1–2, September 3, 1945, p. 2, citing Robert DeRoos; and Matthias, "Journal," August 14, 1945.

18 *Richland Villager,* August 9, 1945, p. 2, September 3, 1945, p. 1 citing Matthias, November 15, 1945, p. 1, January 3, 1946, p. 1, 8, citing *Portland Oregonian, Time* magazine, and Ted Best (editor).

19 Ibid., August 7, 1947, p. 1, September 2, 1948, p. 23, December 23, 1948, p. 1, citing George Prout.

20 Paul Boyer, *By the Bomb's Early Light: American Thought and Culture at the Dawn of the Atomic Age* (New York: Pantheon Books, 1985).

21 Ibid., pp. 7, 14–15, citing *Time* magazine, August 1945, and citing Reinhold Niebuhr.

22 J. Robert Oppenheimer, cited in Rebecca Larsen, *Oppenheimer and the Atomic Bomb* (New York: Franklin Watts, 1988), p. 15. See also J. R. Oppenheimer, cited in Peter Goodchild, *J. Robert Oppenheimer: Shatterer of Worlds* (Boston: Houghton, Mifflin and Co., 1981), p. 174.

23 *Richland Villager,* August 16, 1945, p. 5, citing Reva Matthias.

24 David Lilienthal, *Change, Hope, and the Bomb* (Boston: Little Brown and Co., 1963), pp. 108–9.

25 *Richland Villager,* May 8, 1947, p. 10, citing David Lilienthal.

26 Ibid., January 10, 1946, citing Franklin Matthias, and August 8, 1946, p. 6.

27 *Tri-City Herald,* March 24, 1989, p. A3, citing Frederick Clarke.

28 *Richland Villager,* February 7, 1946, p. 1, February 14, 1946, p. 1, February 21, 1946, p. 1, March 7, 1946, p. 1, citing Carolyn Hageman.

29 Ibid., September 29, 1949, p. 4, citing Ted Best (editor).

30 Silver Anniversary Committee, "Alive," pp. 7–12.

31 *Richland Villager,* August 16, 1945, p. 5, February 2, 1946, p. 1, June 6, 1946, p. 1, February 21, 1946, p. 1, October 3, 1946, p. 1, January 6, 1947, p. 1, August 5, 1948, p. 1, January 19, 1950, p. 1; Seattle First National Bank, "The Hanford Works," pp. 6–7; and *Prosser Record-Bulletin,* May 29, 1947, p. 1.

32 *Richland Villager,* September 3, 1945, p. 2, citing Robert DeRoos.

33 "The Atomic Model City," *Time* 54, no. 24 (December 12, 1949): 21.

34 *Richland Villager,* January 3, 1946, p. 1.

35 Ibid., June 6, 1946, p. 1, 7, January 24, 1946, p. 1, June 5, 1946, p. 1; Richard Hewlett and Oscar Anderson, Jr., *The New World, 1939/1946* (University Park: University of Pennsylvania Press, 1962), pp. 636–37; Nichols, *Road,* p. 231; and Seattle First National Bank, "The Hanford Works," pp. 4–5.

36 *Richland Villager,* January 2, 1947, p. 1,

January 9, 1947, p. 1; and Seattle First National Bank, "The Hanford Works," pp. 4–5.

37 *Richland Villager,* August 7, 1947, p. 1, August 14, 1947, p. 1, August 28, 1947, p. 1, citing David Lilienthal.

38 Ibid., April 21, 1949, p. 1, citing David Lilienthal.

39 Ibid., September 29, 1949, p. 1, citing editor Ted Best.

40 Ibid., September 30, 1948, p. 1, October 21, 1948, p. 12.

41 Matthias, "Journal," April 16, 1945; and *Richland Villager,* September 23, 1948, p. 14, April 7, 1949, p. 9.

42 *Richland Villager,* October 4, 1945, p. 1, April 18, 1946, p. 1; and DuPont, *Operations,* Book VI, "Medical Department, Part I," p. 5.

43 *Richland Villager,* April 4, 1946, p. 1, April 18, 1946, p. 1.

44 "Statement on the Toxicity of DDT," *Journal of the American Medical Association* 139, no. 18 (April 30, 1949): 1285; "Worse Than Insects?" *Time* 53, no. 70 (April 11, 1949): 70; and "The DDT Scare," *Newsweek* 33 (April 18, 1949): 54. See also "DDT Aftermath," *Business Week,* May 14, 1949, p. 26; "Topics of the Times: Scientific Use of DDT," *Audubon Magazine* 51 (May–June 1949): 203; "Possible Hazards from the Use of DDT," *American Journal of Public Health* 39 (July 1949): 925–27; and *Richland Villager,* May 12, 1949, p. 9, citing Dr. William Norwood, January 19, 1950, p. 1.

45 *Richland Villager,* January 9, 1947, pp. 1, 6, February 27, 1947, p. 1, March 20, 1947, p. 1, April 3, 1947, p. 1, August 7, 1947, p. 1.

46 Ibid., September 4, 1947, p. 1, citing David H. Lauder.

47 Hill Williams, "Full Circle," *Seattle Times,* March 31, 1988, p. D2.

48 *Richland Villager,* August 5, 1948, p. 4, citing Dupus Boomer (Dick Donnell). See also *Richland Villager,* August 26, 1948, p. 4, May 26, 1949, p. 4, both citing Dupus Boomer.

49 Ibid., October 21, 1948, p. 9.

50 Ibid., September 16, 1948, pp. 9, 18; and *Tri-City Herald,* August 14, 1988, p. C1, citing Sharon Heisel.

51 *Richland Villager,* January 9, 1947, pp. 1, 6, February 27, 1947, p. 1, March 20, 1947, p. 1, April 3, 1947, p. 1.

52 Ibid., October 30, 1947, p. 1, May 6, 1948, p. 1, March 18, 1948, p. 1, September 23, 1948, p. 1, December 23, 1948, p. 1; and Dick Donnell, *Dupus Boomer: Cartoons and Witticisms* (Kennewick, Wash.: Kennewick Printing Co., 1948), p. 60.

53 *Richland Villager,* March 10, 1949, p. 1, March 17, 1949, p. 1, April 28, 1949, pp. 1, 5, February 23, 1950, p. 1.

54 Van Arsdol, *City,* pp. 49–55. In March 1945, Matthias specifically noted the high degree of "faith of the local population in the engineering ability and public integrity of the Corps of Engineers." See Matthias, "Journal," March 21, 1945.

55 Henry D. Smyth, *Atomic Energy for Military Purposes* (Princeton, N.J.: Princeton University Press, 1945), pp. 139, 149. See also *Richland Villager,* September 27, 1945, p. 1.

56 Matthias, "Journal," August 22, 1945, August 24, 1945.

57 Herbert M. Parker and Simon T. Cantril, "The Status of Health Protection at Hanford Engineer Works," HW-7-2136, CIC-0062016 (RL: HEW, August 24, 1945), pp. 1–6. The document is also located in R. Kathren, R. Baalman, and W. Bair, *Herbert M. Parker* (Columbus, Ohio: Battelle Press, 1986), pp. 306–11.

58 *Richland Villager,* November 29, 1945, p. 3, October 10, 1946, p. 1, citing W. D. Coolidge, October 17, 1946, citing Herbert M. Parker. See also *Richland Villager,* October 25, 1945, citing Leslie R. Groves.

59 Herbert M. Parker, "Health Physics, Instrumentation, and Radiation Protection," reprinted in *Health Physics* 38 (June 1980): 957–96. The original document was written in early 1947.

60 U.S. AEC, "Second Semiannual Report of the Atomic Energy Commission" (Washington, D.C.: U.S. Government Printing Office, July 1947), p. 13.
61 *Richland Villager,* August 14, 1947, p. 1, citing David H. Lauder, August 28, 1947, p. 5, citing David Lilienthal.
62 Ibid., November 26, 1948, p. 5, citing Dorothy Howard, January 20, 1949, p. 20, citing Dr. Ralph Sachs.
63 U.S. AEC, "Sixth Semiannual Report of the Atomic Energy Commission" (Washington, D.C.: U.S. Government Printing Office, July 1949), pp. 55–63.
64 U.S. AEC, "The Handling of Radioactive Waste Materials in the U.S. Atomic Energy Program," AEC 180/2 (Washington, D.C.: U.S. Atomic Energy Commission, October 14, 1949), pp. 12–15.
65 *Richland Villager,* January 19, 1950, p. 1, citing William D. Norwood. For other reassurances during the same period, see *Richland Villager,* October 13, 1949, p. 1, citing AEC General Manager Carroll Wilson, and *Richland Villager,* November 3, 1949, p. 1, citing AEC Hanford Manager Fred Schlemmer.
66 U.S. AEC, "Control of Radiation Hazards in the Atomic Energy Program," in "Eighth Semiannual Report of the Atomic Energy Commission" (Washington, D.C.: U.S. Government Printing Office, July 1950), pp. 140–41, 128–29, 100, 105, 109.
67 Hanson W. Baldwin, "New Atomic Capital," *New York Times Magazine,* July 30, 1950, pp. 17–18.
68 U.S. AEC, "Ninth Semiannual Report of the Atomic Energy Commission" (Washington, D.C.: U.S. Government Printing Office, January 1951), pp. 26, 54, 85–86.
69 Gordon E. Dean, *Report on the Atom,* 2d ed. (New York: Alfred A. Knopf, 1957), pp. 50, 54–56, 151, 191.
70 Lewis L. Strauss, "Atomic Status of the Nation," *Vital Speeches of the Day* 21, no. 8 (February 1, 1955): 1002–4.

71 U.S. AEC, "21st Semiannual Report of the Atomic Energy Commission" (Washington, D.C.: U.S. Government Printing Office, January 1957), pp. 197, 206–7. At this time, radiophosphorus (P-32) levels in Columbia River fish were well above the stated amount. Hanford officials were conducting a secret debate over whether to close large, additional stretches of the Columbia to sport fishing.
72 W. E. Johnson, in *Blue and Gold Memories* (Richland Junior High School yearbook), June 1957, p. 6.
73 J. W. Healy, B. V. Andersen, H. V. Clukey, and J. K. Soldat, "Radiation Exposure to People in the Environs of a Major Production Atomic Energy Plant," reprinted in W. G. Marley and K. Z. Morgan, eds., *Progress in Nuclear Energy,* Series XII, "Health Physics," vol. 1 (New York: Pergamon Press, 1959), p. 457 (address originally delivered September 1958).
74 R. E. Brown, D. W. Pearce, W. DeLaguna, E. G. Struxness, J. H. Horton, and C. M. Patterson, "Experience in the Disposal of Radioactive Wastes to the Ground," in ibid., p. 556 (address originally delivered September 1958).
75 *Tri-City Herald,* September 14, 1958, p. 1, citing John A. McCone.
76 Barton C. Hacker, *The Dragon's Tail: Radiation Safety in the Manhattan Project, 1942–46* (Berkeley: University of California Press, 1987), p. 4; Vincent C. Jones, *Manhattan: The Army and the Atomic Bomb* (Washington, D.C.: U.S. Army Center for Military History, 1985), p. 430; and *Richland Villager,* June 13, 1946, p. 1.
77 *Richland Villager,* May 9, 1946, p. 1, August 22, 1946, p. 1, October 24, 1946, p. 1, February 3, 1949, p. 9.
78 Ibid., March 11, 1948, p. 1.
79 Energy Research and Development Administration, "Waste Management Operations, Hanford Reservation: Final Environmental Statement," ERDA-1538, vol. 1 (Richland: U.S. Energy Research

and Development Administration, December 1975), p. III.2.23. See also U.S. AEC, "Ninth Semiannual," pp. 88–89. In early Richland, public announcements about fire safety and other safety topics did not mention the fact that rangeland in the area was contaminated with radioactivity.

80 *Richland Villager,* February 28, 1946, p. 5, May 9, 1946, p. 1, July 11, 1946, p. 5, August 22, 1946, p. 6, October 3, 1946, p. 6, March 20, 1947, p. 1, May 8, 1947, p. 1, May 22, 1947, p. 4, June 5, 1947, p. 8, June 12, 1947, p. 5, June 19, 1947, p. 4, June 9, 1949, p. 1, June 30, 1949, p. 9, January 5, 1950, p. 1.

81 Ibid., May 26, 1949, p. 13.

82 Ibid., January 15, 1947, p. 1, May 13, 1948, p. 18, citing Herbert Parker. See also *Richland Villager,* January 19, 1950, p. 1, citing William Norwood.

83 Ibid., November 29, 1945, p. 3, June 27, 1946, p. 7, October 31, 1946, p. 1, May 13, 1948, p. 18. See also *Richland Villager,* July 31, 1947, p. 4, November 13, 1947, p. 4, June 3, 1948, p. 10, January 20, 1949, p. 20, May 26, 1949, p. 13.

84 U.S. AEC, "Second Semiannual," p. 15.

85 U.S. AEC, "Third Semiannual Report of the Atomic Energy Commission" (Washington, D.C.: U.S. Government Printing Office, February 1948), pp. 27–28; and U.S. AEC, "Second Semiannual," p. 15.

86 U.S. AEC, "Fifth Semiannual Report of the Atomic Energy Commission" (Washington, D.C.: U.S. Government Printing Office, January 1949), pp. 51–52, 124–26.

87 U.S. AEC, "Report of the Safety and Industrial Health Advisory Board, AEC" AEC-10266 (Washington, D.C.: U.S. AEC, April 2, 1948), p. 6.

88 U.S. AEC, "Control of Radiation Hazards," pp. 227–28. See also Alan Gregg, memo to Carroll Wilson, "Report of Meeting of Advisory Committee for Biology and Medicine, AEC, Washington, D.C., February 12, 1949," CIC-70118 (Washington, D.C.: U.S. Atomic Energy Commission, 1949), p. 2.

89 Pugnetti, *Tiger,* pp. 17–59; and *Tri-City Herald,* December 2, 1947, pp. 1, 3, November 18, 1947, p. 1.

90 Richard Neuberger, "Plutonium and Problems," *Nation* 169 (July 30, 1949): 104–5.

91 U.S. AEC, "Tenth Semiannual Report of the Atomic Energy Commission" (Washington, D.C.: U.S. Government Printing Office, July 1951), pp. 44–45, paraphrasing University of Michigan survey.

92 Laura Lee Bailie, interview with the author, January 14, 1988 (Mesa, Wash.).

93 AEC-10266, pp. 64–65, 72.

94 The technological steps taken in an attempt to contain the radioactive discharges will be discussed in detail in chapters 4, 5, and 6.

95 Simon Cantril and John W. Healy, "Iodine Metabolism with Reference to I-131," HW-7-2604 (RL: HEW, October 22, 1945).

96 *Richland Villager,* August 16, 1945, p. 12.

97 Robert C. Thorburn, "Detection of Plutonium in Flora," HW-7002 (RL: HEW, July 1, 1947); and *Richland Villager,* August 7, 1947, p. 1.

98 A. A. Selders, "The Absorption and Translocation of Several Fission Elements by Russian Thistle," HW-18034 (RL: HEW, June 8, 1950); and *Richland Villager,* May 5, 1949, p. 9.

99 *Richland Villager,* October 10, 1946, p. 2, October 2, 1947, p. 8, March 11, 1948, p. 5; Kenneth E. Herde, "Radioactivity in Upland Wild-Fowl from Areas Surrounding the Hanford Works Project," HW-8668 (RL: HEW, January 26, 1948); K. Herde and J. Cline, "Radioactivity in Pekin Ducks on the Columbia River," HW-12079 (RL: HEW, January 7, 1949); Kenneth E. Herde, "Biological Monitor-

ing of Waste Water From 200 Area . . .
Storage Buildings," HW-12855 (RL: HEW,
March 22, 1949); and R. E. Roberts,
"History of Airborne Contamination and
Control—200 Areas," HW-55569 RD (RL:
HAPO, April 1, 1958). The territory surveyed by Hanford biologists during the
1947 and 1948 hunting seasons ranged
from forty miles west to seventy miles
east of the atomic site. The most contaminated wildfowl were found from four to
seven miles north and northwest of Richland. Site scientists consistently found
that the muscle tissue (flesh) contained
the least amounts of radioactivity. Thyroid, bone, liver, and kidney tissue always contained higher concentrations. In
the case of nonaquatic organisms exposed to I-131, thyroid tissue consistently
demonstrated the most elevated levels.
100 *Richland Villager,* September 29,
1949, p. 3, citing H. W. Strock.
101 John W. Healy, "Accumulation of
Radioactive Elements in Fish . . . in Pile
Effluent Water," HW-3442 (RL: HEW,
February 27, 1946); Kenneth E. Herde,
"Studies in the Accumulations of Radioactive Elements in Chinook Salmon Exposed to a Medium of Pile Effluent
Water," HW-3-5064 (RL: HEW,
October 14, 1946); Kenneth E. Herde, "A
One-Year Study of Columbia River
Fish," HW-11344 (RL: HEW, October 25,
1948); and R. W. Coopey, "The Accumu-
lation of Radioactivity as Shown by a
Limnological Study of the Columbia
River in the Vicinity of Hanford Works:
A Preliminary Report," HW-11662 (Rich-
land: November 12, 1948).
102 *Richland Villager,* January 15, 1948, p.
8.
103 Herde, HW-8668; Frank Adley, "Report of a Study of the Fate of 200 Area
Stack Gases," HW-9864 (RL: HEW,
May 21, 1948), p. 1; Walter Singlevich,
"Radioactive Contamination in the Columbia River and Radiation Levels Measured in the Air at Hanford Works and

Vicinity for 1945, 1946, 1947, and Early
1948," HW-9871 (RL: HEW, May 24,
1948); and Roberts, HW-55569 RD,
pp. 1, 6.
104 *Richland Villager,* October 21, 1946,
p. 1, October 13, 1949, p. 8.
105 Ibid., November 29, 1945, p. 3. The
technology for testing milk specifically
for I-131 had not been developed in the
1940s. However, an estimate of I-131 levels could be discerned from the "gross
beta" radiation level measurements used
by Hanford scientists in those years.
106 Ibid., July 31, 1947, p. 4, August 7,
1947, p. 1.
107 Ibid., June 3, 1948, p. 1, June 17, 1948,
p. 6, June 24, 1948, pp. 6, 18, all citing
Dr. William Norwood.
108 Ibid., September 23, 1948, p. 14, citing Kenneth Lieferman.
109 Ibid., September 30, 1948, p. 6.
110 The potential hazards of Columbia
River water itself, to crops irrigated with
it and to the domestic water supplies of
Pasco and Kennewick, were less severe,
on a concentration basis, than those presented to the food chain by river-based
organisms.

Chapter 4

1 Energy Research and Development
Administration, "Waste Management
Operations, Hanford Reservation: Final
Environmental Statement" ERDA-1538,
vol. 2 (Richland: U.S. Energy Research
and Development Administration, December 1975), pp. II, 1-B-26-27.
2 Simon Cantril and John Healy, "Iodine
Metabolism with Reference to I-131,"
HW-7-2604 (RL: HEW, October 22,
1945); Herbert M. Parker, "Proposed Revision of Tolerance for I-131," HW-7-3042
(RL: HEW, December 17, 1945); R. E.
Roberts, "History of Airborne Contamination and Control—200 Areas,"
HW-55569 RD (RL: HAPO, April 1, 1958),
pp. 6–7; and J. D. Anderson, "Emitted
and Decayed Values of Radionuclides in

Gaseous Wastes Discharged to the Atmosphere," ARH-3026 (Richland: Atlantic Richfield Hanford Co., March 1, 1974), p. 5.

3 D. E. Jenne and J. W. Healy, "Dissolving the Twenty-Day Metal at Hanford," HW-17381 (RL: HEW, May 1, 1950).

4 J. L. Dreher, "Wind Dilution Required to Reduce to Tolerance Levels the Activity Due to Xenon and Iodine in Hanford Engineer Works Dissolver Off-Gases," HW-3-811 DEL (RL: HEW, September 29, 1944).

5 DuPont Corporation, *Operations of Hanford Engineer Works*, HAN-73214 (Wilmington, Del.: E.I. DuPont de Nemours and Co., 1946), Book XII, "S Department," p. 93. See also Dr. William Norwood, in S. L. Sanger and R. W. Mull, eds., *Hanford and the Bomb: An Oral History of World War II* (Seattle: Living History Press, 1990), p. 150; and Robert Thorburn, "Detection of Plutonium in . . . Flora," HW-7002 (RL: HEW, July 1, 1947).

6 DuPont, *Operations*, Book XII, pp. 113–14, 181.

7 Frank Adley, "Report of a Study of the Fate of 200 Area Stack Gases," HW-9864 (RL: HEW, May 21, 1948), p. 1; and Roberts, HW-55569 RD, pp. 1–2.

8 D. P. Ebright, "A History of the Redox Ruthenium Problem," HW-32473 (RL: HAPO, July 16, 1954); J. M. Selby and J. K. Soldat, "Summary of Environmental Contamination Incidents at Hanford, 1952–57," HW-54636 (RL: HAPO, January 25, 1958), p. 8; and Herbert M. Parker, "Status of Ground Contamination Problem," HW-33068 (RL: HAPO, September 15, 1954), pp. 2–12.

9 Some scientists in the 1940s and 1950s believed the kidneys to be the critical organs of biomedical concern with reference to radioruthenium. See Harry A. Kornberg, "The Absorption and Toxicity of Several Radioactive Substances in Plants and Animals," CIC-26514 (Richland: General Electric Co., 1955), p. 8. However the kidneys have not proved to be particularly at risk.

10 Mike Lindblom, "Hanford Zinc Found as Far Away as Willapa Bay," *Tri-City Herald*, September 24, 1988, p. A4, citing Russell Jim.

11 DuPont, *Operations*, Book XII, p. 112.

12 Franklin T. Matthias, "Journal and Notes, 1943–45," unpublished diary (located at Richland, U.S. Department of Energy Public Reading Room), May 27, 1943, June 8, 1943.

13 Ibid., September 7, 1943, October 25, 1943, January 24/25, 1944, February 21, 1944.

14 Ibid., March 1, 1944, July 25, 1944. In late 1944, a meteorology facility (622 Building) was erected between the 200 East and 200 West areas. Wind direction and velocity readings were continuously taken there by the meteorology group.

15 DuPont, *Operations*, Book XII, p. 158.

16 Ibid., pp. 136–41.

17 Ibid., pp. 128–30.

18 Dreher, HW-3-811 DEL, pp. 1–2.

19 Ibid.; and J. L. Dreher, "The Evolution of Iodine During Metal Dissolution," HW-3003 DEL (RL: HEW, August 2, 1945), p. 1.

20 Henry D. Smyth, *Atomic Energy for Military Purposes* (Princeton, N.J.: Princeton University Press, 1945), pp. 136–37. Smyth also informed the public: "Radioxenon and radioiodine . . . are released in considerable quantity when the slugs are dissolved . . . high stacks must be built which will carry off these gases . . . and it must be established that the mixing of radioactive gases with the atmosphere will not endanger the surrounding territory." See Smyth, p. 121.

21 DuPont, *Operations*, Book XII, p. 112.

22 Ibid., p. 158.

23 Matthias, "Journal," November 13, 1944, February 28, 1945, July 6, 1945; and DuPont, *Operations*, Book XII, p. 129.

24 Walter O. Simon, in Sanger and Mull, *Hanford*, p. 125.

25 DuPont, *Operations,* Book XII, p. 167.
26 Ibid., p. 192. During the first six months of 1946, dissolving took place under "unfavorable" conditions 16 percent of the time and under "moderately satisfactory" conditions 16 percent of the time.
27 Ibid., p. 201.
28 Ibid., p. 65.
29 Ibid., pp. 65–66, 130; DuPont, *Operations,* Book VII, "Medical Department: Health Instruments," p. 49; and John W. Healy, "Detection of I-131 in the Body," HW-7-4451 (RL: HEW, July 25, 1946). A few sporadic thyroid checks of 200-Area workers had been done by DuPont beginning in 1944. However, from June 1945 until DuPont finished work on the Hanford Site on August 31, 1946, the checks were done regularly (weekly). The tabulated results of these thyroid checks in general showed few significant dosages.
30 DuPont, *Operations,* Book VII, p. 48; and Matthias, "Journal," November 13, 1944, February 28, 1945, July 6, 1945.
31 DuPont, *Operations,* Book VII, p. 128. Pasco's reading for August 1945 was 1.8 millirads per 24 hours (mr/24 hrs), and Benton City's reading was 2.1 mr/24 hrs.
32 Ibid., p. 50; and Herman J. Paas, Jr., interview with the author, December 7, 1988 (Las Vegas, Nev.).
33 DuPont, *Operations,* Book VII, pp. 50, 151, 146.
34 Herbert M. Parker, "Tolerable Concentrations of Radio-Iodine on Edible Plants," HW-7-3217 (RL: HEW, January 14, 1946).
35 DuPont, *Operations,* Book VII, p. 129.
36 Colonel Frederick Clarke, in *Tri-City Herald,* March 24, 1989, p. A3.
37 DuPont, *Operations,* Book XII, pp. 145, 157, 149, 146.
38 Ibid., pp. 171, 195.
39 Quotation in DuPont, *Operations,* Book VII, p. 165. See also L. D. Turner, "The Trend of Contamination Observed in the Air, Columbia River, and Vegetation at the Hanford Engineer Works for 1946," HW-3-5402 (RL: HEW, March 27, 1947); DuPont, *Operations,* Book VII, pp. 178, 188–89, 197; John W. Healy, "Vegetation Contamination for First Quarter of 1946," HW-3-3495 (RL: HEW, May 1, 1946); L. D. Turner, "Vegetation Contamination for Second Quarter of 1946," HW-3-3603 (RL: HEW, August 6, 1946); and L. D. Turner, "Vegetation Contamination for Period July 2, 1946 to August 31, 1946," HW-3-5055 (RL: HEW, October 22, 1946).
40 L. D. Turner, "Vegetation Contamination for Period September 3, 1946 to December 31, 1946," HW-3-5521 (RL: HEW, May 15, 1947).
41 "For Overactive Thyroids," *Science News Letter* 45, no. 21 (May 20, 1944): 326; Parker, HW-7-3042; and Cantril and Healy, HW-7-2604.
42 "Atoms and Cancer," *Time* 48, no. 16 (October 14, 1946): 54.
43 Amy Porter, "Guinea Pig for Cancer," *Collier's* 121 (June 26, 1948): 30.
44 "Radioisotopes Cancer Aid," *Science News Letter* 54, no. 7 (August 14, 1948): 99.
45 U.S. AEC, "Fourth Semiannual Report of the Atomic Energy Commission" (Washington, D.C.: U.S. Government Printing Office, July 1948), pp. 59–138 (esp. p. 97).
46 DuPont, *Operations,* Book VII, pp. 93–94; and Cantril and Healy, HW-7-2604.
47 Cantril and Healy, HW-7-2604.
48 Parker, HW-7-3042; and DuPont, *Operations,* Book VII, p. 137.
49 Herbert M. Parker, "Tolerance Dose: Interpretation of Permissible Daily Dose," DUH-12, 744 (RL: HEW, February 23, 1946).
50 John W. Healy, "Recovery of I-131," HW-3-3482 (RL: HEW, April 18, 1946).
51 Parker, HW-7-3042; Parker, HW-7-3217; Advisory Committee on

X-Ray and Radium Protection, "X-Ray Protection," HB20 (Washington, D.C.: U.S. Government Printing Office, 1936); and Simon T. Cantril and Herbert M. Parker, "The Tolerance Dose," MDDC-1100, in R. Kathren, R. Baalman, and W. Bair, *Herbert M. Parker* (Columbus, Ohio: Battelle Press, 1986), p. 271 (document originally written January 5, 1945; citation is from p. 4, original document).

52 Leona Marshall Libby, *The Uranium People* (New York: Crane, Russak, 1979), p. 174.

53 Kenneth Herde, "I-131 Accumulation in the Thyroid of Sheep Grazing near Hanford Engineer Works," HW-3-3455 (RL: HEW, March 1, 1946); and Kenneth Herde, "I-131 Deposition in Cattle Grazing on North Margin of Hanford Engineer Works," HW-3-3628 (RL: HEW, August 29, 1946).

54 K. Herde and J. Cline, "Biological Monitoring of Separation Plant Areas by Use of Native and Domestic Rabbits," HW-14085 (RL: HEW, August 8, 1949).

55 Herbert M. Parker, "Radiation Exposure Data," memo to D. G. Sturges (AEC-Hanford operations manager), HW-19404 (RL: HEW, November 8, 1950), p. 2.

56 K. Herde, R. Browning, and W. Hanson, "Activity Densities in Waterfowl of the Hanford Reservation and Environs," HW-18645 (RL: HEW, August 21, 1951).

57 R. S. Apple, "Activities Discharged into the Atmosphere," HW-7-4245 (RL: HEW, June 18, 1946).

58 F. P. Seymour, "A Study of Total Amounts of Active Waste Released in All Manners by the H.E.W. Process to Date," HW-5463 (RL: HEW, December 5, 1946), p. 3.

59 Thorburn, HW-7002.

60 M. L. Mickelson and Staff of the Health Instruments Divisions, "Annual Report of H.I. Divisions, 1950,"

HW-21699 (rev.) (RL: HEW, July 20, 1951), p. 25.

61 Adley, HW-9864, p. 1; Roberts, HW-55569 RD, pp. 1–2; and L. C. Rees, "Particulate Distribution 200-E," HW-8430 (RL: HEW, November 28, 1947).

62 R. S. Bell, "Active Particle Investigation—200 Areas: Installation and Physical Control," HW-08108 (RL: HEW, November 26, 1947).

63 Herbert M. Parker, "Action Taken on Spot Contamination within Separations Plant Areas," HW-7920 (RL: HEW, October 30, 1947); and Herbert M. Parker, "Review of the Stack Discharge Active Particle Contamination Problem," HW-9259 (RL: HEW, March 22, 1948).

64 W. K. MacCready, "Installation of Air Filters—200 Areas," HW-7932 (RL: HEW, November 3, 1947).

65 Herbert M. Parker, "Progress Report on Action taken on the Spot Contamination in the Separations Plant Area," HW-8624 (RL: HEW, January 20, 1948); Adley, HW-9864, p. 4; and O. H. Greager and W. K. MacCready, "Stack Gas Decontamination—Separations Plants," HW-8667 (RL: HEW, January 27, 1948).

66 W. P. Overbeas, "Location of Redox Test Unit," letter to Carleton Shugg (AEC-Hanford manager), HW-9091 (RL: HEW, March 5, 1948). The new location was south and slightly west of the 221U Building.

67 John W. Healy, letter to Dr. Henderson (Atomic Energy Commission, Washington, D.C.), HW-15234 (RL: HEW, November 19, 1949). The other major, outlying particle-monitoring stations were located at Spokane and Walla Walla, Wash.; Meachan, Oreg.; and Lewiston, Idaho.

68 Adley, HW-9864.

69 Roberts, HW-55569 RD, p. 2; and Parker, HW-33068, pp. 1–2.

70 Alan Gregg (chairman, Atomic En-

ergy Commission Advisory Committee on Biology and Medicine), memo to Carroll Wilson (Atomic Energy Commission general manager), CIC-70118 (Washington, D.C.: U.S. Atomic Energy Commission, February 12, 1949), pp. 1–2.
71 Mickelson et al., HW-21699, pp. 24–25; and Parker, HW-33068, pp. 1–2.
72 Carl Gamertsfelder, "Effects on Surrounding Areas Caused by the Operations of the Hanford Engineer Works," HW-7-5934 (RL: HEW, March 11, 1947), p. 4; L. D. Turner and J. W. Healy, "Contamination on Wahluke Slope and Outlying Districts in February 1947," HW-3-5313 (RL: HEW, February 18, 1947; and L. D. Turner, "The Trend of Contamination Observed in the Air, the Columbia River, Vegetation, and Waste at the Hanford Engineer Works for the Period January 1, 1947 to March 25, 1947," HW-3-5511 (RL: HEW, May 9, 1947).
73 Gamertsfelder, HW-7-5934, pp. 2–3.
74 Herbert M. Parker, "Health Physics, Instrumentation, and Radiation Protection," reprinted in *Health Physics* 38 (June 1980): 967 (original document written in early 1947).
75 U.S. AEC, "Report of the Safety and Industrial Health Advisory Board, AEC," AEC-10266 (Washington, D.C.: U.S. AEC, April 4, 1948), pp. 71, 68.
76 Kenneth Herde, "Radioactivity in Upland Wild-Fowl from Areas Surrounding the Hanford Works Project," HW-8668 (RL: HEW, January 26, 1948).
77 Ibid. *Hanford Reach* is a term that was not used in the 1940s and 1950s. Since that time, it has come to designate the stretch of the Columbia River from the foot of Priest Rapids to Richland. This stretch is approximately fifty-two miles long and encompasses the entire river border of the Hanford Nuclear Reservation. Technology to assess each radionuclide separately was not available. The "gross beta" activity was assumed by Hanford scientists to be primarily I-131

because it was concentrated in thyroid tissue.
78 Herbert M. Parker, "Status of Iodine Contamination—Proposed Increase in Cooling Time," HW-9394 (RL: HEW, April 5, 1948).
79 *Richland Villager,* April 10, 1947, p. 3; and U.S. Atomic Energy Commission, "The Handling of Radioactive Waste Materials in the U.S. Atomic Energy Program," AEC 180/2 (Washington, D.C.: U.S. Atomic Energy Commission, September 22, 1949), p. 22. The consultants retained by GE-Hanford Company in April 1947 were Glenn Seaborg (the discoverer of plutonium) and Ernest O. Lawrence of the University of California, Enrico Fermi (the famed Manhattan Project physicist who executed the first controlled, self-sustained, atomic chain reaction), Philip Morrison and T. E. Bethe of Cornell University, and Eugene P. Wigner (director of the Clinton Laboratories at Oak Ridge, Tenn.).
80 Roger S. Warner, Jr. (director, Division of Engineering, U.S. AEC), memo to Carroll Wilson, Jr. (general manager, U.S. AEC), "Decontamination of Stack Gases" (Washington, D.C.: U.S. Atomic Energy Commission, June 4, 1948).
81 Roger S. Warner, memo to Roy B. Snapp (Office of the General Manager, U.S. AEC), "Stack Gas Problem Working Group—Meeting July 20–21" (Washington, D.C.: U.S. Atomic Energy Commission, August 20, 1948), pp. 6, 10, 12.
82 Herbert M. Parker, "Effect of Dissolver Off-Gas Scrubbers on Reduced Cooling Time," letter to W. K. MacCready, HW-10568 (RL: HEW, July 26, 1948).
83 Walter Singlevich, "H.I. Environs Report for the Month of September 1948," HW-11264 (RL: HEW, October 11, 1948); and K. Herde and J. Cline, "Radioactivity in Pekin Ducks on the Columbia River," HW-12079 (RL: HEW, January 7, 1949).

84 E. Teller, M. Benedict, J. Kennedy, J. Wheeler, and A. Wolman, "Review of Certain Operations, Reactor Safeguard Committee Hanford Meeting, June 14, 15, 16, 1948," GEH-14040 (RL: HEW, November 4, 1948), p. 12.

85 Walter Singlevich and Herman Paas, Jr., "Radioactive Contamination in the Environs of the Hanford Works for the Period January, February, March 1949," HW-14243 DEL (RL: HEW, December 23, 1949), pp. 47–49.

86 Roberts, HW-55569 RD, p. 6; Walter Singlevich and Herman Paas, Jr., "Radioactive Contamination in the Environs of the Hanford Works for the Period October, November, December 1949," HW-17003 (RL: HEW, March 2, 1950), pp. 12–15, 18, 21–22, 26, 31; Jenne and Healy, HW-17381; and Maurice A. Robkin, "Experimental Release of Iodine 131: The Green Run, Report to the Technical Steering Panel" (Richland: Hanford Dose Reconstruction Project, December 11, 1989).

87 *Tri-City Herald,* May 6, 1989, p. A1; *Oregonian* (Portland, Oregon), May 13, 1988, citing Carl Gamertsfelder, former Hanford monitoring scientist; and *Tri-City Herald,* April 10, 1988, p. A2, citing Michael Lawrence.

88 *Spokesman Review—Spokane Chronicle,* March 6, 1986, pp. A6, A12, citing Keith Price. Department of Defense documents that might aid in the historical understanding of the Green Run are currently undergoing classification review. It is not possible to gain public access to these documents at this time. The minutes of the meeting of the Atomic Energy Commission, held at Argonne National Laboratory, Lamont, Ill., December 12–14, 1949, do not mention the test at Hanford. However, Roger Anders, a U.S. DOE historian in Washington, D.C., "cannot locate" these minutes. See Roger Anders, letter to the author, February 23, 1989.

89 *Tri-City Herald,* May 6, 1989, p. A1, citing Carl Gamertsfelder.

90 Ibid., April 10, 1986, p. A2, citing Michael Lawrence.

91 Singlevich and Paas, HW-17003, pp. 14–15, 22, 51–54. At Pasco, one rainwater sample contained 69 millimicrocuries (μCi) per liter. "Normal" averages at the time, including rainwater samples that contained Hanford's ongoing I-131 discharges, contained 1.0 to 3.0 μCi/liter. See HW-17003, p. 54.

92 Carl Gamertsfelder, in "Emission at Hanford Part of Cold War," *Portland Oregonian,* May 13, 1986, p. B2.

93 Herde, Browning, and Hanson, HW-18645.

94 Herbert M. Parker, "Feasibility of Reduction of Cooling Time—Separations Process," HW-18049 (RL: HEW, July 25, 1950), pp. 1–4. Occasional vegetation samples in Parker's "reference belt" from early 1949 to mid-1950 (except for the weeks after the Green Run) had reached 0.15 μCi/kg.

95 A. G. Blasewitz, "Iodine Evolution during Metal Dissolution," HW-15367 (RL: HEW, December 9, 1949); C. F. Hill, G. B. Barton, et al., "Symposium on Iodine Problem," HW-39073 (RL: HAPO, August 3, 1955), p. 2; A. G. Blasewitz, R. V. Carlisle, et al., "Decontamination of Dissolver Vent Gases at Hanford," HW-20332 (RL: HEW, February 16, 1951), p. 4; and Parker, HW-18049, p. 4. The caustic scrubbers contained varying concentrations of sodium hydroxide and sodium carbonate in solution and were sometimes called water scrubbers. Other experimental methods of removing or neutralizing I-131 in the separations process also were explored by Hanford chemists during this period. For one example, see R. E. Burns and C. R. McMullen, "Removal of Iodine from Dissolver Solution by Carrier Precipitation," HW-19573 (RL: HEW, November 27, 1950).

96 Herman J. Paas, Jr., and Joseph K. Soldat, "Summary of Measurements for the Activity Density from I-131: For the Period September 1950 to July 1951," HW-21891 (RL: HEW, August 21, 1951), p. 6.

97 J. B. Work, "Efficiency Evaluation of Dissolver Cell Silver Reactor and Fiberglas Filter," HW-19898 (RL: HEW, January 8, 1951).

98 Paas and Soldat, HW-21891, p. 7.

99 Ibid., pp. 8–9; Roberts, HW-55569 RD, p. 6; and Hill, Barton, et al., HW-39073.

100 Roberts, HW-55569 RD, p. 6; W. G. Browne, "I-131 Emission Problem—Bismuth Phosphate Plant," HW-36112 (RL: HAPO, April 6, 1955), pp. 1–2; J. M. Smith "Iodine Contamination of the Hanford Environs," in Hill, Barton, et al., HW-39073, p. 2; and W. G. Browne and H. P. Maffei, "I-131 Control by Two Silver Reactor Units in Series," HW-39485 (RL: HAPO, October 12, 1955). See also A. G. Blasewitz, "Performance of Replacement and Regenerated Silver Reactors—Operated at 375x F," HW-21957 (RL: HEW, August 20, 1951); J. S. Kane and R. E. Burns, "Behavior of Iodine in the Redox Process," HW-23312 (RL: HAPO, January 21, 1952); H. F. Soule and R. E. Taylor, "Review of Silver Reactor Performance in the Separations Facilities," HW-27580 (RL: HAPO, March 27, 1953); L. L. Burger, "Thermodynamics of Iodine Removal," HW-38311 (rev.) (RL: HAPO, July 1, 1955); R. E. Smith, "Flowsheets for Iodine 131 Emission Control at 1961 Power and Enrichment Levels," HW-39261 (RL: HAPO, September 29, 1955); and F. J. Leitz, "Plant Test of Isotopic Exchange for Removal of Radio-Iodine from Dissolver Off-Gas," HW-39835 (RL: HAPO, November 7, 1955).

101 Roberts, HW-55569 RD, p. 6; and Browne, HW-36112, pp. 1–2.

102 Hill, Barton, et al., HW-39073.

103 Smith, HW-39261, p. 2.

104 Roberts, HW-55569 RD, p. 6; and B. V. Andersen, "Monthly Report, Regional Monitoring," CIC-12765 (RL: HAPO), for November 1956 (December 3,
1956), p. 1, and December 1956 (January 3, 1957), p. 1.

105 Staff Report, "Hanford Biology Research Annual Report for 1958," HW-59500 (RL: HAPO, January 5, 1959), p. 141.

106 Robert D. Thompson, "Project Report for ASEE-AEC Summer 1957 Program: Removal of I-131 from Off-Gases," HW-51925 (RL: HAPO, August 16, 1957), p. 1.

107 G. E. Backman, "Summary of Environmental Contamination Incidents at Hanford, 1958–1964," HW-84619 (RL: HAPO, April 12, 1965), p. 8.

108 Mickelson et al., HW-21699, pp. 4, 48; and Paas and Soldat, HW-21891, pp. 21–23, and fig. 8.

109 Mickelson et al., HW-21699, p. 40; Herbert M. Parker, "Quarterly Progress Report—Research and Development Activities for April–June 1950," HW-18371 (RL: HEW, July 19, 1950), p. 12; Herbert M. Parker "Quarterly Progress Report—Research and Development Activities for January–March 1951," HW-20866; and Herbert M. Parker, "Radiological Sciences Department: Quarterly Progress Report—Research and Development Activities for July–September 1951," HW-22576 (RL: HEW, November 1, 1951), p. 16.

110 H. A. Kornberg and J. J. Davis, in Staff Report, HW-59500, pp. 138–39, 141. The 1957 and 1958 spikes in I-131 in jackrabbit thyroids also came partially from fallout produced by atmospheric bomb testing.

111 "Evaluate Atomic Iodine after 10 Years' Use," *Science Digest* 30 (November 1951): 50, citing *American Journal of Roentgenology and Radium Therapy.*

112 Herbert M. Parker, "Radiological Sciences Department, Quarterly Progress Report: Research and Development Activities for January–March, 1952" (RL: HAPO, April 16, 1953), pp. 9–11.

113 U.S. AEC, "Eleventh Semiannual Report of the Atomic Energy Commission" (Washington, D.C.: U.S. Government Printing Office, January 1952), p. 88.

114 "Pheasant Abundant in Columbia Basin," *Tri-City Herald,* October 3, 1958, p. 11.

115 Joseph C. Schoolar, John J. Lane, Robert A. Monroe, John H. Rust, and Bernard F. Trum, "Fractional Total Body Irradiation and Thyroid Function in the Burro," *Science* 120, no. 3129 (December 17, 1954): 1032–33; and H. J. Curtis, "News and Notes: The Thyroid," *Science* 120, no. 3114 (September 3, 1954): 365. See also Robert A. Monroe, John H. Rust, and Bernard F. Trum, "Sublethal Total Body Irradiation and I-131 Metabolism in the Rat Thyroid," *Science* 119, no. 3080 (January 8, 1954): 65.

116 "Thyroid Gland Linked with Decay of Teeth," *Science News Letter* 65, no. 23 (June 5, 1954): 355; and "Radioactive Iodine Gets into Mother's Milk," *Science News Letter* 62, no. 25 (December 22, 1952): 395. For further confirmation of the link to tooth decay, see "Underactive Thyroid Gives Rats Tooth Decay," *Science News Letter* 70, no. 24 (December 15, 1956): 376.

117 S. M. Seidlin, Edward Siegel, A. A. Yalew, and S. Melamed, "Acute Myeloid Leukemia Following Prolonged Iodine-131 Therapy for Metastatic Thyroid Carcinoma," *Science* 123, no. 3201 (May 4, 1956): 800–801; and "Slow Thyroid Can Slow Child's Reading Ability," *Science News Letter* 68, no. 1 (July 2, 1955): 8.

118 Harry A. Kornberg, "The Absorption and Toxicity of Several Radioactive Substances in Plants and Animals," CIC-26514 (Richland: GE Co., 1955), pp. 3–4. I-131 activity levels in the thyroids of Hanford-area jackrabbits ranged from 100 to 1,000 times (averaging 500 times) those of the vegetation eaten by the animals. See Kornberg, CIC-26514, p. 4.

119 Gordon Dunning (U.S. AEC), "Policies of the AEC Regarding Radiological Safety of the Public During Weapons Testing at the Nevada Test Site," CIC-122494 (Washington, D.C.: U.S. Government Printing Office, September 30, 1954), p. 57.

120 Herbert M. Parker, "Health Problems Associated with the Radiochemical Processing Industry," *American Medical Association Archives of Public Health* 13 (May 1956): 454–57.

121 "Britain's Atoms Stage a Scare," *Business Week,* no. 1468 (October 19, 1957), pp. 50–52; and Hartley Howe, "Accident at Windscale: World's First Atomic Alarm," *Popular Science* 173 (October 1958): 92–95.

122 Harold A. Knapp, "Iodine-131 in Fresh Milk and Human Thyroids Following a Single Deposition of Nuclear Test Fallout," TID-19266 (Washington, D.C.: AEC Division of Biology and Medicine, June 1, 1963).

123 Mickelson et al., HW-21699, pp. 41–42; Parker, HW-18371, pp. 12–14; and Herbert M. Parker, "Quarterly Progress Report—Research and Development Activities for July–September 1950," HW-19146 (RL: HEW, October 16, 1950), p. 12. The two highest dosage groups in the original experiment were fed 1,800 and 240 μCi/d, respectively.

124 Herbert M. Parker, "Radiological Sciences Department: Quarterly Progress Report—Research and Development Activities for January–March 1952," HW-24131 (RL: HAPO, April 16, 1952), p. 12.

125 Herbert M. Parker, "Toxicity of I-131 in Sheep," letter to Kenneth L. Englund (AEC, Washington, D.C.), HW-25239 (RL: HAPO, August 9, 1952), p. 3.

126 L. K. Bustad, S. Marks, and N. L. Dockum, "A Comparative Study of Hanford and Utah Range Sheep," HW-30119 (RL: HAPO, November 30, 1953), p. 42.

127 Biology Operation, "Biology Re-

search Annual Report, 1956," HW-47500
(RL: HAPO, January 4, 1957), pp. 84–88.
128 L. K. Bustad, S. Marks, L. A.
George, and L. J. Seigneur, "Thyroid
Adenomas in Sheep Administered
Iodine-131 Daily," *Nature* 179 (March 30,
1957): 677.
129 Kornberg and Davis, in Staff Report,
HW-59500, pp. 52–53.
130 Leo Bustad in H. D. Bruner, M.D.
(chief, Division of Biology and Medicine, Atomic Energy Commission, Wash-
ington, D.C.), "Bio Med Program
Directors Meeting at Hanford, June 7–8,
1959," CIC-25210 (Washington, D.C.:
U.S. Atomic Energy Commission,
June 19, 1959), pp. 3–4. By 1958, Bustad,
Kornberg, and D. E. Warner of GE-
Hanford Company had demonstrated ex-
perimentally that supplying iodized salt
or inorganic iodine (KI) to sheep re-
duced the animals' uptake of single doses
of radioiodine by 30–50 percent. See
L. K. Bustad, D. E. Warner and H. A.
Kornberg, "Effect of Stable Iodine on
Uptake of Radioiodine in Sheep," *American Journal of Veterinary Research* 19, no.
73 (October 1958): 893–94.
131 L. K. Bustad, E. E. Elefson, E. C.
Watson, D. H. Wood, and H. A. Ragan,
"I-131 in the Thyroid of Sheep and in
Food, Thyroid, and Milk of Dairy
Cows," draft report (Richland: General
Electric Co., February 28, 1963).
132 Ebright, HW-32473, p. 1; and Selby
and Soldat, HW-54636, pp. 7–8.
133 Ebright, HW-32473, pp. 3–9.
134 Selby and Soldat, HW-54636, p. 8.
135 Parker, HW-33068, p. 2.
136 U.S. Atomic Energy Commission,
"Advisory Committee on Biology and
Medicine, Notes, January 12, 1951" (Ger-
mantown, Md.: U.S. Department of Energy Archives); and Earnest W.
Goodpasture, letter to Gordon Dean,
December 1, 1951 (Germantown, Md.:
U.S. Department of Energy Archives),
both cited in Majority Staff, Committee

on Governmental Affairs, U.S. Senate,
*Early Health Problems of the U.S. Nuclear
Weapons Industry and Their Implications
for Today,* Senate Print 101-63, 101st
Cong., 1st sess. (Washington, D.C.: U.S.
Government Printing Office, December
1989), pp. 9–10.
137 U.S. AEC, "Sixteenth Semiannual
Report of the Atomic Energy Commission" (Washington, D.C.: U.S. Government Printing Office, July 1954), p. 65.
138 Parker, HW-33068, pp. 4–5.
139 Ibid., p. 2. For X, gamma, and beta
radiation, the term *rem* sometimes is used
interchangeably (albeit somewhat mis-
leadingly) with *rad.*
140 Ibid., pp. 3–12; and Herbert M. Parker, "Control of Ground Contamination," HW-32808 (RL: HAPO, August 19,
1954), pp. 1–2.
141 Roberts, HW-55569 RD, p. 7; D. L.
Uebelacker, "The Source of Activity
Contained in Radioactive Fallout from
the Redox 291-S Stack," HW-67520 (RL:
HAPO, December 9, 1960); and Selby
and Soldat, HW-54636, p. 11.
142 ERDA-1538, 2: II.1-B-26-27, II.1-E-18.
143 Gamertsfelder, HW-7-5934 pp. 1–2.
144 Teller, Benedict, Kennedy, Wheeler,
and Wolman, GEH-14040, pp. 1–2, 14–15.
145 Herbert M. Parker, "Hazards of
Waste Storage at Hanford, Part I,"
HW-14058 (RL: HEW, August 2, 1949);
Singlevich and Paas, HW-14243, DEL,
p. 8; Walter Singlevich and Herman Paas,
Jr., "Radioactive Contamination in the
Environs of the Hanford Works for the
Period April, May, June 1949," HW-17434
DEL (RL: HEW, April 30, 1950); Walter
Singlevich and Herman Paas, Jr., "Radio-
active Contamination in the Environs of
the Hanford Works for the Period July,
August, September 1949," HW-18615 (RL:
HEW, August 30, 1950); and Singlevich
and Paas, HW-17003.
146 D. L. DeNeal, "Historical Events—
Reactors and Fuels Fabrication,"
RL-REA-2247 (RL: HAPO, July 1, 1965).

147 R. K. Hilliard, "Effect of Heating Irradiated Uranium: A Literature Survey," HW-52753 (RL: HAPO, November 1, 1957), citing Recommendation #4 in O. H. Greager, "Recommendations by Advisory Committee on Reactor Safeguards," HW-36621 (RL: HAPO, May 6, 1955), pp. 4–5.

148 R. K. Hilliard, "Oxidation of Uranium in Air at High Temperatures," HW-58022 (RL: HAPO, December 10, 1958); Chemical Effluents Technology Operation, "Chemical Effluents Technology Waste Investigations: January, February, March 1959," HW-56063 RD (RL: HAPO, April 20, 1959), pp. 10–11; W. A. Haney, "Chemical Effluents Technology Waste Investigations: October, November, December 1960," HW-68543 RD (RL: HAPO, March 7, 1961), p. 14; and W. A. Haney, "Chemical Effluents Waste Disposal Investigations—January–June, 1961," HW-70806-RD (RL: HAPO, August 28, 1961), pp. 11–12. As a result of these experiments, the claddings on Hanford's fuel rods eventually were changed to a zirconium alloy known as Zircaloy-2.

149 Edward J. Bloch, "Hanford Production Reactor Power and Exposure Levels," CIC-01075 (Washington, D.C.: U.S. Atomic Energy Commission, July 9, 1958), pp. 1–4.

150 U.S. AEC, "Twenty-first Semiannual Report of the Atomic Energy Commission" (Washington, D.C.: U.S. Government Printing Office, January 1957), p. 143.

151 Bloch, CIC-1075, pp. 1–4. See also J. W. Healy, R. E. Tomlinson, R. L. Dickeman, "Nuclear Safety Discussions with AEC—April 21, 1958," HW-56701 (RL: HAPO, July 10, 1958).

152 U.S. Atomic Energy Commission, "Minutes of Meeting #1392," CIC-1177 (Germantown, Md.: U.S. Atomic Energy Commission, July 29, 1958), p. 564; and John A. McCone, letter to Carl Durham (chairman, Joint Committee on Atomic Energy, U.S. Congress), appended to CIC-1075 (Washington, D.C.: August 4, 1958), p. 1.

153 U.S. AEC, CIC-1177, p. 564, partially citing Commissioner John Graham. See also U.S. Atomic Energy Commission, "Minutes of Meeting #1443," CIC-744 (Germantown, Md.: U.S. Atomic Energy Commission, December 12, 1958), discussion of AEC #40/16; and U.S. Atomic Energy Commission, "Minutes of Meeting #1444," CIC-745 (Germantown, Md.: U.S. Atomic Energy Commission, December 17, 1958), p. 953, discussion of AEC #40/16.

154 Leslie Silverman (chairman, ACRS), "Hanford Reactor Power Levels," memo to John McCone, CIC-518 (Washington, D.C.: U.S. Atomic Energy Commission, March 14, 1960), p. 1.

155 U.S. Atomic Energy Commission, "U.S. Atomic Energy Commission Annual Report to Congress, 1963" (Washington, D.C.: U.S. Government Printing Office, January 1964), p. 163.

156 Matthias, "Journal," July 1, 1944, July 20, 1944, July 29, 1944, August 15, 1944, June 6, 1945.

157 *Richland Villager,* April 3, 1947, p. 11.

158 Ibid., May 6, 1948, p. 1, citing General Mark Clark.

159 Ibid., May 13, 1948, p. 16, October 28, 1948, p. 1, April 28, 1949, p. 1; and Seattle First National Bank, "Pacific Northwest Industries: The Hanford Works" (Seattle: Seattle First National Bank, December 1948), p. 5.

160 *Richland Villager,* July 14, 1949, p. 1, September 1, 1949, p. 1, November 24, 1949, p. 1, January 26, 1950, p. 1, February 23, 1950, p. 1.

161 "Army to Spend Huge Sum at No. Richland," *Columbia Basin News* (Kennewick, Wash.), May 4, 1950, p. 1; "Historic Names from World War Familiar to 518th AAA Battalion," *Columbia Basin News,* May 5, 1950, p. 1; "N. Richland Army Units in Convoy," *Columbia Basin*

News, May 12, 1950; "More Troops to Arrive in North Richland Wednesday," *Columbia Basin News,* July 3, 1950, pp. 1, 8; "More Anti-Aircraft Troops Added to Richland Force," *Columbia Basin News,* August 18, 1950; "Extensive Construction Projects Scheduled at North Richland Base," *Columbia Basin News,* March 24, 1951, p. 1; *U.S. Army 83rd Missile Battalion, Camp Hanford, Washington* (Camp Hanford, Wash.: U.S. Army, April 1955); "Army Spending Here Six Million Annually," *Tri-City Herald,* October 24, 1958, p. 3; and Tom Scanlon, ed., *Guide to Army Posts* (Harrisburg, Penn.: Stackpole Co., 1963), p. 88. See also U.S. AEC, "Eighth Semiannual Report of the AEC" (Washington, D.C.: U.S. Government Printing Office, July 1950), p. 178.

162 In seeking information about Camp Hanford, the author contacted the National Archives and Records Service (Military Reference Branch), the Pentagon Library, the Presidio of the Sixth Army, the *Army Times,* the Washington State Library, the Defense Nuclear Agency, and the U.S. Army Military History Institute. Only the last agency could provide any source material. The brochure provided was "83rd AAA Missile Battalion, Camp Hanford Washington," April 1955, 40 pp.

163 "It Pays to Increase Your Word Power," in *83rd AAA;* Ronald Utz (MP, Hanford, 1946), letter to the author, November 13, 1989 (Coeur d'Alene, Idaho); ten Camp Hanford veterans, group interview with the author, March 30, 1989 (Richland); and Kurt Bocian (Camp Hanford veteran), letter to the author, October 20, 1989 (Kent, Wash.).

164 Utz, letter to the author, November 13, 1989. In 1987, Ronald Utz was diagnosed as having thyroid cancer that had metastasized in his lungs and throat. His surgeon stated in 1989, "While it is difficult to prove what actually caused Mr.

Utz to develop metastatic thyroid cancer, one has to be highly suspicious that Mr. Utz was subjected to a carcinogenic dose of radioactive iodine during his time in the service." Kenneth G. Kraemer, M.D. (University of Washington Medical School), letter to Whom It May Concern, January 3, 1989 (Spokane, Wash.).

165 Group interview with the author, March 31, 1989; and Bocian, letter to the author, October 20, 1989.

166 Eugene Plock, in "AEC Kept Quiet on Hanford Health Risk," *Tri-City Herald,* December 19, 1989, p. A2.

167 David F. Shaw, teletype to R. W. Cook (AEC-Washington, D.C.), CIC-62187 (RL: HEW, April 23, 1951), pp. 1–3.

168 Herman Paas, Jr., and Walter Singlevich, "Radioactive Contamination in the Environs of the Hanford Works for January, February, March 1951," HW-21214 (RL: HEW, June 1, 1951), pp. 35–37.

169 Herman Paas, Jr., "Radioactive Contamination in the Environs of the Hanford Works for the Period April, May, June, 1952," HW-26493 (RL: HAPO, December 15, 1952), p. 30; Herman Paas, Jr., "Radioactive Contamination in the Hanford Environs for the Period April, May, June, 1953," HW-29514 (RL: HAPO, October 2, 1953), p. 42; Herman Paas, Jr., and G. E. Pilcher, "Radioactive Contamination in the Hanford Environs for the Period April, May, June, 1954," HW-33896 (RL: HAPO, November 24, 1954), p. 42; Biophysics Section, "Monthly Reports: Regional Monitoring Unit, 1955," CIC-12753 (HW-40693) (RL: HAPO, 1955), January report; B. V. Andersen, "Regional Monitoring Activities," CIC-12765 (RL: HAPO, 1956), January report, Table IX, and June report, Table IX; and B. V. Andersen, "Regional Monitoring Activities," CIC-12722 (RL: HAPO, 1957), December report. This list of references is not a complete one. It is a representative sample.

312

170 Parker, HW-32808, p. 2; and Parker, HW-33068, p. 11.

171 Andersen, CIC-12765, November report (December 3, 1956), and December report (January 3, 1957); and B. V. Andersen, "Regional Monitoring Activities," HW-55724 (RL: HAPO, April 14, 1958), p. 3.

172 George Sundborg, *Hail Columbia: The Thirty Year Struggle for the Grand Coulee Dam* (New York: Macmillan and Co., 1954), pp. 376–77, 398–417; David Lavender, *Land of Giants: The Drive to the Pacific Northwest, 1750–1950* (Garden City, N.Y.: Doubleday and Co., 1958), pp. 434–46; Cecil Dryden, *Dryden's History of Washington* (Portland: Binfords and Mort, 1968), pp. 328–33; and U.S. Department of the Interior, Bureau of Reclamation (BOR), *Columbia Basin Irrigation Project, Project History, 1946*, vol. 14 (Ephrata, Wash.: U.S. BOR, August 1, 1947), part II, pp. 26–32.

173 BOR, *Columbia Basin*, vol. 14, part II, pp. 33–224; Walter Oberst, *Railroads, Reclamation, and the River: A History of Pasco* (Pasco, Wash.: Franklin County Historical Society, 1978), p. 72; and BOR, *Columbia Basin Irrigation Project, Project History, 1947*, vol. 15 (Ephrata, Wash.: U.S. BOR, 1948), part II, pp. 232–36.

174 BOR, *Columbia Basin*, vol. 14, part II, pp. 169–70; and Sundborg, *Hail*, pp. 410–17.

175 BOR, *Columbia Basin Irrigation Project, Project History, 1955*, vol. 23 (Ephrata, Wash.: U.S. BOR, 1956), part I, p. 6; BOR, *Columbia Basin Irrigation Project, Project History, 1958*, vol. 26 (Ephrata, Wash.: U.S. BOR, 1959), part II, pp. 32–36; and BOR, *Columbia Basin Irrigation Project, Project History, 1959*, vol. 27 (Ephrata, Wash.: U.S. BOR, 1960), p. 29.

176 BOR, *Columbia Basin Irrigation Project, Project History, 1949*, vol. 17 (Ephrata, Wash.: U.S. BOR, 1950), part II, pp. 340–47; BOR, *Columbia Basin Irrigation Project, Project History, 1952*, vol. 20 (Ephrata, Wash.: U.S. BOR, 1953), part I, pp. 1–6; BOR, *Columbia Basin* vol. 21, part I, pp. 5, 17, 37; BOR, *Columbia Basin*, vol. 22 (Ephrata, Wash.: U.S. BOR, 1955), part I, p. 5; and BOR, "Irrigation Blocks, Acreage, and Farm Units, CBP, 1948–1987" (Ephrata, Wash.: U.S. BOR, January 1987).

177 BOR, *Columbia Basin*, vol. 16, part II, pp. 58–59; and *Richland Villager,* July 8, 1948, p. 1.

178 Herde, HW-3-3455; Herde, HW-3-3628; Libby, *Uranium*, p. 174; and Turner and Healy, HW-3-5313.

179 Teller, Benedict, Kennedy, Wheeler, and Wolman, GEH-14040, pp. 10, 13.

180 *Richland Villager,* January 12, 1949, p. 10, citing U.S. AEC, December 17, 1948. An early 1949, secret Hanford vegetation-monitoring survey again found average radioactivity levels on the Wahluke Slope to be higher than those in Richland and other areas near the atomic plant. This survey reconfirmed the existence of "hot spots" of I-131 deposition that were "significantly higher than the overall average." See Singlevich and Paas, HW-14243, p. 47. These same "hot spots" were noted again after the Green Run in December 1949. See Paas and Singlevich, HW-17003, p. 15.

181 U.S. AEC, "Thirteenth Semiannual Report of the Atomic Energy Commission" (Washington, D.C.: U.S. AEC, January 1953), pp. 24–25.

182 R. Dickeman, J. W. Healy, and R. Tomlinson, "Report for Advisory Committee on Reactor Safeguards," HW-55756 (RL: HAPO, April 16, 1958), pp. 13–14.

183 R. Dickeman, J. W. Healy, and R. Tomlinson, "Nuclear Discussions with AEC—April 21, 1958," HW-56701 (RL: HAPO, July 10, 1958), pp. 12–13; and U.S. AEC, CIC-1177, p. 564.

184 U.S. AEC, CIC-744; and U.S. AEC, CIC-745, p. 953; and BOR, *Columbia Basin*, vol. 26, part I, p. 12.

185 BOR, *Columbia Basin Irrigation Proj-*

ect, *Project History, 1965,* vol. 33 (Ephrata, Wash.: U.S. BOR, 1966), p. 18, and vol. 34 (1967), p. 15, and vol. 35 (1968), p. 23.

186 "Saddle Mountain National Wildlife Refuge" (Othello, Wash.: U.S. Department of the Interior, Fish, and Wildlife Service, n.d.).

187 Institute of Agricultural Sciences, "The Columbia Basin Settler: A Study of Social and Economic Resources in New Land Settlement," Bulletin #566 (Pullman: State College of Washington, May 1956), pp. 5–6, 17–18, 35–36, 12.

188 Settlers' round table discussion with the author, August 1, 1989 (Pasco, Wash.).

189 Settlers' round table discussion, April 30, 1989 (Pasco, Wash.).

190 Leo Vogel, *Years Plowed Under* (Spokane, Wash.: University Press, 1977), pp. 30–32.

191 Settlers' round table discussion with the author, August 1, 1989 (Pasco, Wash.) At this meeting several early settlers of the Columbia Basin Irrigation Project farm blocks emphasized their love and attachment to the land, even in the earliest, hardest years. They recalled that in the mid-1950s, two of the winters were "open" (the ground did not freeze), and work went forward. And for only three months during the winter of 1956–57 was the ground frozen solid enough that leveling stopped. During the remainder of that year, the dusty work of land leveling was constant.

192 Kenneth Herde and John Cline, "Radioactivity in Pekin Ducks on the Columbia River," HW-12079 (RL: HEW, January 7, 1949).

193 Edward Berry and John Cline, "First Annual Report of the Botany Field Station," HW-16056 (RL: HEW, January 20, 1950), pp. 14–15, 21; and John Cline and J. W. Porter, "Second Annual Report of the Botany Field Station," HW-20999 (RL: HEW, May 1, 1951), pp. 7–11.

194 Parker, HW-18371, p. 11; Herbert M. Parker, "Quarterly Progress Report: Research and Development Activities for April–June 1951," HW-21511 (RL: HEW, July 6, 1951); Herbert M. Parker, "Radiological Sciences Department, Quarterly Progress Report: Research and Development Activities for October–December 1951," HW-23332 (RL: HAPO, 1952); and Parker, HW-20866.

195 Parker, HW-33068, pp. 3–12.

196 John W. Healy, "A Preliminary Estimate of Wind Pick-Up and Erosion of Particles," HW-35542 (RL: HAPO, March 1, 1955).

197 G. R. Hilst, "Measurement of Relative Wind Erosion of Small Particles from Various Prepared Surfaces," HW-39356 (RL: HAPO, October 5, 1955), pp. 4–5, 8–9, 23–25.

198 See also James J. Fuquay, "Meteorology as Related to Waste Disposal and Weapons Tests," HW-47721 (RL: HAPO, January 15, 1957), pp. 6–7, 9–11, 14–15.

199 R. F. Foster and R. L. Junkins, "Off-Project Exposure from Hanford Reactor Effluent," HW-63654 and HW-63654 (rev.) (RL: HAPO, February 1, 1960, and March 15, 1960); Iral C. Nelson, "Evaluation of Radiological Conditions in the Vicinity of Hanford," HW-73366 (for January–March 1962), p. 9, HW-74398 (for April–June 1962), p. 11, and HW-75431 (for July–September 1962), pp. 4–5 (RL: HAPO, 1962, various quarters); and Iral C. Nelson and Richard F. Foster, "Ringold—A Hanford Environmental Survey," HW-78262 (rev.) (RL: HAPO, April 3, 1964), pp. 7, 12.

Chapter 5

1 P. A. Olson, "Fish and Fish Problems of the Hanford Reservation," HW-11642 (RL: HEW, November 23, 1948), pp. 1–7; Richard F. Foster, "The Effect on Fish of Increasing the Temperature of the Columbia River," HW-54858 (RL: HAPO, March 14, 1958), pp. 3, 16–18; Franklin T.

Matthias, "Journal and Notes, 1943–45," unpublished diary (located at Richland, U.S. Department of Energy Public Reading Room), April 23–24, 1943, August 9, 1943, August 28, 1943; DuPont Corporation, *Operations of Hanford Engineer Works*, HAN-73214 (Wilmington, Del.: E.I. DuPont de Nemours and Co., 1946), Book XI, "P Department, Part II," pp. 90–101; and S. L. Sanger and R. W. Mull, eds., *Hanford and the Bomb: An Oral History of World War II* (Seattle: Living History Press, 1990), pp. 181–86, partially citing Leslie R. Groves and Richard L. Foster. During the mid-1940s, the wholesale economic value of the salmon industry along the Columbia River was approximately $10 million per year. See Olson, HW-11642, p. 1.

2 Until 1963, Richland obtained its water supply from wells located in the southwest quadrant of the city.

3 C. W. Wende, "Radiation a Fish Would Receive in Water Containing Radioactive Material," DUH-10, 165 (RL: HEW, March 30, 1943).

4 Lauren A. Donaldson, "Annual Report of the Laboratory of Radiation Biology, University of Washington, July 1, 1957–June 30, 1958," CIC-50059 (Seattle: University of Washington, June 20, 1958), p. 1; and Matthias, "Journal," May 27, 1943, June 1, 1943. In 1958, the Applied Fisheries Laboratory was renamed the Laboratory of Radiation Biology. Throughout the first twenty years of its existence, this laboratory participated in aquatic and marine biological investigations of territory surrounding atomic weapons test sites, streams, and water environments around proposed Operation Plowshare programs in Alaska and elsewhere, as well as in studies of the Columbia River near the Hanford Site.

5 R. L. Hames (chief counsel, Department of Energy, Richland Operations Office), letter to Charles B. Roe, Jr. (assistant attorney general, State of Washington), October 20, 1983.

6 *The Atomic Energy Act of 1946, Public Law 585*, 79th Cong., 2d sess. (Washington, D.C.: U.S. Government Printing Office, 1946), section 12:a:2; and *The Atomic Energy Act of 1954, Public Law 703*, 83d Cong., 2d sess. (Washington, D.C.: U.S. Government Printing Office, 1954), chapter 1, section 2:d.

7 Herbert M. Parker, "Permissible Limits—Release of Reactor Effluent to the Columbia River," HW-24356 (RL: HAPO, May 6, 1952), pp. 1–2.

8 R. B. Hall and P. C. Jerman, "Reactor Effluent Water Disposal," HW-63653 (RL: HAPO, February 1, 1960).

9 General Electric Company, "Manual of Radiation Protection Standards," HW-25457 (rev. 2) (RL: HAPO, March 1, 1960), pp. 4.5, 1.5; H. V. Clukey, "The Hanford Atomic Project and Columbia River Pollution," HW-54243 (rev.) (RL: HAPO, December 20, 1957), p. 7; and R. L. Junkins and M. W. McConiga, "Hanford Mid-Year Report to the Columbia River Advisory Group—through June 1959," HW-61029 (rev.) (RL: HAPO, August 11, 1959), p. 3. See also H. V. Clukey and M. W. McConiga, "Hanford Mid-Year Report to Columbia River Advisory Group," HW-56623 (RL: HAPO, July 7, 1958), p. 2.

10 T. H. Essig, G. W. Enders, J. K. Soldat, and J. F. Honstead, "Concentrations of 65 Zn in Marine Foodstuffs and Pacific Coastal Residents," BNWL-SA-4206 (Richland: Battelle Pacific Northwest Laboratory, 1972).

11 Washington State Department of Health, "Project Proposal for a Radiological Health Study on the Columbia River, Puget Sound, Washington Seacoast, and Other Surface Waters," CIC-161754 (Olympia: Washington State Department of Health, February 20, 1961); and Oregon State Board of Health, "Project Proposal for a Radiological Health Study on the Lower Columbia River, Its Tributaries, and the

Oregon Seacoast," CIC-161755 (Salem: Oregon State Board of Health, February 15, 1961).

12 E. C. Tsiveglou and M. W. Lammering, "Evaluation of Pollutional Effects of Effluents from Hanford Works" (Cincinnati: Robert A. Taft Sanitary Engineering Center, U.S. Public Health Service, March 1961), p. 24.

13 Matthias, "Journal," September 20, 1943, November 16, 1943, March 30, 1944, May 10, 1944.

14 Ibid., January 5, 1944.

15 Ibid., May 27, 1943.

16 Ibid., March 31, 1944, February 17, 1945, March 6–7, 1945, March 13, 1945, May 12, 1945. After World War II ended, an MED public relations officer, Milton Cydell, briefed UW officials on the true nature of Donaldson's and Foster's fish irradiation studies. At that time, President Lee Paul Seig told Cydell that UW officials had "felt for a long time that the work was being done with little regard" for them and their administrative offices. See Matthias, "Journal," October 13, 1945.

17 DuPont, *Operations,* Book XI, p. 91; Matthias, "Journal," June 14, 1945; and Richard F. Foster, interview with Spencer Hines (reporter), *Portland Oregonian,* May 12, 1986, p. 1. There is extreme seasonal variation in the volume of flow of the Columbia River. In the Hanford Reach, seasonal differences can vary by as much as a factor of six. Therefore, as Hanford aquatic biologists would learn later, "average" dilutions are almost meaningless in this stretch of the Columbia.

18 Leona Marshall Libby, *The Uranium People* (New York: Crane, Russak, 1979), p. 169.

19 Foster, *Portland Oregonian,* May 12, 1986, p. 1.

20 Matthias, "Journal," October 15, 1945.

21 War Department, "Statements Signed by Hanford Engineer Works Personnel Agreeing Not to Divulge Information

Relative to the Effect of Plant Operations on Fish Life in the Columbia River," CIC-62060 (Pasco, Wash.: U.S. Engineer Office, 1946).

22 DuPont, *Operations,* Book XI, p. 98.

23 Richard F. Foster, "Fish Life Observed in the Columbia River on September 27, 1945," HW-7-2514 (RL: HEW, September 27, 1945), pp. 2–3; and DuPont, *Operations,* Book XI, pp. 99–101.

24 John W. Healy, "Accumulation of Radioactive Elements in Fish . . . in Pile Effluent Water," HW-3442 (RL: HEW, February 27, 1946); and Kenneth Herde, "Studies in the Accumulation of Radioactive Elements in Chinook Salmon Exposed to a Medium of Pile Effluent Water," HW-3-5064 (RL: HEW, October 14, 1946).

25 DuPont, *Operations,* Book XI, pp. 103–4.

26 Healy, HW-3442.

27 Herbert M. Parker, "Status of Problem of Measurement of the Activity of Waste Water Returned to the Columbia River," HW-7-2346 (RL: HEW, September 11, 1945).

28 DuPont, *Operations,* Book VII, "Medical Department: Health Instruments," pp. 79, 115, 155, 183.

29 John W. Healy, "Leaks in 107-F and 107-D Basins," HW-3-3259 (RL: HEW, November 26, 1945); and Walter Singlevich, "H.I. Environs Report for the Month of October, 1948," HW-11534 (RL: HEW, November 3, 1948).

30 Singlevich, HW-11534.

31 U.S. Energy Research and Development Administration, "Waste Management Operations, Hanford Reservation: Final Environmental Statement," ERDA-1538, vol. 2 (Richland: U.S. Energy Research and Development Administration, December 1975), p. II.1-B-27. These basin breaks and overflows occurred at 107-B in 1954 and 107-F in 1955.

32 Chemical Effluents Technology Operation, "Chemical Effluents Technology

316

Waste Disposal Investigations—April, May, June, 1959," HW-61197 RD (RL: HAPO, July 22, 1959), p. 15.

33 Hall and Jerman, HW-63653, pp. 2, 5; and W. N. Koop, "The Effects of Reactor Purges When River Temperature Exceeds 15C," HW-50601 (RL: HAPO, June 10, 1957), pp. 2–3.

34 F. P. Seymour, "A Study of Total Amounts of Active Waste Released in All Manners by the HEW Process to Date," HW-7-5463 DEL (RL: HEW, December 5, 1946).

35 Herbert M. Parker, "Health Physics, Instrumentation, and Radiation Protection," reprinted in *Health Physics* 38 (June 1980): 967. The document was originally written in early 1947.

36 Kenneth Herde, "Radioactivity in Various Species of Fish from the Columbia and Yakima River," HW-3-5501 (RL: HEW, May 14, 1947).

37 For a discussion of the CBP, please see chapter 4.

38 K. Herde and J. Cline, "Radioactivity in Pekin Ducks on the Columbia River," HW-12079 (RL: HEW, January 7, 1949); R. W. Coopey, "The Accumulation of Radioactivity as Shown by a Limnological Study of the Columbia River in the Vicinity of Hanford Works: A Preliminary Report," HW-11662 (RL: HEW, November 12, 1948); and Kenneth Herde, "A One-Year Study of Radioactivity in Columbia River Fish," HW-11344 (RL: HEW, October 25, 1948).

39 Herde and Cline, HW-12079.

40 Herde, HW-11344.

41 Coopey, HW-11662, pp. 1–12.

42 Lauren R. Donaldson, "Problems in Liquid Waste Disposal," CIC-50004 (UWFL-15) (Seattle: University of Washington, November 10, 1948), pp. 4–6; and Olson, HW-11642, p. 2.

43 Richard F. Foster, "Radiobiological Problems in the Columbia River, Rough Draft," HW-25793 (RL: HEW, April 1949), pp. 4–9. At that time, a maximum level

of 7.5 μCi/kg (gross beta radioactivity) had been found in plankton in the Hanford Reach. See HW-25793, p. 8.

44 L. D. Turner, "The Trend of Contamination Observed in the Air, the Columbia River, Vegetation, and Wastes at the Hanford Engineer Works for the Period January 1, 1947 to March 25, 1947," HW-3-5511 (RL: HEW, May 9, 1947); and John W. Healy, "The Trend of Contamination Observed in the Air, the Columbia River, Vegetation, and Wastes at the Hanford Engineer Works for the Period March 25, 1947 to June 30, 1947," HW-7317 (RL: HEW, August 12, 1947).

45 Carl Gamertsfelder, "H.I. Environs Report for Month of September, 1947," HW-07831 (RL: HEW, October 20, 1947); Walter Singlevich, "The Trend of Contamination Observed in the Air, the Columbia River, Vegetation and Wastes at the Hanford Engineer Works for the Period July, August, September, 1947," HW-08549 DEL (RL: HEW, December 28, 1947); and Walter Singlevich, "Radioactive Contamination in the Columbia River and in the Air and Radiation Levels Measured in the Air at Hanford Works and Vicinity for 1945, 1946, 1947, and early 1948," HW-09871 (RL: HEW, May 24, 1948). Values in river water at Pasco stood near 10×10^{-5} microcuries per liter (μCi/l) in 1947. Values at Richland rose from 5 to 41×10^{-5} μCi/l during 1946–48. Values at the Hanford townsite reached 520×10^{-5} by early 1948.

46 Walter Singlevich, "H.I. Environs Report for the Month of September 1948," HW-11264 (RL: HEW, October 11, 1948), pp. 10–11. September 1948 values in river water at the Hanford townsite reached 842×10^{-5} μCi/l.

47 Parker, HW-24356, partially citing J. M. Smith to K. J. Perkins, "Sizing of Retention Basin 107-C," March 7, 1951.

48 *Richland Villager*, July 21, 1949, p. 2, citing Fred Schlemmer.

49 *Public Law 845,* 80th Cong. 2d sess., in *United States Code,* 1982 ed. (Washington, D.C.: U.S. Government Printing Office, 1983), p. 886.
50 Frank E. Adley and Wendell K. Crane, "Meeting of the Columbia River Advisory Group, November 21–23, 1949," HW-15861 (RL: HEW, February 2, 1950), pp. 6–9, 11–12.
51 Herbert M. Parker, "Quarterly Progress Report—Research and Development Activities for July–September, 1950," HW-19146 (RL: HEW, October 16, 1950), p. 12; Richard F. Foster, "Abnormally High Activity in Aquatic Organisms below the 100H Area," HW-18438 (RL: HEW, July 27, 1950), pp. 2–4; and M. L. Mickelson and Staff of the H.I. Divisions, "Annual Report of the Health Instruments Divisions, 1950," HW-21699 (rev.) (RL: HEW, July 20, 1951), pp. 34–35. In July 1950, some river organisms near 100-H reached concentration levels of 0.1 µCi/g. Plankton concentration levels in December 1950 reached 1.5×10^{-2} µCi/g.
52 Paas and Singlevich, HW-17003, pp. 44–45. River water concentration averages in early 1950 were 2,425 millimicrocuries per liter (uµCi/l) at the Hanford townsite, 900 uµCi/l at the Richland Dock, 480 uµCi/l at Pasco, and 345 uµCi/l at Kennewick.
53 Mickelson et al., HW-21699 (rev.), p. 5; and Herbert M. Parker, "Quarterly Progress Report—Research and Development Activities for April–June 1950," HW-18371 (RL: HEW, July 19, 1950), p. 13.
54 Herbert M. Parker, "Quarterly Progress Report—Research and Development Activities for January–March 1951," HW-20866 (RL: HEW, April 18, 1951); and R. W. Coopey, "Radioactive Plankton from the Columbia River," HW-20668 (RL: HEW, March 29, 1951), pp. 3–9, 21. The half-life of P-32 is 14.7 days. Since P-32 was one of the most important ra-

dionuclides of biomedical concern, Hanford scientists usually chose its half-life as the threshold for referring to "long half-lived" radioisotopes.
55 Joseph K. Soldat and Robert C. Thorburn, "Radiological Survey of the Pasco Washington Water Treatment Plant," HW-22862 (RL: HEW, December 5, 1951), pp. 3, 6–7. Sludge values at the Pasco water-treatment plant rose from 1×10^{-3} µCi/g in November 1950 to 42.5×10^{-3} µCi/g in October 1951.
56 J. Davis and C. Cooper, "Effect of Pile Effluent upon Aquatic Invertebrates in the Columbia River," HW-20055 (RL: HEW, January 19, 1951), pp. 32, 42–43, 61. The benthic fauna surveyed were aquatic months, caddis flies, mayflies, snails, sponges, and their larvae and nymphs.
57 Harry A. Kornberg and Staff of the Biology Section, "Biology Research Annual Report—1951," HW-25021 (RL: HAPO, April 15, 1952), pp. 15, 4; and K. E. Herde, R. L. Browning, and W. C. Henson, "Activity Densities in Waterfowl of the Hanford Reservation and Environs," HW-18645 (RL: HEW, August 21, 1951).
58 Herbert M. Parker, "Radiological Sciences Department: Quarterly Progress Report—Research and Development Activities for July–September, 1951," HW-22576 (RL: HEW, November 1, 1951), p. 7.
59 Harry A. Kornberg, "Special Meeting of the Columbia River Advisory Group, April 14, 1950—Richland, Washington," HW-17732 (RL: HEW, April 27, 1950), pp. 9–10, 14, 16, 38, 41. All of the PHS scientists obtained "Q" clearances—the highest AEC security clearances—before beginning the Columbia River study.
60 Ibid., p. 44, citing CRAG memo to Fred Schlemmer (manager, Atomic Engineer Commission, Hanford Operations Office), April 19, 1950, pp. 1–2.
61 Herbert M. Parker, "Columbia River Situation—A Semi-Technical Review," HW-32809 (RL: HAPO, August 19, 1954), pp. 4–7.

62 Ibid., pp. 17, 5–7, 10; and Columbia River Advisory Group (CRAG), U.S. Public Health Service, Atomic Energy Commission, General Electric Company, "Summary Report of Joint Quarterly Meeting, October 22–23, 1951," GEH-19226 (RL: HEW, n.d.), appendix A, appendix B, p. 12.

63 Gordon G. Robeck, Croswell Henderson, and Ralph C. Palange, "Water Quality Studies on the Columbia River," Special Report, U.S. Public Health Service, GEH-21328 (also PB-229-103) (Cincinnati, Ohio: Robert A. Taft Sanitary Engineering Center, U.S. Public Health Service, 1954), pp. 87, 83–84, 4, 6–7. According to the U.S. Environmental Protection Agency, the preliminary draft of this report is not available.

64 John F. Honstead, "Columbia River Survey, 1951, 1952, 1953," HW-32506 (RL: HAPO, July 21, 1954).

65 G. E. Pilcher and H. T. Norton, "The Calculation of Beta Particle Emitter Concentration in Hanford Reactor Effluent Water," HW-27584 (RL: HAPO, August 15, 1953), pp. 21–28.

66 R. W. Coopey, "Preliminary Comparison of Nannoplankton and Net Plankton of the Columbia River," HW-29298 (RL: HAPO, September 10, 1953), pp. 4–5.

67 J. J. Davis, D. G. Watson, and C. C. Palmiter, "Radiobiological Studies in the Columbia River through December 1955," HW-36074 (RL: HAPO, November 7, 1956), p. 69.

68 Hall and Jerman, HW-63653, pp. 2, 5; and Parker, HW-24356, pp. 3–6.

69 Hall and Jerman, HW-63653, pp. 2, 5; and CRAG et al., GEH-19226, pp. 1–3.

70 Chemical Effluents Technology Operation (CETO), "Chemical Effluents Technology Waste Disposal Investigations— October, November, December 1957," HW-54848 (RL: HAPO, January 30, 1958), p. 9; Hall and Jerman, HW-63653, pp. 2, 5; and Richard F. Poston, "Radioactive Waste Disposal Practices at Hanford," CIC-80866 (Portland: U.S. Public Health Service, May 13, 1964), citing R. G. Geier (Hanford Atomic Products Operation).

71 General Electric Company, HW-25457, pp. 4.5, 1.5; Clukey, HW-54243, p. 7; and Junkins and McConiga, HW-61029, p. 3. See also Clukey and McConiga, HW-56623, p. 2: Hanford Laboratories Operation, "December Monthly Report: Contamination Control—Columbia River," HW-72065 (RL: HAPO, December 20, 1961); R. G. Geier, "December Monthly Report: Contamination Control—Columbia River" (RL: HAPO, December 20, 1962); and R. G. Geier, "December Monthly Report: Contamination Control—Columbia River" (RL: HAPO, December 20, 1963). Hanford's all-time high of beta release to the Columbia River may have occurred in May 1963, when a serious fuel rupture occurred at KE reactor. Specific curie amounts from this release are not available. As a comparison, 9,610 curies of beta-emitters per day were released to the Columbia River in mid-1957. This figure represents four hours of decay time after entering the river. During the same months, effluent just leaving the retention basins and discharging into the river, with no decay time other than that in the 107 basins themselves, contained 50,000 curies of beta-emitters. By late 1959, reactor flow rates themselves had increased tenfold over early 1948. Between mid-1957 and late 1959, the rates of release of the five radionuclides of prime concern in effluent jumped as follows (expressed as curies per day):

	Mid-1957	Late 1959
As-76	38.3 Ci/d	99.0 Ci/d
P-32	21.3 Ci/d	90.4 Ci/d
Zn-65	53.3 Ci/d (January 1958)	152.2 Ci/d
Cr-51	128.0 Ci/d (January 1958)	145.2 Ci/d
Np-239	89.9 Ci/d	112.0 Ci/d

72 P. A. Olson and R. F. Foster, "Accumulation of Radioactivity in Columbia River Fish in the Vicinity of the Hanford Works," HW-23093 (RL: HAPO, July 1952), p. 39.

73 Hall and Jerman, HW-63653, pp. 2, 5; and Parker, HW-24356, pp. 3–6.

74 Kornberg and Staff, HW-25021, pp. 15, 4.

75 Technical Section, Engineering Department, "Process Specifications, Reactor Cooling Water Treatment," HW-28505 (RL: HAPO, July 15, 1953), pp. 6-1/2, 7-1, 9-1. Sulfuric acid, sodium hydroxide, aluminum sulfate, and ammonium hydroxide were the most abundant chemicals added to the Columbia River in reactor effluent. See ERDA-1538, vol. I, p. V-43.

76 R. F. Foster, J. J. Davis, and P. A. Olson, "Studies on the Effect of the Hanford Reactors on Aquatic Life in the Columbia," HW-33366 (RL: HAPO, October 11, 1954), p. 13.

77 Parker, HW-32809, p. 6.

78 John Bugher, M.D., memo to Kenneth D. Nichols (general manager, Atomic Energy Commission, Washington, D.C.), November 17, 1954, p. 1, appended as Enclosure D to "Columbia River Contamination," CIC-30598 (Washington, D.C.: U.S. Atomic Energy Commission, November 22, 1954), p. 14.

79 P. R. McMurray, "Columbia River Aspects of Increased Production," HW-41049 (RL: HAPO, January 25, 1956).

80 D. G. Watson, "Chinook Salmon Spawning in the Vicinity of Hanford 1947–55," HW-41500 (RL: HAPO, February 16, 1956), pp. 29–34.

81 D. L. DeNeal, "Historical Events—Reactors and Fuels Fabrication," RL-REA-2247 (RL: HAPO, July 1, 1965).

82 Richard F. Foster, "Aquatic Biology Research," in H. V. Clukey, "Minutes of the Columbia River Advisory Group Meeting, February 7–8, 1957," HW-48469 (RL: HAPO, February 12, 1957), p. 5; and Richard F. Foster, "Recommended Limit on Addition of Dichromate to the Columbia River," HW-49713 (RL: HAPO, April 17, 1957), pp. 2, 5.

83 Richard F. Foster, "The Effect on Fish of Increasing the Temperature of the Columbia River," HW-54858 (RL: HAPO, March 14, 1958), pp. 16–18.

84 R. T. Jaske, "An Evaluation of the Use of Selective Discharges from Lake Roosevelt to Cool the Columbia River," BNWL-208 (Richland: Battelle Northwest Laboratories, February 1966," pp. 47–65; and R. T. Jaske and M. O. Synoground, "Effect of Hanford Plant Operations on the Temperature of the Columbia River: 1964 to Present," BNWL-1345-UC-70 (Richland: Battelle Northwest Laboratories, November 1970), pp. 2, 16. See also H. A. Kramer and J. P. Corley, "Use of Lake Roosevelt Storage to Lower Temperatures," HW-SA-2301 (RL: HAPO, 1961), pp. 1–20; H. A. Kramer, "Artificial Cooling of the Columbia by Dam Regulation—1959," HW-65767 (RL: HAPO, 1960); H. A. Kramer, "Artificial Cooling of the Columbia River by Dam Regulation—1960," HW-68337 (RL: HAPO, 1961); H. A. Kramer, "Artificial Cooling of the Columbia River by Dam Regulation—1961," HW-73707 (RL: HAPO, 1962); H. A. Kramer, "Artificial Cooling of the Columbia River by Dam Regulation—1962," HW-76887 (RL: HAPO, 1963); and R. T. Jaske, "Temperature Studies on the Columbia above Hanford," in Richard F. Foster, "Report to the Working Committee for Columbia River Studies on Progress since September, 1962," HW-80649 (RL: HAPO, February 1964), p. 5. All eight single-pass reactors at Hanford closed between 1964 and 1971. For a complete list of shutdown dates, see further in chapter 5.

85 D. G. Watson, "Chinook Salmon Spawning in the Vicinity of Hanford—1959," in "Biology Research Annual Report for 1959," HW-65500 (RL: HAPO,

1960), pp. 180–82. In 1958, 1,485 salmon redds (nests) had been observed in the Columbia between Priest Rapids and Richland. This number was the highest in seventeen years. See D. G. Watson "Chinook Salmon Spawning near Hanford—1963," in HW-80649, p. 19.

86 D. G. Watson, "Salmon Spawning in the Vicinity of Hanford Atomic Products Operation—1960," in "Biology Research Annual Report for 1960," HW-59600 (RL: HAPO, 1961), pp. 156–58.

87 H. A. Kornberg and E. G. Swezea, "Hanford Biology Research Annual Report for 1961," HW-72500 (RL: HAPO, 1962), pp. 148–50. By 1967, 3,100 spawning salmon were counted, a twenty-year high, and 4,500 redds, a record number, were counted in 1970. See R. C. Thompson et al., "Pacific Northwest Laboratory Annual Report, 1966: to the U.S. AEC Division of Biology and Medicine, Volume I, Biological Sciences," BNWL-480 (Richland: Battelle Northwest Laboratory, July 1967), pp. 181–83; and R. C. Thompson et al., "Pacific Northwest Laboratory Annual Report for 1969: to the U.S. AEC Division of Biology and Medicine," BNWL-1306 (Richland: Battelle Northwest Laboratory), pp. 321–22.

88 P. A. Olson, Jr., and R. F. Foster, "Accumulation of Radioactivity in Columbia River Fish in the Vicinity of the Hanford Works," HW-23093 (RL: HAPO, July 1, 1952), pp. 4, 45–46, 21.

89 Foster, Davis, and Olson, HW-33366, pp. 8, 11.

90 Parker, HW-32809, pp. 5, 7.

91 Charles Dunham, M.D., memo to Frank Pittman (deputy director of production, Atomic Energy Commission), October 26, 1954, appended as Enclosure C to CIC-30598, pp. 12–13. See also National Committee on Radiation Protection, "Maximum Permissible Amounts of Radioisotopes in the Human Body and Maximum Permissible Concentrations in Air and Water," NBS-52 (Washington, D.C.: U.S. Government Printing Office, March 20, 1953).

92 David F. Shaw, memo to Edward Bloch (director of production, Atomic Energy Commission), "Transmittal of Information on Columbia River Situation," September 17, 1954, appended as Enclosure B to CIC-30598, p. 4.

93 Kenneth D. Nichols, memo to Lewis Strauss (chairman, Atomic Energy Commission), "Columbia River Contamination," November 18, 1954, appended as Enclosure A to CIC-30598, p. 2.

94 Richard Foster and Royal Rostenbach, "Distribution of Radioisotopes in Columbia River," *Journal of the American Water Works Association* 46, no. 7 (July 1954): 640.

95 Davis, Watson, and Palmiter, HW-36074, p. 15. Resident fish species such as whitefish, bass, suckers, carp, and freshwater trout (not steelhead) are differentiated from anadromous fish such as salmon and steelhead. The latter fish are hatched in the Columbia and later return there to spawn and die. However, their primary feeding and growth is done in the ocean.

96 Ibid., pp. 68–70.

97 Ibid., pp. 68–70; and D. G. Watson and J. J. Davis, "Concentration of Radioisotopes in Columbia River Whitefish in the Vicinity of the Hanford Atomic Products Operation," HW-48523 (RL: HAPO, February 18, 1957), pp. 29–34. Hanford scientists did not take into account the fact that "traditional fishers," particularly Native Americans, often have dietary practices that do involve eating many fish organs and tissues other than the flesh. Between 1955 and 1957, average radioactivity levels in fish at Ringold and Priest Rapids rose from 2–3 × 10⁻⁴ μCi/gm to 4 × 10⁻⁴ μCi/gm.

98 Davis, Watson, and Palmiter, HW-36074; and Watson and Davis, HW-48523, pp. 2–5, 29–35. In 1955, a Hanford biologist, Harry A. Kornberg, disclosed in a paper presented at a nonsecret conference that small fish, plankton, and insect larvae in the Columbia River concentrated P-32 from forty thousand to eight hundred thousand times that of the water. He added, "In none of these organisms studied was there noted any deleterious effect due to production [of reactor effluent]." Kornberg did not address the food-chain effects but simply stated that the organisms themselves, in terms of their ability to thrive and reproduce, were not harmed. He also affirmed, "In no case does the river exceed permissible concentrations for drinking water." See Harry A. Kornberg, "The Absorption and Toxicity of Several Radioactive Substances in Plants and Animals," CIC-26514 (Richland: General Electric Company, 1955), pp. 1–3.

99 U.S. AEC, "Twenty-first Semiannual Report of the Atomic Energy Commission" (Washington, D.C.: U.S. Government Printing Office, January 1957), pp. 176–84; and U.S. AEC, "Twenty-second Semiannual Report of the Atomic Energy Commission" (Washington, D.C.: U.S. Government Printing Office, July 1957), p. 186. The NCRP changes were published first as an NBS Technical News Bulletin in 1957. Later, they were printed as NCRP, "Maximum Permissible Body Burdens and Maximum Permissible Concentrations of Radionuclides in Air and Water for Occupational Exposure," NBS-69 (Washington, D.C.: U.S. Government Printing Office, June 5, 1959).

100 R. F. Foster and R. L. Junkins, "Off-Project Exposure from Hanford Reactor Effluent," HW-63654 (RL: HAPO, February 1, 1960), pp. 23–28. See also R. L. Junkins, E. C. Watson, I. C. Nelson, and R. C. Henle, "Evaluation of Radiological Conditions in the Vicinity of Hanford for 1959," HW-64371 (RL: HAPO, May 9, 1960), p. 20.

101 Staff of the Biology Operation, "Biology Research Annual Report for 1958," HW-59500 (RL: HAPO, January 5, 1959).

102 R. C. Pendleton, "Absorption of Cs 137 by an Aquatic Community," in "Biology Research Annual Report for 1957," HW-53500 (RL: HAPO, 1958), pp. 35–43; and R. C. Pendleton and W. C. Hanson, "Absorption of Cesium-137 by Components of an Aquatic Community," *Proceedings of the Second Annual Conference on Peaceful Uses of Atomic Energy*, vol. 18 (Geneva, Switzerland: International Commission on Radiological Protection, September 1958), pp. 419–22.

103 Richard F. Foster, "The Need for Biological Monitoring in Radioactive Waste Streams," *Sewage and Industrial Wastes* 32, no. 12 (1959): 1409–15, cited in G. D. Becker, "Aquatic Bioenvironmental Studies in the Columbia River at Hanford, 1945–71," BNWL-1734-UC-48 (Richland: Battelle Northwest Laboratories, February 1973), p. 56.

104 Lauriston S. Taylor, "The Influence of Lowered Permissible Dose Levels on Atomic Energy Operations in the United States," in W. G. Marley and K. Z. Morgan, eds., *Progress in Nuclear Energy*, Series XII, "Health Physics," vol. 1 (New York: Pergamon Press, 1959), pp. 10–16.

105 Richard F. Foster, "The Significance of Uptake of Radioisotopes by Fresh-Water Fishes," in "Biological Problems in Water Pollution," TD 420.S4 (Cincinnati, Ohio: U.S. Public Health Service, 1960). The paper was originally presented at the Robert A. Taft Sanitary Engineering Center, U.S. Public Health Service, April 1959.

106 R. H. Schiffman, "The Uptake of Strontium from Diet and Water by Rainbow Trout," HW-72107 (RL: HAPO, December 1961), p. 6.

107 Foster and Junkins, HW-63654, pp. 23–28; Junkins, Watson, Nelson, and Henle, HW-64371, p. 20; Richard F. Foster, "Summary of Radiological Data for the Month of December 1961," HW-72338

(RL: HAPO, January 15, 1962), p. 4; Richard F. Foster, "Radiological Studies of the Hanford Environs for October 1962," HW-74307-10 (RL: HAPO, November 12, 1962), pp. 3–4; Ted Poston and Roger Dirkes, "Environmental Measurements—Columbia River," draft presentation (Richland: Hanford Dose Reconstruction Project [HEDR], December 13, 1989); and R. F. Foster and D. McConnan, "Relationships between the Concentration of Radionuclides in Columbia River Water and Fish," HW-SA-2688 (RL: HAPO, July 25, 1962), p. 18.

108 H. V. Clukey and M. W. McConiga, "Calculation of Drinking Water Radiation Exposures from Columbia River Water Sources," HW-57411 (RL: HAPO, September 16, 1958), pp. 1–2; and Foster and Junkins, HW-63654. The amount of hunting, fishing, swimming, or boating in the Columbia, and home gardening and canning done by an individual or family, became the important variables in "life-style." Whether or not individuals drank milk from backyard cows and whether they worked outdoors also became key determinants in amounts of exposure.

109 General Electric Company, "Manual of Radiation Protection Standards," HW-25457 (rev. 1) (RL: HAPO, July 1957), pp. 3.1, 7.2. See also Clukey, HW-54243, p. 9.

110 General Electric Company, "Manual of Radiation Protection Standards," HW-25457 (rev. 2) (RL: HAPO, March 1, 1960), pp. 4.5, 1.5.

111 Foster and Junkins, HW-63654, pp. 31–36. In 1959, Zn-65 levels in oysters at Willapa Bay stood at 5×10^{-5} μCi/g, as compared with 2×10^{-7} μCi/g for Chesapeake Bay oysters. By January 1970, values for the Willapa Bay oysters had fallen only to 30×10^{-6} (or 3×10^{-5}) μCi/g. By July 1974, three years after the shutdown of the last single-pass reactor

at Hanford, these levels stood at 0.2×10^{-6} μCi/g for Zn-65. See ERDA-1538, 2: III-G-13.

112 Foster and Junkins, HW-63654, pp. 22–30.

113 Charles L. Dunham, M.D., letter to Senator Wayne Morse, CIC-70025 (Washington, D.C.: U.S. Atomic Energy Commission, March 29, 1960), p. 2.

114 Junkins, Watson, Nelson, and Henle, HW-64371, pp. 25, 56, partially citing Herbert M. Parker.

115 Herbert M. Parker, "Statement: Radiation Standards, Including Fallout," Testimony to the Joint Committee on Atomic Energy, June 1962, in R. Kathren, R. Baalman, W. Bair, *Herbert M. Parker* (Columbus, Ohio: Battelle Press, 1986), p. 433.

116 R. B. Hall and R. H. Wilson, "Evaluation of Discharging Radioactive Wastes into Fresh Water Streams," HW-SA-2748 (Richland: Hanford Laboratories Operation, October 1962), p. 16.

117 U.S. AEC, "Annual Report to Congress, 1962" (Washington, D.C.: U.S. Government Printing Office, January 1963), p. 229.

118 I. C. Nelson, "Evaluation of Radiological Conditions in the Vicinity of Hanford, July–September, 1961," HW-71203 (RL: HAPO, September 29, 1961), pp. 2, 8; I. C. Nelson, "Evaluation of Radiological Conditions in the Vicinity of Hanford, January–March, 1962," HW-73366 (RL: HAPO, April 23, 1962), pp. 2, 4, 8–9, 20; J. W. Vanderbeek, "Evaluation of Radiological Conditions in the Vicinity of Hanford, April–June, 1962," HW-74398 (RL: HAPO, July 23, 1962), pp. 2, 9, 11, 17–24; J. W. Vanderbeek, "Evaluation of Radiological Conditions in the Vicinity of Hanford, July–September 1962," HW-75431 (RL: HAPO, October 12, 1962), pp. 1–2, 4–7, 20, 23; and I. C. Nelson and Richard F. Foster, "Ringold—A Hanford Environmental Survey," HW-78262 (rev.) (RL: HAPO, April 3, 1964), pp. 7, 12.

119 Parker, HW-24356, pp. 2–5.
120 Hall and Jerman, HW-63653, pp. 12–13, 2–4. The total curies per day figure had increased from that of 2,030 curies per day in early 1951. The flow rate had risen from about 75,000 units per minute in 1948.
121 John Healy and Royal Rostenbach, "Influence of Hanford Reactors on Domestic Use of Columbia River Water," HW-36862 (RL: HAPO, May 25, 1955), pp. 10, 12.
122 Hall and Jerman, HW-63653, pp. 12–13; and J. D. McCormack and L. C. Schwendiman, "Significance of Rupture Debris in the Columbia River," HW-61325 (RL: HAPO, August 17, 1959), pp. 6, 15.
123 Foster, HW-80649, p. 28; and G. E. Backman, "Summary of Environmental Contamination Incidents at Hanford, 1958–64," HW-84619 (Richland: Battelle Pacific Northwest Laboratory, April 12, 1965). See also J. P. Corley, "Rate of Transport of Effluent Downstream," in HW-80649, p. 31.
124 Poston, CIC-80866, p. 18. Information available in the late 1980s placed the number of fuel element failures at Hanford as follows:

1955	188
1956	167
1957	200
1958	173
1959	74
1960	138
1961	88
1962	93
1963	69

125 Davis, Watson, and Palmiter, HW-36074, p. 15.
126 W. A. Haney, "Dilution of 300 Area Uranium Wastes Entering the Columbia River," HW-52401 (RL: HAPO, September 9, 1957), p. 3.
127 G. E. Backman, "Dispersion of 300 Area Liquid Effluent in the Columbia River," HW-73672 (RL: HAPO, May 25, 1962), pp. 1–3. In early 1964, Richard

Foster analyzed river water contamination near the Richland municipal plant. He found that, even in terms of beta-emitters, "the outlook" was "for an annual exposure to the gastrointestinal tract of Richland residents approximating four times that . . . experienced at Pasco." This condition existed, he reported, because Richland was closer to the reactor outfalls (and thus experienced less radioactive decay) and because it used a new and quicker water-treatment process. See Foster, HW-80649, pp. 27–28.
128 John W. Healy, "The Effect of Purging during Pile Operation on the Effluent Water," HW-24578 (RL: HAPO, May 27, 1952), pp. 1, 6–7; and Hall and Jerman, HW-63653, p. 13.
129 W. Y. Matsumoto, "The Effect of Reactor Power Purges on Radioactive Contamination of Coolant," HW-43830 (RL: HAPO, June 20, 1956), pp. 2, 6, 13–14; Chemical Effluents Technology Operation (CETO), "Chemical Effluents Technology Waste Disposal Investigations—April, May, June, 1957," HW-53225 (RL: HAPO, September 25, 1957), pp. 9–10; and Koop, HW-50601, pp. 2–3, foreword citing D. W. Pearce (manager, CETO).
130 CETO, HW-53225, pp. 8–9; and K. C. Knoll, "Effect of Detergents upon Absorption of Radioisotopes by Soils," HW-52055 (RL: HAPO, August 1, 1957).
131 CETO, HW-54848, p. 8; and W. N. Koop, "Disposal of Decontaminating Agents for Reactor Rear-Face Piping," HW-53372 (RL: HAPO, November 20, 1957), pp. 5–6.
132 Chemical Effluents Technology Operations (CETO), "Chemical Effluents Technology Waste Disposal Investigations, for October, November, December, 1958," HW-58811 RD, p. 10, and "October, November, December 1960," HW-68543 RD, pp. 12–13 (RL: HAPO, January 9, 1959, and March 7, 1961). See also W. W. Sabol and M. N. Myers, "Proposed Laboratory Experiments in

324

Support of Direct Cycle Effluent Problems," DC-60-3-723 (Idaho Falls, Idaho: General Electric Aircraft Propulsion Department, March 2, 1960).

133 Poston, CIC-80866, p. 14.

134 H. W. Heacock, "Adaption of a Recirculating Water System to 100-H Area—Interim Feasibility Report," HW-40837 (RL: HAPO, January 9, 1956), p. 5.

135 J. M. Atwood, M. W. Cook, and H. E. Hanthorn, "Organic Reactor Coolant Survey," HW-44054 (RL: HAPO, July 9, 1956).

136 Honstead, HW-32506, p. 36; and Healy and Rostenbach, HW-36862, p. 52.

137 John F. Honstead, "Dispersion of Dissolved Material in the Columbia River," HW-49008 (RL: HAPO, March 12, 1957); and H. T. Norton, "The Turbulent Diffusion of River Contaminants," HW-49195 (RL: HAPO, March 25, 1957), pp. 2–7.

138 R. H. Bogan, "Review and Analysis of Hydrological and Radiochemical Columbia River Surveys," HW-45124 (RL: HAPO, August 29, 1956), pp. 23–24.

139 J. M. Nielsen and R. W. Perkins, "The Depletion of Radioisotopes from the Columbia River by Natural Processes," HW-52908 (RL: HAPO, October 4, 1957), pp. 3–5, 15–17. The half-lives of Cu-64, Sc-46, and Ba-140 are 12.8 hours, 85 days, and 12.8 days respectively. A 1963–64 survey conducted by the U.S. Geological Survey (USGS) and the General Electric–Hanford Company found that the bottom of McNary Dam reservoir and estuary, about thirty-five miles downstream from Richland, contained the most "major deposits" of radioactive particulate material. See J. M. Nielsen, "Transport and Deposition of Radionuclides in the Columbia River," in Foster, HW-80649, p. 35.

140 Foster and Junkins, HW-63654, pp. 22–30.

141 Royal E. Rostenbach, "Columbia River Survey—1954–1955," HW-43529 (RL: HAPO, May 10, 1956), p. 6.

142 Foster and Junkins, HW-63654, pp. 3–9, 14.

143 J. P. Corley, "Rate of Transport of Effluent Downstream," in Foster, HW-80649, p. 31.

144 In 1950–51, a secret Hanford study of Pasco's water-treatment system found rapidly increasing, but still relatively low, levels of water contamination. See Soldat and Thorburn, HW-22862.

145 Healy and Rostenbach, HW-36862, pp. 2, 14–19, 26; H. V. Clukey and M. W. McConiga, "Calculation of Drinking Water Radiation Exposure from Columbia River Water," HW-57411 (RL: HAPO, September 16, 1958), p. 1; and Clukey, HW-54243, p. 9. HW-36862 reported that average radionuclide concentrations in raw river water rose as follows (expressed as microcuries times E-6 per cubic centimeter):

	July 1952	December 1954
Pasco Pumping Plant	0.19 μCi/cc	2.5 μCi/cc
Kennewick Pumping Plant	0.82 μCi/cc	3.0 μCi/cc
Pasco-Kennewick Bridge	0.60 μCi/cc	2.8 μCi/cc

In early 1955, Healy and Rostenbach measured average radioactive contamination in raw river water at Pasco (inlet) at 2.5×10^{-6} μCi/cc; they found 0.35×10^{-6} μCi/cc in the sanitary (outlet) water.

146 B. V. Andersen, "Monthly Reports, Regional Monitoring, 1956," CIC-12765 (RL: HAPO, 1956), November 1, pp. 2–3, January 3, 1957, p. 2. Mrad per hour refers to, and quantifies, exposure from beta-emitting radiation, whereas mr per hour measures exposure from gamma-emitting radiation. The maximum high activity density reading in river water near 100-D in October 1956 was 6×10^{-5} μCi/ml. At Pasco and Kennewick in December, untreated river water concentration stood at 2.4×10^{-6} μCi/ml.

147 H. V. Clukey, "Radiation Aspects for River Navigation through Hanford Project," HW-47152 (RL: HAPO, December 7, 1956), pp. 2, 7.

148 Ibid. Although some limited commercial barge traffic was allowed, the Hanford Reach remained prohibited to recreational use until the early 1970s. By the early 1960s, however, its islands and north (east) bank were in common, albeit unauthorized, use by picnickers, boaters, and swimmers.

149 Tsiveglou and Lammering, "Evaluation," pp. 3–6, 9–14, 24.

150 Washington State, CIC-161754; and Oregon State, CIC-161755. See also Oliver R. Placek, Memorandum to the Files, CIC-160993 (Washington, D.C.: February 23, 1961). These studies did proceed. See Kenneth H. Spies, "Lower Columbia River Environmental Radiological Survey Progress Report," CIC-161945 and CIC-161946 (Salem: Oregon State Board of Health, June 11, 1960 and July 13, 1966); and Washington State Department of Health, "Radioecological Survey of Surface Water Environment in the State of Washington: First Annual Report" (Olympia: State of Washington, 1962).

151 Leonard B. Dworsky (pollution control officer, Portland, Oreg.), memo to Murray Stein (Public Health Service, Washington, D.C.), "Pollution of the Columbia River Resulting from the Atomic Energy Commission's Hanford Atomic Works," CIC-161744 (Portland: U.S. Public Health Service, Region XI, January 11, 1962). Laboratory work to study and develop feasible methods for reducing the amount of radioactivity released to the Columbia River were funded by the AEC from 1962 to 1965. See Poston, CIC-80866, p. 17.

152 D. McConnan, "Dose-Rate Measurements of Beaches and Islands on the Columbia River between Ringold and Richland," HW-72229 (RL: HAPO,

August 10, 1962), pp. 9–20. Dose rates on the beaches between the 300 Area and Ringold averaged 0.05–0.43 mrep/hr, with a maximum of 1.1 mrep/hr.

153 U.S. AEC, "Annual Report to Congress—1964" (Washington, D.C.: U.S. Atomic Energy Commission, January 1965), pp. 17–21.

154 Poston, CIC-80866, pp. 3, 16–22; and Richard F. Poston, "Report on Radioactivity Waste Discharges from Hanford Plant," CIC-80865 (Portland: U.S. Public Health Service, May 12, 1964), pp. 3, 5–10.

155 D. G. Watson, C. E. Cushing, C. C. Coutant, and W. L. Templeton, "Radioecological Studies on the Columbia River, Part II," BNWL-1377 (Richland: Battelle Northwest Laboratories, 1970), pp. 29–32.

156 T. H. Essig, "Hanford Waste Disposal Summary—1970," BNWL-1618 (Richland: Battelle Northwest Laboratories, September 1971), p. 11.

157 Becker, BNWL-1734-UC-48, p. 37, citing C. E. Cushing, "Concentration and Transport of 32P and 65Zn by Columbia River Plankton," *Limnology and Oceanography* 12, no. 2 (1967): 330–32.

158 C. E. Cushing, D. G. Watson, A. J. Scott, and J. M. Gurtison, "Decline of Radionuclides in Columbia River Biota," PNL-3269-UC-11 (Richland: Pacific Northwest Laboratories, March 1980), p. 19. See also ERDA-1538, 1:II.3-64.

159 ERDA-1538, 1:II.3-64.

Chapter 6

1 R. C. Routson, "A Review of Studies of Soil-Waste Relationships on the Hanford Reservation from 1944 to 1967," BNWL-1464 (Richland: Battelle Northwest Laboratories, March 1973), p. 9. See also F. P. Seymour, "Radioactive Waste Disposal," Lecture XXI in "H.I. Lecture Series," HW-7184, part II (RL: HEW, July 1, 1947), pp. 2, 4.

2 Routson, BNWL-1464, p. 2; and

William H. Bierschenk, "Techniques for Estimating the Specific Retention Properties of Hanford Soils," HW-61644 (RL: HAPO, 1959).

3 W. A. Haney and J. F. Honstead, "History and Discussion of Specific Retention Disposal of Radioactive Liquid Wastes in the 200 Areas," HW-54599 (RL: HAPO, April 18, 1958), pp. 4–6. See also W. A. Haney, "Disposal of High Cobalt-60 Scavenged Wastes," HW-48862 (RL: HAPO, March 4, 1957), p. 4.

4 Routson, BNWL-1464, p. 7.

5 Herbert Parker, "Speculations on Long-Range Waste Disposal Hazards," HW-8674 (RL: HEW, January 26, 1948), pp. 3–4; R. E. Brown and H. G. Ruppert, "The Underground Disposal of Liquid Wastes at the Hanford Works, Washington," HW-17088 (RL: HEW, February 1, 1950), pp. 46–48, 93; Frank E. Adley and Wendell K. Crane, "Meeting of the Columbia River Advisory Group, November 21–23, 1949," HW-15861 (RL: HEW, February 2, 1950), p. 12; and G. G. Parker and A. Piper, "Geologic and Hydrologic Features of the Richland Area, Washington, Relevant to the Disposal of Waste at the Hanford Operations of the Atomic Energy Commission," USGS-W-P-7 (Washington, D.C.: U.S. Geological Survey, July 1949), pp. 5a, 71.

6 Chemical Effluents Technology Operations (CETO), "Chemical Effluents Technology Waste Disposal Investigations, July, August, September 1956," HW-49465 (RL: HAPO, April 12, 1957), p. 13; CETO, "Chemical Effluents Technology Waste Disposal Investigations, April, May, June 1957," HW-53225 (RL: HAPO, September 25, 1957), pp. 6–8; William H. Bierschenk, "Aquifer Characteristics and Groundwater Movement at Hanford," HW-60601 (RL: HAPO, June 9, 1959), pp. 36–42; and U.S. Energy Research and Development Administration, "Waste Management Operations, Hanford Reservation: Final Environmental Statement," ERDA-1538, vol. I (Richland: U.S. Energy Research and Development Administration, December 1975), pp. II-3.64, 3.66, VIII-1, I-5-6.

7 CETO, HW-49465, pp. 1, 8–9; Haney, HW-48862; and ERDA-1538, 2:1-F-1-3.

8 CETO, "Chemical Effluents Technology Waste Disposal Investigations, October, November, December 1958," HW-58811 RD (RL: HAPO, January 9, 1959), p. 10; R. W. Harvey and N. T. Karagianes, "Hanford Radioactive Waste Management Plans," CPD-220 (rev. 1) (Richland: Atlantic Richfield Hanford Co., November 1970), pp. 6–8; and Routson, BNWL-1464, p. 2.

9 CETO, HW-53225, p. 8; CETO, "Chemical Effluents Technology Waste Disposal Investigations, July, August, September 1957," HW-54655 (RL: HAPO, December 27, 1957), p. 8; CETO, "Chemical Effluents Technology Waste Disposal Investigations, October, November, December 1957," HW-54848 (RL: HAPO, January 20, 1958), p. 7; CETO, "Chemical Effluents Technology Waste Disposal Investigations, January, February, March 1959," HW-60163-RD (RL: HAPO, April 20, 1959), p. 12; W. A. Haney, "Chemical Effluents Technology Waste Disposal Investigations, July, August, September 1960," HW-67753-RD (RL: HAPO, December 9, 1960), pp. 12–13; ERDA-1538, 1:II.1-74; and Harvey and Karagianes, CPD-220, pp. 58–59.

10 O. F. Hill, C. D. Corbit, E. E. Voiland, and R. H. Wilson, "Radioactive Solid Waste Management at Richland," ARH-1596 (Richland: Atlantic Richfield Hanford Co., February 20, 1970); and N. P. Willis, "Hanford Site Radioactive Solid Waste Acceptance Criteria," WHC-EP-0063-2 (Richland: Westinghouse Hanford Co., September 1990).

11 ERDA-1538, 2:II.1-C-80-83, 1:iii, VIII-1, I-6, X-1-91.

12 John A. Alwin, *Between the Moun-*

tains: A Portrait of Eastern Washington
(Bozeman, Mont.: Northwest Panorama
Publishing Co., 1984), pp. 14–16, 20–43;
and William H. Bierschenk, "Hydraulic
Characteristics of Hanford Aquifers,"
HW-48916 (RL: HAPO, March 3, 1957),
pp. 8–10. The categories of grains defined by the AGU were "very fine," "fine,"
"medium," and "coarse" for clay, silt,
sand, and gravel. In the case of sands and
gravels, the category of "very coarse" was
added. Clay grain sizes ranged from
0.0000096 to 0.00015 inch, silt grains
ranged from 0.00025 to 0.079 inch, and
gravel grains ranged from 0.079 to 2.52
inches. "Cobbles" ranged from 2.52 to
10.08 inches. See ERDA-1538, 2:II.1-C-51,
citing National Research Council, "Report of the Subcommittee on Sediment
Terminology," *Trans American Geophysics
Union* 28, no. 6 (December 1947).
13 Alwin, *Between*, pp. 14–16, 20–43;
Bierschenk, HW-48916, pp. 8–10; A. M.
Tallman, K. R. Fecht, M. C. Marratt,
and G. V. Last, "Geology of the Separa-
tions Areas, Hanford Site, South-Central
Washington," RHO-ST-23 (Richland:
Rockwell Hanford Operations, 1979);
A. M. Tallman, J. T. Lillie, and K. R.
Fecht, "Suprabasalt Sediments of the
Cold Creek Syncline Area," in C. W.
Myers and S. M. Price, "Subsurface
Geology of the Cold Creek Syncline,"
RHO-BWI-St-14 (Richland: Rockwell
Hanford Operations, 1981); and S. P.
Reidel, K. R. Fecht, M. C. Hagood, and
T. L. Tolan, "The Geologic Evolution of
the Central Columbia Plateau," in S. P.
Reidel and P. R. Hooper, eds., *Volcanism
and Tectonism in the Columbia River
Flood-Basalt Province,* Geological Society
of America Special Paper No. 239 (Boul-
der, Colo.: Geological Society of Amer-
ica, 1989), pp. 247–64.
14 Ted Van Arsdol, *Desert Boom and
Bust: The Story of Irrigation Efforts and
Town Building in Benton County, Washington, 1888–1904* (Vancouver, Wash.:

Published by the author, 1972), p. 57, citing *Report of the Investigations Made during 1904 in Yakima Valley under the
Direction of T. A. Noble and G. H. Bliss*
(Yakima, Wash.: U.S. Bureau of Reclamation, 1904); Mary Powell Harris,
Goodbye, White Bluffs (Yakima, Wash.:
Franklin Press, 1972), pp. 104–9, 117–20;
and Walter A. Oberst, *Railroads, Reclamation, and the River: A History of
Pasco* (Pasco, Wash.: Franklin County
Historical Society, 1978), pp. 61–71. For
further discussion of the experiences of
early farmers and ranchers, see chapter 1.
15 A. E. Kocher and A. T. Strahorn
(U.S. Department of Agriculture, Bureau
of Soils), "Soil Survey of Benton County,
Washington" (Washington, D.C.: U.S.
Government Printing Office, 1919),
pp. 6–7.
16 Olaf P. Jenkins (Washington State Department of Conservation and Development, Division of Geology), "Underground Water Supply of the Region
about White Bluffs and Hanford," Bulletin #6, Geological Series (Olympia,
Wash.: Frank Lamborn, Printer, 1922),
pp. 18–21, 32.
17 Ibid., pp. 28–33; and A. T. Strahorn,
E. J. Carpenter, W. W. Weir, S. Ewing,
and H. H. Krusekopf (U.S. Department
of Agriculture, Bureau of Chemistry and
Soils), and A. F. Heck and H. A. Lunt
(Washington State College), "Soil Survey
(Reconnaissance) of the Columbia Basin
Area, Washington" (Washington, D.C.:
U.S. Government Printing Office, 1929),
pp. 54–55.
18 Franklin T. Matthias, "Hanford Engineering Works, MED: Early History," address delivered at the Department of
Energy Technical Exchange Program,
Richland, Wash., January 14, 1987, pp. 7,
10. Much of the concrete used in Hanford's construction was, in fact, made on
site.
19 L. C. Chestnut and C. W. Wright,
"Gross Appraisal: Gable Project" (Wash-

ington, D.C.: U.S. War Department, January 21, 1943), pp. 2–5.

20 Ibid.; U.S. Army Corps of Engineers, "Basic Data on Hanford Engineer Works, Pasco, Washington" (Washington, D.C.: Office of the Chief of Engineers, May 19, 1943), p. 2; Atomic Energy Commission, "Manhattan District History, Book IV—Pile Project X-10" (Washington, D.C.: U.S. Government Printing Office, December 1947), vol. 4, "Land Acquisition, Hanford Engineer Works," p. 52; and DuPont Corporation, *Construction History—Hanford Engineer Works: History of the Project,* vols. 1–4 (Wilmington, Del.: E.I. DuPont de Nemours and Co., 1945), 1:2–3, 103, 3:814. A year later, the DuPont Corporation conducted another cursory survey, but a thorough investigation of subsoil properties was not undertaken.

21 DuPont, *Construction,* 3:636, 812–13; Franklin T. Matthias, "Journal and Notes, 1943–1945," unpublished diary (located at Richland, U.S. Department of Energy Public Reading Room), March 25, 1944; Paul J. Shippy (DuPont Corporation Atomic Energy Division), letter to the author, June 30, 1988; and Randall E. Brown, interview with the author, July 19, 1989. Camp Hanford was home to approximately fifty thousand construction workers between 1943 and late February 1945. It was located at the old Hanford townsite, a few miles from the 100 and 200 areas.

22 Parker, HW-8674, p. 9; U.S. Atomic Energy Commission, "The Handling of Radioactive Waste Materials in the U.S. Atomic Energy Program," AEC 180/2 (Washington, D.C.: U.S. Atomic Energy Commission, September 22, 1949), p. 22; Walter O. Simon, letter to the author, December 12, 1988 (Fort Lauderdale, Fla.); D. W. Rhodes, "Preliminary Studies of Plutonium Adsorption in Hanford Soil," HW-24548 (RL: HAPO, May 29, 1952), p. 1; Brown, interview, July 18,

1989; and Brown and Ruppert, HW-17088, p. 10, citing R. S. Bell, "Request for Preparation of Project Proposal—Engineering Studies of Active Waste Concentration Methods—200 Areas," HW-10779 (RL: HEW, 1948).

23 "Hanford Technical Manual, Section C, Separations," HW-10475C (RL: HEW, 1948) (this document is a GE Company reprint of a May 1, 1944, MED document); and S. M. Stoller and R. B. Richards, *Reactor Handbook,* 2d ed., vol. 2 (New York: Interscience Publishers, 1961), pp. 227–29.

24 Brown and Ruppert, HW-17088, pp. 8–10; and DuPont Corporation, *Operations of Hanford Engineer Works,* HAN-73214 (Wilmington, Del.: E.I. DuPont de Nemours and Co., 1946), Book XII, "S Department," p. 106.

25 Brown and Ruppert, HW-17088, pp. 8–10; and DuPont, *Operations,* Book VII, "Medical Department: Health Instruments," p. 53, and Book XII, "S Department," p. 108.

26 Brown and Ruppert, HW-17088, pp. 8–10; DuPont, *Operations,* Book VII, p. 166, and Book XII, pp. 107–8, 122, 178, 196; and Edward C. Berry, "Radio-Autographs of Russian Thistle," HW-9241 (RL: HEW, March 19, 1948).

27 W. L. Kay, "Retention Characteristics of 200-Area Soil for Product," HW-3-3427 (RL: HEW, February 2, 1946).

28 John W. Healy, "Adsorption and Retention of Plutonium by 200-Area Topsoil," HW-7-4776 (RL: HEW, August 31, 1946), pp. 1–5.

29 DuPont, *Operations,* Book VII, pp. 52, 132, 166; Carl C. Gamertsfelder, "H.I. Environs Report for Month of September 1947," HW-7831 (RL: HEW, October 29, 1947); and W. A. Haney, "Dilution of 300 Area Uranium Wastes Entering the Columbia River," HW-52401 (RL: HAPO, September 9, 1957).

30 Herbert M. Parker, "Health Physics, Instrumentation, and Radiation Protection," reprinted in *Health Physics* 38 (June 1980): 967. The original document was written in early 1947.

31 Brown and Ruppert, HW-17088, pp. 1–10, 31.

32 Parker, HW-8674, pp. 3–9; and Parker and Piper, USGS-W-P-7, p. 5b.

33 Parker, HW-8674.

34 Ibid., pp. 3–9; and Brown and Ruppert, HW-17088, p. 10.

35 Brown and Ruppert, HW-17088, pp. 46–48, 93; Parker, HW-8674, p. 3; and Adley and Crane, HW-15861, p. 12.

36 E. Teller, M. Benedict, J. Kennedy, J. Wheeler, and A. Wolman, "Review of Certain Hanford Operations: Reactor Safeguard Committee Hanford Meeting, June 14, 15, and 16, 1948," GEH-14040 (Richland: General Electric Hanford Co., November 4, 1948), pp. 10, 13.

37 Parker and Piper, USGS-W-P-7, pp. 5a–5b, 6, 67, 70–71, 74; and Brown and Ruppert, HW-17088, pp. 46–48, 93.

38 Brown and Ruppert, HW-17088, pp. 46–48, 93; and Parker, HW-8674, p. 3.

39 Chemical Development Section, Separations Technology Division, "REDOX Technical Manual," HW-18700-DEL (RL: HAPO, July 10, 1951).

40 Fred Claggett, "Equilibria of Uranium in Nitric Acid between Waste Metal Solutions and TBP and Hydrocarbon Diluents," HW-17339 (RL: HEW, March 24, 1950); and D. P. Granquist and E. T. Merrill, "Uranium Phase Equilibria in the TBP Process," HW-17747 (RL: HEW, March 1, 1951).

41 D. A. Zimmerman, A. E. Reisenauer, G. D. Black, and M. A. Young, "Hanford Site Water Table Changes 1950 through 1980—Data Observations and Evaluation," PNL-5506 (Richland: Battelle Pacific Northwest Laboratories, April 1, 1986), pp. 4–10; and C. W. Thomas, D. L. Reid, and H. A. Treiba, "Cobalt-60 in Ground Water and Separations Waste Streams," HW-42612 (RL: HAPO, April 20, 1956).

42 M. Mickelson and Staff of the H.I. Divisions, "Annual Report of the Health Instruments Divisions, 1950," HW-21699 (rev.) (RL: HEW, July 20, 1951), pp. 8, 51–52, 61.

43 W. H. Bierschenk and M. W. McConiga, "Changes in Hanford Water Table, 1944–57," HW-51277 (RL: HAPO, July 9, 1957), pp. 10–11. Under 200-E Area, the groundwater level had risen from 390 to 405 feet above mean sea level. Under 200-W Area, it had risen from 395 to 450 feet.

44 Herbert M. Parker, "Quarterly Progress Report—Research and Development Activities for January–March 1951," HW-20866 (RL: HEW, April 18, 1951), p. 26; and Herbert M. Parker, "Radiological Sciences Department: Quarterly Progress Report—Research and Development Activities for July–September 1951," HW-22576 (RL: HEW, November 1, 1951), p. 29. See also Bierschenk and McConiga, HW-51277, pp. 13–14.

45 Bierschenk and McConiga, HW-51277, p. 14. Tests performed at that time with fluoresein tracer found average travel velocities of waste water from the 200-W Area of between 350 and 770 feet per day.

46 Rhodes, HW-24548.

47 Bierschenk, HW-48916, pp. 25–27. The 1952 test cited was done on well site 199-K-10, and the 1954 test was performed on well site 699-62-43.

48 John W. Healy, "Release of Radioactive Wastes to Ground," HW-28121 (RL: HAPO, May 20, 1953), pp. 2–3, 9, 14, 19.

49 J. R. McHenry, "Adsorption and Retention of Cesium by Soils of the Hanford Project," HW-31011 (RL: HAPO, March 2, 1954).

50 J. R. McHenry, "Adsorption and Retention of Strontium by Soils of the Hanford Project," HW-34499 (RL: HAPO, February 1, 1955), pp. 6, 33.

51 D. W. Rhodes, K. R. Holtzinger, and J. R. McHenry, "Adsorption of Radioactive Isotopes by Soil from a Bismuth

Phosphate Waste," HW-32978 (RL: HAPO, September 1, 1954). No specific concentration values are given in this document for Ru-106 because, according to the authors, "the data for ruthenium were very erratic and served only to indicate that adsorption by soil was very low."

52 CETO, HW-49465, p. 13; Zimmerman, Reisenauer, Black, and Young, PNL-5506, pp. 4–10, 13–14; and Bierschenk and McConiga, HW-51277, pp. 16–17.

53 Chemical Development Sub-Section, Separations Technical Section, Engineering Department, "PUREX Technical Manual," HW-31000-DEL (RL: HAPO, March 25, 1955).

54 CETO, HW-49465, p. 13; and Zimmerman, Reisenauer, Black, and Young, PNL-5506, pp. 4–14; and Bierschenk and McConiga, HW-51277, pp. 16–17. By mid-1956, groundwater levels beneath 200-E Area ranged from 408.65 feet under the PUREX plant to 395 feet under other parts of this area. Beneath 200-W Area, mid-1956 levels ranged from 471.89 feet in the northern sector to a peak of 475.8 feet in the southern sector.

55 B. V. Andersen, "Monthly Reports, Regional Monitoring, 1956," CIC-12765 (RL: HAPO, 1956), July (July 31, 1956), p. 1, and December (January 3, 1957), p. 1.

56 CETO, "Chemical Effluents Technology Waste Disposal Investigations, for October, November, December 1956," HW-50186 (RL: HAPO, May 14, 1957), pp. 4–6.

57 CETO, HW-49465, p. 13.

58 CETO, "Chemical Effluents Waste Technology Investigations January, February, March, 1957," HW-51095 (RL: HAPO, June 26, 1957), pp. 9, 1–3, 15. The highest concentrations of radioactivity were found in wastes draining from the 216-A-8 crib. Concentrations in groundwater beneath that crib reached 10^{-2} μCi/cc, whereas the limit for subsurface water stood at 1.5×10^{-7} μCi/cc.

59 CETO, HW-53225, pp. 4–5; CETO, HW-54848, p. 4; and William H. Bierschenk, "Effect of Ground-Water Mounds on the PUREX Operations," HW-49728 (RL: HAPO, April 18, 1957), pp. 3–4, 9–11. Disposal swamps in the 200 Area received activated water that had been used to cool the chemical separations plants themselves. This liquid was less contaminated than the actual processing waste solutions.

60 V. W. Wood, "Change of Scope: Relocation of PUREX Cooling Water Swamp—Project CA-683," HW-46396 (RL: HAPO, October 26, 1956), p. 3.

61 CETO, HW-53225, pp. 4–5; and CETO, HW-54848, p. 4.

62 Bierschenk, HW-60601, pp. 4–13, 36–42. Hanford policy at this time allowed for "contamination of the ground waters by significant amounts of Ru-106, Ru-103," since these isotopes have half-lives under three years. See R. E. Brown, D. W. Pearce, et al., "Experience in the Disposal of Radioactive Wastes to the Ground," in W. G. Marley and K. Z. Morgan, eds., *Progress in Nuclear Energy*, Series XII, "Health Physics," vol. 1 (New York: Pergamon Press, 1959), pp. 556–62. This policy stemmed from recommendations made in 1953 in Healy, HW-28121.

63 R. E. Irish, "A Comparison of Ground Waste Disposal Status at Hanford, 1959–61," HW-SA-2236 (RL: HAPO, August 2, 1961), pp. 2–5; CETO, HW-60163-RD, pp. 9–12; CETO, "Chemical Effluents Technology Waste Disposal Investigations, for April, May, June 1959," HW-61197-RD (RL: HAPO, July 22, 1959), pp. 8–15; CETO, "Chemical Effluents Technology Waste Disposal Investigations, for October, November, December 1959," HW-64094-RD (RL: HAPO, March 1, 1960), pp. 3–7.

64 W. A. Haney, "Chemical Effluents Waste Disposal Investigations, for January, February, March 1960," HW-65464-RD (RL: HAPO, May 19,

1960), pp. 4, 6, 8; Haney, HW-67753-RD, pp. 7–11; and W. A. Haney, "Chemical Effluents Waste Disposal Investigations, for October, November, December," HW-68543-RD (RL: HAPO, March 7, 1961), pp. 2–4, 18–21. See also A. E. Reisenauer, "A Procedure for Estimating Capacity of a Ground Disposal Facility for Radioactive Waste," HW-57897 (RL: HAPO, May 4, 1959). The "detection limit" for gross beta radiation in test wells drilled to groundwater was 8 × 10^{-8} μCi/cc in 1960. One well below 200-E Area registered 1.6 × 10^{-3} μCi/cc that year.

65 Thomas, Reid, and Treiba, HW-42612, pp. 2, 7; and CETO, HW-49465, pp. 1, 8–9. Actual measurements showed Co-60 concentrations in groundwater samples below 200-W at 7.2 × 10^{-4} μCi/cc on January 16, 1956, 0.3 × 10^{-2} μCi/cc on March 5, 1956, and 1.3 × 10^{-2} μCi/cc on March 12, 1956.

66 Haney, HW-48862, p. 4; and Haney and Honstead, HW-54599, pp. 4–5.

67 CETO, HW-49465, pp. 1, 8–9; and CETO, HW-51095, pp. 9, 1–3, 15. The allowable concentration level for Co-60 was raised tenfold, from 4 × 10^{-5} μCi/cc to 4 × 10^{-4} μCi/cc. The radiocobalt concentrations in Hanford's groundwater already far exceeded this limit. See Thomas, Reid, and Treiba, HW-42612.

68 CETO, HW-53225, pp. 4–5; and CETO, HW-54655, pp. 4–8.

69 CETO, HW-53225, pp. 6–8; and CETO, HW-54848, p. 6. Gross beta concentrations in groundwater east and southeast of REDOX stood at 1.7 × 10^{-5} μCi/cc in mid-1957, at 7.8 × 10^{-5} μCi/cc in the autumn, and at 2.6 × 10^{-3} μCi/cc in December. The mid-1957 level of Sr-90 in groundwater stood at 1.1 × 10^{-6} μCi/cc.

70 CETO, HW-58811-RD, pp. 5–8; Irish, HW-SA-2236, pp. 2–5; CETO, HW-60163-RD, pp. 9–12; CETO, HW-61197-RD, pp. 8–15; CETO, HW-64094-RD, pp. 3–7; Haney,

HW-65464-RD, pp. 4, 6, 8; Haney, HW-67753-RD, pp. 7–11; and Haney, HW-68543-RD, pp. 2–4, 18–21. The 1958 high in gross beta concentration in groundwater below REDOX reached 1.1 × 10^{-2} μCi/cc. In 1960, one test well below REDOX registered 2.6 × 10^{-2} μCi/cc.

71 "Monitoring Well Anomalies in Vicinity of U-1 and U-2 Cribs, 200-W Area," Unusual Occurrence Report 85-17 (Richland: Rockwell Hanford Operations, March 4, 1985).

72 Bierschenk, HW-48916, pp. 10, 19, 36.

73 CETO, "Chemical Effluents Technology Waste Disposal Investigations, for January, February, March 1957," HW-51095 (RL: HAPO, June 26, 1957), p. 6.

74 J. R. McHenry and J. F. Honstead, "Evaluation of Sites for the Disposal of Radioactive Waste Solutions," HW-53219 (RL: HAPO, November 15, 1957), pp. 5–6.

75 CETO, HW-54655, p. 12.

76 Bierschenk, HW-60601, pp. 4–13, 36–42.

77 Haney, HW-65464-RD, pp. 4, 6, 8; Haney, HW-68543-RD, pp. 2–4; and Reisenauer, HW-57897.

78 CETO, HW-53225, p. 8; and C. E. Linderoth, "Economics of Disposing of Coating Waste as a Gel—Preliminary Estimates," HW-50198 (RL: HAPO, May 14, 1957).

79 CETO, HW-54655, p. 8.

80 C. E. Linderoth, "Thermal Considerations in the Disposal of Gelled High Level Radioactive Wastes," HW-51682 (RL: HAPO, September 10, 1957), p. 3.

81 CETO, HW-54848, p. 7; and W. A. Haney, "Status Report—Disposal of Aluminum Bearing Wastes by Gelation," HW-58211 (RL: HAPO, November 24, 1958), p. 3.

82 K. C. Knoll, "Effect of Detergents upon Absorption of Radioisotopes by Soils," HW-52055 (RL: HAPO, August 1, 1957); and CETO, HW-60163-RD, p. 12.

83 Haney, HW-67753-RD, p. 13.

84 D. E. Braden, "Design Scope, Process Waste Disposal Facility, PRF, Z Plant," HW-79068 (RL: HAPO, 1963); B. F. Judson, "Semi-Works Operation of the RE-CUPLEX Facility," vols. 1, 2, HW-44776 (RL: HAPO, 1956); J. D. Ludowise, "Report on Plutonium Mining Activities at 216-Z-9 Enclosed Trench" RHO-ST-21 (Richland: Rockwell Hanford Operations, 1978); R. B. Kasper, "216-Z-12 Transuranic Crib Characterization: Operational History and Distribution of Plutonium and Americium," RHO-ST-44 (Richland: Rockwell Hanford Operations, 1982); and U.S. Department of Energy (DOE), "Hanford Waste Management Plan," DOE/RL 87-13 (Richland: U.S. DOE, 1987), appendix A.

85 Chemical Development Operation, Hanford Laboratories, "Hot Semiworks Strontium-90 Recovery Program," HW-72666 (RL: HAPO, July 17, 1963); Chemical Processing Department, "Specifications and Standards—Strontium Purification at the Strontium Semiworks," RL-SEP-20 (RL: HAPO, February 15, 1965); and U.S. DOE, DOE/RL 87-13, appendix A.

86 Donald J. Brown, "Chemical Effluents Technology Waste Disposal Investigations, January–June, 1961," HW-70806-RD (RL: HAPO, August 28, 1961), p. 20; W. A. Haney, "Chemical Effluents Technology Waste Disposal Investigations, January–June, 1963," HW-78951 (RL: HAPO, September 16, 1963), pp. 9, 16; and Donald J. Brown, "Chemical Effluents Technology Waste Disposal Investigations, January–December 1964," HW-84549 (RL: HAPO, December 31, 1964), p. 13. The highest gross beta contamination reading under 200-W Area was 1.8×10^{-2} μCi/cc in well W22-14. Under 200-E Area, the contamination in well E24-1 averaged 6,100 picocuries (pCi) per cc throughout 1963. In 1964, well E24-2 averaged 1,800 pCi/cc; 1,800 pCi/cc is equivalent to 1.8×10^{-3} μCi/cc.

87 Zimmerman, Reisenauer, Black, and Young, PNL-5506, pp. 10, 21; Irish, HW-SA-2236, p. 12; and D. J. Brown and W. A. Haney, "Chemical Effluents Technology Waste Disposal Investigations, July–December, 1963—The Movement of Contaminated Ground Water from the 200 Areas to the Columbia River," HW-80909 (RL: HAPO, February 18, 1964), p. 8.

88 Donald J. Brown, "Chemical Effluents Technology Waste Disposal Investigations, July–December, 1961," HW-72645-RD (RL: HAPO, February 1962), pp. 9–10; and Donald J. Brown, "Chemical Effluents Technology Waste Disposal Investigations, January–December 1964," HW-84549 (RL: HAPO, December 31, 1964), pp. 11, 13–23.

89 Brown, HW-70806-RD, pp. 6–9.

90 Donald J. Brown, "Chemical Effluents Technology Waste Disposal Investigations, January–June, 1962," HW-74915-RD (RL: HAPO, September 10, 1962), pp. 11–13; and Haney, HW-78951, p. 15.

91 Brown, HW-74915-RD, pp. 4–11.

92 Haney, HW-78951, pp. 11–13; and Brown, HW-84549, pp. 9–11, 21.

93 Haney, HW-70806-RD.

94 Brown and Haney, HW-80909, pp. 3–14.

95 Richard F. Poston, "Radioactive Waste Disposal Practices at Hanford Plant," CIC-80866 (Portland: U.S. Public Health Service, May 13, 1964), pp. 1–4, 9–11.

96 E. M. Shen, W. L. Bunch, and M. R. Wood, "Neutron Soil Moisture Monitor," HW-82009 (RL: HAPO, May 1964).

97 Glenn T. Seaborg, letter to Senator M. B. Neuberger, CIC-161705 (Washington, D.C.: U.S. Atomic Energy Commission, August 13, 1965), p. 2.

98 Routson, BNWL-1464, p. 8.

99 ERDA-1538, 1:X-67, X-64, X-49, I-5, 2:II.1-C-53.

100 "The Huge and Ever Increasing Problem of Radioactive Wastes," *Con-*

NOTES TO PAGES 159–166

sumer Reports 25, no. 2 (February 1960): 66–67, partially citing National Academy of Sciences.

101 David Lilienthal, *Change, Hope, and the Bomb* (Princeton, N.J.: Princeton University Press, 1963), pp. 135–36.

102 National Academy of Sciences, National Research Council, "Report to the Division of Reactor Development and Technology, U.S. AEC Committee of Geological Aspects of Radioactive Waste Disposal, Division of Earth Sciences" (Washington, D.C.: National Academy Press, 1966).

103 ERDA-1538, 1:X-48-49, citing U.S. Department of the Interior.

104 Ibid., 1:X-65-66, citing U.S. Environmental Protection Agency.

105 Zimmerman, Reisenauer, Black, and Young, PNL-5506, p. 21.

106 T. H. Essig, "Hanford Waste Disposal Summary-1970," BNWL-1618 (Richland: Battelle Pacific Northwest Laboratories, September 1971), p. 15.

107 E. J. Wheelwright and W. H. Swift, "The Recovery of Fission Product Rare Earth Sulfates," HW-63051 (RL: HAPO, May 10, 1961); "AEC Seeks Interest in Fission Product Recovery," *Hanford Project News* (Richland: General Electric Co., November 15, 1968), p. 3; U.S. DOE, *Atomic Power in Space,* DOE/NE/32117-H1 (Washington, D.C.: U.S. DOE, March 1987); and U.S. DOE, "Final Environmental Impact Statement: Disposal of Hanford Defense High-Level Transuranic and Tank Wastes," DOE/EIS/0113 (Richland: U.S. DOE, December 1987), vol. 1, section 3, and appendices A and B.

108 DOE/EIS/0113, 1:II.1-74; and Harvey and Karagianes, CPD-220, pp. 58–59.

109 For an explanation of the construction of the original storage tanks during World War II, see chapter 2.

110 Matthias, "Journal," December 29, 1944. See also January 7–8, 1945.

111 DuPont, *Operations,* Book XII, p. 110.

112 Ibid., p. 151.

113 Ibid., pp. 153, 178–80.

114 Parker, HW-8674, pp. 3–9.

115 U.S. Atomic Energy Commission, "Report of the Safety and Industrial Health Advisory Board," AEC-10266 (Washington, D.C.: U.S. AEC, April 2, 1948), p. 70.

116 DuPont, *Operations,* Book XII, pp. 111, 151, 179.

117 R. E. Tomlinson, "Storage of High-Activity Wastes," HW-37207 (RL: HAPO, July 8, 1955); and D. W. McLenegan, "Temperature Transients in Underground Tanks Storing Nuclear Process Residues," HW-56821 (RL: HAPO, July 28, 1958).

118 W. W. Koenig and L. L. Sanborn, "Corrosion of REDOX Waste Storage Tank Construction Material," HW-18595 (RL: HEW, August 21, 1950), pp. 5–6, 15–16; and N. Endow and K. L. Sanborn, "A Laboratory Study of the Extent of Pitting and General Corrosion of SEA-1010 Steel in Simulated Neutralized PUREX Process Waste Solution," HW-32734 (RL: HAPO, August 6, 1954).

119 M. C. Fraser, "Corrosion of Stainless Steel and Titanium in PUREX WW," HW-43986 (RL: HAPO, March 24, 1958), pp. 2, 12.

120 L. E. Brownell, "Instability of Steel Bottoms in Waste Storage Tanks," HW-57274 (RL: HAPO, August 29, 1958), pp. 1, 15–18. The tank examined in the preparation of this report was 113-SX.

121 Shen, Bunch, and Wood, HW-82009, p. 2.

122 Rhodes, Holtzinger, and McHenry, HW-32978. The tank in question was 112-T.

123 ERDA-1538, 2:II.1-C-82-83; and CETO, HW-58811, p. 10.

124 G. E. Backman, "Summary of Environmental Contamination Incidents at Hanford, 1958–1964," HW-84619 (RL: HAPO, April 12, 1965), p. 9; ERDA-1538, 2:II.1-C-83; R. W. McCullough and J. R.

Cartmell, "Chronological Record of Significant Events in Separations Operations," ARH-780 (Richland: Atlantic Richfield Hanford Co., August 30, 1968); A. G. Fremling and Investigation Committee, "Report on the Investigation of the 106-T Tank Leak at the Hanford Reservation, Richland, Washington," TID-26431 (Richland: U.S. AEC, July 1973); and Research and Engineering Division, "241-T-106 Tank Leak Investigation," ARH-2874 (Richland: Atlantic Richfield Hanford Co., November 1973). The 1971 leak took place at tank 102-BX, and the largest 1973 leak occurred at tank 106-T.

125 R. C. Newcomb and J. R. Strand, "Geologic and Groundwater Characteristics of the Hanford Reservation of the Atomic Energy Commission, Washington," USGS-WP-8 (Richland: AEC-Hanford Operations Office, December 1953), p. 100.

126 U.S. AEC, "Twenty-first Semiannual Report of the Atomic Energy Commission" (Washington, D.C.: U.S. Government Printing Office, January 1957), pp. 15–57.

127 C. R. Anderson, "Seven-Year Waste Program, Chemical Processing Department," HW-53829 (RL: HAPO, December 15, 1958).

128 Herbert Parker, in *Industrial Radioactive Waste Disposal: Hearings before the Special Subcommittee on Radiation of the Joint Committee on Atomic Energy, Congress of the United States,* January 28, 29, and 30, and February 2 and 3, 1959, vol. 1 (Washington, D.C.: U.S. Government Printing Office, 1959), p. 177.

129 Poston, CIC-80866, pp. 8–9, 11–12; and Richard F. Poston, "Report on Radioactivity Waste Discharges from Hanford Plant," CIC-80865 (Portland: U.S. Public Health Service, May 1964), pp. 4, 10.

130 Laura Fermi, *Atoms for the World* (Chicago: University of Chicago Press, 1957), pp. 185–88.

131 Ibid., p. 188, citing Dr. Abel Wolman.

132 Gordon E. Dean, *Report on the Atom,* 2d ed. (New York: Alfred A. Knopf, 1957), pp. 350–51.

133 James G. Terrill, Jr., "Some Public Health Aspects of Radioactive Wastes," *Bulletin of the Atomic Scientists* 14 (January 1958): 44.

134 Routson, BNWL-1464, pp. 37–40. For a brief discussion of the soil cycle in relation to fallout deposition, see chapter 7.

135 "News of Science: Congressional Atomic Energy Group Studies Waste Disposal Problem," *Science* 129, no. 3346 (February 13, 1959): 375–76; and "Hot Problem in Atomic Wastes," *Science News Letter* 75, no. 5 (January 31, 1959): 74–75.

136 "Study Radioactive Wastes," *Science News Letter* 76, no. 4 (July 25, 1959): 51; "One Out of 14 Barrels Leaks in AEC Disposal Test," *Science News Letter* 76, no. 5 (August 1, 1959): 72; and "The Huge," *Consumer Reports,* February 1960, pp. 66–67. As of the end of 1959, 14,000 curies of radioactive waste had been dumped purposely in the Atlantic Ocean, and 8,000 curies had been dumped deliberately in the Pacific Ocean. These amounts do not include those flushed from the mouths of the Columbia, Savannah, and other rivers, the amounts from nuclear weapons tests, or any amounts deliberately dumped by foreign countries.

137 David Lilienthal, *Change, Hope, and the Bomb* (Princeton, N.J.: Princeton University Press, 1963), pp. 129–30.

138 Poston, CIC-80866, pp. 8–9, 11–12; and Poston, CIC-80865, pp. 4, 10.

139 ERDA-1538, 2:II.1-C-80-83, 1:X-1-91, iii, VIII-I-5-6.

140 "Atomic Entombment," *Life* 38, no. 19 (May 9, 1955): 101; and "Burial Tunnel for Hanford's 'Hot' Equipment," *Science Digest* 41, no. 3 (March 1957): 52.

141 Essig, BNWL-1618, p. 20; Backman, HW-84619, pp. 5–7; and Hill, Corbit, Voiland, and Wilson, ARH-1596.

Chapter 7

1 "News from the Field: Physicians Advise Atomic Energy Commission," *American Journal of Public Health* 37, no. 11 (November 1947): 1507.

2 Paul S. Henshaw, M.D., "Roentgen Rays and Gamma Rays: Biologic Effects," in Otto Glassner, ed., *Medical Physics* (Chicago: Year Book Publishers, 1944), 1:1352, 1356–59.

3 DuPont Corporation, *Operations of the Hanford Engineer Works,* HAN-73214 (Wilmington, Del.: E.I. DuPont de Nemours and Co., 1946), Book VII, "Medical Department: Health Instruments," p. 18.

4 Herbert M. Parker, "Health Physics, Instrumentation, and Radiation Protection," reprinted in *Health Physics* 38 (June 1980): 966 (document originally written in early 1947).

5 DuPont, *Operations,* Book VII, pp. 18, 94–95. Throughout World War II, the permissible concentration of plutonium in the air at Hanford was 5×10^{-10} ug/cc (cubic centimeters). The limit through cuts or abrasions, or by percutaneous absorptions, was set at 0.004 ug on each side of a hand. See DuPont, *Operations,* Book VII, p. 95.

6 Richard Abrams, Henri Seibert, Lyman Forker, David Greenberg, Hermann Lisco, Leon Jacobson, and Eric Simmons, "Acute Toxicity of Intubated Plutonium," CH-3875 (Chicago: University of Chicago Metallurgical Laboratory, June 1946), pp. 1, 33–34, 27.

7 Hermann Lisco, Miriam Finkel, and Austin M. Brues, "Carcinogenic Properties of Radioactive Fission Products and of Plutonium" (Chicago: University of Chicago Metallurgical Laboratory, 1946).

8 Joseph G. Hamilton, M.D., "The Metabolism of the Fission Products and the Heaviest Elements" (Berkeley: University of California Division of Medical Physics), publicly presented at the Radiological Society of North America, 32nd

Annual Meeting, December 1–6, 1946, pp. 325, 328–29, 333–39, 342.

9 Ray S. Snider, "Histopathological Studies on Mice Following External Beta Ray Treatment," MDDC-583 (Oak Ridge, Tenn.: Manhattan Engineer District, 1946), published by the U.S. Atomic Energy Commission, pp. 1, 16–17, 10.

10 Parker, "Health Physics," pp. 964–74; and Herbert M. Parker, "H.I. Lecture Series," HW-07184 (RL: HEW, July 1, 1947), part I, Lecture XII, "Tolerance Dose," p. 3.

11 Parker, "Health Physics," pp. 971–72. See also P. A. Fuqua, in HW-07184, part I, Lecture X, "Effects of Radiation in the Body," pp. 1–12.

12 "First A-Bomb Survivors Live 'Life of Reilly,'" *Science News Letter* 63, no. 10 (March 7, 1953): 156, citing Dr. Cyril T. Comar. See also U.S. AEC, "Fourteenth Semiannual Report of the Atomic Energy Commission" (Washington, D.C.: U.S. Government Printing Office, July 1953), p. 52.

13 U.S. AEC, "Annual Report of the AEC for 1964" (Washington, D.C.: U.S. Government Printing Office, January 1965), p. 218. Although funding for the ABCC came from the Atomic Energy Commission, it was supervised academically by the National Research Council of the National Academy of Sciences.

14 "Radiation Sickness," *Life* 22, no. 4 (January 27, 1947): 82; "Secrets of Atom Bomb Tests," *United States News* 22, no. 19 (May 9, 1947): 24–25; Ralph Lapp, *Must We Hide?* (Cambridge, Mass.: Addison Wesley Press, 1949), pp. 21–26; and U.S. AEC, "Sixth Semiannual Report of the Atomic Energy Commission" (Washington, D.C.: U.S. Government Printing Office, July 1949), p. 53.

15 U.S. AEC, "Tenth Semiannual Report of the Atomic Energy Commission" (Washington, D.C.: U.S. Government Printing Office, July 1951), p. 42. See also "Fertility of A-Bomb Victims Returns,"

Science Digest 30, no. 5 (November 1951): 51.

16 U.S. AEC, "Eleventh Semiannual Report of the Atomic Energy Commission" (Washington, D.C.: U.S. Government Printing Office, January 1952), pp. 38–39; and "Leukemia and Abnormalities Show in A-Bomb Children," *Science News Letter* 61, no. 18 (May 3, 1952): 280.

17 U.S. AEC, "Fifteenth Semiannual Report of the Atomic Energy Commission" (Washington, D.C.: U.S. Government Printing Office, January 1954), p. 45.

18 James V. Neel, William J. Schull, et al., *The Effect of Exposure to the Atomic Bombs on Pregnancy Termination in Hiroshima and Nagasaki* (Washington, D.C.: National Academy of Sciences, National Research Council, 1956).

19 "Radiation Injury Study," *Science News Letter* 49, no. 19 (May 11, 1946): 294.

20 David Bradley, *No Place to Hide* (Boston: Little, Brown and Co., 1948), pp. 102–4.

21 *Richland Villager,* June 20, 1946, p. 1, citing "Operation Crossroads," and August 6, 1946, citing Frederick Clarke; and Bradley, *No Place,* pp. 102–64.

22 Bradley, *No Place,* pp. 121–41.

23 "What Science Learned at Bikini," *Life* 23, no. 16 (August 11, 1947): 86–88, citing Stafford Warren; and Lapp, *Hide?* p. 129, citing J. Robert Oppenheimer.

24 Richard Dempewolff, "The Sleepy Hot Lagoon," *Science Illustrated* 4, no. 3 (March 1949): 52–55.

25 Ibid., pp. 52–65; Bradley, *No Place,* pp. 140–64; and A. H. Seymour, "Summary of Activities for the Calendar Year 1950," UWFL Report #23, CIC-50053 (Seattle: University of Washington Fisheries Center, 1951). According to a U.S. Navy RSS physician, even the hazardous levels of radioactivity detected at Operation Crossroads in 1946 may have been very low compared with the actual amounts. "G.M. counters only measured 1 of 6 kinds of radiation . . . There were few of them [Geiger-Müller counters] in working order . . . many of [the RSS task force were] . . . hastily readied to read a G.M. counter but [did] not have more than a cursory knowledge of the meaning . . . Radiation (Baker mainly) tended to dump into 'hot spots' . . . [gamma] emitters (Plutonium, polonium, etc.) we couldn't test for but was always present . . . [and] urine and water canisters were so contaminated the counts [urinalysis] were meaningless— and often made 4–6 weeks later." David Bradley, letter to the author, October 27, 1988.

26 "Secrets of Atom Bomb Tests," *U.S. News* 22, no. 19 (January 27, 1947): 24–25.

27 Dempewolff, "Sleepy," pp. 52–55. See also "What Science Learned," pp. 86–88.

28 "What Science Learned," p. 88. Hanford Site and University of Washington biologists participated together in some of these same studies. See Seymour, CIC-50053.

29 Dempewolff, "Sleepy," p. 55.

30 "Atoms Alter Heredity," *Science News Letter* 58, no. 12 (September 16, 1950): 188, citing Dr. Meta S. Brown.

31 "Radiation," *Life,* January 27, 1947, p. 82.

32 Carl Dreher, "The Weirdest Danger in the World," *Popular Science* 149, no. 4 (October 1946): 86–90.

33 Andrew H. Dowdy, "Safe and Beneficial Utilization of Nuclear Energy," *American Journal of Public Health* 37, no. 10 (October 1947): 1292–93 (originally delivered as an address to the conference of the American Public Health Association, Cleveland, Ohio, November 13, 1946).

34 C. A. Tobias, P. P. Weymouth, L. R. Wassermen, and G. E. Stapleton, "Some Biological Effects Due to Nuclear Fission," *Science* 107 (January 30, 1948): 115–17.

35 "The A-Bomb's Children," *Life* 27, no.

24 (December 12, 1949): 59–60, 65; "Atomic Eye Injury," *Newsweek* 34, no. 24 (December 12, 1949): 51–52; U.S. AEC, "Eighth Semiannual Report of the Atomic Energy Commission" (Washington, D.C.: U.S. Government Printing Office, July 1950), p. 174; and U.S. AEC, "Ninth Semiannual Report of the Atomic Energy Commission" (Washington, D.C.: U.S. Government Printing Office, January 1951), p. 21. In early 1949, Herbert Parker reassured Hanford workers that they had not been subject to such overexposure. See *Richland Villager,* January 20, 1949, p. 3.

36 U.S. AEC, "Twenty-first Semiannual Report of the Atomic Energy Commission" (Washington, D.C.: U.S. Government Printing Office, January 1957), p. 250.

37 U.S. AEC, "Fifth Semiannual Report of the Atomic Energy Commission" (Washington, D.C.: U.S. Government Printing Office, January 1949), pp. 100, 96.

38 U.S. AEC, "Sixth Semiannual," pp. 19–25.

39 "Atom Radiation: How Much Can We Take?" *Science Digest* 27, no. 3 (March 1950): 56–57. This article was condensed from U.S. AEC, "Handling Radioactive Wastes in the Atomic Energy Program," AEC 180/2 (Washington, D.C.: U.S. Atomic Energy Commission, October 14, 1949).

40 Ibid., p. 23.

41 Francoise Giroud, *Marie Curie: A Life,* trans. Lydia Davis (New York: Holmes and Meier, 1986), p. 241.

42 "Phosphorus 32 for Cancer," *Science News Letter* 50, no. 1 (July 6, 1946): 2; and "The Progress of Medicine: First Victory in Atoms—Cancer War," *Science Digest* 20, no. 3 (September 1946): 48–49.

43 "X-Ray for Cancer without Radiation Sickness," *Science News Letter* 49, no. 7 (April 27, 1946): 265.

44 "Atoms and Cancer," *Time* 48, no. 16 (October 14, 1946): 52–54.

45 Robley D. Evans, "The Medical Uses of Atomic Energy," *Atlantic* 177, no. 1 (January 1946): 68.

46 U.S. AEC, "Fourth Semiannual Report of the Atomic Energy Commission" (Washington, D.C.: U.S. Government Printing Office, July 1948), pp. 16, 5.

47 U.S. AEC, "Sixth Semiannual," pp. 100–101, 90.

48 U.S. AEC, "Ninth Semiannual," p. 20.

49 E. N. Lockard, "Atomic Weapons against Cancer," *Science Digest* 29, no. 1 (January 1951): 16–19. The Lockard article was published in *Annual Report of the Board of Regents of the Smithsonian Institution for 1951* (Washington, D.C.: Smithsonian Associates, 1952), pp. 267–69. See also "Radioactive Gold Helps," *Science News Letter* 60, no. 15 (October 13, 1951): 230; and "Gold Wash for Cancer," *Newsweek* 39, no. 10 (March 10, 1952): 94.

50 "Atomic Explosion to Save Life," *Science Digest* 30, no. 1 (July 1951): 72–73; and "Cobalt 60 Therapy," *Newsweek* 37, no. 22 (May 28, 1951): 44–45. See also "Ready Cobalt 60 Machine for Treatment of Cancer," *Science News Letter* 60, no. 14 (October 6, 1951): 213.

51 "18 Months of Betatron," *Time* 57, no. 9 (May 7, 1951): 80–81; and *Newsweek* 40, no. 17 (October 27, 1952): 66.

52 Gordon E. Dean, *Report on the Atom,* 2d ed. (New York: Alfred A. Knopf, 1957), pp. 192–93 (first printed in 1953).

53 Lewis A. Strauss, "Atomic Status of the Nation," *Vital Speeches of the Day* 21, no. 8 (February 1, 1955): 1002–4 (speech delivered as an address to the National Press Club, Washington, D.C., January 11, 1955). See also Duncan Norton-Taylor, "The Controversial Mr. Strauss," *Reader's Digest* 66, no. 396 (April 1955): 142–46.

54 "Radiation Hazard Grows in Industry," *Science Digest* 33, no. 5 (May 1953): 52.

55 "After a Rat Race," *Newsweek* 33, no. 2 (January 10, 1949): 62–63. See also

"Helpful Isotopes," *Business Week,* no. 887 (August 31, 1946), pp. 31–32.

56 "Radiation Hazards—Invisible but Real," *Consumers' Research Bulletin* 25, no. 3 (March 1950): 24–26.

57 Roy M. Chatters, memo to O. S. Willham, "Practical Applications of Isotopes" (Pullman: Washington State College, January 23, 1953). See also C. C. Hassett and D. W. Jenkins, "Production of Radioactive Mosquitos," *Science* 110, no. 2848 (July 29, 1949): 109–10; Dale W. Jenkins and Charles C. Hassett, "Radioisotopes in Entomology," *Nucleonics* 6, no. 3 (March 1950): 5–14; Dale W. Jenkins and Charles C. Hassett, "Dispersal and Flight Range of Subarctic Mosquitos Marked with Radiophosphorus," *Canadian Journal of Zoology* 29 (June 1951): 178–87; C. C. Hassett and D. W. Jenkins, "The Uptake and Effect of Radiophosphorus in Mosquitoes," *Physiological Zoology* 24, no. 3 (July 1951): 257–66; Charles C. Hassett and Dale W. Jenkins, "Use of Fission Products for Insect Control," *Nucleonics* 10, no. 12 (December 1952): 42–46; L. C. Terriere and Robert D. Schonbrod, "The Excretion of a Radioactive Metabolite by House Flies Treated with Carbon Labeled DDT," *Journal of Economic Entomology* 48, no. 6 (December 1955): 736–39; and J. M. Davis and R. H. Nagel, "A Technique for Tagging Large Numbers of Live Adult Insects with Radioisotopes," *Journal of Economic Entomology* 49, no. 2 (April 1956): 210–11.

58 "Atomic Meat Packing," *Scientific American* 191, no. 5 (November 1954): 50.

59 "New Era for the Atom," *U.S. News and World Report* 36, no. 24 (June 11, 1954): 30–32; and David Cavers, "The Atomic Energy Act of 1954," *Scientific American* 191, no. 5 (November 1954): 32–35.

60 "Radiation Hazards," pp. 24–26.

61 "No Radioactive Cosmetics," *Science News Letter* 63, no. 19 (May 9, 1953): 290.

62 "Plutonism, Atomic Disease, Greys Hair, Causes Cancer," *Science News Letter* 51, no. 11 (March 15, 1947): 172.

63 "A-Bomb Can Speed Cancer," *Science News Letter* 56, no. 1 (September 10, 1949): 171.

64 A. K. Solomon, "Cancer: Biophysics," in Otto Glassner, ed., *Medical Physics,* 2d ed., vol. 2 (Chicago: Year Book Publishers, 1950), pp. 150–58.

65 Austin M. Brues, "Isotopes: Radioactive; Toxicity," in ibid., 2:467–68.

66 "Radiation Exposure Told," *Science News Letter* 63, no. 3 (January 17, 1953): 46.

67 "Creeping Suicide," *Science News Letter* 67, no. 3 (January 15, 1955): 35, citing Dr. Henry Quastler.

68 National Academy of Sciences–National Research Council, "The Biological Effects of Atomic Radiations" (Washington, D.C.: National Academy of Science, 1956), pp. 34–38; British Medical Research Council, "The Hazards to Men of Nuclear and Allied Radiations" (London: Her Majesty's Stationery Office, 1956); and "Leukemia Danger," *Science News Letter* 70, no. 1 (July 7, 1956): 3.

69 U.S. AEC, "Twenty-first Semiannual," p. 232.

70 "Small Radiation Doses Cause Blood Changes," *Science News Letter* 71, no. 6 (February 9, 1957): 91. At that time, the permissible dose for human exposure to gamma and X radiation per week was 300 milliroentgens per week (mr/w). The University of California experiments used dosages of 200 mr/w.

71 U.S. AEC, "Twenty-fourth Semiannual Report of the Atomic Energy Commission" (Washington, D.C.: U.S. Government Printing Office, July 1958), p. 193.

72 A. Lacassagne, "The Risks of Cancer Formation by Radiations," *Bulletin of the Atomic Scientists* 13, no. 4 (April 1957): 135.

73 "Report Radiation Harm," *Science News Letter* 74, no. 4 (July 26, 1958): 53.

74 "Hot Problem in Atomic Wastes," *Science News Letter* 75, no. 5 (January 31, 1959): 74. See also "Report Radiation Harm," p. 53.

75 National Academy of Sciences—National Research Council, "The Biological Effects of Atomic Radiation" (Washington, D.C.: NAS, May 1960), pp. 29–30, 35–37. This report was commonly referred to as the BEAR-II report.

76 "With Man as with Mice?" *Science Illustrated* 1, no. 3 (June 1946): 51–52.

77 Raymond E. Zirkle, "Relationships between Chemical and Biological Effects of Ionizing Radiations," *Radiology* 52, no. 6 (June 1949): 846.

78 H. J. Muller, "The Menace of Radiation," *Science News Letter* 55, no. 24 (June 11, 1949): 374, 379–80.

79 U.S. AEC, "Sixth Semiannual," pp. 38–39, 41.

80 "Radiation Produces Freaks," *Science News Letter* 57, no. 9 (March 4, 1950): 131.

81 U.S. AEC, "Eleventh Semiannual," pp. 40, 39.

82 Stanley H. Macht and Philip S. Lawrence, "National Survey of Congenital Malformations Resulting from Exposure to Roentgen Radiation," *American Journal of Roentgenology and Radium Therapy* 73, no. 3 (March 1955): 457–66; and "Radiologists' Children Studied for A-Bomb Hints," *Science News Letter* 60, no. 11 (September 15, 1951): 174.

83 U.S. AEC, "Thirteenth Semiannual Report of the Atomic Energy Commission" (Washington, D.C.: U.S. Government Printing Office, January 1953), p. 123.

84 U.S. AEC, "Seventeenth Semiannual Report of the Atomic Energy Commission" (Washington, D.C.: U.S. Government Printing Office, January 1955), p. 54.

85 "Creeping Suicide," p. 35, citing Drs. Eugene Rabinowitch and Henry Quastler.

86 "Radiation Can Harm Race," *Science News Letter* 67, no. 4 (January 22, 1955): 52, citing Dr. A. H. Sturtevant.

87 Laura Fermi, *Atoms for the World* (Chicago: University of Chicago Press, 1957), pp. 171–80, 57–59.

88 Louis S. Osborne, "The National Academy and Medical Research Council Reports," *Bulletin of the Atomic Scientists* 14, no. 1 (January 1958): 46, citing NAS, "BEAR-I"; and Bentley Glass, "The Hazards of Atomic Radiation to Man—British and American Reports," *Bulletin of the Atomic Scientists* 12, no. 8 (October 1956): 314. See also "Danger . . . Radiation," *Popular Science Monthly* 109, no. 3 (September 1956): 92; and "Radiation Danger Grows," *Science News Letter* 71, no. 18 (May 4, 1957): 279.

89 U.S. AEC, "Twentieth Semiannual Report of the Atomic Energy Commission" (Washington, D.C.: U.S. Government Printing Office, July 1956), p. 107.

90 "Radiation and Heredity," *U.N. Review* 4, no. 1 (July 1957): 7, citing U.N. Scientific Committee on the Effects of Atomic Radiation, "World Health Organization Report," 1957.

91 "Radiation Limits Unsafe," *Science News Letter* 72, no. 10 (September 7, 1957): 147, citing Dr. Michael A. Bender.

92 A. M. Kuzin, "Some Current Problems in Radiobiology," and James F. Crow, "Genetic Effects of Radiation," both in *Bulletin of the Atomic Scientists* 14, no. 1 (January 1958): 48–51, 20; "No 'Safe' Radiation Dose," *Science News Letter* 74, no. 9 (August 30, 1958): 133; James F. Crow, "Ionizing Radiation and Evolution," *Scientific American* 201, no. 3 (September 1959): 138, 160; George W. Beadle, "Ionizing Radiation and the Citizen," *Scientific American* 201, no. 3 (September 1959): 224–32; Alexander Hollaender and George Stapleton, "Ionizing Radiation and the Living Cell," *Scientific American* 201, no. 3 (September 1959): 100; and U.S. AEC, "Annual Report for 1959" (Washington, D.C.: U.S. Government Printing Office, January 1960), p. 198; and NAS-NRC, "BEAR-II," p. 3.

93 ICRP, "International Recommendations on Radiological Protection," *Annals of the ICRP* 56 (March 1951): 431.
94 U.S. AEC, "Sixteenth Semiannual Report of the Atomic Energy Commission" (Washington, D.C.: U.S. Government Printing Office, July 1954), pp. 59–60.
95 U.S. AEC, "Nineteenth Semiannual Report of the Atomic Energy Commission" (Washington, D.C.: U.S. Government Printing Office, January 1956), p. 76.
96 NAS-NRC, "BEAR-I," pp. 34–35.
97 U.S. AEC, "Twenty-first Semiannual," January 1957, pp. 48–49.
98 "Radiation Shortens Life," *Science News Letter* 71, no. 20 (May 18, 1957): 309, partially citing Dr. W. L. Russell. See also "Radiation Danger Grows," p. 279.
99 Dean, "Part of the Way," epilogue to *Report on the Atom,* p. 349.
100 U.S. AEC, "Twenty-first Semiannual," pp. 247, 111. See also pp. 220–57.
101 U.S. AEC, "Thirteenth Semiannual," pp. 42–43; "Brain Radiation Damage," *Science News Letter* 70, no. 4 (July 28, 1956): 53; and A. M. Kuzin, "Some Current Problems in Radiobiology," *Bulletin of the Atomic Scientists* 14 (January 1958): 48–50.
102 U.S. AEC, "Report for 1959," p. 219.
103 U.S. Atomic Energy Commission, "Atomic Energy Research: Life and the Physical Sciences, Reactor Development, Waste Management" (Washington, D.C.: U.S. Government Printing Office, December 1961), p. 81.
104 "Now There's a Warning about Too Much X-Ray," *U.S. News and World Report* 40, no. 25 (June 22, 1956): 60–70, citing NAS-NRC, "BEAR-I."
105 *Readers' Guide to Periodical Literature,* March 1957–February 1959, pp. 1594–95. See in particular Austin M. Brues, "Somatic Effects of Radiation," *Bulletin of the Atomic Scientists* 14, no. 1 (January 1958): 12–13; U.S. AEC, "Twenty-fourth Semiannual," pp. 174–

77; Willie W. Smith and Jerome Cornfield, "Extending the Range of Dose Effect for Irradiated Mice," *Science* 128, no. 3322 (August 29, 1958): 473–74; "Pathologic Effects of Radiation," *Science* 129, no. 3346 (February 13, 1959): 377–78; U.S. AEC, "Report for 1959," pp. 187–89; and "New Data on Radiation and Body Defenses," *Science News Letter* 77, no. 21 (May 21, 1960): 328.
106 Herbert M. Parker, "Quarterly Progress Report—Research and Development Activities for July–September 1950," HW-19146 (RL: HEW, October 16, 1950), pp. 9–19; Herbert M. Parker, "Quarterly Progress Report—Research and Development Activities for January–March 1951," HW-20866 (RL: HEW, April 18, 1951), pp. 2–16; and Herbert M. Parker, "Radiological Sciences Department, Quarterly Progress Report—Research and Development Activities for July–September 1951," HW-22576 (RL: HEW, November 1, 1951), pp. 4–21.
107 Kenneth E. Herde, "Deposition of Radioactivity in Rats Drinking Pile Effluent Water," HW-20102 (RL: HEW, January 24, 1951), pp. 7–15; Parker, HW-22576, p. 15; Herbert M. Parker, "Radiological Sciences Department, Quarterly Progress Report—Research and Development Activities for October–December 1951," HW-23332 (RL: HAPO, January 1952), pp. 9–12; Biology Section, "Biology Research—Annual Report 1951," HW-25021 (RL: HAPO, April 15, 1952), pp. 4–5; Herbert M. Parker, "Radiological Sciences Department, Quarterly Progress Report—Research and Development Activities for January–March 1952," HW-24131 (RL: HAPO, April 6, 1952), pp. 6–9; and Spencer Hines and Linda Monroe, "Hanford's Early Researchers Not Intimidated by Unknown," *Portland Oregonian,* May 12, 1986, p. A1, citing Carl Gamertsfelder.
108 Keith Price, "A Critical Review of Biological Accumulation, Discrimina-

tion, and Uptake of Radionuclides Important to Waste Management Practices, 1943–71," BNWL-B-148 (Richland: Battelle Northwest Laboratories, December 1, 1971), pp. 2, 4, 8.

109 Kenneth E. Herde, R. L. Browning, and W. C. Hanson, "Activity Densities in Waterfowl of the Hanford Reservation and Environs," HW-18645 (RL: HEW, August 21, 1951).

110 Harry A. Kornberg, "The Absorption and Toxicity of Several Radioactive Substances in Plants and Animals," CIC-26514 (Richland: General Electric Co., 1955), pp. 1–3.

111 J. E. Ballou and R. C. Thompson, "The Long-Term Retention of Cesium in the Rat following a Single Peritoneal Injection," HW-46150 (RL: HAPO, April 1, 1957), pp. 5–15.

112 Kornberg, CIC-26514, pp. 7–9.

113 William J. Bair, "Calculation of Maximum Permissible Concentration in the Air, MPC (air), for Ru-106 Particles," HW-52287 (RL: HAPO, October 1, 1957), p. 4. Bair's studies actually used ruthenium oxide (Ru-106 O_2) particulates. Seeking to arrive at an average dose rate of 0.3 rem per week to the lung of man, Bair calculated an MPC of 5–8 × 10^{-9} μCi/ml of air under chronic conditions.

114 J. E. Ballou, "Metabolism of Zinc-65," in "Biology Research Annual Report for 1958," HW-59500 (RL: HAPO, January 5, 1959), pp. 81–86.

115 N. L. Dockum, E. J. Coleman, and G. Vogt, "Detection of Plutonium Contamination in Humans by the Audioradiographic Method," HW-51754 (RL: HAPO, September 3, 1957), pp. 5–8.

116 J. E. Ballou, "Effects of Age and Mode of Ingestion on the Absorption of Plutonium," HW-52895 (RL: HAPO, October 7, 1957), p. 2.

117 William J. Bair, "Translocation and Excretion of Pulmonary Deposited Plutonium Oxide," HW-56636 (RL: HAPO, May 1, 1958); H. D. Bruner, "Biomedical

Program Directors Meeting at Hanford, June 7–8, 1959," CIC-25210 (Washington, D.C.: U.S. Atomic Energy Commission, June 19, 1959), pp. 2–3; and W. J. Bair and D. H. Willard, "Plutonium Inhalation Studies III: Effect of Particle Size and Total Dose on Retention and Translocation," HW-68645 (RL: HAPO, March 1961), p. 3.

118 H. A. Kornberg, "On the Passage of Pairs of Elements through Food Chains," HW-60127 (RL: HAPO, May 1, 1959), pp. 9–20. See also D. H. Willard and W. J. Bair, "Behavior of I-131 following Its Inhalation as a Vapor or as a Particle," HW-58221 (RL: HAPO, December 24, 1958), pp. 10–12.

119 "With Mice," p. 52.

120 Herbert M. Parker, "Quarterly Progress Report—Research and Development Activities for April–June, 1950," HW-18371 (RL: HEW, July 19, 1950), pp. 11–12; Parker, HW-19146, pp. 9–10; Herbert M. Parker, "Quarterly Progress Report—Research and Development Activities for April–June 1951," HW-21511 (RL: HEW, July 6, 1951), pp. 12–15; and Parker, HW-22576, pp. 8–12.

121 Parker, HW-23332, pp. 10–11.

122 "Atom Alters," *Science News Letter* 58, no. 12 (September 16, 1950): 188.

123 Luther Smith, "Effects of Atomic Bomb Radiations and X-Rays on Seeds of Cereals," *Journal of Heredity* 41, no. 5 (May 1950): 125–30. See also C. C. Moh and Luther Smith, "An Analysis of Seedling Mutants (Spontaneous, Atomic Bomb-Radiation-, and X-Ray-Induced) in Barley and Durum Wheat," *Genetics* 36, no. 6 (November 1951): 629–40; and C. C. Moh and Luther Smith, "Three Coincidental Changes in Atom-Bombed Barley," *Journal of Heredity* 43, no. 4 (July–August 1952): 183–188.

124 U.S. AEC, "Ninth Semiannual," p. 25; and Richard G. Hewlett and Francis Duncan, *Atomic Shield, 1947/1952: A History of the U.S. Atomic Energy Commission,*

Vol. I. (University Park: University of Pennsylvania Press, 1969), p. 501.

125 U.S. AEC, "Eleventh Semiannual," pp. 100, 89.

126 Ibid., pp. 71–100. See also U.S. AEC, "Sixth Semiannual," p. 101; and U.S. AEC, "Tenth Semiannual," pp. 43–44.

127 U.S. AEC, "Sixteenth Semiannual," p. 57.

128 U.S. AEC, "Nineteenth Semiannual," p. 81.

129 Harry A. Kornberg, "The Absorption and Toxicity of Several Radioactive Substances in Plants and Animals," CIC-26514 (Richland: General Electric Co., 1955), p. 10; U.S. AEC, "Twenty-second Semiannual Report of the Atomic Energy Commission" (Washington, D.C.: U.S. Government Printing Office, July 1957), p. 117; Keith Price, "A Critical Review of Biological Accumulation, Discrimination, and Uptake of Radionuclides Important to Waste Management Practices, 1943–71," BNWL-B-148 (Richland: Battelle Northwest Laboratories, December 1971), pp. 1, 5–7, 22–24; and Kornberg, HW-60127, pp. 9–10.

130 Robert A. Nilan, "Factors That Govern the Response of Plant Tissues to Ionizing Radiation," *Genetica Agraria* 12, Fasc. 3–4 (1960): 283–96; R. A. Nilan and C. F. Konzak, "Increasing the Efficiency of Mutation Induction," *Mutation and Plant Breeding,* Pub. #891 (Washington, D.C.: NAS-NRC, 1961), pp. 437–60; C. F. Konzak, R. A. Nilan, R. R. Legault, and R. E. Heiner, "Modification of Induced Genetic Damage in Seeds," *Effects of Ionizing Radiations on Seeds* (Vienna, Austria: International Atomic Energy Agency, 1961), pp. 155–69; S. A. Qureshi, F. C. Elliott, R. A. Nilan, and C. F. Konzak, "Natural and Radiation-Induced Recombination," *Journal of Heredity* 52, no. 3 (May–June 1961); 113–17; C. F. Konzak, R. A. Nilan, J. R. Harle, and R. E. Heiner, "Control of Factors Affecting the Response of Plants to Mu-

tagens," *Fundamental Aspects of Radiosensitivity,* Brookhaven Symposia in Biology #14 (Upton, N.Y.: Brookhaven National Laboratory, 1961), pp. 128–57; R. A. Nilan, C. F. Konzak, E. Froese-Gertzen, and N. S. Rao, "Analysis of Radiation-Induced Genetic Damage in Seeds," *Abhandlungen der Deutschen Akademie der Wissenschaften* (Berlin: Akademie-Verlag, 1962), pp. 141–52; and R. A. Nilan, C. F. Konzak, J. R. Harle, and R. E. Heiner, "Interrelation of Oxygen, Water, and Temperature in the Production of Radiation-Induced Genetic Effects in Plants," *Strahlenwirkung und Milieu* (Berlin: Verlag Urban and Schwarzenberg, 1962), pp. 172–81.

131 Walter Singlevich, "Radioactive Particles in the Atmosphere, January 1951–March 1951," HW-20810 (RL: HEW, April 12, 1951); and H. J. Paas and W. Singlevich, "Radioactive Contamination in the Vicinity of the Hanford Works for the Period January, February, March, 1951," HW-21214 (RL: HEW, June 1, 1951), pp. 35–37. The new particle stations were at Denver, Durango, and Grand Junction, Colorado, Salt Lake City, Utah, Albuquerque, New Mexico, and Arco and DuBois, Idaho.

132 U.S. Department of Energy—Nevada Operations Office, "Announced U.S. Nuclear Tests, July 1945 through December 1987," NVO-209 (rev. 8) CIC-67689 (Las Vegas: U.S. Department of Energy, 1988), pp. 2–10; Donald Sturges (AEC-Hanford), "High Offsite Particle Counts," letter to R. W. Cook (U.S. AEC, Washington, D.C.) CIC-26016 (Richland: U.S. Atomic Energy Commission, August 8, 1951), pp. 1–2; Lauren Donaldson, "Annual Report of the Laboratory of Radiation Biology, University of Washington, July 1, 1957–June 30, 1958), CIC-50059 (Seattle: University of Washington, June 20, 1958), pp. 1–6; Leo K. Bustad, "A Comparative Study of Hanford and Utah Range

Sheep," HW-30119 (RL: HAPO, November 30, 1953); and Leo K. Bustad, "Biological Implications of Atomic Test Fallout" CIC-143448 (Las Vegas: U.S. Atomic Energy Commission, February 26, 1955).

133 A. A. Selders, J. H. Rediske, and R. F. Palmer, "The Absorption and Translocation by Plants of Radioactive Elements from 'Jangle' Soil," HW-27620 (RL: HAPO, February 16, 1953); Biology Operations Staff, "Biology Research Annual Report for 1952," HW-28636 (RL: HAPO, 1953), pp. 117–20; and R. C. Routson, "A Review of Studies of Soil-Waste Relationships on the Hanford Reservation from 1944 to 1967," BNWL-1464 (Richland: Battelle Northwest Laboratories, March 1973).

134 Singlevich, HW-20810; Paas and Singlevich, HW-21214, pp. 35–37; and H. J. Paas, "Radioactive Contamination in the Environs of the Hanford Works for the Period October, November, and December 1951," HW-24203 (RL: HAPO, April 22, 1952), pp. 13, 20, 34–35. To better track the fallout, scientists changed particle-sampling from weekly to daily in the last quarter of 1951 at eight Hanford-based monitoring stations in Washington, Oregon, and Idaho.

135 H. J. Paas, "Radioactive Contamination in the Environs of the Hanford Works: For the Period April, May, June 1952," HW-26493 (RL: HAPO, December 16, 1952), pp. 4–5, 36; Richard Miller, *Under the Cloud: The Decades of Nuclear Testing* (New York: Free Press, 1986), pp. 449, 169; J. F. Honstead, "Monitoring Survey—Richland to Arco, Period May 9–11, 1952," HW-24727 (RL: HAPO, June 20, 1952), pp. 3–7, 10–12; H. J. Paas, F. R. Adley, P. L. Eisenacher, D. L. Reid, J. J. Fuquay, and D. E. Jenne, "Radioactive Particle Fallout in the Hanford Environs from Nevada Nuclear Explosions, Spring 1953," HW-28925 (RL: HAPO, August 4, 1953), pp. 3, 5–10, 28–

37, 40–45; and R. S. Paul, "Gamma Activity from 'Hot' Rain of May 26, 1953," HW-28403 (RL: HAPO, June 6, 1953), pp. 1–3.

136 Philip Fradkin, *Fallout: An American Nuclear Tragedy* (Tucson: University of Arizona Press, 1989), pp. 2–17; Subcommittee on Oversight and Investigations, Committee on Interstate and Foreign Commerce, U.S. House of Representatives, *The Forgotten Guinea Pigs,* 96th Cong., 2d sess. (Washington, D.C.: U.S. Government Printing Office, August 1980), pp. iii–iv, 5, 13–21; "The Ashes of Death," *Time* 63 (March 29, 1954): 17; "Science and the Citizen," *Scientific American* 190, no. 5 (May 1954): 46–48; James R. Arnold, "Effects of the Recent Bomb Tests on Human Beings," *Bulletin of the Atomic Scientists* 10, no. 9 (November 1954): 347–48; "Radiation: Glimpse into Hell," *Newsweek* 51, no. 2 (January 13, 1958): 78; Ralph E. Lapp, *The Voyage of the Lucky Dragon* (New York: Harper and Brothers, 1958), p. 197; "Atomic Light on the Desert," *Newsweek* 45, no. 12 (March 21, 1955): 3–31; and Z. M. Bacq, "The U.N. Radiation Committee," *Bulletin of the Atomic Scientists* 14, no. 1 (January 1958): 55. The controversy over fallout is a huge topic that cannot be dealt with in depth in this analysis. These citations represent only a sample.

137 B. V. Andersen, Biophysics Section, "Monthly Reports: Regional Monitoring Unit, 1955," CIC-12753 (RL: HAPO, 1955), May: p. 2, June: p. 2; and H. M. Parker, memo to James Travis (AEC-Hanford), CIC-17673 (RL: HAPO), p. 1. Particle counts at Boise, Idaho, in the third week of May 1955 rose from the normal level of 20 × 10⁻³ particles per cubic meter (p/m3) to 1,400 × 10⁻³ p/m3.

138 A. T. Gifford (AEC-Hanford), telex to Gordon Dunning (AEC-Washington, D.C.), CIC-11946, CIC-11943, CIC-11952 (RL: HAPO, May 29, June 13, May 25, 1956); B. V. Andersen, "Fallout Data,"

CIC-74771 (RL: HAPO, June 6, June 21, July 12, July 19, July 26, September 19, 1956); B. V. Andersen, Biophysics Section, "Monthly Reports: Regional Monitoring Unit, 1956," CIC-12765 (RL: HAPO, 1956), May–September; Kenneth Englund, memo to Gordon Dunning, CIC-11952 (RL: HAPO, July 26, 1956); Shelby Thompson (AEC-Hanford), "Response to Queries—Possible Fallout from Tests in Hanford Area," CIC-32146 (RL: HAPO, July 27, 1956); and W. C. Hanson, "Accumulation of Radioisotopes from Fallout by Terrestrial Animals at Hanford, Washington," *Northwest Science* 34, no. 3 (1960), also CIC-1537, pp. 91–92.

139 C. W. Thomas, D. L. Reid, L. F. Lust, "Radiochemical Analysis of Marine Biological Samples following the 'Redwing' Shot Series—1956," HW-58674, CIC-19514 (RL: HAPO, December 29, 1958), p. 6.

140 B. V. Andersen, "Monthly Reports: Regional Monitoring, 1957," CIC-12722 (RL: HAPO, 1957), June 28, pp. 1–2; and Hanson, CIC-1537, pp. 91–92.

141 Andersen, CIC-12722, October 31, p. 1.

142 B. V. Andersen, "Regional Monitoring Activities for September 1958," HW-57644 (RL: HAPO, October 7, 1958), p. 4; and B. V. Andersen, "Regional Monitoring Activities for October 1958," HW-58072 (RL: HAPO, November 7, 1958), p. 4.

143 "Science and the Citizen: The Test Conference," *Scientific American* 201, no. 2 (August 1959): 60–61.

144 J. J. Davis, in "Project Chariot Progress Report," AEC-M-4/0, CIC-16857 (RL: HAPO, September 23, 1959), pp. 1–3; J. J. Davis, D. G. Watson, W. C. Hanson, "Hanford Phase II Report of Project Chariot Studies—1959," CIC-0173280 (RL: HAPO, May 31, 1960), pp. 1–6; and J. J. Davis, D. G. Watson, W. C. Hanson, "Hanford Progress Report of Project

Chariot Studies—1961," CIC-16855 (RL: HAPO, 1961), pp. 1–3. See also *Tri-City Herald,* October 29, 1958, p. 1. Eventually, the Kotzebue Harbor project, part of Operation Plowshare, was abandoned. Underground atomic tests conducted at the NTS in 1962 demonstrated that the radioactivity generated by planned explosions in northern Alaska and at the Panama Canal would spread contamination throughout those areas. See Fradkin, *Fallout,* pp. 135–36.

145 Hal Holister and Alfred Klement, Jr. (U.S. AEC, Division of Biology and Medicine), memo to Dr. Charles Dunham, "Visit to Radioecology Group, Hanford," CIC-25359 (Washington, D.C.: U.S. Atomic Energy Commission, February 11, 1960); and R. W. Neill, "Air Sampling Networks for Radioactivity," CIC-160996 (Washington, D.C.: U.S. Public Health Service, March 3, 1960), p. 4.

146 U.S. DOE, NVO-209 (rev. 8), CIC-67689, pp. 10–17; and Miller, *Under the Cloud,* pp. 336–53.

147 U.S. DOE, NVO-209 (rev. 8), CIC-67689, pp. 12–14; Miller, *Under the Cloud,* pp. 470–71; Fradkin, *Fallout,* p. 135; R. F. Foster, "Summary of Radiological Data for the Month of May 1962," HW-72691-5 (RL: HAPO, June 11, 1962), p. 4; R. F. Foster, "Radiological Status of the Hanford Environs for June 1962," HW-74307-6 (RL: HAPO, July 16, 1962); J W. Vanderbeek, "Evaluation of Radiological Conditions in the Vicinity of Hanford, July–September 1962," HW-75431 (RL: HAPO, October 12, 1962), pp. 2–7, 18–23; and R. F. Foster, "Radiological Status of the Hanford Environs for December 1962," HW-74307-12, and "For . . . January . . . February . . . March . . . April 1963," HW-76525-1, -2, -3, -4 (RL: HAPO, January 10, February 12, March, April, May 1963), pp. 3–4 (all months).

148 T. F. McCraw, "Notes on Recent

Hanford Data for Cesium-137 Whole Body Burdens in Alaskan Eskimos," CIC-65646 (Washington, D.C.: U.S. Atomic Energy Commission, September 22, 1964), pp. 1–3; and Donald L. Snow, letter to Wayne C. Hanson, CIC-56341 (Washington, D.C.: U.S. Public Health Service, June 20, 1965), pp. 1–2.

149 Lisco, Finkel, and Brues, "Carcinogenic Properties," p. 361.

150 U.S. AEC, "Report on Project Gabriel" (Washington, D.C.: U.S. Atomic Energy Commission, 1954), p. 1.

151 Selders, Rediske, and Palmer, HW-27620, pp. 7, 10; Biology Operations Staff, HW-28636, pp. 117–21; and Routson, BNWL-1464, pp. 37–40.

152 U.S. AEC, "Eleventh Semiannual," p. 87.

153 Bustad, CIC-143448, p. 5.

154 Kornberg, HW-60127, pp. 9–10. See also Kornberg, CIC-26514, pp. 10, 3.

155 Kornberg, HW-60127, pp. 21, 33.

156 U.S. AEC, "Fifth Semiannual," pp. 95–96.

157 "Secrets of Atom Bomb Tests," p. 25.

158 Parker, "Health Physics," p. 958.

159 J. Fuqua, "Effects of Radiation," in Health Instruments Division, "H.I. Lecture Series," HW-07184 (RL: HEW, July 1, 1947), part I, Lecture X, p. 8.

160 U.S. AEC, "Fifth Semiannual," pp. 95–96.

161 "Study Radiation Immunity," *Science News Letter* 55, no. 13 (March 26, 1949): 197; U.S. AEC, "Sixth Semiannual," pp. 27–28; and U.S. AEC, "Seventh Semiannual Report of the Atomic Energy Commission" (Washington, D.C.: U.S. Government Printing Office, January 1950), pp. 21–22.

162 *Richland Villager,* July 14, 1949, p. 3.

163 Parker, HW-19146, p. 9; and Parker, HW-24131, pp. 15–16. See also Parker, HW-18371, HW-20866, HW-21511, HW-22576.

164 U.S. AEC, "Tenth Semiannual," p.
41; and U.S. AEC "Eleventh Semiannual," pp. 36–38.

165 U.S. AEC, "Ninth Semiannual," pp. 20–21; and U.S. AEC, "Tenth Semiannual," pp. 40–41. See also "New Blood Factor May Aid A-Bomb Protection," *Science News Letter* 59, no. 2 (January 13, 1951): 25.

166 U.S. AEC, "Tenth Semiannual," p. 41; and U.S. AEC, "Eleventh Semiannual," pp. 36–38.

167 Henry A. Schlang, Eugene P. Cronkite, and George Brecher, "Some Experimental Approaches to the Therapy of Whole Body Irradiation" (Bethesda, Md.: Naval Medical Research Institute, February 20, 1953), p. 7.

168 U.S. AEC, "Eighteenth Semiannual Report of the Atomic Energy Commission (Washington, D.C.: U.S. Government Printing Office, July 1955), pp. 84–85; "Treatment before and after Radiation Works," *Science News Letter* 67, no. 19 (May 7, 1955): 296; and U.S. AEC, "Twentieth Semiannual," July 1956, p. 111.

169 U.S. AEC, "Twenty-second Semiannual," p. 116; U.S. AEC, "Twenty-fourth Semiannual," pp. 163–65; and "Premature Pill Talk," *Time* 72, no. 8 (August 25, 1958): 52.

170 "Radiation Antidote," *Science News Letter* 69, no. 17 (April 28, 1956): 270.

171 "Radiation Repair," *Time* 48, no. 6 (August 6, 1956): 32.

172 "Irradiated Blood Gives Radiation Immunity," *Science News Letter* 70, no. 10 (September 8, 1956): 149.

173 "Find Oxygen Gives Radiation Protection," *Science News Letter* 65, no. 14 (April 3, 1954): 217; U.S. AEC, "Eighteenth Semiannual," p. 84; Austin M. Brues and Harvey M. Patt, "Mechanisms of Protection against Mammalian Radiation Injury," *Physiological Review* 33, no. 1 (January 1953): 85–89; and Theodore M. Tahmisain and Rosemaries L. Divine, "Repression and Enhancement of Irradiation Effects on Grasshopper Cells by

Metabolic Poisons and Oxygen," *Radiation Research* 3, no. 2 (October 1955): 182–90. See also R. A. Nilan, C. F. Konzak, R. R. Legault, and J. R. Harle, "The Oxygen Effect in Barley Seeds," *Proceedings* (Vienna, Austria: International Atomic Energy Agency, 1961), pp. 139–54.

174 Bruner, CIC-25210, pp. 4, 6.

175 Clyde M. Williams and George M. Krise, "Inhibition of Postirradiation Diuresis in Rats by Pitressin," *Science,* 128, no. 3322 (August 29, 1958): 475–76.

176 U.S. AEC, "Report for 1959," pp. 192–98; and "AEC Has Busy Year," *Science News Letter* 77, no. 7 (February 13, 1960): 102.

177 Simon T. Cantril and Herbert M. Parker, "The Tolerance Dose," MDDC-1100, reprinted in R. Kathren, R. R. Baalman, and W. Bair, *Herbert M. Parker* (Columbus, Ohio: Battelle Press, 1986), p. 270 (document originally written on January 5, 1945, 19 pp.). See also Parker, "Health Physics," p. 969; and Lauriston S. Taylor, "Roentgen Rays, Protection," in Glassner, *Medical Physics* (1944), 1:1382.

178 For a discussion of the earliest biomedical experiences with ionizing radiation and the formation of protection organizations and standards, see chapter 1.

179 H. Wintz and W. Rump, "Protective Measures against Dangers Resulting from the Use of Radium, Roentgen, and Ultraviolet Rays," League of Nations, C.H. 1054 (Geneva: League of Nations, 1931); and Cantril and Parker, "The Tolerance Dose."

180 Brues, "Isotopes," in Glassner, *Medical Physics* (1950), 2:466–67.

181 Cantril and Parker, "The Tolerance Dose."

182 Parker, "Health Physics," p. 974.

183 C. M. Patterson, in Parker, HW-07184, part I, Lecture I, "Scope of Health Instrumentation," p. 4.

184 P. A. Fuqua, in ibid., Lecture X: "Effects of Radiation on the Body," pp. 3–4.

185 Herbert M. Parker, "The Squares of the Natural Numbers in Radiation Protection," in Kathren, Baalman, and Bair, *Herbert M. Parker,* pp. 22–23.

186 Parker, Ibid., p. 974.

187 Parker, "Health Physics," pp. 969–70.

188 Harry A. Kornberg, "Columbia River Symposium Second Meeting, 21–22 May, 1951—Richland, Washington," HW-22181 (RL: HEW, July 5, 1951), pp. 17, 5–7, 10.

189 Cantril and Parker, "The Tolerance Dose," pp. 18–19; *The Atomic Energy Act of 1946, Public Law 585,* 79th Cong. 2d sess. (Washington, D.C.: U.S. Government Printing Office, 1946); and *The Atomic Energy Act of 1954, Public Law 703,* 83d Cong., 2d sess. (Washington, D.C.: U.S. Government Printing Office, 1954).

190 Lauriston S. Taylor, *Radiation Protection Standards* (Cleveland, Ohio: CRC Press, 1971), pp. 13–15 and entire book; Parker, "The Squares," pp. 672–99. Originally delivered as the First Annual Lauriston S. Taylor lecture on Radiation Protection and Measurements, NCRP, Washington, D.C., December 17, 1977, p. 40; and Parker, HW-07184, part I, Lecture XII: "Tolerance Dose," p. 7.

191 Herbert M. Parker, "Toxicity of I-131 in Sheep," HW-25239 (RL: HAPO, August 4, 1952), p. 4; Parker, "The Squares"; and NCRP, "Maximum Permissible Body Burdens and Maximum Permissible Concentrations of Radionuclides in Air and in Water for Occupational Exposure," NBS-69 (Washington, D.C.: U.S. Government Printing Office, June 5, 1959), pp. 1–4.

192 U.S. AEC, "Report of the Safety and Industrial Health Advisory Board, AEC," AEC-10266 (Washington, D.C.: U.S. AEC, April 2, 1948), pp. 74–75, 63.

193 U.S. AEC, "Thirteenth Semiannual," p. 113.

194 NCRP, "X-Ray Protection," HB20 (Washington, D.C.: U.S. Government Printing Office, 1936); and NCRP, "Radium Protection," HB23 (Washington, D.C.: U.S. Government Printing Office, 1938).

195 ICRP, "International Recommendations for X-Ray and Radium Protection" (Oxford, England: International X-Ray and Radium Protection Commission, 1937).

196 During 1945–49, Herbert Parker referred to a wartime NCRP standard of one rad per day to the thyroid gland. As various radioisotopes were isolated, the NCRP discussed them and offered guidelines. Based on the standard of one rad per day to the thyroid, Parker calculated I-131 exposure limits at Hanford. He revised these downward in 1946.

197 "Atom Radiation: How Much Can We Take?" *Science Digest* 27, no. 3 (March 1950): 56–57; U.S. AEC, "Eighth Semiannual," pp. 12–13; U.S. AEC, "Ninth Semiannual," pp. 18–19; and Hanson Blatz, ed., *Radiation Hygiene Handbook* (New York: McGraw-Hill, 1959), pp. 14, 10–12.

198 ICRP, "Recommendations of the International Commission on Radiological Protection," NBS47 (Washington, D.C.: U.S. Government Printing Office, June 29, 1951).

199 NCRP, "Maximum Permissible Amounts of Radioisotopes in the Human Body and Maximum Permissible Concentrations in Air and Water," NBS52 (Washington, D.C.: U.S. Government Printing Office, March 20, 1953).

200 John W. Healy, "Proposed Revision in Computation of MPC's for Long-lived Radioisotopes," HW-35662 (RL: HAPO, March 1, 1955), pp. 1–6.

201 H. V. Clukey, "Minutes of the Columbia River Advisory Group Meeting," HW-48469 (RL: HAPO, February 12, 1957), p. 4.

202 U.S. AEC, "Twenty-first Semiannual," pp. 176–84; U.S. AEC, "Twenty-

second Semiannual," pp. 186; GE Co., "Manual of Radiation Protection Standards," July 1957 Revision, HW-25457 (rev. 1) (RL: HAPO, July 1957); and U.S. AEC, "Twenty-third Semiannual Report of the Atomic Energy Commission" (Washington, D.C.: U.S. Government Printing Office, January 1958), pp. 400, 289–91.

203 Lauriston S. Taylor, "The Influence of Lowered Permissible Dose Levels on Atomic Energy Operations in the United States," in W. G. Marley and K. Z. Morgan, eds., *Progress in Nuclear Energy*, Series XII, "Health Physics," vol. 1 (New York: Pergamon Press, 1959), p. 14.

204 U.S. AEC, "Twenty-third Semiannual," pp. 400, 289–91.

205 "Reports Disagree on Radiation Hazards," *Science* 129, no. 3361 (May 29, 1959): 1473–74.

206 U.S. AEC, "Twenty-first Semiannual," pp. 176–82; and Lauriston S. Taylor, "Brief History of the National Committee on Radiation Protection (NCRP) and Measurements Covering the Period 1929–1946," in *Health Physics*, vol. 1 (New York: Pergamon Press, 1958), pp. 3–8, and vol. 13, 1967, pp. 301–302; and ICRP, "The Origins of the ICRP . . . ," in *ICRP Catalog* (New York: Pergamon Press, 1989); and U.S. AEC, "Annual Report for 1960" (Washington, D.C.: U.S. Government Printing Office, January 1961), pp. 234–35, 266–67.

207 U.S. AEC, "Report for 1959," pp. 243–45; NAS-NRC, "BEAR-II"; and "President Will Review Radiation Standards," *Science News Letter* 78, no. 10 (September 3, 1960): 150.

208 U.S. AEC, "Annual Report of the Atomic Energy Commission for 1961" (Washington, D.C.: U.S. Government Printing Office, 1962), pp. 234–35, 266–67.

Chapter 8
1 See *Tri-City Herald,* 1986 (entire year); *Spokesman-Review Spokane Chronicle,* 1986

(entire year); *Seattle Post-Intelligencer* and *Seattle Times,* February–September 1986; and *Portland Oregonian,* February–May 1986. In most cases, the Hanford stories were carried on page A1. See also Office of Radiation Protection, Department of Social and Health Services, "Special Report: Preliminary Dose Assessment of Hanford Historical Releases, 1944–1956" (Olympia: State of Washington, September 22, 1986); and James Ruttenber and Robert Mooney, eds., "Report of the Hanford Health Effects Review Panel and Recommendations of the Sponsoring Agencies" (Olympia: State of Washington, October 1987). In April 1987, another batch of approximately twenty thousand pages of Hanford historical documents was released by the DOE. Between 1987 and 1991, another thirty thousand pages were released in smaller batches.

2 David E. Lilienthal, *Change, Hope, and the Bomb* (Princeton, N.J.: Princeton University Press, 1963), pp. 70, 64.

3 Wanda Briggs, "Panel to Review Plan for Hanford Radiation Study," *Tri-City Herald,* July 21, 1988, p. B1; and Wanda Briggs, "Dosage Study Won't Be Rushed," *Tri-City Herald,* May 19, 1989, p. A4, citing Dr. John Till.

4 Wanda Briggs, "Preliminary Thyroid Inquiry Has Few Answers, Panel Members Say," *Tri-City Herald,* June 18, 1990, p. A2, citing Mary Lou Blazek.

5 Associated Press, "Thyroid Study Bill Signed by President," *Tri-City Herald,* September 23, 1988, p. A4; and Wanda Briggs, "Team to Study Hanford Area Ailments," *Tri-City Herald,* September 28, 1989, p. A8.

6 Hanford Education Action League, "Mission Statement and Goals" (Spokane, Wash.: Hanford Education Action League. 1985 and 1989).

7 June Stark Casey, "Hanford Downwinders Chapter Forms" (San Francisco: National Association of Radiation Survivors, July 1988).

8 Don Carter, "Downwinder Organization Forming," *Hanford Downwinder Monitor* (Seattle) 1, no. 1 (September/October 1989), p. 1; and Judith Jurji, "December 1949," exhibit at the Fremont Fine Arts Gallery, December 2–16, 1989.

9 Chris Sivula and David Whitney, "'Cold Standby' for N," *Tri-City Herald,* February 17, 1988, pp. A1–A2, citing Michael Lawrence.

10 David Whitney, "Nevada Picked for Repository," *Tri-City Herald,* December 18, 1987, p. A1.

11 Larry Lange and Darrell Glover, "N Reactor to Stay Closed—A Big Blow to Tri-Cities," *Seattle Post-Intelligencer,* February 27, 1988, pp. A1, A4.

12 David Whitney, "Congressional Split Rules Out Hanford," *Tri-City Herald,* August 4, 1988, p. A1.

13 National Academy of Sciences— National Research Council (NAS-NRC), "Safety Issues at the DOE Test and Research Reactors" (Washington, D.C.: National Academy Press, 1988), p. 17.

14 U.S. DOE, Office of the Assistant Secretary for Environmental Management (Leo Duffy), presentation (Washington, D.C.: U.S. Department of Energy, April 2, 1990), p. 1.

15 Barbara Melber et al., "Nuclear Power and the Public: Analysis of Collected Survey Research," PNL-2430 (Seattle: Battelle Human Affairs Research Center, 1977), pp. 129–33, 170–77; and Spencer Weart, *Nuclear Fear: A History of Images* (Cambridge, Mass.: Harvard University Press, 1988), pp. 317–18. See also Joseph P. Tomain, *Nuclear Power Transformation* (Bloomington: University of Indiana Press, 1990).

16 Chris Sivula, "N's Life One of Constant Controversy," *Tri-City Herald,* February 17, 1988, p. A7; NAS-NRC, "Safety Issues at the Defense Production Reactors" (Washington, D.C.: National Academy Press, 1987), pp. 25–27, 35–38, 51–55, 63–65, 192–207; and U.S. Energy

Research and Development Administration, "Waste Management Operations, Hanford Reservation: Final Environmental Statement," ERDA-1538, vol. 1 (Richland: U.S. Energy Research and Development Administration, December 1975), pp. XI–X94. The PUREX plant was completed in 1956.

17 NAS-NRC, "Safety Issues at the DOE Test," p. 18.

18 "Nuclear Danger and Deceit," Newsweek 112, no. 18 (October 31, 1988): 29; and "Crisis Brewing in Nuclear Waste Storage," Tri-City Herald, November 28, 1988, p. A4.

19 Associated Press, "Gardner Urged to Reject Nuclear Waste Shipments," Tri-City Herald, February 13, 1989, p. A1; and Associated Press, "Idaho Accepts Last Load of Waste," Tri-City Herald, August 19, 1989, p. A7.

20 Associated Press, "States Refuse to Take Nuclear Waste from U.S. Arms Plant near Denver," Arizona Republic, October 12, 1989; Eloise Schumacher, "Gardner One of 7 Governors Praised for N-Waste Stance," Seattle Times, November 5, 1989, p. D7; and Associated Press, "New Search on for Nuclear Waste Site," Tri-City Herald, December 6, 1989, p. D3.

21 Associated Press, "Rocky Flats Finds Space for Year More of A-Waste," Tri-City Herald, February 27, 1990, p. A2.

22 "House Committee Seeks to Delay Use of WIPP," Nuclear News 34, no. 5 (April 1991); and "Bills Introduced on WIPP, NES Waste Provisions," Nuclear News 34, no. 9 (July 1991): 105–6.

23 Associated Press, "Low-Level Waste a High-Level Puzzle," Tri-City Herald, March 20, 1989, p. A1.

24 Erik Smith, "State Bans D.C., Rhode Island from Waste Site," Tri-City Herald, February 20, 1990, p. A1, citing Dan Silver.

25 Chris Sivula, "Gardner Bars Michigan's A-Waste from Hanford," Tri-City Herald, November 14, 1990, p. A3; and Associated Press, "State Eyes Cutoff of 5 States' A-Waste," Tri-City Herald, December 8, 1990, p. A7.

26 Associated Press, "Nuclear Waste Dump Tears Nebraska County Apart," Tri-City Herald, October 23, 1990, p. A12; Associated Press, "Nuclear Waste Opponents Say Movement Still Strong," Tri-City Herald, February 4, 1991, p. A8; and "N.Y. Siting Body Advice: Offer Incentive Payments," Nuclear News 34, no. 3 (March 1991): 76.

27 Wanda Briggs, "DOE to Reward States Willing to Store High-Level A-Waste," Tri-City Herald, April 11, 1990, pp. A1–A2.

28 Erik Smith, "State Officials Balk at Plan to Use Hanford for Waste Test," Tri-City Herald, May 16, 1990, p. A8.

29 New York Times News Service, "A-Site Salesman Has Customers Running Away," Tri-City Herald, February 17, 1991, p. A3.

30 Chris Sivula, "Community Rallied to Save N in 1971," Tri-City Herald, January 30, 1988, p. A5.

31 Tri-City Herald, April–May 1979, editorial pages.

32 Ibid., July–September, 1973.

33 "1954 Hanford 'Leak' Comes to Light," Tri-City Herald, April 29, 1979, p. 1; and Editor, "The Atom and the Public," Tri-City Herald, May 2, 1979, p. 6.

34 "Fallout from the Nuke-In," Newsweek 93, no. 21 (May 21, 1979): 34–35; and Editor, "The New Cause," Tri-City Herald, May 11, 1979, p. 6.

35 Jim Dullenty, "Security Tight for Tonight's Debate," Tri-City Herald, May 18, 1979, p. 1; and Todd Crowell, "Nader Greeted by Pro-Nuke Demonstrators," Tri-City Herald, May 20, 1979, p. 1.

36 Kelso Gillenwater, "Preserving a National Resource," Tri-City Herald, January 31, 1988, p. E1.

37 Wanda Briggs, "Peace Alters Hanford's Role," *Tri-City Herald,* August 30, 1989, pp. A1, A2, partially citing James Watkins; Les Blumenthal, "New Hanford Manager Aims for New Focus," *Tri-City Herald,* July 14, 1990, p. A1; and Chris Sivula and Wanda Briggs, "Watkins Pledges Job Security," *Tri-City Herald,* October 16, 1990, p. A1.

38 "The Hanford Update" (Olympia: Washington State Department of Ecology), quarterly editions throughout 1989, 1990, and 1991.

39 Associated Press, "Report Predicts Pressures to Close DOE Plants," *Tri-City Herald,* July 20, 1989, p. B4.

40 Associated Press, "Watkins Criticizes Safety Violations," *Tri-City Herald,* February 6, 1990, p. A12; and Associated Press, "Error Gives Glimpse into A-Plants," *Tri-City Herald,* May 4, 1990, p. A9.

41 Majority Staff, Senate Governmental Affairs Committee (GAC), *Early Health Problems of the U.S. Nuclear Weapons Industry and Their Implications for Today,* 101st Cong., 1st sess., S. Print 101-63 (Washington, D.C.: U.S. Government Printing Office, December 1989), pp. 1–16; and "AEC Kept Quiet on Hanford Health Risk," *Tri-City Herald,* December 12, 1989, p. A1.

42 Robert Milliken, "Australia's Nuclear Graveyard," *Bulletin of the Atomic Scientists* 43, no. 3 (April 1987): 28–44.

43 Andrew Revkin, "Plutonium in Paradise," *Discover* 10, no. 5 (May 1989): 38–42; Bengt Danielsson, "Poisoned Pacific: The Legacy of French Nuclear Testing," *Bulletin of the Atomic Scientists* 42, no. 2 (March 1990): 22–31; and Tilman Ruff, "Bomb Tests Attack the Food Chain," *Bulletin of the Atomic Scientists* 42, no. 2 (March 1990): 32–34.

44 Robert A. Conrad, M.D., "Review of Medical Findings in a Marshallese Population Twenty-Six Years after Accidental Exposure to Radioactive Fallout" (Long Island, N.Y.: Brookhaven National Laboratory, 1980); Washington Post, "DOE Misled Residents on '54 Radiation, Group Says," *Tri-City Herald,* June 1, 1988, p. A7; "Fallout from Pacific Tests Reaches Congress," *Science* 245, no. 4914 (July 14, 1989): 123–24; and Majority Staff, Senate GAC, *Early Health Problems,* p. 13.

45 Thomas H. Cochran and Robert S. Norris, "Soviet Nuclear Warhead Production," NWD 90-3 (Washington, D.C.: Natural Resources Defense Council, August 1, 1990).

46 David Dickson, "Details of 1957 British Nuclear Accident Withheld to Avoid Endangering U.S. Ties," *Science* 239, no. 4836 (January 8, 1988): 137; and David Dickson, "Doctored Report Revives Debate on 1957 Mishap," *Science* 239, no. 4840 (February 5, 1988): 556–57.

47 "Does a Father's Dose Cause Childhood Leukemia?" *Nuclear News* 33, no. 5 (April 1990): 70–71, citing Martin Gardner et al., United Kingdom Medical Research Council, Environmental Epidemiological Unit, Southampton University, 1990.

48 Philip J. Hilts, "Higher Cancer Risk Found in Radiation," *New York Times,* December 20, 1989, p. A22; and Wanda Briggs, "Report Shifts Focus to Tighter Radiation Rules," *Tri-City Herald,* December 21, 1989, p. A3. The first two such reports in this series, issued in 1956 and 1960, were entitled, "Biological Effects of Atomic Radiations." They were known as BEAR-I and BEAR-II. Subsequent reports in the series were entitled "Biological Effects of Ionizing Radiations." Some experts maintain that the BEIR-V estimates of when radiation damage can begin are too low. See Chris Sivula, "Expert Critical . . . ," *Tri-City Herald,* March 16, 1991, p. A1–2.

49 Glyn G. Caldwell, Delle B. Kelley, and Clark W. Heath, Jr., "Leukemia among Participants in Military Maneuvers at a Nuclear Bomb Test," *Journal of the American Medical Association* 244, no. 14 (October 3, 1980): 1575–78; Glyn G. Caldwell, Delle B. Kelley, Matthew Zack, et al., "Mortality and Cancer Frequency among Military Nuclear Test (Smoky) Participants, 1957 through 1979," *Journal of the American Medical Association* 250, no. 5 (August 5, 1983): 620–24; and Glyn G. Caldwell, Delle B. Kelley, Clark W. Heath, Jr., and Matthew Zack, "Polycythemia Vera among Participants of a Nuclear Weapons Test," *Journal of the American Medical Association* 252, no. 5 (August 3, 1984): 662–64. (These references represent only a sampling of the articles and studies that led to the passage of the Atomic Veterans Compensation Act.) See also Associated Press, "'Atomic Vet' Benefits OK'd," *Tri-City Herald*, May 3, 1988, p. A6.

50 Keith Schneider, "Uranium Miners Inherit Dispute's Sad Legacy," *New York Times*, January 9, 1990, pp. A1, A20; and Associated Press, "Congress Approves Funding for Victims . . . ," *Sun City* (Ariz.) *News-Sun*, September 28, 1990. See also "U.S. Uranium Miners Escaping Lung Cancer," *Science News Letter* 67, no. 18 (April 30, 1955): 277; U.S. AEC, "Twenty-fourth Semiannual Report of the AEC" (Washington, D.C.: U.S. Government Printing Office, July 1958), p. 192; and U.S. AEC, "Annual Report for 1963" (Washington, D.C.: January 1964), p. 181. The 1990 legislation also benefits people exposed to fallout from atomic bomb tests.

51 William Bequette, "Journal: DOE Losing Trust of Nuclear Workers," *Tri-City Herald*, January 1, 1989, p. D1.

52 William Bequette, "Perspectives: Nuclear Injuries Shrouded in Secret," *Tri-City Herald*, January 21, 1990, p. D1.

53 Wanda Briggs, "Hanford Clean-Up Pact Signed," *Tri-City Herald*, May 16, 1989, p. A1, citing Lawrence. See also U.S. DOE, U.S. EPA, Washington State Department of Ecology, "Hanford Federal Facility Agreement and Consent Order," 89-10 (Richland: U.S. Department of Energy, May 1989).

54 Washington Post News Service, "DOE to Put Safety before Production," *Tri-City Herald*, June 17, 1989, p. A1; and Lee Bandy, "Watkins Admits DOE Mistakes," *Seattle Times,* June 28, 1989, p. A1, partially citing Henson Moore and James Watkins.

55 U.S. DOE, "Environmental Restoration and Waste Management Five-Year Plan," DE89-015619 (Washington, D.C.: National Technical Information Service, 1989), p. 4.

56 Wanda Briggs, "Peace Alters Hanford Role, Says Watkins," *Tri-City Herald,* August 30, 1989, p. A1.

57 Wanda Briggs, "Tri-Cities Weathers Ghost-Town Forecast," *Tri-City Herald,* November 5, 1989, p. A1; Wanda Briggs, "Businesses Eye Jobs, Profits from Hanford Clean-Up," *Tri-City Herald,* November 16, 1989, p. A3; Associated Press, "Hanford Focus Turns from Defense to Clean-Up," *Tri-City Herald,* December 25, 1989, p. A4; and Wanda Briggs, "Tri-Cities Robust, Report Says," *Tri-City Herald,* April 5, 1990, p. A1.

58 Westinghouse Hanford Company, "Vitrification Plant to Handle Hanford Wastes," *Tri-City Herald,* April 3, 1990, p. E14; and Les Blumenthal, "FFTF Could Cut Cleanup Cost, Panel Told," *Tri-City Herald,* March 8, 1990, p. A1.

59 Associated Press, "Officials Call for Bigger Role in Defense Waste Clean-Up," *Tri-City Herald,* May 11, 1989, p. B2; and Associated Press, "Governors Urge Independent Oversight at Nuclear Plants," *Tri-City Herald,* May 2, 1990, p. A7.

60 Ken Morgan (DOE-Richland public affairs officer), "Comments from Public Workshops on Hanford Cleanup Five-Year Plan" (Richland: U.S. Department of Energy, 1990), pp. 1–5. See also Ronald Lerch, "Hanford Clean-Up Pact Ushers in New Era," *Tri-City Herald,* March 3, 1990, p. E4.

61 James D. Watkins, "Setting the New Course," SEN-11-89 (Washington, D.C.: Department of Energy, September 5, 1989), pp. 1–5.

62 Wanda Briggs, "DOE Oversight, Not Studies, 'A Mess,'" *Tri-City Herald,* August 4, 1989, p. A5, citing James D. Watkins. A complete review of DOE (formerly AEC and ERDA) health studies is beyond the purview of this manuscript. At issue in debates over this is whether an agency charged with production of nuclear materials, and responsible for overseeing plant operations, could also objectively judge its own performance in terms of health protection. In terms of Hanford workers, the most significant controversy began in 1978, when Dr. Thomas Mancuso, a chief researcher at the University of Pittsburgh School of Public Health, found excess cancer rates in Hanford workers. About 5 percent of cancer deaths among these employees, Mancuso concluded, were radiation-related. His federally funded research contract was terminated, but his conclusions were supported by Dr. John Gofman, head of the biomedical division at Lawrence Livermore Laboratory (part of the University of California but funded by the DOE). Ethel Gilbert, a biostatistician with the Hanford Site contractor, Battelle Northwest Laboratories, disagreed with Mancuso, but Dr. Alice Stewart, a British radiologist, argued that Gilbert's findings were statistically biased in favor of the "healthy worker effect." See Rita Hibbard, "Contradictions Cloud Cancer Studies," *Seattle Post-Intelligencer,* May 13, 1986, p. C1; "Hanford Programs Protect Workers' Health," profile (Richland: Battelle Pacific Northwest Laboratories, Winter 1988); and Richard Miller, *Under the Cloud: The De-*

cades of Nuclear Testing (New York: Free Press, 1986), pp. 373–89.

63 New York Times News Service, "Panel to Call for Release of DOE Medical Records," *Tri-City Herald,* November 23, 1989, p. A1, citing Kristine Gebbie; and Keith Schneider, "Panel Questions Credibility of Nuclear Health Checks," *New York Times,* February 28, 1990, p. A11.

64 J. D. Watkins and L. W. Sullivan, "Memorandum of Understanding between Department of Energy and Department of Health and Human Services," January 7, 1991; and "DOE Cedes Worker Studies to HHS Department," *Nuclear News* 34, no. 2 (February 1991): 88.

65 Les Blumenthal, "DOE Sees No Future for FFTF," *Tri-City Herald,* January 27, 1990, p. A1; Blumenthal, "FFTF Could Cut"; and Briggs, "Peace Alters," citing James Watkins.

66 Wanda Briggs, "FFTF Teams Draft Reactor Marketing Plan," *Tri-City Herald,* April 12, 1990, p. A1; Wanda Briggs, "FFTF Teams Hear Praise Worldwide," *Tri-City Herald,* May 18, 1990, p. A1; Les Blumenthal, "House Assigns Corps Role to Hanford," *Tri-City Herald,* June 20, 1990, pp. A1, A2; and "FFTF Marketing Bill Introduced in Congress," *Tri-City Herald,* February 8, 1991, p. A3.

67 Wanda Briggs, "Hanford on a Growth Curve, Lawrence Says," *Tri-City Herald,* June 21, 1990, p. A4.

68 Technical Steering Panel, HEDRP, "Initial Hanford Radiation Dose Estimates" (Olympia: Washington Department of Ecology, July 1990); Technical Steering Panel, HEDRP, "Hanford Radiation Dose Study Preliminary Results Released," press release, Richland, Wash. (located at U.S. DOE Public Reading Room), July 12, 1990; Pacific Northwest Laboratory, "Draft Summary Report: Phase I of the Hanford Environmental Dose Reconstruction Project," PNL-7410

HEDR UC-707 (Richland: Pacific Northwest Laboratory, July 1990); Pacific Northwest Laboratory, "Draft Air Pathway Report: Phase I of the Hanford Environmental Dose Reconstruction Project," PNL-7412 HEDR UC-707 (Richland: Pacific Northwest Laboratory, July 1990); Pacific Northwest Laboratory, "Draft Columbia River Pathway Report: Phase I of the Hanford Environmental Dose Reconstruction Project," PNL-7411 HEDR UC-707 (Richland: Pacific Northwest Laboratory, July 1990); and John Till, press conference, Richland, Wash., July 12, 1990.

69 Wanda Briggs, "Downwinders Receive Study with 'Sorrow, Relief,'" *Tri-City Herald,* July 13, 1990, p. A2; Karen Dorn Steele, "Downwinders Finally Hear Truth," *Spokesman-Review Spokane Chronicle,* July 13, 1990, p. A4; and Associated Press, "A-Bomb Plant 'Guinea Pigs' Angry about Exposure," *Arizona Republic,* July 13, 1990, p. A14.

70 Wanda Briggs, "21 File Suit over Hanford Releases," *Tri-City Herald,* August 7, 1990, p. A1; Rob Taylor, Paul Shukovsky, and Larry Lange, "Second Lawsuit Due over Hanford," *Seattle Post-Intelligencer,* August 9, 1990, p. A1; Associated Press, "Hanford Hurt Fishing, Indians Claim in Suit," *Tri-City Herald,* October 24, 1990, p. A1; and Associated Press, "Oregonians File Suit against Hanford," *Tri-City Herald,* October 25, 1990, p. A9.

71 Kelso Gillenwater (publisher), "Swimming in Hogwash: DOE Headquarters Is the Major Problem," *Tri-City Herald,* July 15, 1990, p. D1.

72 Kelso Gillenwater (publisher), "Nuclear Pioneers Did All They Could," *Tri-City Herald,* July 23, 1990, p. A6.

73 Erik Smith, "Redress Slow in Coming for Radiation Victims," *Tri-City Herald,* July 13, 1990, p. A3, citing Sidney Morrison.

74 Ibid., citing Kristine Gebbie.

75 Les Blumenthal and Gale Robinette, "Clean-Up Puts Hanford Budget on High," *Tri-City Herald,* February 5, 1991, p. A1; Chris Sivula, "Hanford's First Superfund Work Starts Next Week," *Tri-City Herald,* February 21, 1991, p. A3; and Chris Sivula, "Hanford Cleanup Plan to Change," *Tri-City Herald,* May 17, 1991, p. A1.

76 Henry D. Smyth, *Atomic Energy for Military Purposes* (Princeton, N.J.: Princeton University Press, 1945), p. 226.

77 J. Robert Oppenheimer, "Physics in the Contemporary World," Arthur Dehon Little Memorial Lecture, Massachusetts Institute of Technology, Cambridge, November 25, 1947; and J. Robert Oppenheimer, "Atomic Energy as a Contemporary Problem," lecture to the Foreign Service, U.S. Department of State, Washington, D.C., September 17, 1947. Both lectures are reprinted in J. Robert Oppenheimer, *The Open Mind* (New York: Simon and Schuster, 1955), quotations from pp. 101, 37.

78 U.S. AEC, "Report of the Safety and Industrial Health Advisory Board, AEC," AEC-10266 (Washington, D.C.: U.S. AEC, April 2, 1948), pp. 74, 88–89, 63.

79 U.S. AEC, "Fourth Semiannual Report to Congress" (Washington, D.C.: U.S. Government Printing Office, July 1948), p. 5.

80 Herbert M. Parker, "Speculations on Long-Range Waste Disposal Hazards," HW-08674 (RL: HEW, January 26, 1948), p. 9.

81 Norbert Wiener, *I Am a Mathematician* (Garden City, N.Y.: Doubleday and Co., 1956), pp. 307–8.

82 Gordon E. Dean, *Report on the Atom,* 2d ed. (New York: Alfred A. Knopf, 1957), epilogue, p. 350.

83 Graham DuShane (editor), "Radiation and Public Health," *Science* 127, no. 3301 (April 4, 1958): 3. In the late 1950s, enlarged funding for the PHS was designed almost exclusively for programs that monitored foodstuffs exposed to fallout from atmospheric atomic bomb testing. Even in this limited area of investigation, the PHS was bound by the AEC to silence. See *Deseret News* (Salt Lake City), April 5, 1979, citing 1954 AEC-PHS agreement.

84 Lilienthal, *Change*, pp. 20, 23, 126, 60.

85 "Science, Press, Public Need Nuclear Rapport," *Portland Oregonian*, September 2, 1973, forum p. 1.

86 Horace Busby, cited in "Points to Ponder," *Reader's Digest* 136, no. 818 (June 1990): 51.

87 John Till, press conference, July 12, 1990, Richland, Wash.

88 *The Atomic Energy Act of 1946, Public Law 585*, 79th Cong., 2d sess. (Washington, D.C.: U.S. government Printing Office, 1946), Sec. 10(a) (2); and *The Atomic Energy Act of 1954, Public Law 703*, 83d Cong., 2d sess. (Washington, D.C.: U.S. Government Printing Office, 1954), Ch. 12, Sec. 141(b).

89 Wanda Briggs, "Preliminary Thyroid Study Has Few Answers, Panel Members Say," *Tri-City Herald*, June 18, 1990, p. A2, citing John Till.

Epilogue

Additional Abbreviations Used in Notes:

BHI—Bechtel Hanford, Inc.
BNI—Bechtel National, Inc.
DNFSN—Defense Nuclear Facilities Safety Board
EPA—Environmental Protection Agency
FDH—Fluor Daniel Hanford, Inc.
FH—Fluor Hanford, Inc.
HAB—Hanford Advisory Board
HEDL—Hanford Engineering Development Laboratory
HNF—refers to documents generated by various Hanford Site contractors beginning in 1996

IAEA—International Atomic Energy Agency
NIOSH—National Institute for Occupational Safety and Health
NRC—National Research Council
ORP—Office of River Protection
PHMC—Project Hanford Management Contract
PNNL—Pacific Northwest National Laboratory
RL—Richland and/or Richland Operations Office
RPP—River Protection Project
USDI—U.S. Department of the Interior
WDOE—Washington Department of Ecology
WHC—Westinghouse Hanford Company

1 C. Krauthammer, "The End of Heroism," cited in R. K. Kolb, "VFW Cold War Memorials, Medals and Museums," www.vfw.org/magazine/may98/22.shtml, p. 1.

2 G. Lobsenz, "Expert Panel Warns DOE on Re-Use, Stewardship of Contaminated Sites," citing "Long Term Institutional Management of U.S. Department of Energy Legacy Waste Sites," in *Energy Daily* (Washington, D.C.), August 14, 2000, pp. 1–2.

3 M. S. Gerber, "A Brief History of the PUREX and UO3 Facilities," WHC-MR-0437 (RL: WHC, November 1993); R. W. Bailey and M. S. Gerber, "PUREX/UO3 Plant Deactivation Lessons Learned History," HNF-SP-1147, Rev. 2 (RL: PHMC, October 1997).

4 U.S. DOE, "B-Plant Deactivation Completed Four Years Early," RL/OEA-98-127 (RL: U.S. DOE, October 19, 1998).

5 Bailey and Gerber, HNF-SP-1147, Rev. 2.

6 J. Long, "Hanford A-Bomb Plant Shuts Door 4 Years Early," *Oregonian* (Portland), August 15, 1998, p. C5.

7 M. S. Gerber, "Getting Ready to Tackle the Famous Five," *Nuclear Engineering International* (London), August 1994.

8 W. G. Jasen, "PUREX/UO3 Deactivation Management Plan," WHC-SP-1011 (RL:

WHC, August 1994); Bailey and Gerber, HNF-SP-1147, Rev. 2.

9 "N Area Deactivation Project, www.wch-rcc.com/N Area/N Area; U.S. DOE, "Environmental Assessment for the De-activation of N Reactor Facilities," DOE/EA-0984 (RL: U.S. DOE, May 1995); U.S. DOE, "Deactivation of Final Hanford Reactor Completed," RL/OEA-98-114 (RL: U.S. DOE, September 25, 1998).

10 M. S. Gerber, "Deactivation Completed at Historic Hanford Fuels Laboratory," WHC-SA-2366–FP (RL: WHC, March 1994); S. A. Dawson, "Fuel Supply Facilities Shut Down," WHC-SD-FL-SSP-002 (RL: WHC, March 31, 1994); B. C. Cornwell, "309 Building Transition Plan," WHC-SD-SP-SSP-001, Rev. 1 (RL: WHC, May 3, 1995); W. Briggs, "Hanford Landmarks Tower No More," *Tri-City Herald* (Kennewick, Wash.) July 22, 1996, p. A1; FH, "324/327 Buildings Stabilization/Deactivation Project, Project Management Plan," HNF-IP-1289, Rev 3 (RL: FH, January 2000).

11 "C Reactor Interim Safe Storage," www.wch-rcc.com/Creactor/c-reactr; U.S. DOE, "Hanford's 'C' Reactor Transformed," RL/OEA-98-120 (RL: U.S. DOE, October 14, 1998).

12 A. Cary, "N Reactor Demolition Begins," *Tri-City Herald*, February 15, 2005, pp. B1–2; U.S. DOE, "Engineering Evaluation/Cost Analysis for the 105–KE and 105–KW Reactor Facilities and Ancillary Facilities," DOE/RL-2005-086 (RL: U.S. DOE, 2005).

13 G. Tyree, T. Orgill, J. Ridelle, A. Harper, "More Hanford Firsts: Demolition of a Major Hanford Plutonium Facility," *Radwaste Solutions* (La Grange Park, Ill.), July/August 2004, pp. 11–14.

14 U.S. DOE, "DOE Completes Demolition of Former Plutonium Incinerator at Its Hanford Site," RL-06-009 (RL: U.S. DOE, June 26, 2006); "Last Incinerator Debris Removed from Hanford," *Tri-City Herald*, August 3, 2006.

15 U.S. DOE, "Hanford Site River Corridor Cleanup," DOE/RL-2000-66 Draft (RL: U.S. DOE, November 2000), www.hanford.gov/docs/rl-2000-66.

16 J. E. Stang, "Hanford Test to Mix Waste Cleanup, Economic Development," *Tri-City Herald*, April 10, 1999, p. A6; J. E. Stang, "Old Hanford Fuel Plant Called Too Contaminated to Use," *Tri-City Herald*, October 16, 1999; A. Cary, "DOE Names Contractor for $1.9B Cleanup," *Tri-City Herald*, March 24, 2005, pp. B1–2.

17 FH, "Hanford Site 300 Area Accelerated Closure Project Plan," HNF-6465 (RL: FH, June 29, 2000).

18 A. Cary, "300 Area Cleanup ahead of Schedule," *Tri-City Herald*, September 4, 2006, pp. B1–2.

19 "At Richland . . . Soil Cleanup Begins along Columbia River," *Weapons Complex Monitor* (Washington, D.C.), August 14, 2000, p. 13; "At Richland . . . 100 Area Soil Cleanup Nearing Half-Way Mark," *Weapons Complex Monitor*, June 24, 2002, pp. 8–9; J. E. Stang, "Bechtel Removes Contaminated Soil ahead of Schedule, *Tri-City Herald*, June 26, 2003, p. B3.

20 A. Cary, "Nuclear Graveyard," *Tri-City Herald*, March 18, 2005, pp. A1–2.; A. Cary, "Workers Hunt for Hanford Mercury," *Tri-City Herald*, June 27, 2006, p. B1; WDOE, EPA, and U.S. DOE, "Last Big Liquid Waste near Columbia River Cleaned Up," *Hanford Update* (Olympia, Wash.), Summer 2006; A. Cary, "Hanford's Animal Waste Cleanup Likely to Get Smelly," *Tri-City Herald*, April 25, 2006.

21 The three corporations are CH2M-Hill, Inc., Washington Group, Inc., and Bechtel, Inc.

22 The Central Plateau refers to the central part of the Hanford Site, 8–10 miles from the Columbia River. It is high above the groundwater table (250–300 feet) in relation to the rest of the Site, and is often called "the hill," "the plateau," or "central Hanford."

23 U.S. DOE, DOE/RL-2000-66 Draft; J. E. Stang, "DOE Aims to Speed Rivershore Cleanup," *Tri-City Herald*, August 11, 2000, p. A1.

24 M. S. Gerber, "Past Practices Technical Characterization Study, 300 Area, Hanford Site," WHC-MR-0388 (RL: WHC, December 1992) Section 3; "Another Hanford Surprise," *Seattle Post-Intelligencer*, October 3, 2000, p. B4; J. E. Stang, "Bottomless Containers Could Be Source of Tritium," *Tri-City Herald*, September 30, 2000, p. A3.

25 P. Pettiette, "Corridor Contract First Step in Hanford Closure," *Tri-City Herald*, March 4, 2006, p. F15.

26 M. S. Gerber, "Dramatic Change at T-Plant," WHC-MR-0452 (RL: WHC, April 1994); "First Batch of K Basin Sludge Treated," *Weapons Complex Monitor*, June 19, 2006, pp. 9–10.

27 L. L. Weaver, "222–S Laboratory Interim Safety Basis," WHC-SD-CP-ISB-002, Rev. 1 (RL: WHC, July 10, 1996).

28 "Westinghouse Re-Starts Upgraded HLW Waste Evaporator at Hanford Site, *Nuclear Waste News* (Silver Spring MD), April 21, 1994.

29 U.S. DOE, "Waste Processing Underway at Hanford's WRAP Facility," RL-99-013 (RL: U.S. DOE, November 12, 1998).

30 "Environmental Restoration Disposal Facility," www.wch-rcc.com/erdf; "Hanford Cleanup Marks Milestone," *Inside Energy* (Washington, D.C.), July 28, 2003, pp. 17–18; WDOE, EPA, and DOE, "ERDF Expansion Complete," *Hanford Update*, Winter 2005.

31 U.S. DOE, "Energy Secretary Hazel O'Leary to Dedicate Environmental Molecular Sciences Laboratory at Hanford," RL-96–102 (RL: U.S. DOE, October 16, 1996); "Environmental Molecular Science Laboratory," www.emsl.pnl.gov; "HAMMER's Capabilities Needed in War on Terror," *Tri-City Herald*, January 25, 2004, p. F3.

32 A. L. Brandt, "Hanford Cleanup Effort Reaches First Milestone," *Spokesman-Review* (Spokane, Wash.), June 30, 1995, citing D. Sherwood; "Liquid Effluents Program Hits Major Milestone," *Hanford Reach* (Richland, Wash.), October 6, 1997; "Success Story at Hanford," *Oregonian*, June 17, 1996.

33 U.S. DOE, "Draft Reports Confirm Hanford Tank Farm Leaks Contributing Source of Groundwater Contamination," RL/OEA-97-096 (RL: U.S. DOE, November 25, 1977).

34 J. Ritter, "Nuclear Plant's Neighbors Lose Patience with Cleanup," *USA Today* (Washington, D.C.), December 18, 1997, pp. A4, A6; K. Murphy, "Radioactive Waste Seeps toward Columbia River," *Los Angeles Times*, March 12, 2000.

35 J. E. Stang, "Contaminants from Nuclear Reservation Seep toward the River," *Tri-City Herald*, August 30, 1998, pp. A1, A6, citing D. Dunning.

36 The vadose zone is the area of substrata between the ground surface and the top of the groundwater table.

37 U.S. DOE, "Management and Integration of Hanford Site Groundwater and Vadose Zone Activities," DOE/RL-98-03 (RL: U.S. DOE, April 1998).

38 M. S. Gerber, "Battling Groundwater Contamination at Hanford," *Radwaste Solutions*, September/October 2006.

39 K. D. Steele, "Salmon Close to Radiation," *Spokesman-Review*, June 27, 1999, p. A1; J. E. Stang, "Hanford's Experiment to Dilute Contaminant Seems to Be Working," *Tri-City Herald*, August 3, 1999, p. A1.

40 M. J. Hartman, L. F. Morasch, W. D. Weber, "Hanford Site Groundwater Monitoring for Fiscal Year 2005," PNNL-15670 (RL: PNNL, March 2006).

41 Hartman, et al., PNNL-15670.

42 Gerber, "Battling Groundwater."

43 A. Cary, "DOE Looking at 2 Contaminated Areas at Hanford," *Tri-City Herald*, October 26, 2005, p. B3.

44 N. Netherton, "Hanford Contractor

to Use New Method to Block Strontium Movement into River," *BNA Environment Reporter* (Washington, D.C.), June 6, 2006.

45 S. Dininny, "Hanford Seeks Ways to Treat Contaminated Groundwater," *Tri-City Herald*, February 6, 2005, p. B3.

46 J. E. Stang, "Dangerous Vapor Prompts Removal of Waste Barrels," *Tri-City Herald*, September 2, 2002, p. B2; J. E. Stang, "Hanford Dilutes Trench Vapors," *Tri-City Herald*, November 23, 2003, p. B3.

47 Hartman, et al., PNNL-15670.

48 A picocurie is one-trillionth of a curie.

49 A. Cary, "Hanford Pumping Hits Early Objective," *Tri-City Herald*, February 6, 2005, pp. B1–2; A. Dworkin, "Hanford Scores Successes, Setbacks amid Criticism," *Oregonian*, October 26, 2005, pp. A1, A14.

50 A. Dworkin, "Scientists Take Aim at Hanford's Dirty Past," *Oregonian*, October 26, 2005, pp. A13–14.

51 Hartman, et al., PNNL-15670; and Cary, "DOE Looking."

52 S. Dininny, "Report Faults U.S. over Hanford Wells," *Seattle Times*, January 7, 2005, p. B2.

53 U.S. DOE, "Memorandum: Pollution Prevention Best-in-Class Awards" (Washington, D.C.: U.S. DOE, July 9, 2004).

54 L. Stiffler, "Hanford Water Cleanup Not Working, Report Says," *Seattle Post-Intelligencer*, July 28, 2004, p. B2, partially citing G. Friedman; and L. Blumenthal, "Report Critical of Hanford Cleanup," *Tri-City Herald*, March 30, 2004, pp. B1–2.

55 Dworkin, "Hanford Scores Successes."

56 U.S. GAO, "Columbia River Contamination from the Hanford Site," GAO-06-77R (Washington, D.C.: U.S. GAO, November 4, 2005); "At Richland . . . GAO Faults Groundwater Remedies," *Weapons Complex Monitor*, November 7, 2005, p. 10; and A. Cary, "Hanford Cleanup Ef-

forts Faulted," *Tri-City Herald*, May 12, 2006, pp. B1–2.

57 "Lethal and Leaking," *60 Minutes* (New York: CBS News), April 30, 2006, C. Gregoire.

58 U.S. DOE, "EM-21 Technical Proposals," www.hanford.gov/cp/gpp/sience, em21.

59 A. Cary, "More Data Needed on Hanford Soil," *Tri-City Herald*, September 6, 2006, p. B1; U.S. GAO, "Nuclear Waste: DOE's Efforts to Protect the Columbia River from Contamination Could Be Further Strengthened," GAO-06-1018 (Washington, D.C.: U.S. GAO, August 2006).

60 T. E. Bergman, "Plan for Central Plateau Closure," CP-22319–Del (RL: FH, September 2004).

61 M. B. Lackey, T. E. Bergman, B. J. Kerr, B. A. Austin, J. R. Robertson, "Comprehensive Closure Plan for the Central Plateau," ICEM05-1291, *Proceedings of the 10th International Conference on Environmental Remediation and Radioactive Waste Management* (New York: American Society of Mechanical Engineers, 2005).

62 Lackey, et al., ICEM05-1291, pp. 4–5.

63 U.S. EPA, "Record of Decision, 221–U Facility (Canyon Disposal Initiative), Hanford Site, Washington" (RL: U.S. EPA, 2005).

64 U.S. DOE, "Hanford Site Receives National Recognition" (RL: U.S. DOE, May 11, 2006); "Hanford's U-Plant Cleanup Honored," *Tri-City Herald*, May 20, 2006, p. B6.

65 WDOE, EPA, and DOE, "First-Ever Record of Decision for Disposition of a Processing Canyon," *Hanford Update*, Fall 2005, pp. 1–2; Lackey, et al., ICEM05-1291.

66 T. Martin, "Central Plateau Cleanup Must Be a Priority in Tri-Party Agreement," *Tri-City Herald*, March 4, 2006, p. F6.

67 The Tri-Party Agreement or TPA is an agreement that sets enforceable milestones for Hanford Site cleanup among the Washington State Department of Ecology (or WDOE), the U.S. Environmental Protection Agency (EPA) and the DOE. Signed in May 1989, it was the first such agreement in the nation.

68 U.S. DOE, "Hanford Waste Shipment Departs for Waste Isolation Pilot Plant," RL-00-071 (RL: U.S. DOE, July 12, 2000).

69 U.S. DOE, "WIPP Shipment Figures," www.wipp.energy.gov/shipments.htm.

70 Suspect TRU waste essentially is that waste for which the records are unclear or incomplete, but the time and place of origin cause knowledgeable people to think they might contain TRU elements. From 1970 to 1987, Hanford segregated such wastes in a few specific burial trenches.

71 J. E. Stang, "DOE Taps Hanford to Become Receiving Site for Federal Wastes," *Tri-City Herald*, February 26, 2000, p. A1; G. Lobsenz, "Low-Level Waste Turns Politically Toxic at Hanford," *Energy Daily*, March 2, 2000, pp. 1–2.

72 R. Wyden, "Clean Up, Don't Fill Up Hanford," *Oregonian*, July 27, 2002, p. B5.

73 "Hanford's Taken Enough," *Oregonian*, July 30, 2002, p. B8.

74 G. Lobsenz, "State Regulators Rip DOE Plan on Hanford Waste," *Energy Daily*, August 27, 2002, pp. 1, 3.

75 "Charge DOE to Store, Not Just Ship, Wastes," *Tri-City Herald*, November 20, 2002, p. A8.

76 J. E. Stang and C. Mulick, "Radioactive Waste Agreement Reached," *Tri-City Herald*, December 17, 2002, p. A1.

77 A. Galloway and L. Stiffler, "Suit Filed to Block Hanford Waste," *Seattle Post-Intelligencer*, March 5, 2003, pp. A1, A16; J. E. Stang, "DOE Sues State Ecology," *Tri-City Herald*, April 10, 2003, pp. A1–2.

78 J. E. Stang, "Shipments Halted in State-DOE Feud," *Tri-City Herald*, May 13, 2003, pp. A1–2.

79 "Hanford Waste Cleanup EIS Offers 'Pessimistic Assumptions,'" *Inside Energy*, July 28, 2003, pp. 17–18.

80 C. Mulick, "Initiative Filed to Halt Hanford Shipments," *Tri-City Herald*, June 10, 2003, p. B2; C. Mulick, "Hanford Initiative Heading for Ballot," *Tri-City Herald*, February 19, 2004, p. B1; G. Lobsenz, "Initiative Turns Hanford Cleanup into 2004 Political Football," *Energy Daily*, January 7, 2004, pp. 1–2.

81 "Washington Reps Enter Ballot Fray over Blocking Waste to Hanford," *Weapons Complex Monitor*, September 6, 2004, pp. 4–5; E. Sanders, "Effect of Waste Vote, Not Outcome, Is at Issue," *New York Times*, October 17, 2004, pp. A1–2.

82 "I-297 Is Bad Law," *Seattle Times*, September 26, 2004, p. D2.

83 "Reject Hanford Initiative," *Oregonian*, October 21, 2004, p. D10.

84 S. Dininny, "U.S. Wants Wash. Nuclear Waste Ban Tossed," *Seattle Post-Intelligencer*, December 1, 2004; S. Dininny, "Hanford Initiative Injunction Retained," *Seattle Post-Intelligencer*, December 8, 2004; E. Pryne, "Federal Judge Strikes Down Hanford N-Waste Initiative," *Seattle Times*, June 13, 2006, pp. B1, B4; Associated Press, "State Appeals Ruling Tossing Hanford Ban," *Seattle Times*, July 13, 2006, p. B3.

85 Battelle Memorial Institute is the parent organization of a company that operates Pacific Northwest National Laboratory for the U.S. DOE. PNNL was writing the Hanford Solid Waste EIS for DOE, while a Battelle Memorial Institute laboratory in Ohio was seeking to send its TRU waste to Hanford.

86 J. E. Stang, "HAB Rebukes Waste Study," *Tri-City Herald*, June 9, 2003, p. B2.

87 J. E. Stang, "Environmental Impact Statement Faulty, State Says," *Tri-City Herald*, June 12, 2003, p. B3; J. E. Stang, "Regulators Say DOE Waste Plans in 'Disarray,'" *Tri-City Herald*, March 18, 2003, p. B3.

88 WDOE, "Ecology Department Orders Cleanup of Hanford's Buried Waste," 03-079 (Olympia: WDOE, April 30, 2003.

89 L. Stiffler, "Hanford Cleanup Delayed," *Seattle Post-Intelligencer*, May 10, 2003, p. B2; "DOE's Risky Posturing Unacceptable Threat," *Tri-City Herald*, May 11, 2003, p. F2; "Skip the Tantrum, Get Hanford Working," *Seattle Times*, May 14, 2003, p. B6.

90 "State Officials Move to Defuse Hanford Cleanup Confrontation," *Energy Daily*, May 16, 2003; S. Dininny, "Breakthrough in Hanford Waste Dispute," *Seattle Post-Intelligencer*, October 25, 2003, p. B2; U.S. DOE, "Retrieval of Hanford's Buried Transuranic Waste Begins," RL-04-2002 (RL: U.S. DOE, October 27, 2003; S. Dininny, "Hanford Workers Unearthing Barrels," *Seattle Times*, March 10, 2004, pp. B1, B17; WDOE, EPA, and U.S. DOE, "2004: A Year of Cleanup Progress," *Hanford Update*, Winter 2005.

91 U.S. DOE, "Final Hanford Site Solid (Radioactive and Hazardous) Waste Program Environmental Impact Statement, Richland, Washington," DOE/EIS-0286F (RL: U.S. DOE, January 2004); "DOE Issues Final Plan for Hanford Site, and Wash. Critics Line Up in Opposition," *Inside Energy*, February 9, 2004, p. 10; S. Dininny, "A Dumping Ground? Report Raises Concerns," *Seattle Times*, March 10, 2004, p. B3; U.S. DOE, "Retrieval of Hanford's Buried Transuranic Waste Begins," RL-04-0024 (RL: U.S. DOE, October 27, 2003); "DOE Drastically Cuts Sending Off-Site Waste to Hanford," *Weapons Complex Monitor*, June 28, 2004, pp. 4–5; A. Cary, "State Plans Suit to Bar Waste Shipments," *Tri-City Herald*, July 17, 2004, pp. A1–2; A. Cary, "DOE Stops Waste Shipments to Hanford," *Tri-City Herald*, July 23, 2004, p. A1.

92 WDOE, "State Issues Record Fine for Nuke-Waste Mismanagement at Hanford," 04-175 (Olympia: WDOE, September 1, 2004).

93 "DOE Loses Hanford Site Waste Case, Told to Comply with Wash. State Law," *Inside Energy*, January 31, 2005, p. 9.

94 A. Cary, "Ruling Lets State Bar Some Waste," *Tri-City Herald*, January 25, 2005, pp. A1–2, partially citing S. Hutchison.

95 N. Geranios, "Hanford Required to Take Limited Waste, Judge Rules," *Seattle Times*, May 14, 2005; U.S. DOE, "Statement of Charles Anderson Regarding the Hanford Solid Waste Environmental Impact Statement" (Washington, D.C.: U.S. DOE, July 22, 2005); "DOE Halts Shipment of TRU Waste to Hanford Due to EIS Errors," *Weapons Complex Monitor*, August 1, 2005, pp. 3–4; A. Cary, "Review Finds Problems in Hanford Study," *Tri-City Herald*, January 10, 2006, p. B1.

96 U.S. DOE, "Energy Secretary Bodman Statement on Hanford Solid Waste Settlement Agreement" (Washington, D.C.: U.S. DOE, January 9, 2006).

97 WDOE, EPA, and U.S. DOE, "Integrated Disposal Facility Update," *Hanford Update*, Winter 2005; A. Cary, "Landfill Moves Forward," *Tri-City Herald*, May 3, 2006.

98 DNFSB, "Improved Schedule for Remediation," Recommendation 1994-1 (Washington, D.C.: DNFSB, May 26, 1994), J. Conway, Letter of Transmittal, p. 1.

99 R. Jim, G. Pollett, G. deBruler, T. E. Carpenter, L. M. Stembridge, P. Knight, "Letter to H. O'Leary" (Seattle: Confederated Tribes and Bands of the Yakama Nation, Heart of America Northwest, Columbia River United, Government Accountability Project, Hanford Education Action League, Northwest Advocates and Hanford Watch, April 22 1993); G. Lobsenz, "DOE Signs New Hanford Pact with State," *Energy Daily*, January 26, 1994.

100 M. S. Gerber, "History and Stabilization of the Plutonium Finishing Plant (PFP) Complex, Hanford Site," HNF-EP-0924 (RL: PHMC, March 1997).

101 U.S. DOE, "Citizen Bulletin: Stabilizing Reactive Plutonium at Hanford's Plutonium Finishing Plant" (RL: U.S. DOE, June 1993).

360

102 M. S. Gerber, "Turning the Corner at Hanford," *Radwaste Solutions*, January/February 2005.

103 J. Hunter, "Good News Emerges from Hanford, Not Just Gloom and Doom," *Tri-City Herald*, December 5, 1994, p. A6.

104 U.S. DOE, "Plutonium Finishing Plant Stabilization, Final Environmental Impact Statement," DOE/EIS-0244–F (RL: U.S. DOE, May 1996); "Hanford: ROD Calls for Stabilization of Plutonium Finishing Plant by 2004," *Nuclear Waste News*, July 3, 1996.

105 DNFSB, "Stabilization and Storage of Nuclear Material," Recommendation 2000-1 (Washington, D.C.: DNFSB, January 14, 2000); J. Conway, Letter of Transmittal, p. 5; DNFSB, Recommendation 1994-1; "New Plan in Place for Materials Stabilization Work," *Weapons Complex Monitor*, June 26, 2000, p. 9.

106 U.S. DOE, "Hanford's Plutonium Finishing Plant Starts Up New Automated Packaging System," RL-00-099 (RL: U.S. DOE, October 2, 2000); Associated Press, "Hanford Begins Storing Plutonium in More Stable Form," *Seattle Times*, September 20, 2000, p. B5.

107 J. E. Stang, "PFP Cleanup Well Ahead of Schedule," *Tri-City Herald*, March 13, 2003, p. B1.

108 U.S. DOE, "Hanford's Plutonium Plant First to Meet New Department of Energy Plutonium Packaging Standard," RL-01-053 (RL: U.S. DOE, April 11, 2001).

109 "At Richland . . . Residues Stabilized at Plutonium Finishing Plant," *Weapons Complex Monitor*, August 11, 2003, p. 8.

110 J. E. Stang, "Plutonium-Laced Liquids Converted to Safer Powder," *Tri-City Herald*, June 27, 2002, p. B1.

111 Gerber, "Turning the Corner."

112 A. Cary, "Celebrating a Milestone: Hanford Recognizes Plutonium Stabilization as 'Grand Jewel,'" *Tri-City Her-ald*, February 21, 2004, pp. A1–2; "Hanford Finishes Plutonium Stabilization," *Energy Daily*, February 23, 2004, p. 3.

113. Gerber, "Turning the Corner."

114 A. Cary, "DOE Honors Hanford Project," *Tri-City Herald*, August 26, 2004, pp. B7–8.

115 Gerber, "Turning the Corner," partially citing G. Locke, K. Niles, N. Ceto, and R. Hastings.

116 "At Richland . . . D&D of Pu Finishing Plant Moving Forward," *Weapons Complex Monitor*, March 14, 2005, p. 7; "Hanford Decommissioning Projects Update," *Decontamination, Decommissioning and Reutilization Division Newsletter* (La Grange Park, Ill.: American Nuclear Society), May 2005, pp. 22–24; and U.S. DOE, RL-06-0009.

117 M. A. Reilly, "Spent Nuclear Fuel Project Technical Data Book," HNF-SD-SNF-TI-015, Rev 6 (RL: FDH, October 23, 1998); R. L. Miller and J. M. Steffes, "Radionuclide Inventory and Source terms for the Surplus Production Reactors at Hanford," UNI-3714 (RL: United Nuclear Industries, Inc., June 1986); M. S. Gerber, "Spent Fuel Removal Concludes at Hanford's K Basins" *Radwaste Solutions*, January/February 2005; K. Klein, "In 2004, DOE Eliminated 2 of Hanford's 3 Urgent Risks," *Tri-City Herald*, March 5, 2005, pp. F4–5.

118 G. Lobsenz, "DOE Begins High-Profile K Basin Cleanup," *Energy Daily*, December 8, 2000, pp. 1–2; M. S. Gerber, "Hanford Cheers as Spent Fuel Moves," *Hanford Reach*, December 18, 2000, pp. 5–8.

119 A. Cary, "Spent Fuel Removal Finished at K Basins," *Tri-City Herald*, October 23, 2004, pp. A1–2; S. Dininny, "Nuclear Fuel Removed from Hanford Basins," *Seattle Times*, October 25, 2004, p. B2; A. Dworkin, "Basins Clear of Spent Nuclear Fuel at Hanford," *Oregonian*, October 24, 2004, p. D2.

120 Gerber, "Spent Fuel Removal Concludes," citing N. Ceto and K. Niles.

121 B. Hunsberger, "Hanford Cleanup Starts Slowly," *Oregonian*, December 8, 2000, p. BI.

122 J. E. Stang, "Westinghouse Says It Will Take 2 Years to Seal Leak," *Tri-City Herald*, March 2, 1993, p. A7; W. Briggs, "K-Basin Concerns Top Cleanup Priority List," *Tri-City Herald*, May 25, 1994, p. AI; WDOE, EPA, and U.S. DOE, "Safety Concerns Accelerate Work at K-Basins," *Hanford Update*, February 1996.

123 U.S. DOE, "Department of Energy Programmatic Spent Nuclear Fuel Management and Idaho National Engineering Laboratory Restoration and Waste Management Programs, Final Environmental Impact Statement, DOE/EIS-0203 (Washington, D.C.: U.S. DOE, April 1995); U.S. DOE, "Management of Spent Nuclear Fuels from the K-Basins at the Hanford Site: Final Environmental Impact Statement," DOE/EIS-0245 (RL: U.S. DOE, January 1996).

124 P. LeRoy, "Spent Nuclear Fuel Project, Project Execution Plan," HNF-3552, Rev. 1 (RL: FH, June 22, 2000).

125 Gerber, "Spent Fuel Removal Concludes."

126 Reilly, HNF-SD-SNF-TI-015, Rev. 6; K. D. Gibson, "K Basins Safety Analysis Report," HNF-SD-WM-SAR-062, Rev. 4 (RL: FH, June 28, 2000); L. J. Garvin, "Spent Nuclear Fuel Project, Annex A Canister Storage Building Final Safety Analysis Report," HNF-3553, vol. 2 (RL: FH, May 11, 2000); J. R. Brehm, J. Carrell, S. F. Kessler, C. Krahn, "Spent Nuclear Fuel Project, Annex B Cold Vacuum Drying Facility Safety Analysis Report," HNF-3553, vol. 3 (RL: FH, August 9, 2000).

127 J. Long, "Hanford's Hot Rods," *Oregonian*, November 11, 1994, p. AI6.

128 Gerber, "Spent Fuel Removal Concludes," p. 19, citing T. Ruane.

129 Gerber, "Spent Fuel Removal Concludes," p. 13, citing C. Lucas.

130 "Glauthier Tightens Controls over Department Projects," *Weapons Complex Monitor*, June 28, 1999, pp. 2–3.

131 K. A. Klein, "Approval of Safety Analysis Report (SAR) Revision (Rev.) 3K, and Technical Safety Requirement (TSR) Rev. 0–G," Letter to R. G. Hanson, 00–SFO-059 (RL: U.S. DOE, December 22, 1999).

132 A. Cary, "K Basin Concrete Likely Holding," *Tri-City Herald*, February 17, 2005, pp. BI–2.

133 Gerber, "Spent Fuel Removal Concludes," p. 20, citing M. Peres.

134 J. E. Stang, "Tackling the K Basin Sludge Problem," *Tri-City Herald*, July 6, 1999, p. A3; "K Basin Spent Fuel Removal Done; But Challenges Remain for Sludge," *Weapons Complex Monitor*, November 1, 2004, p. 4.

135 R. Michal, "Cleaning Up Hanford's K Basins Is Hard Work," *Nuclear News* (La Grange Park, Ill.), July 2005, pp. 53–56.

136 G. Lobsenz, "DOE Threatens to Take Hanford Cleanup Job Away from Fluor," *Energy Daily*, September 9, 2003, pp. 1–2; A. Cary, "DOE Faces Fine for K Basins Sludge," *Tri-City Herald*, March 25, 2004, pp. BI–2; "DOE Mulls Removing Fluor from Hanford K-Basin Sludge Project," *Weapons Complex Monitor*, March 29, 2004, p. 2.

137 "At Richland. . . . First Batch of K Basin Sludge Treated," *Weapons Complex Monitor*, June 19, 2006, pp. 9–10.

138 C. R. Anderson, "Seven Year Waste Program, Chemical Processing Department," HW-58329 (RL: Hanford Atmic Products Operation, December 15, 1958).

139 U.S. DOE, "About Us," www.hanford.gov/orp.

140 Note that in late 2006, Hanford's underground tanks contained about 53 million gallons of waste. The lower number has occurred due to engineered evaporation in the 242–A Waste Evaporator. New wastes from deactivation projects and other cleanup work have also been added to the tanks.

362

141 "DOE to Get $5.18 Billion for Cleanup," *Defense Cleanup* (Arlington, Va.), October 22, 1993.

142 H. D. Harmon and M. C. Druby, "Hanford's Latest Achievement: Mixer Pump and New Long-Term Waste Treatment Plans," *Radwaste*, January 1994, pp. 36–41.

143 S. M. Blush and T. H. Heitman, "Train Wreck along the River of Money" (Washington, D.C.: Senate Committee on Energy and Natural Resources, March 1995).

144 T. Aeppel, "Untidy Cleanup: Mess at A-Bomb Plant Shows What Happens if Pork Gets into Play," *Wall Street Journal* (New York), March 29, 1955; G. Lee, "Nuclear Plant Cleanup Assailed," *Washington Post*, March 15, 1995; J. Lynch, "Hanford Dollars Squandered, Report Concludes," *Spokesman-Review*, March 15, 1995.

145 "DOE to Be Cut by $1.6 Billion, EM Program to Focus on Risks," *Nuclear Waste News*, December 22, 1994, p. 1.

146 Note that safety concerns over flammable gases and the need to install flammable gas monitors were other reasons that single-shelled tank pumping slowed in 1995.

147 M. S. Gerber, "TPA Praised at 10–Year Anniversary Celebration," *Hanford Reach*, July 12, 1999, p. 3, citing M. Lawrence and D. Silver.

148 Gerber, "TPA Praised," citing D. Silver, R. French, M. Gearheard; J. Lynch, "Hanford Cleanup Isn't All Great News," *Seattle Times*, July 5, 1999, pp. 1–2.

149 T. Martin, "Frustration with the Tank Waste Treatment Project" (Portland: Hanford Watch, April 1999), pp. 1, 4, www.hanfordwatch.org/archive/martin-tank%20waste.

150 WDOE, "Protecting the Columbia River: The Need to Retrieve and Immobilize Hanford's High-level Radioactive Tank Waste" (Olympia: WDOE, March 1999), p. 2.

151 Note that there is no evidence that Tank C-106 ever leaked. However, the potential for leakage made tank remediation an urgent need.

152 J. E. Stang, "High Heat Tank Saga Should Be Over Today," *Tri-City Herald*, October 6, 1999, citing S. Dahl; G. Lobsenz, "In Cleanup Milestone, DOE Empties First Hanford Waste Tank," *Energy Daily*, October 18, 1999, pp. 1, 3.

153 "Two Hanford Tanks Removed from Watch List; Burping Tank May Be Next," *Inside Energy*, September 11, 2000, pp. 5–6; "DOE Closes the Books on HLW Tank Ferrocyanide Safety Issue," *Nuclear Waste News*, November 28, 1996, pp. 463–64; Associated Press, "18 Tanks off Hanford Hazard List; 28 Remain," *Spokesman-Review*, December 18, 1998, p. B3; V. S. Rezendes, "Letter to Honorable R. Wyden," B-271613 (Washington, D.C.: U.S. GAO, April 10, 1996); H. L. Boston, "Closure of the Flammable Gas Safety Issue and Removal of 24 Tanks from the Flammable Gas Watch List," 01-SHD-077 (RL: ORP, August 1, 2001); J. H. Roberson, "Approval to Close the Flammable Gas Safety Issue and Remove 24 Tanks from the Flammable Gas Watch List," Memorandum to H. L. Boston (Washington, D.C.: U.S. DOE, November 19, 2001).

154 U.S. DOE, "Cross-Site Transfer Line Ready to Operate," RL 98-056 (RL: U.S. DOE, June 17, 1998).

155 U.S. DOE, "Major Ventilation Project Completed on Two Hanford Tank Farms," RL/OEA 98-033 (RL: U.S. DOE, April 7, 1998); "Good Maintenance Helps Slow Leaks from Aging Single-Shell HLW Tanks," *Nuclear Waste News*, August 30, 2001, p. 355; "CH2M Hill Uses Polyurea Foam to Seal Tank Farm Process Pits," *Nuclear Waste News*, December 20, 2001, p. 510.

156 L. Ashton, "Nuclear Blob Rises in Hanford Radioactive Waste Tank," *Oregonian*, September 28, 1999, p. B11.

157 M. S. Kazimi, "RE: April 12–14 1999 TAP Meeting Comments Regarding SY101," Letter to R. French (Cambridge: Massachusetts Institute of Technology, May 3, 1999).

158 J. E. Stang, "Worries over Hanford 'Burping' Tank Appear to Be at End," *Tri-City Herald*, March 9, 2000, p. A7; G. Lobsenz, "Taming of 'Burping' Tank Signals Turning Point for Hanford Tanks," *Energy Daily*, February 24, 2000, pp. 1–2.

159 C. O. Gregoire and G. Locke, "Notice of Intent to Sue for Violation of the Hanford Federal Facility Agreement and Consent Order," Letter to F. Pena and J. D. Wagoner (Olympia: State of Washington, June 8, 1998); "Lawsuit Might Result in Cleanup," *Seattle Post-Intelligencer*, June 10, 1998, p. A12; "We Need Action: Not Paper Shuffling," *Spokesman-Review*, June 9, 1998, p. B4; "State Right to Sue DOE: Enough Is Enough," *Tri-City Herald*, June 9, 1998, p. A6.

160 J. E. Stang, "State, DOE Reach Cleanup Agreement," *Tri-City Herald*, March 4, 1999, pp. A1–2, citing C. Gregoire.

161 A. Cary, "DOE Empties Liquid from Old Tanks," *Tri-City Herald*, August 13, 2004, pp. A1–2; A. Cary, "Hanford Tanks Cleared," *Tri-City Herald*, August 24, 2004, pp. A1–2; "No Sleeping Chernobyl," *Seattle Times*, August 25, 2004, p. B8; "Tanks a Lot," *Tri-City Herald*, August 30, 2004, p. A12.

162 S. Dininny, "Hanford Reaches Milestone in Cleanup of Tanks," *Seattle Post-Intelligencer*, August 24, 2004, p. B2, partially citing C. Gregoire.

163 G. Lobsenz, "Enviros Sue over DOE Plans to Leave Nuke Waste in Storage Tanks," *Energy Daily*, July 5, 2001, pp. 1–2; G. Lobsenz, "Hanford Contractor Proposes Burying Nuke Waste in Tanks," *Energy Daily*, January 4, 2002, pp. 1–2; M. I. Wald, "Energy Department Is Challenged over Waste Disposal Methods," *New York Times*, March 4, 2002, p. A15.

164 A. Cary, "State Tries to Join Suit against DOE," *Tri-City Herald*, July 17, 2002, p. B1; L. Blumenthal, "Hanford Regulators Still Concerned about Cleanup," *Tri-City Herald*, July 20, 2002, p. B3.

165 U.S. DOE, "Hanford Prepares to Close 26 Waste Tanks within Four Years," ORP-03-001 (RL: U.S. DOE, October 8, 2002).

166 J. E. Stang, "DOE Unveils Plans for Site's Tank Wastes," *Tri-City Herald*, January 10, 2003, pp. B1–2.

167 WDOE, "Negotiations Start on Tank Waste Retrieval and Closure Milestone M-45-00C" (Olympia, WDOE, November 18, 2003).

168 CH2MHill Hanford Co. is the tank management contractor for the DOE at Hanford.

169 "At River Protection . . . Pumping Begins on First Tank Slated for Closure," *Weapons Complex Monitor*, April 7, 2003, p. 8; A. Cary, "Another Hanford Tank Being Emptied," *Tri-City Herald*, July 28, 2006; "New Vacuum System Showing Promise in Hanford Tank Farms," *Weapons Complex Monitor*, December 12, 2005, pp. 7–8; A. Cary, "Robot Blasting Away Tank Waste," *Tri-City Herald*, August 22, 2006, pp. B1–2.

170 Associated Press, "Corrosion Found in Hanford Radioactive Waste Storage Tank," *Seattle Post-Intelligencer*, October 4, 1999, p. B4; J. E. Stang, "DOE to Pay for Missed Deadline," *Tri-City Herald*, June 14, 2000, p. A1.

171 Associated Press, "Hanford Waste Contains Toxic PCBs; Tank Cleanup Could Be Complicated," *Seattle Post-Intelligencer*, March 7, 2000, p. B3; U.S. DOE, ORP, "Path to Resolving PCB Issue Agreed Upon for Hanford's Tank Waste—Significant Hurdle Cleared for Tank Waste Treatment" (Richland, Wash.: U.S. DOE, May 14, 2000). Vitrification is the process of heating and hardening tank wastes into solid blocks.

364

172 A. Cary, "Vapor Concerns Halt Work at Portion of Tank Farms," *Tri-City Herald*, March 25, 2004, pp. B1–2; A. Cary, "Tank Farms under Review," *Tri-City Herald*, March 30, 2004, pp. A1–2; A. Cary, "NIOSH Concerned over Tank Farms Risks," *Tri-City Herald*, July 17, 2004, pp. B1–2; NIOSH, "Health Hazard Evaluation Report: CH2M Hill Hanford Group, Inc. and United States Department of Energy, Office of Rover Protection, Richland, Washington," HETA 2004-0145-2941 (Cincinnati: NIOSH, July 2004); and A. Cary, "CH2MHill Upgrading Ventilation Systems," *Tri-City Herald*, December 23, 2004, p. B1; A. Cary, "Respirator Rule Lifted at Hanford," *Tri-City Herald*, May 1, 2006, pp. B1–2.

173 U.S. DOE, "Final Environmental Impact Statement for the Tank Waste Remediation System," DOE/EIS-0189–F (RL: U.S. DOE, August 1996).

174 "Draft EIS Reflects Hanford Tank Plan," *Defense Cleanup*, April 12, 1996; U.S. DOE, DOE/EIS-0189–F; "DOE Privatization Proposal Begins New Era in Waste Cleanup," *Energy Daily*, February 23, 1996; DOE Issues RFP for Tank Waste Solidification," *Nuclear News*, April 1996, p. 40; "More on Hanford: DOE Tank Waste EIS Calls for Two-Phased Privatized Cleanup," *Environmental Remediation Technology* (Silver Spring MD), April 17, 1996.

175 U.S. DOE, "DOE and BNFL, Inc. Sign Contract for Hanford Tank Waste Treatment," RL-98-166 (RL: U.S. DOE, August 24, 1998); "Delay and Promises on Hanford Cleanup," *Seattle Post-Intelligencer*, August 2, 1998, p. E2.

176 "Energy Department Fires Hanford Cleanup Firm," *Seattle Post-Intelligencer*, May 9, 2000, pp. A1–2; "Energy Department Ends BNFL Contract," *Tri-City Herald*, May 9, 2000, citing W. Richardson.

177 "Latest Delays Must Not Put Hanford Cleanup Project on Hold," *Yakima Herald-Republic*, October 11, 2000.

178 N. Geranios, "Federal Judge May Direct Hanford Nulcear Cleanup," *Seattle Times*, May 11, 2000, p. B2.

179 C. Mulick, "Gregoire Fed Up with DOE," *Tri-City Herald*, October 18, 2000, p. A7, citing C. Gregoire.

180 U.S. DOE, "Integrated Management Plan for the Hanford Tanks Waste Remediation System," DOE-RL-99-06 (RL: U.S. DOE, January 1999).

181 J. E. Stang, "Bechtel Team Wins Vit Plant Contract," *Tri-City Herald*, December 11, 2000, p. A1; J. E. Stang, "Hanford Regulators Worry about Future Cleanup Budget," *Tri-City Herald*, March 8, 2001, p. A4.

182 J. E. Stang, "DOE OKs Plan to Delay Glassification," *Tri-City Herald*, May 9, 2003, p. B1; J. E. Stang, "State OKs DOE's Vitrification Schedule," *Tri-City Herald*, July 12, 2003, pp. A1–2.

183 U.S. GAO, "Nuclear Waste: Absence of Key Management Reforms on Hanford's Cleanup Project Adds to Challenges of Achieving Cost and Schedule Goals," GAO-04-611 (Washington, D.C.: U.S. GAO, June 2005): "At River Protection . . . Uncertainty Remains for Vit Plant, GAO Says," *Weapons Complex Monitor*, July 19, 2004, pp. 6–7; A. Cary, "Rebar Errors Turn Up Again at Vit Plant," *Tri-City Herald*, January 30, 2004, pp. B1–2.

184 A. Cary, "Vit Plant Put on Hold," *Tri-City Herald*, June 29, 2005, pp. A1–2; G. Lobsenz, "Cost of Hanford Waste Plant Going Up Again," *Energy Daily*, May 17, 2005, pp. 1–2.

185 "Army Corps Sheds Light on Serious Problems with Hanford Vit Plant," *Weapons Complex Monitor*, September 12, 2005, pp. 2–4, partially citing U.S. ACE.

186 "DOE Silent Treatment Getting Very, Very Old," *Tri-City Herald*, September 19, 2005, p. A10; W. Cornwall, "Secretive Study Paints Dire Picture at Hanford," *Seattle Times*, December 1, 2005, pp. A1, A17.

187 W. Cornwall, "U.S. Unveils Report on Problems at Hanford," *Seattle Times*, December 7, 2005, pp. B1, B3; "New Bechtel Cost Estimate for Hanford Vit Plant Tops $10B," *Weapons Complex Monitor*, February 13, 2006, pp. 3–4.
188 "Miscues on Hanford Vit Plant Draw Strong Rebuke from Appropriators," *Weapons Complex Monitor*, April 10, 2006, pp. 2–3; H. Bernton and W. Cornwall, "Lucky Find Reveals Nuke-Tank Flaws," *Seattle Times*, May 1, 2005, pp. B1, B4; "Lethal and Leaking," citing C. Gregoire.
189 S. Dininny, "Contractor at Hanford Ordered to Give Back Fee," *Seattle Post-Intelligencer*, June 8, 2006; "DOE Formally Releases Bechtel's New Cost Estimate for Vit Plant," *Weapons Complex Monitor*, June 27, 2006, pp. 3–4.
190 A. Cary, "Estimated Cost of Hanford's Vitrification Plant May Increase," *Tri-City Herald*, July 18, 2006, p. B1; S. Dininny, "Hanford Plant Now $1.2 Billion," *Seattle Post-Intelligencer*, September 8, 2006. p. B5.
191 A. Cary, "Vit Plant to Stay Paused, DOE Official Says," *Tri-City Herald*, August 23, 2006, pp. A1–2.
192 J. E. Stang, "Hanford Explores Alternate Methods," *Tri-City Herald*, April 15, 2003, p. B1; Associated Press, "Cheaper Plan for N-Waste Storage Studied," *Seattle Times*, September 2, 2004, p. B2.
193 A. Cary, "Permit Allows Facility to Test Vitrification," *Tri-City Herald*, April 15, 2003, pp. B1–2; A. Cary, "Test Goes Smoothly as Glass Blocks Produced," *Tri-City Herald*, September 18, 2005, p. B1.
194 TRIDEC, "Bulk Vit Design Completed—Ecology Commended," *TRIDEC News* (Kennewick, Wash.: TRIDEC, August 9, 2006), p. 2.
195 J. E. Stang, "HAB OKs Plan to Ship Tank Wastes," *Tri-City Herald*, August 13, 2003, p. B1; A. Cary, "DOE, Ecology Discuss Sending Waste to WIPP,"

Tri-City Herald, September 17, 2003, p. B2; A. Cary, "Audit Faults DOE Disposal Project," *Tri-City Herald*, December 1, 2005, pp. A1–2; U.S. DOE, "Management Controls over the Hanford Site Transuranic Mixed Tank Waste," OAS-M-06-01 (Washington, D.C.: U.S. DOE, November 2005).
196 J. H. Roberson, "Environmental Management Priorities," Memorandum to Director (Washington, D.C.: U.S. DOE, November 19, 2001); Associated Press, "Report Suggests 2 Solutions for Revising Hanford Cleanup Plans," *Seattle Post-Intelligencer*, December 12, 2001, p. B4.
197 G. Lobsenz, "Judge Rules Against DOE in Nuclear Waste Disposal Case," *Energy Daily*, August 13, 2002, pp. 1–2.
198 "Idaho, S.C., Ore., Wash., Challenge DOE HLW Reclassification Rule," *Weapons Complex Monitor*, March 31, 2003, p. 4.
199 M. I. Wald, "Judge Voids Cleanup Plan for Wastes at Bomb Plants," *New York Times*, July 4, 2003, p. A12; J. E. Stang, "Abraham Takes Reclassification to Lawmakers," *Tri-City Herald*, August 15, 2003, pp. A1–2; "Abraham Defends Proposal to Hold Back $350M from HLW Cleanup," *Weapons Complex Monitor*, March 15, 2004, pp. 2–3.
200 "Richardson Aims to Head Off Any Plan by DOE to Ship Tank Waste Residue to WIPP," *Inside Energy*, November 3, 2003, pp. 9–10.
201 J. H. Hebert, "Feds Issue Threat over Money for Cleanup," *Seattle Times*, April 8, 2004, pp. B1, B4; "DOE Pulling a Fast One at Hanford," *Seattle Post-Intelligencer*, April 12, 2004, p. B7.
202 "DOE Still Using Politics to Get Its Way on Tanks," *Tri-City Herald*, June 1, 2004, p. A10.
203 "A Sneaky Ploy over Nuclear Waste," *Seattle Times*, June 12, 2004, p. B6.
204 "Short Cut on Nuclear Waste," *New York Times*, June 3, 2004, p. A26.
205 G. Lobsenz, "Congress Backs DOE

on Residual Waste, Advanced Nukes," *Energy Daily*, January 7, 2004, pp. 1–2.

206 A. Cary, "N. Mexico Won't Take High-Level Wastes," *Tri-City Herald*, November 4, 2004, pp. B1–2.

207 J. H. Hebert, "Scientists against Removing All Nuke Waste from Defense Sites," *Las Vegas Sun*, March 1, 2005; "Research Council Backs DOE's Basis for Waste Reclassification," *Weapons Complex Monitor*, March 7, 2005, p. 5; NRC, "Risk and Decisions about Disposition of Transuranic and High-Level Radioactive Waste" (Washington, D.C.: National Academy of Sciences, 2005).

208 NRC, "Tank Waste Retrieval, Processing and On-Site Disposal at Three Department of Energy Sites: Final Report" (Washington, D.C.: National Academy Press, 2006).

209 R. Vartabelian, "Errors, Costs Stall Nuclear Waste Project," *Los Angeles Times*, September 4, 2006, citing S. Dahl.

210 A. Cary, "Core Drilling Starts at FFTF," *Tri-City Herald*, April 30, 2005, pp. A1–2, partially citing C. Oliver.

211 "FFTF's Loss Still Proves Community's Potential," *Tri-City Herald*, May 4, 2005, p. A10.

212 "Pull Plug on FFTF," *Seattle Times*, April 2, 2003, p. E10.

213 A. Cary, "DOE to Permanently Shut Down FFTF," *Tri-City Herald*, November 22, 2000, pp. A1–2.

214 WHC, "Priority Message: FFTF to be Placed in 'Cold' Standby" (RL: WHC, January 12, 1993).

215 WHC, "Fast Flux Test Facility Transition Project Plan," WHC-SD-FF-SSP-004, Rev. 2 (RL: WHC, November 1995); U.S. DOE, "Fast Flux Test Facility" (RL: U.S. DOE, 1996).

216 "New Life for DOE's Fast Flux Test Facility," *Energy Daily*, December 4, 1995; "Tritium Production FFTF's Hope for a Mission," *New Technology Week* (Washington, D.C.), December 11, 1995; L. Blumenthal, "Panel Hears FFTF Tritium

Plan," *Tri-City Herald*, July 16, 1996, p. A5; J. E. Stang, "Panel Recommends FFTF for Production of Tritium," *Tri-City Herald*, August 1, 1996, p. A1.

217 J. E. Stang, "FFTF Could Have Role in Making Nuclear Space Batteries," *Tri-City Herald*, October 29, 1998, p. A3; P. Knight, "Proposal for New Nuclear Missions Imperils Cleanup at Hanford," *Oregonian*, December 22, 1998, p. D13.

218 U.S. DOE, "Fast Flux Test Facility Will Not Be Used for Tritium Production," RR-98-201 (Washington, D.C.: U.S DOE, December 22, 1998).

219 U.S. DOE, "Final Programmatic Environmental Impact Statement for Accomplishing Civilian Nuclear Energy Research and Development and Isotope Production Missions in the United States, Including the Role of the Fast Flux Test Facility," DOE/EIS-0310D (Washington, D.C.: U.S. DOE, August 30, 2000).

220 "P-I Opinion: Kill the FFTF before It Produces More Waste," *Seattle Post-Intelligencer*, December 2000, p. B6; "Focus on Cleanup at Hanford," *Seattle Times*, September 18, 2000, p. B6; H. Buskirk, "Coverup Charged as DOE Probes FFTF Reactor Restart," *Energy Daily*, August 30, 2000, pp. 1–3.

221 J. E. Stang, "Richland FFTF Meeting Draws about 325," *Tri-City Herald*, September 1, 2000, p. A1; P. McMahon, "Cancer Survivors Support Reactor," *USA Today*, October 23, 2000, p. A3.

222 A. Cary, "Cost Report Sets FFTF Restart as Solid Move," *Tri-City Herald*, August 26, 2000, p. A1; A. Cary, "Restart of FFTF Fares Well in Report," *Tri-City Herald*, September 6, 2000, p. A1.

223 U.S. DOE, "DOE Announces Preferred Alternative for Nuclear Infrastructure," RL-00–291 (Washington, D.C.: U.S. DOE, November 1, 2000).

224 U.S. DOE, DOE/EIS-0310–F.

225 A. Cary, "DOE Suspends FFTF Shutdown," *Tri-City Herald*, April 26, 2001,

p. AI; L. Ashton, "Watchdog Groups Urge Shutdown of Test Reactor," *Seattle Post-Intelligencer*, May 16, 2001, p. B2; "There's No Time to Waste on Reprieve for FFTF," *Tri-City Herald*, May 1, 2001, p. A8; National Association of Cancer Patients, "Cancer Patients Applaud Energy Secretary's Decision to Review FFTF Commercialization Option" (La Jolla, Calif.: NACP, August 9, 2001); Associated Press, "Groups Seek to Close Reactor at Hanford," *Oregonian*, September 28, 2001, p. C2; A. Cary, "DOE Investigating Proposal for FFTF," *Tri-City Herald*, June 12, 2001, p. B3.

226 U.S. DOE, "Department of Energy to Permanently Deactivate Fast Flux Test Facility Research Reactor" (Washington, D.C.: December 19, 2001); M. I. Wald, "Plug Pulled on Nuclear Plant That Had Simmered for Years," *New York Times*, December 20, 2001, p. A20.

227 U.S. DOE, "Department of Energy's (DOE's) Office of Environmental Management Takes Over Fast Flux Test Facility Decommissioning and Dismantlement Activities," R-02-0040 (RL: U.S. DOE, September 18, 2002); A. Cary, "Dismantling of FFTF Starts Today," *Tri-City Herald*, September 19, 2002, p. AI.

228 "At Richland . . . Communities to Fight FFTF Closure," *Weapons Complex Monitor*, November 2, 2002, p. 8; J. E. Stang, "FFTF Sodium Draining Begins," *Tri-City Herald*, April 8, 2003, pp. AI–2; N. Geranios, "Reactor Project Passes Point That Any New Use Is Unlikely," *Oregonian*, July 17, 2003, p. D4.

229 "Flowers for FFTF Don't Change Past," *Tri-City Herald*, November 25, 2005, p. FI2.

230 Associated Press, "Hanford Research Reactor Named Historic Landmark," *Seattle Post-Intelligencer*, April 19, 2006; "FFTF's Contributions Worth Remembering," *Tri-City Herald*, April 16, 2006, p. AIO.

231 A. Dworkin, "Public Has Chance to Help Treat Hanford Headache," *Oregonian*, March 27, 2006, pp. BI, B8.

232 Hanford Engineering Development Laboratory, "HEDL Facilities Catalog—400 Area," HEDL-MG-189 (RL: HEDL, June 1985); G. F. Larson, A. B. Webb, M. W. Benecke, I. L. Metcalf, R. K. Hulvey, W. I. Clark, R. C. Reinmann, "Fuel Cycle Plant Final Safety Analysis Report," HEDL-TC-2679 (RL: HEDL, November 1986).

233 "Hanford Facility up for Sale," *Defense Cleanup*, March 24, 1995; W. Briggs, "Hanford Laboratory Eyed by Hollywood, Others," *Tri-City Herald*, March 20, 1995; "Hanford Fuel Fab Facility: DOE Will Accept Best Offer," *New Technology Week*, January 16, 1996.

234 U.S. DOE, "Record of Decision for the Storage and Disposition of Weapons-Usable Fissile Materials, Final Programmatic Environmental Impact Statement," DOE/EIS-0229 (Washington, D.C.: U.S. DOE, January 1997); M. S. Gerber, "Plutonium Disposition: Will Hanford Have a Role?" *Hanford Reach*, June 30, 1997.

235 G. Lobsenz, "New PEACE Group Seeks to Burn DOE's Cold War Residue," *Energy Daily*, February 26, 1977; Hanford Communities, "Hanford's FMEF: The Potential for Significant Savings" (RL: Hanford Communities, March 1997).

236 D. McManman, "Public Goes Critical on DOE Plan to Burn Plutonium," *Tri-City Herald*, June 23, 1997, p. A4; and U.S. DOE, "Surplus Plutonium Disposition Environmental Impact Statement Public Scoping Meeting Comment Summary," DOE/MD-0006 Washington, D.C.: U.S. DOE, September 1997).

237 Note that in April 2000, the two Virginia reactors withdrew from the MOX burn program.

238 J. Beattie, "Domenici Bill Would Paint Nuclear Power Green," *Energy Daily*, March 8, 2001, p. 4; J. Beattie, "Cheney Backs New Nukes to Fight Global Warming," *Energy Daily*, March

368

23, 2001, pp. 1–2; G. Lobsenz, "Two Ontario Reactors Get Restart Nod," *Energy Daily*, April 9, 2001, pp. 1–2; M. Means, "Everybody Wants Power, but Nobody Wants Nuclear Waste," *Tri-City Herald*, April 15, 2001; L. Hawkins, "Concerns over Nuclear Waste Disposal Linger," *Oregonian*, July 4, 2001, p. C1.

239 C. Holly, "Bush Administration Report Changes Tune on Global Warning, Cites Fossil Fuel Link," *Energy Daily*, June 4, 2002, pp. 1, 4; J. Beattie, "DOE Seeking Industry Partners for New Nukes," *Energy Daily*, November 24, 2003, p. 4; "Nuclear Advocates Prepare Strategy for Expansion," *Inside Energy*, July 19, 2004, pp. 1, 11; G. Lobsenz, "Abraham Calls for Doubling of U.S. Nuclear Power," *Energy Daily*, October 12, 2004, pp. 1, 4.

240 C. Holly, "McCain: Global Warming Fight Requires Nukes," *Energy Daily*, June 6, 2005, p. 4; "Reid Says He'll Support N-Power," *Inside Energy*, June 13, 2005, p. 1; "U.S. and Russia Push Nuclear Power," *BBC News* (London), March 20, 2006; "Renaissance Watch: An Update on Developments That May Lead to New Power Reactor Orders and Construction," *Nuclear News*, January 2006, pp. 20–21.

241 P. Moore, "Nuclear Salvation: Green Makes Case for Going Nuclear," *Tri-City Herald*, April 23, 2006, pp. F1, F3.

242 B. Weinstein, "America Needs to Get Up and Atom, Folks," *Fort Worth Star-Telegram*, July 21, 2006; J. Gertner, "Atomic Balm?" *New York Times Magazine*, July 16, 2006, pp. 34–45, 56–64; "Bush Budget Reveals More Details on Reprocessing Plan; Critics Emerge," *Nuclear Waste News*, February 9, 2006, p. 24.

243 "Hanford: The Long Cleanup," *Seattle Post-Intelligencer*, May 1, 2006, p. B7.

244 "The Greening of Nuclear Power," *New York Times*, May 13, 2006.

245 "That Eerie Green Glow," *Washington Post*, August 16, 2006, p. A24.

246 A. Cary, "Plan Would Recycle Used Nuclear Fuel," *Tri-City Herald*, August 31, 2006, pp. A1–2.

247 PNNL, "United States/Russian Federation Core Conversion Project" (RL: PNNL, January 10, 2000), www.pnl.gov.2080/?coreconv; PNNL, "Cessation of Plutonium Production through Core Conversion of the Sversk and Zheleznogorsk Reactors" (RL: PNNL, September 2, 1999), www.pnl.gov.2080/?coreconv/coreprojects.

248 M. S. Gerber, "Historic Visit: Russians Tour Hanford Plutonium Plant," *Tri-City Herald*, July 24, 1994, p. D1, citing J. Keliher.

249 PNNL, "United States/Russian Federation Core"; PNNL, "Cessation of Plutonium Production"; J. F. Fuller, "PNNL Ensures Global Security Around the World" (RL: PNNL, March 2000) www.pnl.gov/news/back/security; J. E. Stang, "Russian Representatives Seek PNNL's Help in Dealing with Job Cuts," *Tri-City Herald*, September 1, 1998, p. A4; "DOE Labs, U.S. Industry Collaborate to Employ Ex-Soviet Scientists," *Inside Energy*, July 31, 2000, pp. 7–8; PNNL, "Ukraine Energy Center Steps Out on Its Own" (RL: PNNL, November 18, 1998), www.pnl.gov/news/1998/bnw98_42.htm; U.S. DOE, "Safety Improvements at the Chornobyl Reactor" (Washington, D.C.: U.S. DOE, February 1998).

250 PNNL, "Pacific Northwest to Host Forum on Chornobyl" (RL: PNNL, February 6, 1997), www.pnl.gov/news/1997/bnw97_03.htm.

251 PNNL, "DOE, Kazakhstan Government Launch Aerial Imaging Project" (RL: PNNL, June 19, 1997), www.pnl.gov/news/1997/bnw97_18.htm; PNNL, "New Training Program to Help Countries Stop Smugglers" (RL: PNNL, September 4, 1997), www.pnl.gov/news/1997/bnw97_29.htm; PNNL, "Tracking a Legacy of Waste in Western Siberian Basin" (RL: PNNL, December 4, 1998), www.pnl.

gov/news/1998/siberia; PNNL, "Research Highlights from Pacific Northwest National Laboratory: Dress Rehearsal for Nuclear Weapons Detection" (RL: PNNL, Spring 2000), www.pnl.gov/news/notes/spring00.

252 PNNL, "PNNL and UW Form Institute for Global and Regional Security Studies," *PNNL Global Security* (RL: PNNL, December 2001), pp. 1, 14.

253 "U.S.–Russian Federation Sign Pact to Demilitarize Excess Plutonium," *Defense Cleanup*, September 8, 2000, p. 278; "Gore, Kasyanov Sign Plutonium Pact, Agree to Major Conversion Facilities," *Nuclear Waste News*, September 7, 2000, p. 355.

254 "DOE Head Pushes Campaign to Aid Russian Nuke Cleanup," *Defense Cleanup*, September 8, 2000, p. 278; "Richardson Unveils Plans for Two Pacific Fleet SF Storage Facilities," *Defense Cleanup*, September 7, 2000, p. 355.

255 U.S. DOE, "Secretary Pena Announces Preferred Sites for Key Plutonium Disposition Facilities," RL-98-108 (RL: U.S. DOE, June 23, 1998); J. E. Stang, "DOE Plutonium Plan Rules Out Hanford," *Tri-City Herald*, June 24, 1998, p. A1; G. Lobsenz, "DOE Awards $130 Million Contract for Plutonium Disposal through MOX," *Energy Daily*, March 23, 1999, pp. 1, 4; G. Lobsenz, "Virginia Power Drops Out of DOE Plutonium Program," *Energy Daily*, April 11, 2000, pp. 1, 4; "U.S. Deal with Russia on Plutonium Called Prime Example for World," *Inside Energy*, June 12, 2000, p. 7.

256 "DOE Offers $1.2M to IAEA, Announces New Nuclear Pact with Russia," *Inside Energy*, December 3, 2001, p. 8; "Abraham Announces Nonproliferation Effort with Kazakhstan," *Inside Energy*, July 8, 2002, p. 8; "Closure of Russian Plutonium Reactors to Take Years," *Energy Daily*, March 14, 2003, p. 4; "Russian Stonewall Stalling DOE on Nuke Safeguards," *Energy Daily*, March 25,

2003, pp. 1–2; PNNL, "Enhancing Russian ADE Reactor Safety," *PNNL Global Security*, May 2003, pp. 3, 6.

257 "Nuclear Cities Initiative Faces End without Russian Response on Liability," *Inside Energy*, July 28, 2003, pp. 17–18; "Russian Disputes Rice on U.S. Inspections of Nuclear Sites," *Energy Daily*, April 21, 2005, p. 3.

258 Y. Humber, "Plutonium Reactors to Be Shut by 2010," *Moscow Times*, August 15, 2006, p. 7.

259 M. J. Scott, D. B. Belzer, R. J. Nesse, R. W. Schultz, P. A. Stokowski, D. C. Clark, "The Economic and Community Impact of Closing Hanford's N Reactor and Nuclear Materials Production Facilities," PNL-6295 (RL: PNL, August 1987).

260 T. Cozzens, "It's Fluor," *Hanford Reach*, August 12, 1996, p. 1.

261 FDH, "Economic Transition and Outsourcing Plan for Project Hanford," HNF-MP-006, Rev. 0 (RL: FDH, 1997).

262 J. E. Stang, "K Basins Contract Realigned," *Tri-City Herald*, August 5, 1999, p. A3; J. E. Stang, "Fluor Corporate Shuffle to Bring Subcontractor Shuffles," *Tri-City Herald*, September 2, 1999, p. A3; J. E. Stang, "Fluor Shifting Economic Development Focus," *Tri-City Herald*, September 23, 1999, p. A1; "DOE Contractor Teaming Turns from Polygamy to Monogamy," *Weapons Complex Monitor*, February 21, 2000, p. 9; J. E. Stang, "4 Hanford Contract Companies in Business for Five Years," *Tri-City Herald*, October 21, 2001, p. B1.

263 J. E. Stang, "Fluor Exceeds Job Creation Goals," *Tri-City Herald*, September 20, 2001, p. B6.

264 M. O'Neil, "Building Surges in 1999: Housing Starts Strong in Mid-Columbia," *Tri-City Herald*, January 27, 2000, p. C1; W. Culverwell, "Tri-City Job Rate Near Top in State," *Tri-City Herald*, May 17, 2000, p. A1; U.S. DOE, "Tri-Cities Economy Continues Strong Growth," RL-00-059 (RL: U.S. DOE, June 6, 2000);

W. Culverwell, "Tri-City Jobs Come Close to Record," *Tri-City Herald*, June 14, 2000, p. A1; W. Culverwell, "Apartments in Tri-Cities Nearly Full," *Tri-City Herald*, October 5, 2000, p. C1.

265 M. O'Neil, "Entrepreneurial Spirit in Tri-Cities Survives Hanford Downsizing," *Washington CEO* (Seattle), February 2000.

266 "Tri-Cities Ranks 9th as One of the Hot Top Small Cities for 2005," *RRC Project News* (RL: Washington Closure Hanford), November 1, 2005, p. 2.

267 J. St. John, "Tri-Cities Ranks 7th in Job Growth Study," *Tri-City Herald*, February 26, 2006, p. B6.

268 G. Sibold-Cohn, "Tri-Cities Adds 20,000 People in Past Decade," *Tri-City Herald*, October 20, 2000, p. A1; W. Culverwell, "Tri-City Economy Continues to Grow," *Tri-City Herald*, October 18, 2000, p. A5; N. Isaacs, "Economist: Employment Picture Flat," *Tri-City Herald*, June 14, 2006. pp. B1–2; M. O'Neil, "Hanford Workers Cashing In: Hanford Salaries Far More Than Tri-City Median," *Tri-City Herald*, March 9, 2000, p. C1; "Fiscal Year 2006 U.S. Department of Energy Budget Tracker," *Weapons Complex Monitor*, November 9, 2005, p. 3; "Budget Cuts Might Force More SRS Layoffs," *Augusta Chronicle*, April 26, 2006.

269 Hanford Advisory Board (HAB), "Tracking the Cleanup, FY 1995" (RL: U.S. DOE, EPA, WDOE, 1995); Hanford Future Site Uses Working Group, "The Future for Hanford: Uses and Cleanup" (RL: U.S. DOE, December 1992).

270 J. E. Stang, "Environmental Consultant to Head Up HAB," *Tri-City Herald*, November 4, 2000, p. A3.

271 HAB, "Tracking the Cleanup"; HAB, "Progress Report, Fiscal Year 1998" (RL: U.S. DOE, EPA, WDOE, 1998); HAB, "Progress Report Fiscal Year 1999" (RL: U.S. DOE, EPA, WDOE, 1999); HAB, "Progress Report Fiscal Year 2005" (RL: U.S. DOE, EPA, WDOE, 2005); HAB, "Ad-

vice and Responses," www.hanford.gov/public/boards/hab/?hab=advice.

272 U.S. DOE, "Openness Press Conference Fact Sheets" (Washington, D.C.: U.S. DOE, December 7, 1993, and June 27, 1994); "DOE Releases First Installment of Formerly Classified Information," *Nuclear Waste News*, December 19, 1993; National Research Council (NRC), "A Review of Department of Energy Classification Policy and Practice" (Washington, D.C.: National Academy Press, 1995).

273 NRC, "A Review of," pp. 3–9.

274 U.S. DOE, "Drawing Back the Curtain of Secrecy: Restricted Data Declassification Decisions 1946 to the Present," RDD-4 (Washington, D.C.: U.S. DOE, January 1, 1998); U.S. DOE, "Nearly 2 Million Pages of Documents and Materials Declassified at Hanford," DOE/RL-99-069 (RL: U.S. DOE, August 18, 1999); L. Ashton, "Declassified Photos Depict Hanford Life," *Oregonian*, August 27, 2000, p. A26.

275 "Energy Dep't Review of Published Works Raises Fears of Censorship," *Weapons Complex Monitor*, November 5, 2001, pp. 2–3; "Interest Groups Voice Concern over Information Restrictions," *Weapons Complex Monitor*, December 3, 2001, pp. 3–4.; R. Herschaft and F. Bass, "Update 5: Archives OK'd Removing Records, Kept Quiet," *Forbes* (New York), April 12, 2006, www.forbes.com/home/feeds/ap/2006/04/12/ap2664897.html.

276 A. Cary, "GAO Report Puts DOE to Task," *Tri-City Herald*, March 15, 2006, pp. B1–2; "Report, Legislation Drive Push to End Pseudo-Classification of Information," *OMB Watch* (Washington, D.C.), April 18, 2006, www.ombwatch.org/article/articleprint/3382/-1/1; U.S. GAO, "Information Sharing: The Federal Government Needs to Establish Policies and Processes for Sharing Terrorism-Related and Sensitive but Unclassified Information," GAO-06-385 (Washington,

D.C.: U.S. GAO, March 2006); S. Shane, "National Archives Says Records Were Wrongly Classified," *New York Times*, April 27, 2006.

277 C. Lee, "Cold War Missiles Target of Blackout," *Washington Post*, August 21, 2006.

278 U.S. DOE, "U.S. DOE Environment, Safety and Health Public Meeting, February 3, 2000, 6:30 PM, Federal Building, Richland, Washington," Transcript, tis.eh.doe.gov/benefits/meetings/000203hanford; A. Galloway, "Hanford Workers Break Silence," *Seattle Post-Intelligencer*, February 4, 2000, p. A5; L. Ashton, "Tearful Hanford Workers Describe Ailments," *Spokesman-Review*, February 4, 2000, p. B3; K. Murphy, "Government Finally Hears a Nuclear Town's Horrors," *Los Angeles Times*, February 5, 2000; "Acknowledgement of Hanford's Dangers Tardy, but Hopeful," *Tri-City Herald*, February 11, 2000.

279 A. Cary, "DOE Report Long on Horizon," *Tri-City Herald*, February 27, 2000, p. A1; J. Warrick, "U.S. Admits Harm from Radiation," *Spokesman-Review*, January 30, 2000, p. A1, citing W. Richardson; M. I. Wald, "Hanford Exposure Admitted," *Seattle Post-Intelligencer*, January 31, 2000, p. A1; G. Lobsenz, "Draft Federal Report Finds Radiation-Cancer Link among DOE Workers," *Energy Daily*, February 1, 2000, pp. 1–2.

280 "DOE to Compensate Thousands of Sick Workers," *Hanford Reach*, April 17, 2000, pp. 1, 8, citing A. Gore.

281 K. Rizzo, "House Approves Payments for Nuclear Workers," *Oregonian*, October 12, 2000, p. A11; A. Cary and J. E. Stang, "Clinton Signs Bill for Sick Workers," *Tri-City Herald*, October 31, 2000, p. A1; A. Cary, "More Eligible for Nuclear Compensation," *Tri-City Herald*, December 18, 2001, p. A1.

282 A. Cary, "Hanford Claims Program Criticized," *Tri-City Herald*, April 26, 2001, p. A1; A. Cary, "Lack of Radiation

Data Troubles Feds, *Tri-City Herald*, August 4, 2002, p. B1; A. Cary, "Meeting Held for Ill Nuclear Workers," *Tri-City Herald*, August 8, 2002, p. A1.

283 H. Bernton, "Compensation, at Last, for Some Hanford Workers," *Seattle Times*, May 1, 2005, pp. B1, B4; A. Cary, "Hanford Workers Seek Compensation Answers," *Tri-City Herald*, February 17, 2004, pp. B1–2; "Dep't of Labor Officially Takes Over DOE Sick Worker Program," *Weapons Complex Monitor*, November 8, 2004, p. 4.

284 Associated Press, "Complaints on Hanford Health Bills," *Seattle Post-Intelligencer*, June 20, 2005, p. B4; "House, Senate Lawmakers Raise Concerns about Sick Worker Rule," *Weapons Complex Monitor*, August 8, 2005, p. 6.

285 A. Cary, "Hanford Data Needs Review, Cantwell Says," *Tri-City Herald*, October 5, 2005, pp. A1–2; A. Cary, "Hanford Program Frustrating Users, Ombudsman Office Says," *Tri-City Herald*, February 21, 2006, pp. B1–2; N. Zuckerbrod, "Rep. Probes Nuclear Compensation Program," *Seattle Post-Intelligencer*, April 10, 2006; R. Snodgrass, "Nuclear Workers Compensation Program Faces Cuts" *L.A. Monitor* (Los Alamos, N.M.), May 8, 2006.

286 "House Bill Would Prevent Changes to Sick Nuke Worker Program," *Weapons Complex Monitor*, July 30, 2001, pp. 6–7.

287 A. Cary, "Medical Claims Near $1 Million," *Tri-City Herald*, July 23, 2006, pp. B1–2.

288 S. Wing, "Epidemiology of Multiple Myeloma at Four DOE Sites" (Chapel Hill: University of North Carolina, 1999).

289 NIOSH, "Mortality among Female Nuclear Weapons Workers" (Cincinnati: NIOSH, 2000), www.cdc.gov/niosh/2001-133g.html; G. S. Wilkinson, N. Trieffe, R. Graham, and R. L. Priore, "Final Report: Study of Mortality among Female Nuclear Weapons Workers" (Buffalo: State University of New York, May 19, 2000).

290 NIOSH, "Protocol: Multi-Site Case-Control Study of Lung Cancer and External Ionizing Radiation" (Cincinnati: NIOSH, September 1999); NIOSH, "Hanford Site Mortality Update: Age at Exposure to Ionizing Radiation" (Cincinnati: NIOSH, June 2005, www.cdc.gov/niosh/oerp/pdfs/GRNT_HANF_05-13-2005.pdf.

291 M. I. Wald, "Study Disputes Downwinders' Claims," *Tri-City Herald*, January 28, 1999, p. A1; A. Cary, "Despite Study, Downwinders Still Feel Hanford to Blame," *Tri-City Herald*, January 28, 1999, p. A1; A. Cary, "Thyroid Study Sound, Peers Say," *Tri-City Herald*, December 15, 1999, p. A1; A. Cary, "Cancer Rates Don't Increase near Hanford," *Tri-City Herald*, April 25, 2006.

292 U.S. DOE, "Beryllium Awareness Group Formed at Hanford," RL-99-046 (RL: U.S. DOE, May 10, 1999); Associated Press, "Tests Show Hanford Workers at Risk of Lung Disease," *Tri-City Herald*, November 6, 1998, p. C5; A. Cary, "2nd Chronic Beryllium Disease Diagnosed," *Tri-City Herald*, December 12, 1999.

293 A. Cary, "Study Links Hanford, Disease," *Tri-City Herald*, July 25, 2006, pp. A1–2; Associated Press, "Study Ties Thyroid Ills to Hanford," *Seattle Times*, July 27, 2006, pp. B1–2.

294 W. Briggs, "21 File Suit over Hanford Releases," *Tri-City Herald*, August 7, 1990), p. A1; Associated Press, "Second Damage Suit Filed against Hanford Operators," *Tri-City Herald*, August 10, 1990, p. A3; Associated Press, "Hanford Hurt Fishing, Indians Claim in Suit," *Tri-City Herald*, October 24, 1990, p. A1; Associated Press, "Oregonians File Suit against Hanford," *Tri-City Herald*, October 25, 1990, p. A9; Associated Press, "Judge Combines Radiation Lawsuits," *Tri-City Herald*, March 1, 1991, p. A8; Associated Press, "Downwinders Sue for Medical Care," *Tri-City Herald*, July 11,

1993, p. A3; Associated Press, "Suit Targets Hanford Health Hazards," *Tri-City Herald*, July 12, 1993, p. A1.

295 "DOE Issues Interim Policy Regarding Huge Legal Fees," *Report on Defense Plant Wastes* (Silver Spring MD), September 12, 1994; K. D. Steele and J. Lynch, "See You in Court," *Spokesman-Review*, November 16, 1994, p. A1; "DOE Tightens Controls on Contractors' Legal Fees," *Energy Daily*, April 8, 1996; "DOE Complex: GAO: DOE Should Do More to Reduce Costs of Lawsuits against Contractors," *Nuclear Waste News*, May 9, 1996.

296 A rad is a measure of absorbed dose of radiation.

297 Associated Press and staff of the *Tri-City Herald*, "Judge Dismisses Most of Claims of Downwinders," *Tri-City Herald*, August 26, 1998, p. A1.

298 A. Cary, "Judge Puts More Limits on Claims for Downwinders," *Tri-City Herald*, September 2, 1999, p. A1.

299 The "Superfund" law is part of the Comprehensive Environmental Response, Compensation and Liability Act (CERCLA).

300 A. Cary, "Federal Judge Dismisses Downwinders' DOE Suit," *Tri-City Herald*, April 1, 1999, p. A4; Associated Press, "Judge Dismisses Downwinders Suit," *Spokesman-Review*, April 3, 1999, p. B1.

301 J. E. Stang, "$100 Billion Lawsuit Filed against 13 Hanford Contractors," *Tri-City Herald*, July 13, 2000, p. A4; Associated Press, "Hanford Lawsuit Seeks $100 Billion," *Oregonian*, July 14, 2000, p. B2.

302 L. Siffler, "Hanford 'Downwinders' Win a New Day in Court," *Seattle Post-Intelligencer*, May 10, 2002, p. B2; C. Welch, "Hanford Lawsuits Given New Life," *Seattle Times*, June 19, 2002, p. A1.

303 Associated Press, "Judge Takes Leave of Hanford Downwinder Suit," *Oregonian*, March 12, 2003, p. D2.

304 A. Cary, "Some Downwinder Cases May Be Heard," *Tri-City Herald*, May 30, 2003, pp. B1–2.

305 Associated Press, "Judge Sells General Electric Stock to Hear Radiation Case," *Tri-City Herald*, March 12, 2003, p. D2.

306. A. Cary, "Health to Be Key Issue in Downwinder Trial," *Tri-City Herald*, November 5, 2004, pp. B1–2; A. Cary, "Judge Limits Ex-Contractors' Defense," *Tri-City Herald*, March 31, 2004, p. B2.

307 J. Wiley, "Hanford Health-Effects Trial Opens," *Seattle Post-Intelligencer*, April 26, 2005, p. B2; W. Cornwall, "Hanford Likely Caused Cancer Downwind, Jury Decides," *Seattle Post-Intelligencer*, May 20, 2005, pp. A1, A16; Associated Press, "No New Trial for Hanford Downwinder," *Seattle Post-Intelligencer*, January 23, 2006, p. B3; S. Dininny, "Government, Plaintiffs Wait through Downwinder Appeals," *Seattle Post-Intelligencer*, June 10, 2006.

308 U.S. Bureau of Reclamation, "Columbia Basin Project, Project History" (Ephrata, Wash.: U.S. Bureau of Reclamation, 1966), vol. 34, p. 15; Bureau of Reclamation, "Columbia Basin Project, Project History" (Ephrata, Wash.: U.S. Bureau of Reclamation, 1965), vol. 33, p. 23.

309 U.S. DOE, "New Plant and Animal Species Previously Unknown to Science Found at Hanford," RL-98-054 (RL: U.S. DOE, May 21, 1998).

310 L. Blumenthal, "River Wild: Cold War Leaves Free-Flowing Legacy," *Tri-City Herald*, October 9, 1994, p. D1; J. Long, "The Hanford Land Rush," *Oregonian*, April 17, 1996, pp. A1, A2.

311 E. Smith, "Preserve Reach, Lowry Says," *Tri-City Herald*, November 7, 1993, p. A1; J. E. Stang, "Make Reach Scenic, Park Service Offers Recommendation," *Tri-City Herald*, July 13, 1994, p. A1; "Save Hanford Reach," *Seattle Post-Intelligencer*, July 15, 1994, p. A12; "Protect Hanford Reach," *Oregonian*, April 18, 1996, p. E10; M. Lee, "Catholic Bishops Release Letter on Columbia River," *Tri-City Herald*, May 14, 1999, p. A3; E. Smith, "Hastings Sees Little Hope for Reach Bill," *Tri-City Herald*, January 17, 2004, p. A1; U.S. DOE, "Final Hanford Comprehensive Land-Use Plan Environmental Impact Statement," DOE/EIS-0222–F (RL: U.S. DOE, September 1999).

312 M. Lee, "A Monumental Decision," *Tri-City Herald*, June 10, 2000, pp. A1, A8.

313 U.S. FWS, "Babbitt Lauds Arid Lands Ecology Reserve Management Agreement" (Washington, D.C.: U.S. DI, August 27, 1997).

314 "Reach Declaration Good for Tri-Cities," *Seattle Post-Intelligencer*, June 13, 2000, p. B6.

315 "Wasteland to Treasure: Scientists Have Long Valued Hanford; Now, National Monument May Draw Tourists," *Spokesman-Review*, June 11, 2000, p. B1; Associated Press, "Monument Status Could Boost Tourism for Hanford Reach," *Seattle Post-Intelligencer*, June 13, 2000, p. B3; "Hanford Reach: Get Over It, Grant County," *Tri-City Herald*, October 6, 2000, p. A6; R. Thompson, "Richland Will Work with All to Build Reach Center," *Tri-City Herald*, June 18, 2000, p. D2.

316 M. S. Gerber, "Huge Fire Sweeps through Hanford," *Hanford Reach*, July 10, 2000, p. 1; M. S. Gerber, "2000 Fire Most Intense, but Not Biggest," *Hanford Reach*, July 17, 2000.

317 A. King, "Reach Restoration Wraps Up," *Tri-City Herald*, December 9, 2004, pp. A1–2; "Sagebrush Perfume," *Tri-City Herald*, December 16, 2004, p. A10.

318 J. E. Stang, "Hanford Reach Plan Taking Shape," *Tri-City Herald*, December 5, 2003, pp. B1–2; USFWS, "Hanford Reach National Monument Comprehensive Conservation Plan, Planning Update 5" (RL: USFWS, September 2005); G. Hughes, "Reach Focusing on Restoration, Helping Visitors," *Tri-City Herald*, February 25, 2006, p. F15.

374

319 "A Milestone for Reach," *Tri-City Herald*, December 7, 2003, p. F2; "On Common Ground," *Tri-City Herald*, July 26, 2004, p. A12; R. Hicks, "Reach Visitors Center a Benefit to Entire Community," *Tri-City Herald*, February 25, 2006, p. F13.

320 Uranium cracks and warps when exposed to water. Therefore, B Reactor's uranium fuel had to be jacketed, coated, or "canned" in a thin veneer of other metals to preserve the precise shape of the uranium elements.

321 U.S. DOE, "Historic American Engineering Record, B Reactor (105–B Building)," DOE/RL-2001-16 (HAER No. WA. 164) (RL: U.S. DOE, December 2000).

322 PNNL, Parsons Environmental Services, P. W. Griffin, "105–B Reactor Facility Museum Phase I Feasibility Study Report," BHI-00076, Rev 1 (RL: BHI, September 1995); BHI, "105–B Reactor Museum Feasibility Assessment (Phase II) Project," BHI-01384 (RL: BHI, June 2000); P. W. Griffin and L. M. Douglas, "105–B Reactor Museum Phase II Project Supplemental Cost Estimate," BHI-01385 (RL: BHI, June 2000).

323 N. Kerr, "Preliminary Hazards Classification for the 105–B Reactor," BHI-01085 (RL: BHI, August 1997); N. Kerr, "Surplus Reactor Auditable Safety Analysis," BHI-01172 (RL: BHI, June 1998); P. W. Griffin and J. J. Sharpe, "Hanford B Reactor Building Hazard Assessment Report," BHI-01282 (RL: BHI, June 1999); U.S. DOE, "Engineering Evaluation, Cost Analysis for the 105–B Reactor Facility," DOE/RL-2001-09 (RL: U.S. DOE, June 2001); S. P. Kretzschmar, "B Reactor Structural Analysis," BHI-01672 (RL: BHI, December 2002).

Glossary of Technical or Specialized Terms, Acronyms, and Abbreviations

activation Induction of radioactivity in a material by irradiation with neutron radioactive material, a radiation-generating machine, or a nuclear reactor.

activity A measure of the rate at which a material is emitting nuclear radiation, usually given in terms of the number of nuclear disintegrations occurring in a given quantity of material over a unit of time; the standard unit of activity is the curie (Ci).

AEC Atomic Energy Commission.

alpha-emitter A radioisotope that emits alpha radiation.

alpha radiation An emission of particles (helium nuclei) from a material undergoing nuclear transformation; the particles have a nuclear mass number of four and a charge of plus two.

alpha waste Waste material that is contaminated by radionuclides that emit alpha particles, particularly transuranic elements.

aquifer A subsurface formation containing sufficient saturated permeable material to yield significant quantities of water.

ARHCO Atlantic Richfield Hanford Company, the chemical-processing and waste-management contractor at the Hanford Site.

atomic number The number of protons in the nucleus of each chemical element.

background radiation The level of radioactivity that is produced by sources other than the one of specific interest; in the Hanford region, the background radiation is produced by naturally occurring radioactive materials in the crust of the earth, cosmic radiations, and the fallout from nuclear weapons tests.

benthic organisms Organisms dwelling on the bottom of a body of water.

beta-emitter A radioisotope that emits beta radiation.

beta radiation Essentially weightless charged particles (electrons and positrons) emitted from the nucleus of atoms undergoing nuclear transformation.

bioconcentration (bioaccumulation) The process whereby an organic system selectively removes an element from the environment and accumulates that element in a higher concentration.

biota The plant and animal life of a region.

BNWL The Pacific Northwest Laboratories of Battelle Memorial Institute, commonly known as Battelle-Northwest; BNWL has conducted environmental-monitoring operations at the Hanford Site since 1965; in 1977, a corporate separation resulted in a name change to Pacific Northwest Laboratories.

body burden The amount of a specified radioactive material (or the sum of the amounts of various radioactive materials) present in an animal or human body.

boiling waste High-level, liquid radioactive waste containing radionuclides (principally Sr-90 and Cs-137) that provide sufficient decay heat to be near the liquid's boiling point; such liquid usually requires some supplemental means of cooling.

BOR Bureau of Reclamation.

bottoms (tank) The more concentrated material remaining in Hanford high-level liquid radioactive waste tanks after the bulk of the contents has been pumped out for solidification or transfer to other storage tanks; the term also refers to specific tanks used to collect such "bottoms waste" from several other tanks.

burial ground An area set aside for the subsurface disposal of solid waste or excess materials.

BWIP Basalt Waste Isolation Project.

by-product material Radioactive materials produced in a nuclear reactor, ancillary to the reactor's main purpose of producing power or fissile materials; fission products are usually considered the by-product material.

cask A container for transporting radioactive materials, usually with special shielding, handling, and sealing features.

chemical processing Chemical treatment of materials to separate usable constituents; at Hanford, chemical means separate plutonium from uranium and fission products resulting from irradiation of the uranium in a nuclear reactor.

Ci Curie.

cladding Metal coating bonded to a metal core.

confined aquifer A subsurface water-bearing region having relatively impermeable upper and lower boundaries and held by pressures greater than that of the atmosphere.

CBP Columbia Basin Irrigation Project.

crib An excavation approximately fifteen feet deep with a perforated pipe at the bottom, which is then filled with broken rock or other loose material, topped with a membrane impermeable to liquid, and layered with soil at the top. Cribs are used to store intermediate-level liquid wastes, which enter through the pipe.

critical The condition in which a material undergoes nuclear fission at a self-sustaining rate; the minimum critical mass is the amount of a fissile isotope that will self-sustain nuclear fission when placed in optimum conditions.

Cs Cesium (atomic number 55).

curie (Ci) A unit of radioactivity defined as the amount of a radioactive material that has an activity of 3.7×10^{10} disintegrations per second (d/s); millicurie (mCi) = 10^{-3} curie; microcurie (μCi) = 10^{-6} curie; nanocurie (nCi) = 10^{-9} curie; picocurie (pCi) = 10^{-12} curie; femtocurie (fCi) = 10^{-15} curie.

deactivated The condition of a facility after operations have ceased, or of a disposal site when no further waste materials are accepted.

decay (radioactive) The process in which radioactive isotopes emit particles or gamma rays until a stable balance of electrons and protons is reached.

decommissioning The process of removing a facility or area from operation and decontaminating and/or disposing of it or placing it in a standby condition.

decontamination The selective removal of radioactive material from a surface or from within another material.

disintegrations per minute (dpm) The number of radioactive decay events in a given amount of material per minute.

disposal The planned release or placement of waste in a manner that precludes recovery.

DOE U.S. Department of Energy.

dose A general term indicating the amount of energy absorbed from incident radiation by a specific mass.

dry well A bore hole that does not sink deep enough to reach groundwater and is used to monitor the movement of liquid waste released near the surface and to check for leaks in underground storage tanks.

DuPont E.I. DuPont de Nemours and Co.

environmental monitoring A monitoring of the impact on the surrounding region of the discharges from industrial operations.

EPA Environmental Protection Agency.

ERDA Energy Research and Development Administration.

erg A centimeter-gram-second unit of energy.

fallout Radioactive materials released into the atmosphere and deposited on the earth's surface by the detonation of nuclear weapons.

FFTF Fast Flux Test Facility.

fission (nuclear) The division of a nucleus into two nuclides of lower mass, usually accompanied by the expulsion of gamma rays and neutrons.

fissionable Material capable of undergoing fission by slow neutrons.

fission products The nuclides formed by the division of a heavier nucleus, most usually in a nuclear reactor.

food chain The successive utilizations of nutrient energy by a series of species, beginning with plants and lower animal species and progressing through fish, birds, and other mammals, sometimes to man.

fractionization The process of removing specific constituents (such as strontium and cesium) from liquid waste.

fuel (nuclear, reactor) Fissionable material used as the source of power when placed in a critical arrangement in a nuclear reactor.

fuel separation (fuel reprocessing) The processing of irradiated (spent) nuclear reactor fuel to recover useful materials such as plutonium, uranium, and fission products.

gamma radiation Electromagnetic energy emitted in the process of a nuclear transition.

gastrointestinal dose (GI) The dose to the stomach and lower tract of humans and animals via external exposure or internal transport of radioactive material.

GE General Electric Co.

Geiger-Müller Tube A gas-filled tube used to detect radiation events by the ionization pulse produced in the gas; the tube is used in a Geiger-Müller (GM) counter.

glacio-fluviate Pertaining to streams flowing from glaciers, or the deposits made by such streams.

gpd Gallons per day.

gpm Gallons per minute.

half-life The time required for the activity of a radionuclide to decay to half its value; the term is used as a measure of the persistence of radioactive materials; each radionuclide has a characteristic constant half-life.

HAPO Hanford Atomic Products Operation.

HEPA High Efficiency Particulate Air: an air filter capable of removing at least 99.97% of the particulate material in an air stream.

HEW Hanford Engineer Works.

H.I. Health Instruments Division.

high-level liquid waste Fluid materials from Hanford Operations, disposed of by storage in underground tanks, which are contaminated by greater than 100 μCi/ml of mixed fission products or more than 2 μCi/ml of Cs-137, Sr-90, or long-lived alpha-emitters.

HW Hanford Works.

hypothetical average individual A postulated person who is assumed to receive an average credible radiological dose through each of the exposure pathways being considered (for example, eating average amounts of fish from a body of water, swimming or boating occasionally in that same water).

hypothetical maximum individual (max man) A postulated person who is assumed to receive the maximum credible radiological dose through each of the exposure pathways from the source being considered (for example, swimming often in a body of water, eating large quantities of fish obtained from that water, and drinking large amounts of the same water).

ICRP International Commission on Radiological Protection, an international organization devoted to studying the physiological effects of radiation and recommending protection standards.

INEL Idaho National Engineering Laboratory, originally called the Reactor Testing Station, currently a Department of Energy Site near Idaho Falls, Idaho.

intermediate-level liquid waste Fluid waste materials in Hanford operations which contain from 5×10^{-5} μCi/ml to 100 μCi/ml of mixed fission products, including less than 2 μCi/ml of Cs-137, Sr-90, or long-lived alpha emitters.

inversion Weather condition in which the temperature of the atmosphere increases with height above ground.

ion exchange A process for selectively removing a constituent from a waste stream by reversibly transferring ions between an insoluble solid and the waste stream; the exchange medium (usually a column of resin or soil) can then be washed to collect the waste or taken directly to disposal; for example, a hot-water softener works on this principle.

irradiation Exposure to radiation by being placed near a radioactive source—usually, in the case of fuel materials, being placed in an operating nuclear reactor.

isotope Nuclides with the same atomic number (the same chemical element) but with different atomic masses; although chemical properties are the same, radioactive and nuclear properties may be quite different for each isotope of an element.

ITS-1 and -2 In-Tank Solidification, Units 1 and 2.

kw Kilowatt.

long-lived isotope A radioactive nuclide that decays at such a slow rate that a quantity of it will exist for an extended period; usually refers to radionuclides whose half-life is greater than three years.

low-level liquid waste Fluid materials, disposed of at Hanford, which are contaminated by less than 5×10^{-5} μCi/ml of mixed fission products.

mCi Millicurie (see curie).

MED Manhattan Engineer District.

MPC Maximum permissible concentration.

mrad Millirad (see rad).

mrem Millirem (see rem).

NAS National Academy of Sciences.

NCRP National Committee on Radiation Protection, an American organization devoted to studying physiological radiation effects and recommending protection standards.

NPH Saturated kerosene, having a straight molecular chain of 12 units (like dodecane).

partitioning The process of separating liquid waste into two or more fractional solutions.

pCi Picocurie (see curie).

penetrating radiation Forms of radiant energy that are capable of passing through significant thicknesses of solid material; these usually include gamma rays, x-rays, and neutrons.

permissible dose That dose of ionizing radiation that, in the light of present knowledge, carries negligible probability of causing severe somatic injury or genetic defect.

pH A measure of the relative acidity or alkalinity of solution; a neutral solution has a pH of 7; acids have a pH of from 1 to 7; bases (alkalies) have a pH of from 7 to 14.

power reactor A nuclear reactor designed to produce heat for conversion into electrical energy or mechanical propulsion.

production reactor A nuclear reactor designed for transforming one nuclide into another—usually, a conversion of natural uranium into plutonium.

Pu Plutonium (atomic number 94).

PUREX The facility, as well as the process, that uses steps of solvent extraction and ion exchange for the separation of plutonium and uranium from irradiated production fuels.

rad A special unit of measure for the absorbed dose of radiation; one rad equals 100 ergs absorbed per gram of material.

radiation (ionizing) Particles and electromagnetic energy emitted by nuclear transformations that are capable of producing ions when interacting with matter; gamma rays and alpha and beta particles are primary examples in Hanford waste.

radiation survey Evaluation of an area or object with instruments in order to detect, identify, and quantify radioactive materials and radiation fields.

radioactive decay Spontaneous nuclear transformation in which nuclear particles or electromagnetic energy is emitted.

radioiodines Radioactive isotopes of iodine.

reactivity A measure of the capability of a system to maintain criticality; systems with high reactivity are capable of undergoing rapid excursions of increasing power; systems with low reactivity will undergo slower excursions; systems with negative reactivity will not become critical.

redd Spawning grounds or nests of salmon.

RECUPLEX Acronym for Recovery of Uranium and Plutonium by Extraction; a facility that operated at the Hanford Site from 1955 to 1962.

REDOX A facility and the process for separating plutonium and uranium from irradiated reactor fuels by using successive steps of chemical *Red*uction *Ox*idation, with solvent extraction.

release limit (release guide) A control number that regulates the concentration or amount of radioactive material released to the environment in an industrial situation; usually the dose to people in the environment is derived from the environmental behavior of this released material so that the dose can be kept below a selected control value.

rem A unit of measure for the dose of ionizing radiation that gives the same biological effect as one roentgen of X rays; one rem is approximately equal to one rad for X, gamma, or beta radiation.

rep An acronym for *R*oentgen *E*quivalent *P*hysical, a term no longer used; rep is roughly equivalent to rem.

reprocessing Chemical processing of irradiated nuclear reactor fuels to remove desired constituents.

retention basin An excavated and lined area used to hold contaminated fluids until radioactive decay reduces activities to levels permissible for release.

roentgen A unit of measure of ionizing electromagnetic radiation (X and gamma); one roentgen corresponds to the release by ionization of 83.8 ergs of energy.

rupture A breach of the metal cladding of a production reactor fuel element, thereby releasing radioactive materials to reactor cooling streams.

salt cake The solid residue from a concentration of high-level liquid waste in Hanford underground waste-storage tanks.

self-boiling waste High-level liquid radioactive waste whose constituent radionuclides contribute sufficient decay heat to cause the solution to boil and/or self-concentrate.

semiworks A pilot plant or small-scale plant sufficient to test the actual operating capabilities of a new technique or process.

shielding Bulkheads, walls, or other construction used to absorb radiation in order to protect personnel and equipment.

short-lived isotope A radioactive nuclide that decays so rapidly that a given quantity is transformed into its daughter products within a short period (usually those with a half-life of days or less).

slug A fuel element for one of the Hanford production reactors.

solid wastes (radioactive) Either solid radioactive material or solid objects that contain radioactive material or bear radioactive surface contamination.

source material Uranium or thorium or any ore that contains at least 0.5 percent of uranium or thorium.

special nuclear material (SNM) Plutonium, U-233, U-235, or uranium enriched to a higher percentage than normal of the 233 or 235 isotopes.

special work permit (SWP) A formal, written permit delineating time, clothing, equipment, and conduct of work involving radioactive materials; at the Hanford Site and at many U.S. nuclear sites, the term SWP has come to refer to special protective clothing designed to shield against radioactivity.

Sr Strontium (atomic number 38).

SRP Savannah River Plant, currently called the Savannah River Site, a site in the Department of Energy complex.

standby The condition wherein a facility or location is placed in a nonoperating condition but is maintained in readiness for subsequent operation.

storage basin A water-filled facility for holding irradiated reactor fuels, with the water acting as a shield.

sump A hole or catch basin at the lowest point of a drainage system, into which liquids are drained in order to be pumped out.

tank farm An installation of interconnected containers (tanks) for storage of high-level waste.

tracer A radionuclide(s) or chemical introduced in minute quantities into a system or process in order to use radiation- or chemical-detection techniques to follow the behavior of the process or system.

transmissivity A coefficient relating the volumetric flow through a unit width of groundwater to the driving force (hydraulic potential); transmissivity is a function of both the porous medium, fluid properties and the saturated thickness of the aquifer.

transmutation The process whereby one nuclide changes (or is changed) into another, usually by the addition of nuclear particles.

transuranics Nuclides having an atomic number greater than that of uranium (greater than 92).

trench A ditch used for the disposal of solid radioactive waste or low-level liquid waste.

Tri-Cities The area occupied by the cities of Richland, Pasco, and Kennewick, Washington.

U Uranium (atomic number 92).

unconfined aquifer An aquifer that has a water table or surface at atmospheric pressure.

UNH Uranyl nitrate hexahydrate, the liquid uranium product stream generated by many radiochemical processes.

vadose zone The unsaturated region of soil between the ground surface and the water table.

water table Upper boundary of an unconfined aquifer surface below which saturated groundwater occurs; the water table is defined by the levels at which water stands in wells that barely penetrate the aquifer.

WPPSS Washington Public Power Supply System.

Index

DATE DUE
